10 $\frac{50}{1}$

THE
BRITISH OVERSEAS

The fault of our going was our own. What could be thought fitting or necessary we had; but what we should find or want we were all ignorant.
Such actions have ever since the World's beginning been subject to accidents, and everything of worth is found full of difficulties; but nothing so difficult as to establish a Commonwealth so far remote from men and means.
But to proceed . . . CAPTAIN JOHN SMITH

THE
BRITISH OVERSEAS

Exploits of a Nation of Shopkeepers

BY

C. E. CARRINGTON

SECOND EDITION

Part I: Making of the Empire

CAMBRIDGE
AT THE UNIVERSITY PRESS
1968

Published by the Syndics of the Cambridge University Press
Bentley House, P.O. Box 92, 200 Euston Road, London, N.W.1
American Branch: 32 East 57th Street, New York, N.Y. 10022

First edition, complete   1950
Second edition of Part 1   1968

Standard Book Numbers:
521 07174 7 *clothbound*
521 09514 X *paperback*

First printed in Great Britain at the University Printing House, Cambridge
Reprinted in Great Britain by Hazell Watson & Viney Ltd, Aylesbury, Bucks

CONTENTS

LIST OF ILLUSTRATIONS

MAPS

GRAPHS

PORTRAITS

PREFACE TO THE SECOND EDITION

A plan for a book on the subject of *The British Overseas* took shape in my mind during the year 1937. When I had already made some progress, the onset of the Second World War obliged me to lay my task aside for several years; and when I returned to it, the phenomenon I proposed to describe had taken a new shape.

My intention had been to display the growth of the Empire and the emergence of the Commonwealth Ideal from the point of view of the British pioneers. Who were they, I asked; why did they go overseas; and what did they suppose themselves to be doing? In the nineteen-thirties, I thought that I could find an answer to these questions. The Empire-Commonwealth seemed to have surmounted an obstacle, to have reached a stage of equilibrium and to be moving steadily on a course which might be charted. The ' Old Dominions ' had achieved virtual independence without disrupting the Imperial system, thus inaugurating a new style in international co-operation. There was still hope that Dominion status might solve the perennial problem of Anglo-Irish relations; and men of progressive views in Great Britain were not dismayed by the far more exacting crisis of Empire in Asia. Burma was well on the way towards Dominion status; Ceylon with its ingenious ' Donoughmore ' constitution, was moving in the same direction; and the Government of India Bill (1935) seemed to open the way for Indian political progress, if only it could be made to work. The notion if not yet the name of ' de-colonisation ' was already familiar, and, in the circles where I moved, no one doubted that the destiny of all the larger colonies was to move methodically towards self-government; though, to the best of my knowledge, no one supposed in 1937 that the whole Empire would be de-colonised within thirty years, and mainly by an orderly process. The acceleration of social change is a feature of twentieth-century life which had not been foreseen.

My book was completed in November 1949 and published in
1950. The later chapters (how could they not?) revealed doubts
and uncertainties that had not been evident in 1937, many raw
edges and loose ends. But there comes a time for every author
when he must draw the line and I drew it at the Commonwealth
Conference of 1949, which, unlike the Statute of Westminster,
was the beginning of a new phase, not the end of an old one. I
indicated the direction of future change by some dedicatory
verses on the theme, ' Look to Africa '.

The continuing demand for my book, though gratifying, places
the author in a quandary. Some of the judgments I made twenty
years ago are quaintly old-fashioned; a few of my historical
statements have been proved wrong by information that has
since come to light; and several friends have drawn my attention
to errors in detail which are almost inevitable in the first edition
of so large and comprehensive a book. I do not think the time is
yet ripe for a new work on the whole subject of Colonisation and
De-colonisation. Yet, if I begin to revise my book, I find that
nothing short of re-writing every chapter will suffice. I have
therefore decided to re-issue the first half with a minimum of
change. While a number of factual errors have been corrected, I
have not, as a rule, revised matters of judgment and opinion,
except—rarely—in footnotes. As for the conclusion, I have
endeavoured to describe the Commonwealth as it was in the
momentous years 1947–9. The book, then, with its weaknesses,
is a historical document. This is what the story of the Empire
looked like about the time of the Second World War. The only
mercy I beg of the critics is that they will allow for development
in me as well as in my subject; and will not suppose that I have
remained since 1949 in what John Stuart Mill called ' the deep
slumber of a decided opinion '. It is my intention to complete
the story of de-colonisation in a second volume.

Proper names are spelt in the familiar anglicised form, if there
is one, without regard to the pedantry of recent orthographers.

When such phrases occur as ' the treaty is still effective ', or the
coins ' still pass current ', it should be understood that they refer
to what was effective or current in 1949.

I have added a few acknowledgments in footnotes.

December 1967   C.E.C.

I

EARLY VENTURES OVERSEAS

Argument: Little is known of the earliest English voyages. Certainly in the fifteenth century and increasingly after the Reformation, English merchant-venturers visited the Atlantic Islands and West Africa, sometimes with the connivance of the Spanish and Portuguese, sometimes in spite of their hostility. Before 1583 the Newfoundland fisheries were frequented and regulated by customary law.

Settlement in North America was promoted by a group of political theorists who stimulated religious and philanthropic bodies to plant many systematic colonies between 1607 and 1733. Their record in treatment of the Indians shows an improvement throughout the period. The earlier ideological struggle of Dutch and English against the Spanish monopoly ended at the Treaty of Utrecht which virtually admitted the principle of spheres of influence in the New World. It left England supreme at sea on both sides of the North Atlantic.

1. INTRODUCTORY

THE tale begins with the migration of certain tribes known somewhat indiscriminately as Saxons or Angles from Angeln in Germany to that part of the island of Britain which they renamed England. The cause and the method of this migration and the number of persons who migrated are quite unknown. All that we know is that the English first appear in history as a wandering and colonising race. They had to fight hard for their foothold for more than three hundred years before driving away or subduing the native Britons and fixing the English as opposed to the British frontier. With their backs to the sea they had become and remained for many centuries a race of land-lubbers. We know no reason for the change. They were now woodmen, ploughmen, swineherds, shepherds; they cleared the forests, drained the fens, multiplied and replenished the land until, a thousand years after the first migration from Angeln to England, there was a stirring in the hearts of the English who turned again to the sea and before long were sending out their sons to found another New England, and after that many more.

During the thousand sedentary years, two new strains of blood were crossed with the Anglo-Saxons. First the Norsemen, a nation of sea-traders and buccaneers, invaded and overran England. It is perhaps not fanciful to ascribe to them the emergence of a taste for commerce. Then came the Normans who damped down national patriotism for some generations, but brought to England the spirit of chivalry. Though Knight-errantry and Crusading were an outlet for the adventure-seekers, the English were still land-bound. Their exploits at first hardly carried them farther than the opposite shores of the English and the Irish Channels. There were raids and conquests, and feudal lordships won and lost in Scotland, Ireland, Wales and France; there was between the eleventh and the sixteenth centuries only one clear example of permanent English colonisation, the planting of 'Little England' among the Welsh of Pembrokeshire.

In Tudor times there was much talk of Empire, but of Empire in a sense quite different from that which fascinated Disraeli in the reign of Queen Victoria. The Statute of Appeals, by which the Parliament of England threw off the jurisdiction of the Pope, began with a magniloquent declaration in the preamble that this realm of England is an Empire and is so described in 'divers sundry old authentic histories and chronicles'. But in that context, and when Milton wrote, a hundred years later, of 'this Britannick Empire with all her daughter-islands about her' the English were not thinking of the Dominion over palm and pine that later imperialists applauded; their eye was fixed upon the large island Britain, with its satellites, Ireland, the Hebrides, Jersey, Man and the others. According to the mythical histories of King Arthur, which in Elizabethan England were accepted as true, the British Isles had successfully asserted their independence of Rome and formed an imperial realm, a thousand years before King Henry VIII. Remote as the fictions of Geoffrey of Monmouth may seem to be from modern colonial expansion, they have this nominal connexion. To the Elizabethan adventurers the word Empire conveyed suggestions of Arthurian romance; to the constitutional lawyers it suggested the old relation of the Crown to the Estates of Jersey, to the dependent kingdom of Man, and to the Dominion of Ireland. It is this that should be called the First British Empire; the American colonies came second, when feudal gave way to commercial expansion.

England slowly became an exporting country, her staple product being wool. For this the first of English trading companies, the Merchants of the Staple, set up a depot at Calais. Later a rival company, the Merchant Adventurers, established themselves at Bruges and Antwerp. There was, so long as victories over the French allowed, an import trade from Bordeaux which made claret, for a time, as cheap as beer in England; but a more profitable import was fish. The English sailors were not yet as active as the Portuguese, the Normans, or the Biscainers, and for long their progress was less than that of the Dutch, but the English fisheries had begun in the North Sea and occasionally had reached as far as Iceland. This industry came to be regarded as the nursery of English naval power and the school of navigation. Other foreign trade was chiefly in the hands of German and Italian shippers.

Small as these English undertakings were, there is other evidence that the English had a taste for voyaging. When spring returned, wrote Chaucer:

> Then priketh them nature in hir corages
> Then longen folk to goon on pilgrimages
> And palmers for to seken strangë strandës
> And fernë halwes couth in sondry landës.

The knight in Chaucer's day might go to Prussia and to Tunis, the Squire to 'chivachye' in Artois and in Flanders, the shipman to Spain; nor was the wife of Bath the only one who had 'passëd many a strangë stream' on the tourists' road to the Holy Land.

2. EARLY ENGLISH VOYAGES

CHAUCER's Dartmouth skipper knew all the 'creeks from Brittany to Spain', the natural direction of west-country commerce in the Middle Ages. The old alliances between the English and the Christian principalities of Portugal and Castile were long-established when John of Gaunt renewed them in Chaucer's day. English knights had fought in the twelfth-century crusades against the Moors and had assisted at the birth of the Portuguese kingdom. History records no time when English seamen did not frequent their seaports. Among the petty kingdoms of the Iberian Peninsula, as the Moors were driven southwards, Castile

predominated, except over Portugal, which retained its independence with English help. John of Gaunt had interests in
both camps; but, having designs of his own upon the Castilian
throne, he led an army of English archers to help the Portuguese
against the reigning king of Castile. He negotiated the Anglo-
Portuguese Treaty of Windsor (1386), so often renewed and
still, after 580 years, effective. Sturdy Portugal was England's
ally, but diplomatic and commercial links with Castile were also
strong. During the Age of Exploration, English seamen were
associated with their fellows of both nations, but, when Spain
and Portugal fell out, aligned themselves with the Portuguese.

According to an unconfirmed though quite credible tradition,
it was an Englishman, Robert Machin (or Macham) of Bristol,
who made the first advance into the Atlantic. The story is not as
familiar as it should be:

In the year 1344 [Hakluyt quotes from a Portuguese chronicle] the island
of Madeira was discovered by an Englishman, which was named Macham,
who, sailing out of England into Spain, with a woman that he had stolen,
[Anne D'Arcy according to another version] arrived by tempest in that
island, and did cast anchor in that haven or bay which now is called Machico,
after the name of Macham. And because his lover was seasick, he went on
land with some of his company, and the ship with a good wind made sail
away, and the woman died for thought. Macham, who loved her dearly, built
a chapel or hermitage to bury her in, calling it by the name of Jesus and
caused his name and hers to be written or graven upon the stone of her tomb,
and the occasion of their arrival there. And afterwards, he ordained a boat
made of one tree (for there be trees of a great compass about) and went to
sea in it, with those men that he had and were left behind with him, and came
upon the coast of Afrika without sail or oar. And when the Moors which
saw it took it to be a marvellous thing, and presented him unto the king of
that country for a wonder, that king also sent him and his companions for a
miracle unto the king of Castile. In the year 1395 . . . the information which
Macham gave of this island . . . moved many of France and Castile, to go and
discover it, and also the great Canaria.

Had the general outline of the African coast ever been quite
unknown to medieval seamen? Probably not, since Levantine
merchants dealt with Arabs whose commerce ran right down the
east coast of Africa from the Gulf of Aden to Madagascar; and,
on the west coast, followed the trade wind from Morocco down
to Cape Verde. But the Atlantic islands, though known and
described in antiquity and marked on Ptolemy's map, can only
have received the most casual of visits from travellers; or so it

appears from the state of their inhabitants when rediscovered in
the fifteenth century. The 'Guanches' of the Canaries were an
aboriginal white race, tall, fair-haired and blue-eyed, still living
in palaeolithic simplicity as cave-dwellers, dressed in skins, with
stones as their only weapons. The name Canaria was given to
the principal island because of the great dogs which 'served the
islanders instead of sheep for victual'. Perhaps Horace was right
in declaring that Phoenician traders had never reached these
islands:

> non huc Sidonii torserunt cornua nautae,
> laboriosa nec cohors Ulixei.

A voyage to so primitive a land reads like a chapter from
Herodotus, or like one of the Labours of Hercules, who was
indeed renowned for having reached these 'fortunate isles'.
Under that name, the crown of the Fortunate Isles was conferred
upon a Castilian prince (1360) by a grant from Pope Clement VI,
the source of all later Spanish claims and papal arbitrations upon
the dominion of the New World. Thirty years later a Norman
knight, with some legal pretension to administer this 'crown',
led an expedition to explore and subjugate the Canaries. His
right eventually lapsed to the kings of Castile, who intermittently sent expeditions to the islands during the fifteenth century.
These Spaniards, says Hakluyt, 'had divers English gentlemen in
their company whose posterity at present lives in the islands'.

The English also took part in the early Portuguese voyages.
'English merchantes and Almains' helped the Portuguese at the
siege of Ceuta in 1415, their first foothold in Africa and 'the first
occasion of all Portuguese discoveries'. The alliance was, in that
generation, firmly knit, its pledge being the great Prince Henry
the Navigator, the son of John of Gaunt's daughter. But, during
the systematic exploration of West Africa which he organised,
though French interlopers challenged and sometimes preceded
the Portuguese expeditions, we have no record of English intervention until the end of the period. In 1481 King John of Portugal
appealed to his good ally Edward IV to restrain his English
subjects from encroaching on the Portuguese 'seigneurie of
Guinea' where the strong castle of Sao Jorge al Mina (known to
the English as Elmina) had just been founded. Edward IV willingly agreed to put a stop to an expedition which William
Fabian and John Tintam were fitting out under Spanish patronage,

by an embargo which seems to have deterred Englishmen from other than clandestine trade with West Africa for two generations.

What part was taken by English mariners in the Discovery of the New World cannot be stated precisely, but it was not spectacular. The Bristol voyages to Labrador and Newfoundland originated in the North Atlantic fisheries of which no written record exists. As well as the Danes and Norwegians who voyaged to Iceland and beyond, the Bretons, Normans and Biscainers, English and Irish worked the deep-sea fisheries perhaps as far as the Newfoundland Banks without publishing their logs. They knew, and Columbus probably knew, the tale of Eric the Red, of the Danish settlements in Greenland still surviving in the fifteenth century, and of the voyages thence southward to a land where vines grew wild and the savages had copper-coloured skins. The Atlantic seaboard rang with similar stories of islands discovered in the west by Welsh princes, Irish monks and Norman adventurers long before the celebrated Spanish voyages. But the rough north-western seas revealed no Gold Coast, no Mexico or Peru, to tempt the cupidity of the kings of Europe as did the voyages south-westward from Portugal and Spain.

One series of early explorations only, that of John Cabot, has been recorded, and scantily. He was an Italian resident in Bristol whose ships made a landfall on some part of North America in 1497. Little more is known but that the parsimonious King Henry VII gave him a gratuity ('to him that found the new isle, £10') and retained him and his son Sebastian on a pension. Many years later at the court of Henry VIII, Sebastian Cabot was reputed an expert in geography and navigation and may have exaggerated his own youthful exploits. Further voyages from Bristol, from one of which, in 1502 some Indians were brought to England, led to no settlement in America, but originated the Newfoundland fisheries. John Rut in a king's ship, in 1527, found Normans, Bretons and Portuguese fishing for cod off the Newfoundland Banks. The French and Portuguese were deep-sea fishermen who brought home their catch packed in salt, but the English, who had no abundance of salt, preferred to fish off-shore and to preserve their fish by drying it on the beach. At some date unknown, seasonal fishermen's settlements appeared at St John's and other Newfoundland anchorages. By the end of Queen Elizabeth's reign there were reckoned to be engaged in the fisheries 9,000 seamen, the main force of the Royal Navy in time of war.

Trading ventures in those days were usually carried out by chartered companies of merchants, organised as guilds, that is to say trading associations, not financial companies. Within the guild each adventurer traded on his own account, investing his own goods, a great or small stock according to his means. If he had nothing better, Whittington the apprentice might even venture out his cat.[1] The Crown, for a consideration, extended its protection to the guildsmen, endowing them with a monopoly and the right to exclude interlopers. The guildsmen made their own conditions of trade. The system, with variations, was world-wide. In all countries within and without Christendom merchants endeavoured to obtain, from the rulers of foreign countries to which they traded, 'capitulations', that is the right to establish depots in which their resident agents enjoyed self-government under their own laws. The capitulation often included the right to raise a guard of soldiers for the defence of the settlement. The system was very ancient, having its origin in Roman law; it had been common throughout the history of Islam; it was still flourishing in many parts of the world in the twentieth century, and relics still survive here and there. The British Capitulations in China were relinquished only in 1943. At the period of the exploration of the New World several companies of Merchant Adventurers traded from English ports in this way, and new ventures tended to take this form. In 1530, King Henry VIII chartered the English merchants in Spain, long-established family firms like the Thornes of Bristol and the Hawkinses of Plymouth, who had resident agents not only in Spain but in the Canaries and at least one, a certain T. Tison, in the Spanish West Indies (1526).

But the middle of the sixteenth century was a time of financial instability. The introduction of bullion from America, especially

[1] There was a market for cats in Africa. On John Lock's voyage (1554) an English sailor stole a 'muske cat' from the natives who were 'very wary people in the bargaining'. They declined to trade any more and when the ship made sail along the coast to another market, the sailors found that the story of the cat had preceded them. No trade could be done until the cat was restored or paid for (Hakluyt). Von Harff, a German pilgrim of the fifteenth century, also reported that cats were still held sacred in Moslem Egypt as they had been in the days of the Pharaohs.

of silver from Mexico in the fifteen-forties, produced a great expansion in the currency and a corresponding rise in prices. At the same time the seizure of Church lands in the Protestant countries unsettled agriculture, glutting the market with land at knock-down prices and with unemployed labourers. Finally, the wars of religion broke the commercial links between the farming and fishing communities of north-western Europe and the trading and commercial cities of Flanders and the Rhineland. The loss of Calais to the French and the occupation of Antwerp by the Spaniards seemed to spell ruin to the English sheep-farmer.

From all these changes the profit came to the moneyed man. This is the period of the emergence of capitalism, in continental Catholic countries as much as in the Protestant countries around the North Sea. Wealth now came to consist of money rather than of goods, and money was available for investment overseas. The English capitalists were at first small men compared with the financiers who backed the King of Spain and the Emperor, but they made their market in the end. The first recorded joint-stock enterprise in English history is the Muscovy Company, incorporated in 1553. Nicholas Thorne of Bristol, a wealthy man who had been to America in 1502, long resided in Seville and wrote from there, in 1527, a letter to Henry VIII urging the despatch of voyages to find the North-east and North-west Passages. During the reign of Edward VI, Sebastian Cabot, now an old man, was again in England stimulating interest in exploration. Rivalry with the Hanse merchants of the Baltic suggested a new direction for adventure. As Edward VI lay dying, the ships of Willoughby and Chancellor were putting down London River for the discovery of a North-east Passage to the riches of the East. The Portuguese had found the South-east Passage round the Cape of Good Hope; the Spaniards the South-west Passage through Magellan Strait, and in searching for that had stumbled across the mines of Mexico and Peru; it was now the dream of the English to find a way north-east or north-west about. Willoughby and his men were lost in the ice, but Chancellor reached the White Sea and the Court of Czar Ivan the Terrible at Moscow. Diplomatic relations and a sporadic trade followed, but these belong to the history of commerce rather than the history of empire, though groups of English merchants settled in Novgorod and Moscow and have descendants there to-day. The significance of the Muscovy Company is that it was a financial company, not a mere trading association. The adventurers pooled their capital in a 'joint-stock', risking it all and agreeing to share the profits.

The outburst of activity in 1553 seems to have been a symptom of Protestant enthusiasm. The Wars of Religion in France and Holland began with privateering against the Catholic and maritime powers of Spain and Portugal. The English voyages to the north were matched by voyages, at the same time, into the forbidden waters of our old ally Portugal. In August 1553, Captain Thomas Windham sailed from Portsmouth with the *Primrose* and *Lion*, under guidance of a renegade Portuguese pilot, on a 'voyage unto Guinea and Benin, at the charges of certain merchant adventurers of London,...before never enterprised by Englishmen, or at least so frequented as at this present they are and may be...if the same be not hindered by the ambition of such, as for the conquering of forty or fifty miles here or there, and erecting of certain fortresses, think to be lords of half the world'. Accordingly, the avoidance of these 'certain fortresses' and especially of the Castle of Elmina was necessary to the voyage. Not many miles away they made a landfall and bought from the natives eighty tons of pepper which should have made a trading profit for an otherwise unfortunate venture. Windham and the pilot quarrelled perpetually and both died of fevers before the ships came home.

Next year Captain John Lock made a voyage to the Coast in the *Trinity*, a London ship. A long account of his voyage was published by Hakluyt with a wealth of geographical and other information, containing many wonders and much useful knowledge. He noted that the Africans above all things coveted brass wire for anklets and 'manilios';[1] and expatiated on the trade in 'Oliphants' teeth'. According to rumour, he brought home 5000 ounces of gold dust, 'certain black slaves, whereof some were tall and strong men, and could well agree with our meats and drinks'.

[1] 'Manilios', now known as 'manillas', are bracelets which recently passed for currency in South-eastern Nigeria. Two hundred years ago, the Bristol firm of R. and W. King (long since merged into the United Africa Company) was manufacturing hoops of bronze for export to the Coast, as Manilla currency.

William Towerson, who made two voyages to the Coast (1555 and 1556), was much impressed with the hard bargaining of the natives and already noted the influence of the European slave-trade. 'The Portugales were bad men,' said the natives, 'and made them slaves if they could take them.' Towerson preferred to make an effect with his panoply and then to barter 'manilios' for gold dust. He sent boats up some steamy African estuary, tricked out with Renaissance pageantry: twelve men 'with their morions and corslets; four trumpets, a drum and a fife; and a boat all hanged with streamers of silk'. He sent his men ashore with English longbows to shoot before an African king who 'with all his people wondered to see them shoot so far, and assayed to draw their bows and could not'. He also set out to hunt elephants with swords and longbows, but the elephants had the best of it.

The succession of voyages lapsed while Philip of Spain, as Queen Mary's husband, was England's ruler, and affronts to the Catholic powers were frowned on but, with the accession of the young Elizabeth, ventures to the Coast were soon renewed. In 1561 plans were set afoot for building a fort at Kormantin, a few miles from Elmina. William Rutter brought home 1750 lb. of ivory from thereabouts in 1562. There were tales of English merchants who had gone up-country farther to the east in the Bight of Benin. In 1566 George Fenner bought 'civet, musk, gold and grains' far to the west near Cape Verde, where he found the natives so suspicious of slave-raiders that they would not traffic without first exchanging hostages. A few years later Towerson was again on the Coast at Kormantin getting ivory and gold dust by the ounce, in exchange for basins and pots of tin, beads, blue coral, horse-tails, red cloth and kersey, brass basins and ewers, bells, gloves, and leather bags, but above all for 'manilios' of Brummagem wire. Every voyage found the Africans more suspicious and the Portuguese more active against these interlopers, until the voyages of John Hawkins led to diplomatic action. Three times between 1561 and 1564 embassies came from the court of Portugal to protest to Queen Elizabeth. In 1562 Hawkins picked up a cargo of 300 slaves off the African coast, by piracy the Portuguese alleged, from a Portuguese ship, and looked around for a market, which he found at Hispaniola in Spanish America. The trade, in our eyes infamous in itself, seems not to have been thought morally wrong; diplomatically it was audacious. The slave-traders broke the Portuguese law by exporting from Africa, and the Spanish law by importing to America, but the Spanish authorities at first turned a blind eye. Hawkins's third voyage (1567) ended in disaster, for there had arrived a new Spanish governor who treated the English interlopers as pirates. Their ship, crew and cargo were trapped at St Juan d'Ulua (near Vera Cruz in Mexico) and taken after a bloody fight, from which one of the few to escape was young Francis Drake, thereafter the lifelong enemy of Spain.

By the Papal Bull of 1493 and its later amendments, all the newly discovered lands west of a meridian in mid-Atlantic had been allotted to the King of Spain and those east of the line to the King of Portugal, but from the beginning the English never admitted the claim of Spain and Portugal to exclude all other nations from these territories and even from adjacent seas. They might have objected on the grounds that Free Trade had been established by treaty with both Portugal and Spain, or on the ground that Protestant Englishmen now rejected the international jurisdiction of the Pope. In fact they stood on other grounds. Queen Elizabeth never subscribed to the doctrine put forward by most other sovereigns, English and foreign, that there could be national dominion over the sea. 'The use of the sea and air', she said, is 'common to all.' As for the land, she and her advisers soon developed the useful principle that there could be no dominion without 'effective occupation'. Merely to proclaim the annexation of a territory was insufficient; a ruler who asserted his dominion should be in a position to enforce it. The Portuguese had a fine castle at Elmina on the Gold Coast. Very well, that and the region controlled by it were lawful territory of the Portuguese King. But if the English were gladly received a hundred miles away by a native prince who was anxious to exchange gold dust for trade goods the Portuguese King should not complain. His remedy was to forbid his subjects to trade with the English and to enforce his orders, if he could. Queen Elizabeth took shares in several African ventures and found them very profitable; she rather enjoyed the ensuing diplomatic exchanges with the Portuguese ambassador.

A new turn in the negotiations came in 1580 when King Philip of Spain asserted his right to the Portuguese throne on the death of the king, and proceeded to the conquest of Portugal. Then for sixty years the New Worlds in the east and west were united under one despotic ruler, in economic and religious enmity to the petty Protestant states of northern Europe. When the old alliance between England and Portugal parted after wearing thin in the preceding years, Elizabeth could harass Philip of Spain by cherishing Don Antonio, her pretender to the Portuguese throne, and could make trouble for Spain by stirring conspiracies in Portugal. As for the adventurers, they could now enrich themselves in the lands the Portuguese affected to call their dominion, treating that as they treated the dominions of Spain.

In 1585 letters-patent were issued to 'noblemen and merchants of London for a trade to Barbary' within the dominions of the Emperor of Morocco; and in 1588 a charter to merchants of Exeter and London for a trade to 'the river of Senega and of Gambia in Guinea'. The latter, for the first of the African Companies, was a stroke in Anglo-Portuguese politics. 'The traffique' would 'in time be very beneficial to these our realms and dominions,...also a great succour and relief unto...those Portugals who live here under our protection'. The merchants were to have a monopoly, which was justified on the grounds that the 'adventuring and enterprising of a new trade cannot be a matter of small charge and hazard to the adventurers in the beginning'.

English trade was spreading south and east. The Levant Company, whose merchants ran the gauntlet between Barbary rovers and Spanish galleys, was chartered in 1581 and soon made figs, dates and currants and muslin cloth from Mosul better known in England.

The first Englishman, so far as we know, to visit India was Father Thomas Stevens, a Jesuit, who was sent to the Portuguese establishment at Goa in 1579. He was a man of science, who wrote home to explain the method of finding the longitude by studying the variation of the compass, and became so proficient in Indian languages as to compose vernacular poems which are still admired. No doubt this good man welcomed the sight of a fellow-countryman's face when, in 1582, Ralph Fitch, with two other Englishmen, appeared at Goa and threw themselves on Stevens's mercy. Ralph Fitch was a merchant who had made earlier voyages in the Near East. In 1582 he set off for Aleppo in the *Tiger* (the ship cursed by the witches in *Macbeth*) with a party of merchants of the Turkey Company, carrying a letter from Queen Elizabeth to the Great Mogul Akbar, whom they addressed as the King of Cambay. John Newbery led the expedition, their intention being, it seems, to trade in gems with the help of William Leeds, a jeweller; but there were others in the party including James Story, a portrait-painter, who joined them on his own account as a private venture.

The party came to Goa by sea from Ormuz, having passed from one Portuguese post to another, often finding a friendly reception. But at Goa they were imprisoned and threatened with expulsion from the Portuguese dominions; and with worse treatment when King Philip, now King of Portugal as well as of Spain, came to hear of their arrival. However, with the good offices of Stevens, since all three professed to be papists, they were released on bail and allowed to escape over the frontier. In 1584 or 1585 they reached Akbar's court at Agra, though their letters say little of what they achieved there. It is not known whether they succeeded in delivering the Queen's letter to the Mogul. Leeds settled at the Mogul's court, where a jeweller would not lack business. Fitch went on alone to Bengal, Arakan, Bassein, and the kingdom of Pegu, where he was mightily impressed by the Shwe Dagon Pagoda, 'the fairest place, as I suppose, that is in the world'. He even reached the Portuguese station of Malacca and brought back news of the Chinese trade at Macao. He returned home in 1591 by the Portuguese sea-routes, after an absence of eight years. His companions vanished from the pages of history.

Fitch concluded his report by 'declaring some of the things which India and the country further eastward do bring forth': pepper, ginger, cloves, nutmegs, mace, sandalwood, camphor (which is sold 'dearer than golde') aloes, benjamin, long pepper, musk, ambergris, rubies, sapphires, 'spinelles', diamonds, pearls and many kinds of drugs. He described the places where they are found and the method of obtaining them like a tradesman, with accuracy, and no doubt expatiated on these subjects when, eight years later, he was summoned to advise the founders of the East India Company.

At least one private adventurer anticipated the East Indian merchants. A disreputable free-lance named John Mildenhall found his way to the court of Akbar in 1603, asserting that he had a commission from Queen Elizabeth. Later he reappeared in England saying that he had obtained concessions from the Mogul, for which he demanded large payments from the Company. His whole story lacked confirmation beyond the fact that he had been to Agra where he antagonised the Portuguese agents, and, apparently, had spoken with the great Akbar, the only Englishman who claimed to have done so. In 1611 he was again in India selling what was said to be stolen merchandise. He died in 1614 and was buried at Agra where his tomb is shown, the oldest existing relic of the British in India.

The outbreak of war with Spain led to an extension of the privateering war into the eastern seas. James Lancaster with three ships, *Penelope*, *Marchant Royal* and *Edward Bonaventure* led a commerce-raiding expedition into the Indian Ocean in 1591. He called at the Cape, not yet occupied by the Dutch, to buy cattle and fat-tailed sheep from 'very brutish black salvages', at the rate of a beast for a knife of Sheffield steel, and saw besides 'divers sorts of wild beasts unknown to us and great store of overgrown monkeys'. At Zanzibar he attempted negotiation with the Portuguese on the score that 'we were Englishmen come from Don Antonio [the Pretender] upon business to his men in the Indies', but met such plain evidence of hostility as to justify reprisals in the Indian Ocean.

All through 1592, after sending home one ship for lack of men and parting company with another, Lancaster cruised in the Indian Ocean, from Galle in Ceylon to Penang in Malaya, taking two large prizes and several smaller ones; but more valuable than his plunder, which he was not fated to bring home, was the news of the trade the Portuguese had tapped with 'the Maine of India': 'Pavilions for beds and wrought quilts' from 'Bangala', Calicut cloth, rice from Tenasserim, rubies and diamonds from Pegu. What prospects of wealth might not lie beyond since 'the Portugals have discovered the coast of China to the latitude of 59°, finding the sea still open to the northward and giving great hope of the Northeast and Northwest Passage'?

On his way home in 1593, Lancaster put in at the lonely island of St Helena to take up a maroon, John Segar of Bury, who had been left there fifteen months earlier by one of the other ships. The unfortunate man was found 'in good plight of body but half out of his wits...'. Whether in fright or of sudden joy at seeing Lancaster's ship he became 'idle-headed' and soon died.

Lancaster's voyage ended in disaster. His crew, turning mutinous, deserted him in the West Indies so that he arrived home empty-handed and almost alone, as a passenger in a French ship. The news he brought of the riches of the East opened prospects for trade on a vaster scale than Guinea, Barbary or Newfoundland afforded, and led to the foundation of the East India Company on the last day of the sixteenth century.

3. THE WEST-COUNTRY ADVENTURERS

THE group of west-countrymen who founded Virginia began their careers with the French and Dutch Protestant rebels. Such a mixture of motives is rarely to be found as that of the Gilberts, the Grenvilles and their kind, Devon and Cornwall squires, aristocrats by birth, scholars by breeding, pirates and wreckers by local tradition. A quixotic knight-errantry, exemplified in the last fight of the *Revenge*, was in their blood:

> Who seeks to wear the laurel crown
> Or hath the mind that would aspire,
> Let him his native land eschew,
> Let him go range and seek a new.

These were verses of the elder Richard Grenville, and this was the spirit in which Nicholas Thorne of Bristol said to Henry VIII, 'I judge there is no land unhabitable nor sea innavigable.'

Politically they were of the anti-Spanish party at a time when appeasement of Spain was the aim of Queen Elizabeth's government. They were Protestant leaders in the west country and opposed to the old religion which lingered there. They are largely responsible for the English prejudice against the Pope and the King of Spain, whom they most inaccurately represented as inseparable allies sworn to destroy the prosperity, the freedom, and the religion of England. The leader of this group was Humphrey Gilbert; young Walter Ralegh (1552–1618) was his half-brother. The Grenvilles, a dynasty of splendid adventurers, were headed in this generation by Sir Richard of the *Revenge*, one of Gilbert's associates. Richard Hakluyt (1552–1616) devoted a laborious life, as chronicler of the group, to recording *The*

Principal Navigations, Voyages, Traffiques and Discoveries of the English Nation made by sea or over Land to the Remote and farthest Distant Quarters of the Earth at any time within the compass of these 1600 years. Francis Drake (1540–96), the curate's son from Tavistock, the greatest sailor of them all, was an outlier, associated in some of their enterprises but hardly to be counted one of their number.

Since about 1560 the French Huguenots had been attempting to found colonies in America; again and again the settlers were dispersed and massacred by the Spaniards. Thus the west-country privateers, who were friends of the Huguenot leaders, turned their attention to the Spanish Main. As early as 1574 Grenville had petitioned the Queen for a Charter to plant 'certain rich lands fatally and it seemeth by God's providence reserved for England', in the direction of the River Plate. Drake's voyage round the world (1577–80), the second such voyage following the path taken by Magellan sixty years earlier, was authorised by those members of the English government who desired to limit the expanding frontiers of the Spanish Empire and to encroach upon the Spanish power. Walsingham, the Secretary of State, supported him; the Queen and Burleigh were believed to favour, in public at least, the policy of appeasing Spain. Hence some mysterious features in Drake's story; Drake had his private wrongs to avenge upon the Spaniards. He was a merciful man, most unlike his fellow-adventurers in being not at all addicted to bloodshed, but he would take his reprisal for the loss of his ship and cargo at St Juan d'Ulua. It was probably for some political difference between the peace party and the war party among his officers that he denounced his friend Doughty as a traitor, and executed him after court-martial on the bare coast of Patagonia.

Not till he had passed Magellan Strait and entered the Pacific did Drake cease to be a peaceable free-trader and begin to wage private war against the commerce of the King of Spain. The treasure ship *Cacafuego* which, said Drake, should have been named Spit-silver not Spit-fire, the pile of silver ingots quietly removed from the care of a sleeping Spanish sentry at Valparaiso, the mule-train of silver seized on the Isthmus of Panama, with some smaller prizes, satisfied his cupidity and made the name of El Draque, the dragon, renowned as the worst of all pirates in

Plate I A

SIR FRANCIS DRAKE
(1540?–96)

This and the following portraits of Gilbert and Frobisher are taken from *Heroologia*, an illustrated series of biographies edited by H. Holland, 1620. The engravings are based upon contemporary portraits. *See p. 16.*

Plate I B

SIR HUMPHREY GILBERT
(1539?–83)

Projector and pioneer of British expansion overseas. *See p. 17.*

Plate 2A

CAPTAIN JOHN SMITH
(1580–1631)

Aged 37. The frontispiece to his description of New England. *See p. 21.*

Plate 2B

SIR MARTIN FROBISHER
(1535?–94)

'Very valiant but withal harsh and violent.' *See p. 18.*

Spanish story. Later in the voyage came his work as empire-builder. He sailed north along the American coast as far as California, to latitude 38° N., landed and proclaimed 'New Albion' a dominion of Queen Elizabeth. No Englishman went there again for 200 years, but the doctrine of effective occupation, which we found so useful against Portugal and Spain, was now conveniently overlooked and, in the eighteenth century, the lands known later as California, Oregon and British Columbia were claimed for Britain by right of Drake's annexation.

This was for the future. More immediately valuable was his descent upon the Spice Islands across the Pacific from the East. It was no slight blow to Portuguese pretensions and no small advantage in Queen Elizabeth's eyes that in the Moluccas he made a treaty of friendship and commerce with the Sultan of Ternate. Drake returned westward about the Cape of Good Hope. The Queen's share in the profits of his voyage was £80,000, of which she invested half in the stock of the Levant Company.

Drake's later voyages against Spain and the Indies fall outside the scope of this book. His character was true English. An affable, short, stocky, bullet-headed man with reddish hair, he was practical, business-like, plain-spoken, and no theoriser; a good citizen and benefactor of Plymouth in the time of his prosperity. He had his pride, and dined alone at sea off silver to the sound of violins, but showed an honest contempt for idle gallants. He 'would have the gentlemen to pull and haul with the common sailors'. Drake's legendary drum sounded again in 1939, in Exeter Guildhall, to record another triumph for the men of Devon in action off the River Plate against a different foe. The old trade is still plying.

Sir Humphrey Gilbert (1539–83) was an indefatigable writer and projector. His *Discourse of a Discovery for a New Passage to Cataia* led to the founding of the abortive Company of Cathay and to at least fifteen voyages in search of the North-west Passage (Frobisher 1576, 1577, 1578; Davis 1585, 1587; Waymouth 1601; Knight 1606; Hudson 1610, 1611; Button 1612; Baffin 1615, 1616; Fox 1631; James 1631, 1632). Their little ships pried into the icy straits and sounds, searching for an ice-free route to the west, and searching also for the gold and silver mines that other voyagers to the Americas had found. The maps based upon

Baffin's charts showed a knowledge of the lie of the land that rather decayed during the next 200 years. Hudson Strait, Frobisher Bay, Davis Strait, James' Sound and, in the farthest north, Smith Sound named after Sir Thomas Smythe (or Smith), the patron of so many ventures, were charted by these early explorers, who contributed mightily to the literature of travel. James's voyages provided much of the local colour used by Coleridge's *Ancient Mariner*.

Sir Martin Frobisher (1535–94), who brought home accounts of the Red Indians of Newfoundland, was the first adventurer to proclaim the annexation of American ground to the English Crown, in 1576, on the frigid coast of Baffin Land. Entering Frobisher Bay, which he called Frobisher Strait, he supposed that the land on his right hand was a projection of North-east Asia and that his strait was the long-sought passage. His later voyages were treasure-hunts, since he was allured by the mineral wealth of the Arctic. Though he mistook pyrites for gold he pioneered better than he knew, by discovering the riches that lay unused in Northern Canada until our own age. Frobisher was 'very valiant', says Hakluyt, 'but withal harsh and violent (faults which may be dispensed with in one of his profession)'. Having commanded a Queen's ship against the Spanish Armada he was killed in one of the later battles of the war.

In 1578 Gilbert obtained from the Queen a charter authorising him 'to discover, find, search out and view such remote heathen and barbarous lands not actually possessed by a Christian prince or people...and the same to have, hold, occupy and enjoy for ever with all commodities, jurisdiction and royalties both by sea and by land', a generous donation, as extravagant as anything ever granted by the Pope to the King of Spain. But this comprehensive plan included something more than peaceful settlement. The colony was to be a base from which to harass the Spaniards without open declaration of war, and to stake out claims in the New World.

In 1583 Gilbert set out to found his colony, intending, as he wrote, to find a cure for unemployment by planting labourers in America where their needs would make a market for English manufactured goods. Trade with our own colonies would reduce the necessity of importing from foreign lands and thus adjust the balance of trade in our favour; such was the economic theory of the age. On his way to America, he put in at St John's Bay, Newfoundland, where he ceremoniously proclaimed its annexation 'two hundred leagues every way' before the crews of thirty-six English, French and Portuguese fishing craft. After a short stay he set off 'to annoy the Spaniards', promising to return next year with greater force. Bearing away southward in stormy weather, Gilbert proudly shifted his flag into the smaller of his two vessels, a mere fishing-smack of ten tons, which vanished in a squall. The last who saw him from the larger ship described him sitting in the stern-sheets, wrapped in a cloak, reading in More's *Utopia*, and crying out through a lull in the storm More's words: 'we are as near heaven by sea as by land'.

An earlier visitor to Newfoundland, Anthony Parkhurst, had told Hakluyt in 1578 that Spanish and Portuguese ships outnumbered English and French on the Banks, although the English who landed to dry their fish were 'commonly lords of the harbours'. He was for occupying and fortifying the island in order to monopolise the fisheries. Gilbert did not stay to carry out this project, which was not revived for another thirty years. But when war broke out with Spain in 1585, one of the opening moves was a raid upon the Spanish Newfoundland fleet by Sir Bernard Drake, a kinsman of the great Sir Francis. The Spanish ships were seized or scattered and did not again frequent the Newfoundland coast. The first permanent settlement of Newfoundland, in 1610, may be reserved for a later chapter.

On the death of Gilbert, his half-brother Ralegh took up the cause. He remains after a hundred criticisms an inexplicable and fascinating figure. 'He was a tall handsome bold man but...he was damnable proud.' His colony of Virginia was to have been no mere trading post or dependency but a new home for Englishmen. His colonists were to 'enjoy all the privileges of free denizens of England' and were conceived as substantial yeomen, 'the least that he hath granted being 500 acres'. But the first Virginia colony at Roanoke failed. The settlers were ill-chosen and lacked capital and the site on Chesapeake Bay was unlucky. Two settlements were attempted, but all came to nothing. The settlers disappeared.

Next year (1585) came the open breach with Spain and a host of other activities for Ralegh. His contemporary fame rested more on his Guiana voyage of 1595 and the rolling eloquence with which he wrote of it. Guiana, the land between the Orinoco and the Amazon, was a land of wonders and treasures which the Spaniards had not grasped. Ralegh's fatal search for the Golden City of Manoa was a more romantic quest than the Virginia expedition. Yet who need set limits to his imagination after reading what the Spaniards had already found in Mexico and Peru? There was sound sense as well as vision in the quest for Eldorado, even for the Amazonian women whom Ralegh hoped to bring under the protection of a Virgin Queen. There was gold, as he proved, but no gilded cacique, rich city or tribe of women-warriors so far as he could find, yet a country where the Spaniards might be forestalled. Even though his second voyage, twenty years later, did embroil him with a Spanish force, Guiana was never a Spanish Dominion. Many attempts to colonise it were made by English, French and Dutch during the next hundred years, the only lasting settlements being the Dutch colony at Essequibo (1616) and the French at Cayenne (1665).

The later years of Ralegh's active life before his disgrace and imprisonment were given to another colonising project, the 'plantation of Ireland'. From the days of Elizabeth to those of Cromwell the language of colonisation—'natives', 'settlers', 'plantations'—is habitually used by Englishmen of Ireland. The 'wild Irish' were to be subdued, expropriated in favour of English settlers and confined to certain districts; they were, in short, to be treated as the American Indians were treated, according to the social morality of the age. Not only the proud, fierce Ralegh but such mild humane men as the poet Spenser wrote in this strain. The organisation of the first American colonies owes something to experience gained in the plantation of Derry.

Ralegh is traditionally reputed to have introduced the potato from America to Ireland. He is also remembered as the man who made tobacco-smoking fashionable in England. These two homely results of his American undertakings would alone have made the name of a lesser man. After the accession of James I (who among many fads hated the smell of tobacco) Ralegh fell into disfavour. He was imprisoned and attainted and, largely to curry favour with the Spanish ambassador, was at last beheaded. Before his death a new Virginia colony had begun to flourish. 'I shall yet live to see it an English nation', he had prophesied in his dark days.

4. THE FIRST ENGLISH COLONIES

(1) VIRGINIA

WHEN in financial difficulties in 1589 Ralegh assigned his interests in Virginia to a group of adventurers among whom were Hakluyt, Sir Thomas Smythe a rich merchant, and two returned settlers named White and Dare. After the Peace with Spain in 1604 they revived the old schemes. Hakluyt's efforts brought in the political support of the Earl of Southampton, Shakespeare's patron, and Smythe aroused the interest of the city. In 1606, when Ralegh was a prisoner in the Tower, a Royal Council for Virginia was created in London, to administer the trade and plantation of the American coast between the thirty-fourth and forty-fifth parallels of latitude. Two colonies were to be established, a 'London' and a 'Plymouth' colony. Both were founded in Virginia in 1607, and both were financial failures. In the whole history of colonisation, then and for many generations thereafter, it was never appreciated that a steady continuous flow of capital and labour was required in the early years of a new settlement. The 'Plymouth' colony on the Kennebec River was abandoned; the 'London' colony at Jamestown was like to have been until the settlers were disciplined, organised and set to work by the redoubtable Captain John Smith (1580–1631).

Smith had been everywhere and claimed to have tried his hand at everything. The evidence about his adventures in the Turkish wars and about his experiences with the Red Indians depends solely upon his own sensational narratives; the facts are that he bullied and cajoled the Jamestown colonists through the critical winter of 1608–9, and set up friendly relations with the Indians, exchanging trade goods for food. Pocahontas, the Indian princess who, according to Smith's narrative, saved his life from her father Powhatan really lived and befriended the English. She married an Englishman named John Rolfe, the first settler to cultivate tobacco in Virginia, and died at Gravesend during a brief visit to England, where she was long remembered as 'la belle sauvage'.

In 1609 and again in 1612 the Virginia charter was remodelled. The general government was placed in the hands of the shareholders in London, with Sir Thomas Smythe as treasurer. Membership was extended to those who invested £12. 10s. in the common stock, and to the 'planters' whose contribution was their labour and that of their servants. In the colony there was no prosperity until the original communism was abandoned and individual holdings of twelve acres of land allotted. Labouring servants, who might eventually work out their indentures and join the class of free planters, were also imported. This system of indentured labour was used to rid the home country of undesirables and unemployables. As well as the few men of high blood whom the 'First Five Hundred Families' of Virginia now proudly claim as their ancestors there were also convicted felons and insolvent debtors. Gondomar, the Spanish ambassador, reported to his master a tale of three condemned felons who were offered the choice of Virginia or the gallows. Two seized the chance of life, but the third heartily preferred to be hanged and stood to his decision.

Rarely in colonial history has a satisfactory solution been found of the problem how and when to turn over the administration from the founders at home who provide the capital to the settlers abroad who employ it. Originally the intention had been for the settlers to elect a local council with authority to make grants of land in the name of the Crown and to prepare local by-laws which should be 'not repugnant to the laws of England'. The hardships and failures of the first few years made a sterner rule necessary. From 1609 to 1618 the colony was under the military rule of powerful governors sent out to represent the shareholders. In 1618 political changes at home led to an attack on the privileges of the Company and to the displacement of Smythe. The Company lingered on till 1632 but never paid a dividend. Meanwhile a new era of free trade began in Virginia where there were now 1000 white settlers. Instructions were sent out for the governor to summon a 'house of burgesses', the first offspring of the Mother of Parliaments, in 1619. Prosperity was now in sight. An export trade was at last established in tobacco, and already a cargo of negro slaves had been imported to work for the planters.

(2) CALIBAN'S ISLAND

One of the early governors of Virginia brought out in his train Sir George Somers who, in 1609, was cast ashore on a beautiful unknown island in mid-Atlantic, where his men lived for months on turtles and wild pigs. Somers's nephew, who succeeded to the command on his uncle's death, persuaded the Virginia Company to plant this isle, Bermuda, the third British colony after Virginia and Newfoundland. In 1612 they sent out a modest company of fifty settlers under Richard Moore, a ship's carpenter, who found, when they reached Bermuda, three maroons in residence, deserters from Somers's ship. Like most founders of colonies Moore met with mutiny and discontent at his settlement of St George's in the first years, until the plantation became self-supporting. A subsidiary company was formed in 1615, the 'London Company for the Somer Islands', which played the unpopular role of absentee proprietor until 1684 when, at the petition of the colonists, it was dissolved. Otherwise their life was of Arcadian simplicity. In 1629 their numbers had reached 2000 and in 1679, 8000, by which time they had been reinforced with political exiles and some negro slaves; but slavery in Bermuda was of a mild domestic character. Some puritan malcontents, under William Sayle (d. 1670), moved on from Bermuda in 1656 to found another island community at Eleuthera in the uninhabited Bahamas.

From 1684 Bermuda was a royal colony; its Assembly, elected since 1620 by representatives of the nine parishes, is second only to the Assembly of Virginia in seniority among the Parliaments overseas.

This delightful land, an isle
full of noises
Sounds and sweet airs that give delight and hurt not

caught the popular imagination. The English discoverer named the group the Somers Islands, but two great poems in the seventeenth century fixed upon the Islands their Spanish name, Bermuda, 'in the Ocean's bosom unespied', 'an isle far kinder than our own', as Andrew Marvell wrote. To the mature mind of Shakespeare the 'Bermoothes', the magic isle of Ariel and Caliban, gave the occasion for his last masterpiece, perhaps the most deeply philosophical and the most purely poetical of all his works, a closely constructed symphony on the subject of calm after storm and shipwreck. Among the strains that build up the harmony the themes of sea-adventure and discovery, the nobilities and the meannesses of empire-builders, the Utopian dreams of projectors, the well-intentioned paternal government that overreaches itself, the grossness of savagery with its sudden surprising gleams of grandeur, and the great design like to be marred by the beastliness of the drunken underlings, 'the poor whites', all occur and recur in the music till, 'like this insubstantial pageant faded', the projects and the projectors pass away leaving the sea-girt island to its aboriginal inhabitants.

The Tempest is not a treatise on the art of colonisation, but it contains a notable portrait of a savage. The first quite primitive, quite barbarous nation encountered by the English mariners were the Caribs of the West Indies, now almost extinct. They were fierce in defence of their liberties and untamable. Neither Spaniards nor English could make either slaves or converts of them. They stood condemned in Christian eyes because they occasionally practised the rite of sacrificing and eating human flesh, a custom which inspired our ancestors with superstitious horror. Caribs or Cannibals, the name is spelt either way, were beyond the bounds of pity. Shakespeare's monster, Caliban, offspring of the devil and a witch, whose name is but a poetic variant of 'cannibal', presents the savage as an Elizabethan audience expected to see him. He learns to speak intelligibly only from his white master, yet he will not

> ...fetch in firing
> At requiring,
> Nor scrape trencher,
> Nor wash dish.

In return for kindness he only plots to murder his master and ravish his master's daughter. But the universal sympathy of Shakespeare went deeper than that, and was exercised to draw a subtle parallel between the savage and the renegade white sailor. The savage was the better man.

The horror of barbarous rites lasted long even among Europeans who were themselves indifferent Christians. A hundred years later the writings of Defoe are full of violent denunciations of cannibalism. Crusoe on his island, for all his piety and all his

natural tenderness towards Man Friday, could not refrain from
slaying at sight those other Indians whom he believed guilty of
eating human flesh. Other barbarisms might be eradicated and
forgiven, but not that. This abomination, this European taboo
on a practice which has been world-wide, remained in full force
until the present age, and, no doubt, still exists, though the analysis
of primitive customs by modern anthropologists has thrown a
new light upon it.

Savages who practised these 'abhorred', 'inhuman' customs
got no consideration at law. The scholastic philosophers had
written and argued on the civil rights of pagans in conflict with
Christians, but this did not become a practical problem until the
age of colonisation. The early Spanish missionaries, especially
Las Casas, in vain demanded legal protection for their actual and
potential converts. Greed for land and contempt for the habits
of the Indians alike swayed the settlers in the other direction.
The common form of colonial charters was to allow the adventurers to occupy at will 'lands not actually possessed by any
Christian prince or people': which suited the settlers very well
when it was a question of expropriating a few naked barbarians,
but which they did not see fit to attempt if they happened upon
the shores of a monarch as powerful as the Sultan of Turkey or the
Great Mogul.

Among the mixed motives of the English voyagers the impulse
to extend the Christian religion was not wanting. It is very
prominently given as a motive in the Virginia charter of 1606.
One of the projectors was the celebrated pietist Nicholas Ferrar.
'In all places where I came,' wrote one of Ralegh's staff, 'I did
my best to make God's immortal glory known.' 'Reducing
heathen people to civility and true religion' is mentioned by
Captain John Smith as a more important object than 'gaining
provinces' for the King's crown. Drake's chaplain wrote that
when the Californian Indians seemed to worship the voyagers as
gods, 'we fell to prayers and singing of psalms whereby they
were allured to forget their folly'. But these slight evidences of
intention are poor indeed beside the heroic zeal of the Spanish
Jesuits in America and Asia.

The English were not yet a missionary people. It was by ruder
qualities that they were beginning to make their mark. 'The

English', wrote a Venetian ambassador, 'would never yield and though driven back and thrown into confusion they always return to the fight.' As with the men so with their ships: 'for strength, assurance, nimbleness and swiftness of sailing there are no vessels in the world to be compared with them', wrote another contemporary. A thousand lesser men like these are forgotten while a few great names are recorded. A commonplace of colonial history is the arrival of a chartered and renowned expedition at the goal to find some nameless squatter or interloper already in possession. To identify the first settler, even the first discoverer of a new island, is rarely an easy task. Especially in the West Indies, voyages of exploration overlap, charters regrant what has unknowingly been granted to another claimant, settlers with designs on one island plant another, claims are jumped, or schemes anticipated. Ralegh's Guiana voyage and first Virginia colony were followed by scores of English expeditions and projects. Soon the merchant adventurers were flocking to these islands which contained at least two British settlements before King James died.

Among obscurer men should not be forgotten those forerunners of overseas expansion who sailed under foreign flags, such men as Chambers, the English sailor of whom we know nothing but that he sailed with Magellan; Henry Hudson who commanded a Dutch ship to the river and bay that bear his name; and William Adams of Gillingham who found his way to Japan, also in a Dutch ship, and ended his days there building ships for the Mikado.

(3) NEW ENGLAND

Captain John Smith first drew attention to the land he called New England. After leaving Virginia he went on several whaling voyages off the North American coast. 'Of all the four parts of the world that I have yet seen not inhabited,' he wrote in 1616, 'I would rather live [there] than anywhere....New England is great enough to make many kingdoms and countries, were it all inhabited.' The proprietary rights over New England were disputed between two authorities in London, the Virginia Company and a new 'Council for New England' over which presided the Duke of Buckingham. Against both of them the west-country fishing interests were arrayed since it was thought

THE 'MAYFLOWER'   27

that access to the Newfoundland fisheries would be restricted by
settlers on adjacent shores. These barren quarrels may now be
forgotten, for a colonising influence of a new and stronger kind
was at work.

For many years small groups of uncompromising English
puritans had been settled in Holland, the only European state
where there was complete religious toleration. In 1617, one such
congregation determined to plant a new state in the New World
far from all corrupting influences. Their agents were received
favourably by the Virginia Company who made them a grant of
land 500 miles to the north of the previous Virginian settlements.
They obtained the permission of the Crown to go overseas, and
had little difficulty in raising capital from a group of London
merchants who saw possibilities in the New England fur trade and
the fisheries.

Thus began the voyage of the *Mayflower* which left Plymouth
on 6 September 1620, and anchored off Cape Cod two months
later. Of the 102 passengers thirty-five were the original Puritan
congregation; the remainder were casual emigrants including, as
all companies of settlers included, a proportion of wastrels.

During the voyage the colonists, who were saddled with no
Lord Proprietor and no governing council, drew up a 'social
contract', one of the few actual examples of such a document in
the history of the world. Admitting themselves to be already
members of a civil society they formally constituted it a state.
Forty-one signatures were appended, on 11 November 1620, to
this declaration: 'In the name of God, amen. We whose names
are underwritten, the loyal subjects of our dread sovereign King
James, having undertaken, for the glory of God and advancement
of the Christian faith and honour of our King and country, a
voyage to plant the first colony in the northern parts of Virginia,
do, by these presents, solemnly and mutually in the presence of
God and of one another, covenant and combine ourselves together into a civil body politic, for our better ordering and
preservation and furtherance of the ends aforesaid; and by
virtue thereof to enact, constitute and frame such just and equal
laws, ordinances, acts, constitutions, and offices, from time to time,
as shall be thought more convenient for the general good of
the colony, unto which we promise all due submission and
obedience.'

This admirable document, the first written constitution in the history of the Anglo-Saxon peoples, did not imply that New England was to be a free state, but quite the contrary. The original Puritan settlers held themselves to be a chosen people who had withdrawn from the world and did not propose to allow its corruptions to seep in. Their little commonwealth was an exclusive oligarchy ruled by the elders of the Church with ferocious intolerance. They had not gone out into the wilderness to indulge freedom of thought but to ensure a rigid uniformity. Let us forgive them that. They starved in the snow of a New England winter, survived to sow and reap their first harvest and made for it a yearly festival of Thanksgiving to the God who sent Abraham and Moses by faith into the wilderness. In faith they built 'a city with foundations'.

The little colony of the Pilgrim Fathers drew small attention at the time. The second Puritan colony was a much larger affair. The Rev. John White of Dorchester was a coloniser on a great scale. His *General Considerations for Planting New England* appeared in 1629 when the dispute between King Charles I and the Puritans had reached its first crisis. He desired to make a city of refuge in America for the righteous, 'to raise a bulwark against the Kingdom of Antichrist which the Jesuits labour to build up in all parts of the world . . . to avoid the plague while it is foreseen and not to tarry'. When it came to the point, however, White did not find it necessary to go there, nor did the authorities of the Kingdom of Antichrist show hostility to the righteous. The process of plantation took the usual form. With the help of the Puritan Earl of Warwick a grant of land was got from the Council for New England, and the Massachusetts Company was formed under a charter from the Crown. It differed from the trading companies of earlier days in the essential feature that so soon as the legal forms were complete, and an advance party had prepared the ground, the whole Company, its members and their families with their patent from the Crown, transferred themselves in a body to New England. The advance party had consisted of 300 settlers; in 1630 John Winthrop led the main body of 1000 settlers to the new colony. Their numbers rapidly increased until, ten years later, they were 14,000. As among the Pilgrim Fathers, political power was strictly confined to Church members, who were not more than one in five of the adult males.

Religious orthodoxy was imposed with far more rigour than in royalist England. Religious persecution of minorities broke out almost at once.

Comfort, though not luxury, quickly came to New England. The English were in those days still a rustic agricultural people. The New Englanders came from a frugal, industrious and enterprising branch of that farming stock. Land was to be had for the taking in Massachusetts without the irksome restrictions of English customary tenure. Here there were no common fields to lower the standard of the best farmer to the standard of the worst, no surviving feudal dues and restrictions, no law of settlement to prevent an honest man from seeking to better himself. In New England began the outward drift to the frontier, the encroachment upon the wilderness by the most daring of the new settlers who left their original plantations near the coast to be eagerly taken up by newly-arrived settlers from London. Everywhere in New England farming paid its way. Within seven years from the landing at Cape Cod the Pilgrim Fathers had been able to buy out the stock-holders in London and to become the owners of the land they tilled.

The rigid form of Church government in Massachusetts soon enough produced rebels, who were treated with much greater harshness in New England than the original settlers had been in Old England. From Massachusetts there broke off, against the will of the rulers of the Church, colonies of a still more radical type. In 1636 Thomas Hooker led away to the Banks of the Connecticut River a body of settlers who formed there a completely democratic republic with religious toleration. The Constitution of Connecticut gave no recognition of the superior power either of the Massachusetts government or of the English King.

Another rebel in Massachusetts was Roger Williams, an extreme democrat, who asserted among other alarming propositions that grants of land made in the name of King Charles were invalid because they ignored the rights of the Indians, the true owners of the soil. Williams was tried for his heresies and was banished. He fled for refuge to the Indians of the district later called Rhode Island where he was joined by other malcontents. In 1637 the Pequot Indians, whose lands had been seized by Connecticut settlers, retaliated with war. The

Massachusetts preachers cried out for vengeance and massacre. Williams demanded peace and conciliation. Before these troubles were concluded the Long Parliament had assumed the executive power so that Rhode Island received its first charter[1] from a parliamentary commission. Another colony with a completely democratic form of government was founded at Newhaven, where even the common law was abandoned and the 'Word of God' was the only rule.

5. PROPRIETARY AND ROYAL COLONIES

(i) GENERAL PRINCIPLES

When the New England colonies took root and flourished, there was one respect in which they proved disappointing to political theorists at Whitehall: they produced no staple, no product or crop for export which could not as easily be found or cultivated at home. They drew off men from Old England without providing any visible advantage to balance the account. Since the fear of over-population and unemployment vanished with the sixteenth century, the export of good citizens required some justification. From the earliest time the utility of planting Massachusetts was questioned. By some opinions such colonies were useful only because they eased the morbid humours of the commonwealth. Puritans with their republican fancies might be transported for the public good, as might popish recusants and, in later time, Quakers, Scottish and Irish rebels, and undesirables of all sorts. This sort of colonisation had been denounced by Francis Bacon, the most eminent follower of Gilbert and Hakluyt, as being no better than planting a field with thistles.

Bacon's essay, *Of Plantations*, reveals a change in the approach of enlightened men to the problem after a generation of painful experiment. Colonisation is now regarded as an affair of high policy, not a mere profit-making venture. He assumes that the settlers will first take measures to become self-supporting and then concentrate upon the 'maine business', the provision of staple for export to England, which must not be expected too

[1] Toleration was permitted in Rhode Island on the ground that the colony was too remote to make any breach in the 'unity and uniformity established in this nation'.

soon. 'The destruction of most plantations hath been the base and hasty drawing of profit in the first years.' From this wise lesson, which has proved its truth in every succeeding generation, Bacon derived the principle that the 'undertakers' of a new colony should be 'rather noblemen and gentlemen than merchants, for they [the merchants] look ever to the present gain'.

Accordingly attempts were made under the Stuart kings to frame a systematic colonial policy, bringing the Plantations more directly under control of the Crown. The settlers were to enjoy the rights and liberties of Englishmen living abroad, instead of being merely the resident agents of financiers in London. On the whole the new policy was surprisingly liberal, though here and there attempts were made to entail upon the New World the feudal notions that were already obsolescent in the Old. Virginia, under the constitution which became effective in 1624, with its Royal Governor, its Assembly elected by the freeholders, its established Anglican Church, and its use of English common law, was the model upon which fifty or sixty colonies have been based. Several British colonies to-day are governed much as the Old Dominion was governed 300 years ago. And Virginia could export tobacco.

As Bacon had recommended, 'noblemen and gentlemen' were engaged in the task of empire-building by devolving the royal prerogative upon certain lords of the Council and their associates as Lords Proprietor of new plantations. They were to exercise the functions of government, either in person or by deputy, and to reimburse themselves from the profit of unappropriated land which by common law was reputed the property of the Crown. It would be both the duty and the interest of the Lord Proprietor to bring in settlers, so that the 'maine business' of exporting some commodity required in England would follow in due course. The prerogative of the Lords Proprietor was described in some charters as being equivalent to that enjoyed by the Prince-Bishops of Durham in their palatinate, which sounded formidable but did not amount to much, since the guarantees of civil liberty under the common law were, in every case, in the hands of the colonists. Furthermore, a large part of the Lord Proprietor's revenues depended upon the votes of the assembly which soon came into existence in every colony. His real advantage lay in patronage and in control of the undeveloped land.

(2) NATIONAL RIVALRY AND THE LEEWARD ISLANDS

After 1618, the world was deeply divided by the widening
struggle of the Thirty Years War. Beginning as a struggle
between the Catholic and Protestant powers, the issues were
confused by the intervention of Catholic France on the Protestant
side. The original cause of quarrel was lost in the ruthless fight
for world power between Richelieu and his Protestant allies on
the one hand and the Hapsburg dynasties of Spain and Austria
on the other. The part played by England was as insignificant
as ignoble. At first intervening feebly on the Protestant side she
then withdrew, and blundered into a separate and again a feeble
campaign against France. In 1632 England retired from the war
and was not a party to the negotiations which produced the Treaty
of Westphalia, 1648, after the first general peace conference held
by the European nations.

In the New World the hostilities were reflected by three-
cornered fights between English, French and Spanish colonists.
Plantations were made, and dispersed, and sometimes reformed
at less conspicuous sites after long intervals, so that 'effective
occupation' was indeed the only good title to dominion. Such
murmurs of these little wars as reached the ear of European
statesmen were much confused by ignorance of geography. No
one in Whitehall knew where the islands really were. Barbados
was frequently confused with Barbuda and sometimes even with
Bermuda, a thousand miles away.

The adventurers who made free with the coasts and islands of
the Spanish Empire found that the lure of gold had drawn the
Spaniards on to the central group of the Greater Antilles (Porto
Rico, Jamaica, San Domingo, Cuba) and to the Main, leaving the
outer chain of smaller islands, the Lesser Antilles, unoccupied.
Claims were staked out upon these islands by English, French,
and Dutch men who abandoned their rivalry with one another
only to combine occasionally against the overweening Spaniards.
All the islands were fertile and beautiful; some were inhabited
by hostile Caribs; the 'desert' islands, that is the uninhabited
islands, were the first to be settled.

In 1623 Captain (afterwards Sir) Thomas Warner landed with
a small party upon St Christopher, the island which Columbus
had named after his own patron saint, built a fort and grew a crop

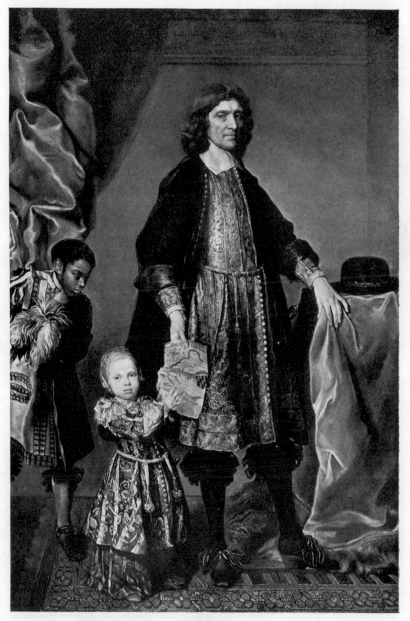

Plate 3

CECIL CALVERT, 2ND LORD BALTIMORE (1605–75)

Baltimore ('the wisest and most successful of English colonisers', according to Gibbon Wakefield) passes a map of Maryland to his infant son Charles, afterwards 3rd Lord Baltimore. From a painting by Gerard Soest, about 1640. *See p. 36.*

Plate 4A

GENERAL JAMES
OGLETHORPE
(1696–1785)

Founder of Georgia, soldier and philanthropist. *See p. 80.*

Plate 4B

WILLIAM PENN
(1644–1718)

Founder of Pennsylvania, late in life. After a portrait by Kneller. *See p. 52.*

of tobacco. Next year he returned to England to engage the patronage of some courtier for a more ambitious colony. In 1625 he crossed the seas again with a commission as governor not only of St Christopher, which the English called St Kitts, but of a large group of West Indian islands which were very imperfectly known. On the very day of his landing, a party of French settlers came ashore in another part of the isle. With unusual good sense French and English came to terms, agreeing to divide the little realm, which is smaller than the Isle of Man.

Meanwhile, in England, great confusion had been caused by overlapping grants to rival colonising syndicates. After negotiation, an overriding charter was given to King James's favourite, the Earl of Carlisle (1627), as Governor of all the 'Caribbee Islands' with powers similar to those of the 'Bishop of Durham in his Palatinate'. The Carlisle grant, the first of the great proprietary charters, was treated as the foundation of English rights in the Lesser Antilles for many years.

St Kitts prospered exceedingly, receiving thousands of adventurous settlers who soon began to swarm off to neighbouring islands within the Carlisle concession: to Nevis in 1628, to Antigua and Montserrat in 1632, to the Virgin Islands in 1650. Yet there were still said to be 4000 Englishmen at St Kitts in 1640. Warner retained his post as governor through the Civil War until his death at St Kitts in 1649.

At about the same time the French settled in Guadeloupe and Martinique (1635) and the Dutch in St Eustatius (1632). The jewel of the group, St Thomas with its admirable harbour, fell to the Danes (1670) and stood neutral in the wars.

(3) BARBADOS

Outside the ring of islands, farther to windward—that is exposed to the first breath of the trade-wind—lies Barbados, a fertile healthy island as large as the Isle of Wight, not too mountainous for settlement, but unfortunately without a natural harbour. It was quite uninhabited when annexed in 1624 by a merchant captain named John Powell who called there on his way home from an unsuccessful voyage to Guiana. In the following year a London merchant of Flemish origin, Sir William Courten (1572–1636), invested £10,000 in a design of trading to the Dutch settlements in Guiana from Barbados, with his fleet of twenty ships. He sent out Captain H. Powell, a brother of the discoverer, with a band of forty settlers who founded Jamestown early in 1625 and attracted 1600 colonists in three years. Courten's highly profitable schemes provoked competition in London from other projectors, especially from Lord Carlisle, the Proprietor of 'the Caribees', who despatched a rival group of sixty-four settlers under a Captain Charles Wolferston, to found a colony which they called Bridgetown (1628).

After intricate negotiation the rival claims were put to arbitration which went in favour of Lord Carlisle. The two colonies coalesced and, by 1636, there were said to be 6000 Englishmen in Barbados. Some of them, in their first year, had gone farther afield to settle in Tobago, but that colony withered away.

The great age of Barbados was when Captain Philip Bell was governor (1641–50). The population was swollen by great numbers of political exiles who seemed to find in that equable island a refuge from the political animosities of England. Barbados was royalist but calm. By 1643 there were said to be 8000 English landholders in the island, making with their families a white population of 18,000 and employing no more than 6000 slaves. Their wealth at first lay in tobacco plantations until, after 1640, a glut on the London market led the settlers to look about for an alternative crop. In those years Bell introduced the sugar-cane from Brazil, a plant which was to multiply the financial wealth of the island while destroying its Utopian social system. Whereas tobacco was cultivated on small-holdings by working proprietors, sugar required large estates, capital, and gangs of slaves. Thirty years later there may have been 20,000 whites in Barbados—the figures sometimes quoted are unreliable—but 50,000 slaves, and thereafter the proportion of slaves to freemen steadily rose. The number of holdings had dropped, by 1676, from 8000 to 800. Yet Barbados was richer, better cultivated, more populous, more civilised, and socially more stable than any of the other islands. Philip Bell had given it a constitution which still (1949) survives, dividing it into nine parishes from each of which two representatives were elected to the Assembly. Before 1650, though the exact date is unknown, the first Assembly had met.

The proprietary government of Lord Carlisle had lapsed when he died, insolvent, in 1636. After long dispute his right passed to Francis, Lord Willoughby of Parham (1613?–66), whose career will be considered in a later chapter (see page 49).

(4) NOVA SCOTIA

An attempt to found a colony of a different sort was made to the northward of New England. From an early period in his reign King James I had given his countenance to Scottish plantations in Ulster. A somewhat shabby device for attracting capitalists had been the creation of a hereditary order of knighthood, the baronetcy, and the open sale of Ulster baronetcies to those who took up a plantation. In the same way, when a poetical courtier, Sir William Alexander, proposed an American plantation by Scotsmen, to be named Nova Scotia (1621), the King allowed capital to be raised by the sale of Nova Scotia baronetcies. The system was neither so corrupt nor so irregular as it seems to modern ears, since knighthood was in the seventeenth century a social duty rather than an award for honourable services. Rich men were occasionally fined for refusing to take up knighthood and the public responsibilities it implied. The proprietor of a large grant of land in a plantation might well be expected to take up knighthood and to pay the price. Rebellion against all such feudal inequalities was in the seventeenth century a new and tiny spark kindled in the breast of some few mutinous soldiers in Cromwell's army and of some Connecticut and Rhode Island farmers, and nowhere else.

Nevertheless the grant provoked the wits to draw comparisons between Sir William Alexander, a poet who wanted to be a king, and James I and VI, a king who wanted to be a poet. In effect, no more than one or two of Alexander's knights-errant visited their province. For, in spite of the grant, the French were already in possession. As early as 1605, before the foundation of Virginia or Quebec, a small French settlement had been formed at Port Royal in the Bay of Fundy and a claim established to the district which they loosely called Acadie. A piratical expedition from Virginia scattered the Acadians in 1613, but they re-assembled, the first of many such episodes. For 150 years the dispute dragged on, the Acadian French clinging to their land, the British colonials, by virtue of some paper charter or treaty, trying to evict them. A handful of Scottish settlers who landed in 1623 withdrew on finding themselves outnumbered by the French.

The Nova Scotia grant was renewed by Charles I and exploited, on Alexander's behalf, by Sir David Kirke, an adventurer who engaged in a long series of plots with Huguenots of uncertain allegiance, and in campaigns against the French-Canadians. In his time (1628) a Scottish colony was founded near the site of the modern town of Granville. In 1629 he captured Quebec, but, when Canada and Acadie were receded at the Peace Treaty of 1632, he withdrew with his settlers to Newfoundland.

But the Nova Scotia claim in the abstract was maintained by the New England colonies. Cromwell sent a force which seized Port Royal again in 1654, but did not colonise the country. Being empty and unprofitable—except to the handful of Acadian peasants—it was a second time receded to France in 1667.

(5) MARYLAND

The colony of Maryland was founded in 1632 as a place of refuge for English Roman Catholics. Sir George Calvert (1578–1632) was a hardworking civil servant and Secretary of State to James I, until he disagreed with the King over his decision to break relations with Spain. Calvert then declared himself a papist and was allowed to retire from the King's service with a pension and, a year or two later, a peerage. He took the Irish title of Lord Baltimore. While in office he had sent a relative, Captain Edward Wynne, with some Welsh settlers to found a colony at Ferryland in Newfoundland and in 1632 was given a charter for his new province which he called Avalon. He visited the colony in 1627 and returned with his family in 1629 intending to remain. A contemporary praises his stone house and his 'brood of horses, cows and other bestial'; he had done more 'for building and planting than was ever performed of any in so short time', at a cost of £25,000. But before long he was petitioning the King for a province in a better climate. He died while on a visit to England, in 1632, before the patent for his new 'palatinate' had passed the Great Seal.

Cecil Calvert, second Lord Baltimore, the traditional founder of Maryland, acted for the most part by deputy, sending his

younger brother, Leonard Calvert, to represent him (1632).
Leonard set sail with 'twenty gentlemen of very good fashion and
three hundred labouring men', to the shore of Chesapeake Bay,

ENGLISH SETTLEMENTS AND
DISCOVERIES IN AMERICA
BEFORE 1640

Miles
0   250   500   750   1000

French Settlements
Dutch Settlements
Spanish Settlements

Baffin Land
Davis Strait
Frobisher Bay
1576
Hudson Strait

St. John
1583
Ferryland 1610
Nova Scotia
1628
Boston
1630
Plymouth 1620
Maryland 1633
Virginia 1607
Bermuda
1612

New Albion ?
1578

Tortuga
St. Kitts 1625
Barbados
1625
Belize
1638
Old
Providence
1630
Guiana

George Philip & Son, Ltd.

Map 1

which King Charles I named Maryland after his Queen; and from
the beginning met trouble because settlers from Virginia, especially
Richard Clayborne, claimed the land by right of earlier possession.
The struggle between Calvert and Clayborne lasted nearly

twenty years, the period of the Great Rebellion in England. Calvert drew help from his brother Lord Baltimore who, although a royalist, managed to maintain his chartered rights except for a short period. Clayborne continually renewed his objections, drawing support from Virginia and the Protestant interest. In 1646 Clayborne took arms, seized the government, and destroyed the early records of the colony. The Calverts reasserted their rights, after a little scuffling, but were ejected by parliamentary commissioners from England between 1654 and 1658. As in other colonies an assembly of the colonists to legislate within the terms of the charter came early into existence. These primitive struggles may be regarded as an eddy from the English Civil War, but were confused by two cross-issues, the fierce rivalry for land between Calvert and Clayborne, and Protestant hatred of the Maryland papists.

Lord Baltimore had first intended a papist colony and then, at least, toleration for his own religion, though the first charter imposed the ecclesiastical laws of England. An Act of toleration, passed in the colonial Assembly in 1649, permitted free exercise of religion to Protestants and Catholics alike. By 1660 the population had risen to 8000, mostly Protestants, and, for the next thirty years, Maryland was assimilated to the type of proprietary colony, though with the outstanding merit of toleration to papists, and with a papist Lord Proprietor.[1]

[1] As the Lords Proprietor of Maryland survived longer and were more distinguished than those of any other province it may be worth while to trace their later history. Charles Calvert, the third Lord Baltimore, governed his province in person from 1661 to 1676 and again from 1679 to 1684. As a papist lord he was denounced by Titus Oates and fell into disfavour with the Whigs. At the Revolution the Proprietorship was cancelled. Not only was Baltimore deprived, but his Roman Catholic fellow-subjects in Maryland were disfranchised in the colony founded for their relief. On his death in 1714 the Proprietorship was revived in favour of his infant son Benedict, the fourth Lord Baltimore, who was brought up as a Protestant. In his time (1729) the town of Baltimore was founded. The fifth Lord Baltimore also governed his province in person for a short period in the 1730's. The line ended with Frederick, the sixth baron, a dilettante and a rake, who lived on the Continent, having got into disrepute. Dying, without a lawful heir, at Venice in 1772 he bequeathed his rights in America to his natural son, a minor, by a will which gave great offence to the people of Maryland. These dues and perquisites, estimated to be worth more than 35,000 dollars a year were, however, soon extinguished by the onset of the American Revolution.

At the census of 1790 there were reported to be 25,000 Roman Catholics in the United States of whom 16,000 were in Maryland. Like the Protestant Episcopalians they had no bishop until John Carroll, one of a celebrated Maryland family, was consecrated Bishop of Baltimore in 1789.

A proprietary government that failed was that which some Puritan lords founded on the island of Providence (1627). The patrons of the Massachusetts Bay Company, Lord Brooke, Lord Saye and Sele, and others, with John Pym as their business agent, desired to found a colony from which to harry the Spaniards and, in the same year as they despatched the peaceful Plymouth colony, they attempted a settlement near the Honduras Coast. Its history is obscure and disreputable. From the island unaptly named Providence, the Englishmen settled in Tortuga, which was merely a pirates' lair. The Spaniards drove them out of Tortuga in 1635 and Providence in 1641. These proceedings established an English interest in a region to which Cromwell laid claim some years later. As a young man he had been one of the promoters and, in 1641, even thought of emigration. English traders frequented the Honduras Coast from early times, certainly from the time of the Providence Company, perhaps long before. About the year 1638 the settlement of Belize (traditionally a corruption of the name of Wallis, an English pirate) was founded by traders who landed to cut log-wood from which a fast black dye was extracted. Treaties with the Moskito Indians, often renewed in later times, date from these first contacts. The log-wood cutters of the Moskito Coast who hunted the wild cattle for ships' victuals were known as the buccaneers, that is eaters of dried beef.

6. THE FREEDOM OF THE SEAS

'THE use of the sea and air', said Queen Elizabeth, 'is free and common to all', an enlightened doctrine far more liberal than the common thought of her age, or of ours. Philosophers long wrangled about *jus naturale*, God's Law of Nature revealed by reason to every rational being, and *jus gentium*, the Law of Nations, that least common denominator of the laws of all civilised nations which they applied in their dealings with one another. But the common practice and common sense of world-wide humanity proved that these laws, where there was no effective sanction, were empty words. International authority there had been and international sanctions had been imposed, but not often and not far afield. Normally in the fifteenth century such international authority as was admitted was exercised by the Pope. All nations had tacitly accepted the award of 1360 by which a Castilian Prince was given the crown of the 'Fortunate Islands' and, with the progress of discoveries during the following century, a series of awards and arbitrations came without question from the papal court. When in 1493, after Columbus's first voyage, Pope Alexander VI decided that the new islands east of a certain meridian should pass to Portugal and west of that meridian to Spain, no new precedent was created nor had any of the parties the least conception of what they were dividing. Columbus had found what he believed to be a group of islands off the coast of Asia. The American continent was neither named nor thought of. Nor was it clear whether the Pope was acting as an international sovereign or as a mere arbitrator. The award was several times amended by direct negotiation between Spain and Portugal.

With the progress of exploration, as the vast extent of the New World was revealed, uncertainties arose as to the relative positions of some new lands, especially because, then and long after, there was no accurate method of fixing the longitude, and therefore no accurate map. There were negotiations and further arbitrations, first over the division of South America and, thirty years later, over the continuation of the meridian on the other side of the world where it passed through the Spice Islands themselves. At last the Treaty of Barcelona in 1529 made the decision, which stood for about 200 years, and determined some frontiers which still remain. In the Atlantic the dividing line allotted the sea coast of Brazil to Portugal and the whole American continent excluding Brazil to Spain; in the Pacific the Philippines were allotted to Spain and the rest of the East Indies—as then known—to Portugal. The Spanish hemisphere was gradually construed to include not only the Islands and the 'Spanish Main' of South America, but the surrounding seas and the whole of the Pacific, or Great South Sea, which the Spaniard Balboa had first observed from a Peak in Darien, and which Magellan had first navigated in a Spanish ship. From all this empire of land and water on which, as the kings of Spain boasted, the sun never set, they claimed to exclude all foreign trade and settlement. Nor was it an empty title for they backed their claim with the sanction of strong fleets and armies.

Queen Elizabeth's response to the Spanish imperial policy has already been mentioned. She would respect Spanish sovereignty only when there was effective occupation and she would not admit any principle of dominion over the sea. It was not until the following century that a clear legal doctrine of the freedom of the seas was evolved. Not only did the Spaniards and Portuguese assert their rights over certain oceans, but the English, in other reigns than Queen Elizabeth's, were no less assertive. As long ago as the reign of King John the demand had been made that every foreign ship should salute the ships of the English king in the Narrow Seas, a claim that was only at last waived in 1872. During the early seventeenth century this pretension to rule the Narrow Seas led to fishery disputes between England and the Netherlands. The Dutch lawyer Hugo Grotius put out the first systematic treatise on the freedom of the seas in his *Mare Liberum* which he afterwards incorporated into his general work *De Jure Belli et Pacis* (1625). A learned lawyer's controversy followed, the best known English exposition being the *Mare Clausum* of John Selden (1635). The English were now taking a higher line and demanding the right to levy tolls, even to exclude foreign ships from trading and fishing in the British Seas, whereas Grotius had declared that by natural law the fisheries of all seas should be free to all. From these discussions emerged the first principles of a newborn science of international law, which guided the Peace Conference at the end of the Thirty Years War, and every European Conference until the Germans overthrew all law and restraint in our own age. The greater Grotius founded the whole science; the lesser Selden enunciated the proposition, which has been generally accepted, of Dominion over Territorial Waters, 'so much as was capable of being controlled from the land'. It is curious that the Spanish jurists contributed powerfully to these academic discussions on the side of freedom of the seas, though their own King in diplomatic negotiation paid no attention to their arguments.

The Dutch claimed free fishing rights in vain from the English; the English, Dutch, and French together claimed free trading rights from the Spaniards, in vain. But in the course of the long changes of war and diplomacy the Spanish statesmen devised a new principle. Treaties made before the discovery of the New World applied to the Old World only. New treaties were to be

drawn with reference to the Old World and should leave consideration of the New World out of court. Hence as early as 1559
Spain had made a treaty of peace with France with the exception
that beyond the Pope's line of demarcation 'might should make
right and violence done by either party to the other should not be
regarded as a breach of the treaty'. The principle that whether
there were peace or war this side there should be 'No peace
beyond the line' cropped up in negotiations all through the
seventeenth century. This it was that justified at law Drake's
exploits and those of the Buccaneers a hundred years later.

All this logic-chopping in the grave chancelleries and universities
of Europe worked out very differently on the high seas, where
every captain was supreme judge on his own quarter-deck. Was
there any law of the sea above that of the stronger hand and the
swifter blow? Had not seamen since crafty Ulysses been a lawless race? Were not the English voyagers true successors to the
vikings who brought home whatever harvest the ocean furrows
bore?

> Some we got by purchase,
> And some we had by trade,
> And some we found by courtesy
> Of pike and carronade...
> At midnight midsea meetings,
> For charity to keep,
> And light the rolling homeward-bound
> That rode a foot too deep!

Were not all Bristol men slave-traders, all Cornishmen wreckers,
all Sussex men smugglers, all Manxmen pirates since time out of
mind? If rumour lied in saying so, there was no denying that
every ship went armed and every shipman, like Chaucer's, was
prepared to defend his craft and lading, neither giving nor asking
quarter:

> If that he fought and had the higher hand
> By water he sent them home to every land.

Even in the British seas, in time of peace, the Barbary rovers
might seize an English ship to carry her crew into captivity in
Algiers. An injured sea-captain might take out Letters-of-
Reprisal from the king to avenge his private wrongs by making
war on his private enemies though the kingdom was at peace;
and when the king went to war he would issue Letters-of-

Marque to sea-captains authorising them to wage war on his enemies at their own charges and for their own profit. So obscure was the line between plunder and reprisal, between piracy and privateering under letter-of-marque, so weak was the control of kings over their more distant subjects that, in effect, there was no law beyond the limits of strong government; and, by the King of Spain's admission, no law but that of violence 'beyond the line'.

7. THE COLONIES IN THE INTERREGNUM

THE English Civil War had but a slight effect and that a retarding effect on the progress of the colonies. Emigration fell off since shipping was restricted. As for political changes the colonial assemblies on the whole treated the Long Parliament and Cromwell with the same degree of passive obstruction that they had shown to James I and Charles I. King and Parliament in turn failed to bring them under a proprietary government. So far from taking sides with the English Puritans the Massachusetts Assembly rejected the legislative authority of Parliament: 'Our allegiance binds us not to the laws of England any longer than while we live in England.' Parliamentary sovereignty could not be accepted 'lest in after times...hostile forces might be in control, and meantime a precedent would have been established'. The New England States combined, in 1643, into a confederation which foreshadowed their republican future.

When King Charles was beheaded there was a royalist reaction in the southern colonies as in Scotland and Ireland. Virginia under Governor Berkeley, and Barbados under Governor Willoughby, with Antigua and Bermuda, declared for Charles II. After a year or two the Parliamentary navy, reorganised and led by Blake, was able to detach a squadron to reduce them by blockade. There was no fighting worth recording. One by one, in 1652, the colonies submitted and were reinstated in their former liberties, some royalist governors having been superseded.

The Commonwealth governments had an exalted view of the rights of the Sovereign People of England. They attempted to monopolise the profit of the seas they claimed as their own and at the same time to resist similar claims advanced by other empires, thus forcing certain issues at international and commercial law. A new code of commercial law for the Empire was inaugurated in the Navigation Acts passed by the Rump Parliament. 'Whereas there are in divers places in America colonies which were planted and settled by the people, and by authority of this nation, which are and ought to be subordinate and dependent upon England;...be it enacted...' and so on; thus runs the preamble of the Act of 1650. The second Act of 1651 begins: 'For the increase of the shipping and encouragement of the navigation of this nation which, under the good providence and protection of God, is so great a means of the welfare and safety of this Commonwealth, be it enacted....'

The effect of the two Acts was absolutely to prohibit the ships of foreign nations from trading with the colonies; to ensure that no goods should be brought from any part of Asia, Africa or America into England or the colonies except in English ships manned by crews of which the greater part were English; and to ensure that with certain named exceptions no European goods were to be brought into England save in English ships or ships of the country whence the goods were brought.

The aim of these acts was naval and political. They were intended to subordinate the colonies, to maintain the merchant navy, and to deprive the Dutch of the carrying trade between Asia and England. They were hardly concerned with the increase of trade and not at all with the free growth of the colonies.

The Acts of Navigation remained in force, though many times amended, for 200 years. They achieved their main object by forcing an issue with the Dutch shippers and depriving them of their carrying trade to England. They did in fact preserve and develop England's world-wide sea power. As for the subordination of the colonies, the Navigation Acts had but a slight effect. Over long periods and vast areas they were ignored; they were never in any colony effectively enforced; and when a serious attempt was made in the eighteenth century to enforce them on thirteen of the American colonies the attempt led to the disruption of the Empire.

The Dutch who at last, by the Treaty of 1648, had won their independence and a foothold in Spanish America, were at the height of their commercial greatness in 1652. During the Thirty Years War they had captured from the Portuguese the greatest prize of the Age of Discovery, the Spice Islands. Theirs was the wealth of the East Indies. In every sea they were the successful rivals of the English, in the Caribbean, in the Baltic, in the Iceland fisheries, in the coastal trade of New England, in the Gulf of Guinea, and in the East, where they had completely ejected the English East India Company from its 'factory' at Amboyna. The Navigation Acts were bound to bring to a crisis the fever heat which antagonised Englishmen and Dutchmen in all parts of the world. But the *casus belli* was sentimental not economic; it was Tromp's refusal to salute the English flag in the Narrow Seas, which the English claimed as their own dominion, as proudly as ever the King of Spain claimed the Pacific Ocean. The first Dutch War (1652–4), though of great interest strategically, had no profound effect on the colonies. The Dutch were more concerned with trade than with plantations; their settlements in America and Africa and Asia were trading posts not colonies; and it was their trade that suffered by Blake's victories and the seizure of 1500 Dutch ships.

The end of the first war was hastened by the rise to supreme power of Oliver Cromwell who had a totally different imperial policy. He was of the old school, and favoured alliance with all the Protestant powers against the Pope and the King of Spain, whom he would attack at their most sensitive point, in the West Indies. Before peace with the Dutch was concluded Cromwell was proposing a joint attack by both powers on the Spanish Empire. As Spain and Portugal had shared the world in 1493, now Holland might take Asia, England might take America, and the power of Spain be overthrown. Though this grandiose and truculent plan came to nothing, Cromwell persevered alone with a 'Western Design'. He presented Spain with a quite unacceptable series of demands and, on her refusal, reopened the buccaneering type of war, which had been so successful in the first half of Queen Elizabeth's reign but so unsuccessful in her later years, after the Spaniards had made preparations to defend themselves. Blake showed the English flag in the Mediterranean and captured the treasure fleet at Santa Cruz, while another expedition sailed against Hispaniola as in the days of Drake.

Cromwell's experiment in empire-building showed little appreciation of realities. It was based upon an anti-Spanish foreign policy that was fifty years behind the times, and was carried out with utter neglect of fifty years' experience of colonisation. He supposed that a Spanish army could be defeated by a mob, and that a successful colony could be planted with London unemployables. The expedition that he sent against San Domingo was disgracefully defeated and as a consolation seized the island of Jamaica where there was but a weak Spanish garrison (1655).

For about sixty years the Portuguese dominions had been incorporated with those of Spain so that the greater part of the New World, east and west, had been in the hands of those whom English Protestants held to be their natural enemies. At the time of the English Civil War the Portuguese had regained their freedom. Charles II completed one of Cromwell's designs by renewing the ancient treaty with Portugal. The alliance was cemented by the King's marriage with a Portuguese princess, who brought to England as her dowry the sovereignty of Bombay and Tangier. Bombay will be considered in a later chapter; Tangier provided a European complication. King Charles found himself master of two fortresses, Dunkirk, which Cromwell had captured from the Spaniards, and now Tangier, commanding one gate of the Mediterranean. He rid himself of Dunkirk which was expensive and useless, but retained Tangier for twenty years. It served as a cantonment for a small standing army which he wished to maintain though his people disapproved. The time had not yet come when England had the necessity or the strength to stretch her sea-power so far south. It was no strategic loss and a saving of revenue when, in 1683, Tangier was evacuated.

8. THE AMERICAN COLONIES UNDER CHARLES II

CHARLES II, his brother James, Clarendon, Shaftesbury and other leading statesmen actively concerned themselves with the colonies and brought into their counsels such eminent advisers as John Locke and William Penn. Broadly, it may be said that their chief concern was with trade and shipping, the mainstays of the nation. Colonial trade, it was assumed, was subordinate to the interest of the English market; the colonists were conceived as Englishmen living overseas for the purpose of increasing

English trade, but entitled to the protection of the same laws and the enjoyment of the same liberties as if they were living at home.

The Navigation Acts of 1650 and 1651 were therefore re-enacted and amended, as conditions required, into a code of commercial law known as the Acts of Trade. Much argument took place over the schedule of 'enumerated commodities' which were to be reserved for the home market. These were tropical products such as 'sugar, tobacco, cotton-wool, indigo, ginger, fustic, logwood and braziletto', which were always scarce and of which it was thought desirable that there should be an English monopoly. Alterations in the schedule led to much legislation at home and much litigation in the colonies, where all attempts to enforce the law through revenue officers or to prosecute offenders in the Courts of Admiralty provoked fierce legal struggles in the colonial courts. From the beginning the colonists resented the intrusion of royal officers into the colonies as a breach of their chartered rights. For the present little harm was done, because the Acts could not be enforced. Smuggling was common through the Dutch settlement at Manhattan and through the buccaneering ports in the West Indies.

While the colonists were beginning to nourish a grievance against the mother-country over trading restrictions they could have no complaint over political rights. They enjoyed a far higher degree of self-government than Englishmen at home. The three New England provinces were confirmed in their liberties even to the extent of being authorised to elect their own governors.

(1) JAMAICA

Cromwell's last years had been spent in the ill-conducted war with Spain by which Jamaica had come into British hands. When the war ended in Europe it dragged on 'beyond the line' since Charles II was unwilling to restore the island. Thus for years Jamaica was at war while the rest of the world was at peace. It was most notably the island of the buccaneers, a great haunt of smugglers and a receiving house for stolen goods. Where the line was to be drawn between smuggler, pirate, privateer, buccaneer and man-of-war's man in Jamaica was indeed hard to say. The age has its hero in the Welshman Henry Morgan (1635–88), who led a raid across the Isthmus to the city of Panama

(1670), where Drake himself had failed. He looted and burned the town, seizing a vast treasure from the baroque church which still stands in ruins near the entrance to the Panama Canal. Though cruel and rapacious Morgan was a privateer not a pirate. Recalled to England to give an account of himself, he was exonerated, knighted and appointed Lieutenant-governor of Jamaica by Charles II.

The Spanish power was now fast declining; the cities of the Isthmus fell into decay after 150 years of greatness and were of little account until their resurgence in the twentieth century.

Although a large island, nearly as extensive as Wales, with a good harbour, Jamaica had been neglected by the Spaniards. When it was captured, the population did not exceed 1500 Europeans and about as many negro slaves. Some of the latter escaped into the wooded interior which rises in altitude to 7000 feet, reverting there to savagery. A desultory war was waged for many years against these wild negroes (known as Cimaroons, or Maroons—that is, 'men of the mountains') until, in 1738, they were pacified and 'settled' on the land. The Europeans at first were not remarkable for civilised virtues. Mutinous soldiers, Irish prisoners-of-war, vagrants and convicts made bad colonists, who lived in idleness and despondency until most of them died of yellow fever. The best were the overflow from the other colonies, 1500 from Nevis and even more from Barbados. By 1658 the population was said to be 4500 whites, 1500 slaves, and the Maroons.

During Cromwell's time the island was kept under military rule which proved as expensive as inefficient. Little real progress was made until King Charles II set up a colonial government of normal type with a royal governor, and an elected assembly, bound by English common law (1663). A long constitutional wrangle with the home government over the revenue ended, in 1728, with the voting of a permanent civil list. The Captain-general of Jamaica was a great personage, sometimes an English duke.

Cocoa was the first crop to be grown and marketed by small-holders, but, as in Barbados, sugar plantations organised on a larger scale soon prevailed. Jamaica sugar and rum fetched a higher price than the produce of the other islands. Though sugar was profitable, war and buccaneering made the real wealth of Jamaica. During the eighteenth century piracy was gradually suppressed and slave-grown sugar became ever more important. The population grew, and changed in character, from 8500 whites and 9500 slaves in 1673 to about 30,000 whites and 300,000 slaves in 1800. As slavery increased, so the slaves grew more restive, sometimes and notably in 1760, rising in revolt. Nature, too, was restive; a new town built at Kingston, after the destruction of Port Royal in an earthquake (1692), eventually became the capital.

(2) LEEWARD AND WINDWARD ISLANDS

The tangled claims of rival proprietors to the lordship of West Indian islands were again canvassed after the Restoration of Charles II. Lord Willoughby got the reversion of the Carlisle grant, subject to compensation for the other claimants, after appeals and counter-appeals to the Privy Council. In 1663, the financial obligations of the colonies were consolidated by an act of Parliament which levied an export duty of 4½ per cent on all the exports from the islands in the Carlisle Grant (Barbados and the Leeward Islands), to raise a fund from which the claims of the Crown and the Proprietors were to be satisfied. This duty is the sole example in the history of the British Empire of a tribute levied by the mother-country upon its dependencies, the sole example, that is to say, of that profit-making imperialism which all other empires in the history of mankind had regarded as the purpose for which dependencies were brought into existence; and this modest little revenue tariff was imposed only in order to liquidate legal liabilities. It survived for 170 years until, after strong remonstrances from the colonial assemblies, it was repealed by an act of 1838.

With a revenue guaranteed from his share of the export duty Willoughby returned to his proprietary lordship. His two periods as Governor (1650–2 and 1663–6) were full of activity. He had founded a thriving little colony of 100 settlers at Surinam in British Guiana (1650), had sent Sir Thomas Warner's half-breed son to come to terms with the Caribs of St Lucia, and was encouraging the expansion of all the island settlements, when the war against French and Dutch (1664–7) brought him to a halt. He beat off de Ruyter from Barbados, but lost Surinam to the Dutch, and temporarily lost St Kitts. On an expedition to its relief in 1666 he was drowned.

After the death of the fifth Lord Willoughby, his brother the sixth baron carried on his work with spirit and energy. In 1671 the great area of 'the Caribees' was split into two governments of the two geographical regions windward and leeward of the French colony of Guadeloupe. An early attempt to federate the Leeward Islands was made in 1698, but the General Assembly at St Kitts lapsed during the wars. Their greatest figure was Christopher Codrington (1668–1710), born in the West Indies, son of the Captain-general of the Leeward Islands. The Codrington family owned Barbuda and made the prosperity of Antigua, where lesser planters were jealous of their pre-eminence. Young Codrington, a gallant soldier and an Oxford man, succeeded his father as Captain-general in 1698 and governed the islands well. At his death, in addition to his legacy of £10,000 for founding the Codrington Library at Oxford, he left two plantations in Barbados to the Society for the Propagation of the Gospel, for the foundation of Codrington College which has a remarkable history. For a hundred and twenty years the Society managed these slave-plantations while educating the slaves and treating them benevolently. They founded a grammar-school for white boys and, in 1830, a college which trained white and coloured students for the ministry.

The Windward Islands, excluding Barbados, were not much settled in the seventeenth century. They were the home of the most numerous and ferocious of the Caribs. The French from Martinique and the English from St Kitts had made some attempts at settlement but without success. A strange story is that of 'Indian' Warner, Sir Thomas Warner's half-breed son, who was sent by Lord Willoughby to colonise Dominica, the most beautiful and fertile of the islands. More Carib than Englishman he became a chief in the island and, having quarrelled with his father's people, was treacherously killed by Philip Warner, his English half-brother. After this failure French and English mutually agreed to leave the Caribs alone. Except Martinique (French) and Barbados (British), all the Windward Islands, south of Guadeloupe, were treated as independent and declared so in several treaties, even as late as the Treaty of Aix-la-Chapelle, 1748. Nevertheless some infiltration of white settlers took place. Dominica and St Lucia, on either side of Martinique, acquired a French-speaking population.

(3) NEW YORK, PENNSYLVANIA, CAROLINA

In 1664, when the English and the Dutch were again at war, a plan of campaign against the Dutch settlements on the American coast was devised by James, Duke of York, and carried out by a small force of English and colonial troops without bloodshed. At the Peace Treaty of 1667 the Dutch retained the English colony of Surinam which they had captured, and ceded 'New Amsterdam' as they called their colony in North America.

Thus fell into English hands, in 1664, the island of Manhattan, the estuary of the Hudson river and the coast-line between New England and Virginia. The captured region was reorganised as two proprietary colonies under the names of New York and New Jersey. The Duke, as Proprietor of New York, established a civil government with liberty of worship and trial by jury, but without an elected assembly. Some Dutch traders had been settled on the coast since 1609, the year when Henry Hudson explored the river that bears his name. In 1626, in spite of English protests, they had bought from the Indians for a parcel of trade goods the rocky tip of the island of Manhattan in the mouth of the river, the best anchorage on the coast and the best line of advance into the interior. Here on the island they had built a trading post which grew into a little town. The anchorage was commanded by a fort at what is still called Battery Point. Wall Street to-day marks the site of the stockaded wall cutting off and protecting the tip of the island against the English who regarded the Dutch settlers as interlopers in their province of New England. Outside the wall the Governor like a true Dutchman planted a pleasure-garden which he called the Bowery. The estuary of the Hudson they called, as it is still called, the North River, the South River being the Delaware 200 miles away.

At the British conquest there were about 7000 Dutchmen in the colony, most of whom remained as British subjects. From the beginning the Manhattan colony was cosmopolitan; it included some Swedes from an earlier Swedish settlement which the Dutch had captured and incorporated, besides the Dutch and English. French Huguenots fled there for refuge and before the end of the century there was also a colony of Jews. It was never and is not now a typical American town, but a doorway from

Europe, a port of call. Of the many races that have come ashore in the Hudson none has left a stronger impress of personality than the sturdy Dutch originals. Stuyvesants and Rensselaers, Cortlandts and Van Burens, Schuylers, Vanderbilts and Roosevelts, the old 'knickerbocker' families, have been New York's leading citizens.

More remarkable was the Quaker colony of Pennsylvania, which arose from the odd friendship between the papist Duke of York and William Penn the Quaker leader. At several stages in his career the Duke attempted to build up a political party by reconciling all the dissident minorities in England against the central stronghold of the Anglican Church. Of the minorities the two most bitterly hated in Old and New England were the Papists and the Quakers. The quietism and pacifism which mark the Quakers to-day did not distinguish them in their first generation. Their contempt for rank and ceremony in an orderly society, their refusal to adopt conventional manners and customs led to their being regarded as dangerous revolutionaries. They were bitterly persecuted everywhere, but nowhere so harshly as in Massachusetts. The world was glad to see the last of them and to get them safely disposed in the Duke's new colony. Penn was a rich aristocrat to whom the Crown owed money. The debt was discharged in 1681 by a grant of land in the southern part of New Jersey where Philadelphia, the City of Brotherly Love, was founded. King Charles himself invented the name Pennsylvania for the Utopia which Penn was to found in the woods. It was described in one of its advertisements in London as 'a very unusual society for it is an absolutely free one and in a free country. Every one may be concerned that will, and yet have the same liberty of private traffique as though there were no society at all.' His colonists were drawn from many sources, not only Welsh and Irish Quakers but members of pietist sects from Germany and Switzerland. In 1683 arrived the first shipload of German Mennonites, better known to European readers as the Anabaptists of Munster. About 20,000 German Protestant refugees came to America, mostly to Pennsylvania, during the next forty years. In the 1730's another sect, the Bohemian Hussites generally known as Moravians, came to America under their leader Zinzendorff. They, too, found a home in Pennsylvania which became the most German part of the New World, preserving the frugal piety of old rural Germany, which was destined to be destroyed and perverted in the Fatherland.

Though many of Penn's schemes proved to be impracticable, he has two striking achievements to his credit. He laid out the city of Philadelphia on a rational plan based upon Wren's rejected plan for rebuilding London; and he established honest and friendly relations with the Indians. Penn was a slave-owner; it was only in later times that the Quaker state took the lead in the fight against slavery. The frontier between Pennsylvania and Maryland was long in dispute and finally came to be known as the Mason-Dixon line, from the names of its two surveyors. This line was to be the northern boundary of ' Dixie ', the land of negro slavery.

Early in Charles II's reign a fantastic project was begun for a large proprietary colony to be planted to the southward of Virginia, under the name of Carolina. Among the numerous courtiers who formed the proprietary body, the leader was Lord Shaftesbury the Whig. He employed John Locke to draft a constitution (1668) for the colony, an extraordinary document which bears no mark of the liberal principles associated with its author's name. Locke supposed that the colonists could be subjected to a rigid feudal system, as vassals of their absentee landlords, without self-government and without common-law rights. No effort was made to put this absurd scheme into practice, and not much effort to enforce the authority of the Proprietors. Carolina (or Carolana), the unexplored wilderness between Virginia and Spanish Florida, was already inhabited by a few interlopers from Virginia and the West Indies. Ignoring the vapourings of the Proprietors they formed an assembly in 1668 and elected their own governor. Charleston, afterwards capital of South Carolina and the largest city in the old South, was founded in 1670. During the next few years the Proprietors attempted, with slight success, to assert their authority. They could not prevent the growth of free institutions like those of all the other colonies. On the whole their influence was negative and Carolina a backward area until the development of the cotton plantations, a century later. The Carolina grant, which also covered the Bahama Islands, was the cause of endless frontier disputes with Spain.

The Atlantic seaboard between French Canada and Spanish Florida, though there were disputes at both extremities, was effectively occupied by the English in the seventeenth century. The settlements still, in 1700, lay along a coastal fringe communicating with one another by water. Inland lay unexplored forests from which the Indians occasionally emerged, in strange attire, to barter furs for gunpowder or rum, and to indulge in sudden inexplicable fits of violence.

9. THE RED INDIANS

WHAT every schoolboy knows about America is the myth of the noble red man, the American Indian. Like other legends it has grown with time. Those whom the Virginia colonists first met were forest Indians settled in villages and clearings along the shores and creeks of Chesapeake Bay. They were never numerous and soon outnumbered by the immigrants. On the whole, they were friendly disposed towards the pale-faced newcomers until, finding their plantations encroached upon, their forests cleared, their game driven off, they retaliated by a raid on the settlers, in 1622. Thereafter they were treated as enemies. In the North they traded with the Dutch and the French for furs, but found little friendly dealing among the Puritans of New England to whom they were like the Amalekites, idolatrous heathen, to be smitten hip and thigh; worshippers of Baal whose blood was to be shed without remorse, so that the Lord's chosen people might inherit the land; or in the homely idiom of the frontier 'the only good Indian was a dead Indian'. Against these harsh words and harsher measures good Roger Williams of Rhode Island and William Penn of the City of Brotherly Love protested in vain.

The Indians, according to the frontiersmen, were treacherous, implacable, bloodthirsty and crafty. But those men of peace who laboured among them found them also generous, honourable and nobly eloquent. They could be both in turn or both at once, like other human beings. Their pride and simplicity, their stoic courage, their mastery of woodcraft, their swift changes from silent dignity to unbridled passion, their aquiline beauty and picturesque adornments soon became the property of every romantic writer. A legend which began in the forests fringing the Atlantic shore gained new life in later days, when the frontiersmen encountered the horse-riding Prairie Indians of the far west.

The Indians who captured, threatened, and at last befriended
Captain John Smith were not acquainted with the wheel, forged
no metals, wove no textiles, plaited no cords. Their dress was
a hunting shirt, leggings and sandals made of soft deerskin
fringed and patterned with lines of sea-shells. Their axes and
knives and arrows were tipped with jade, their bows were strung
with deer-sinews, their ropes were strips of bark. They warmed
themselves in robes of beaver and bearskin; they crowned their
chiefs and warriors with a headdress of wild-turkey feathers.
They lived in gypsy tents of skins or, in their older settlements,
made sheds of slanting poles. The women worked in their small
gardens tilling sweet potatoes and maize (which the Americans
came to know as Indian corn); the men idled and gamed when not
engaged in hunting or in war.

Like contemporary Scottish clans each Indian tribe occupied a
small plantation and claimed a common right over vast ill-defined
hunting-grounds. Some neighbouring tribes were hereditary
enemies, others hereditary friends, but war was the exception and
peace the normal state; even though some young brave might
think fit to advance his private prowess by prosecuting the blood
feud against a neighbour and taking his scalp when there was no
public war. The young men lived together in clubs bound by a
secret freemasonry to which they could be admitted only by
passing terrific tests of courage and endurance in initiatory rites.
When tribal quarrels boiled over, after the harvest and the cele-
bration of the Corn-dance, or when the young braves forced
the hand of their more cautious elders, the tribe with solemn
dedication went on the war-path. All fleshly pleasures were
renounced. The warriors shaved their heads, leaving a single
tuft of long, black hair, the scalp-lock, which an enemy—if he
were man enough to do it—might cut, bleeding scalp and all,
and claim as the trophy of personal victory. Naked to the waist
and daubed with war-paint, that is with patterns of soot and red
ochre, the braves maddened themselves in the frenzied war-dance
and followed the trail to battle.

War was fought under strict rules, and resolved itself into
Homeric single combats between champions whose renown was
measured by the number of scalps taken. Honour and glory once
sated, the warriors were ready to meet in conference, to make
long speeches enlivened with miming and dancing and to declare

truce by the solemn smoking of the pipe of peace and the burying of the hatchet, until the urge for war should stir again. All this pomp with a very moderate amount of actual fighting was altogether different from the ruthless endless war of extermination, without quarter on either side, which arose when the white man drove the red man from his tribal hunting-grounds.

Like their cousins the Aztecs, who immolated human victims to their gods by hundreds, the Indians of the north had some notions of human sacrifice. They took delight in torturing and killing their prisoners of war, partly out of a perverted lust for cruelty, but chiefly for an obscurer reason, a half-understood theory of expiation. They cleaned the land from the guilt of blood by the ceremonial shedding of the blood of a victim, a scapegoat. This calculated cruelty provoked horror and hatred among the pale-faces who did not stay to reflect that their own persecution of heretics and witches derived from the same psychological impulse.

The Indians were also capable of nobler conceptions. The great world-spirit, the distant, uncomprehended *Manitou* had revealed himself to the red men through a culture-hero, a gay, smiling youth, who came among the people from the unknown and returned to the unknown again. He had taught them the arts of peace, to fish with lines, and to construct frail craft from sheets of birch-bark, to plant the maize whose sheath-like leaves of delicate green and golden tasselled head were the robes of the corn-spirit sacrificed, buried and brought to life again by the secret rite of the Corn-dance, which represented and stimulated the yearly miracle of the life and death of the corn. In the end of things he would return to lead the red men to happy hunting-grounds beyond the shining, unknown levels of the Great Lakes in the land of the Setting Sun. Longfellow's *Hiawatha* is an idealised version of one such (Ojibway) myth.

This was the life of the Indians before the coming of the white men, that dread invasion against which Hiawatha himself had forewarned them, or so that life has been dramatised by the pale-faced storytellers. But the red man has been so much written up by poets and novelists, and so much written down by practical men who were concerned with stealing his property that the plain truth is overlaid and lost. Some such generalisation as is here attempted will serve to show what the Indians have been thought to be. This picture of a doomed way of life has had a profound effect on the progress of America and on the attitude of the white men to the coloured races in all parts of the world.

The very language in which it has been described, the war-path and the pipe of peace, the braves with their gruesome trophy of bleeding scalps, the trail and the happy hunting-grounds are now the current coin of the English language, the common-places of Anglo-Saxon thought, which perpetually mould ideas. Even the primitive speech of the savages has been called in to enrich the Anglo-Saxon vocabulary with *canoes* and *tomahawks* and *moccasins* and *wigwams*; with the *squaw* and the *papoose*; with the tribal *totem*; with the *pow-wow* where the *sachems* meet in solemn debate concluded by the passing of the *calumet*[1] from lip to lip, in token of peace concluded with the *Yankees*[1] who had penetrated their forests.

In Virginia and in Maryland the invading white men came as farmers whose concern with the Indians in the first instance was the acquisition of land. Before the seventeenth century was over the Indians were driven back from the coastal plain into the wooded foothills of the Appalachians. They had not retired without many bloody struggles nor without getting some material gains from the pale-faces. They now used guns from Birming-ham and knives of Sheffield steel and embroidered their leather work with English glass beads instead of the lines of shells called *wampum* which had been their currency. Coin was still scarce in America where much retail trade was done by barter. Among the white men, Virginia tobacco and Jamaica rum were commonly used as currency so that before long the fire-water of the pale-faces was traded with the Indians for beaver-skins. From the days of Caliban to the last days of the frontier in the 1880's the curse of the red men was the trader who supplied them with fire-water and fire-arms; their ferocious tendencies were mad-dened to frenzy by the one and their power to take vengeance on the white man multiplied by the other. At first the Indian traders were mostly Dutchmen from Manhattan and Frenchmen from Quebec whose settlements commanded the routes into the interior, through country controlled by a powerful confederacy of tribes.

The Five Nations (Mohawks, Cayugas, Senecas, Oneidas, Onandagas), known to the French as the Iroquois, who roamed

---

[1] *Calumet* probably French-Indian, *yankee* probably Dutch-Indian patois.

through all the lands about the River Hudson and west as far as
the Great Lakes, were combined into a confederacy ruled by a
council of fifty sachems. Even when a sixth nation (Tuscaroras)
joined the league their numbers probably did not exceed 30,000.
A muster of 940 braves who accompanied the British to Fort
Niagara was described as 'all the Mohawks and almost all the
Six Nations'. By 1644 they were in alliance with the Dutch to
whom they supplied beaver-skins in exchange for muskets, with
which the Iroquois drove the French Indians (Hurons and
Algonquins) north across the Great Lakes. When the English
came to New York they took over the alliance and the trade.

The penetration of the Indian country by French traders and
missionaries began when Frontenac was Governor of Quebec
(1673–82 and again 1689–98), and made Fort Frontenac, now
Kingston, his advanced post on Lake Ontario. His invasion of
the province of New York during the war which began in 1689
definitely confirmed the Iroquois in their alliance with Great
Britain. By the Treaty of 1701, made with commissioners from
New York, they placed themselves under protection of King
William III, acknowledging themselves tenants of the Crown for
the whole of their vast territories, an area of 800 miles by 400
miles, extending from Albany to the site where Chicago now
stands and including 'the great falls of Oakinagaro'. To this
treaty which still protects some of their descendants the Iroquois
on the whole remained loyal, especially the Mohawks whose
chief, 'King Hendrick', was the most powerful in the league.
They were reputed as British subjects 'appendant to the colony
of New York'.

The Society for the Propagation of the Gospel (S.P.G.) first
sent missionaries among the Iroquois in 1704 and for long with
small results. Their first success was the conversion of some
Mohawk chiefs and among them King Hendrick, who was then
escorted in great state to London, a triumph for the missionaries
and a guarantee that the alliance would be maintained in the
French War which had again flared up on the frontier. Hendrick
was presented to Queen Anne and protested his gratitude and
friendship in the name of the three Mohawk totems, Bear, Wolf
and Turtle.

10. WAR AND COMMERCE, 1688–1721

(1) THE REVOLUTION OF 1688

THE reign of Charles II is marked in British imperial history as a period of expansion in every part of the world in accordance with a comprehensive and, on the whole, an enlightened policy. Those years saw the acquisition of Bombay and New York, the foundation of Philadelphia and Charleston, the building of Cape Coast Castle and of Fort James on the Gambia, the development of the African slave trade (against which as yet no protest was made in any quarter) and the Hudson Bay fur trade, the attempted grouping of small colonies into dominions, the preparation of a commercial code for the whole Empire in the Acts of Trade, and the direction of policy through a single department, the Board of Trade and Plantations, which was permanently established in 1696. In all these undertakings the Duke of York had played a part, which he continued to play when, as James II, he succeeded his brother on the throne. His hand was felt in the administration of the American colonies and when his policy collapsed in the English Revolution of 1688, the imperial system in the colonies was sorely shaken. But with moderation the same imperial policy was renewed under his supplanter.

James was for firm efficient administration in each colony by a strong executive which might draw support from some elective assembly but would never submit to being controlled by it; foreign foes and domestic faction alike would be curbed by a standing army and navy; but within the frame of this autocratic rule common-law rights and religious toleration were to be ensured. Sir Edmund Andros, a conscientious and experienced administrator and a Protestant, was selected as the instrument of this policy. He was appointed successively governor of several colonies and, in 1686, Governor-General of New England, in partnership with a Surveyor-general of customs who was to enforce the Acts of Trade. The scattered factious Puritan commonwealths were to be united into a loyal dominion where even Quakers and Papists, even Indians, might enjoy their own. But the New Englanders were as determined as the men of Old England that they would not have legal equality on those terms. They plainly saw where jesuitry had led the Huguenots who trusted the paternal rule of Louis XIV. When Andros attempted to call in and revise their precious charters he met resistance in every colony. The news of the overthrow of James II reached Boston in 1689. Without hesitation and without violence the citizens rose and deposed his servant Andros, restoring the former governor. For the next few years there was confusion in several colonies; in Maryland where Catholics and Protestants again came to blows; in New York where rival factions alternately seized power; and in Boston. Meanwhile, a war had broken out in Europe. The French seized St Kitts in the West Indies and, with Indian help, encroached on every frontier: Newfoundland, Canada, Hudson Bay.

King William's War (1690–7) and Queen Anne's War (1702–13) were fought by Grand Alliances pledged to restrain the overwhelming power of Louis XIV of France. In each war the English government was the mainspring of the alliance and from the two wars the commercial and naval power of England derived great advantages. The trading interests regarded these as their war aims, but the governments were more concerned with political plans: in the first war with resisting King Louis' intention to restore King James II to the throne of Great Britain and Ireland, and in the second with preventing King Louis from seizing possession of the moribund Spanish Empire. These wars, of the English and Spanish Succession, are among the few examples in our history of a predominant part taken by British generals and armies in the land campaigns on the main continental front. But the political and strategic genius of Marlborough went far beyond the direction of his own battles in Bavaria and Flanders. He, first of Englishmen, conceived and inspired the plan of naval control of the Mediterranean in order to threaten what his descendant, Winston Churchill, called 'the soft underbelly of Europe'. After 1704 a decisive factor in all British strategy was the maintenance of a fleet in the Mediterranean, to prevent a combination between the enemy squadrons based on the ports of southern Europe and those based on the Atlantic ports. To make this strategy aggressive, to carry the war to the enemy's coast has required advanced bases far deeper into the Mediterranean than Gibraltar Bay. Hence the Balearic Isles, Corsica, Sicily, Malta, Corfu, Crete and Cyprus have at one time and another been occupied by British fleets and armies.

Gibraltar was seized from the French party in Spain by a neat little combined operation, in 1704, and was then retained in spite of counter-attacks by French fleets and Spanish armies, the first of many such attempts at siege. The Rock has now been in British hands for 240 years, a period of time rather longer than the former period during which it was subject to the united Spanish monarchy. Its population, of mixed Mediterranean descent, has hitherto shown no desire to return to Spanish rule.

Four years after the capture of Gibraltar a further step forward was taken by the seizure of the land-locked harbour of Port Mahon in Minorca, the most suitable base in the Balearic Islands for operations against the southern coast of France. Throughout the eighteenth century, British Mediterranean strategy was based upon Gibraltar for defence and Minorca for attack.

From the merchants' point of view these operations had the intention and the effect of defending our trade with the Levant. Protection for the Smyrna convoys meant as much to the merchants of London as protection for the treasure fleets to the merchants of Seville. The presence of a British squadron in the Mediterranean also had a restraining effect on the 'Barbary Pirates', the Moslem states of North Africa which lived by plunder and slave-raiding. The petition in the Litany for God's pity on 'all prisoners and captives' serves to recall our ancestors' perpetual fear of being kidnapped into slavery in Algiers or Tunis.

Outside Europe the campaigns were unimportant and for the most part unheroic. Even the greater naval operations were treasure-hunts, the only true-blue hero being the stout, old 'tarry-breeks' Admiral Benbow who died of wounds after an ill-fated action off Santa Marta. What seafaring men remembered of these wars was the plundering and destruction of a Spanish fleet worth fifteen millions sterling off Cartagena, and the burning of the treasure fleet in Vigo Bay (1702) when millions of pieces-of-eight went to the bottom, and lie there still. In the West Indies there were raids and plundering expeditions, mostly around the island of St Kitts which was lost to the French and retaken. 'Trade in general seems at a stand and nothing on foot but privateering', wrote a Jamaican in 1708. 'The war will leave to the world a brood of pirates to infest it.'

The northern colonies made a poor showing against the French, since their affairs were in great confusion after the overthrow of Andros, while French Canada was strong and united under Governor Frontenac. A champion arose at Boston in the person of Sir William Phipps, a rough, honest fellow, who got the confidence of the townsmen. He led a colonial expedition against Port Royal in Acadie, but achieved nothing beyond sacking the papist church. 'Not a blow was struck,' he said, 'for want of courage and conduct in the officers.'

In that year (1691) a new charter was issued making Massachusetts a royal colony with Phipps as Governor. He repeatedly tried to organise combined attacks on Quebec, that failed, mainly because of the unwillingness of the New Englanders to co-operate or to contribute funds. Three years later their pride had been so humbled by Indian raids and bankruptcy that they threw themselves on King William's mercy: 'we implore your royal aid...for the rescuing of a languished province...we prostrate ourselves at your feet'. But they remained republicans at heart.

Meanwhile the French with their Indian allies came down from Lake Champlain to raid New York Province. The most brilliant figure in the war was d'Iberville, a French-Canadian, who ranged the whole interior of America from Hudson Bay to the mouth of the Mississippi, harassing the English. He drove away the agents of the newly established Hudson's Bay Company, and captured the English settlements in Newfoundland. But his exploits were barren since the victory of the allies in Europe obliged the French to give up all their conquests at the end of the war.

(2) THE TREATY OF UTRECHT

In the public history of Europe the Treaty of Utrecht, 1713, showed some disreputable features, but it was epoch-making for the British Empire. It gave the British navy control of the Mediterranean Sea, it made the first breach in the closed economy of Spain, and it narrowed and defined the French holdings in North America. In the first place Gibraltar and Minorca were ceded by Spain to Great Britain. Valuable as these fortresses were for naval operations, they made sore spots in the sensitive Spanish pride. Since the Treaty also placed a Bourbon Prince upon the Spanish throne it was almost inevitable that in any future war the King of Spain would join with France in the hope of recovering his lost fortresses; hence the concern felt in England over the repeated Family Compacts, in the eighteenth century, between the kings of France and Spain.

It will be necessary to pursue at some length the effect of the other clauses of the Treaty:

(1) France ceded her territory in Newfoundland and Nova Scotia to Great Britain with certain reservations, which will be discussed in a later chapter.

(2) Spain gave formal permission for a limited English trade with the Isthmus of Panama. She also admitted the right of British to cut logwood on the Moskito Coast.

The Treaty of Utrecht thus put an end to the old days of uncontrolled warfare against Spain 'beyond the line'. For a hundred years the kings of Spain had fought for their monopoly with pertinacity and courage. On the whole they had provided naval protection by concentrating the commerce of their Empire in armed convoys which converged each year at Porto Bello. There the manufactured goods of the Old World were exchanged for the luxuries of the New World and especially for bullion which was conveyed to Europe in the annual treasure fleet. Neither Drake nor Grenville had succeeded in grasping this prize, which only once fell into British hands, when Admiral Blake captured it at Santa Cruz (1657). Designs to seize the treasure fleet dominated our strategy in each successive war, but in vain; it was too well guarded.

While giving this naval protection to their ships the Spaniards had failed in giving economic protection to the commerce on which those ships lived. Not gold and silver, but sugar, rum, molasses, tobacco, indigo, and logwood were the true wealth of the Spanish Indies and the Spanish Main. The most valuable import that could be exchanged against these exports was a steady flow of negro slaves to work the plantations. It was not the naval raids against the treasure fleet that broke the power of Spain, but economic penetration. The Dutch, the French and the English had occupied and planted many of the most profitable islands in spite of Spanish resistance. They had built up in those islands a trade that flourished largely because it was unrestricted. Not that the Kings of England and France were less anxious than their brother of Spain to control and monopolise their own colonial trade; they tried but had not the power to do it.

The interlopers were often buccaneers and smugglers, occasionally pirates, but primarily traders. They came to import goods that the Spaniards sorely needed, English manufactured stuffs and negro slaves from Africa. They sought a market and if necessary would fight for it, but not often, because nothing suited the Spanish settlers better than to buy. The Spanish officials and even governors often connived at the free trade. Jamaica, where the best sugar was grown and the best rum distilled, was the smugglers' market for the two commodities so potentially demoralising, rum and slaves.

The eighteenth century was to see a more humdrum struggle for the West Indian sugar trade, a prize of greater value than chests of doubloons or pieces-of-eight. For this trade France and England fought five great wars over the prostrate limbs of the fallen Spanish Empire, but wars of a quite different character from the Protestant crusade of Drake and Ralegh against the 'inquisition-dogs and the devildoms of Spain'. That had been total war, 'ideological' war, with no respite and no quarter. The struggle with France was commercial and political with occasional resort to force when diplomacy failed. The wars were limited in duration and in violence by the principles of international law which, since Grotius, the nations had begun to apply. When legitimate war had been distinguished from lawless violence, piracy could be defined. It flourished among the unnumbered reefs and bays and islands of the Caribbean, above all in the Bahamas, which contained so many hiding-places for rogues. But pirates after Utrecht were denounced, pursued and punished, by all honest governments alike, as enemies of the human race.

(3) THE BAHAMAS: PIRATES

The Bahamas had been included in the grant to the influential proprietors of Carolina (1670) but without much effect. The Cloud-cuckoo land which John Locke devised for Lord Shaftesbury and his associates remained in the air, hardly even taking root at Charleston, while the numerous sandy islands of the Bahama group were exploited by adventurers on their own account. The island of New Providence [1] was settled in 1666 by a

---

[1] New Providence in the Bahamas is to be distinguished from the older colony of Providence off the coast of Honduras.

party of pioneers from Bermuda who elected J. Wentworth as their governor and maintained him in spite of the Carolina grant. Their port at Nassau was a rallying point in the irregular perpetual war with Spain and, as buccaneering declined into piracy, so Nassau became a free port where not too many questions were asked. A convenient centre for blockade-running in all the wars, it has been noted for contraband trade until recent times.

Not all governors were honest. John Avery, who captured the Great Mogul's daughter in the Indian Seas (1695), returned to disperse his crew and realise his gains in the Bahamas, where he was in league with the Governor. The wealth of Asia slipped through his fingers leaving him to die a beggar at Bideford in Devon. William Kidd, whom the government of Massachusetts hired to fight the pirates, concealed in the Bahamas some part of the loot of six French ships before returning to London to face the charge of having himself turned pirate. Some unsavoury tales of official collusion came to light, and more were smothered away, before he was hanged at Execution Dock (1701). Edward Teach, known as Blackbeard, was a pirate from Jamaica who made his base at New Providence. The terror of the Carolina coast, he held Charleston to ransom, exploiting a rivalry between two governors. Teach's treasure is probably mythical though his orgies and his bloodthirsty habits are recorded facts. A change for the better came when Captain Woodes Rogers, the circumnavigator, acquired the governorship of the Bahamas from the *fainéant* Lords Proprietor. In 1718 Teach was killed in a seafight and the pirates' lairs routed out. The celebrated Captain England went to Mauritius where his crew marooned him, others to Madagascar. Several who 'declared war on the human race' began to operate from Sierra Leone, so that their exploits blacken the history of Africa rather than America.

(4) THE ASIENTO AND THE TRADING COMPANIES

As part of the general settlement which accompanied the Treaty of Utrecht, France surrendered to England the 'Asiento', the profitable contract for supplying negro slaves to the Spanish colonies, a bargain which revolted the consciences of the Victorian English, but which rejoiced the harder hearts of their ancestors in the reign of Good Queen Anne. For the southern Spanish colonies a British slave-market was to be established at Buenos Ayres;[1] for the Indies the depot for the trade in human flesh was at Jamaica. The management of the trade was eagerly contested. It was already a privilege of the Royal African Company to buy negroes in West Africa and to ship them overseas. The distribution at the forward end was now allotted to the newly formed South Sea Company which before long was importing 5000 negroes a year through the main depots of Vera Cruz, Panama, Cartagena, Havana, Porto Bello and Caracas. But this happy state of affairs was destined not to last. The obstruction of free-traders and smugglers, British and Spanish, many of them officials of the colonial governments, was too strong. In 1750 the Spaniards withdrew the Asiento, buying out the South Sea Company for £100,000 and throwing the market open. British merchants and shippers flocked to this desirable trade and soon made the port of Liverpool, from which the slavers sailed, second only to London among British seaports.

In spite of the attitude of the City of London, where monopolies were disliked, four great chartered companies were formed or reformed in these years. The East India Company (see below, chapter III, 3) was refounded, after a fierce commercial struggle, in 1696. The Hudson's Bay Company, first chartered in 1670, suffered severely in Queen Anne's War and was saved by the Treaty of Utrecht; it will be more fully considered in the next chapter. The Royal African Company (1664) and the South Sea Company (1711) enjoyed a boom created by the Asiento Treaty. The decline of Spain produced a new wave of commercial adventure on the Spanish Main and in what were loosely described as the South Seas. The name properly belonged to the Pacific Ocean, the unknown waste of water seen to the southward from the Isthmus of Panama, containing, it was believed, the Antarctic continent and the fabled gold mines of King Solomon. Adventure at sea was the subject of the two greatest romances of the age, *Gulliver's Travels* and *Robinson Crusoe*, books which from that day to this have never lost the attention of 'the best audiences in the world, the children and the wise men'. Robinson Crusoe's island was not in the South Sea but off the Atlantic Coast of the Spanish Main; and the great 'bubble' company, though it placed the name of the South

[1] Probably the origin of the British commercial colony on the River Plate.

Sea in the prospectus, actually traded to the Caribbean and the River Plate.

The treaty permitted the British South Sea Company to send each year one ship, laden with British goods, to the annual fair at Porto Bello. This system, having once opened the door, gave every opportunity for further illicit trade in the commodities which the Spaniards so earnestly desired. The first such ship, the *Royal Prince*, laden with goods to the value of £256,000, made a successful voyage in 1717. But the limitation to a single voyage proved unworkable. Not more than ten of these annual voyages were made before the method was abandoned.

The Asiento agreement and the sailing of the first ship to Porto Bello sent South Sea shares soaring from £100 on issue in 1711 to over £1000 in 1718. Then a financial scandal involving the directors and two members of the cabinet broke the market. The shares came tumbling down, but were held at a figure above par by the skilful intervention of Robert Walpole, who at this crisis became what was beginning to be called 'prime minister'. The Company was saved, and survived in obscurity till 1853, providing in its later years a clerical post for Charles Lamb.

The South Sea Bubble was one of three great financial disasters caused by a phenomenon then new but now familiar, a hysterical rush to invest and play the market at a time when money was cheap, followed by an inevitable slump when the actual trade proved insufficient to justify the high price of shares. It had its counterparts in the Darien Scheme (1698), a Scottish venture in trading and colonisation, and the similar French Mississippi scheme (1720). In each of these instances the financial collapse involved the livelihood and even the lives of confiding settlers, a far more deplorable affair than the losses of the speculators.

The Darien scheme was the classic example of folly in colonisation. Although individual Scots had begun to make their mark in the colonies, no successful Scottish settlement had been planted and Scotland was excluded by the Acts of Trade from the benefits of commerce with the English colonies. The newly formed Board of Trade (1696), and Randolph its surveyor-general in America, resisted all attempts of the Scots to share these benefits, with the result that the Scottish merchants pressed for a colony of their own. In 1698 William Paterson, the founder of the Bank of England, floated a company for Scottish emigration to the

Isthmus of Darien, a quite unsuitable location, which was hampered by the nullifying stipulation in the charter that there should be no settlement in Spanish territory. The shares were taken up with avidity in Edinburgh while the project was denounced in London. William III, as Kings of Scots, had carelessly approved the scheme; as King of England he carelessly allowed his parliament to repudiate it. No protection against the Spaniards was to be afforded for this Scottish rival to the English trading ventures. About 2000 settlers and most of the scanty floating capital of Scotland were launched and sunk in the expedition to Darien. No adequate site was found and no market for the profusion of trade goods. The settlers, marooned on an unhealthy shore, met bitter opposition from the Spaniards to whom they eventually surrendered. Their funds were exhausted and the jealous English government made no move to help them. Some died, others drifted to the other colonies, and the colony came to an end, or rather failed to come into existence. This lamentable affair was a principal factor in persuading the Scots to forgo their independence in order to accept a commercial union with England. An indemnity from the English Treasury to the Scottish investors in the Darien Company was an article of the Act of Union.

(5) 'THE CITY'

Trade, shipping, the Navy—not colonisation—were the true imperial interests of Englishmen in the hundred years after the Restoration of Charles II. By 1688 the annual tonnage of ships cleared from English ports outward bound was 190,000; by 1701, 273,000; by 1738, 476,000; by 1763, 561,000. Money to invest was growing ever more plentiful and the great complex of financial interests which we call 'the City' had come into existence. Joint-stock companies were being formed for every sort of undertaking and especially for banking and insurance which gave a new stability to the market. Nothing contributed more to this stability than the funding of the national debt. In earlier times the greatest problem in every large national undertaking was that of providing a continuous flow of ready money other than on short-term loan. How could cash be found to repay the cash borrowed? The financier William Paterson arranged in 1694 to advance large credits to the government on a long term, the sum to be borrowed from subscribers who were to be repaid with terminable life annuities. In course of time the annuities were converted to payments of interest at a fixed rate which, long after, stood for generations at 3 per cent. This was the origin of the Bank of England which kept national credit firm through wars and slumps and made London the money-market of the world. Good credit in its turn secured the 'three-per-cents' as the stock for the cautious investor. Every landed man could now have a stake in the national finances as well as in his county and would find an interest in overseas trade, the foundation of national wealth. The whole solid system enabled 'the City' to invest its growing surplus in trading ventures.

Hardly less important was the system of marine insurance. Ned Lloyd's coffee-house was a favourite rendezvous in Charles II's reign for sea-captains and for shipping merchants. Here investors gambled on the chance of shipwreck by guaranteeing, for a price, to repay the value of vessels or cargoes lost. Before the end of the century the *habitués* of Lloyd's had formed a ring of underwriters who examined and classified ships and cargoes and insured them at agreed rates. The name of Lloyd's which has been absorbed into every European language, the regularity of insurance, the firmness of the London markets, the cautious management which, for 250 years, has justified the phrase 'Safe as the Bank of England', and especially the integrity of the London merchants, form the solid base on which trade and empire have been built. They would never have grown and endured had not 'the word of an Englishman', *palabra inglés* actually stood for honest dealing and prompt payment the world wide, a reputation enjoyed by the English individually but not by their government which has more commonly been described as *Albion perfide*.

'The City' was strongly protectionist. It presumed, perhaps rightly, that our commercial greatness had sprung from the Navigation Laws, and fought bitterly to retain these advantages for the home country, opposing the extension of free trade to the colonies and to Ireland. But within the frame of the laws protecting English trade, privilege was unpopular. 'The City' did not approve of royal monopolies or chartered companies, but desired freedom for all English merchants. There were, however, powerful 'interests' which sometimes overruled the preference for free competition. From the earliest times individual colonies retained their agents in London to look after their commercial and other interests.

Walpole was in office from 1721 to 1742, a long period of peace and prosperity. While trade flourished with the East and West Indies, while 'moderate men grew big' in the City of London, the American colonists were imperceptibly growing into a nation, were extending their pioneering labours into the wilderness, and were finding themselves confronted by a new military and naval power even more formidable than that of Spain. The French government was carrying out a set policy of limiting the English frontiers by ringing them round with naval and military posts.

(6) HUDSON'S BAY COMPANY

On 25 October 1666 a Huguenot adventurer named Chouart had audience of King Charles II. He had been to Canada where he acquired a seigneury from which he took the title of Sieur des Groseillers. In the City of London they called him 'Mr Gooseberry'. He had been fined by the Governor of Quebec for illicit trading in the far west and therefore brought his expectations to another market, offering to lead an English expedition from Canada to Hudson Bay, a proposal which was well received at court. When the Dutch War ended, in 1667, a holding company, in which the Duke of York, Prince Rupert, and half the King's ministers took shares, was formed to finance a preliminary expedition. In June 1668 two ships set sail; one went astray, the other, the *Nonesuch* with Mr Gooseberry on board, reached Prince Rupert's River in Hudson Bay, made a pact with the Cree Indians, built Fort Charles, and wintered in the Bay with 'nature looking like a carcase frozen to death'.

The voyage appeared to justify the King in issuing a charter to the Hudson's Bay Company on 2 May 1670: 'having undertaken an expedition...for a discovery of a new passage into the South Seas, and for the finding of some trade for furs, minerals, and other considerable commodities, and by such their undertakings have already made such discoveries...the Governor and Company of Adventurers of England trading into Hudson Bay [are granted]...the whole trade of all those seas, streights, and bays, rivers, lakes, creeks, and sounds...that lie within the entrance of the streights commonly called Hudson's Streights together with all the lands...upon the coasts and confines of the seas aforesaid...which are not now actually possessed by any of our subjects, or by the subjects of any other Christian prince or state....' The whole of this unknown tract of land was given away to the officers of the Company 'in free and common socage', with authority 'to judge all such persons as shall live under them according to the laws of this country' and to 'make war or peace with any prince or people that are not Christian'. While thus disposing of one-third of a continent, the King had no more notion of the extent of his grant than the Pope had in giving half the world to the King of Spain.

The Directors, with Prince Rupert in the chair, soon set to work. From 1671 they despatched three ships annually, in June, laden with some such cargo as '200 fowling pieces and powder and shot, 200 brass kettles; twelve gross of knives, and 900 hatchets' which were to be exchanged for beaver-skins against the return of the ships in October. The trade boomed at the rate of one beaver for a pound of tobacco, six for a laced coat, and twelve for a fowling piece. Five forts, at which landing parties could meet the Indians and, if necessary, pass the winter were established at Albany River, Hayes Island, Rupert's River, Port Nelson and New Severn. The Duke of York succeeded Prince Rupert as second Governor, the third was John Churchill (afterwards Duke of Marlborough), whose name was given to Fort Churchill in 1686. By that time the Company was paying a huge annual dividend, sometimes 50 per cent. In 1690 they watered the stock to three times its former value and still paid 25 per cent. But the French now began to react sharply against this attempt to penetrate western America from the northern seas. The French-Canadian, d'Iberville, was sent overland from Quebec to resist their progress, with no small success. During King William's and Queen Anne's wars the Hudson's Bay Company lost much of its trade, and all its forts except one, to the French. The Treaty of Utrecht restored the trade and territory of the Hudson's Bay Company though without compensation for war damage.

The following fifty years (1713–63) saw the struggle between France and England for the hinterland of North America. While the English had begun to move inland in great numbers from the eastern seaboard and had now established trading posts on the

northern seaboard, the French, until their defeats in the Seven
Years War, held the inland waterways. In 1684 they had reached
Niagara. In 1682 La Salle sailed down the Mississippi. In 1717
De La Noue reached the head of Lake Superior. In 1731 Veren-
drye pushed westward as far as Lake Winnipeg. In 1743 one of
his parties had a distant view of the Rocky Mountains. In 1751
they built a fort on the Saskatchewan not far from the site of
Calgary. Meanwhile the Hudson's Bay Company was sharply
criticised in London for failure to carry out the terms of the
charter; they had been content to collect beaver-skins without
searching for the North-west Passage. A public inquiry
justified their actions. The share-capital had been increased from
£10,000 to £100,000 upon which they annually exported trade
goods worth £4000 and imported furs worth £12,000. What
more could be asked of a trading company in the unromantic age
of Walpole and the Pelhams?

11. NEWFOUNDLAND

THE history of Newfoundland is unlike that of any other colony.
For 300 years fish and the fisheries constituted its only topic.
The Newfoundlanders turned their backs upon the interior of
their island, dismissing it contemptuously as the 'barrens',
and looked outwards to the offshore fisheries. A 'plantation' in
Newfoundlander's jargon was the name given to a fishing establishment; a 'fishing-room' meant the claim over a strip of beach
on which fish could be dried; and fish meant cod. All the English
settlements were fishing villages along the shores of the south-
eastern corner of the island, and the Avalon Peninsula, with no
connexion by land better than steep footpaths through rocks and
woods. There was no carriage-road in the island before the
nineteenth century.

The seasonal fishing-fleet from the west of England arrived in
May as soon as the ice was thawed and left in October or November before the winter storms set in. As early as 1549, an Act of
Parliament was passed, making admiralty regulations for the
'better encouragement of the fisheries of Iceland and Newfoundland'. Even before Gilbert's ill-fated voyage (1583), which is

taken as the substantial claim to sovereignty over the island, a naval officer had been sent to adjudicate the quarrels of the fishermen. Before the end of the century a customary practice had grown up that the skipper of the first ship to arrive at Ferryland, on the eastern shore, should be recognised as the 'Fishing Admiral' for the season. In 1633 the custom of the fishing-fleet was authorised by Star Chamber in the form of a Fishing Charter issued to the Mayors of Southampton, Weymouth, Melcombe, Lyme, Plymouth, Dartmouth, East Looe, Fowey and Barnstaple, the nine west-country ports from which the ships sailed. Under supervision of the nine mayors the fishing-fleet was a floating republic with the Fishing Admiral as President and judge. The charter was based upon the customary law of the sea as prescribed in the ancient codes of Oléron and Wisby.

During the next few years three separate attempts were made to colonise Newfoundland by projectors working in the tradition of Sir Humphrey Gilbert. A fortified settlement would enable the British to monopolise the fisheries, excluding ships of other nations from the use of anchorages and 'fishing-rooms'. Such a plan for conducting the fisheries from a base in the island provoked hostility from the holders of the Fishing Charter who worked from bases in England. In spite of their activity a charter for a colony was obtained through the influence of Francis Bacon. John Guy, William Colston and others were incorporated, in 1610, as the Company of Adventurers and Planters of London and Bristol[1] for the Colony or Plantations in Newfoundland. The first party of settlers, led by John Guy of Bristol, wintered at Cuper's Cove in Concepcion Bay in 1610–11, founding there the oldest British colony which still survives; they numbered about a hundred. There was little progress until the plantation was reinforced by the support of Sir George Calvert (see above, page 36) who settled with his family at Ferryland in 1629. On his departure for Maryland, the colony languished. Some colonists, however, remained when the reversion of the Company's charter was given to Sir David Kirke in 1637. For some years Kirke lived in the stone house built by Calvert at Ferryland, with a few

[1] J. D. Rogers, the historian of Newfoundland, points out the recurrent dualism of the charters in this age. The rivalry between London and the west-country ports appears frequently in the titles of the companies. The west country resented London interference.

Scottish emigrants whom the French had driven out of Nova Scotia. He first fortified the narrow entrance to the harbour of St John's. The triumph of Cromwell in England led to Kirke's recall and a return to the principles of the Fishing Charter. Cromwell would have removed the Newfoundlanders to his new colony of Jamaica and, after the Restoration, the Council of Trade and Plantations continued in that mind.

The colony was saved by the influence of the Navy. When at last a decision was taken, in 1675, to remove the settlers, a report was rendered on the island by the naval officers who convoyed the annual fishing-fleet. In their opinion it was necessary for strategic reasons to maintain a base in Newfoundland. The report showed that there were then twenty-eight distinct settlements on the coast between Cape Race and the south-east corner of the island. The settled population engaged in the fisheries was 523, of whom 361 were women and children. To these were added a casual population of 1342 visitors who stayed in the island over a winter or two, fur-trading, boat-building or growing vegetables for the fishing-fleet. In consequence of this report the Council of Trade reversed their decision in 1680, allowing the settlers to remain. The new status of the island was regulated by an Act of 1699 establishing a double government. The fisheries were still to be governed by the Fishing Admiral in accordance with the charter of 1633, but the Convoy Captain, that is the senior naval officer, was to be governor of the settlements. In the winter, when both the Fishing Admiral and the Convoy Captain had departed, the Newfoundlanders were left ungoverned.

Fear of the French had caused the Navy to take an interest in the problem. In 1662 Louis XIV had founded the settlement of Placentia on the ice-free southern coast where he stimulated the French fishers with bounties and a more liberal Fishing Charter than the English enjoyed. Newfoundland suffered much in the ensuing wars. In 1696 the celebrated French frontiersman, d'Ilberville, raided and sacked St John's at midwinter with a band of men who crossed the island from Placentia on snow-shoes. Too late, the War Office spent £3000 on fortifying St John's in the following year. Twice again, in Queen Anne's War, the French overran the English settlements, taking advantage of the fogs which interfered with naval support. In 1711, the Convoy Captain summoned a General Assembly of the islanders to organise a militia, the first beginnings of a formal administration in the island. Since that date Newfoundland has been securely held as a British possession, with a peculiar status recognised in the eleventh clause of the Utrecht Treaty (1713). The French King admitted British sovereignty over the whole island, promising to withdraw the French settlers from Placentia. While abandoning the southern shore the French fishermen were still allowed a concession to 'take and dry fish' on the unoccupied northern and western shores, a concession productive of many disputes since these coasts were unsurveyed and were defined in the Treaty by reference to places not marked on any map. The Treaty also had the effect of concentrating the French settlements and shipping around the Straits of Belle Isle and the St Lawrence Gulf. The settlers from Placentia were removed to Cape Breton Island which became a French fortress.

12. PHILANTHROPY IN AMERICA

THE early New Englanders were a dour race, addicted to a frugal industrious way of life and indifferent if not hostile to the more genial virtues. Like their 'unco guid' fellow-calvinists in Scotland against whom Robert Burns railed, their religion, their laws, their habits were exclusive and intolerant. They were strict sabbatarians with little liking for cakes and ale, and were much inclined to impose civil penalties for breaches of the moral law. Theirs was not a missionary creed. The children of light withdrew themselves from the darkness of the outer world. The heathen were to be rooted out of the land; heretics and schismatics were driven into the wilderness. They were bitter in their hostility to all other Christian sects, especially to the Church of England. Papists were persecuted in New England and Quakers were hanged. It is not surprising that they shared the prevalent horror of witchcraft, as the most blasphemous of all heresies. One of the last and worst examples of the legal persecution of supposed witches in any Protestant country occurred at Salem, Massachusetts, where nineteen victims were executed in 1692. When Sir William Phipps became the first Royal Governor he shared the prevalent hysteria but soon came to his senses (perhaps because the witchfinders laid accusations against his wife), and put a stop to the legal proceedings, for which he was warmly commended by King William.[1] Tolerance was a bitter pill for the Boston Puritans, and another was the enlarged franchise under the new royal charter.

With their defects the New Englanders had corresponding strength of character. Like the Scots they were far ahead of the English in public education, having provided a school for every township of fifty householders. Church and school formed the basis of village life, their management being the nucleus of the New England town meeting, the assembly of all the citizens for direct democratic government. They elected their officers annually and voted them a salary, a system quite unlike that of the English townships where the local officers served, gratis, in rotation. Hence the status and function of justices, sheriffs and the lesser village officers differ profoundly in Old and New England.

One in 200 of the early Massachusetts settlers, forty of their eighty ministers, were graduates of Oxford or Cambridge, but scholarship inevitably declined in the hard pioneering age. There was a printing-house at Boston in 1639, and a strict censorship of the press, in a society with no disposition towards polite literature. Its first important production was an Algonquin Bible produced in 1661-3, the first bible printed in America. This was the work of the Rev. John Eliot (1604-90) of Jesus College, Cambridge, the 'apostle of the Indians'. In 1646 he began his mission to the Algonquins and at first received moral and financial support both from the General Court of Massachusetts and from the Long Parliament in England. The great sum of £11,000 was raised on both sides of the Atlantic for his work which culminated in the foundation of a Christian-Indian township (1651). He claimed 4000 converts. Later came the inevitable struggle by the Indians to retain their hunting-grounds. In the Indian war of 1674, known as 'King Philip's War' his converts were killed or scattered and his work brought to an end.

The beginning of a more humane culture derives from the legacy bequeathed by John Harvard of Emmanuel College, Cambridge, in 1636, £1000 and a library of books for the foundation of a college in New England. It began in a very small way as a training college for the ministry and, during the eighteenth

[1] *Calendar of State Papers (American)*, 12 Jan. 1692-3.

century, grew slowly into a small provincial university with a strictly classical curriculum. It should be remembered that Harvard College was unimportant when compared with the contemporary Spanish University of Mexico which already included faculties for classical studies, anthropology and native Mexican culture; but it played a part in forming the American nation. By 1693, 107 out of 123 of the clergy in New England were Harvard men. In the course of 200 years Harvard created the characteristic Boston School of writers and philosophers, austere, lucid, restrained in thought and style, the first native literature to appear on the American continent. After 300 years the modest foundation of John Harvard has grown into one of the greatest, wealthiest and most learned of the world's universities, notable for research and still retaining at Cambridge, Massachusetts, some faint flavour of the older Puritan university where Milton and Cromwell spent their youth in the placid English Fenland.

The next American university was founded at Williamsburg, Virginia, in 1691, where the original buildings have been piously preserved. Yale followed in 1716 and from that time colleges for higher education have kept pace with the growth of the American nation. The later universities, especially Princeton (1746) followed the Scottish rather than the English model.

The general sense of the American colonists favoured the free churches and most commonly those with Calvinist principles. But free-churchmen, Anglicans, infidels, all alike shared a hatred of 'popery', a prejudice even more virulent among the Americans than among the English. While there were as yet few Roman Catholics in the colonies, and no Catholic Irish vote, the colonists were becoming increasingly restive over French penetration into the hinterland of North America and its corollary, the spread of French Jesuit missions among the Indian tribes.

By a typically English legal fiction all colonists, for purposes of English law, were deemed to be freemen of the county of Middlesex who happened to be residing abroad. Like other Englishmen they were presumed to be members of the established Church unless they rejected its services by some legal form of dissent or recusancy. Though most colonists were, if they observed any religious forms, Dissenters, they came under the ecclesiastical jurisdiction of the Bishop of London who had commissaries in several of the colonies to exercise a spiritual control over the Church established by law in New York, Maryland, Virginia, and the Carolinas, and the principal West Indian islands, according to the usages of the Church of England. It must be admitted that the Anglican clergy in these colonies were lax and indolent on the whole. The Church flourished only among the aristocrats of Virginia who affected an English way of life, and in the cosmopolitan town of New York. The facts that the Church was losing ground, that it failed to reconcile the Puritans of New England, that it showed no missionary fervour to convert Indians or negroes were recorded by all observers. The first attempts at reform were made under the auspices of Queen Anne, 'the Church of England's Glory', by the foundation of the Society for the Propagation of the Gospel (1701) and the Society for the Promotion of Christian Knowledge (1698), the former concerned with missionary efforts and the latter with Christian education. The S.P.G. made notable progress especi-ally in the Carolinas, in reviving churchmanship and in missions to the Indians, which aroused much suspicious hostility among the New England Puritans. Schools for the sons of chiefs were an early necessity; for this purpose Dartmouth College (New Hampshire) was founded in 1749. The S.P.C.K. concerned itself with issuing versions of the Bible in the Indian languages. But equally useful was the protection which the missionaries tried hard to get for the Indians against the unrestricted trade in rum, the cause of their worst misfortunes. Rum, it was universally agreed, perverted the most civilised Indian into a bloodthirsty savage. So vital was this restriction and so dangerous was the trade in rum that even the moderate use of strong liquors has been denounced as vice, in America, for two centuries.

Church activity was as yet on a small scale. The Anglican Church in America consisted of a few isolated parishes 3000 miles away from their diocesan bishop. It was recruited by occasional immigrant clergymen, in many cases poor representatives of their order. It could not flourish until rooted in American soil. Since the earliest days Churchmen had recognised this and had desired the establishment of a bishopric, a proposal that produced the most violent political reactions. In Georgian England a bishop was conceived as a political at least as much as a pastoral function-ary. The days were not forgotten when proud prelates had ruled the land from high places in government. They still enjoyed wealth and patronage, advised the Crown, presided in ecclesi-astical courts. Puritans, who had fled to New England to escape from this accursed thing, and Whiggish aristocrats in the southern colonies, who were not at all desirous to buttress the power of the Crown, alike objected. The conception of a bishop who had merely spiritual authority and that only over his own flock was unfamiliar. The Board of Trade was unlikely to move in this troublesome controversial matter. The Anglican Church in America had no bishop until after the Revolution; its activities were regarded with hostility by most colonists, who suspected that its sympathies lay with the King's royal prerogative rather than with colonial rights, even with justice for the red man rather than with unlimited progress for the white.

A persistent and noble effort was made by the idealist philo-sopher Berkeley to raise the standard of religion and learning in the colonies. As a rising young Irish clergyman he was launched into Society by Dean Swift (1724) with the odd testi-monial that Berkeley's heart would break if his Irish benefice were not taken away from him. Swift added to his letter the recommendation that it would be more useful to 'keep one of the first men in the Kingdom at home'. He was determined to found a college in Bermuda both for white settlers and for the sons of Indian chiefs who were to be trained as clergy and teachers for the New World. Berkeley persevered so far as to get from the House of Commons an almost unanimous resolution that it would be proper to endow the proposed college with £20,000 from Crown property in the West Indies which had been allotted to the colonial Church by Queen Anne. So promising a begin-ning encouraged Berkeley to migrate to America with his own small fortune and a sum of £3000 raised by private subscription. After waiting for some years in Rhode Island, he was at last con-vinced that the Whig government had no intention of releasing good money for any such quixotic purpose. Walpole, the Prime Minister, characteristically, after subscribing £200 to Berkeley's private fund, let him know that the Treasury had no intention of issuing the grant of £20,000; Berkeley 'had better give up his expectations'. A bishop was heard to say at Westminster that the resolution had been a mere compliment: 'all was done out of regard for the man, not the design'. Another 'very good lord' went further: 'learning', he said, 'tended to make the colonies independent of their mother-country...the ignorance of the Indians and the variety of sects in our plantations was England's security'.

After a ten years' struggle Berkeley lost hope of getting the money. He had spent his private funds for the benefit of the Anglican Church in Rhode Island and for the new college at Yale, and had assisted in the foundation of a college at New York which was destined to become the University of Columbia, before returning to a philosophic career and an Irish bishopric. His contribution to the future of America was faith in a New World where no longer 'infidels would pass for fine gentlemen, and venal traitors for men of sense'. Among his papers there exists a copy of verses containing the celebrated lines:

> Westward the course of empire takes its way,
> The four first acts already past,
> A fifth shall close the drama with the day,
> The world's great effort is the last.[1]

Though Berkeley, perhaps from modesty, described these lines as 'wrote by a friend of mine', they declare his hope, his vision.

Another philanthropist in London tried to get the reversion of the money promised to Berkeley. This was General James Oglethorpe, a Tory soldier and suspected Jacobite. He devoted many years to relieving the condition of insolvent debtors who were confined, in great numbers, in English prisons. In 1732 he and others, including good Captain Coram of the Foundling Hospital, were appointed by the Crown as 'Trustees for the Colony of Georgia' which was to be planted between the Savannah and the Altamaha rivers. Philanthropy, the motive of the founders, was backed in this instance by prudence on the part of Walpole's government which judged that a British outpost so far south would serve to check the northward progress of the Spaniards from their fort at St Augustine in Florida, and that at small cost to the Crown. In this instance, therefore, £10,000 was voted and actually paid out.

In 1733 Oglethorpe led his first colony of 114 settlers to Georgia intending to direct their settlement with paternal benevolence. 'The Society will use their utmost endeavours to

---

[1] Correspondence of Berkeley with John Perceval, who acted as London agent to him and to General Oglethorpe.

prevent luxury and oppression in the officers, idleness and vice in the people. They intend to send no governor, to prevent the pride that name might instil. The power of the government they intend to invest in an overseer and council of honest and discreet men.... They [the settlers] are to be regularly armed and exercised yet the lands where they establish are to be regularly purchased from the Indians and all measures used to keep peace and friendship with them.... The Indians shall upon all occasions be treated with the strictest justice and utmost humanity. No rum...will be allowed to be sold to the Indians....All men are from the beginning to be established as freemen and not as servants....Mankind will be obliged for the enlarging civility, cultivating wild countries, and founding of colonies, the posterity of whom may, in all probability, be powerful and learned nations.'

In spite of these excellent intentions the ne'er-do-wells of London were ne'er-do-wells still in Georgia. Few men were found 'honest and discreet' enough to put down luxury and idleness alike except Oglethorpe himself, a born dictator. His colonists, small-holders each occupying a fifty-acre allotment, found work in a sub-tropical climate, without negro labour and without rum, so uncongenial that their unhappy fate was selected by Goldsmith in his *Deserted Village* to illustrate the horrors of emigration. Oglethorpe alone kept the colony going. He was on excellent terms with the Indians and successfully fended off Spanish encroachment, fighting a brilliant little campaign with his colonials against a column of Spanish regulars from St Augustine in the War of 1739. He attracted industrious Scottish emigrants from the Carolinas, and German Protestant refugees expelled from Salzburg by a persecuting archbishop, so that, when he retired in 1743, his colony was taking root. By 1752, when the charter was revoked and normal colonial government instituted, Georgia had assimilated to its northern neighbours. Besides 5000 white settlers there were now 2000 blacks and no embargo on slavery or rum.

But Georgia made one distinct contribution to American life by providing the cradle of the Methodist Revival. Oglethorpe, like many of the reformers of the age, was a Tory High Churchman and took with him to Georgia two young Oxford clergymen of good abilities and unimpeachable High Church principles,

John and Charles Wesley. Though they did not remain long in Oglethorpe's Utopia their life-work was directed and formed by their American experiences. Berkeley, Oglethorpe and the Wesleys had much in common, the intention to regenerate an old corrupt society in the pure air of the New World whether by education, by enlightened government, or by evangelism.

Wesley's successor as Oglethorpe's secretary was George Whitefield (1714–70) another Oxford parson. While the Wesleys returned to reinvigorate the moral life of the English, Whitefield remained as the apostle of Methodism in America. He soon left Georgia and preached 'at large', during six visits to the colonies, quite breaking with the Anglican system. His was salvationist doctrine of a simpler type than that of the Wesleys whose religion was flavoured with German mysticism and the pietism of William Law. John Wesley was a scholar and a precisian, George Whitefield an evangelist who spoke like a prophet from the Old Testament. His message spread far beyond the narrow conventicles of Boston, beyond the musty loyalties of tide-water Virginia. He, not the Puritans of Massachusetts, created American Protestantism with its moral fervour, individualism, and self-reliance, a proper religion for frontiersmen. He made a deep impression even on Benjamin Franklin. Before Whitefield's death his Methodists far outnumbered the New England Independents, who have dwindled to a small minority even in the City of Boston. It may be mentioned that he gratified his colonial audiences by justifying negro slavery from the Old Testament.

II

BRITISH NORTH AMERICA IN THE
EIGHTEENTH CENTURY

Argument: The compact group of English colonies on the Atlantic sea-board was hemmed in by French settlements at strategic points on the waterways to the interior. Friction in Acadie, western Virginia, and also in Newfoundland, was a contributory cause of the great wars which ended in the triumph of the British at the Treaty of Paris, 1763.

When the French had been expelled, the English colonists in America became conscious of their opportunity and their destiny. They resisted attempts by the British government to reorganise the whole Empire on a rigid though enlightened plan with a common fiscal policy, local self-government, and safeguards for subject races. Invoking a coalition of the European powers against the mother-country, they won independence. A substantial minority of loyalists laid the foundations of a new British Commonwealth in Nova Scotia and Canada.

for term paper

1. ENGLISH AND FRENCH IN
NORTH AMERICA

AFTER twenty years of peace England drifted into war with Spain in 1739. Walpole, after skilfully avoiding earlier adventures, was at last hounded into a martial policy, by the Opposition leaders who hoped to make it a means of replacing him in office, and by the ignorant who hankered after the old days of Protestant warfare and treasure-hunting on the Spanish Main. There was no lack of matters for contention: occasionally the Inquisition still claimed an unwary English heretic as its victim; the King of Spain objected to the English settlement of Georgia; there were smugglers everywhere, and endless legal disputes over the Asiento. What followed was known derisively as the War of Jenkins' Ear from the tendentious story, put out as propaganda by the Opposition leaders, of an English skipper whose ear had been cut off by a Spanish coastguard.

This disreputable struggle at sea was the first phase of a general European war precipitated by the rapacity and treachery of Frederick the Great of Prussia. In Macaulay's glowing words: 'The whole world sprang to arms. On the head of Frederick is all the blood which was shed in a war which raged during many years, and in every quarter of the globe, the blood of the Column of Fontenoy, the blood of the mountaineers who were slaughtered at Culloden. The evils produced by his wickedness were felt in lands where the name of Prussia was unknown; and, in order that he might rob a neighbour whom he had promised to defend, black men fought on the Coast of Coromandel, and red men scalped each other by the Great Lakes of North America.' Wicked as Frederick was, this accusation is not fair to him. All the causes of war between French and English had long previously been recorded and each party in North America had often already played off against the other the ferocity of the red men; while in Southern India civil wars already raged among the black men before French and English were drawn into the strife (see page 161).

The war had one positive effect upon the growth of the empire, through the pacification of the Scottish Highlands. The break-up of the clan system led to the first emigrations of landless high-landers to America, a great loss to Scotland and a great gain to America. It also led to the formation of the highland regiments which have taken so heroic a part in the colonial campaigns of the British Army from Ticonderoga in 1758 to Tunis in 1943.

An uneasy feeling that the French were encircling the colonies by establishing a chain of posts to the westward had been in the minds of the English colonists for many years. Their own settlements had been formed in the Atlantic estuaries, and for long clung to tide-water. Inland lay trackless forests full of wild Indians. The westward movement had at first been made by systematic colonisation. In New England groups of approved settlers had been assembled to occupy, clear, and cultivate selected sites, they had gone in parties and had provided for themselves churches, schools, and town-meetings. In the southern colonies the advance inland had been by the surveying of large estates which were granted or sold under authority of the Lord Proprietor. On the fringe beyond the farthest clearances social life was unrestrained by the conventions of the tide-water settlements. Far inland, hunters, trappers and traders followed the Indian trails up to the passes of the Alleghanies and beyond to the headwaters of the unknown rivers that flowed westward. There neither King George's writ ran nor the writ of the Colonial Assembly. The frontiersmen, despising the square-toed citizens of Boston and Philadelphia, wore a deerskin dress not unlike that of the Indians, lived in the woods, and rivalled the Indians in woodcraft. Of these pioneers the most celebrated was that model hero of a hundred boys' adventure stories, Daniel Boone (1734–1820) who explored Kentucky. There were wilder characters than Boone, runaway sailors and servants breaking their indentures, who took to the woods to live entirely with the Indians. Such 'renegades' were often held in wretched slavery, but sometimes by practising a useful handicraft made themselves indispensable to their Indian masters as intermediaries and interpreters between the white and the red men. The trader, the missionary, and the government agent often got their first foothold in Indian tribal society by the help of some demoralised renegade. Occasionally these unfortunates cultivated an insane fury against the civilisation from which they were outcasts, went on the war-path with the Indians and got vengeance with the scalping-knife for the injuries they supposed themselves to have suffered.

By the year 1750 the frontiersmen at a hundred points found themselves in opposition to similar pioneers from the French colonies. It was vain to talk of legal rights. French-Canadian and half-breed, Yankee hunter and renegade, alike accepted no law but the law of might, and all encroached upon the hunting-grounds of the Indian when strong enough to defy him. There was, however, growing up a body of legal principles which were much discussed by lawyers in Boston and in London. It was beginning to be agreed that, in opening up new country, effective occupation of a coastline gave the occupier a prescriptive right to the hinterland. Some colonial charters, vaguely foreseeing the problem, had granted the Proprietors a strip of land running inland from the known Atlantic Coast right across unknown America to the Pacific. But whereas this westward limit of the colonies was legally uncertain, nature had given them a definite geographical limit in the watershed of the Alleghany Mountains, a barrier to settlement for more than a hundred years.

The story of the French settlements in North America had been very different. It began, as did the story of the English, with the fisheries off the Newfoundland coast and the search for the North-west Passage. In 1534 Cartier had sailed up the broad estuary of the St Lawrence to the point where the gulf narrows into a river channel and on to the limit of navigation. The first of these points is Quebec; the second, where Cartier was taken by friendly Indians to survey the prospect from the Hill of Hochelaga, he renamed with enthusiasm Mont-royal (now Montreal). Beyond claiming sovereignty little more was done by the French until the reign of Henri IV when the first attempts were made at colonisation. Port-royal in Acadie was settled in 1605 and Quebec in Canada by Champlain in 1608.

La nation canadienne, that very tough and homogeneous entity, was made by two great men, Frontenac who served two terms as governor (1673–82 and 1689–95), and Laval, bishop from 1662 to 1681. At first the policy of Louis XIV's government was to concentrate the colonists; but, later, Colbert instructed Frontenac to find a passage westward into the 'South Seas'. Hence, La Salle's voyage down the Mississippi, in 1682, was a disappointment; the stream did not flow west. And hence the frontier farm, a few miles west of Montreal, was derisively called *La Chine* (China). The first wealth of Canada proved to be in the fur trade which drew both French and English traders to traffic with the Indians far in the interior. Frontenac's campaigns against the English, in his second term of office, might more properly be described as French-Indian campaigns against the English-Indians of the Hudson Bay posts and of New York province. At this time the French and French-Indians established themselves on the Great Lakes, at Fort Frontenac (Kingston, Ontario).

From 1664 onwards French colonial policy was directed to the object of building up an empire upon the basis of certain selected strategic points which were to be seized and held by naval and military power. Where necessary, colonists from France would be imported by direct action of the home government and when planted they would be kept under strict political control. This was to be a political empire quite unlike the sprawling individualist expansion of the nation of shopkeepers. Only in naval policy in the Mediterranean can we find anything in English history at all resembling the French occupation of Pondicherry, Mauritius and Goree, of Martinique and Guadeloupe, of Quebec, Montreal and Acadie. The weakness of the plan lay in the difficulty of attracting home-loving Frenchmen overseas. No more than a dribble of emigrants arrived in Canada, mostly Norman peasants, docile, pious and industrious, who cultivated small-holdings on the banks of the St Lawrence. French-Canadian society showed marked characteristics, all of them evident at the present day.

The settled peasantry, the *habitants* lived in village communities at the water's edge from which a narrow strip of land running back into the forest was cleared and cultivated. Each of these strips was a *seigneurie* granted to some French gentleman and organised on the model of a Norman manor. Life in a French-Canadian village was the repetition of life in France under the *ancien régime*, and retains today more survivals of that way of life than does village life in France. The seigneurial system survived in full strength into the nineteenth century. The *habitants* were as prolific as they were frugal. From an estimated 60,000 in 1750 they have increased to 2,000,000 in six generations, almost without reinforcement by immigration, and by slow progress have formed innumerable free village settlements inland from the original *seigneuries*.

But Canada too had its frontier and its frontiersmen. There were settled *habitants* and there were nomadic *coureurs-de-bois*. These latter like the hunters of New England, went long journeys into the woods. They had less colour-prejudice than the English, intermarried freely with the Indians and after a few generations were mostly half-breeds. Their commerce was in furs of beaver, racoon and bear; their skill was in rivers rather than in the trail and the packhorse. Their way to the interior was by canoe up to the headwaters of the rivers, then by carrying their canoes across the watershed or *portage* to another river down which they could descend to the next trading post. It must be admitted that the French were far more successful than the English in their relations with the Indians. Long afterwards, in 1826, a Chippewa chief said of the French: 'They never mocked at our ceremonies and they never molested the places of our dead. Seven generations of men have passed away and we have never forgotten it.'

The French government, then in close alliance with the Jesuit Order, was quick to see the advantage of planting French missionaries among the Indians. With the most enterprising traders, and even ahead of them, were to be found the French Jesuit priests whose zeal and heroism even to martyrdom do honour to human history. They were the first Europeans to see

Niagara Falls and the Great Lakes, or at least to record that they
had seen them. But to the English colonists, with their hatred
and horror of Roman Catholics, they were merely French spies
of a peculiarly sinister sort. Against this background of *habitants*,
coureurs-de-bois and Jesuit missions the ministers of King Louis
XIV composed their designs for the mastery of North America.

French trading posts and mission stations appeared at numerous
strategic points along the waterways of the interior. The year
1720 saw the foundation of Louisburg on Cape Breton Island at
one end of the chain, of Fort Niagara in the centre of it, and of
New Orleans at the mouth of the Mississippi forming the other
end, 3000 miles away. Between 1720 and 1730 French and
English settlers came into direct contact at the head of the Hudson
River. Here there were two ways inland, west by the Mohawk
Gap to Lake Ontario, and north by Lake Champlain to Canada.
The English occupied the Mohawk gap with trading stations at
Saratoga and Oswego; the French came down Lake Champlain
and built military posts at Crown Point and Ticonderoga. Even
when French and English were at peace, French Indians were at
war with English Indians in this region. In the 1740's the French
rapidly pushed on, occupying with brilliant strategic insight what
have proved to be the sites of the cities of the Middle West, Fort
William at the head of Lake Superior, Sault Ste Marie between
Lakes Superior and Huron, Detroit between Lakes Huron and
Erie, Chicago on the *portage* from Lake Michigan to the Illinois
River, St Louis at the junction of the Missouri with the Mississippi, and finally at the head waters of the Ohio, the Fort
which the French named Duquesne after the Governor of
Canada, but which the Virginians renamed Pittsburg, after the
great English commoner.

All this fertile, well-wooded land between the Hudson River,
Lake Ontario, and the head of the Ohio was the hunting-ground
of the Iroquois, who showed the greatest political abilities and
the greatest faculty for civilised progress of all the Indians;
acted as a single unit; and were even disposed towards peace and
the arts of peace. This does not of course imply that, when they
went on the war-path, they were any less intent than their fellow-
savages upon plundering, scalping and torturing their victims;
this was the code of war as they conceived it. The Mohawks,
whose lands lay along the Mohawk River, at the vortex of the

struggle were *par excellence* the 'English Indians'. They have
been the loyal friends of the British for over 250 years. In the
wars the Mohawks always, and by their influence the whole Six
Nations as a rule, have fought on the British side. During
negotiations at Albany, when each of the other tribes buried a
hatchet, the Mohawks refused, saying: 'We bury none, for we
have never broken the ancient links.'

The problem of rights over the hinterland should be considered as triangular. Land-hunger, the motive that brought
French and English into strife between Fort Ticonderoga and
Fort Duquesne, was a hunger to occupy the little plantations and
the vast hunting-grounds of the Six Nations. Penetration inland
was a matter of supreme interest to the colonial assemblies of
Massachusetts, New York, Pennsylvania and Virginia, but Indian
wars were quite another matter. Each colony might reluctantly
raise its militia and vote a sum of money for repelling an Indian
raid on its own frontier, but one and all consistently refused to
combine in any joint scheme for defending the whole region, for
administering the whole area of undeveloped land, for settling the
Indians, or for resisting the French. On several occasions the
governors met in conference, but their good intentions were
nullified by lack of soldiers, by lack of funds, and by the narrow
view of the assemblies which refused to provide them. The
fiercest strife was on the northern frontier of New England.

In the French War of 1690–7 ferocious fighting between bands
of French and British partisans in Nova Scotia ended in the
recognition for the third time of the French rights in Acadie.
Since the country was neither mapped nor explored this recognition did not mean much. During the previous thirty years
fisheries had been established by New Englanders in the harbours
of the Atlantic coast, while the French had drained and cultivated
their holdings at the head of the Bay of Fundy. Some of the
younger Frenchmen, according to the custom of Canada, took
to the woods as *coureurs-de-bois*, mingling with the Indians and
joining in their raids against the Puritan Yankees. For the most
part the *habitants* of Port-Royal, Grand-Pre, and the other
settlements were a pious and tranquil peasantry who had no
politics other than obedience to their priests.

In Queen Anne's War Port-Royal was captured (1710) by an
expedition from New England and was renamed Annapolis. To

the delight of the New Englanders, Acadie, 'including Port-
Royal', was at last ceded to Great Britain at the Treaty of Utrecht,
though the boundaries of the province remained a subject of
dispute. The British asserted that the act of cession covered the
whole of Nova Scotia, with much of what is now New Brunswick; the French protested that the special mention of Port-
Royal implied that Acadie was something else and smaller, merely
the Atlantic coast of the peninsula. The status of the Acadian
habitants in the Bay of Fundy thus became the crux of an international quarrel. The new British governor at Annapolis offered
them protection, the use of their own laws and religion, and a
representative assembly on condition of their taking an oath of
allegiance to King George. Some hundreds, living near Annapolis, took the oath; the great majority ignored the appeal and
stood neutral.

Beyond the confines of Annapolis and the fishery harbours
King George's writ did not run. The woods were infested by
French Indians and 'neutral' Acadians with whom there was no
peace. It was the real or supposed influence of the French priests
over the Indians that roused the anger of the New Englanders.
Religious bigotry added to the barbarity of Indian warfare.
Both sides offered rewards for scalps; each party accused the
other of atrocious murders.

Mutual animosities increased when, about 1720, the French
design to control the waterways of North America took shape.
The outer bastion of the French strategic line from the St
Lawrence to the Mississippi was Cape Breton Island, separated
from Nova Scotia by a narrow strait. There the French founded
the fortress of Louisburg, building up its strength, over a period
of five and twenty years, at a cost of three million *livres*. When
war broke out again in 1740, renewed Indian fighting and a
French raid on Annapolis provoked the great expedition of the
New Englanders against Cape Breton Island. They raised a force
of 4000 colonials under a militia officer, Colonel Pepperall;
formed their own fleet of transports; and landed on the island in
April 1745, as soon as its shores were free of the winter's ice.
A British naval squadron, under Commodore Warren, following
somewhat tardily, came too late to cover the landing, but supported the assault on Louisburg. When some outer forts had
been taken, batteries were mounted to bombard the main works

and the siege was vigorously pressed, against strong resistance, for forty-nine days. At last the capture by Commodore Warren of a seventy-four-gun ship carrying essential stores obliged the French to capitulate. The garrison of 650 veteran troops and 1300 militiamen surrendered on condition of being carried back to France, with the 4000 civilian inhabitants. The plan 'for the reduction of this regularly constructed fortress was drawn up by a lawyer and executed by a body of husbandmen and merchants'. The motive force that impelled this army of civilians was to a large extent religious; they marched beneath a banner for which George Whitefield had provided the motto: *Nil Desperandum, Christo Duce*; their chaplain bore an axe with which to destroy the images in the popish Churches. They justified themselves as Protestant crusaders.

But the English government as yet had little interest in Canada. Macaulay has preserved an anecdote, perhaps apocryphal, of the appreciation of the campaign by the Duke of Newcastle, then Secretary of State. 'Oh—yes—yes—to be sure—Annapolis must be defended—Troops must be sent to Annapolis—Pray, where is Annapolis?' And again: 'Cape Breton an island! Wonderful!—My dear sir, you always bring us good news. I must go and tell the king that Cape Breton is an island.'

At the Treaty of Aix-la-Chapelle, 1748, the conquests made by the colonials in America were restored to France in exchange for Madras (see page 162), a bargain which both affronted and alarmed the New Englanders. Louisburg was a nest of privateers, an American Dunkirk; a fortress commanding the Inland Sea, an American Gibraltar, as great a threat to the New Englanders as was Fort Duquesne to the Virginians.

2. FORT DUQUESNE, ACADIE, AND QUEBEC

THE war of 1739–48 and the interval of uneasy peace that followed it brought to the fore three of the greatest figures in early American history, Benjamin Franklin (1706–90), Sir William Johnson (1715–74) and George Washington (1732–99). Franklin first appeared in politics as forcing the hands of the Quaker Assembly of Pennsylvania which would not vote funds for its own defence even when the Indians were raiding the colony. Franklin raised a corps of volunteers and paid for it by a lottery. In 1754 he laid before a Conference of Governors at Albany a plan for a Union of the American Colonies with a central authority to control Defence, Indian Trade and Indian Lands; but this plan which might have destroyed the causes of the American Revolution at their root came to nothing. The colonies were far too jealous of one another to make any such agreement. Responsibility for defence of the frontier was firmly handed back to the British government, which called upon the British tax-payer to provide £200,000 and an army for the defence of New York province.

Johnson was a wild Irish lad who had been shipped to New York to seek his fortune. In 1738 he opened a store for Indian trade on the Mohawk River and threw himself with avidity into the life of the frontier. He hunted with the Indians, excelled them at their own warlike sports, and in the end married an Indian princess. He was initiated into the Mohawk tribe as a warrior, was given an Indian name, and appeared wearing Indian dress with war-paint to represent the Indian cause at the Con-ference at Albany. The State of New York appointed him a salaried Native Commissioner. In the war of 1739–48 he com-manded bands of Iroquois against the French Indians with the rank of colonel. During the interval of peace he built himself a great house, Johnson Hall, on an estate granted to him beside the Mohawk River. There he lived like a squire, planting orchards and wheatfields, building his flour-mill and his saw-mill, and settling his lands with hardworking Germans and Dutchmen and Highland Scots. He kept open house for his Indian friends who camped about his estate by hundreds. It was his labour to keep them at peace, to protect them from exploitation, and to encourage the work of the missionaries among them. However, he quarrelled with the parsimonious Assembly at New York and resigned, until his Indian friends persuaded him to become their agent again, and their leader when, the colonial war with France broke out again, in 1754, as the result of a skirmish on the Virginian frontier.

By 1750 pioneers from Virginia had crossed the passes of the Alleghanies and were beginning to establish themselves in the Ohio valley in rivalry with the French. The Virginian govern-ment employed a young man of good cavalier family, George

Washington, to survey these lands for development. In 1753 he was sent with a party of frontiersmen to establish himself on the headwaters of the Ohio, thus claiming dominion over this region by 'effective occupation'. He was expelled in the following year by a superior French force under Governor Duquesne, who then built the stockaded fort which was to bear his name. France and England were still at peace. This frontier scuffle had little effect on the leisurely proceedings of the European powers where the 'Diplomatic Revolution' or 'Reversal of Alliances' was leading to a new war between England and Prussia on the one part and France and Austria on the other. It was not thought that a final breach in Europe would be forced, even by the sending of General Braddock with four regiments of regular troops to restore British control over the Virginian frontier. Braddock marched over the hills and through the forest defiles with a column in close order and a train of baggage until he was ambushed by French-Indians and his column was thrown into confusion. Braddock was carried to the rear, wounded and dying, muttering 'better luck next time'. Young Major Washington brought off the retreating column with credit, learning some useful lessons both about the weakness of regular troops in guerrilla fighting and their steadiness in disaster. 860 men were lost out of a strength of 1460, including 61 out of 87 officers.

The affair at Fort Duquesne which made the name of George Washington is better known than contemporary events in Nova Scotia. For some years past schemes proposed by Captain Coram and others for the colonisation of Nova Scotia had been discussed. In 1749 a plan for a military settlement on this troublesome frontier was approved by Lord Halifax,[1] the President of the Board of Trade. The Bay of Chebucto, which differed from Louisburg in being ice-free except in the severest winters, was selected for the settlement. Just at the time when the French were reoccupying Louisburg (June 1749), Governor Edward Cornwallis arrived with a colony of 3760 settlers to found the city of Halifax in Chebucto Bay. Most of the settlers were discharged soldiers to whom grants of land were promised according to their rank: 50 acres for soldiers or seamen, 300 for lieutenants, 600 for senior officers. Parliament had voted £40,000 for preliminary expenses and undertook to supply a free issue of

[1] George Dunk, Marquess of Halifax (1716–71).

rations, arms and implements until the plantation should take root. Further grants-in-aid were voted during the next seven years, the whole cost to the British tax-payer of founding Halifax being £415,000.

The site was covered with virgin forest to the water's edge. At first no thought of cultivation could be entertained. The Governor set the men to work for wages, clearing the town-site, laying out streets, contructing a wharf and a saw-mill, and building 300 log houses inside a strong stockade, against the approach of winter. In 1750 the garrison was withdrawn from Annapolis to Halifax which became the capital of Nova Scotia. A second settlement at Lunenburg (1753) was planted by a colony of 1430 Germans collected by public advertisement and shipped from Rotterdam. During the interval between the wars (1749–55) Halifax was strictly a military post maintained by its soldier-settlers in opposition to the great fortress of Louisburg which the French made stronger even than before. The British were so annoyed and restricted by the raids of French-Indians that they made little progress inland from their settlements.

When the news came from Virginia of Braddock's disaster at Fort Duquesne the provincial governments at Boston and Halifax were convinced that they must remove the perpetual threat from the Acadians and their Indian allies. The decision was promptly taken to clear the country of the 'neutrals' who had refused to take the Oath of Allegiance. All those who could be caught, to the number of 7000 or 8000, were forcibly deported (1755) in transport-ships to New York, Pennsylvania and Georgia. Some had been taken in arms against the British but most were the peaceful *habitants* of Grand-Pré and other villages in the Bay of Fundy. The searches and deportations, mostly carried out by colonial troops from Boston, continued for some years. Meanwhile the inevitable Seven Years War had broken out in Europe (1756). The second capture of Louisburg, by Wolfe in 1758, and the subsequent conquest of Canada removed the necessity for further persecution. When the whole of New France was ceded to the British in 1763, the surviving Acadians were allowed to remain in the few villages from which they had not been evicted. About 1300 of them settled in the district of Clare in the extreme south-west of Nova Scotia; some have drifted back from their place of exile to their old homes, other to the Magdalen Islands.

No excuse will suffice to justify the barbarous method of deporting these simple peasants whose land and stock were simply confiscated. Their case has, however, been sentimentally overstated in *Evangeline*, which so deeply moved the pity of our grandparents. The Acadians, who may or may not have been the innocents described by Longfellow, had brought about their own ruin by passive resistance against a lawful (and liberal) administration. While they refused British protection, the French blandly repudiated all responsibility for them. Neither subjects, combatants, nor rebels, they suffered the fate of the stateless, in the no-man's-land between the warring powers.

The year 1758 brought the war in Nova Scotia to an end. Since that date the province has been at peace except for privateering raids in the two American wars. The Naval dockyard at Halifax dates from that year (1758) as does representative government in Nova Scotia. Peace with the French at once led to peace with the Indians who made a treaty with the government of Nova Scotia in 1761 by solemnly burying the hatchet in the presence of the Provincial House of Assembly.

The Seven Years War (1756–63) raised the glory of British arms higher than ever before or since. The four central years of the war, 1757–61, when Pitt was in high office, form the only period in British history when national policy has been systematically directed to imperial ends, and when combined operations have been based on a true strategic initiative. Neither Cromwell nor Marlborough nor William Pitt the younger nor Lloyd George nor Winston Churchill has had the will and the power and the strategic insight and the understanding of imperial necessities to fight a war as the governments of France in the eighteenth century and of Germany in the twentieth century have planned and fought. The elder Pitt is the only British statesman who has made war an instrument of policy, almost the only 'imperialist' premier in British history, using that word in its derogatory sense.

The war had caught us, as usual, unprepared. After the pin-prick at Fort Duquesne there had been a series of greater defeats, the loss of our 'factories' in Bengal, the loss of Minorca, the loss of Hanover. Montcalm, the French Governor of Canada, was winning successes about Lake Champlain. French-Indians were raiding into New York State, where they plundered the Mohawk

Valley. Only the influence of William Johnson steadied the Six Nations and prevented a general Indian rising. The first good news was to come from Bengal where Clive, in 1757, won the Battle of Plassy, but victory did not take shape until the combined naval and military operations under officers of Pitt's choice were begun in 1758. The outworks of French Canada were simultaneously assaulted by three widely separated columns. In the west, as Braddock's dying words had foretold, Fort Duquesne fell to 'better luck', or better management; in the centre, not so luckily, the British were bloodily repulsed from Fort Ticonderoga. In eastern Canada young General Wolfe's army landed under fire on an open beach and took the fortress of Louisburg, the decisive stroke of the campaign. The year of Victories, 1759, saw naval successes in the Bay of Biscay, the Mediterranean, and the Caribbean, military successes in Germany, and especially the threefold advance on Canada. In July, Johnson took Fort Niagara, and what is more remarkable prevented his Indians from committing outrages after the victory. Amherst, the Commander-in-Chief, at last stormed Ticonderoga and passed Lake Champlain, but the judgment of history has rightly adjudged to Wolfe the decisive part, and the greater honour. The two resounding volleys and the charge of the Highlanders, at sunrise on 13 September 1759, decided the battle on the Heights of Abraham, the campaign for control of the St Lawrence Valley, the future of the English-speaking nations. North America was to be English not French, and economic mastery of the world for at least 200 years went with the decision. This was the cause in which the two young champions Wolfe and Montcalm both had died. Wolfe's dying eyes saw that his was the victory.

Though the decisive battle had been won, there was much hard fighting before the conquest of Canada was complete. In 1760 all the columns converged on Montreal where the French capitulated. In Europe, too, the greater campaigns on the continental front were, for quite separate reasons, drawing to a close. There were desultory negotiations in which Pitt was ready to consider a peace of compromise, exchanging Canada for the West Indian Island of Guadeloupe, and even Gibraltar for the lost fortress of Minorca. But the war was renewed when Spain injudiciously revealed its alliance with the toppling power of France. At once Pitt's pugnacious instincts revived, and he urged an immediate declaration of war in order to seize the yearly treasure fleet.

It was on this issue that he quarrelled with the young King George III who consistently worked for peace on generous terms. 'Let any war be ever so successful,' wrote the King, 'it will be found upon examination that it has impoverished the nation, enriched individuals, and raised the name only of the conquerors.' However, into war with Spain we drifted without the guiding hand of Pitt at the helm. During the last two years of the war while peace negotiations dawdled on, at the ponderous gait of eighteenth-century diplomacy, British fleets were acquiring French and Spanish possessions in all quarters of the globe; from Spain Havana in the West Indies, and Manila in the East; from France the Sugar Islands of St Lucia, Guadeloupe and Martinique, and the African slave stations of Senegal and Goree. While the King and his minister Bute steadily worked for peace and reconciliation, without crippling annexations, the City, through the mouths of Alderman Beckford and the demagogue John Wilkes, demanded a crushing final triumph over French commerce. This was the 'interest' that supported Pitt and from which he won his title of the Great Commoner. It was, said Beckford, 'the West Indies where all our wars must begin and end'. We must be satisfied with nothing less than a complete exclusion of the French from the Newfoundland fisheries and from the West Indian sugar trade. We must retain Havana, Guadeloupe and Goree. Pitt, who two years earlier had been moderate, was now flushed by victory and vindictive against France and Spain.

It thus appears strange to posterity that the Treaty of Paris (1763), which left the British masters of all North America and with their rule firmly planted in Bengal, should have appeared to the City and the Whigs a shameful diplomatic defeat, a betrayal of Pitt's achievements by Bute and the young king. 'The Peace of Paris is like the Peace of God,' wrote Wilkes profanely, 'it passeth all understanding.' To retain Canada but to give up Guadeloupe seemed as absurd to commercial men of that age as a contrary decision would seem to-day to us. The future wealth of Canada was hidden from all but a few visionaries, while sugar was good for cash and credit on change in Lombard Street. Voltaire wrote that the nations were at war 'pour quelques arpents de neige vers le Canada, et qu'elles dépensent pour cette belle guerre beaucoup plus que tout le Canada ne vaut'.

France ceded to Great Britain by the Treaty of Paris Canada with Acadie and Louisiana, and admitted the English claims over Bengal. Great Britain restored to France her Newfoundland fishing rights, most of her West Indian Islands, Goree in Africa; she restored to Spain all the recent conquests. Minorca again passed to Great Britain.

3. THE AMERICAN COLONIES IN 1763

To those who study the tides and currents of human history no phenomenon can be of more lasting interest than the gradual separation of two great nations, two streams derived from a single source, flowing at first together in one channel, then parting, dividing their course, varying their character, as they pass through different environments, absorbing tributary streams that increase the distinction between them, until the original resemblance is faint and distant. No simple explanation can be given, nor can any final conclusion be reached to account for the causes, the occasion, the beginning, or the completion of the cleavage. To generalise is to give a false impression. This hiving-off, or casting-off, or breaking away of the United States from the British Empire can be and has been reduced to a formula and inflated into a myth, but the causes lie deeper. The successive political crises, when set against their psychological, economic and geographical backgrounds, provide a plan of historical causation leading to an almost inevitable schism.

Not so has the story of the American Revolution been presented to the world. A potent and lasting force in American history has been the revolutionary myth. To create the revolutionary fervour in 1776 it was necessary to invent and to propagate a legend of resistance against tyranny and oppression, and this legend has become part of the American heritage. Long ago American historians with painstaking sincerity set themselves to disentangle the truth from this fantastic tale; but history is of little interest to the public except where it creates enthusiasm, and the myth will never be destroyed until some more compelling political event is inflated by a new political artist into a myth of greater power. Whatever the profound historians may demonstrate in their works of learning, the people of America will continue to be nourished upon the anti-British tirades of the Declaration of Independence, the nursery tales of Paul Revere and Patrick Henry and the Boston Tea-Party, the allusions in a thousand songs and speeches to the glorious escape from the jaws of the tyrant King. This is not a sentimental trifle, it is the deeply-rooted almost instinctive foundation of the American national character, which must be appreciated if America is to be understood. That their own historians should have proved the legend of the downtrodden colonists and the wicked King George III to be a fable is a matter of very slight importance. The tale of Troy was a fable and that too built the character of a nation. What matters is that the Americans believe themselves to have come into existence fighting for liberty, no unworthy faith, and in that faith they stand for liberty to-day.

It is, however, less lucky for us that we should be cast as the villains of this drama. Though the British cause in 1776 has been largely rehabilitated by the efforts of American historians, the mud that was originally thrown sticks. Naturally the British are less powerfully affected by the myth than are the Americans, because what was the birth of America was a mere episode in British history; but so far as there is a traditional tale of the Revolution about which Britons have felt deeply, that tale is told exclusively from the American point of view. The Whig historians of the nineteenth century excelled their transatlantic colleagues in propagating the American myth, and to-day every allusion to the American War on a public platform or in a newspaper in this country is expected to be apologetic and slightly shamefaced. The attitude is symbolised in the erection of a monument to our great adversary, Washington, in Trafalgar Square. The time is likely to be far distant when the Americans, in a mood of magnanimity, will erect a monument to George III, as evidence that old scars are healed and old scores forgotten. Here, in short, is living history, old enthusiasms that still cause the heart to glow, old quarrels that still divide, old passions that are not resolved by logical demonstrations, old faiths that are still fruitful in works.

A neglected aspect of the story is the consideration that thirteen only out of the twenty-seven British dependencies in the West broke out into rebellion. Though there were mutterings of complaint in several others they remained loyal when put to the test. The island colonies were influenced by their sense of dependence on the Royal Navy. Canada had particular reasons for adhering to Great Britain. The significant cases are the two youngest of the mainland colonies. Georgia in the extreme south threw in her lot with the Revolution late and reluctantly, while Nova Scotia in the north remained triumphantly loyal.

Immediately after the pacification of 1763 steps were taken to allure settlers from New England to Nova Scotia with promises of land. The cultivated fields of Grand Pré, protected by dykes against the roaring tides of Fundy were occupied by settlers from Connecticut who founded the township of Horton in 1760. The fishing port of Yarmouth was developed, in 1761, by seamen from the Massachusetts coast. A projector named Alexander McNutt settled the Acadian lands at the head of the Bay with colonists from New England, largely Irishmen (1761–7). This district, Onslow, alone of the Nova Scotian settlements, favoured the Revolutionary party in the American Revolution. The abandoned site of Annapolis, marked by ruinous stone walls and orchard trees, was reoccupied in 1764. As early as 1765 Highlanders from Scotland were settling in the district of Pictou. The whole population of Nova Scotia, in 1764, was estimated at 13,000. The island of Saint John (known as Prince Edward Island after 1799) was granted away by the Crown in 1767 to a group of absentee proprietors. In spite of this handicap 150 families had settled there by 1770 when it became a separate colony.

In 1763 there were no accurate statistics of the population either of the British Isles or of the colonies on the American mainland. It was estimated that there were between eight and nine millions in Great Britain and Ireland. Though the fact was not fully appreciated, the population was beginning to increase very rapidly, and where the fact was conjectured it was not ascribed to the correct cause, a fall in the annual death-rate. Improved hygiene and sanitation and greater variety of diet were imperceptibly conquering diseases produced by dirt and malnutrition, especially among children. The rapid rate of increase was even more noteworthy in the colonies where conditions of life were healthier. Although natural increase in America was assisted by immigration, the former was by far the greater factor.

The population of the mainland colonies in 1760 was estimated at about 70,000 French-Canadians, about 1,200,000 colonists of British origin, and about 400,000 negro slaves, three-quarters of them south of the Mason-Dixon Line. There was no reliable estimate of the Red Indian population, but they were not numerous.

The four New England colonies were a compact group in which Massachusetts, containing Boston the only large town, took the lead over its smaller associates, New Hampshire, Connecticut, and Rhode Island. Their peoples were of entirely English Protestant stock. This region was self-supporting in foodstuffs but not much more. The Acts of Trade prevented New England from developing manufactures, but craftsmanship flourished in the smaller village trades, and the New Englanders were already renowned as skilful shipbuilders. The Navigation Acts which restricted them in other directions protected them in this, so that they monopolised the American coastal trade and were active in the fisheries.

The middle colonies, New York, New Jersey and Pennsylvania, contained two large towns, New York city and Philadelphia, and the best routes to the interior. New York was, as it still is, the most cosmopolitan city in America, and was the centre of English mercantile interests. Wheat, Indian corn and pork were produced in the middle colonies in quantity to allow a surplus for export. Among the inhabitants of the middle colonies were many Protestant Dutchmen and Germans, but the Irish Roman Catholics had not yet begun to make their appearance. The Roman Catholic Church was everywhere persecuted except in Pennsylvania—even in Maryland, once a Catholic sanctuary.

Delaware and Maryland in a small way, and Virginia in a large way were the tobacco colonies. The London merchants sent their ships up the navigable creeks of Chesapeake Bay to buy tobacco in bulk direct from the estates of the growers, so that the tobacco-planters needed no commercial centre and used little currency. Though they lived a liberal life in their manor houses surrounded by ill-conditioned easy-going families of slaves, their wealth was less solid than it appeared, and suffered all the disadvantages of dependence on a single crop. If the market failed, Virginia had to live on scanty credit.

The Carolinas and Georgia were beginning to develop a vicious slave economy far different from the household slavery of Virginia. The planters were capitalists who had found a profitable crop in rice, and were soon to find one still more profitable in cotton. Slaves were bought and sold like cattle, were worked in gangs, and deprived of all protection by the laws, the slave-code being far more atrocious than those of the French and Spanish colonies. Rewards in money were offered for the recapture of runaways, the figure being sometimes as high as £50, if alive, and, if dead, £10 each for scalps.

The only large town in the south was Charleston, the market and the pleasure-resort of the planters. Of the four principal towns in the colonies, Boston, New York, Philadelphia, Charleston, none had a population exceeding 30,000.

The external trade of the colonies which had been both fostered and restricted by the Navigation Acts had developed largely on the 'triangular' route. New England ships carried the foodstuffs of the northern and middle colonies to the sub-tropical southern and West Indian colonies. They in their turn sent their tobacco, sugar, rice, indigo and other 'enumerated commodities' to the English market, and the returning trade brought English manufactured goods to Boston and New York from where they were distributed through America.

The administrative control of colonial commerce by the Acts of Trade was less real than its secondary consequence, financial control by the 'City'. Since the whole volume of colonial exports passed to England and since new supplies of capital for colonial development came from England also, many of the greater properties were owned by English capitalists or mortgaged to English banks. There was a perpetual shortage of currency in the colonies, and no money-market. Spanish dollars —pieces-of-eight—passed current everywhere, but local trade was largely by barter, rum or tobacco being the usual mediums of exchange. Little local banks issued notes, on doubtful security, until Parliament intervened with an Act for restraining note-issues. Though intended to prevent inflation and fraud it was an item in the account booked up against the Imperial Government. Another was control of the frontier.

4. TAXATION AND REPRESENTATION

CANADA was no sooner conquered than the colonies began to grow restive, even before peace was concluded with France. During many years every observant visitor to America, every designing foreign statesman, and several political philosophers had prophesied a breach between Old and New England as soon as the French menace should be removed. It has been recorded in John Wesley's *Journal*, and in the dying words of Montcalm that the sole link between England and her colonies was fear of the French on the frontier. The saying of the French economist Turgot was accepted as a commonplace that colonies are destined to drop off from the parent tree like fruit when ripe. The time of maturity had come and was first recognised by ambitious lawyers who had always found it easy to get notoriety in the colonial courts by twisting the lion's tail. The year 1761 is marked by several court cases in which irresponsible advocates, such as James Otis of Massachusetts and Patrick Henry of Virginia, challenged the authority of the British government to intervene in colonial affairs. Otis, in particular, fought a test case on the legality of search-warrants, a curious parallel to the case which the irresponsible demagogue, John Wilkes, fought in England a year or two later.

These cases stood upon historical precedent. 'What we did', wrote Jefferson, the Virginian democrat, 'was with the help of *Rushworth* [editor of legal documents of the Cromwellian period] whom we rummaged over for the Revolutionary precedents of those days.' The appeal was to the old principles of the constitution, to the seventeenth-century Whig writers, especially John Locke, and to the conveniently elastic 'Laws of Nature', an appeal which was strictly in line with that of the contemporary English radicals. From beginning to end every phase of the American Revolution had its counterpart in England. The constitutional struggle was fought throughout the Empire and almost came to civil war in England and in Ireland as well as in America; but far deeper than these pedantic lawyers' quarrels were the true issues, the emergence of a new nation that could no longer be held in subordination, and the failure on either side of the Atlantic to devise an adequate imperial constitution.

At the end of the Seven Years War the British government found itself in possession of vast conquered territories which perforce were held under martial law. Canada, with its French-speaking Roman Catholic population, was kept in that status for some years. The little-known wilderness called Louisiana, lightly populated by primitive nomadic Indians, was a more difficult problem, as the Indian lands had been encroached upon by French-colonial pioneers from the north and English-colonial pioneers from the east for several years past. It was, after 1761, controlled by British regular troops and their Indian allies. The intention of the British government was to form an extensive Indian reservation in the Ohio basin and to protect the Indians from exploitation by rum-runners and land-sharks. The immediate practical solution was to proclaim (1763) the whole hinterland between the watershed of the Alleghanies and the Mississippi a reserve for the Indian nations, to be administered by the military Governor of Canada, a well-intentioned policy which unfortunately pleased nobody but the French politicians. The English colonists were infuriated at finding their westward march again blocked by a military power far greater than that of Governor Duquesne; the Canadian *coureurs-de-bois* disliked the proclamation which limited their activities also; the Indian tribes resented transference from the French to the British allegiance without consent or consultation; and the French found it easy to plant agents among the Indians to foment the irritation. No display of force, no cunning of statecraft could have availed to prevent the frontiersmen from percolating into these fertile and almost empty lands, or to restrain the Indians from savage reprisals on the intruders. In 1763 and 1764 the whole frontier was ablaze from Lake Ontario to Georgia. The Indian tribes, capable at times of a high degree of political organisation, had found a leader in the Ottawa chief, Pontiac, who even succeeded in detaching the Senecas, one of the six tribes of the Iroquois, from their alliance with the British. Uncounted families of pioneers were driven from their settlements, robbed and scalped, until the Indian confederacy was broken up by two columns of British regulars who had been trained and equipped for Indian warfare. They were clothed, for protective coloration, in dark green, armed with rifled guns, and trained to fight in open order. The regiment is now called the King's Royal Rifles. In these campaigns the colonial assemblies far away in safety by the tide-water showed their worst form. With secure complacency they thrust the financial burden of the campaign upon the British exchequer and, in general, refused to allow their local militia to join in any united operation. Each colony would defend its own frontier and grudgingly vote funds for that alone. It was the last service of Sir William Johnson to pacify the tribes after Pontiac's war. He travelled far and wide through the Indian reserve, penetrating to the Mississippi and to Detroit and finally presided at an assembly of the Indians at Fort Stanwyx in 1768. Johnson died in 1774, and his work for the Indians hardly survived him.

The British government was now at peace with the world and disposed towards economy. The national debt had reached the figure of £130,000,000, a sum on which the annual interest amounted to one-half the national revenue, and this sum had been spent on the conquest of French North America. Canada and Louisiana had been conquered by British arms and British money; they were still defended by these agencies alone. The yearly cost of the army of occupation was estimated at £400,000, spent in the colonies. The case put forward by George Grenville, as Chancellor of the Exchequer in 1764, was that a part of this additional liability should be collected from the colonies, and in equity his case was unanswerable. But to demand the repayment of a debt of honour and to endeavour to collect the debt by force are rarely the acts of a wise statesman. After courteously consulting the colonial agents in London and rejecting their advice, Grenville introduced into Parliament a bill for collecting a small revenue in the colonies in the form of a stamp duty on legal documents. As is the way with colonial measures the bill attracted little attention and was passed by a 'languid' House. At the same time Grenville took measures to enforce the customs regulations which were authorised by the 'Acts of Trade'.

The outbreak of protest and obstruction with which these moderate measures were greeted in America came as a complete surprise. They had the effect which neither the French nor the Indian wars, neither the ingenuity of Franklin nor the policy of the British military commanders could produce; they crystallised American opinion and at last formed the disjointed colonies into a single nation. All the politically-minded among the settlers believed themselves to have a legitimate grievance and were more united in opinion than ever before. A 'continental' congress to concert joint measures against the Stamp Act was at once convened, and the history of the United States was begun.

At the root of their new-found hostility to Great Britain was a conviction that the western lands should be their own, both by the moral law which entitled a pioneer to the lands he has discovered, planted, and converted to the use of man, and by constitutional law declared in the charters which the Stuart kings had granted. They saw the establishment in their midst of a standing army—in itself, they believed, unconstitutional—for the express purpose of limiting their westward expansion. They observed the new decision to enforce and to stiffen the code of commercial restrictions which had been so laxly administered, so easily evaded for a hundred years. These tendencies seemed to have been drawn by the Stamp Act into a general aim, to subject the colonies to the British Parliament, at the moment when their national destiny of freedom and expansion lay at last open before them.

There was as yet no outcry for independence; the colonies demanded their chartered rights, which were derived immediately from the King and not from Parliament. They resisted the attempt by Parliament to override their own assemblies and appealed against Parliament to the King, claiming very much what has come to be known in the twentieth century as Dominion Status. The form of the struggle thus became direct disagreement on a point of principle, whether Parliament could legally impose a direct tax on the colonies. The Americans summarised their case in the slogan, 'No Taxation without Representation', which was hotly discussed in both Houses of Parliament. The case for the Government was stated by Lord Chief Justice Mansfield in terms of 'virtual representation'. Democracy was no part of the British Constitution. Eight of the nine million inhabitants of Great Britain were without votes, but none the less had their interests upheld in Parliament. The House of Commons represented shires and boroughs and corporations not flocks of voters; it virtually represented all substantial interests, and through them every British subject could make his voice heard. This was plain fact. The fisheries interest, the shipping interest, the tobacco interest, the sugar interest, the slave interest were powerful in both Houses and, as for the general interest of the

American people, that was virtually represented by a range of talent such as Parliament has rarely known. By what system of suffrages could they have elected such men as Pitt, Shelburne, Burke, Fox and Wilkes, who ranging from the right to the left wing of politics defended the American cause from the Opposition benches. But the interplay of English politics at that moment, unhappily for America, had placed all the talent with the Opposition and all the votes of the dumb back-benchers with the Government. Let the disreputable Wilkes talk democracy; it was out of the question then and for another hundred years in aristocratic Britain. Let the sentimentalist Burke preach generosity rather than legality: 'It is not a question whether it is your right to make these people miserable but whether it is not your interest to make them happy'; it had no effect on the votes of the Government supporters. It was Pitt who swayed the opinion of the House. He proclaimed and gloried in the absolute sovereignty of Parliament, which could legislate for all parts of the Empire and in all cases, with this one Whiggish exception, that it could not 'take a man's money out of his pocket without his own consent'.

This was but one issue in a political struggle and not the crucial issue which led to the fall of Grenville's government, a few months after the passing of the Stamp Act. The next government, under Rockingham, a feeble, inept politician, repealed the Stamp Act but tacked to the repeal a general Declaratory Act, asserting the legislative authority of Parliament over all colonial assemblies, though it took no steps to implement it. The colonists had won the first round, having defied Parliament and resisted the tax. But the Declaratory Act served to confirm them in the suspicion that the British government had further tyrannical designs. The Act is one of the few examples in English history of an attempt to define constitutional principles by statute, to convert our unwritten constitution to a formal written model. It remained as a cause of friction with various colonial legislatures until, in 1931, the substance of it was repealed by the so-called ' Statute of Westminster '.

The problem of paying for the defence of the American frontier remained, and a new administration which shortly replaced that of Rockingham set about solving it in a way suggested by the Declaratory Act. The next Chancellor of the Exchequer, Townshend, admitted that he thought the distinction between direct and indirect taxation 'nonsensical', but since the colonists accepted the legality of the latter and rejected that of the former he would proceed to raise a little revenue, all of it to be spent in and for the colonies, by way of customs duties on tea, glass, paint and other articles of secondary importance—the colonists had always agreed in theory to the Acts of Trade and why not to this? Having introduced his imprudent Budget he died shortly after.

Three or four years of revolutionary education had meanwhile made colonial opinion much firmer, so that the opposition to these duties was more systematic than that to the Stamp Act. The anti-British agitation had never died down in New England; it now broke out in Virginia under the leadership of Patrick Henry. Again a Continental Congress was summoned and again a series of resolutions was voted, protesting loyalty to the King, but determination to resist the encroachments of Parliament. An Association was formed on the model of the Scottish Covenanters' League to resist the payment of duties and to denounce those American 'Tories' who were obedient to the British Government. There rapidly spread through the colonies a system of local committees who organised a boycott of dutiable goods and, what is less justifiable, a boycott of all those persons who took the loyal side. As in all revolutions those who shouted loudest for liberty were the first to deny it to those who differed from them.

At this juncture there was a violent change in the balance of British politics. The young King George III had spent the first years of his reign in breaking up the domination of the Whig noblemen who for two generations had monopolised the spoils of office. A series of political manoeuvres had served to divide them into smaller factions, to split up their voting power, and to build a national party in opposition to them. He had succeeded, at least so far as to place in office (1770) the amiable, loyal, and pliant Lord North with a sufficient majority in both Houses of Parliament. The vacillations of the 1760's now gave place in the 1770's to a clear, consistent, and firm policy which might perhaps have produced some effect if it had been begun ten years sooner.

King George and his minister North were determined upon the principles of the Declaratory Act. The imperial sovereignty of Parliament must first be enforced and acknowledged. Secondly, order must be restored in the colonies; the unquestionable duty of a sovereign government was to maintain public tranquillity and due process of law. Thirdly, if the colonies would submit and place themselves under his protection, the King would assure them their chartered rights and would make any reasonable accommodation in the matter of the cost of their defence. This attitude was a great disappointment to the colonies; they were now not complaining about a tax of ninepence in the pound on tea, but about something which had become a point of honour with them, a matter of prestige. They had appealed to the King for protection against the demands of Parliament, but the King had taken his stand with his Parliament against them.

5. INDEPENDENCE

THE years 1770 to 1774 were largely taken up with unsuccessful attempts to restore order in Boston, where the town mob was systematically urged to riot and sedition. It was not difficult to inflame a sea-faring population, renowned for smuggling, against the officers of the revenue. The task was skilfully done by Samuel Adams, a radical lawyer with a fiercely anti-English bias. He was apt at provoking riots and inventing tales of atrocities against the officers whose duty it was to suppress them. At first the British government behaved with restraint and conciliation. After a riot in which a handful of soldiers were obliged to fire on a mob in self-defence, the so-called 'Boston Massacre', the government withdrew the soldiers from the town to avoid other incidents. Order reigned again in New England until the agitators provoked a mob to loot and burn the King's ship *Gaspée*, the most disgraceful of their actions, and finally to stage the riot known as the 'Boston Tea-Party', in December 1773. This arose from the last attempt to implement the Declaratory Act by imposing a token customs-duty on the colonies. The obnoxious duties levied by Townshend had been withdrawn, excepting that on tea which was retained as a test case. In order to oblige the East India Company which had large stocks of tea on hand, shipments were to be sent direct to America, thus avoiding the duties payable in English ports. The colonies were to pay a nominal duty of ninepence in the pound as a matter of principle and would get their tea nevertheless far cheaper than before. But to admit the principle was just what they would not do. The tea was refused everywhere in America and remains a little-used commodity there to this day. The Boston consignment was destroyed in a riot which exhausted the patience of King George's government. It was decided to restore order in New England by coercive measures. Without much difficulty North got through Parliament a series of bills for closing the Port of Boston, for suspending the charter of Massachusetts, and for placing New England under the military rule of General Gage, the Commander-in-Chief.

This desultory quarrel had now been going on for more than ten years, a long period in the history of party politics. On the British side, the rights and wrongs of the American colonists had taken their turn for the public notice with other imperial problems. Riots incited by radicals in Boston had not loomed so large as riots incited by radicals in London over the Middlesex Election. The constitutional relation between Parliament and the colonial assemblies was no more urgent a problem than the relation between Parliament and the East India Company. This last was much before Parliament in the early 1770's when Burke and Pitt (now Earl of Chatham) had more to say about Bengal than Boston.

At the time when their Empire in the West was dissolving into revolution, though they did not yet appreciate the danger, the Lords and Commons of England had their eyes fixed upon the East. A liberal policy for India, the new doctrine of 'trusteeship' for subject races, were the topics of debate. Even the Treasury was moved to co-operate when an enlightened Chancellor, ranging from one end of the imperial landscape to the other, thought to help Indian trade by importing to America, under a special tariff, the tea which the Americans chose to throw into Boston Harbour.

Canada, too, was taking up Parliamentary time. By the Quebec Act of 1773 the boundaries of Canada were confirmed as including the Ohio Basin, and the French-Canadians were permitted to retain their own civil law and religion. The last clause gave great offence in Protestant New England.

The coercion of New England by statute did not at first seem to be either a difficult undertaking or a desperate measure; but the colonists felt it as the latter and were resolved to make it the former. Suppression of chartered rights, martial law, the iron hand withdrawn from the velvet glove, these were the signs of tyranny which they had long dreaded and now saw revealed.

During the autumn of 1774, civil war rapidly drew on. Gage and his small army found themselves blockaded in Boston where they were dependent for supplies upon a hostile rural neighbourhood. The dispossessed Massachusetts Assembly, nearby at Salem, was in regular correspondence with the Congress at Philadelphia and both were openly concerting measures of resistance. No overt act of war took place however until April 1775, when Gage sent a column of troops to destroy a rebel magazine at the unhappily named village of Concord. On the way back the troops were attacked by armed bands at Lexington. They fought their way through to Boston with a loss of sixty-five men killed. A few weeks later the colonists boldly took the initiative by occupying and entrenching Bunker Hill which overlooks the harbour. On 17 June, Gage ordered out a brigade of British regulars to clear the hilltop. He so much under-estimated the fighting qualities of the Americans as to neglect both the superior power of manoeuvre possessed by his trained troops and the help which the warships of the fleet might have given him. He counted on dislodging the Americans by a display of force in a frontal attack. The Americans were dislodged, but only at the third assault and after inflicting 1200 casualties on the British, a loss they could not afford. This, if anything, should be remembered as the Boston Massacre.

A few days earlier, Congress had voted authority for raising a Continental Army to be commanded by George Washington; but even as late in the struggle as this its full implications were not understood. It was on either side an attempt to establish a principle by direct action and not yet an absolute war. The news of Bunker Hill was an effective solvent of sentimental ties. The British realised they must fight relentlessly if they were to retain the colonies, and the Americans, having killed so many redcoats, felt that they were capable of victory.

During these months, belated attempts at conciliation were made by both sides. A final petition known as the Olive Branch, in the form of an appeal from his American subjects for protection against his British subjects, was sent to the King, who refused to receive it since it came from Congress which was in armed rebellion against him. Simultaneously he offered peace and protection to any colony which should propose its own plan for the cost of its own defence; but this proposal was rejected out of hand by Congress as an insidious attempt to sow dissensions between the colonies. The news of Bunker Hill had put an end to hopes of conciliation.

It was the aim of the British government and of their generals in America to crush the rebellion in New England before it should spread to the other colonies. This policy might have been attained in one of two ways: the rebels might have been crushed by superior military force, punished by martial law, and reduced to such misery as would have obliged them to submit, for the time at least; or they might have been confronted by some magnanimous stroke of policy, a generous offer of concessions which would have reconciled the moderate men and left the convinced revolutionaries in a small minority. Neither of these paths was taken. The King's proposal of 1775 offered too little and arrived too late; on the other hand, General Gage had neither the power nor the inclination to terrorise the country. The Army was helpless in Boston; when concentrated there it achieved nothing, when dispersed in detachments it was destroyed piecemeal by the guerrilla bands. New England proved to have an ideal social system for carrying on partisan warfare. Every able-bodied man was a hunter accustomed to the use of arms; every township was self-supporting and self-governing. The occupation of the capital, Boston, by a hostile army made almost no difference to the farmers who grew their own food and managed their own affairs in the town-meeting. The British commanders might have attempted to clear the country, hanging all men found in possession of arms, but no such drastic measure was ever proposed. On the contrary, several of the generals, especially Howe, who succeeded Gage as Commander-in-Chief in 1776, were much inclined to political sympathy with the rebels. They would have welcomed an accommodation and hated, as soldiers always do, this active service in aid of the civil power, a war against their fellow-subjects. It was with relief that they decided to withdraw from Boston and conduct a campaign from a more suitable base, the loyal city of New York.

The British government conceived the plan of isolating the incorrigible New Englanders and of rallying the friendly elements in all the other colonies. In Nova Scotia these were a safe majority; in Canada it was to be hoped that the toleration recently granted by the Quebec Act would at least tend to keep the *habitants* tranquil; New York, whose life and commerce depended on the British connexion, was pretty well secured; in Virginia, the Old Dominion, though there was much disloyal talk, surely there were many loyal sons of the cavaliers; in the Carolinas and in Georgia there seemed to be little sign of rebellion. Meanwhile a contrary policy was adopted by the Congress leaders whose interest it was to spread the revolution into every colony. By means of their network of corresponding committees they gained control of the organs of government in the twelve adjacent colonies from New Hampshire to South Carolina and at last in Georgia, the thirteenth. Where they had constitutional power they used it to disfranchise the loyalists and to confiscate their property; where there was no legal authority they incited mobs to plunder and ill-use the loyalists; and where this method was beyond their strength they levied guerrilla war. In 1776, Canada was invaded by an army from New England. The Governor, Sir Guy Carleton, defended the ramparts of Quebec, eventually driving off the invaders with the help of Scottish and French-Canadian loyalist volunteers. Since Congress had fiercely protested against the grant of religious toleration to the Canadian Roman Catholics it is not surprising that an appeal to the Canadians to rise in revolt against the government that guaranteed this toleration was a failure.

The loyalists in the Thirteen Colonies were numerous but unorganised. They included in their ranks the majority of royal officials, of Anglican clergy and their families. Among those who may be classed as officials were many whose duties took them among the Indians. Missionaries, Native Agents and officers of the irregular corps which guarded the frontiers were disposed to see the Indian point of view in the struggle for the hinterland and to favour the imperial policy of creating Indian reserves. Sir William Johnson's death in 1774 was a loss to moderate and British interests; his son Sir John was a loyalist leader. Robert Rogers, the most celebrated frontiersman of his day, whose Rangers have been an inspiration to all later practicians of irregular warfare, was a loyalist.

In the cities all that connexion which nowadays is called 'Big Business' tended to the British side. Those who had interests on both sides of the Atlantic felt the advantage of the Acts of Trade and could afford to scoff at the pettiness of colonial politics. At the end of the war they withdrew with their wealth to the comforts of Old England, and maintained their personal contacts and their commercial dealings with the new America. In this class there was an ebb and flow with the fortunes of war. Alexander Hamilton was not the only loyalist who ended as a revolutionary nor Benedict Arnold the only revolutionary who reverted to the loyalist side. Families were divided; Franklin's son was a loyalist.

These were distinguished individuals. The great bulk of the loyalists was composed of recent emigrants to America and was to be found in the newer colonies. The Highlanders in Nova Scotia and the Scottish elements in the other colonies in general withheld their support from the Revolution. The inland settlements of the Carolinas and Georgia had been planted by Jacobite emigrants after the failure of the '45. Their traditional politics were Tory and, by a strange reversal, they had transferred their loyalty to the Tory King George, though his grandfather had been their enemy and his uncle, Cumberland, the destroyer of the Highland clans. Among the Scottish loyalists who fled from the fury of the American Whigs, as she had fled thirty years before from the fury of the English Whigs, was Flora MacDonald, the saviour of Prince Charlie.

On the other hand the Scotch-Irish, as Ulstermen were called in America, were solidly on the revolutionary side. They had begun to move across the Atlantic in Charles II's time when the Navigation Laws bore as hardly on Irish as on colonial manufactures. By 1750 it was estimated that they numbered about 50,000, from whose number Washington drew the best regiments of his Continental Army. The Scotch-Irish provided a high proportion of the political leaders in the early years of the Republic.

Ten years earlier there had been no suggestion of independence in any colonial assembly or in the correspondence of any responsible American leader. Every petition and remonstrance has been expressed in the language of legality and of loyalty. But the long struggle over the Stamp Act, the Declaratory Act, the Acts of

Trade, and the Tea Duties had forced thousands of simple colonists to re-examine the fundamentals of their politics. Gradually and reluctantly they discovered that their loyalty to the King of Great Britain had died. The stalk had withered, the fruit was ripe and ready to fall from the tree. The Americans roused themselves and awoke a nation of republicans and democrats, actively hostile to the Court of St James's and to the whole galaxy of social, legal and ecclesiastical lights that circulated around it. This change of heart was not made casually, nor absolutely, nor without moments of weakness and regret. In 1775 and 1776 there were many hesitants. Even after his appointment as general, Washington declared that he 'abhorred the idea of Independence'. But when the change came, when the inhibition was released, the conversion produced a flow of energy and power and a bitter hatred of the divorced partner in the broken alliance. The inhibition, the mental struggle, the release and the compensating violence are all clearly expressed in the preamble to the Declaration of Independence, which was chiefly the work of Thomas Jefferson:

When in the Course of human events, it becomes necessary for one people to dissolve the political bands which have connected them with another, and to assume among the powers of the earth, the separate and equal station to which the Laws of Nature and of Nature's God entitle them, a decent respect to the opinions of mankind requires that they should declare the causes which impel them to the separation.

The Declaration next proclaims the 'self-evident truths' that all men are 'created equal', are endowed with 'inalienable rights' to 'Life, Liberty and the Pursuit of Happiness', and have instituted governments to secure these rights. But 'whenever any Form of Government becomes destructive of these ends, it is the Right of the People to alter or to abolish it and to institute new governments'.

Prudence, indeed, will dictate that Governments long established should not be changed for light and transient causes; and accordingly all experience hath shown, that mankind are more disposed to suffer, while evils are sufferable, than to right themselves by abolishing the forms to which they are accustomed. But when a long train of abuses and usurpations, pursuing invariably the same object evinces a design to reduce them under absolute Despotism, it is their right, it is their duty, to throw off such Government....

No doubt the Americans persuaded themselves that there was in fact a direct design in Great Britain to establish 'an absolute Tyranny over these States', though it is hard to reconcile the evidence they adduced with the melancholy tale of fumblings and vacillations in British colonial policy then and thereafter; in George Grenville's parsimonious book-keeping, or in the illogical compromise with which it had been overruled, or in the experimental tariff of custom duties levied and varied and counter-manded by Townshend, Grafton and North, or even in the stubborn determination of King George to suppress sabotage and riot.

'Let facts', say the authors of the Declaration, 'be submitted to a candid world.' The King of Great Britain has 'obstructed the administration of justice'; 'has erected a multitude of new offices and sent hither swarms of officers to harass our people'; 'has kept among us, in time of peace, standing armies'; 'has affected to render the military independent of the civil power'; 'has combined with others [i.e. Parliament] to subject us to a jurisdiction foreign to our constitution'. He has given his 'assent to their Acts:...for cutting off our trade...for imposing taxes on us without our consent...for abolishing the free system of English laws in a neighbouring Province [Quebec],...and enlarging its boundaries so as to render it...a fit instrument for introducing the same absolute rule into these colonies,...for taking away our Charters,...for suspending our Legislatures. He had abdicated Government here by...waging war against us ...has plundered our seas, ravaged our coasts, burnt our towns. ...He is at this time transporting...mercenaries to complete the works of death, desolation, and tyranny...and has endeavoured to bring on the inhabitants of our frontiers the merciless Indian savages.' The violent rhetoric of this document shows how far the revolutionary sentiment had moved in America between 17 June 1775 and 4 July 1776.

6. WASHINGTON AND FRANKLIN

AFTER the failure to extend the Revolution to Canada the American cause languished and the quarrels between the various colonies revived. The mere show of force by the British Army in New York and by the Navy at many points in American waters appeared to be breaking the spirit of the rebels so that a restoration of the old order was confidently expected. The members of Congress seemed as unwilling to make sacrifices for the American as for the Imperial cause, and occupied themselves largely with obstructing the needs and questioning the authority of General Washington who now bore the whole burden of responsibility for the Campaign. It was his intention and his achievement to make his ragged 'Continentals' into an army and to keep that army in being as a nucleus for the national revolt. He must pin the British down, harass their outposts, and threaten their flanks, but avoid a pitched battle in which he was likely to be defeated. While the Continental Army remained in the field, the British regulars could not be dispersed to pacify the country, and the country would remain in the possession of the colonial guerrilla bands.

Washington was a strange leader for a people's war. High birth and breeding, a coat-of-arms which is to be seen quartered with the coats of the noblest houses on several English heraldic monuments,[1] great wealth which made him by repute the richest man in America, and a cold haughty manner seemed to have designed him for command over the loyalists; but from the moment when he accepted the generalship of the Continental Army he never wavered. His character and his purpose were fixed, his resolution was unchangeable. When he made up his mind for independence thousands of moderate men followed his decision. When he offered his sword for the protection of the Boston rioters, accepting their part as better justified than that of their opponents, thousands of respectable men who had shrunk from the onset of violence took side with him. By temper a

---

[1] Argent, three mullets gules, three bars azure. A well-known story tells how this design was worked into the first American flag by Washington's household. The mullets (stars) replaced the Union Jack in a flag based on that of the East India Company, a red ensign with six horizontal white stripes.

conservative aristocrat he set himself to impose discipline on his
ill-found soldiery and to acquire for them the status of regular
combatants. Lack of money, lack of equipment, and an inclination shown by his men to desert every summer at harvest-time
hampered him more than the unenterprising movements of the
English generals. Though there were 700,000 adult males in
America his army never reached a strength of 25,000; he never
put as many as 18,000 in the field; he ended the war with a mere
6000 regulars; and this from a population of nearly two millions.
He overcame all difficulties, partly by employing Prussian
soldiers of fortune as drill-masters, mostly by the force of his own
rock-like personality. He cared nothing that his dignity and
reserve destroyed his popularity. The ribald soldier's song,
'Yankee Doodle', in one of its early versions ridiculed him for
being so 'tarnal proud', for being a 'macaroni with a feather in
his hat', but he ignored the criticism. His army never won a
battle but it won the war.

After the defiant challenge of the Declaration of Independence
(4 July 1776) the Americans for more than a year achieved very
little. There was an indecisive campaign about New York from
which Washington retired, having had the worst of every engagement, to winter quarters south of the Delaware, a wretched winter
and the lowest ebb of American hopes.

While he and his men shivered, keeping up their spirits by
occasional raids on the British outposts, King George's government was preparing plans and providing troops to bring the war
to a crisis. But though there were loyalists in America there were
also rebel sympathisers in England, and in general the cause and
the campaigns were unpopular. Lack of recruits, never too plentiful in Old England, forced upon the government the hateful
expedient of building up the strength of the Army with German
mercenaries, sold into slavery by their unnatural monarch, the
Duke of Hesse. The hiring out of conscripts was normal among
the kings of Europe but aroused horror among the republicans
of the New World who did not always pause to recollect that
they too were slave-traders.

The conduct of the war was largely in the hands of Lord
George Germain, the holder of a new office, the Secretaryship of
State for Trade and the Colonies. A shallow clever man, he had
never quite lived down the imputation of cowardice made against

him many years before when he was serving as a young officer
at the Battle of Minden. He was now prolific of grandiose plans
and optimistic forecasts, and much inclined to interfere with the
puzzled, unwilling generals, though his information was by
necessity two or three months out of date. It was alleged, perhaps
unjustly, that the campaign of 1777 failed because he forgot to
post a despatch to General Howe before going away for a holiday,
an occurrence amusingly described in Mr Bernard Shaw's *Devil's
Disciple*.

Two alternative plans were proposed for the year's operations.
One was the assemblage of a force in Canada to march down by
Lake Champlain, the path so often fought over in the French wars,
to occupy the line of the Hudson. New England would thus be
cut off from the interior and from the other nine colonies, and
might be reduced at leisure. The other plan was for a march south
from New York to complete the recovery of the middle colonies
by dispersing the Congress and its supporters from Philadelphia,
and to rally the southern loyalists. Owing to a confusion of
plans, the fault partly of Germain but partly of the rival generals,
both plans were simultaneously attempted. Howe marched
south, captured Philadelphia, and sent the Congressmen flying
helter-skelter into Virginia, while Burgoyne came down from
Canada as far as Saratoga on the Hudson, where he found himself threatened on all sides and with no prospect of help from
Howe. His little force of about 1900 British regulars and 1600
Hessians had cut themselves off from their base and could not now
reach their goal. After gallant and costly attempts to fight his
way through the American militiamen, who outnumbered him
three to one, Burgoyne surrendered on terms. His men were to
be marched to the coast with the honours of war, the officers
remaining with their men, and were to be repatriated to England.
Every clause of the convention was broken by the American
Congress. The rank and file were separated from their officers
and held as prisoners while inducements were offered them to
desert to the Revolutionary side, a policy which had some
success with the German mercenaries.

The news of Saratoga (October 1777) changed the face of the
war. It revived American hopes; it shattered British complacency; it served to persuade the Bourbon Kings of France and
Spain to give recognition, military aid, and eventually open

alliance to the Americans. Carleton wrote from Canada on hearing the news, 'this unfortunate event, it is hoped, will in future prevent Ministers from pretending to conduct operations of war in a country at three thousand miles distance', but his hopes were

THE THIRTEEN COLONIES
AND NOVA SCOTIA
1763-83
Miles
0   100   200   300

States of Vermont and Maine not organized till after Independence. Frontiers of Nova Scotia disputed.

George Philip & Son, Ltd.

Map 2

not realised. Lord North did, however, make a final attempt at conciliation in order to reunite the empire against the French. He sent commissioners to America with almost unlimited powers to offer any concessions short of Independence, but Congress refused to make any reply.

Benjamin Franklin had been for many years the London agent
of several of the colonies, holding also a salaried post as deputy
Postmaster-General for the Colonies. In this capacity he had suggested some useful modifications in the Stamp Act. Like other
Americans he had shared in the exultation over Pitt's victories
and like King George had 'gloried in the name of Britain'. As
far back as 1754 he had proposed the plan at Albany for uniting
the colonies within the Empire, and twenty years later he was
still engaged in discussions and negotiations to this end. As
Washington was the most eminent among the colonists in
America, so Franklin was the most eminent American in the eyes
of the polite world of Europe. But though he favoured a rugged,
colonial simplicity and appeared to be bland, expansive, even
jocular, his was a subtle scheming nature. He had got the better
of the mealy-mouthed Quakers in the petty politics of Pennsylvania, and was quite capable of outwitting the counsellors of
King George and of King Louis. His reputation stood, in 1770,
on his researches into electrical phenomena which had led to the
invention of the lightning-conductor, and on his endeavours to
promote popular education. He had founded an academy, a
public library, and a newspaper in Philadelphia; and the series of
moral aphorisms which he issued under the pseudonym of 'Poor
Richard' were forming the character of the American business
man. He was the industrious apprentice turned philosopher.

At what point he ceased to work for imperial reform and
began to work for American independence it is hard to say. In
1763 he had fully approved of 'some revenue arising out of the
American trade to be applied towards supporting troops', that
is, the plan of the Tea Duties which, ten years later, he resisted.
During the Stamp Act debates he spoke ominously at the Bar
of the House of Commons of resisting 'by force of arms' the
payment of direct taxes. He was at all times exasperated by the
supercilious tone of condescension which so many Englishmen
adopted (and still adopt) in speaking of the Empire. 'Every man
in England', he said bitterly, 'seems to consider himself as a piece
of a sovereign over America; seems to jostle himself into the
throne with the King, and talks of *our subjects in the colonies*.'
His antipathy increased as the dispute dragged on, until an event
in January 1774 made him an open republican. The Assembly of
Massachusetts, shortly before its suppression, petitioned for the

removal of the Governor, employing Franklin to argue their case
before the Privy Council. The evidence against the Governor
was based upon some stolen letters which had come into Franklin's possession, and had been published in spite of Franklin's
promise that they would remain private. The Solicitor-General
roundly called Franklin a thief, not without some justification.
From that moment Franklin became a dangerous and powerful
enemy to Great Britain.

After the Declaration of Independence, Franklin was sent with
two other agents to represent the American Congress in Paris.
The court of France had been watching the troubles in America
with malicious delight. The French defeats in the Seven Years
War still rankled and the humiliation of England seemed desirable.
Accordingly the French government adopted what is known in
the diplomatic jargon of to-day as a 'non-belligerent' policy.
They gave the Americans open goodwill and easy terms for
obtaining munitions. French volunteers, among whom the most
celebrated was Lafayette, were encouraged to join the Continental Army. Paris became the centre of a network of underground activities, conducted in a highly melodramatic style by
Beaumarchais, the author of *Figaro*. Gun-running, the equipment
of privateers in French ports, *espionage* and *sabotage* were
organised on the largest scale. False reports of British atrocities
were invented and put out as propaganda. An elaborate and unsuccessful plot was contrived to introduce into England spies
who were to burn the Naval dockyards, but the ringleader was
caught and hanged. Franklin threw himself into these activities
and reinforced them with diplomatic measures. The news of
Saratoga enabled him to persuade the French court that the time
had come for revenge on England. In February 1778 he negotiated a treaty of military alliance with France which thereby
recognised the independence of the United States. In the
following year Spain, which also had scores to pay off against
England, joined the alliance. France and Spain were to fight for
American freedom, but Franklin had not the slightest intention
of allowing them to compensate themselves at America's expense.

7. GREAT BRITAIN FIGHTS THE WORLD

WITH the appearance of the Bourbon powers upon the scene the interest of the war shifted from the land to the sea. As is usual in the interval between major wars, the Navy had been stinted of supplies and was quite unequal to a struggle with France and Spain, while the First Lord of the Admiralty, Sandwich, was perhaps the weakest member of Lord North's mediocre admini-stration. On the other hand, the French Navy had been enlarged and re-equipped with more powerful ships and was commanded by the most able admirals in French history. The loser in the last war is often the best equipped at the beginning of the next. While the main theatre of naval operations was, as before, the West Indies, fleets, armies and supplies were also diverted from America to protect the coast of England from threatened in-vasion, to defend Gibraltar which was besieged by the Spaniards, and to fight the French in India. England itself was in such peril that the unpopular campaign in North America fell into a secondary place, as was recognised by Pitt whose last speech in the House (1778) was a rousing appeal to the nation to forget past differences and unite against the French.

Nevertheless, the British forces were firmly based, by land and sea, on Halifax and New York and were not dismayed by the defeat at Saratoga and its consequences. General Clinton began the methodical recovery of the southern colonies, where very numerous loyalists rose in arms to join the British wherever they appeared. Georgia was subdued in 1778, the Carolinas in 1779 and Charleston the capital of the south in 1780. Even as late in the war as this, there was a drift of disheartened colonials to the loyalist side, the most noted example being Benedict Arnold, one of Washington's trusted generals, who, like the French Admiral Darlan in 1940, suddenly decided on co-operation with the enemy. Even Washington wrote, in April 1781, 'we are at the end of our tether, now or never our deliverance must come'. It was coming. In South Carolina civil war was raging between loyalist and revolutionary bands, the former steadied by a force of British which Clinton had detached under Cornwallis, the latter by an army of French regulars under Rochambeau who had landed in Virginia. This reappearance of the French in America meant that command of the sea was lost. When Cornwallis fell back to Yorktown on the shore of Chesapeake Bay intending to ship his army to Charleston, he found the French Admiral De Grasse blockading the entrance to the Bay, instead of the expected British squadron.

After a short siege by a force twice as large as his own and half composed of French regulars, Cornwallis was obliged to capitulate with 7000 British soldiers on 17 October 1781, the fourth anniversary of Burgoyne's surrender at Saratoga. The British officers, studiously ignoring the 'rebel' officers of the Continental Army, handed their swords to Rochambeau's French staff; but the gesture was vain. Though the decisive manoeuvres had been made by a French admiral and a French general it was the stability of Washington that had maintained the American cause through so many waverings, and the subtlety of Franklin that united Europe against the British. These two were the makers of American Independence.

The news of Yorktown reached London in November 1781. It led to an immediate agitation for the overthrow of Lord North's government, and for an end to 'this unnatural and unfortunate war' with America. The King, who believed his royal honour involved in maintaining the unity of the Empire, was the last to yield. North himself had long been anxious to resign, but was not allowed to do so until March 1782. The new government under Rockingham opened preliminary negotiations with Franklin in Paris, while the war with France and Spain was prosecuted with vigour. The campaign in America had lapsed, leaving the British in possession of Canada, Nova Scotia and New York.

Until 1779 the naval war in the West Indies had been indecisive; fleets had manoeuvred, fought and parted; islands had changed hands. These actions, which then seemed vital are, for posterity, but distractions from the campaign on the American coast. They had the effect of quieting the unrest among the self-governing West Indian colonies who had agreed with the Thirteen Colonies in resisting the Stamp Act and the Tea Duties. Under the menace of the French fleet they remembered their debt to the British Navy, and their revolutionary fervour died away.

The war had taken a turn for the worse in 1779, when Spain joined the alliance against Great Britain with the avowed intention of regaining Gibraltar and Minorca. The great siege of Gibraltar, which was gallantly, defiantly, defended for three years by Sir George Eliott, focused the patriotic sentiments of the British.[1] In December 1779, Rodney fought his way in with a fleet to revictual the garrison, then sailed for the West Indies. All through 1780 the fortress was blockaded while the general prospects of the war worsened. In 1781 another convoy fought its way in with supplies for the besieged garrison of Gibraltar, but Minorca, too far away for relief, surrendered to the Spaniards. The northern nations banded together in an armed neutrality to resist the British claim to search neutral ships for contraband, that corollary of sea power which in every European war has embroiled the British with the neutral powers. In particular the Dutch had carried on so brisk a trade in what the British held to be contraband, and had given such unconcealed support to the American privateer Paul Jones, that Britain declared war against Holland (1780) and now faced the open or secret enmity of all Europe. Rodney's operations in the West Indies were then turned against the Dutch West Indies, the centre of the contraband trade with America. It was at this crisis, when the eyes of the British government were on the Rock of Gibraltar and the West Indies, that De Grasse sailed for Chesapeake Bay, bringing Washington the deliverance he desired.

Then came Yorktown, the fall of Lord North's government, and the first overtures for peace. But while preliminary proposals were exchanging between agents who were not fully accredited, before even the slow processes of diplomacy had been set in motion, the tide of victory turned. On 12 April 1782, Rodney's smashing victory over De Grasse near the island of Dominica quite altered the complexion of the negotiations, though it caused some confusion among the English Whigs who had been denouncing Rodney as an incompetent creature of the Tories. English politics were intolerably obscure and factious. The different groups who had combined to oust Lord North had no clear political aim except to scramble for the spoils of office. The death of the mild sentimentalist Rockingham led to another scuffle from which Shelburne rose to the top for a few months until he was displaced by an indecent coalition of two life-long opponents, Fox and North, who agreed only in dislike for

[1] It may very fairly be compared with the great siege of Malta, 1940–3.

Shelburne. Shelburne was responsible for the peace terms with America, France, Spain and Holland, but the definitive treaties were not signed until September 1783, by which time Fox and North were in office.

The terms of peace with Spain, also, were modified by the last actions of the war. When the diplomatic struggle was already far advanced the Spaniards endeavoured to achieve their war aims by a direct assault on Gibraltar. The attack was launched in September 1782 by a huge fleet of warships, by a powerful army on the landward side, and by specially constructed floating batteries carrying heavy artillery. Eliott destroyed the batteries with red-hot shot and repelled every assault. Next month Rodney appeared, drove away the Spanish fleet and raised the siege. Thus the war ended with a flicker if not a blaze of glory. The hearts of oak had fought again, and again conquered the fleets of Spain and France, even if the soldiers had failed in a war fought reluctantly against their own kinsmen.

The Thirteen Colonies were lost, but much had been saved largely by the efforts of four men, Rodney in the West Indies, Eliott at Gibraltar, Carleton in Canada and Warren Hastings in India.

The discussions in Paris were prolonged and complicated, not least by the successive political changes in England. All parties agreed that the thesis of the Declaratory Act was now untenable; American independence must be admitted, but the boundaries of the United States were a troublesome problem. The British were anxious to detach the Americans from the French alliance and to prevent the French from re-establishing their power in North America. Franklin was not at all disposed to exchange English for French patronage, but was bound by treaty with France not to make a separate peace. Having scored his point on American independence he welcomed the British victories over France and Spain which enabled him to play off his enemies against his allies. He presented four principal conditions: independence, definition of boundaries, restriction of the limits of Quebec to what it was before the Quebec Act, and freedom of fishing on the Newfoundland Banks; and these became the basis of the treaty. He also added a number of 'desirable' conditions, some merely facetious such as the cession of Canada, an indemnity and an admission of error on the part of Great Britain; but these were not taken seriously. The British negotiators stoutly held out for the rights of the loyalists, demanding personal security for them and legal possession of their property, to which Franklin blandly replied that Congress had no authority to overrule the decisions of the separate colonies on this point. The British had to be content with a recommendation to the colonies to end the persecution.

France got very little from the war except her revenge. The rights of fishing off Newfoundland with the use of St Pierre and Miquelon, which had been in dispute since the Treaty of Utrecht, were defined in a form favourable to France. She recovered two islands in the West Indies and several trading posts which the British had captured in India and Africa. The Dutch actually lost by their intervention in the war; they were obliged to admit the right of the British to trade without interference in the Eastern Seas.

The Spaniards failed to get what they wanted, Gibraltar, but otherwise got considerable advantages. They retained possession of Minorca but returned to Great Britain some captured West Indian islands. After long three-cornered discussions and much finessing, the Spaniards were confirmed in their possession of Florida, including what was then called West Florida at the mouth of the Mississippi and, in addition, the whole unexplored region beyond that river. No one, least of all the Spaniards, realised what wealth lay hidden in that vast domain. The United States, though possessed of the Ohio basin, were again obstructed in their westward march.

The definitive treaties of Versailles which ended the story of the first British Empire were signed on 3 September 1783. At the complimentary banquet, or so the wits alleged, the French plenipotentiary proposed the health of King Louis comparing him, with traditional flattery, to the Sun in splendour. The Englishman who followed turned the compliment by proposing King George who 'like the Moon rules the waves'. 'And I give you', said Benjamin Franklin, 'the health of General Washington who, like Joshua of old, bade the Sun and the Moon to stand still and they obeyed him.' He was right, the kings of Europe were all losers. King George had lost something but King Louis more. France had bankrupted herself in fighting other people's battles, had gained nothing solid, and had infected herself with a contagious disease fatal to the system of *le roi soleil*. Liberty,

Equality and Fraternity acquired in the forests of the New World were soon to raise the blood of France to fever heat. Spain, too, was to learn that it was not only English colonies in America that fall off like ripe fruit from the parent tree.

8. THE UNITED STATES AND CANADA

MANY tangled problems remained to be solved in America when the treaties were ratified: financial settlements between merchants with interests on both sides of the Atlantic, the survey of the new frontiers, the evacuation of the loyalists and the withdrawal of the British garrisons. Sir Guy Carleton, then commanding at New York, was unwilling to leave that loyal city until, in November 1783, he had arranged for the removal to Nova Scotia of all loyalists who sought his protection.

The American Congress which had urged the thirteen colonial governments, in 1777, to disfranchise and expropriate the loyalists now did nothing to restore their property and civil rights, nor made any gesture of conciliation. The heats engendered by civil war are not quickly cooled. The revolution, like all revolutions, had been the work of an active politically-minded minority. A large part of the population, as in all civil wars, stood neutral until the war forced itself into notice. John Adams, the revolutionary leader, estimated the active revolutionaries as one-third and the active loyalists as one-third also. A large number, more or less willingly, volunteered to serve King George in those areas where the King's soldiers were in control and, like the guerrilla fighters on the other side, melted away, when the fortunes of war changed. A surprisingly large number in the North, where they could put themselves under Carleton's protection, decided to go into exile with him and remain under the British flag. Throughout the war the British generals had been hampered by increasing crowds of loyalist refugees who, as the British cause deteriorated, were gradually concentrated in New York. About 30,000 were transported by sea to Nova Scotia.

The settlement of Shelburne was founded, not without many setbacks, by an organised party of 471 families who sailed in eighteen ships from New York. Douglas was founded by the 84th (New York) Loyalist Regiment. Montagu's and Tarlton's

Regiments from Carolina settled at Guysborough. Many legal and administrative officials from New York settled along the St John and Miramichi rivers, where a few immigrants from Scotland had already broken the ground. In 1784 this region was formed into the separate colony of New Brunswick which, though a small province, has taken a notable part in Canadian history, its founders having had a high level of political and intellectual ability.

Cape Breton Island was also made a separate colony (but reunited with Nova Scotia in 1820). While the site of Louisburg remained a deserted ruin, a new settlement was founded at Sydney (1783) and was soon attracting immigrants from Scotland at the rate of a thousand a year. New Edinburgh, another Scottish colony, was planted by Andrew Stewart in the same year. A steady emigration of discharged highland soldiers, to the Pictou district of Nova Scotia, followed the Peace of 1783.

Halifax remained the social and commercial centre of the Maritime Provinces. A leader among the newcomers there was the Rev. Charles Inglis, ejected from his rectory of Trinity Church, New York. In 1787 he was consecrated Bishop of Nova Scotia, the first creation by the Crown of an Anglican bishopric in the colonies. Politics in Nova Scotia in the next generation turned on denominational rivalries between the Anglican loyalists, the Acadian Roman Catholics and the Scottish immigrants. This, and a laudable interest in education, provided the little colony eventually with four rival University Colleges.

The loyalists were refugees from persecution, emigrants of another type from any hitherto described. Many whose political principles had driven them into the wilderness were unwilling pioneers, some were elderly professional men, some were infirm and old, most had been robbed of all their property. To the hardships and obstacles always encountered by the settlers in a new colony was added much personal misery for the loyalists in the Maritime Provinces. The Nova Scotians took a pride in overcoming these misfortunes, accepted the jocular nickname of 'blue-noses', and took as their motto the defiant words: 'We bloom amid the snow.'

When Pitt became Prime Minister in December 1783, he appointed a Royal Commission which sat from 1783 to 1790 and spent over £3,000,000 in making 'a liberal and a handsome compensation' for the loyalists, the poorest among them receiving the largest grants. Carleton, who was active in the organisation of the new settlements, obtained from the Crown, as a mark of royal favour, the distinction that the loyalists and their descendants should write after their names the letters, 'U.E.', to record their devotion to the cause of a United Empire.

Another group of immigrants were loyalist negroes from the southern colonies. From Nova Scotia they sent delegates to consult the Anti-Slavery Society about their future. Clarkson urged them to migrate again to Sierra Leone (see page 225), the new home for liberated slaves. Eleven hundred of them took his advice in 1792. Seven years later, some hundreds of Maroons from Jamaica (see page 225) also arrived in Nova Scotia. They too preferred to go on to Sierra Leone in 1800.

It fell to Carleton's successor, Haldimand, to provide for another loyalist emigration by land into the province of Quebec. It has been claimed that 20,000 loyalists of New York State found their way by Lake Champlain to the St Lawrence or through the Mohawk Gap to the shores of Lake Ontario. These were mostly settlers of another type, farmers from Sir William Johnson's great estate, led by his son Sir John; Gaelic-speaking Highlanders, twice-exiled, who had no more love for Whigs in New England than for Whigs in Edinburgh; time-expired soldiers; Rangers from the frontier who had fought under Robert Rogers. Sir John Johnson brought with him two whole regiments, the Royal Greens, which he had raised and commanded; and with him came large numbers of British Indians, including most of the faithful tribe of the Mohawks, who were granted lands at Brantford and Quinté and own them to this day.

Much attention was paid to surveying townships and to allotting equitable grants of land. Soldiers might be allotted up to 200 acres free, and civilians 100 acres, but, in order to concentrate the settlers, the normal grant was sixty acres of virgin land and a town lot. The townships were surveyed in strips running back from the water's edge, along the Upper St Lawrence and on the banks of the Great Lakes. Thus began the British settlement of Upper Canada, later known as Ontario. It contained some strongly-marked Scottish areas where the kilt, the bagpipes and the Gaelic speech have never fallen into disuse.

Fair these broad meads, these hoary woods are grand,
But we are exiles from our native land.

From the lone sheiling in the misty island,
Distance divides us, and the waste of seas;
But still the blood is strong, the heart is Highland,
And we in dreams behold the Hebrides.

Scotsmen continued to migrate in parties to Canada and the
Maritime Provinces, throughout the whole period of the Highland clearances. A notable emigration was that of the Glengarry
Fencibles, a Highland Regiment brought out by their commanding officer at the Peace of 1802. They were Gaelic-speaking
Catholics and their leader, Alexander Macdonell, became the
first Roman Catholic Bishop of Upper Canada (1826).

The appearance of a large British population in part of the
province of Quebec led to a demand on their part for revision of
the Quebec Act. The French-Canadians, however, desired no
such change; the Act was their charter of liberties ensuring them
their own religion and civil laws. The immigrant loyalists wanted
political rights like those enjoyed by the Maritime Provinces,
where there was normal colonial self-government. They petitioned Parliament for these advantages, which Pitt conceded,
deliberately. Though a reformer he had no sympathy with the
advanced democracy of the United States and was anxious to
establish a 'mixed' form of government in Canada, avoiding the
errors which had led to the American Revolution. Carleton, now
Lord Dorchester, who returned to North America in 1786 as
Governor-General over all the surviving British provinces, was of
a like opinion. He was of a cautious soldierly temper, suspicious
of agitating politicians, and concerned above all to maintain a
strong central government. In his long Canadian service he had
grown to sympathise with the French point of view. 'This
country', he wrote, 'must to the end of Time be peopled by the
[French] Canadian race who have already taken such firm root.'
After consulting Carleton, Pitt brought forward a proposal
which was thus described in the House of Lords: 'Parliament
are about to communicate the blessings of the English Constitution to the subjects of Canada because they are fully conscious
that it is the best in the world.'

By the Canada Act, 1791, the Province of Quebec was split
in two, Lower (or French) Canada, and Upper (or British)

Canada. Each was to have its own assembly, laws, language, and established Church, but the Governor-General, with more than royal powers, was supreme over both. Members of the lower house were elected as in the English shires by all freeholders with lands worth forty shillings a year. The nominated upper house was to have been composed of hereditary peers; but this intention, as Carleton warned Pitt, would never work and was quietly left unfulfilled. The French Canadians were not much pleased with the elective assembly which was alien to their traditions, but they were strengthened in their local patriotism by the establishment and endowment of the Roman Catholic Church. The Anglican Church was similarly established and endowed with one-seventh of the undeveloped waste land of the province. English common law was introduced into Upper Canada. 'To avoid the occasion of a misunderstanding similar to that which had formerly taken place,' said Pitt, 'no taxes were meant to be imposed by the Parliament respecting Canada, but such as might be necessary for the purpose of commercial regulation.'

The two provinces of Canada and the four Maritime Provinces may now be left in a stage of quiet development for twenty years. The 'Maritimes' grew their own food and exported masts and timber; Canada as yet exported little besides furs. All six provinces were weak and poverty-stricken, compared with the United States now in their boisterous youth. The destiny of Canada, its wealth in the north-west, lay hidden in the future. Many English and all American observers believed that sooner or later these sickly infant provinces would come to maturity under the Stars and Stripes.

Meanwhile relations between Great Britain and America continued to be very unfriendly. Owing to the unsettled condition of the Indian frontier, the British refused to evacuate some frontier posts in the Ohio region. During the twenty years of revolution the population of the Thirteen Colonies had increased almost to three million and had overflowed westward into the disputed territories of the Ohio basin. Raids and reprisals by Indian bands, by loyalist rangers and by guerrilla fighters who were neither one nor the other, had deluged the advancing frontier with bloodshed and 'atrocity' stories. Never was a struggle nor its outcome more inevitable. By the end of the war the projected

Indian reserve contained a million scattered American settlers
who hardly laid aside the rifle to take up axe and plough-rein.
Gone for ever were the hunting-grounds and the domain of the
redskins, but from this domain the British refused to withdraw
their outposts at Oswego, Niagara, Detroit.

When war against the French Revolution broke out in 1792,
and American hotheads urged Washington to renew the military
alliance with France against England, he preferred to send Chief
Justice Jay to negotiate a settlement of outstanding disputes.
The Treaty of 1794, known as Jay's treaty, ends the struggle for
North America. The frontier as far west as the source of the
Mississippi, beyond which the Spanish territories lay unexplored,
was agreed and surveyed as it remains to-day. The British withdrew their garrisons into Canada. Jay also hoped to gain concessions on the disputed question of the right to search neutral
ships in time of war; but here he made no progress and the dispute
has been a fruitful source of ill-will in every succeeding war.
There were Americans so naïve as to suppose that Great Britain
could be persuaded to admit the United States to all the economic
advantages of the Acts of Trade even though they had contracted
out of the Empire. Such a triumph would have been beyond the
powers of any negotiator and was far beyond the powers of John
Jay. He was thought to have failed in his mission when he got
no more than a limited right for American ships to trade directly
with the surviving British colonies. The final severance between
the two branches of the English-speaking race was thus accomplished in a niggling spirit with a complete absence of magnanimity on either part. Dignity was shown almost alone by
George III in his reception of John Adams, the first American
minister at the Court of St James's. He said that as 'he had been
the last to consent to the separation so he would be the first to
meet the friendship of the United States as an independent
power'.

9. A RETROSPECT

WHAT justifiable complaints could have been made by the colonies in the eighteenth century against the mother-country? Not tyranny but neglect and condescension. For long years they were left to themselves until their problems happened to force the attention of the home government. A simple well-meant regulation was then imposed upon the colonies by officials who never doubted that they were superiors providing for their inferiors. When the propriety of the regulation was challenged by the colonists, the superior officials were so obliging as to recall it and substitute another, but never so critical as to question their own superiority. Not only were the colonial governments inferior jurisdictions, the colonists themselves were socially inferior people, a subordinate class. London society was unwilling to believe that Washington could be a gentleman or that Franklin would not be patronised. Too frequently the stay-at-home English have regarded the colonies as a refuse heap for misfits and failures, from the governor, often the feckless member of some political grandee's family, to the 'remittance man', that well-known figure in every colony, the black sheep paid to go abroad and stay abroad. As James Mill said, the colonial service was regarded as 'a system of outdoor relief for the upper classes'. Far worse was the disposition to export the vicious dregs of the old country, on Dogberry's principle that the best police report was to 'thank God you are rid of a knave'. The English penal laws were then the severest in the world, crimes classed as felony and punishable by death being numerous. Jeremy Bentham's model prisons had not yet imposed upon society a universal belief in solitary confinement as the proper treatment for convicted criminals. If not hanged, it seemed reasonable and cheap to dispose of felons by selling them into slavery for a term of years or for the term of their natural life. From 1707 till 1770 convicted felons were transported, by contract with ship-owners who placed them as indentured labourers in the American colonies. There was a brisk demand for the labourers but a very well-justified series of complaints against the practice from colonial statesmen.

Hardly less irksome than this low conception of colonial life was the 'Treasury Point of View'. Moneyed men in the City, and their political associates in Downing Street assessed the colonies as items in a balance-sheet. The plantations themselves, financed indeed by capital raised and owned in the City, were estates which ought to show a net annual profit. The colonists, very commonly mortgaged deeply, were the financial dependants of merchants at home and should be proud to act as their agents. The Treasury, keeping a watchful eye on the balance of trade, would favour any colony showing a healthy figure of raw materials sent home and a healthier figure of English manu- factured goods brought out; but a colony that called for a grant- in-aid was worthless and should be written off.

It was, however, recognised, in the eighteenth century, that every colony had one concealed asset which might be turned to the advantage of the Treasury, its undeveloped 'waste lands'. These by custom were the domain of the Crown, when effective occupation of any part of the region had been established by subjects of the Crown. The limitations of that hinterland were uncertainly defined, a problem which had already arisen in the case of the Ohio basin and which would arise again in each new colony on the coast of an unexplored continent. Fruitful in trouble was the inevitable clash between the frontiersmen, urged by restless ambition to go up and occupy the land, and the projectors of Whitehall making grants and restrictions on small- scale maps. Land-hunger was more powerful than distant, ill- informed, civil servants with no more than a languid interest in the ways of the wilderness.

When intervening to allot the 'waste lands', on whatever principle, it has always been the part of the Crown to protect the aborigines against frontier lawlessness. No solution was found in the history of the Thirteen Colonies, nor has it yet been found, to the problem of imposing a higher civilisation upon a primitive race without exposing the latter to exploitation and demoralisation. To assert that the 400,000 or 500,000 Indians were the rightful possessors of America and that by some law of nature it should have been reserved for them rather than for the 200,000,000 who now live there is ridiculous. Perhaps, as men lived and thought in the seventeenth and eighteenth centuries, no other fate than racial war was possible for the American Indians. Their expulsion from the fertile eastern lands was but one episode in the 5000 years' struggle between the predatory, nomadic tribes of the Stone Age and the agricultural peoples who have learned to be civilised by the use of metal implements. Let Englishmen be proud that their government attempted to protect and to civilise the savages; and let them not be surprised that they got no thanks from the settlers who lived under the threat of the Indian scalping-knives.

Philanthropic endeavour among the Indians was conducted by missionaries and largely by those of the official Anglican Church. Just as the Jesuits in Canada were regarded as the political agents of the French King, so in the Thirteen Colonies the Anglican clergy, and especially the missionaries of the S.P.G., were King George's men. There was more than a suspicion in America, as in later colonies, that missionary work among the savages was itself politically reprehensible; it stirred them to rebellious sentiments and acts. At the period of the American Revolution the authority of the clergy was slight; in the next age it was too much enlarged. As a class the clergy were loyalists, and the Tory party in England was soon to come under the influence of a religious revival. During the succeeding fifty years, when the Tories were almost continually in office, colonial policy was to be swayed by the missionary 'interest' more strongly than by any of those commercial 'interests', in the fisheries, in sugar, in cotton or in oil, which at other times have formed the motives of the Colonial Office.

Downing Street has fought many colonial campaigns, some arising out of, and some leading towards, greater wars in Europe. In all these campaigns the settlers in the colonies concerned have played a gallant part when it was their interest to do so. The colonists willingly shed their blood and somewhat less willingly spent their money to conquer Louisburg and Fort Duquesne. It was not until late in the nineteenth century that any colony saw fit to take part in an imperial campaign beyond its own frontier. Overseas trade, sea-power, and, by the same token, the expenses of the Navy were imperial concerns. The King's ships would naturally defend the trade which the King directed to his own advantage. As in England so in the colonies, the jolly tars were regarded with affection, but the soldiers were on another footing. All the old English dislike of militarism, the fear of martial law, flourished in the colonies which were as proud of their own 'constitutional' militia as they were suspicious of King George's red-coats. They had no control over these soldiers and were unwilling to pay their expenses. On the other hand, Downing Street had no liking for campaigns fought in the interests of colonists who would not meet the bill. Thus in each colonial war there was rivalry and friction, as young Washington found in his first campaigns under Braddock, between the formal regular officers with their ponderous stereotyped art of war and the undisciplined militia, so apt at a guerrilla skirmish on their own ground, so ineffective in a pitched battle.

All these causes of friction were essentially English; the traditions, the prejudices they had inherited from their English forefathers produced the mental atmosphere of the American Revolution; an equally English complacency and narrow-mindedness in the House of Commons produced the resistance to it. These ingredients, on one side and the other, have recurred in every later imperial crisis, though not always with such deplorable results. The foundation of the Irish Free State and of the Union of South Africa give evidence of the effect of 'magnanimity', a quality for which Burke called in vain in the 1770's, to dissolve prejudices and restore peace.

When the Americans had got their independence they made no clean break with the past. Their new constitution was not founded upon any Utopian design nor upon any historical precedent other than the existing colonial forms of government. The Thirteen Colonies, when they became sovereign states, retained the chartered rights they had received from English kings. Supreme control over some aspects of government they surrendered to a President and a Congress who were to play the part which the King and Parliament of England, as they supposed, should have ideally played under the old regime. Written constitutions, so unfamiliar to the home-staying English, came naturally to Americans accustomed as they were to chartered rights; and the veto over unconstitutional legislation assumed by the Supreme Court of the United States was but a repetition of the former right of the Crown to disallow Acts of colonial legislatures. The English common law remained, with all its imperfections, the basis of American law, though very differently administered in the United States. New England influence spread throughout the Union the concept of direct democracy, the people's justice. So much was power decentralised that in the backwoods, where the writ of the state could hardly run, the town-meeting usurped all the functions of government. Judges were directly chosen by the citizens, and if no other judge, then 'Judge Lynch'. Politics were strictly local; in a new country with bad communications, though there may be wide open spaces, there is often a narrow mental outlook. The township means more than the state, the state more than the Union. In these little, remote, self-governing communities, direct democracy sometimes degenerated into mob-rule or dwindled into anarchy. This primitive struggle to preserve the people's justice is the tradition of the 'Wild West'.

American political ideas and prejudices were derived from English sources; and in many other ways the United States was long dependent upon the British Empire. A flag, a president, a constitution could not alter the fact that the external trade of America was still in the hands of the British. Almost the whole tonnage of shipping entering American ports sailed under the British flag, the whole of it under protection of the British Navy. More than one-half of American exports went to Great Britain. The Americans were a nation of primary producers still backward in industrial development; for all manufactured goods, other than those produced in village workshops, they were obliged to rely upon the British, the one industrialised nation. This dependence tended to increase rather than to decrease as the Age of the Machines drew on. The southern states, enlarging the scope of their agriculture, sold increasing quantities of raw cotton to the English market; the northern states, eager to mechanise their crafts, bought their heavy machinery in Great Britain. While the Americans never lacked inventiveness, coming early into the field with labour-saving devices such as the harvester and the sewing-machine, they came late into the field of pure scientific research (excepting the work of the many-sided Franklin).

When the fringe of cultivation was not far inland, when no part of the United States was far removed from the life of the frontier, the struggle with nature occupied men's minds and produced appropriate practical qualities. Not in the first generations after independence could an indigenous school of Art or Letters be expected to arise. The culture of New England, which came nearest to it, was still provincial, not quite sure of itself, though it had the merit of being rooted in the soil. Elsewhere there was long a tendency, which has been repeated in more recent British colonies, for men of talent like the painters Copley and West, the writers Washington Irving and Fenimore Cooper, like Franklin himself, like Whistler, Sargent and Henry James a hundred years later, to settle in the more congenial society of Europe.

The American miracle was not their War of Independence, nor their constitution nor—what now seems remarkable—their technical ability; it was the conquest of a continent. No other event in the nineteenth century is so important as the westward march and expansion of the Americans. No other record exists in human history of colonisation on so gigantic a scale. The million and a half of white colonists, advancing in a hundred years from the Ohio to the Pacific Ocean, had multiplied seventeenfold to constitute the 26,000,000 white Americans of 1860. In these hundred years the bulk of the increase was caused by the natural fertility of the original English colonists and by the steady flow of immigrants from Great Britain. The new-comers were drawn in the first eighty of these hundred years mostly from England and Scotland, in the last twenty from Ireland. The American population, excluding negroes, drew level in 1860 with the population of the British Isles, though that too had been increasing at a surprising rate. The daughter had achieved an equality of stature with the mother-country. But even then the colonial period was not concluded. The flow of emigration continued; America was still a 'plantation' requiring new settlers to break the virgin ground, and attracting an increasing proportion of them from continental Europe. Again, the population doubled itself in a generation and continued to rise, though less steeply, until in 1930 there were 109,000,000 white men in the United States against 45,000,000 in Great Britain; but of the emigrants in the first years of the twentieth century only about one-quarter had come from the British Empire.

The western wilderness had now been subdued; the United States was highly industrialised; world markets other than the

English market invited American raw materials and manufactured goods; American social customs, jargon, hobbies,
beliefs, no longer derived from Europe, were in their turn
changing the character of European society. The American
universities, once the pale copies of unreformed Cambridge and
Glasgow, now devoting their boundless wealth and zeal to
research, experiment and record, were as well able to teach as to
learn from Europe. The colonial age ended when, in 1921, the
door was shut to European emigrants. The last link of dependence on Great Britain was financial subordination to the City of
London. America had been developed in its earlier heroic age by
British emigrants and through all its history by British capital.
At the beginning of the First German War the United States was
still a debtor nation with much of its resources mortgaged to the
City, to those same 'interests' which 150 years earlier had backed
the policy of the Elder Pitt. The two German Wars liquidated
these British capital investments, leaving the United States at last
mature and free. England had called the New World into existence to redress the balance against oppression in the Old, at the
cost of her own supremacy.

Note: When this chapter was written, I had not fully accepted Dr Namier's new
interpretation of politics in the reign of George III. Valuable though it is, it does
not oblige me to re-cast colonial history.

Two other books which I recommend to my readers have, however, been
published since I first wrote this book, and both carry my argument on the
American Revolution to greater lengths. One is *Empire* (1961) by the late
Richard Koebner, my honoured friend, who first elucidated what Americans and
Englishmen meant when they talked of ' empire ' in the eighteenth century; the
other is *The Founding of the Second British Empire* (2 vols., 1952, 1964), by
Vincent T. Harlow, who, for the first time, makes sense of British colonial policy
under George III.   C.E.C.

III

THE EAST INDIA COMPANY, 1600–1833

Argument: The Mogul court was more powerful and luxurious, in some ways more civilised, than that of any contemporary European king. At the end of the seventeenth century the attempt of the Mogul emperors to unite India had failed, largely because of a Hindu reaction led by the Maratha chiefs.

Early European visitors, deeply impressed by the wealth of Asiatic rulers, could at first effect little except in buying oriental luxuries for cash. The rivalry between Portuguese, Dutch and English was a struggle for sea-power and concessions at sea-ports. About the year 1740 French and British adventurers were drawn into the anarchic struggles of a dissolving empire. Sepoys led and trained by Europeans dominated every battle-field, but in the general course of world-affairs sea-power gave the British party victory over the French.

At a late stage Parliament intervened to curb the irresponsible 'nabobs' who had enriched themselves in the general anarchy. British India was thereafter governed by contract. The Company, withdrawing from trade, provided an administrative service under the control of a royal governor-general who ensured that public morality should conform to Western standards.

1. THE INDIAN BACKGROUND

'EVERY schoolboy knows', wrote Macaulay a hundred years ago, 'who imprisoned Montezuma and who strangled Atahualpa, but we doubt whether one in ten, even among English gentlemen of highly cultivated minds can tell who won the Battle of Buxar, who perpetrated the massacre of Patna, whether Sujah Dowlah ruled in Oude or in Travancore, or whether Holkar was a Hindu or a Mussulman. It might have been expected that every Englishman who takes an interest in any part of history would be curious to know how a handful of his countrymen, separated from their home by an immense ocean, subjugated, in the course of a few years, one of the greatest empires in the world. Yet unless we greatly err, this subject is, to most readers, not only insipid but positively distasteful.'

By the eloquence of his essays on Clive and Warren Hastings Macaulay himself has done much to remedy the fault. Though few now read Prescott's *Conquest of Mexico, and Peru* every schoolboy has heard at least of the Siege of Arcot, the Black Hole of Calcutta, and the Trial of Warren Hastings, some of the most familiar episodes in our imperial history. But English knowledge seldom goes deep enough to understand the British Raj as an episode in the age-long history of India, one in a series of foreign dominations. Perhaps the most extraordinary chain of events in all political history is that by which, almost imperceptibly, a company of English merchants crept into the throne of Aurangzeb as residuary legatees to the Mogul Empire. The pomp of Indian princes, among whom the English took their place, dazzled their eyes, giving them a false view of Indian prosperity. It was long before they realised that India, in fact, was miserably poor, a country where millions lived on the edge of starvation, where the Malthusian checks of war, famine and disease intermittently operated to prevent the natural increase of population and to force down the standard of living. The Indian social system which it fell to the English to maintain was already stratified with deposits from the remote past.

Modern archaeological research has revealed the ruins of civilisations in the valley of the Indus as old as Ur of the Chaldees and not dissimilar in culture. What dark-skinned nations dwelt in them it is hard to say, but they were long-established and far removed from barbarism when, in the second millennium before Christ, the Aryan invaders came through the passes of the Himalayas. All that is known of the Aryans is derived from some poetic fragments, the oldest surviving literature in the world. Sanskrit, the language of these ancient writings, had for many centuries been known only to indigenous scholars when Sir William Jones (1749–96), the Chief Justice of Bengal, brought it to the notice of the academies of the West. Warren Hastings encouraged the study of the Ancient Laws of India and founded the Bengal Asiatic Society (1784). In his presidential address (1786) Sir William Jones declared that Greek, Latin and Sanskrit had a common origin. Jones's translations from the Sanskrit led to the comparative study of grammar and mythology by a line of industrious German scholars, from Schlegel and

Jacob Grimm to Max Müller, who classified the Indo-European group of languages.

The Aryans, as described in the *Vedic Hymns*, were a nomadic, pastoral, fair-haired conquering race which had occupied the plains of north-western Hindustan; later they spread south into the tableland of the Deccan, and east to the Ganges delta. They devoted themselves to hunting, war and poetry. Their heroes were of divine origin and kept their blood pure from admixture with the dark-skinned aboriginals. At an early period their rigid marriage customs led to a division into three exclusive castes of the 'twice-born' conquering race—the Brahmins, the Warriors, the Merchants, and a lower caste of the conquered labourers, all of whom were restricted to marriage within their caste. In the course of centuries the lower castes have been infinitely subdivided, a process which caused progressive racial degeneration by in-breeding weakly types. The caste system was maintained by a system of stultifying taboos prescribing limits to the actions and habits and customs of every caste, and quite preventing rational improvements in the arts of life. Since many common functions and articles were tabooed as 'unclean' the structure of Hindu society required a class of universal slaves, *pariahs*, to perform the necessary menial tasks. These depressed classes, together with the heathen aboriginals of the jungle, and the foreigners who ignored the taboos, were deprived of social rights in this world and hopes of salvation in the next, but were none the less necessary if the world's work was to be carried on.

Hindu reformers of the present day very properly point out that the caste-system is no original or essential feature of their religion, but an accretion of some later age; yet this monstrosity exists, though with infinite local variations as the rigid frame of Indian society, and has its defenders. A sense of fraternity and a rule of self-government bind the members of each caste into a social unit, all together constituting the frame of a corporative state. The industrial castes are highly organised as craft guilds, maintaining wage-rates and standards of work, and allowing none of their members to starve. The village communities are ruled by councils of elders representing all castes, high and low. Caste has given such complete stability to society that the history of India has been a mere military pageant. Armies marched, kingdoms rose and fell, but the laws of caste and the lives of the caste-

ridden remained unchanged. The incidence of good or bad kings
was like the incidence of good or bad harvests, an event from
which no other than the immediate consequences were to be
expected or desired; there was no political or constitutional progress and, until the nineteenth century, hardly any economic
change. Before the coming of the English, the rulers of India
were without exception despots, having no check upon their
whims and lusts except the check imposed by irrational taboos.
There have been great and benevolent monarchs in Indian
history such as Asoka in the third century B.C. and Kanishka in
the second century A.D., but their influence was merely personal.

Our knowledge of Indian history is, however, incomplete.
The Sanskrit classics, though they constitute one of the world's
great literatures are limited in scope. Unlike other early literatures they are singularly poor in chronology; they are rich in
poetry but not in history. The tendency of Hindu philosophy
has been increasingly towards the contemplative and away from
the active virtues, a tendency much strengthened by the system of
Buddhism which originated in Hindustan during the sixth century
before Christ. Though there are now few adherents of the
Buddhist religion in India proper, the cosmology ascribed to
Prince Gautama has been largely absorbed into the Hindu
religion. Nothing has done more to mould the character of
modern India than the doctrine of *Karma* with all its implications; its submissiveness, its quietism, its renunciation of power
and will, its picture of human life as an unbroken chain of rein-
carnations leading forward to *Nirvana*, negation, the nihilist
heaven.

But the religion of the Brahmins was capable of far more
surprising accretions. Every godling could be adopted into the
Hindu pantheon. Where every act of life was hedged round with
caste taboos there was fertile soil for coarser superstitions. All
sorts of fetishism and idolatry flourished, from the cult of
the cow, the totem animal of the cattle-breeding Aryans, to the
bloody rites of Kali and the masochistic festival of Juggernaut.
Suttee and *Thuggee*, temple prostitution, female infanticide and
human sacrifice were practised in the name of the Hindu cult.
These rites were but the earthy symbols of a transcendental
religion comprehended only by the refined whose purity of life
and integrity of motive were above reproach. Not many *mahat-*

mas were to be expected in a single generation. They breathed a rarefied air where religion was defended by every sophisticated argument, for Hindu metaphysicians, like Hindu lawyers, were remarkable for intellectual subtlety.

So catholic is the multiplicity of shrines, ceremonies and idols admitted into the Hindu cult that the Portuguese who came to Calicut in 1498 entered a Hindu temple to pray, supposing from the images, the lights, the bells, the incense and the shaven priests that they were in one of their own churches. Such were the standards of Christianity when Rodrigo Borgia was Pope.

The worst deterioration in Hindu society was their treatment of women, who originally had equal rights with men. Child-marriages and premature child-bearing were enjoined by Brahmin law. Child-widows, if not forced to perform *suttee*, were the most wretched of slaves. This was and is the charge that must be laid in the balance against the virtue and charm of Indian domestic life where the wife and mother is supreme in her own household. *Purdah*, the seclusion of women, is a modern custom in India and due to Moslem influence. The evils of child-marriage, added to the effects of malnutrition, an enervating climate, the dysgenic effects of caste, and the insanitary customs imposed by superstition have all combined to keep physical standards in India among the lowest in the world.

Between the eleventh and the eighteenth centuries many armies of Afghans, Turks, Persians and Mongols invaded India through the Khyber Pass. All were Moslems and, flooding into the plains of Hindustan, brought successive waves of Moslem influence to submerge or at least to wash over the Hindu culture. In the foothills of the Himalayas, in the Indus Valley, and in the plains of Bengal, Moslems settled or Hindus were forcibly converted to Islam. Throughout India, Moslems won lordships and estates with the sword and often retained them in the midst of a Hindu population. Elsewhere there were Hindu revivals and recoveries, so that all India is full of religious anomalies. Hyderabad, a Hindu state, had a Moslem ruler; while Kashmir, a Moslem state was ruled by a Hindu. The Moslems, believers in one God, one faith, one law, iconoclasts and puritans, active to propagate their faith, intolerant of alien customs, rationalists, democrats in religion, despised the Hindus as mere idolaters; on the other hand, the Hindus condemned the Moslems as *mlechchas*, unclean cow-eaters without caste. Much could be absorbed into the Hindu cult but not the religion of Islam. The moral systems of the two cults are so radically opposed, the cleavage so absolute between the two societies that strife has been inevitable and recurrent. Several attempts from one side and the other to reconcile them in some comprehensive system have failed, but what is more remarkable is, by contrast, the amity in which Moslems and Hindus have often lived together for long periods in some Indian provinces. In particular Moslem rulers have been obliged to depend upon the skill and intelligence of Hindu administrators.

The Mogul Empire which at last provided India with an effective administrative system, was founded by Babur, the King of Cabul. By a victory won in 1526 at Panipat, the scene of several of the decisive contests of Indian history, Babur became master of the Jumna valley with its cities of Agra and Delhi. Among the spoils was the jewel called the Koh-i-noor, the symbol of imperial power. Babur left written memoirs which reveal him as a man of culture and observation; he composed verses, enjoyed good living, and was much more than a conquering tyrant. He thought little of the dreary plains of Hindustan compared with his own cool mountain kingdom. The people were ugly and unsociable, without genius or courtesy, they had 'no good horses, no good flesh-meat, no grapes or melons, no ice or cold water, no good bread, no baths or colleges'. But at Agra his descendants lived and reigned, built magnificently and astonished the world.

His grandson Akbar (1556–1605) extended his sway over the whole of Hindustan, imposed peace and organised his conquests. The Empire was divided into fifteen provinces each ruled by a feudal governor know as the *Nawab*, a word vulgarised by the English as 'nabob'. Since time immemorial the Hindu village communities had paid a fee or tax to the King of at least one-sixth and sometimes one-half of the annual value of the land. The original payment in kind had often been commuted for cash. Akbar attempted, but with only partial success, to convert this vague customary arrangement into a feudal-system by assigning the farm of villages or districts to his feudatories who undertook in return to support him in the field with an assigned number of armed horsemen. Within his province the Nawab was supreme and, like a feudal vassal in Christendom, might on occasion assert himself by force against his sovereign. The provinces were composed of smaller fiefs held by princes known as *rajahs*, or by some other title. Many of the rajahs were Hindus, the successors of ancient monarchs now tributary to the Moguls; but others were new fiefs created at the Emperor's will. The rajahs in turn claimed military service from their tenants, the 'landed gentry' of India whose feudal obligation and status varied locally as in medieval Europe. The *zemindars* of Bengal may be taken as typical. They lived upon a revenue drawn from the village communities, whose patrons and protectors they were, and passed on a proportion of that revenue, perhaps through some intermediate rajah, to the nawab who in his turn passed on a proportion to the court of the Great Mogul. Whether the zemindars should be regarded as the actual proprietors whose revenue was rent or whether they were government officials collecting a tax is a question for political economists. The provincial system and the method of collecting revenue in the form of a rent or tax on land outlived the Mogul Empire and were taken over by the East India Company.

Though the revenue system, like all systems of tax-farming, was oppressive it had the merit of regularity; and throughout Akbar's reign Hindustan was, by Asiatic standards, well and peaceably governed. Akbar was a sagacious politician and a cultured man of the world. As he grew older he lapsed from Moslem orthodoxy and developed a sceptical curiosity about other cults. He attempted a synthesis of Hindu, Christian and Zoroastrian theologies, held round-table conferences of religious leaders, invited the Jesuits from Goa to expound their doctrines at his court and married three wives—a Moslem, a Hindu and a Christian. India seemed to be drawing towards national unity, even to be developing a national language in *Urdu*, the language of the 'horde', its structure being Hindustani, its vocabulary largely Persian. But Akbar's successor, Jahangir (1605–27), drifted back to Moslem orthodoxy. The Empire reached its greatest extent and magnificence under the succeeding Emperor Shah Jahan (1627–58), the builder of the Taj Mahal, who ruled all India excepting the southernmost tip, now the state of Travancore. The long reign of Aurangzeb (1658–1707), a bigot and a persecutor, was largely spent in wars against rebellious Hindu vassals. The culture of the Mogul court was Persian; all the

Mogul princes loved gardens and landscape, they spent the hot weather in Kashmir; all were patrons of painting and architecture in a Persian style.

Moslem domination, intensified by the intolerance of Akbar's successors, had produced a noteworthy Hindu reaction. A puritanical Hindu sect known as the Sikhs had arisen among the warlike peoples of the Punjab. The high-born Hindu princes of Rajputana were restive, and a new military power, the Maratha confederacy, had appeared in the western Deccan. The most useful mounted troops in the polyglot armies of the Moguls had been drawn from the Maratha tribesmen, light cavalry who lived by war and plunder. During Aurangzeb's reign a Maratha general, Sivaji, conceived the plan of building up the Maratha tribes into a nation that might control or defy the Emperor. By making raids on all their neighbours and by exploiting the progressive weakness of Aurangzeb's successors the Maratha chiefs extended their power across central India from the Arabian Sea to the Bay of Bengal, keeping all India in terror for a hundred years. Though they set up a political administration over the provinces they subdued and looted, and though the Maratha principalities had long histories, it is almost impossible to describe their system in a few words. Sivaji founded the kingdom of Sattara near Bombay. It maintained a dynasty of rajahs but, in a single generation, their authority lapsed into the hands of their chief ministers, whose office also became hereditary in another dynasty known as the Peshwas of Poona. So far as anyone was head of the Maratha confederacy it was the Peshwa. His unruly vassals, or colleagues, were Scindia of Gwalior, Holkar of Indore, Bhonsla of Berar, Gaekwar of Baroda and others, in each case the bearer of a name which became a hereditary title. It was fear of the Marathas that drove the East India Company to remove their mainland factory from Surat to the safer island of Bombay; a few years later Calcutta, a thousand miles away, was fortified against their raids by what is known as the Maratha Ditch. They destroyed the peaceful administration of the Empire, allowing, if not obliging, the Nawabs to act as independent rulers in their provinces. While destroying the central government they failed to defend Hindustan against the disastrous Persian and Afghan invasions from the north-west.

2. THE PORTUGUESE AND DUTCH IN ASIA

Asia, in the sixteenth century and long after, was pictured in Europe as a series of fantastic monarchies, the farther the more fabulous.

The myth had some foundation; at Constantinople, the world's most populous city, the Caliph of Islam known in Europe as the Grand Signior, or more simply as the Grand Turk, ruled over dominions far wider and perhaps as well-governed as those of the Holy Roman Emperor. Beyond the Turkish dominions the Soldan of Egypt reigned until, in 1517, the Turks added his kingdom to their own; beyond Egypt were the lands of the 'Sophy', the Shah of Persia. Hindustan was ruled by a king whose court at Agra surpassed in magnificence the most ambitious dreams of Rome or Paris. Sir Thomas Roe's description of Jahangir provided the model for Milton's description of Satan enthroned in Hell: 'High on a gallery, with a canopy over him and a carpet before him, sat in great and barbarous state the GREAT MOGUL.' Eastward of Mogul territories lay the 'Celestial' Empire of the Great Khan of Cathay about which Marco Polo had woven tales which sober men treated as gross exaggeration; his statistics of cities and their populations, of armies, and fortifications, and offices of state, though modern enquiry has verified them, outran belief. Even stranger tales were told of outlying kingdoms, such as the forbidden island realm of Cipangu, or Japan, which only in the twentieth century revealed its true character to the western world. Laputa and Brobdingnag seemed almost as likely to exist.

Early travellers from Europe approached these strange lands in a mood of childlike wonder, without the least sense of racial superiority, and rightly. In law and medicine and mathematics the Asiatics, and especially the Brahmins, were the masters of European scholars until the Revival of Learning in Europe. But to the unlearned travellers from the west, cruelty, wealth and power seemed to distinguish those regions where

> the gorgeous East with richest hand
> Showers on her kings barbaric pearl and gold.

To be sure the peoples of Asia were for the most part heathen and many of them worshippers of the false Mahound, but in

social refinement and political organisation they were not conceived as being inferior to the peoples of Christendom. The
colour-line had not yet been drawn on the map. Whites and
blacks wondered at one another and on occasion developed a
physical repugnance, but the lightly pigmented Saracens of the
Levant, who were the most familiar of Asiatic peoples, were not
'black-a-moors' and were not classed with them. Religion not
race set up the barrier.

The Saracen kings barred the way to the more distant, more
exotic lands, filled with hypothetical treasures, where certain
luxuries much desired in Christendom could actually be pro-
cured: the silks of China, the fine cottons and muslins of Bengal,
the shawls of Cashmere, the rubies of Golconda, the pearls of
Ormuz, ivory from East Africa—cinnamon from Ceylon, pepper
from Malabar, cloves and nutmeg from the Moluccas. What
reached Christendom of these delights was paid for in cash, a
steady drain of silver from west to east which lasted throughout
the Middle Ages and helped to build up the treasure hoards of the
Asiatic princes. The desire for a short-cut to the supposed riches
of the East, outflanking the Turks northward or southward, was
the motive of all the Renaissance explorations, especially of
those two voyages which Adam Smith described as the two
'greatest and most important events recorded in the history of
mankind', the discovery of America by Columbus in 1492 and the
rounding of the Cape of Good Hope by Vasco da Gama in 1497.

The Spaniards in discovering America had missed their aim.
Deluded at first by some resemblances between the Spice Islands
and the new-found lands which they called the West Indies, they
were consoled, when the error was revealed, by the actual
treasures of Mexico and Peru. After these had been looted, the
sons of the conquistadores slowly learned what was the true and
lasting wealth of the New World. Meanwhile the Portuguese
had begun to exploit the fabled riches of Asia, with motives
which, though mixed, were not so much commercial as quixotic.
They were a nation of sailors and sea-crusaders, seeking power
and glory, though not disdaining gold as a means to those ends.
Throughout their two centuries of greatness their policy was
concerned with opposition to the Turks and their Moslem allies.
South about Africa there must be a way to the sea-ports of
southern Asia which Marco Polo had described; and there a

Christian empire might be founded upon sea-power, to grasp the wealth of the Indies and to rally the Christian communities of the East against the Moslems. Were there not Christian Copts in Egypt, and Nestorians in India planted by St Thomas the Apostle? Was there not a Christian kingdom in Ethiopia, and might there not be a greater in the land of Prester John, could men but find the way there?

When Vasco da Gama landed at Calicut in 1498 he had the luck to find himself on the shore of a Hindu kingdom, in his eyes a friendly state because hostile to the Moslems. Successive Portuguese expeditions engaged themselves in the politics of western India with the object of establishing a base from which to operate against Moslem trade in the Arabian Sea. To this end, the greatest of Portuguese empire-builders, Albuquerque, made his capital city at Goa, in 1510, and spent his force in getting a foothold in the Persian Gulf. The trade of Asia largely went in Arab ships from the Malabar Coast to the Red Sea and the Persian Gulf, whence it passed overland through the dominions of the Soldan of Egypt. The Portuguese gradually extended their power from Goa to Ormuz, Mozambique, Colombo and Malacca, four points from which they could control all the sea-routes of the Indian Ocean. Building fortresses and maintaining fleets against the Soldan they made little effort to spread inland or to develop their own commerce. The trade remained in the hands of Asiatics who already made use of a complete system of commercial banking, bills of exchange and marine insurance, more highly developed than anything of the kind in Europe. Albuquerque encouraged his men to marry Asiatic wives and breed soldiers; he was more desirous of conquering and converting the heathen than of buying and selling with them. Before many years Goa contained more priests than merchants, and naval expeditions to the Red Sea were equalled in heroism by the expeditions of the Jesuit missionaries. At Goa St Francis Xavier died and was buried in 1542. But the power and pride of the Viceroyalty and Archbishopric of Goa declined with Portuguese sea-power, when, from 1580 to 1640, Portugal was subjected to Spain and was accordingly involved in the disastrous naval wars against the English and the Dutch.

The sixteenth century which saw the rise of the Portuguese maritime empire in the East saw too the rise of the equally foreign Mogul dynasty. Babur, the first of the Mogul emperors, from his kingdom of Kabul, was forming designs for the conquest of northern Hindustan while his contemporary, Albuquerque, was getting control of its western seaboard. Akbar, the contemporary of Queen Elizabeth, was the greatest monarch and the most enlightened statesman of his age. While he dominated the Indian mainland, and the Portuguese the Indian seas, Dutch and English interlopers appeared upon the scene.

In the east the Dutch outstripped their English rivals by an initial investment of capital five times as great. During the first ten years of its existence the English East India Company sent seventeen ships to Asia, the Dutch sent 134. The Dutch East India Company, a powerful trading corporation unhindered by state control, determined at an early date upon a policy far more ambitious than that of the English and different in design from that of the Portuguese. The Dutch traders sought to control and exploit the populous regions in which the desired tropical products were produced. By the year 1607 they had established themselves in Java and the Moluccas; in 1609 they made their headquarters at Batavia, the capital of their eastern empire for more than 300 years. In 1641 they seized Malacca from the Portuguese and after years of sporadic fighting expelled them from Ceylon in 1658. In 1652 they formed the first settlement at the Cape of Good Hope. These establishments did not involve them in the politics of the great Asiatic empires but were firm bases for commercial power. Their political strategy was intended to exclude their rivals, the English and the Portuguese, rather than to triumph over infidel monarchies. In despite of Portuguese armadas and Dutch commercial skill, the English began, in a small way, to seek a share in the trade of Asia.

3. THE EAST INDIA COMPANY, 1600–1709

THE voyages of Fitch and Lancaster stimulated sufficient interest in London for the foundation of a trading company. Accordingly a body of merchants, under the presidency of the Lord Mayor, petitioned the Queen to charter a project 'for the honour of their native country, and the advancement of trade and merchandise within the realm of England, and to set forth a voyage this year to the East Indies and other islands and countries thereabouts'. The charter was issued on 31 December 1600, granting to the 'Governor and Company of Merchants of London, trading to the East Indies', an exclusive right 'to traffic with any countries, islands, or ports beyond the Cape of Good Hope to the Straits of Magellan, not yet occupied by any friendly power'. The Governor and Directors, who were to be elected annually, were given authority 'to hold court and make ordinances and impose penalties...not contrary to the laws of this our realm', presumably within the limits of such 'factories' as they should establish.

The first Governor, Sir Thomas Smythe, whose interest in Virginia has already been mentioned, set his face against colonisation. 'The Portuguese,' he wrote, 'notwithstanding their many rich residences, are beggared by keeping of soldiers. They never made advantage of the Indies since they defended them. It has also been the error of the Dutch who seek plantations here by the sword. Let this be received as a rule, that if you will profit seek, seek it at sea and in quiet trade.' For the beginning of this quiet trade a joint stock of £30,133. 6s. was raised by 101 subscribers.

The first three voyages of the Company were made to Java, Sumatra, and the Moluccas, but after the peace with Spain and Portugal in 1604 it was decided to seek a concession from the Great Mogul for trade with the Indian mainland. The Portuguese, without doubt, would raise objections but perhaps might not, now that peace was restored, resist the English merchants forcibly.

The Company had rejected Mildenhall's advances (see above, page 14), with the intention of sending their own accredited agent, William Hawkins, to the Mogul court, in sufficient state to impress the Indians. His ship, the *Hector*, the first vessel to show the English flag on the Indian coast, anchored at the mouth of the Tapti River on 24 August 1608. After many months of negotiation with the local governor and in spite of counter-efforts by the Portuguese, Hawkins at last went up-country to Agra in April 1609. Jahangir (1605–27), who had succeeded to the throne but not to the greatness of his father Akbar, was a jolly toper, brutal, virile and obstinate. Though he had abandoned Akbar's heresies in favour of at least an external loyalty to Islam, he still extended toleration to the Portuguese Jesuits and appreciated the effects of Portuguese sea-power. While Hawkins could not break down the Portuguese influence at court, he achieved something by becoming the tyrant's boon companion, conversing with him fluently in Turkish. He lived three years at court in Asiatic style, married an Armenian Christian wife at Jahangir's behest, and was invested with a feudal fee 'of four hundred horse'.

Though Hawkins could get no *firman* from the Emperor, trade began in a small way. In 1613 the English were allowed to found an agency ('factory') for trade at Surat, to the chagrin of the Portuguese and their friends among the Surat merchants. Within a few months, though there was peace in Europe, English and Portuguese came to blows. An English fleet in 'Swally Hole' at the mouth of the river blockaded the Portuguese in Surat and drove off a punitive squadron sent by the Viceroy of Goa. The English ship *Hope* brought home the first Indian cargo, of indigo and cotton, in 1614. Jahangir took offence at Portuguese pretensions, favouring the English on the whole, especially when Sir Thomas Roe, a scholar, courtier and wit, arrived in 1616, as ambassador from King James I. To the further annoyance of the Portuguese the English also extended their trading activities into the Red Sea.

All accounts emphasise that nothing was done at the Mogul's court without an inducement, the difficulty being to provide any sort of present which would take the fancy of the richest ruler in the world. To compete with rajahs who brought their lord trains of elephants harnessed with gold was difficult for the factors of a London company. Jewels were out of the question; the Mogul appeared in a new outfit of them every day in the year. Broadcloth, though unrivalled in its own market, was not much in demand in the hot weather. The Englishmen racked their brains to think of ingenious 'toys'. Whereas a set of virginals was a total failure, a cornet proved such a success with Jahangir, who blew through it for an hour on end, that the cornet-player was persuaded to stay at court and turn Mohammedan. English mastiffs, fierce enough for baiting tigers found favour, but Sir Thomas Roe concluded that nothing went down so well with the Emperor as a few cases of Burgundy wine. It was not these things but the robust character of the strangers that made their fortune. Jahangir used to say, or so the English reported, that 'one Portugal will beate three of them [Hindus], and one Englishman three Portugals'.

Since Hawkins's time there had been several English residents at Agra, not only a 'factory' of the Company's agents, but also other visitors. Several voluminous accounts survive, in *Purchas's Pilgrimes* and elsewhere of Hindu ceremonies, of the feudal government of the Mogul's Moslem lords, and of the bidding against the Portuguese for commercial favours. The most amusing of the tourists was the eccentric Tom Coryat who walked to India overland for a wager laid in the Mermaid Tavern and, thanks to the tolerance extended in the East to those whom Allah has afflicted, went where he liked, talking whimsical paradoxes in any one of a dozen languages at an average expense of twopence a day. His ambition was to ride an elephant but he performed greater feats. He had the courage to climb a minaret at Agra and mimic the muezzin's cry with his own invocation: 'La Alla, illa Alla, Hazaret-Eesa, Ebn-Alla.' 'There is no God but the one God, and the Lord Jesus Son of God.' Coryat's adventures, until his death at Surat in 1617, were chronicled in letters to his friends at the Mermaid with special messages for Ben Jonson, Donne and Inigo Jones. Shakespeare cast a side-glance at him in *Measure for Measure*.

The trade of the Company was at first very profitable. One cargo of cloves bought in Amboyna for £2948 was sold in London for £36,827. Profits averaged 150 per cent on each successful voyage, that is, if the ships returned at all. But the trade was carried out in the teeth of opposition from all sides; the Company was one of those hated royal monopolies against which Parliament continually protested. Interlopers crept in, among them Sir William Courten—whom we have already noted as an interloper in the West Indies—with a special licence from King Charles I to trade with Asia, the Company's charter notwithstanding. There was strife with the Portuguese in the Indian Ocean and with the Dutch in the Spice Islands. There the Dutch prevailed, after the incident known as the 'Massacre of Amboyna'. The English dogged the heels of the Dutch traders and intrigued for a share of the trade which the Dutch claimed as their monopoly. In 1623 the Dutch merchants on the island brought a charge of conspiracy against the agents of the English Company, examined them under torture, in accordance with Roman-Dutch law, and executed the ten Englishmen of the party, with their leader, Towerson.[1] This was a shocking episode, even in a trade war where no hands were clean, and led to much bad blood. The tale of Towerson's torture and death lost nothing in the telling and was brought up again and again as propaganda against the Dutch Republic. It was a principal cause of the First Dutch War, thirty years later, and was only allowed to be forgotten when an indemnity of £88,000 was paid by the Dutch at the Peace Treaty of 1654.

Nevertheless the English were effectively excluded from the Spice Islands. They maintained a precarious foothold at Bantam in Java until 1682, but mainly depended for their oriental goods upon middlemen in Indian seaports. Hence the East India Company concentrated its efforts upon its 'factories' on the Indian mainland where it negotiated with Indian rulers for concessions.

The volume of trade, though it was sufficient to pay a good dividend on the capital of the Company, was never large. The Company imported indigo from Agra, saltpetre and sugar from Bengal, Malabar pepper, cotton yarn and piece-goods from Madras, calico from Calicut, and raw silk from Persia. The difficulty was to find a market for European goods with which to balance the trade. English broadcloth, which the Company was obliged by charter to carry abroad for sale, was welcomed by those few who could afford to buy it. Some was sold in Agra, but it was in small demand among the naked impoverished millions of Hindustan. Most of the imports were paid for in silver bullion sent out in bars or coined as Spanish pieces-of-eight, the universal currency of that age. This system of exchange encouraged the English merchants to speculate in secondary trading ventures from Indian ports to Persia and to China which, among other consequences, had the effect of introducing coffee and tea to the English market. 'That excellent and by all Physitians approved China Drink called by the Chineans Tcha, by other nations Tay alias Tee' was advertised for sale in London in 1658.

Groups of agents representing the Company were settled in the 1630's and 1640's in 'factories' at numerous points in India;

[1] Gabriel Towerson, probably the son of William Towerson, the West African trader (see page 10). Gabriel married William Hawkins' widow, the Armenian lady given him by Jahangir.

at Agra, at Masulipatam, at Balasore, and elsewhere, the principal establishment, or Presidency, being at Surat. On the eastern coast, though there was trade to be done in cotton cloth, there was no good harbour. As useful an anchorage as any was the roadstead off the village of Madras. In September 1641 the factory at Masulipatam was removed to this site where a walled settlement was built by Francis Day, on land leased from a Hindu princeling, and named the Presidency of Fort St George. That part of India was then disputed between rival rulers; in 1647 it fell into the hands of the Sultan of Golconda who confirmed the English in their possession of Fort St George, granting them the right to administer the port and district of Madras, on condition of paying him a fixed tribute from the revenues. Thus the East India Company became the feudal vassal of an Indian ruler.

Meanwhile the rivalry between England and Portugal had ended. A truce was agreed in 1634 between the Viceroy of Goa and the English merchants at Surat. A few years later Portugal regained its independence from Spain and at once began to draw towards its old alliance and friendship with the English government. Cromwell restored and Charles II confirmed the ancient treaties in such terms as to admit English trade to those seas and seaports in the East which the Portuguese had formerly claimed as their own. It was as part of a plan for combined resistance against the Dutch that the Portuguese ceded the island and castle of Bombay to England, in the marriage treaty between Charles II and Catherine of Braganza. The English fleet needed a base on the Malabar Coast from which to co-operate with the fleet from Goa. The status of the East India Company was so much raised in that decade that King Charles showed practical good sense in handing over the administration of Bombay, in 1669, to the East India Company for a nominal rent. The Presidency was removed from Surat to Bombay in 1687.

In Bengal the merchants welcomed the English buyers, though Dacca muslins and Agra saltpetre were subject to restrictions and charges imposed by the Mogul's governors. Several attempts were made to occupy some vantage point in the Ganges delta from which the trade of the Bay of Bengal could be controlled by blockade, but unsuccessfully until Job Charnock occupied the site where now is the city of Calcutta (August 1690). In 1691 he negotiated an agreement to pay the Nawab of Bengal an annual fee in return for an exemption from customs duties. In 1696 the Company acquired the right to fortify the factory, and in 1698 bought the *zemindari* or feudal authority over three neighbouring villages, which involved the collection of the land-tax and the payment of a share of it to the Nawab. On this ground was built Fort William, which became a Presidency in 1700 and grew rapidly into a city under English rule.

The three Presidencies of the Company were placed in fortified factories or depots, at Fort St George, Fort William, and Bombay Castle, the nuclei around which grew the new cities of Madras, Calcutta and Bombay. In each the primary function of the Company, to sell English wares in exchange for the wares of India, was replaced by the more exacting and more profitable task of administering the government and the revenues of a rapidly expanding sea-port town. The Indian peninsula, at the end of the seventeenth century, had been reduced to anarchy by internal wars, and offered no security for peaceful trade outside the European factories. Traders and ships gathered at Calcutta and Bombay, leaving Surat and Masulipatam and even Goa to wither away, until the customs collected by the English merchants outstripped in value the profit of their trading ventures. The three English factories were cities of refuge.

This change in the character of the Presidencies in India, though its full effect was not appreciated, was reflected by changes in the organisation of the East India Company. Like other royal foundations it had seen bad times during the Civil War, had made some recovery in Cromwell's later days, and had been re-established in its privileges at the Restoration of Charles II. A new charter, issued in 1661, was several times revised during the next few years, always with a grant of extended powers to the Company. The Directors were authorised to coin money, to appoint governors of fortresses, to enlist soldiers, to arm ships, to hold Courts of Admiralty, to enforce martial law within proper limitations, even to levy war and to negotiate treaties 'with any people that are not Christians'. In short the three Presidents in India might exercise powers wider than those of a royal governor in North America.

On the other hand the effective control of the shareholders over the Directors was limited by restricting the right of voting to those proprietors who held shares exceeding £500 in nominal value. Actually the shares, which maintained a steady annual profit of 20 per cent or 25 per cent, were at a high premium. John Evelyn recorded that he bought a share for £250 in 1657 and sold it to the Royal Society in 1682 for £750. Ten years later he would have got a higher price.

Sir Josiah Child, the goldsmith and banker, was Governor of the Company during the years of expansion, and dictated the new policy. 'The increase of our revenue', he wrote in 1688, 'is the subject of our care as much as our trade. 'Tis that must make us a nation in India.' It was his object to establish 'such a polity of civil and military power and to create such a large revenue. . . as may be the foundation of a well-grounded English dominion in India for all time to come'. Though the reader should not be misled into supposing that the words 'nation' and 'dominion' meant to Child what they meant to us, there is no mistaking here a new sense of imperial destiny.

But the Company by no means enjoyed tranquil progress. It was a Tory stronghold and was hotly attacked by the Whigs after the Revolution of 1688. The House of Commons carried a motion in 1694 resolving that the Crown could not deprive Englishmen of the right to trade with the Indies; only an Act of Parliament could do that. Accordingly a new statutory East India Company was chartered by Parliament, 1698, in opposition to the old royal Company. For several years the two companies were in competition, all the advantage going to the old Company which had capital and credit and bases in India. It also scored a tactical victory by buying up a block of shares in the new Company, thus acquiring a controlling interest. The Government, hard put to it for money with which to finance Marlborough's Wars, favoured whichever of the two would make the larger investment in war loan. Eventually, after long negotiation, the companies amalgamated, in 1709, in a form which lasted for about sixty years.

The impact of India upon English public opinion took the form of a growing rumour about the great fortunes which were to be made in the East. Among the first of the wealthy upstarts known as 'nabobs', was Governor Thomas Pitt, the grandfather of the Great Commoner, and the owner of the largest diamond in the world. Many strange tales were told of its origin in the Golconda mines. As far as Governor Pitt was concerned, the facts are plain. With a set purpose of investing his fortune in jewels he bought the diamond in the open market for 48,000 *pagodas* (say £16,000), smuggled it home in 1701, and sold it some years later to the Regent of France for 2,000,000 francs (say £125,000). With the proceeds of this shrewd deal he acquired possession of the pocket-borough of Old Sarum, a wise provision for his family.

4. DUPLEIX AND CLIVE

WHEN Aurangzeb died at a great age, in 1707, the Mogul Empire began to disintegrate. The most powerful of the Nawabs, Nizam-al-mulk, Viceroy of the Deccan, converted much of his fief into the independent state of Hyderabad, with difficulty maintaining his position against the Marathas who terrorised all central India. In the North the Sikhs made, lost and made again a kingdom about Lahore. Meanwhile at Delhi a series of puppets preserved the state and title of Mogul Emperors. Even so they existed only on sufferance after the Persian invasion of 1739. A great army led by Nadir Shah came through the Khyber Pass, scattered the worthless soldiers of the Mogul, annexed all provinces west of the Indus, plundered Delhi of £100,000,000 and withdrew contemptuously with the state jewels, the Peacock Throne and the Koh-i-noor. After Nadir Shah's death his eastern conquests were seized by a Durani chief who formed them into the kingdom of Afghanistan, whence four times in the next twenty years his men raided India as far eastward as Delhi. The sole power that might have restored some stable rule by resisting them was that of the Marathas; but in 1761 the Afghans inflicted on the Marathas a crushing defeat which they followed with the massacre of 200,000 men at Panipat, so often the field of India's decisive battles. All hopes that the Marathas might form a predominantly Hindu empire ended at Panipat. India was partitioned between Moslems and Hindus, although for almost another hundred years the lineal descendant of Timur, Babur, Akbar and Aurangzeb maintained a shadowy precedence over the other princes of the Empire. During these years the new seaport towns garrisoned by the merchants of the various trading companies from Europe enjoyed peace and attracted commerce.

Inevitably the restless rivalry of French and English induced them to take a hand in the political struggle.

As in Canada, so in India the first enterprises of the French had been made under Henri IV, but with little success until, fifty years later, Colbert produced his comprehensive schemes for building up naval and commercial power. The French factory at Pondicherry not far from Madras was founded in 1673, and that at Chandernagore not far from Calcutta in 1690. During the wars of King William's and Queen Anne's reigns, hostilities did not break out between English and French in India, though there was fighting between the French and Dutch; but the succeeding age, when all India was lapsing into anarchy and the Mogul Emperor was unable to offer any pretence of protection, was the age of French colonial expansion. The same years which saw the penetration of Louisiana from New Orleans to Fort Duquesne saw the appearance of French political designs throughout India. A brilliant series of governors, intermittently supported by French naval power, plunged into the chaos of Indian politics with the clear intention of sharing in the partition of the Mogul Empire. Much earlier the prescience of Sir J. Child had proposed a like policy to the English Company, but there was neither naval nor diplomatic support for it. The Directors in Leadenhall Street were anxious for their dividends and the government in Whitehall was in no mood for adventure.

The French appreciated that all their efforts depended on sea-power and to that end occupied the two islands of Mauritius, (1690) and Réunion (1720) then known as Isle de France and Isle de Bourbon. During the short period that Admiral La Bour-donnais was Governor of Mauritius it seemed likely that the French might become the rulers of India.

On land, French political influence dates from about 1735 when the Governor of Pondicherry began to intervene in party strife in the Deccan. In 1740 when the Marathas invaded the Carnatic, a province including both British Madras and French Pondicherry, the ruling prince fled for protection to the French Governor, who won fame throughout India by defying the Marathas. The titular Emperor at Delhi rewarded the Frenchman by raising him to the rank of Nawab which placed him far above the English merchants of Madras in Indian estimation. That was the year when Frederick the Great provoked world-wide war by invading

Silesia. In 1742 Dupleix succeeded as Governor of Pondi-cherry (ranking also as Nawab). It was his studied policy to make French influence supreme by using the forms of government to which Indians were accustomed. He lived magnificently, exploit-ing his imperial rank with more than oriental splendour. He was the titular equal of the Nawab of the Carnatic and even of the greater Nizam, the Viceroy of the Deccan; and behaved as his subjects expected him to do. His army of 7000 native infantry and artillery, trained by European methods, was more than a match for the irregular cavalry which composed the Indian forces. In four years he made himself master of southern India and might have been its legitimate ruler, but for the fortunes of war in Europe.

Meanwhile La Bourdonnais from his base at Mauritius operated off the Coromandel Coast, forcing the surrender of Madras in 1746. The English merchants appealed to their protector, the Nawab of the Carnatic, but in vain, since Dupleix utterly defeated him by land. This was the campaign which established, for 160 years, the superiority of European over Asiatic armies. The French victories, however, were barren since news arrived from Europe, early in 1749, that the Peace of Aix-la-Chapelle had been signed. The French government had renounced its conquests in Asia, restoring Madras to the English in exchange for Louisburg which the English had conquered in Canada.

At that time rival heirs were disputing the succession to both the Deccan and the Carnatic. Dupleix supported a candidate for each, with diplomacy and with force; and seemed likely to restore his control of southern India by establishing his men in these two governments. Again the shadowy authority of the Mogul was invoked to legitimise the power of the Frenchman.

A new English governor, Saunders, who had taken over the Madras Presidency resolved to resist French influence in the Carnatic by suporting the rival prince. In the desultory campaign which broke out, the English sepoys appeared as auxiliaries on the one part and the French on the other. Among the European volunteers was young Robert Clive whose fiery spirit had revolted both against the humiliating position of the English and against his own fate. He had been sent out as a 'writer' to Fort St George, and found himself possessed of other talents which might be made more profitable in India. His seizure and defence of Arcot (September–October 1751) turned the fortune of this

INDIA IN THE
TIME OF CLIVE

Miles
0   100   200   300   400   500

George Philip & Son, Ltd.

Map 3

petty war. The boy was one of those born leaders who could
bend stubborn Englishmen to his will, and whom soldiers of a
more primitive race worshipped as a warlike *avatar*. The spell
of Dupleix's successes was broken. A general sense that Dupleix's

grandiose schemes had proved disappointing, that he had over-reached himself, that his activities were diplomatically embarrassing, such considerations as these led to his recall to France in 1754. This great Frenchman died in disgrace and poverty. The boy Clive also returned to Europe in 1753; he had distinguished himself in several actions after the Siege of Arcot, but as a junior officer, hardly yet to be mentioned in the same breath with Dupleix. In 1755 he went out to Madras again as deputy-governor of Fort St David with the King's commission as lieutenant-colonel. A naval squadron under Admiral Watson was also sent to cruise in the Bay of Bengal carrying with it the 39th Regiment of Foot, now the Dorsetshire regiment (*Primus in Indis*). These precautions were intended to counter-balance French influence in the Deccan where Dupleix's military commander, Bussy, was still active, but the centre of European interest shifted suddenly to Calcutta.

The Nawab of Bengal was a shiftless youth named Siraj-ud-Daula whom nationalist writers have elevated into a patriot hero only by a remarkable display of ingenuity. He made an unprovoked attack on Fort William, where there was no regular garrison and the fortifications had been neglected. The English Governor fled in panic to a ship in the river, leaving one of his counsellors, Holwell, to organise resistance with some European and Asiatic volunteers. These miscellaneous armed civilians soon surrendered and were confined in a guard-house, long remembered as the 'Black Hole of Calcutta', where about 120 of the 140 captives died of suffocation, through the negligence rather than the cruelty of their guards. Holwell survived to write an account which appears substantially true though it has been much questioned. As propaganda it was powerful. When the news reached Madras (August 1756) a punitive expedition was at once dispatched to the Hugli under Clive and Watson, who recovered Calcutta after a little skirmishing, in January 1757. There was nothing in the story of the 'Black Hole' to shock the sensibilities of Indian politicians; the English prisoners were lucky not to be robbed, tortured, and impaled on stakes, the usual fate of defeated armies in the wars of the Moguls. An insistence upon adherence to treaties and to the conventions of civilised warfare was new in India and marked the rising power and prestige of the European nations. Clive and Watson at first demanded no more than a firm undertaking from Siraj-ud-Daula that he would

restore the plunder of Calcutta and guarantee the immunity of
Fort William, but the policies of the place and age were not
conducted so straightforwardly.

There followed six months of intrigue and chicanery during
which Siraj-ud-Daula twisted and turned in endeavours to avoid
making restitution to the English Company. His hopes lay in
stimulating the French at Chandernagore to assist him 'by
neutralising the English at Calcutta; his fears that, while he embroiled himself with these dangerous foes in the Ganges delta, the
Afghan armies would march down from the headwaters of the
Ganges to take him in the rear. The wretched Nawab, who had
proved as untrustworthy to his own subjects as to his English
neighbours, was surrounded by traitors. There was not a courtier
in his palace at Murshidabad, nor a magnate in Bengal, who was
not willing to conspire against him, for a price. Hindu bankers
and bureaucrats who had no love for their Moslem oppressor
were the leaders in the plot. History rarely records such another
web of corruption and treachery, and it must be admitted that
the English lowered themselves almost to the moral level of the
other conspirators. The Council at Calcutta formed the design of
replacing the Nawab by his general Mir Jafar, employing as
go-between a certain Omichund, who then attempted to
blackmail them. Clive and his friends outwitted Omichund by
showing him a falsified copy of the agreement, to which they
had forged the signature of Admiral Watson. Through these
intrigues Clive moved with ruthless insight and decision. The
French problem was solved by the seizure of Chandernagore
after an attack by sea and land. The overthrow of Siraj-ud-Daula
was begun on the day after the signing of the false agreement.
On 23 June 1757, Clive won the Battle of Plassey with 800
Europeans and 2000 sepoys against Siraj-ud-Daula's 50,000 men.
Mir Jafar stood neutral with his contingent, uncertain whether
his treachery was to bring him the prize; and came in to Clive's
camp after the victory in terror of being contemptuously
abandoned. He was, however, installed as Nawab of Bengal,
after Siraj-ud-Daula had been put to death according to the
custom of the country. Clive, who might have taken the loot
of Murshidabad and, like Dupleix, might have made himself
Nawab into the bargain, was contented with a gratuity of
£200,000, and 'stood astonished at his own moderation'.

Mir Jafar found no peace after slaying his master. During his short uneasy reign he began at once to work up an alliance with the Dutch Company at Chinsura as a counterpoise against the English. The Dutch, failing to read the signs of the times, seized some English ships in the Hugli and prepared an attack on one of the lesser English factories (1759). Clive fell upon them and routed their Malayan sepoys, compelling Chinsura to capitulate. Thereafter the Dutch were not permitted to fortify or garrison their factory and remained in Bengal only on English sufferance. Clive returned to England a second time in 1760, in the middle of the Seven Years War.

After the recall of Dupleix there had been uneasy peace between the European settlements in the south. No major act of war took place until, in 1758, Lally, a soldier of Irish extraction, arrived at Pondicherry as French Governor, Commander-in-chief, and Director of the French East India Company. Again it seemed that an audacious compound of diplomacy and military force would make the French supreme. Lally, though endowed with brilliant gifts, was hasty and overbearing and contemptuous of native customs; he failed to reproduce Dupleix's masterly knowledge and use of Indian political methods. But far more significant was the flimsy foundation of his power. The French depended upon diplomatic skill and military prowess while the British now controlled the commerce and shipping of the richest Indian provinces. The basin of the Ganges and the estuary of the Hugli provided men, money, supplies and a base for sea-power, the essentials in which Lally was always deficient. Southern India was too poor and Mauritius too far away to supply his campaigns by land and sea. The naval operations of the war are of slight interest. Though the British fleet won no decisive victory it maintained a sufficient degree of command over the Bay of Bengal. A grandiose attempt by Lally to mount a combined attack by land and sea against Madras broke down when his fleet was obliged to fall back upon Mauritius, after an action with the British squadron from Calcutta. In 1760 Sir Eyre Coote, with some regular regiments, decisively defeated Lally's dwindling forces at Wandiwash, and proceeded to reduce the French factories in the Carnatic, one by one. The land campaigns were not so arduous as in later days. Officers were carried in palanquins at the head of their regiments, which were followed by long trains of camp-followers. At the Treaty of Paris in 1763, the

British restored the French factories, but on condition that they should be unfortified trading posts, as they remained thereafter. The French King undertook not to maintain troops in India, thus ending the great design formed by Dupleix. The suspicion and, if it is rightly so called, the ingratitude which pursued Clive and Warren Hastings to their graves was paralleled in the story of their French rivals. Dupleix, La Bourdonnais, and Lally all died in disgrace, but their influence did not perish in India. For many years French diplomacy was directed towards stirring up resistance against the English, by means of agents and soldiers of fortune at the courts of Indian princes.

While Coote was expelling the French sepoys from the Carnatic, the Council of the Presidency of Bengal were enjoying the privileges of an Indian ruling-class. They were men who had gone to India to make their fortunes and for no other purpose; they found themselves the colleagues of Indian financiers such as Omichund and Nuncomar to whom it had never occurred that government existed for any purpose, but to enrich the governors. It had long been the custom of servants of the Company to augment their meagre salaries by private trade on their own account. Since they enjoyed exemption from all tariffs and restrictions, wealth from private trade was easily got. Latterly they had taken to politics which was still more lucrative since nothing was done in India except for a consideration. Gratuities measured by *lakhs* of rupees, that is amounts of about £10,000, were commonly given to conclude a deal. Twenty *lakhs* had been Clive's reward for making Mir Jafar Nawab. It was afterwards enlarged from Mir Jafar's bounty by a grant to Clive of the quit-rent paid by the Company for the site of Calcutta. Clive thus became ground landlord of Fort William with an estate of about £30,000 a year.

The profitable trade of king-making offered more opportunities when Clive had gone home. Mir Jafar refused to be a puppet of the Company. He was almost as bad a ruler as Siraj-ud-Daula, had played the Company false with the Dutch, and like other traitors had no true friends. He in turn was dethroned in 1760 in favour of Mir Kasim, in spite of the protest of a junior member of Council, Warren Hastings: 'That he is a usurper is certain, and one of our making.' . . . 'We are bound if not in justice, in honour and policy to support him through these troubles. . . .'

The following year, 1761, saw the battle of Panipat where the Maratha power was crushed by the Afghans. India slipped further down towards chaos; there was now no prospect of a Hindu political revival. There was, however, still a Mogul Emperor, Shah Alam II, who was disposed to place himself under protection of the English since the Marathas had failed him. The Company at Calcutta toyed with the idea of placing their own man upon the throne of Delhi but the situation got out of their control. The new Nawab of Bengal, Mir Kasim, resisted their encroachments, limited their trading privileges and allied himself against them with his neighbour, Shuja Daula, the Nawab of Oudh (who as titular Vizier of the Mogul Empire was often called the Nawab Vizier). In 1763 the quarrel came to open war which Mir Kasim conducted on the usual principles. His multitudinous armies fled from every battle and he consoled himself by employing an Alsatian mercenary to kill about 200 English civilians who fell into his hands, at Patna. In October 1764 Major Munro defeated the forces of the two Nawabs at Buxar. Mir Kasim was overthrown and the more serviceable Mir Jafar was restored to his place in Bengal. Relations, with Oudh and with the Emperor were still under negotiation when, in May 1765, Clive returned to India for the third time. While in England, in spite of violent criticism, he had used his wealth to buy sufficient East India shares to control the Court of Directors and had thus been chosen as Governor of Bengal. His third visit to India was for a new object: he was now no longer a fortune-hunter but a reformer.

His first task was to negotiate a settlement between the Mogul and his two vassals, the Nawabs of Oudh and Bengal. Resolving that the Company, which hitherto had made and unmade governments in Bengal without show of legality, should become openly responsible he obtained from the Mogul the cession of the *diwani* of Bengal, that is the management and collection of the revenue. The servants of the Company at Fort William thus ceased to be merchants and became revenue officials with the title of Collectors. Under the feudal system current in the Mogul Empire, rights of jurisdiction naturally grew out of landholding, so that the Collector of a district was also a magistrate. The English Governor now acted constitutionally in Bengal as a business agent for the Nawab to whom he paid a regular civil list from the

revenue. The remainder of the *diwani*, amounting to about
£4,000,000 a year had to provide tribute to the Mogul, the
normal expenses of government, and a dividend for the shareholders in London. A similar cession of the *diwani* to the
Company was made at the same time for some districts in the
Carnatic known as the Northern Circars.

Having secured his position in Bengal Clive was not disposed
to advance further up the country. He undertook to establish the
Nawab of Oudh in his dominions and to support him with the
Company's troops, if the Nawab would foot the bill. The Mogul,
too, was gratified by the restoration of a part of the province to
his direct rule. Oudh was to be a strong protected barrier between
Bengal and the unsettled regions of Upper India.

Bengal now entered upon 170 years of peace and constitutional
government; but corruption, when it is the custom of the
country and when men with very small stipends are habitually
offered very large bribes, is not easily put down. Clive had made
his own fortune and why should not his juniors follow his
example? He was inexorable; private trade and the receipt of
gratuities by the Company's servants were to end. Recalcitrants
were replaced by men from Madras whom Clive could trust,
while newcomers from Europe were obliged to sign a covenant
renouncing these corrupt practices. More difficult was the
management of the Bengal Army, whose officers mutinied when
Clive reduced their allowances. He cashiered and replaced the
mutineers. As an inducement to serve under these altered conditions he assigned that part of the revenue derived from the
monopoly in salt, appropriately, for increasing the salaries of the
Company's officers. Remuneration was at a high rate, though a
mere fraction of the ill-gotten gains of Hindu or English officials
in earlier times. The Governor received about £25,000 a year,
and half-a-dozen other officials sums between £5000 and £10,000.

When the Nawab Mir Jafar died, in 1765, he left the Governor a
legacy of £60,000. Clive devoted the whole of it to a benevolent
foundation, known as Lord Clive's Fund, for assisting retired
servants of the Company. He also paid generous allowances from
his private fortune to deserving friends, especially to his first
patron at Madras, Colonel Stringer Lawrence. Clive finally
retired to England in 1767, to live in gloomy magnificence as the
richest and most deeply suspect of all 'nabobs'.

A great famine which afflicted Bengal in 1770, the first of many such calamities to throw responsibility for relief upon a British-Indian government, drew the attention of Government at home to the incongruous position of the Company and led to Lord North's Regulating Act for the better government of Bengal. When Clive was attacked, he defended himself in his place in Parliament with reckless eloquence, hurling reproaches at his critics and at the Court of Directors. After bitter debates the House of Commons agreed to two resolutions: first, that provinces acquired in war by the forces of the Crown should belong to the Crown alone, and, secondly, that Clive had misused his powers as Commander-in-chief to obtain large sums of money from Mir Jafar. There they paused and, instead of proceeding to deprive the East India Company of its lands and Clive of his money, they resolved with illogical magnanimity 'that Lord Clive had rendered great and meritorious services to his country'. There was a chance that he might render still greater services. The year of the Regulating Act was also the year of the 'Boston Tea-Party' and it was Lord North's intention to send Clive to America to pacify the rebellious colonies, but this was not to be. Clive had suffered throughout his life from fits of depression; he died in 1774, by his own hand—as it is believed—at the early age of forty-nine.

Clive himself had formerly proposed to Chatham that the Crown should take over the government of Bengal; it was indeed absurd that a trading company should rule a province three times more populous than Great Britain, after conquering it with the help of the King's soldiers and the King's ships. But in eighteenth-century eyes nothing was more sacred than the rights of property and no act of state more culpable than confiscation. To rob the East India Company of its possessions was as unjust in the eyes of the Whigs as to tax the Americans without their own consent, a policy which Parliament had just renounced. It was first proposed that the Company should pay a tribute to the Crown, but the debates on Clive's administration led to a demand for more drastic measures. Although there had been a boom in East India stock the truth emerged, to the discomfiture of Burke and Fox who had been speculating in the shares, that the Company was insolvent and required financial backing from the Crown. Two acts were passed: one authorising a Treasury loan of £1,400,000 to the Company; the other, the Regulating Act, reorganising the constitution of the Court of Directors and providing for the appointment of a royal Governor-General for Bengal with a right of supervision over the Presidencies of Madras and Bombay. There was to be a Council of State of four members and a Supreme Court of Justice. For the post of Governor-General Lord North selected Warren Hastings, who was already Governor of Fort William, as 'a person to whom nobody would object'.

5. WARREN HASTINGS

CLIVE and Warren Hastings were both sons of impoverished Tory gentry from the Welsh Marches and both were packed off to India as writers to make their fortunes. There the resemblance ends. Clive, as a boy, was a rude and reckless Tony Lumpkin; as a man, he was harsh, imperious, uncultivated. He never mastered any Asiatic language. So unstable and unhappy was his nature that his faculties were fully extended only when he had battles to fight and obstacles to overcome.[1] Warren Hastings was an elegant classical scholar from Westminster School. In the midst of his wars and political struggles he found time to study the ancient Sanskrit poems, and to read and write in courtly Persian. He corresponded with Dr Johnson, who recommended Sir William Jones to him, patronised Hindu learning, and founded a Moslem College in Calcutta. He was a handsome man though slight in stature, with engaging manners in society. His long, happy, married life had begun with a celebrated love match. But the most striking feature of his character was unshakable resolution, *mens aequa in arduis*. He was icy cool; and it is hard to acquit him of Macaulay's judgment: 'His principles were somewhat lax. His heart was somewhat hard.'

At the time of the passing of the Regulating Act in London, Hastings in India was deeply engaged in the affair of the Rohilla War. Clive had bequeathed to his successors an engagement by which the Nawab of Oudh could claim military assistance from

---

[1] Like T. E. Lawrence, of whom Mr Churchill wrote: 'He was one of those beings whose pace of life was faster and more intense than the ordinary. Just as an aeroplane only flies by its speed and pressure against the air, so he flew best and easiest in the hurricane. He was not in complete harmony with the normal.'

the Bengal Army. The Company's troops had been raised as mercenaries and, like other mercenaries, could be let out on hire, as the Madras Army had been employed during the wars of the Carnatic. In 1773, therefore, Hastings agreed, for a price, to allow his army to be used by the Nawab of Oudh to drive out a predatory tribe, the Rohillas from a fertile valley which they had seized in the north of the province. The *casus belli* was adequate, and the Company's participation was in fulfilment of a treaty, but the hiring-out of British mercenaries to an Asiatic ruler— and that was what the transaction looked like—seemed hardly reputable. It has never been repeated.

Three new members of Council, appointed under the Regulating Act, arrived in India in 1774, when Hastings was just concluding the Rohilla War; they made it clear within a few days of their arrival that they had come to thwart and, if possible, to supplant him. The ablest among them, Sir Philip Francis, was almost certainly the author of the bitter political diatribes known as the *Letters of Junius*. So base was the malignity and the envy shown by Francis towards Hastings that he defeated his own end. He excited the pity of posterity for his victim who, whatever else he may have been, was a most ill-used man. Cruel indeed was the fate of Hastings against whom reckless charges of oppression were framed by the poisoned pen of 'Junius', proclaimed in Westminster Hall with all the eloquence at the command of Edmund Burke, and recorded for the succeeding age by the ponderous philippic of Macaulay. Hastings never flinched. From 1774 until 1776, he was in a minority in his own Council with no overriding power. His achievements in administration and diplomacy were made in the teeth of open avowed opposition from the men with whom he had to do his daily work. The death of one of them, in 1776, eased him by giving him a majority in Council of a single vote. In 1780, he freed himself from criticism by challenging Francis to a duel and severely wounding him. Thereafter he was master and had only to expect the vengeance that his defeated rivals were plotting for the day of his return to England.

The humiliation of the Governor by his own Council had produced a crop of false witnesses eager to ingratiate themselves with the rising power, by slandering that which seemed near its setting. The vilest of them was a certain Nandu Kumar, known to the English as Nuncomar, who supplied Francis with a series of scandalous charges against the Governor. It proved unnecessary for Hastings to refute these charges, since an action for forgery, brought by a Bengali merchant, was already pending against Nuncomar. A bench of English judges, newly appointed under the Regulating Act, took it upon themselves to assert the purity of English justice by making an example of Nuncomar, found him guilty and sentenced him to be hanged. Hastings, not the man to spare an enemy in such a situation, let the law take its course. Francis, on his part, recognising that Nuncomar dead was a far more potent weapon against the Governor than Nuncomar alive, ignored the appeals of his condemned associate for help, and made no move for a respite. It would be more convenient to assert that the Governor and the Chief Justice had conspired to suppress a witness against themselves by a judicial murder. The Chief Justice, Sir Elijah Impey, was impeached on this charge when he returned to England and was acquitted after completely justifying his action, but slander is not easily obliterated and was again used by Macaulay long after Impey's death to besmirch his memory.

The incident has more than political significance. It is an example of the danger of imposing a Western code of laws upon an Eastern people. The judges intended to vindicate honest principles by punishing a liar. The Bengali officials, who regarded forgery and perjury as the merest peccadilloes, drew from the occurrence the lesson that it was highly dangerous to thwart the Governor-General, placing upon the prosecution of Nuncomar a construction that Francis was quick to exploit. The true fault, as Macaulay pointed out, lay with the House of Commons which passed the Regulating Act in a form so carelessly drafted that the judges in Bengal could not know what classes of persons came into their jurisdiction nor what code they were to administer. Nuncomar's case was the first of many legal muddles. All the delays, the picturesque survivals, the quaint anomalies of the English common law, together with its ferocious code of pains and penalties were now entailed upon the Bengali baboos, whose subtle minds were not slow to discover in the system a thousand ways of eluding judgment.

The enduring work of Warren Hastings was to repair the ravages of the famine and to establish a just and economical government in Bengal. Not content with the collection of the revenue, he took over complete control of the *diwani*, removing the administrative capital from Murshidabad to Calcutta, and appointing Englishmen as collectors throughout the province. In repeated journeys he satisfied himself as to the rights of the actual tillers of the soil, preventing unauthorised exactions. He continued to fight against corruption in the government service and against clandestine attempts by the Company's agents to trade on their own account. He simplified customs duties and removed internal *octrois*. He established a civil police. He strove to convert Bengal into a peaceful prosperous province with honest finances and equal laws, and to root out the arbitrary oppression of the peasants, which had long been the bane of India. But he would have done this better if he had not himself been incurably careless about money matters. Some of his own household were allowed to be laxer than himself.

Though he made and kept Bengal an oasis in a waste of confusion, Hastings could not keep the peace without diplomatic adventures and even preventive wars. As administrator of Bengal, the Company's government was tributary to the Great Mogul. Hastings escaped from this ignominious state and saved a large sum annually, by repudiating the tribute when the Mogul again fell into the power of the Marathas. The principle of his foreign policy was 'to extend the influence of the British nation to every part of India not too remote from their possessions without enlarging the circle of their defence or involving them in hazardous or indefinite engagements; and to accept of the allegiance of such of our neighbours as shall sue to be enlisted among the friends and allies of the King of Great Britain'.

Though Hastings surmounted all obstacles in the relations between Bengal and its neighbouring provinces he found it difficult to impose his will upon the junior Presidencies of Bombay and Madras. They involved themselves in wars of which he disapproved and called on him to save them from the consequences of their own folly. However harassed by his disloyal Council, however short of troops and funds, he found means of relieving them.

Bombay, unlike the other Presidencies, was a royal colony, on an island. Nevertheless, the Council had begun to dabble in mainland politics, hoping, by playing off one Maratha prince against another, to get possession of some Portuguese settlements which the Marathas had overrun. The Bombay Army soon found itself engaged in a war which was sadly mismanaged. Though Hastings thought this war 'impolitic, dangerous, unauthorised and unjust', he recognised that he must prevent a triumph of the Marathas over the Company. He sent two columns from Bengal, in 1780, to march across India, one to take charge of the campaign near Bombay, the other to strike at Gwalior, the capital of Scindia who led the Maratha armies. The escalade of the Rock of Gwalior (August 1780), hitherto thought impregnable, relieved the pressure on Bombay, enabling Hastings to look southward where much greater dangers threatened. There was every prospect that the English would find themselves at war with the Nizam and the Sultan of Mysore as well as with the Marathas, and that the whole combination of enemies would be supported by a French fleet. It was a triumph to secure the north by bringing Scindia to terms in October 1781, and to sign a definitive treaty with him at Salbai in 1782.

The trouble in the south began with the tangled finances of the Nawab of the Carnatic (known to the English as the 'Nabob of Arcot'). He was publicly indebted to the Company and privately indebted to some of the Company's servants and to other European adventurers. Like other debtors he found himself in a position to sway the policy of his creditors. Supremacy just then in the Deccan was disputed between the Nizam and a Moslem soldier of fortune named Hyder Ali who had made himself Sultan of Mysore. Though the English at Madras made a very good thing out of advancing money to the Nawab, they made a very sorry show of protecting him against the rival threats of the Nizam and Hyder Ali. A break came over the claim of the Company to the *diwani* of the Northern Circars, which Hyder coveted.

In July 1780, while Colonel Popham on the other side of India was marching on Gwalior, Hyder Ali invaded the Carnatic, plundering and ravishing the whole province to the walls of Fort St George. Here also the Council, which had blundered into war in spite of the Governor-General, appealed to him for help. Here again Hastings promptly sent men and money, with his best officer Sir Eyre Coote, now old and testy. No decisive victory was won, but Coote at least checked Hyder Ali's progress and inspired him with respect for British troops, at the battles of Porto Novo and Pollilore, in 1781.

The resources of the Company were strained to the utmost by the wars of the Bombay and Madras armies, but worse was to come. Hyder Ali had drawn supplies from the French in Mauritius and was to receive far greater assistance. Early in 1782, a well-found French fleet, more powerful than the British squadron and commanded by de Suffren, a first-rate admiral, appeared in Indian waters. Four stubborn actions were fought that year between de Suffren and the British Admiral Hughes, an obstinate fighter with no great talent. De Suffren occupied the Dutch harbour of Trincomali in Ceylon, cruised off the coast, and put a French army ashore in the Carnatic. Hughes achieved no more than keeping his fleet in being. In 1783, by an action off Cuddalore, de Suffren compelled Hughes to put back to his base to refit, abandoning the Madras Army (like Cornwallis at Yorktown a few months earlier) ashore between a hostile army and a hostile fleet. But the luck turned when news arrived in June that preliminary articles of peace had been signed at Versailles. The French again withdrew their armies from India thus forfeiting all chance of exploiting in Asia the prestige their forces had won in America. The Treaty of Salbai had placed the Bombay Presidency in a state of predominance over the Marathas, but in the Madras Presidency there was no such ascendency. There the French had merely withdrawn leaving the Sultan of Mysore supreme. During the war Hyder Ali died leaving his throne to his son, Tipu, an equally ferocious soldier, but a far less able ruler than his father. He made peace with the Company by the Treaty of Mangalore, 1784, after humiliating the envoys who came to discuss terms and, in general, behaving as a conqueror. There was, however, peace throughout India in the last year of Warren Hastings' rule.

The turning-point had been the hot season of 1781, when Scindia was brought to terms with the Bombay Presidency and when Coote checked the progress of Hyder Ali; that too was the crisis of the world war. Ten thousand miles away Cornwallis was turning at bay in the peninsula of Yorktown; Minorca was lost; Gibraltar was closely invested by land and sea. There had been little that Hastings could count on, beyond his own resources.

The Mysore and Maratha Wars cost money which Hastings had no means of supplying except from the treasury of Bengal. So far from helping him to conclude these wars which had been forced on him, the Directors in Leadenhall Street pressed him to send money for dividends and the House of Commons merely passed a vote of censure on his conduct. Hastings was obliged to get money where he could in the manner of other oriental rulers. Like a European king in the Middle Ages he demanded special war-contributions from his richer vassals and did not hesitate to crush his enemies by crippling demands. Two special instances were remembered against him, those of Chait Singh and the Begums of Oudh. In each case money was due and a special contribution not unreasonable. Chait Singh was a noble-man of Benares who had conspired against Hastings in the past and was not to be spared. When his contribution was not forthcoming it was doubled, and further delay led to the imposition of a huge fine. When Chait Singh protested Hastings went with a small escort to arrest him, but was forced to flee from a rising of the townsmen of Benares. He returned to confiscate Chait Singh's fief and property. The Begums were princesses of Oudh, who owed money to the Nawab, who owed it to the Company. Hastings brought relentless pressure on the Nawab to extract the money from these very retentive old ladies by any means. It was at last forthcoming. In each instance the victim had offered Hastings a large personal bribe; in each case he had accepted it, turned the money over to the treasury, and renewed his demand. Such extortion, by English standards, was disgraceful, though the common form of India during the decline of the Mogul Empire.

Meanwhile a tide of criticism had been rising against Hastings in England. After the Treaty of Versailles the state of India was the vortex of party strife in which the Coalition government of Fox and North was swept away. The Younger Pitt, on coming into office, proceeded with the India Bill of 1784, which will be further considered in the next chapter. It led to the retirement of Hastings who arrived in England in June 1785, expecting to be a centre of controversy and quite undaunted. He was an active man of fifty-three who might have hoped for office and honour but, after spending almost all of his adult life as an autocrat in India, he was unacquainted with the ways of English politics.

The Whig leaders slowly mustered their forces. Two years passed before the Commons resolved to impeach Hastings, and another nine months before Parliamentary time could be found for this obsolescent ritual. Such were the delays of procedure and the difficulties of collecting evidence from the other side of the world that the trial dragged on over 148 days in seven sessions of Parliament. Burke and Sheridan, the principal managers for the Commons, opened their case in 1788 with fervid eloquence based upon the model of Cicero's denunciation of Verres, but the proceedings dragged. Charge after charge, the cases of Nuncomar and the Rohilla War, were dropped, as the accusations proved to be mere verbiage. All the more vehemently they pressed the accusations of extortion from Chait Singh and the Begums, but no more could be proved than that, with war threatening on every hand, he had acted with injudicious harshness. At last, in 1795, the Lords who had heard the case with scrupulous attention to law and equity, acquitted Hastings on every charge.

By that time the wars of India had been overshadowed by the nearer catastrophe of the French Revolution. The public had lost interest in Hastings; the membership of the House of Commons had been quite reconstituted by a general election. The spectacle of a great Englishman, baited and abused in public over a period of seven years and ruined by the cost of his defence, had provoked a reaction in his favour, which had been anticipated in the cool judgment of Adam Smith: 'The servants of the East India Company acted as their situation naturally directed, and they who have clamoured the loudest against them would, probably, not have acted better themselves. In war and negotiation, the councils of Madras and Calcutta have upon several occasions conducted themselves with a resolution and decisive wisdom which would have done honour to the Senate of Rome.'

Certainly Hastings had never lacked Roman virtue and could forgo ambition with the piety of Cincinnatus. His lifelong ambition had been to restore the estate and name of his family. What was left of his modest fortune assisted by a pension from the Directors of the Company enabled him to buy and to maintain the lands held by his ancestors since a time before the Norman Conquest. For more than twenty years of retirement he lived a plain country life, content to be Warren Hastings of Daylesford, in the County of Worcestershire, Esquire.

6. CONSOLIDATION OF BRITISH INDIA,
1783–1813

SINCE the Regulating Act had been passed in 1773, a dominion constituted on just principles in America and ruled by just laws had been lost, owing to the dullness and vacillation of its rulers. During the same years a British dominion had been formed in India by methods of doubtful morality, but by men of great vigour and boldness. British India never lacked mighty men of valour. If Hastings had been supported by legitimate sovereign powers what might he not have achieved? But the Regulating Act was a failure: it did not succeed in subordinating the Directors of the Company to Parliament, nor the Governor-General to the Directors, nor the Councils of Madras and Bombay to the Governor-General, nor even in making the Governor-General master in his own Council-chamber. The enormities ascribed to Hastings were largely the fault of the framers of the Act who had burdened him with an impossible task.

Though all agreed that the Crown must take over the supreme government of Bengal, the method was the occasion of a party struggle. When the Coalition government was in office in 1783, Fox brought in a bill for replacing the Court of Directors of the East India Company by a Parliamentary committee, a measure which savoured of confiscation and alarmed the champions of property. King George, who hated him, found means to make a majority against Fox by rallying his own supporters in the House of Lords, and dismissed the Coalition. William Pitt, the King's chosen Prime Minister, produced his India Bill (1784) for setting up an unpaid Board of Control consisting of six cabinet ministers and privy councillors who would have no motive for directing Indian affairs on narrow party lines. A royal governor-general was to be appointed with authority, in case of necessity, to override his council, the commander-in-chief, or the Governors of Bombay and Madras. The Directors were left in possession of all remaining patronage. Under this dual control of the Crown and the Company, British India was administered for seventy years.

The essence of the system was the personal authority of the Governor-General who became not only the greatest subject of the Crown but, for his term of office, the most powerful of the world's rulers. In the days before it was possible for Whitehall to interfere by telegraph, the Governor-General had unrestrained executive power over a population which increased to more than one hundred millions. He was supreme lord of war and peace. It was Pitt's intention that the office should always be held by some great nobleman, exalted by rank and wealth over any temptation to corrupt practices, a man actuated only by honourable motives. Surely, if ever aristocracy is justified it is in this series of great rulers, the most beneficent, the most disinterested dynasty the world has known. No other absolute monarchs have maintained for so long a period such firmness with such moderation, nor has the reputation of the Viceroys of India for honourable dealing declined in the present age which has outlived respect for aristocracy.

First of the line was Charles, Marquess Cornwallis, the general who had been defeated at Yorktown. The reputation he had lost, through no fault of his own in America, he regained many times over by his judicious rule in India. It may be convenient to recall here the roll of his successors: Sir J. Shore (1793), Marquess Wellesley (1798), Sir G. Barlow (1805), 2nd Earl of Minto (1807), Viscount Hastings (1813), Viscount Amherst (1823), Lord W. Bentinck (1828), Lord Auckland (1836), Earl of Ellenborough (1842), 1st Viscount Hardinge (1846), Earl of Dalhousie (1848), Viscount Canning (1856), 8th Earl of Elgin (1862), Lord Lawrence (1864), Earl of Mayo (1869), Lord Northbrook (1872), Earl of Lytton (1876), Marquess of Ripon (1880), Marquess of Dufferin (1884), Marquess of Lansdowne (1888), 9th Earl of Elgin (1894), Lord Curzon (1899), 3rd Earl of Minto (1905), 3rd Viscount Hardinge (1910), Lord Chelmsford (1916), Lord Reading (1921), Lord Irwin (1926), Lord Willingdon (1931), Marquess of Linlithgow (1936), Lord Wavell (1943), Viscount Mountbatten (1947).

Cornwallis, eminently a safe man, was determined to carry out his instructions. His character was beyond reproach, and he was armed with a moral and legal authority unknown to Clive and Hastings. For advice upon the administrative and judicial reforms which he intended, he was able to rely upon Sir John Shore who had long experience of India, and upon Sir William Jones. He was a zealous enemy to patronage and jobbery. The higher posts under government were taken away from survivors of the age of corruption, whether Indians or Englishmen, and given to covenanted servants of the Company, Englishmen of character and of experience.[1] In order to carry on the fight against private trade he found it necessary again to raise the scale of salaries. But the principal reform associated with his name is the Permanent Settlement of the revenue of Bengal (1790), which was carried out after long consideration both by Cornwallis in India and by Pitt in England. In intention it fixed the amount of land-tax payable annually by the *zemindars*, who had previously been subject to arbitrary and variable assessments; in effect it secured them in the freehold possession of the land.

The Act of 1784 had stated that 'the pursuit of schemes of conquest was repugnant to the honour and policy of the British nation', yet Cornwallis found, like his predecessors, that the un-settled state of India obliged him to go to war. There was no appeasing Tipu Sahib who ruled in Mysore by the same right as the English in Bengal, that is by right of conquest and, like them, was determined to be paramount in India. Very soon after the Treaty of Mangalore Tipu was openly urging the French to join him in expelling the English. When, in 1790, he attacked Travancore, an independent Hindu state to which the English had promised friendship and protection, Cornwallis was bound to intervene. After fighting Tipu in two arduous, methodical campaigns he deprived him of some strategic points essential to the defence of the Carnatic and obliged him to surrender two of his sons as hostages for good behaviour. They were honourably treated and well educated in Calcutta.

Cornwallis retired in 1793, leaving Sir John Shore first as his deputy and then as his successor, until the arrival in India of Richard, Lord Mornington (better known as the Marquess Wellesley), who brought with him his two brothers, Henry and Arthur Wellesley. The war against the French Revolution had, by 1798, reached an acute phase so that Wellesley, like Warren Hastings twenty years earlier, was confronted with the problem of maintaining British power in India, while at home the British government stood alone against a world of foes. Tipu was busily inciting the French and Turks, through his agents at Paris and

[1] The new status of Cornwallis as Governor-General, with overriding powers held in reserve but rarely used, was authorised by the Amending Act of 1786 (26 Geo. III, cap. 16). Its importance was elucidated in V. T. Harlow's *Founding of the Second British Empire* (vol. II, 1964). C.E.C.

Constantinople, to carry the war against England into the East, while French adventurers in India formed Jacobin clubs and drank the health of 'citoyen Tipu'. A few weeks later came the news that Bonaparte had landed in Egypt with positive intentions of marching to India in the footsteps of Alexander the Great. Wellesley at once declared war on Tipu, sending several columns into Mysore, one under his brother Arthur (who characteristically thought the French threat to India mere moonshine). On 4 May 1798, Sir David Baird carried the fortress of Seringapatam by storm. Tipu died gallantly defending the breach. All the sea-coast of Mysore, the passes of the Ghats, and the fortress of Seringapatam were placed under the direct administration of the Governor of Madras, to prevent the French from penetrating southern India by sea. Tipu's family was pensioned off, while search was made for the heir of the original Hindu rulers. The legitimate line was then restored to the throne of the compact inland state of Mysore, which became the model native state of British India.

The two Moslem Sultans of Mysore, Hyder Ali and his son Tipu, were alien soldiers of fortune, as was Robert Clive. They staked their swords and their lives on the chance of creating a new independent kingdom with French help. They lost, and no sympathy need be wasted on them. Wellesley was high-handed in his settlement of southern India, but he was also high-minded. The *Pax Britannica* conferred benefits upon all the people of the south, of a kind quite beyond the reach of Tipu's imagination.

The Nizam, too, was firmly attached to the British alliance by the Treaty of Hyderabad, 1798. Unlike the Hindu kings of Travancore who had never been subject to the Great Mogul, and unlike Tipu the soldier of fortune, the Nizam was hereditary viceroy of a group of provinces in the Mogul Empire. The viceroyalty persisted, though allegiance passed from the Mogul Emperor to the Kaisar-i-Hind.

The Nawabs of the Carnatic had once been provincial governors under the Nizam and, like other Indian office-holders, had made the post hereditary. By the end of the century the Nawab had transferred much of the administration, including the *diwani* of several districts to the English at Madras. All his powers were mortgaged to his creditors. Wellesley was determined to provide an honest administration throughout the province, by straightening this tangle. On the death of the Nawab in 1801, he obliged the heir to accept a pension and brought the whole of the Carnatic under the Madras Presidency.

The land-revenue system in the south had been simple during the Mysore Wars. The landlord, with the help of his armed retainers, took all that he could find of the produce of the soil, while the tenant kept all that he could hide. Wellesley ordered a permanent settlement of the revenue, as in Bengal, but luckily his instructions were gradually modified. The man on the spot, Sir Thomas Munro, preferred the more flexible form of tenure known as *ryotwary*, his intention being to revive the authority of the village councils or *panchayets*. By consulting them about the assessment he hoped to increase the confidence of the peasants and so to encourage them to bring more land into cultivation. Security for the tenant was the aim in Madras rather than security for the landlord, which the permanent settlement had achieved in Bengal. The Madras *ryotwary* system prevails also in Bombay and Assam, the Bengal *ʒemindari* system in several other provinces.

The pacification of Mysore was completed by Arthur Wellesley who won his spurs hunting down the armed robber bands into which Tipu's army of mercenaries had disintegrated. All India south of the Godavari River was now at peace and has remained so for 140 years, a great part of it under the rule of legitimate native princes. Law and order have prevailed except for occasional outbreaks of fanaticism among the Moplahs, a turbulent Moslem tribe of the Malabar Coast. The peoples of southern India, in general, are not pugnacious and, for four generations, they have been unused to war. The Madras Presidency, so long in the full current of world politics has been a quiet backwater, the happy land that has no history.

In the north, Wellesley asserted the British claim to supremacy with even greater emphasis. The province of Oudh, largely on account of its partial dependence on the Company, which gave free play to all forms of corruption known to Europeans or Asiatics, was a scandal to lovers of justice. Again, as in the Carnatic, Wellesley made a clean sweep, by obliging the Nawab to cede certain vital frontier districts, to disband his dissolute unruly army, and to accept the Governor's brother, Henry Wellesley, as a general supervisor of the administration. This despotic action, though severely criticised, soon brought unexampled prosperity to the people of the rich Ganges and Jumna valleys.

There was now but one power in India strong enough to challenge the British—the Marathas, who were waging one of. their frequent civil wars, Scindia and Holkar versus the Peshwa. Wellesley renewed old agreements with the Peshwa, by the Treaty of Bassein (1802), and accordingly incurred the hostility of the other princes. The Peshwa undertook to renounce all engagements with other European powers, to exclude all other Europeans from his service, and to restrict his diplomatic activity to intercourse with the British only. His enemies were then driven out of Poona by British arms. Wellesley won a decisive victory at Assaye (1803) over Scindia whose army was trained and commanded by Frenchmen. During the campaign against Holkar, who defended himself with skill, General Lake occupied Delhi (1805) and became the protector of the old blind emperor Shah Alam. Provided that the rites and symbols of monarchy were respected, the Great Mogul seemed indifferent whether Englishmen or Marathas were his guardians.

Holkar still held out in his principality of Indore when, in 1805, the English government recalled Wellesley. The Maratha Wars had proved an unlimited liability which they would not underwrite in times of greater danger nearer home. Cornwallis, now an old man, was sent back to India to patch up peace. He soon died, leaving the incomplete negotiation to a deputy governor of mean abilities, Sir G. Barlow. Wellesley had left the British supreme in eastern and in southern India and by so doing had conferred untold blessings on the peoples of India. The timidity of the home government, which prevented him from completing his task of pacifying the Marathas, condemned central India to thirteen years of misery and rapine. They postponed the inevitable decision between the Maratha hordes who lived by plunder, and the nation of shopkeepers whose representative was now patron and protector of the Great Mogul.

During the later stages of the Napoleonic Wars, when Lord Minto was Governor-General, British India was not much troubled. Though Napoleon's designs on Asia were several times renewed they were countered by naval measures which will be considered in another chapter. The occupation of Mauritius

(1810) from which all French attempts upon India had been launched, put an end to French ambitions in the East.

Lord Hastings (not a relative of Warren Hastings), who was Governor-General from 1813 to 1823, was obliged to renew the wars and to fight throughout his term of office. He had first to secure the northern border of British India against the tribes of Nepal who encroached upon it, village by village. After some severe fighting in which the British by no means had their own way, the Maharajah of Nepal was brought to terms by the Treaty of Sagauli (1816) which restricted his frontiers. Since that day this remote Hindu state has maintained its freedom and its convenanted friendship with British India, excluding all foreigners from admission and exporting men for the celebrated Gurkha regiments, some of the bravest soldiers in the world. The Nepal War gave the British access to the hill station of Simla. Lord Amherst retired there for the hot season of 1827 and, after 1848, Dalhousie went there regularly. It became the summer capital of India in 1864.

Having secured the north Lord Hastings was able to attend to the Maratha frontier. Some thousands of armed brigands known as the Pindaris had taken advantage of the total anarchy of the Maratha states to live by plunder and to raid British India. To subdue the Pindaris required the concurrence of the Maratha princes which meant prolonged negotiation, and probable war with one or other of them. When Scindia was persuaded, unwillingly, to co-operate against the Pindaris, the Peshwa took the opportunity to denounce his treaty with the British and marked the occasion by sacking the British residency at Poona. He was joined by Holkar and the Bhonsla. After two years of fighting (1816–18) the Third Maratha War ended in the reduction of the whole of central India. The confederacy of the Marathas was dissolved. Its titular head, the Rajah of Sattara, was confined within the limits of his small principality; its actual head, the Peshwa of Poona, was deprived of his dominions but gratified with an enormous pension. The other principal Maratha chiefs, Holkar, Scindia, Bhonsla and Gaekwar, were confirmed in the possession of their principalities with straitened frontiers and under British supervision.

The destruction of the Maratha power led to the release from oppression of several Hindu principalities of far more respectable antiquity. These, the Rajput States of Jaipur, Udaipur, Jodhpur, and others, regained their freedom under British protection.

When Lord Hastings became Governor-General he refused to make any show of homage to the Mogul Emperor. He proposed to 'extinguish the fiction'. Thus the imperceptible process was completed by which the King of Great Britain became the sovereign of a great part of India. The Mogul remained as 'King of Delhi'. In the same year, 1813, the monopoly of the East India Company was broken down by the admission of all comers to a share in the trade of British India.

7. 'JOHN COMPANY'

SINCE they had become a political power the Directors of the Honourable East India Company had quite changed the character of their operations. Their profits were derived from the land-tax raised in the provinces they ruled, rather than from the import and export trade with Asia. East India stock was more valuable than ever, but for a new reason; it controlled a share of the patronage of British India. The perquisites of a director-ship were said to be worth £10,000 a year. The twenty-four Directors were elected from the Court of Proprietors, that is of the shareholders, numbering about 1800, who possessed holdings of stock with a nominal value exceeding £1000. By the Regulating Act the annual dividend was limited to 10½ per cent which meant about 3½ per cent on the average cash price of the shares, but it is doubtful whether even this moderate rate of interest was justified by the balance-sheet. Though provinces, when thoroughly pacified, brought in a steady and increasing revenue, it was rarely sufficient to pay the cost of the wars of conquest. The Company steadily increased its indebtedness to the Crown on account of war loans. Its transactions showed a profit in London but an annual deficit in Calcutta which was regularly met by borrowing. Thus there was a great appearance of prosperity even when the Company, on a close scrutiny, would have been found insolvent.

Though not so important as formerly, the trading monopoly still persisted in India until 1813, and in China until 1833. The Company was obliged by its charters to export English woollen goods to Asia and still made a show of doing so. But small was the chance of finding a market among the millions of exploited peasants whose sad experience was that any display of unwonted finery led to an increase in the land-tax. It was this apathetic acquiescence in misery that so appalled Cornwallis and Wellesley, and inspired their efforts to give security of tenure by permanent settlements of the revenue. As in earlier times, the Company still sent bullion to the East, but in declining quantities. Towards the end of the eighteenth century the annual imports from England averaged at about half a million sterling in woollen goods and half a million in silver dollars. To this was added in Calcutta a proportion of the revenue of Bengal and Madras after the cost of administration had been met. The sum of these accounts constituted the Company's 'Investment' with which Indian goods were bought for export. About half of the Investment was spent on saltpetre, fine muslins and cotton piece-goods for direct shipment to England; the remainder was invested in opium for export to China. There it was sold in the Company's factory at Canton, to provide funds for the most important purchases made by the Company, the yearly crop of China tea, amounting sometimes to 27,000,000 lb. weight, and saleable in London for over £4,000,000 sterling. By comparison the shipments of cotton goods were decreasing in value. Lancashire was beginning to spin and weave American cotton, and soon, in the early nineteenth century, would be exporting cheap cotton cloths to India.

Tea was still a secure monopoly because China was still closed to foreigners. The Portuguese, alone of Europeans, occupied a treaty port at Macao. The merchants of the British Company were restricted to a single building at Canton which they approached by water. They might sell opium at the annual fair and buy tea, by contract with the Chinese merchants' guild, but not set foot outside their factory nor hold intercourse with the Chinese people. Though the 'foreign devils' were treated with contempt by Chinese officials, they lived in great luxury inside the factory which was reputed the best place in the Company's gift. The President might make as much as £20,000 a year.

There was luxurious living in all the Presidencies. Calcutta, described by one traveller as 'the most magnificent city in the world', stretched for a league of porticoed villas and lawns along the shores of the Hugli at Garden Reach. Its citadel, Fort William, reputed the strongest fortress outside Europe, had been built by Clive at a cost of £2,000,000. The city contained two Anglican churches, a Government House built by Wellesley on the model of Kedleston Hall in Derbyshire, a library founded by Sir William Jones and enriched with oriental MSS. taken in the sack of Seringapatam, and many merchants' houses designed like English mansions in the classic taste. The population of Calcutta in 1800 may have been 4000 or 5000 British and half a million Indians, the greater part of them huddled in the Black Town, a filthy slum which lay to the north.

Madras had a population of about 2000 British officials and 300,000 Indians. Though the government of the Presidency was conducted in the old buildings of Fort St George, most of the British inhabitants lived outside the walls, or inland at a hill-station. Formerly the capital of British India, Madras, still retained sufficient social prestige to expect that its governor should be a lord. Bombay stood much lower in social estimation. The population was not more than 150,000, many of them Portuguese half-castes. There were not more than 1700 British residents and none so rich and proud as the judges and counsellors at Calcutta with their salaries ranging up to £10,000 a year, or as the 'nabobs' of the Bengal commercial branch who still grew rich on perquisites.

Hardly less important than the commercial interest of the Company was the shipping interest. The East India Docks in London have a long history which began in the reign of Queen Elizabeth. Throughout the eighteenth century they contained several shipyards at which were built the bluff deep-hulled three-masters known as East-Indiamen, the biggest merchant ships afloat. The Company's ship *Hindostan* rated as a 1200 tonner (in 1799) was, by measurement in tons burthen, a larger ship than H.M.S. *Victory*, and five or six ships of not much smaller dimensions were built in London river every year. At war prices they cost £60,000 to build and equip for their first voyage, and after about six voyages were only fit to be sold out of the service. The East Indiamen were armed against pirates, sometimes with as many as thirty guns, mounted in broadside on the main deck and firing through ports painted, man-of-war fashion, in the Nelson chequer of black and white. In general appearance they much resembled frigates of the Navy and were even occasionally mistaken for seventy-fours. In war-time they were sometimes requisitioned for service as ships of the line. Ships of this special class, built and maintained for the East India trade, were retained under charter by the Company during the whole of their useful life, so that the owners inevitably acquired an interest in the Company's affairs. The shipping interest made larger profits than the Company's commercial branch and constituted a solid block of voters in the Court of Proprietors.

The captain of an East Indiaman was an important personage who held a position in society not much inferior to that of a naval officer. He bought his commission for about £8000 and hoped to clear at least £2000 a voyage. His officers were picked men wearing uniforms and swords. Nelson himself as a young man made a voyage as an officer in this service. The maintenance and discipline of ships and crews was as regular as in the Navy, with the advantage of profit from private trade, a surer expectation than the chance of naval prize-money. In addition to the regular lading of the Company's goods, or of troops conveyed at government charge, the captain, and his crew in due proportion, might fill a part of the cargo space with private merchandise. By this means quantities of English comforts and luxuries were carried to Bengal for sale to Englishmen abroad: the heavy wines of Madeira and Oporto that inflamed the legendary Anglo-Indian 'liver', and the special brew for tropical consumption still known as India Pale Ale. On the return voyage the bottom of the hold was filled with the captain's private venture in china-ware, a cargo not liable to damage by leakage of water, above which the Company's purchase of tea was stowed high and dry.

Still more lucrative a perquisite was the captain's right to charge fees for cabin accommodation in accordance with the passenger's rank, £250 for a general, £110 for a subaltern or 'writer'. Special accommodation for ladies might cost £500 or more for each berth. The ships left London crammed with cargo, passengers, and livestock—cows, goats and poultry for the voyage—leaving small space for amenities, even for those who had paid highly. Private berths were spaces in the 'tween-decks screened off with canvas and furnished at the passenger's expense. The only approach to comfort was the captain's after-cabin, opening on to the stern galleries through casement windows. Here honoured passengers were permitted to dine.

The voyage to India was slow, since safety and comfort were more desirable than speed when there was no competition. Four months to Calcutta and six or eight months to Canton was fast enough until, in the nineteenth century, the Yankee clippers broke in on the monopoly and forced the pace. They sailed no better than the old Indiamen but were kept at top speed in all weathers. During the Mutiny when speed was essential for all, the best voyages were made by the old bluff-bowed ships. Even before that an Indiaman had reached England from Ceylon in seventy-seven days.

But the 'Investment' at Calcutta was mostly put into the 'country trade' carried in ships built on the Malabar Coast. Dr C. N. Parkinson [1] has demonstrated that when the British first went to the East their ships were inferior in sailing qualities both to the dhows of the Arabian seas and to the Chinese junks. The shipbuilders of Surat, and in later times of Bombay, turned from their own traditional design to ships modelled on the British Indiamen, and bettered their instruction by building them of teak. They made the change not because they thought British ships more seaworthy but because of the terror of the British name. In seas infested with pirates British ships rode secure, for it was known that British sailors could and would fight. The best protection for less pugnacious mariners was to sail in what looked like a British ship. Hence there grew up a shipbuilding trade in each of the Presidencies, fostered by Indian capital but served by British managers and craftsmen. The Bombay dock-yard, owned by successive generations of the Parsee family of Wadia, built admirable ships for the 'Country trade', the Indian Marine and even for the Royal Navy.

The East India Company had a navy long before it had an army. In the first expeditions to Surat it was found necessary to establish a few ships in the Arabian Sea in opposition to the Portuguese. When Bombay became a presidency it regularly bore on its establishment an 'admiral' with a flotilla of country-built ships. In every war fought east of the Cape of Good Hope this unadvertised force, known at first as the Bombay Marine

---

[1] Author of *Trade in the Eastern Seas* to which I am much obliged for the information given in this chapter.

and later as the Royal Indian Marine, has played an adventurous part. Its ships supported Clive's campaigns, fought beside the Royal Navy against de Suffren, battled with Maratha pirates during the first Maratha War, assisted in the capture of Ceylon and, in later times, made voyages to war-fronts in Persia, China, even as far as New Zealand. Throughout the history of the East India Company the Marine Service never ceased to operate against the pirates of the Persian Gulf. After the abolition of the slave trade a new mission was to hunt down the Arab slavers. Gradually its organisation was merged into that of the Royal Navy. In 1827 its officers were given naval rank and a naval officer became superintendent. When Company rule ended, in 1858, it ceased to be an independent fighting service. The Indian Marine had frequently undertaken more peaceable but equally useful tasks. It established a steam-packet service to Egypt, in 1838, for the carriage of mails to Europe by the Overland Route. It surveyed the coasts and islands of the Indian Ocean. After 1858 it undertook the provision of river and coastal gunboats and the transport of troops between India and England, while the maintenance of sea-power in Eastern waters became a responsibility of the Admiralty.

The Indian Army is of more recent origin than the Marine Service; it can hardly be said to have existed before the days of Clive. There had been guards at the French and English factories from their beginnings but they were *peons*, armed servants, rather than soldiers. Perhaps an exception is the company of Englishmen sent by Charles II to Bombay, in 1662, though they were not, in fact, the nucleus from which the Indian Army grew. *Sepoys, Sipahis, Spahis*, that is, native troops drilled by Europeans, appeared first at Pondicherry about 1720. To meet this new French threat the Company brought out to India a King's officer, Major Stringer Lawrence, who was to organise a force of British sepoys. Since Fort St George was in enemy hands it was at Fort St David that he formed the first Sepoy regiment (1748), in which Robert Clive obtained a captain's commission. Having improvised the army which re-established the English power in the Carnatic, Stringer Lawrence set to work during the interval of peace to organise a permanent force. His plan (1759) was to raise seven battalions of sepoys each established on the model of the British infantry and to attach to each battalion two British subalterns and three serjeants, many of them volunteers from the 39th Foot. This little force, the prototype of many more, won for Stringer Lawrence the name of 'father of the Indian Army'. It also extracted from the Frenchman, Lally, a reluctant compliment: 'Their sepoys will venture to attack our white troops, while ours will not even look at their black ones.'

In his later days in Bengal, Clive commanded an army of this type but three times as large. He built up the units into formations resembling what in a modern army are called Brigade Groups, each consisting of a troop of cavalry, a battery of artillery, a battalion of European infantry and seven battalions of sepoys. In 1805 the strength of the Company's armies was: in Bengal 64,000, in Madras 64,000, in Bombay 24,500. Of these about 22,000 were Europeans, more than two-thirds of the white population of British India.

The European troops were not King's regiments but bands of European adventurers, by no means all Englishmen. They were mercenaries fighting for their fortune. In earlier and worse times their recompense was plunder; in later, better-regulated times it was prize-money such as is still paid to sailors. £13,000,000 was divided among the officers and men who took Seringapatam. 'Loot' was one of the earliest words adopted from Hindustani into English.

The sepoys, also, were miscellaneous soldiers of fortune, flotsam of the tide of troubles that swept over eighteenth-century India, largely Moslem Moplahs in the south, and in Bengal, caste Hindus who were not remarkable for military virtues. Like all mercenaries they grumbled at their wages and mutinied on pretexts their employers thought frivolous: because a new type of shako disarranged their caste-marks, because they suspected they were to be sent overseas, away from the sacred soil of Mother India, because their cartridges were greased with pig's and cow's fat, or simply for a larger share of prize-money. Long before the great mutiny of '57, men told tales of Hector Munro's suppression of the mutiny in the Bengal Army in 1764, of Gillespie's ruthless action against the Madras mutineers who killed 200 Englishmen at Vellore in 1806, and of many other outbreaks.

The British officers were almost equally insubordinate. The very first English soldiers in India had mutinied under their Captain, Richard Keigwin, and had set up a military government

Plate 5 A

ROBERT, LORD CLIVE
(1725–74)

Painted towards the end of his life, by N. Dance. *See p. 162.*

Plate 5 B

WARREN HASTINGS
(1732–1818)

ainted in India, about 1775, y Tilly Kettle. *See p. 171.*

Plate 6A

RICHARD, MARQUES
WELLESLEY
(1760–1842)

By J. Pain Davis. *See p. 1*

Plate 6B

CHARLES, MARQUESS
CORNWALLIS
(1738–1805)

After his return from America,
1783, painted by T. Gains-
borough. *See p. 180.*

at Bombay in 1683. Clive's difficulties with the officers of the Bengal Army have already been mentioned. The 'white mutiny' of the Madras Army, in 1809, revealed their discontent. Now that the years of anarchy were over, they had no prospect of winning wealth or honour or promotion, these favours being reserved for officers of the King's regiments. Officers of the Company's Army were sent out to India very young, without training or supervision, to live in discomfort on meagre salaries, starting at £120 per annum. No share of the fabled riches of the East came their way in time of peace. Sir Thomas Munro wrote, when as a boy he joined the Madras Army, 'my dress grows tattered in one quarter whilst I am establishing funds to repair it in another, and my coat is in danger of losing the sleeves, while I am pulling it off.... I have dined to-day on porridge made of half-ground flour and I shall most likely dine to-morrow on plantain fritters, this simplicity of fare being the effect of necessity, not of choice.' It was no wonder that good officers were scarce.

In the early days Europeans showed little colour-prejudice. Since there were only 250 white women among the 4000 white inhabitants of Bengal it is not surprising that young officers formed connexions, often quite respectably, with the women of the country. An apartment known as the *Bibi-khana*, or women's quarters, is still to be found in the older cantonments, though long since put to other uses. Thus a half-caste population sprang up, contributing to the many Eurasians of modern India, to whom a recent snobbish affectation has attached the inaccurate name of Anglo-Indians. A touch of country blood did not disqualify a man for a commission in the Company's Army, and rightly; but caste prejudice, the custom of India, prevailed even among the English and eventually condemned mixed marriages. The practice of openly keeping Indian women as mistresses was frowned upon as the professional status of the Company's servants was raised. The higher moral tone of English society in the nineteenth century worked against it, and improved communications with Europe permitted Englishmen in India to visit their families on furlough, or to bring out their wives to the East. In the old days a commission to serve the Company in India was a life-sentence, if not a death-sentence. There was no furlough and only about one in four of the cadets who went out as young lads lived to retire at Bath or Cheltenham.

The covenanted servants of the Company, the body which was to grow into the Indian Civil Service, numbered about 2000 in the year 1800. Since they had prospects of power and promotion, if no longer of unlimited wealth, appointments were sought after and candidates were young men of ability. The first effects of intervention by the Crown in the affairs of the Company had been to raise the standard. Cornwallis set his face against the jobbery by which the Directors put their clients into the most highly-paid posts, without regard to talent or experience. All higher officials, excepting the Governors, Counsellors and High Court Judges, who were appointed by the Crown, were to be covenanted servants with sufficient experience of Indian affairs. Incidentally this ruling closed the higher offices against natives of India.

Wellesley lifted the reforms on to a higher plane. His hatred of oppression and dishonesty was equalled by his belief in the need for enlightenment. He supported the Church establishment in the Presidency cities and encouraged the work of the chaplains. It was his desire to raise the moral and intellectual level of the Company's servants, an aim which he hoped to reach by education. No longer adventurers or traders, they were to be statesmen and soldiers worthy to represent a Christian king. In 1800 he founded a college at Calcutta where the young civilians were to be trained in literature, science and oriental languages. When it proved more convenient to carry out this training before the young men left England, the East India College was founded at Haileybury in 1806. For fifty years fifty young men were sent out annually from Old Haileybury to the civil service of 'John Company', as they affectionately nicknamed it; and few educational establishments can boast more eminent pupils. The College was conceived as something like a university, providing courses in Law, History, Political Economy and Oriental Languages, for students who commenced with a public school education. The staff were men of distinction, the most celebrated being the Rev. T. R. Malthus, the Professor of History. Among names remembered in India of men who bore the stamp of Old Haileybury are John Lawrence, the Colvins, father and son, Charles Trevelyan, Bartle Frere; but the College left its stamp on hundreds of others. They were strongly tinged with evangelical Protestantism and, if not all devout men, equally demonstrated the stoic habits of the Puritan. Scrupulously honest and even-handed, conscientious in the discharge of their duties, fearless, ruthless, and insensitive, they gave their lives to the service of India, ruling it with a disinterested fervour that has no parallel in history. This was the spirit, also of the Indian Army, when its officers, after 1812, were trained for their profession at Addiscombe. The spirit survives in many outlying provinces of the British Empire:

> Some beneath the further star
>   Bear the greater burden
> Set to serve the lands they rule,
> Save he serve no man may rule,
> Serve and love the lands they rule,
>   Seeking praise nor guerdon.

Slowly the pattern of English life in India changed. The old corrupt fortune-hunters, the 'nabobs', the men who went to the East, to 'shake the pagoda-tree' (*pagodas* being the gold coins of Golconda), were replaced by new men to whom Empire was a trust and work for it a pious duty. The age of Philanthropy was dawning.

IV

THE SOUTH SEAS: CONVICTS: SLAVES

Argument: The Pacific Ocean, hitherto almost unknown, was explored by rival French and British expeditions in the intervals between the wars of the eighteenth century. Captain Cook's three voyages revealed the general plan of the southern world. Picturesque accounts of the South Sea Islands opened a new field to traders, missionaries, and colonists. The whaling industry was vastly expanded.

Australia provided a sufficiently remote repository for convicts who could no longer be transported to America. By 1820 New South Wales, having attracted pastoral settlers and island-traders, had outgrown its original form as a convict-settlement under martial law.

The evangelical revival produced an agitation against the slave-trade which, since 1713, had been regarded as a staple of British commerce and sea-power. When it had been declared illegal, in 1807, after a long Parliamentary struggle, the British made strenuous efforts for an international agreement to suppress the trade.

The British colonies on the Gambia and the Gold Coast were by-products of the slave-trade. Sierra Leone was founded by the reformers as a refuge for freed slaves.

1. THE EXPLORATION OF THE PACIFIC

THE island-studded southern ocean, covering nearly one-half of the surface of the globe, was explored and mapped during the eighteenth century, but to tell its story it is necessary to hark back beyond the Renaissance voyages, beyond Marco Polo, to the Graeco-Roman geographers who knew very well that the earth was round. They were, however, disposed to guess that the southern hemisphere was likely to resemble the northern in containing more land than water. An unbroken expanse of water through 350° of longitude in the forties and fifties south of the equator seemed so unlikely as to be incredible. All that was known of this southern world for several hundred years was comprised in some vague misunderstood allusions which Marco Polo made, on hearsay, about rich kingdoms in the southern seas.

The first Europeans to penetrate those seas were the Portuguese who reached Malacca in 1511, the China Coast in 1516, and New Guinea in 1526. This progress step by step from places known to places conjectured seemed less significant than the Spanish approach by way of the New World, the vision seen by Balboa in 1513 'upon a peak in Darien'. Six years later Magellan set out to find a south-west passage into the southern ocean and emerged from the western outlet of his Strait on 28 November 1520. His track across the sea, to which he gave the well-omened name of Pacific, lay northerly through the Ladrones Islands to the Philippines where he met his death, leaving to his crew the task of concluding the first voyage round the world.

The great length of Magellan's voyage imposed such hardships on his crew that few attempts were made to repeat his exploit for many years. No ship succeeded in returning to America on an easterly course until 1565, when it was found that favourable winds prevailed in the north temperate latitudes. From that time an annual service of galleons sailed from Panama to Manila and back, rarely altering course from this easy route. Drake's addition to geographical knowledge, after capturing the Manila galleon, was his expedition up the coast to California, presumably undertaken in the vain hope of finding a short way home through the western entrance of some North-west Passage; his route across the Pacific revealed nothing new.

Further noteworthy discoveries made by the Spaniards were the Solomon Islands which were visited by Mendaña in 1565. Thirty years later he set out to plant them with a colony of settlers but, so faulty was the navigation of his day, neither he nor other voyagers could find them again. One of his successors, Torres, passed through the straits which bear his name, in 1606, but the discovery was kept secret, as was usual in that age of jealous, exclusive empire-building. All these discoveries remained hidden for nearly 200 years in the archives at Madrid, and the Solomon Islanders were still some of the most primitive peoples in the world when, in 1942, the clash of civilisations came rudely to their notice.

As the Spanish power faded from the Pacific the Dutch, who had ousted the Portuguese from the East Indies, began to enter the ocean from the western side. About 1611, Dutch skippers, often delayed like the Flying Dutchman himself, by the heavy

weather off the south-east coast of Africa, learned to take the
great circle southerly from the Cape, through the roaring 'forties
where the westerly gales are constant, to the longitude of their
East Indian possessions. Then striking north for Java they
picked up the dry harbourless coast of Western Australia, which
they called New Holland. Traditionally, the first Dutch skipper
to make the landfall was Dirk Hartog, at Shark Bay, in 1616;
though we now know that another ship from the Moluccas had
visited Northern Australia ten years earlier without making much
of it. The Shark Bay landfall became a regular sailing mark, no
more, and though the Dutchmen touched the coast at various
points they found nothing to tempt them to stay.

Van Diemen, the Governor of Java, sent out a number of
voyages of discovery, the principal being that of Tasman, whose
task was to find a way into the Pacific south about New Holland.
His first discovery was the island which he called Van Diemen's
Land, but which posterity has preferred to call Tasmania. Thence
he sailed away easterly until his path was barred by a high rocky
coast running north and south for several hundred miles. Some
of his men, venturing in a small boat, were attacked, killed and
eaten by savages of efficient ferocity. Thus repulsed from what
he thought was the Southern Continent across his path, Tasman
cautiously turned away north for Java, rounding Australia,
though he did not sight its eastern coast, and passing to the
north of New Guinea. He had thus proved New Holland an island,
or a group of islands; but by his ill-fated landfall on the west
coast of New Zealand (13 December 1642) he perpetuated for
another hundred years the legend of the Great Southern
Continent.

There was now a pause in the exploration of the Pacific.
The shape of western America was pretty well known as far north
as California; beyond that there might or might not be the outlet
from the North-west Passage. The China Seas and the East
Indies were known if not charted. North of the latitude of Japan
was a matter of guesswork so that there was nothing to prevent
Dean Swift from locating there the flying island of Laputa,
and Brobdingnag the land of the giants. South of the equator,
from Cape Horn to Tasman's bleak discoveries, the map was
blank; there might be ocean, but it was supposed that there
was land.

THE PACIFIC OCEAN
AS KNOWN ABOUT THE YEAR 1756
Based upon de Vaugondy's map carried by
Captain Cook on his First Voyage, 1769
(Mercator's Projection)

George Philip & Son, Ltd.

Map 4

The renewal of the age of discovery is connected with the growing rivalry between England and France, the imperial nations of the eighteenth century. The literatures of both countries abounded at that time in books of travel and in scientific treatises on geography. This was a noble rivalry, concerned with the increase of knowledge and the extension of civilisation as well as with new opportunities for commerce; it differed greatly from the mean exclusive struggle for monopoly which had marked earlier exploration. A book that stimulated interest was the *Voyages* of Woodes Rogers, whose narratives include the anecdote of Alexander Selkirk, the original of Robinson Crusoe. William Dampier, who had knocked about the world in very shady company, is now remembered as the first Englishman to land in New Holland (1688) and as the discoverer of New Britain, an island of little service until, in 1942, the Japanese made it a naval base. In the Spanish war of 1739 an ambitious voyage was undertaken by Admiral George Anson (1697–1762) with a squadron of six ships and 1000 men. Only his flagship, the *Centurion*, returned round the world and only a sixth part of the crews; the rest had died of scurvy. Anson's intention was two-fold: to raise a rebellion in the Spanish colonies, which came to nothing; and to seize the treasure-galleon, which he did though he had to chase it across the Pacific to Manila. He refitted his ship in the Canton River after the action.

Anson thought poorly of the Portuguese at Macao and of the English merchants at Canton who lived in terror of giving offence to the mandarins. Only one Englishman spoke Chinese, the rest were content to converse in pidgin-English. He resolved to assert his prestige as a King's officer by making a state call upon the Viceroy of Canton, in an eighteen-oared barge with a crew dressed in blue silk waistcoats, scarlet coats, and silver buttons. After every objection had been raised he insisted upon being received, partly by his customary firmness and tact which taught him just how to parley with the subtle Chinese, partly because his jolly tars made themselves popular by putting out a fire in the town, and partly because his equipage included two arguments commanding respect in other ports besides Canton—a broadside that could sink any ship or silence any fort on the China coast, and a Spanish treasure of 1,300,000 pieces-of-eight stowed below hatches. Anson's *Journal of a Voyage Round the World*, 1740–4, stimulated the public interest.

At the end of the Seven Years War many eyes were turned towards the maps of the Pacific Ocean, both in France and England. George Grenville's schemes to organise the Empire included a plan for rediscovering Drake's 'New Albion', an obvious next step after the conquest of Canada. The writings of Alexander Dalrymple, who by some means had learned the Spanish secret of the discovery of Torres Strait, moved the Admiralty and the scientific world to activity. Two naval expeditions under Byron and Wallis crossed the Pacific Ocean between 1764 and 1767; Byron was unfortunate in hitting upon no major discovery, but Wallis in 1767 discovered Tahiti and wrote a stolid account of it. The following year a French expedition under Bougainville again visited the island, and his account profoundly affected the French philosophers by revealing the South Sea Islands as an earthly paradise. The crews of one expedition or the other repaid the easy hospitality of the Tahitians by infecting them with syphilis.

In 1769 a transit of Venus across the Sun was due to occur, a rare astronomical phenomenon which would enable geographers to make some useful corrections in the mathematics of navigation. As these were of practical value to the Navy and of scientific interest to the learned, it was agreed by the Admiralty and the Royal Society to send an expedition, jointly, to a place in the Pacific Ocean from where the transit could best be observed. The backer was a wealthy young amateur, (Sir) Joseph Banks, (1743–1820) who advanced funds, and accompanied the expedition with a team of scientific assistants. The Admiralty provided a ship, a crew and a commander, Lieutenant James Cook (1728–79). Rarely does the historian have the privilege of describing so admirable a career as that of Cook. The son of a Yorkshire farm labourer, he went to sea in a Whitby collier, educated himself, studied his profession and became a master-mariner. At the outbreak of the Seven Years War he volunteered into the Navy before the mast and served with Admiral Saunders' squadron in the combined operations which led to the fall of Quebec. His skilful pilotage in the awkward waters of the St Lawrence under the French guns led to his selection, after the war, to survey the coasts of Newfoundland, a task which he accomplished so accurately and thoroughly that he was marked down by the Admiralty as 'fit for greater enterprises'. In 1768 he was appointed to command the barque *Endeavour* which was to take Sir Joseph Banks and his party to the newly discovered island of Tahiti.

Cook's instructions were, after completing the observations at Tahiti, to search the 'forties for the Southern Continent, to report upon its products and peoples, to cultivate their friendship and to annex convenient trading posts in the King's name. On leaving Tahiti he went away south and then west, intending to come down upon the east side of the inhospitable land discovered by Tasman, and made his landfall on 7 October 1769. For six months he cruised in New Zealand waters surveying the coasts and studying the native peoples. His charts, which remained in use for eighty years, proved that this was no part of a continent but a long and narrow group of islands extending from north to south through a thousand miles.

From New Zealand, Cook bore away west to search for the eastern coast of New Holland. He skirted along a line of cliffs which, from some fancied resemblance to the Welsh coast, he named New South Wales. Further north he found himself in danger between the land and the shoals of the Barrier Reef, which he followed for several hundred miles, a feat of navigation achieved by equal skill and luck. By way of Torres Strait he returned to England where he was loaded with honours. On the coasts both of New Zealand and of New South Wales he had made formal acts of annexation to the British Crown, but these were disregarded by the government at home.

In 1772 Cook was despatched again to search the southern seas for land. Making his base among the savages in a New Zealand harbour he crossed and recrossed the Pacific, as far south as latitude 70° where his way was barred by the Great Ice Barrier. He thus disposed of the ancient myth; there was no continental mass north of the antarctic ice. This second of Cook's voyages round the world was remarkable in that only one man of his crew died of disease, a record indeed when in earlier circumnavigations a crew was lucky if more than a minority came home alive.

In his third voyage Cook disproved the other great myth of Pacific geography, the existence of a navigable North-west Passage in the temperate zone, by cruising along the western coast of North America beyond Drake's 'New Albion', beyond the limit of Spanish exploration and into the Behring Sea. A by-product of the voyage was his discovery of the Hawaiian Group which seems to have escaped the notice of the numerous earlier navigators in the central Pacific. The rest of the tale is well known. His men were at first received at Hawaii with Polynesian liberality, he himself was treated with divine honours as a great chief—all Polynesian chiefs were of divine origin. But the ships outstayed their welcome. Quarrels arose between the rough sailors and the islanders, who had the easiest notions of private property and coveted the iron tools and weapons of the strangers. On 14 February 1779, Cook was killed in a brawl on the beach while trying to recover a stolen ship's cutter. His last word to his boat's crew was to cease firing. When their quick tempers had subsided the Hawaiians regretted his death and endeavoured to make amends.

The publication of the account of Cook's voyages aroused an extraordinary outburst of interest in England. His achievements were greater than those of any earlier navigator; he had outlined on the map the shape of lands and seas, hitherto unknown or hardly known, amounting to one-quarter of the whole surface of the globe; he had charted the coasts of New Zealand, New South Wales, Hawaii and scores of smaller islands; he had disproved the two ancient myths of the navigable North-west Passage and the habitable Southern Continent; he had sailed three times round the world, had taken his ship into the Arctic and the Antarctic regions and, most remarkable of all, had done this almost without loss of life. Cook has been credited with the discovery of a preventive or of a cure for scurvy, but this is beyond his due. It was the common knowledge of his age that scurvy was a disease caused by malnutrition and curable by proper diet. It was Cook's triumph that he prevented its outbreak by enforcing rules of health. He insisted on cleanliness, ventilation, daily exercise, variety in diet and on the use of a decoction of *sauerkraut* when no other fresh vegetables were available. He took great pains to keep his crews cheerful and encouraged dancing on the foc'sle. He was a naval not a medical reformer.

With Cook's death ends the fantastic age of exploration by sea. The general plan of all the oceans was known and only details remained to be discovered. No longer need mariners be lost in uncharted oceans, since Harrison's Chronometer, first used by Cook, at last solved the old problem of finding the longitude. Though his adventures received the widest publicity, though the best society of his day attempted to lionise him, Cook remains personally unknown. Among his voluminous official papers there is hardly an anecdote or a characteristic saying to tell us what kind of man he was. His portrait at Greenwich reveals him as a tall, handsome man with a pleasant expression and a shrewd inquisitive eye; but he had no small talk and no aptitude for letter-writing. All accounts, including those of the Polynesian natives who were mightily impressed by him, agree that he was aloof, dignified and taciturn. His life, as Newbolt pointed out, is summed in the names of the four ships he commanded: *Endeavour*, *Resolution*, *Adventure* and *Discovery*.

The sailors of that age were in general careless of human life and brutally callous in their treatment of primitive peoples. The habit of kidnapping savages as slaves, the universal contempt for their religious and social customs, provoked sudden outbursts of vengeance, which the sailors regarded as treachery and punished with indiscriminate massacre. Among the light-hearted islanders of the Pacific, gaiety and good humour would turn in an instant to fighting frenzy when their honour was offended. Almost alone among the voyagers, Cook spared no effort to make a friendly honourable approach to the islanders. It is then all the more tragic that he should have lost his life in a brawl arising from a misunderstanding.[1]

2. THE SOUTH SEA ISLANDERS

THE aboriginals of New Guinea, and the belt of islands known as Melanesia to the eastward of Australia, are among the most primitive peoples in the world. In person they are tall, slender and negroid, with profuse heads of hair. When first discovered they lived by fishing and hunting, wove no cloth, made no use of metals, domesticated no animals, knew little of agriculture and lived in rude huts of branches. Descent was traced through the

[1] When this and the following section were first written I hoped that they would have been revised by my brother, A. H. Carrington, whose knowledge of the Pacific and of its exploration was, perhaps, unequalled. His death in 1947 deprived me of that advantage. C.E.C.

female line since, as Malinowski asserted of the Trobrianders even in the twentieth century, they had no understanding of the process of paternity. The mysterious sense of unity with some animal totem united the family-group in so close a relationship as to compel marriage outside the group in order to avoid incest. The whole complex of beliefs, varying widely from region to region, but based upon some such folk-belief raised an impassable psychological barrier against European understanding and influence. Their political, their economic, their religious life were utterly unlike ours. The barrier has never been broken down. In general the Australian blacks and the Melanesian islanders have remained at their former level of culture and have not acquired European ways of thought in 200 years of contact. Of late a more enlightened school of colonial administrators has abandoned the attempt to 'civilise' these natives, adopting instead the 'zoological-gardens' policy of isolating them in their mental and physical wilderness. All the experience of colonisation goes to prove this segregation impracticable, although in some instances the islanders themselves have shown signs of welcoming it. But that ancient solvent of fossilised cultures, external war, has of late been at work in Melanesia.

Very different from the primitive negroid Melanesians were and are the gay sophisticated peoples of the zone of volcanic islands and coral reefs stretching through sixty degrees of the central Pacific from Fiji to Easter Island, from Hawaii to New Zealand, the mysterious Polynesians. They, too, used no metals but ground exquisite tools and weapons of a neolithic type from obsidian and jade. In the northern islands they wove cloth on the loom, but through most of the region beat out bark into fabric as fine as cotton cloth, excelled in basket work and patterned mattings of delicate fibre, embroidered their clothing with the gorgeous plumage of tropical birds. They cultivated the yam, the bread-fruit, and the sweet potato. They lived at the sea's edge as expert swimmers, navigators, fishermen; they named and studied the stars, knew the ocean currents, and could plot the map of the Pacific though they knew nothing of even the simplest form of writing.

Yet once, as they knew and told in traditional poems, they had been a greater people. Their culture showed all the signs of degeneration not of progress. For perhaps a thousand years they had lived the life of lotus-eaters in the fortunate isles where the sun was always warm and the earth almost unaided produced her kindly fruits; but they had come from an earlier home in a land which all the islanders alike remember and revere, the fabulous land of 'Hawa-iki'. They had spread through the islands in half-decked double canoes that could beat against the wind. They retained, as priestly secrets, traces of a monotheistic religion, and knew that they had once built holy places of dressed stone. Relics of the lost theogony remain at Easter Island, the farthest and strangest Polynesian outpost where gigantic stone idols and terraces of masonry remain to confound the imaginations both of visiting ethnologists and of the islanders themselves. Everywhere decadent traces of the lost culture remain in the broken-down conventional patterns which all the Polynesians incise on the door-posts of their houses, the figure-heads of their canoes, and the tattooing of their faces; designs containing representations of gods whose names and attributes alone survive after their cult has been forgotten.

The Polynesian migrations ended with the occupation of New Zealand by the Maoris about the year 1350. Then the art of navigation was forgotten, as it seems to have been forgotten by our own Anglo-Saxon ancestors after their invasion of Britain. The Maoris never returned to the north, nor were voyages made across the wider gaps between other island-groups; the ocean-going double canoes fell into disuse and were remembered only in legend. Yet when Bougainville and Cook introduced the Polynesian race to the attention of the learned, comparative studies proved that in the islands which had held no intercommunication for 400 years the same traditional histories were told and the pedigrees of chiefs were consistently traced to the same ancestors, not only as far back as the age of dispersion through Polynesia in the fourteenth century, but to a common origin a thousand years earlier in 'Hawa-iki'.

Descent in Polynesia was traced through the male line and pride of birth was no higher in Scotland. The chiefs were heaven-born and endowed with supernatural powers, especially in having an innate reservoir of force which they called *tapu*, anglicised as taboo. The chief was bound by rules of caste, as strictly as any Brahmin, in order to preserve and insulate this dangerous potential which might strike an intruder dead as with an electric shock. The chief's person and property, his house, food and weapons were *tapu*, polluted if touched by an inferior, and touched only with peril. The chief by a mere word might lay a *tapu* upon any thing or place, charging it, as it were, with a current so that all the magical restrictions attaching to his own person attached to the *tapu*-ed place or thing. No Polynesian dared break a *tapu*, on pain of punishment by the chief whose honour was thereby defiled, but much more for fear of supernatural penalties. The fact that *tapu* was something of which Europeans were quite unappreciative, whether through ignorance or through contempt, was the cause of almost every clash between the two races. The prestige of a chief increased with his triumphs in politics and war, making his *tapu* ever more effective. An intention in battle was to master and acquire and add to one's own the prestige of the opposing chief, an end best achieved by killing and eating him. Thus contests of skill and courage, in war and intrigue, were a natural occupation of chiefs and were concluded by a ritual cannibal feast.

Captain Cook earnestly and generously studied the Polynesians but never grasped their state of mind. They, too, studied him, obviously a great chief, aloof and dignified on his *tapu*-ed quarter-deck. The game ended without malice when they clustered round, each stabbing at his body to share in the prestige they gained by his death, each hoping for a mouthful of that strong meat.

The Polynesians are a tall, strong, stoutly built race varying in colour from light brown in the northern islands to a deeper colour in New Zealand and Fiji where there may be a strain of negroid Melanesian blood. Their language has hardly more than dialectic variations from island to island. Tribes held their land in common and made a festival of harvesting a crop or launching a new boat; no such event passing without feasting and dancing. The men were bold and active, the women graceful and licentious. This idyllic life reached its easy climax in Tahiti, the goal of every sailor sick for the land.

The Maoris who had voyaged to New Zealand found themselves in a temperate climate where the hard necessities of life made them a tougher, fiercer people. The yam would not grow at all and the sweet potato only in the north. There was no edible quadruped in New Zealand and a shortage of all meat after the invaders had killed off the *moa*, the gigantic flightless birds that once abounded there. The lack of other proteins led the Maoris to eat men for food. It made them the most ferocious enemies that the European adventurers have ever encountered.

In spite of their sexual morals which to Puritan sensibilities seemed so degraded, and the cannibalism which was so abhorrent, the Polynesians were shrewd and lively enough to adopt the culture of the invading Europeans. Of all 'coloured' races they have inspired least colour-prejudice and have interbred freely with the whites inside and outside wedlock. Their sea-going propensities led them to enlist gladly as sailors in the ships of the early navigators, and to renew their long-lost contacts with the world. Islanders appeared in London, kept their wits about them, and bought muskets with which to advance their honour in island feuds. When the missionaries came, the islanders welcomed them and made use of them. In the principal groups the people were rapidly converted to Christianity. In short, it took the Polynesians no more than two or three generations to advance a thousand years in culture, but not without misfortunes and mal-adjustments to which I shall refer later.

3. 'BOTANY BAY', 1788–1820

YOUNG Mr Pitt's cabinet in the period of reconstruction after the American War was filled with mediocrities, among them the Secretary of State, Lord Sydney, known to posterity for having given his name to the metropolis of the south Pacific. It was his task to cope with two urgent problems, the settlement of the American loyalists and the provision of a new land of exile for convicted felons since they could no longer be shipped to Virginia by contract. Several plans of colonisation were pro-posed both for the honoured and the dishonoured groups of emigrants, together or separately. Sir Joseph Banks suggested New South Wales for the felons and, after debate, the House of Commons resolved that 'the plan of establishing a colony of young convicts in some distant part of the globe...where the climate is healthy and the means of support attainable, is equally agreeable to the dictates of humanity and sound policy, and might prove in the result advantageous both to navigation and commerce'.

Plate 7

CAPTAIN JAMES COOK (1728–79)

Painted in 1776 by N. Dance, at Greenwich. Another painting in the National Portrait Gallery is strikingly different but this was reputed a good likeness by Cook's friends. *See p. 201.*

Plate 8

CAPTAIN ARTHUR PHILLIP (1738–1814)

Founder of Sydney and New South Wales.
By F. Wheatley. *See p. 209.*

That indefatigable map-maker, Cook, had sprinkled the chart of the Pacific with names of capes, islands and mountains generally selected out of compliment to his patrons in the Navy, but occasionally with a touch of whimsicality. In his voyage along the coast of New South Wales he had noted but not entered an opening in the cliffs which he named Port Jackson, after an admiralty official. He had gone ashore in a marshy cove at a few miles' distance, where long afterwards Sydney built its first airport. Cook's holograph journal, now at Canberra, shows that he first called this landing-place Stingray Harbour, then altered the name to Botanist and then again, by a happy transition, to Botany Bay on account of the variety of unknown plants collected by Sir Joseph Banks. The odd name caught the popular fancy and was to be long used as a general nickname for the convict settlements though, in fact, the site was not occupied by the convicts. 'Botany Bay', and all that it implied, were as well known as Jack Ketch and Tyburn Tree to two whole generations of the criminal classes and those who studied their ways.

Time passed in deliberations, and comparisons with sites in other continents, until the housing of convicts had become a scandal. As there were then no detention prisons they were held, in shocking discomfort, in hulks of ships moored in English harbours. Philanthropists like John Howard and projectors like Jeremy Bentham protested both against their present condition and against the plan to exile them among the savages, but sheer necessity prevailed and Botany Bay was selected. Parliament passed an enabling act and, in 1786, a naval officer, Captain Arthur Phillip, was appointed Governor of New South Wales. On 18 January 1788 he arrived at Botany Bay with a fleet of ten ships containing 529 male convicts, 188 females and a guard of 200 marines. Without hesitation he rejected the chosen site, where there was no anchorage and entered the gap which Cook had named Port Jackson. Phillip instantly recognised the harbour with its hundreds of miles of winding shore and deep sheltered waters as 'the finest in the world, in which a thousand sail of the line may rest in perfect security'. Posterity has justified his choice to which the pride of the free people of New South Wales in their incomparable harbour is an everlasting tribute. On 26 January the flag was broken; the marines fired a *feu-de-joie*, and healths were drunk to the royal family and the success of the new colony; tents were pitched, to be replaced soon by huts built of local stone near the head of the harbour, beside a bay of deep water which Phillip named Sydney Cove.

Early days at Sydney were quite unlike the beginnings of any other British colony. From the first day there was rule and method and strong administration, by a governor who exercised powers little short of dictatorship. He could draw on the Treasury for money with which to import food, and could use the forced labour of the convicts for making wharves and roads and public buildings. The colony was a town rather than a plantation. It cost the Treasury at first about £95,000 a year, which was thought so excessive that proposals were made in Parliament to put an end to the experiment. 'We have lost New England', wrote one political economist, 'but New Wales has started up. How many millions it may cost may be the subject of the calculations of succeeding financiers a century hence, unless by the exertions of some able statesman that source of future waste and extravagance is prevented.'[1] Phillip, however, saw clearly from the beginning that he was laying the foundation of something greater than a convict prison. He insisted on the importance of making a start at agriculture and repeatedly urged the Government to send out free settlers. He is described as a thin, meagre little man; 'intelligent, active, persevering; with firmness to make his authority respected and mildness to render it pleasing'. 'I have no doubt', he said, 'but that the country will hereafter prove a most valuable acquisition to Great Britain.... It will require patience and perseverance.' 'Settlers appear to be absolutely necessary.' When ill-health obliged him to retire in 1792, a number of time-expired soldiers and sailors had begun to cultivate small-holdings about Sydney, with the help of convict servants 'assigned' to them by the Governor. At least one convict had already been set free, with a grant of thirty acres as a reward for good behaviour.

The political history of New South Wales for the next thirty years is a somewhat dismal tale of petty tyranny and its consequences. A succession of retired officers of the Army and Navy held the appointment of Governor, for which they were selected on account of their supposed capacity for disciplining a population of felons. The Governor had no power of pardon, but had

[1] Sir J. Sinclair, *History of the Public Revenue*.

absolute discretion in 'assigning' convict servants to the few free colonists, and absolute control over undeveloped lands; he could thus make any settler at will a rich man or a pauper. There was no representative element in the government, no trial by jury. The discipline imposed upon the convicts was ferocious. Floggings were frequent, hangings 300 times as numerous in proportion to the population as in England; but worst of all was the threat to transport convicts who misbehaved to the punishment camps formed in Van Diemen's Land (1804) and Norfolk Island (1825). The tales of happenings there recalls Buchenwald and Dachau, yet Governors King, Hunter, Bligh, Macquarie and Brisbane were conscientious reasonable men and their powers, except in respect of the punishment camps, were not misused.

The Governors were quite dependent upon the support of the military garrison, a sort of Pretorian Guard, called the New South Wales Corps. The officers of this regiment formed a 'racket', to buy up the entire cargoes of incoming ships and to maintain high prices for their own profit. The liquor trade, both in imported and locally distilled spirits, came entirely into their hands. Thus the government of New South Wales, for some years after the departure of Phillip, was marked by cruelty to the convicts, corruption organised by the warders and arbitrary interventions by well-meaning though despotic Governors. The picture would be black if civil government were the chief concern of colonial history, but the background of the story of New South Wales is of another colour.

All the Governors from Phillip onwards complained bitterly of the poor human material that formed a large part of the population. London pickpockets lacked the physique, the country training and the industrious habits needed for pioneering though some of them, when their time was out, lived well by their wits at urban occupations in Sydney town. There were also country lads in plenty, many of them victims of the iniquitous English game-laws, in exile at Botany Bay, where they often made good and lived to raise respectable families. It has been estimated that four-fifths of the convicts were transported for crimes which would now 'be dealt with by the summary jurisdiction of a police court or possibly pardoned under a First Offenders' Act'. These flattering assumptions must not be carried too far; it was well said of the convicts (though not, as is often alleged, by Barrington, the *doyen* of pickpockets) that:

> From distant climes, o'er widespread seas we come,
> (Though not with much *éclat* or beat of drum);
> True patriots all; for be it understood,
> We left our country for our country's good...
> And none will doubt but that our emigration
> Has proved most useful to the English nation.[1]

During the wars of the French Revolution political prisoners in large numbers swelled the population of Sydney, quite altering its character. Many ardent spirits, whose views were too advanced for Pitt's anti-Jacobins, found themselves interned at 'Botany Bay', among them men of education and virtue, such as the Scottish political 'martyrs' who were sentenced to transportation by Lord Justice Clerk Braxfield, and in later times the Dorset farm labourers known to Trade Union history as the Tolpuddle Martyrs. There were also several hundred Irish rebels who attempted a mutiny in 1800.

Convicts were first worked in gangs on roads or public buildings, then, as their character and abilities became known, assigned to free settlers as labourers, house-servants or even in positions of trust as clerks or secretaries. Then released on ticket-of-leave they were allowed to take up land, and finally became free settlers, 'emancipists'. It is not surprising that social barriers remained. The officers of the New South Wales Corps, the best society of Sydney, mixed only with those who had come to the colony as free men, and frowned on the Governor if he showed favour to an 'emancipist', of whatever degree of personal worth. Among the first free emigrants were the sailors, since Sydney assumed at once its destined place as the centre of south Pacific trade. The ocean swarmed with sperm-whales which, before the end of the eighteenth century, attracted British and American whaling-ships in plenty. By an odd chance the colony lay within the area over which the East India Company claimed trading rights and therefore was outside the restrictions imposed by the British Navigation Acts. The Company assumed no sort of control, leaving Sydney open to the navigation of the world, a great boon to the shipping interest of the United States. As wealth and

[1] The origin of this celebrated satire has been much disputed. It was probably written and first published in London.

commerce grew, the influence of the New South Wales Corps waxed fat with it, all the more when the officers found a natural leader in Captain John Macarthur, the son of a Highland chief who had fought at Culloden. In this very corrupt society, Macarthur retained his personal integrity and, by honest if grasping means, became the richest man in the colony. He was 'keen as a razor and rapacious as a shark'.

In an age when economists were obsessed with the necessity of increasing the acreage of wheat and tended to neglect other forms of productive wealth, Macarthur demonstrated that the future of New South Wales was to be pastoral rather than agricultural. In 1794 he was breeding sheep, in 1797 he imported fine-wooled merinos from South Africa, and in 1806 a ram and five ewes from King George's own model farm at Kew. So rich and progressive a settler, an officer and a gentleman with friends in high places at home, could afford to defy the Governor and did so. Honest Governor Hunter, who did his best to break the monopoly in rum held by the officers of the corps, was himself recalled as a result of their intrigues in London.

The contest between the masterful Macarthur and the administration reached its climax in 1806–8 when the redoubtable Bligh of the *Bounty* was Governor. William Bligh had been with Cook at Hawaii in 1778 and had been given the command of another scientific expedition. He was to collect specimens of the bread-fruit plant in Tahiti and transfer them to the West Indies, where it was hoped that bread-fruit would make cheap food for slaves. The lotus-eating life of Tahiti was too seductive for Bligh's crew who mutinied, setting him adrift with a few companions in an open boat. Bligh's boat-voyage of 1500 miles to Timor is a classic tale of sea-adventure. The mutineers of the *Bounty* after various adventures arrived at Pitcairn Island, one of the remotest islands of eastern Polynesia, with some Tahitian women. Thus was founded in 1789, a few months after the landing at Botany Bay, the second British colony in the Pacific. The mutineers had fled far from the shipping lanes and remained forgotten until 1813, when a warship stumbled across their hiding-place. One of the mutineers was still alive, the ancestor of a numerous progeny which inhabits Pitcairn Island to-day.

Bligh returned to a distinguished career in the Navy, but had the misfortune to be involved in a second outbreak, the Mutiny at the Nore in 1797. This, too, he survived, to fight gallantly at Camperdown and Copenhagen where he was singled out by Nelson for special praise. In 1806 he arrived at Sydney, still a martinet with a truculent manner, and set himself to destroy the corrupt influence of the New South Wales Corps. 'The law, sir! My will is the law, and woe unto the man who dares to disobey it.' 'Damn the Secretary of State! He commands at home. I command here.'

Bligh correctly appreciated that using rum as currency was the vicious principle by which the power of the Corps was upheld. His attempts to suppress the trade in rum led to open hostility and at last to rebellion by the officers. For the third time in his life Bligh found himself a prisoner in the hands of mutineers. Macarthur's influence was so great that he lived down even the offence of deposing and imprisoning the Governor. Two years passed (1808–10), during which Bligh escaped and endeavoured to regain his authority, until Downing Street solved the problem, somewhat meekly, by sending out a new Governor, Macquarie with a new regiment of soldiers. To save Bligh's face he was reinstated as Governor for one day. The New South Wales Corps ended its disgraceful history by returning to England where it was reorganised as the 102nd regiment of the line. Governor Macquarie had many of the same troubles to contend with as his predecessors, but not thereafter a corrupt and mutinous garrison.

While the Governors were struggling with Macarthur's growing influence, there was much to be done away from Sydney town. The first settlement was a natural gaol, bounded by the sea and the rugged chain of the Blue Mountains which no colonist passed for twenty years. The shape of the country was quite unknown. Beyond the Blue Mountains there might be another Mississippi valley, or an arm of the sea dividing New South Wales as an island from the land far in the west known as New Holland. Two young naval officers, William Bass and Matthew Flinders, explored the southern coasts in a tiny private yacht. In 1798 they sailed through Bass's Strait proving that Van Diemen's Land (or Tasmania) was an island separated from New South Wales. Later Flinders, in a sloop provided by the Admiralty, made a survey of the whole south coast of the continent as far as Cape Leeuwin (1801–2), thus proving New

Holland and New South Wales to be parts of a single island continent, to which he gave the name of Australia. His expeditions were intended largely to forestall the French who were supposed to have designs in the South Seas.

At every stage in the exploration of the Pacific, the French and the English ran neck and neck. Wallis at Tahiti, Cook off the New Zealand coast, Phillip at Port Jackson, and Flinders on each of his voyages anticipated a rival French expedition by a few days or months. Back in the polite eighteenth century, the age of reason, national rivalries did not extend into the republic of science. When Cook set out on his last voyage, during the American War, the belligerent powers had issued instructions to their colonies to treat Cook as a neutral, and to afford him every help in a task which was for the interest of humanity; but times were changing. The ideological wars arising out of the French Revolution were precursors of the hideous total war of our time. 'The age of chivalry was gone.' Thus Flinders found the attitude of the French at each meeting less friendly. During the Peace of Amiens, Napoleon stretched out tentacles into every continent and every sea, preparing designs even against Botany Bay and, when the war was resumed, the republic of science took up arms. Flinders put in at the French island of Mauritius in 1804, and was arrested as a spy. Napoleon, to do him justice, intervened by ordering his release, but the French Governor found excuses for detaining Flinders until, in 1810, Mauritius was captured and annexed by a British fleet.

While Bass and Flinders explored the Australian coast, other and less successful pioneers tried to force their way inland. The first great discovery, in 1797, was a coalfield at a place on the Hunter River to which the name of Newcastle was given. It was not till 1812 that Gregory Blaxland found a way across the Blue Mountains. When no path could be found through the steep gullies he made his way over the tops by keeping to the rugged ridges, through sparse woods of eucalypt, into the grassy plains beyond. Governor Macquarie built a road across the ranges, but took care to restrict access to the new territories. The gaol wall had been broken down and he must see that his prisoners should not escape. This he might achieve, but not prevent the march of a nation. The free settlers were on the move as the Americans had moved over the Blue Ridge into the Ohio valley.

MacArthur's merinos were multiplying and eating up the land. Australia was no longer synonymous with Botany Bay, but was becoming a pastoral colony in which wool, not convict labour, would be the source of wealth.

At last Downing Street became aware of the change and sent J. T. Bigge as Royal Commissioner to enquire into the state of New South Wales. He reported that between 1788 and 1820, 22,000 men and 3600 women had been transported to Australia as convicts. The population, in 1820, was 30,000, of whom 2000 had come as free settlers and 1700 had been born in the colony. 12,000 were still serving their sentences while the remainder were 'emancipists' in various stages of release. About one-fifth of the population were at the subordinate settlement in Van Diemen's Land. There were in the districts round Sydney 4000 horses, 68,000 cattle, and 110,000 sheep, but the colony was not yet self-supporting in other foodstuffs. Bigge's Commission was a first step towards the Colonial Reform movement which will be discussed in a later chapter.

4. THE SLAVE TRADE AND THE AFRICA COMPANIES

THE early adventurers in Africa had been gold-seekers; until late in the seventeenth century slave-trading was a side-line. Each of the voyaging nations by that time had established its fortified posts in the Gulf of Guinea, some of them strong stone castles with bastions, turrets and crenellated walls in the best style of Renaissance military architecture. Christiansborg, Kormantin, Cape Coast Castle, Elmina, built respectively by the Danes, the British, the Dutch, the Portuguese stand in majestic decay along the strand of the Gold Coast, like the ruined castles that crown the headlands of North Wales. As in other parts of the world so in West Africa, the original primacy of the Portuguese was overthrown by the Dutch, whose power was again overshadowed by the French and British in the eighteenth-century wars. A changing pattern of factories along the coast has followed the fortunes of war in Europe, the rise and fall of chartered companies, and the influence of individual traders with the native kings. Never has there been a systematic allotment of spheres of influence between the trading nations. The map is still a chequer-board marked out in colonial areas by the chance of history, without reference to geographical or ethnological factors.

The earliest of the British Africa companies was that chartered by Queen Elizabeth in 1588 for 'trade to Senega and Gambra'. It lapsed and, thirty years later, King James issued a charter to certain 'Adventurers of London to Gynney and Bynney'. This company was fortunate in producing a man of parts, Richard Jobson, who went on their third voyage to the Gambia River in 1620 as supercargo. Refusing to trade in slaves he penetrated far up the river in search of a fabulous mountain of gold. Though he never found it he never lost faith, returning to publish a book of travel, *The Golden Trade* (1623) giving an accurate account of the country and promising rich rewards to merchants who would trade to the Gambia. A persistent enthusiast, he continued to spread stories of the golden mountain. Among those he inspired was Prince Rupert who visited the coast in 1652 on his naval campaign and took a Roundhead ship in the Gambia river. After the Restoration Rupert helped to form a new company, the Royal Adventurers (1660), 'for discovering the golden mines'. The first expedition was led by Robert Holmes, the swashbuckling admiral of Pepys's Diary, who seized a fort from some Courlander merchants, on an island in the estuary, naming it Fort James (1661). After three years of negotiation Fort James was ceded by the Duke of Courland to King Charles II and thus may be called the oldest British colony in Africa. It was sublet to a group of traders known as the Gambia Adventurers, who lost their money. Farther up the coast, de Ruyter with a Dutch fleet was esconced at Goree, near Cape Verde, and came to blows with the British in 1664. Thus English and Dutch rivalry in the Gambia was the immediate cause of the Second Dutch War for which some people blamed Robert Holmes. The French succeeded the Dutch at Goree in 1678 and in the next generation war was intermittent between the French at Goree and the English at Fort James.

Meanwhile another company had been formed by Sir Nicholas Crisp (his first endeavours as far back as 1631) to trade with the Gulf of Guinea. His people had formed trading posts at Sierra Leone and Kormantin, which, with Fort James at Gambia, long remained the centres of British interest. Crisp also lost his investment and sold out, in 1657, to the East India Company. These interests were taken up by the Royal Adventurers who occupied and rebuilt an old abandoned fort near Kormantin in 1662. Its name was Cabo Corso which the English corrupted as Cape Coast Castle. It resisted a siege by de Ruyter himself in 1665 and was recognised as British by the Treaty of Breda (1667) at the end of the Second Dutch War. The British settled at Accrà in 1676.

The Royal Adventurers, bankrupt like many such companies, surrendered their charter in 1672 to the Royal African Company of England, which was allowed a monopoly, so far as the King of England could grant it, of the slave trade. This was the African Company which survived for seventy years, maintaining forts and striving to maintain its monopoly in seas where every advantage lay with the free-trader. Except for the Senegal and Gambia estuaries, which faced the broad Atlantic and were strategic bases in the naval wars, the West African coast had neither ports nor cities. Trade was done in little ships which put in at random wherever parcels of gold-dust, ivory, palm-kernels, or slaves could be got by hard bargaining with tribal chiefs. There were no great markets, no openings for big business and every monopolising company, French, Dutch or British, failed to show a profit.

Though the Royal African had turned its attention to slave-trading, the coast still provided what store of gold bullion the English government could get. Some sovereigns, valued at twenty silver shillings, had occasionally been minted since Henry VII's time. With the gold brought by the Royal African, a new gold coinage was struck in 1663 bearing an elephant, the badge of the Company. These coins soon won the familiar name of 'guineas' and tended to increase in value since gold was scarce in the seventeenth century and silver plentiful. When Isaac Newton was Master of the Mint he observed that in popular esteem gold was taking the place of silver as the standard of value, at an enhanced price. Through his efforts a recoinage was effected in 1717 and the guinea fixed at twenty-one shillings, an arrangement which had the effect of making gold a legal tender.

The trade in a commodity so easily alienated as gold-dust, together with the irregularities of interloping trade, made West Africa a favourite haunt of the pirates when the West Indies became too warm to hold them. Sierra Leone, then no-man's-land, was a pirates' anchorage. There harboured Edward Davis in his ship significantly named *Bachelor's Delight*, and there, too, his fellow-Welshman Howel Davis who captured Fort James by a stratagem. The greatest of all pirates was the martinet Bartholomew Roberts who kept naval discipline and, by good management, plundered 400 ships in four years (1719–22) along the Guinea Coast. When he was killed and his ship, the *Royal Fortune*, taken after a formal sea-battle with H.M.S. *Swallow* she was found to contain forty guns, 157 men and £4000 in gold-dust. Fifty-two of these pirates were tried and hanged at Cape Coast Castle.

The slave trade with America was organised as a commercial routine by the Royal African Company in 1672. Beginning with a modest export of 5000 slaves a year they reached a much higher figure, though the statistics are unreliable. From 1698 to 1713 the interlopers succeeded in overreaching the Company, by obtaining an Act of Parliament which took away the monopoly but saddled the Company with the cost of maintaining the forts, from the receipts of a 10 per cent duty on imports. This proved so insufficient that the Company found relief in the Asiento Treaty (see page 66) by which, from 1713 to 1750, the African Company produced the slaves and the South Sea Company shipped them to America. That system in its turn gave way again to free trade in slaves through the last and most prosperous age of the slave trade, from 1750 to 1807. By an Act of 1750 the trade was thrown open to the 'Company of Merchants', a free association which all might join, while a grant-in-aid of £10,000 a year was allotted to the African Company which survived solely to maintain the West African forts.

Buying and selling strong young negroes of both sexes was a matter of hard bargaining in a well-organised market. It depended first on the customary codes of the African kingdoms which defined the status of slavery. Normally the slaves were prisoners of war, though the European buyer rarely studied their origins. They were produced in droves by recognised middle-men at the factories and were sold by auction after a careful physical examination. Three pounds a head was a fair purchase price, in the eighteenth century, for slaves who might fetch thirteen or fourteen pounds in Charleston or Jamaica, if they survived the 'Middle Passage'. Warlike African kings made a good revenue by raiding more primitive tribes for captives who could be sold profitably on the Coast. Never has there been a time in Africa when the more advanced peoples of the coasts have not ravaged the interior for this sort of merchandise; the negro slave trade is depicted on the frescoed walls of temples in ancient Egypt; it is not yet extinct on the shores of the Red Sea. Without doubt the brisk demand from America stimulated the supply and brought into the business the fearless, rapacious Moslem dealers from the north who searched all Africa for heathen 'Kaffirs', fetching them to market in caravans that travelled hundreds of miles, through the deserts of the interior uplands, and the fever-stricken forests of the coastal belt. The young and strong were brought to market with no little care, for they were worth money; the infants, the old, and the infirm got no mercy. When the lordly Saracen emirs of the Niger, and the negro rulers of the ancient kingdoms of Dahomey and Benin and Ashanti, as well as the middlemen on the Coast, had all to get a fair commission on the deal, it was no easy task to buy slaves at an economic price. The trade brought good business to English merchants. In return for exporting men the West Africans bought Brummagem goods, iron pots and kettles, copper and tin, beads and linen and 'manillas'. There was even a brisk demand for English broadcloth.

Liverpool and Bristol grew rich on the slave trade. The Lord Mayor of Bristol said in 1739 that it was 'the great support of our people'. Liverpool boasted of being 'the principal slaving port not only in England, but in Europe'. But the good people of these cities never set eyes on the results of their handiwork. They built ships designed to carry the maximum load of slaves in the minimum deck-space, fitted them out for the 'Coast' but never saw them again until they returned empty from America to refit. The largest ships each carried about 700 slaves, who were occasionally let out in batches on the main deck for air and exercise, since it would not be profitable to let them die, but otherwise were shackled between decks with space to lie at full length but not to stand upright. 'The French, Portuguese and English slave ships', said a Dutch commercial rival, 'are always foul and stinking.' It was the general saying at sea that you could recognise a slaver by the smell if you got to leeward of her. In all long voyages 200 years ago, sickness and mortality were to be expected. The death-rate on the 'Middle Passage' from Africa to America, explains the width of the margin between the buying and the selling price of slaves.

It is not for those who have lived in the 1930's and 1940's to upbraid other generations for callous indifference to human suffering. All men have a strongly developed faculty for ignoring the troubles of unknown remote nations when those troubles put money into their own pockets. The slave trade was regarded in Great Britain for 150 years as the foundation of imperial prosperity. 'The most approved judges...have ever been of opinion that our West India and Africa trades are the most nationally beneficial of any we carry on.... The Trade of Africa is the branch which renders our American Colonies and Plantations so advantageous to Great Britain, that traffic affording our planters a constant supply of negro servants for the culture of their lands.... The Negro-Trade therefore, and the natural consequences resulting from it, may be justly esteemed an inexhaustible Fund of Wealth and Naval Power to this Nation.' So wrote an anonymous essayist in 1749, echoing the general opinion of his contemporaries. In the next generation contrary voices began to be heard until, at the end of the century, the outcries of the philanthropists against the horrors of the slave trade drowned the arguments of the merchants in favour of its continuance.

Humanitarianism was becoming the fashionable cult. The poetic figment of the 'noble savage' had appeared in popular literature, a noteworthy example being Robinson Crusoe's Man Friday (1719). Religious leaders disapproved of slavery and denounced the slave trade. The Quakers petitioned Parliament against it; Wesley preached against it; even that stout Tory, Dr Johnson, startled an Oxford Common Room by drinking a toast to 'the next insurrection of negroes in the West Indies'. These academic objections, however, had little effect upon the moneyed men of the West Indian Interest. Political agitation could only be formed upon some evidence which would stir the political conscience of the nation. It came in the realisation that there were 14,000 negro slaves actually in England, brought there by West Indian 'nabobs', and that the common law was vague about their status. Could slavery exist in this free country?

Long ago when Domesday Book was compiled, there had been considerable numbers of slaves, not to mention that majority of the population held in the semi-servile status of *villeinage*. This feudal slavery had never been abolished by any general law of emancipation, but had imperceptibly dwindled and disappeared. A lingering remnant of villeins had been released from bondage by proclamation of Queen Elizabeth quoting as an authority the old tag of the Stoics 'that all men are by nature born free'; but even in the eighteenth century some vestiges of villeinage survived, especially in Scotland. There seemed to be no rule of law precluding the existence of negro slavery in Georgian England.

The first of the abolitionists was Granville Sharp (1735–1813), a civil servant who undertook the cause of the slaves in England. He made it his business to defend runaway slaves whose masters claimed ownership in the courts. Five such cases were decided on minor points of law before Sharp could oblige the courts to give a decision on the major issue: was slavery recognised by the laws of England? A negro named James Somersett had been brought to England by his master, cast adrift in the streets when ill and useless, and kidnapped back into slavery when his master found that he could be of use again. Sharp applied for Somersett's release on a writ of *habeas corpus*. The case came before Lord Chief Justice Mansfield who tried hard to get it settled out of court, as he was most averse to interfering with property rights, the first consideration of law and politics in that age. But equity prevailed with him to set free James Somersett and 14,000 other slaves, thus destroying property worth half a million pounds, with the decision (1772) that 'the state of slavery was so odious that nothing can be suffered to support it but positive law'. At once the difficulty appeared that the wrong done by slavery is not undone by the act of emancipation. Some thousands of derelict negroes were now thrown upon the world with no means of livelihood, so that Sharp found himself obliged to organise further relief for them. The agitation against slavery now began to gather force, but some years passed before it crystallised into political activity.

In 1785 a young man named Thomas Clarkson (1760–1846), when riding down from Cambridge to London, halted to rest his horse on a green hillside near Ware. As he sat, he reflected on the

University prize he had just won for a Latin essay on *Slavery*,[1] and resolved to devote his life to uprooting its evils. A monument now marks the spot where the resolution was made which he so nobly fulfilled. He made himself known to Granville Sharp and other abolitionists and, in 1787 called, with a copy of his essay, upon William Wilberforce (1759–1833), a Yorkshire Member of Parliament who was thought to be a likely recruit for the cause. This little group of enthusiasts, who were to do battle with the powerful West India Interest, formed part of a large circle which came to be known derisively as the 'Clapham Sect' or the 'Saints'. Society was at that time swept by a wave of religious revival which in the course of a generation permeated and altered the life of the whole nation. Its tendency was evangelical, towards a simple personal devotion and an absolute reliance on the Bible; its aim was to spread religious education at home and abroad. National education, so that every child could read the Bible, and foreign missions, were the main external activities of the Evangelicals; the abolition of slavery, for the spiritual rather than the physical benefit of the slaves, was a by-product. Clarkson, Sharp and Wilberforce met regularly, with other Evangelicals such as Zachary Macaulay, Hannah More, and the converted slave-trader John Newton, at Clapham where one of their number had a villa. Much that concerned the Empire during the next forty years emerged from their discussions.

Clarkson inspired Wilberforce to take up the cudgels in the House against the slave trade, and Wilberforce approached his friend Pitt. Although the first resolution (1788), that the House should take the slave trade into consideration, was moved by Pitt and supported by Burke and Fox, this was but the beginning of the task. The method of the Abolition Committee has become the classic means whereby great progressive movements in England achieve their ends. Clarkson toured the country collecting information from ships' captains at Bristol and Liverpool, interviewing visitors from the colonies, and thus building up a body of evidence on which to base his propaganda. He organised corresponding branches of the Abolition Committee, addressed meetings, published statistical reports, circulated popular appeals including copies of a poem by Cowper and a cameo by Wedg-

[1] *Anne liceat invitos in servitutem dare.*

wood with the motto, 'Am I not a Man and a Brother?' His
correspondents collected signatures for petitions which Wilberforce presented to the House of Commons. Clarkson's outside
agitation was used by Wilberforce to sway opinion inside the
little world of the governing class. Tory members marked the
growing influence of the Evangelicals among their constituents;
Whig members marked the rising voice of democracy, a slightly
discordant note in the abolitionist chorus.

Though Pitt never wavered in his personal hostility to the
slave trade and invariably supported Wilberforce with his own
voice and vote, he was unable to make abolition a Government
measure. It was to him but one necessary reform which must
take its turn among his efforts for the national revival and one
which, pressed too hastily, would split his party and frustrate his
larger policy. If one large section of his supporters were Evangelicals, another constituted the West India Interest. It was the
general opinion in the City among shipping and commercial
men that abolition would spell ruin to trade. They therefore
supported the West Indians, as did the Navy. Rodney defended
the trade in the House of Lords on grounds of strategy. But
among these cautious men there were many who approved of a
regulation of the conditions under which the trade was carried
out, leading to a 'gradual' abolition at some future date. From
1791 onwards several bills were enacted for preventing the over-
crowding of slave-ships and for encouraging with bounties the
humane treatment of slaves at sea. Against these concessions
there were reactionaries of the right wing who foresaw the direst
consequences. The West Indian Assemblies, that of Jamaica
most truculently, resisted every form of change, being convinced that concessions to the negroes would lead not only to
commercial ruin but to mutiny and massacre in the colonies.
'How can we hesitate a moment', asked Pitt in the House, 'to
abolish this commerce in human flesh which has so long disgraced
our country and which our example will contribute to abolish in
every corner of the globe?' Yet the members hesitated: 'The
leaders, it is true, are for abolition', said a back-bencher. 'But
the minor orators, the dwarfs, the pygmies will, I trust, this day
carry the question against them. The property of the West
Indians is at stake; and though men may be generous with their
own property, they should not be so with the property of others.'

All that Pitt could get was a resolution of the House of Commons carried by 193 votes to 125 that 'the Slave Trade ought to be gradually abolished' (1793).

Meanwhile Clarkson had made a tactical error. On the outbreak of the French Revolution, in that enthusiastic dawn when it was 'bliss to be alive', he had visited Paris and established correspondence with committees of advanced democrats. Liberty, Equality and Fraternity made an explosive mixture which the Tories, alarmed by Burke's eloquence, determined to exclude from the British Empire. They were not surprised at the reports from San Domingo where the mulattos, intoxicated with their new-found liberty, had massacred 2000 Frenchmen, and at sympathetic riots in neighbouring British colonies. They succeeded in holding off further action by the abolitionists 'until the end of the war'. Nevertheless, year by year, Wilberforce kept the cause alive by rising in his place in the House to propose immediate abolition. During those years, since the British Navy blockaded French and, for part of the time, Spanish commerce, the British slave trade flourished as never before.

A practical measure undertaken by the abolitionists during these years of struggle was the settlement of emancipated slaves at Sierra Leone, which has the best natural harbour in West Africa. In 1787 Granville Sharp sent out a party of three hundred and forty negroes from London, with some white vagabonds. The first colony aroused the hostility of a local chief who dispersed the settlers and burnt their camp. Nothing daunted, the abolitionists began again on a larger scale, this time obtaining a charter from the Crown for a colonising company, in the old style, with Henry Thornton as president (1791). The settlers were further reinforced by 1,200 negro loyalists who had fled to Nova Scotia from the Thirteen Colonies. Thomas Peters, a Nova Scotian, was the most prominent among them. But the settlement was again destroyed (1794), this time as an act of war by a French Jacobin expedition. The Governor, Zachary Macaulay, one of the Clapham 'Saints', by firm administration set the colony on its feet after this setback until, four years later, Freetown was a little town with 300 houses, 1200 inhabitants and a growing trade with the interior. Yet it required a grant-in-aid that grew year by year. By 1804 the Sierra Leone Company appealed to the Crown for £25,000, having exhausted all its funds. Since,

clearly the settlement was a financial failure, the charter was withdrawn and Sierra Leone was taken over by the Colonial Office
in January 1808.

In addition to the fever and the plagues of insects which per-
vaded all settlements along the Coast, the founders of Sierra
Leone encountered difficulties similar to those which, in the same
years, were hampering the founders of New South Wales. The
negro colonists were quite unfitted for pioneering. Their lives
had been spent as slaves in white men's countries, many of them
in temperate climes, so that they were just as much strangers in
Sierra Leone as were the white officials. They had no knowledge
of African agriculture and, like all freed slaves, a great dislike
for unnecessary exertion. Their contempt for the uncivilised
'bush-niggers' was only equalled by their inferiority at all the
arts of living in tropical Africa. It is a great tribute to the efforts
of Macaulay and his colleagues that anything was made of Sierra
Leone. During the long years when the Navy was engaged in
suppressing the contraband slave trade, cargo after cargo of
negroes from all parts of Africa, at all stages of culture and speaking a hundred different languages, were liberated at Freetown.

A sudden turn in English party politics produced the opportunity
for abolishing the slave trade. Pitt died in January 1806, after
governing by means of a coalition of the right and centre. His
right wing had prevented him from giving unqualified support to
Wilberforce. The succeeding administration which lasted for a
few months only, until the death of Fox its leader, was a government of the centre and left. Several Radical politicians, among
them Henry Brougham, now spoke from the Government
benches in support of abolition. Unlike Pitt who had subordinated all other questions to the necessities of the French War,
Fox regarded the slave trade as a vital problem looming larger
even than the war with Napoleon, in which he was a belated
and reluctant participant. The two groups of abolitionists, the
Radicals who desired political freedom for the negro and the
Evangelicals who desired his moral progress, were united, while
other circumstances at that moment divided the slave-owners.
The conquest of several Dutch and French slave-colonies had
upset the market for slave-grown crops. It seemed clear that the
time had come for a reorganisation of the whole 'interest', since

the moderates were ready for a compromise. When Fox moved a resolution for immediate abolition the defenders of slavery spoke with an uncertain voice and lost the vote in both Houses. The Act prohibiting the 'dealing and trading' in slaves, in British ships, under penalty of fine and confiscation, became law on 25 March 1807. Fox died while the Bill was before Parliament.

Much remained to be done before the trade across the Atlantic could be ended. French, American and Spanish slavers still abounded and seized the trade which the English had abandoned. It therefore became a cardinal principle of British diplomacy in every negotiation to press for international action. The Continental powers found some difficulty in appreciating this obsession of English diplomats.

The long struggle of Great Britain to abolish the international slave trade involved her in difficulties with all the slave-owning powers. At the Congress of Vienna the eight great powers agreed upon a declaration, dictated by the quixotic British to bring the slave trade to an end 'by all the means at their disposal'. The British alone took steps to carry out this undertaking. From 1807 onwards, even in the crisis of the French War about one-sixth of the effective strength of the Navy was diverted to the 'Preventive Squadron' on the African Coast. On that dangerous and unhealthy duty, ships' companies lost 5 per cent by deaths in every cruise, but had the consolation of receiving prize-money at the rate of £5 for every slave they released. The squadron cost the British taxpayer £750,000 annually. Though they rescued over 3000 slaves a year it was soon discovered that the Squadron alone would never solve the problem. The greater the difficulty of transporting slaves to the Spanish and Portuguese colonies, the worse was the treatment of these unfortunates on the Middle Passage. They were stowed tighter in the slave-ships and were ruthlessly thrown overboard if capture by a British cruiser seemed inevitable. Very large numbers still slipped through to the Argentine and Brazil and many were still smuggled into the United States, though Jefferson had forbidden the import of slaves in 1808.

No improvement was possible until the Squadron was given the Right of Search over suspected slave-ships, and this the jealous nations were slow to concede. A mutual arrangement was ineffective since none but the British were making any systematic attempt to hunt the slavers down. Agreements were reached with France in 1831, with Spain in 1835, and with Portugal in 1839. Only after a virtual blockade of the Brazilian ports was that branch of the trade brought under control. Slavers were then obliged to find refuge under the Stars and Stripes, for only that flag resisted the Right of Search. The Abolition of Slavery in the United States itself (1863) marked the end of the Atlantic Slave Trade.

V

WAR, TRADE, AND PHILANTHROPY,
1793–1833

Argument: Adam Smith's *Wealth of Nations* convinced thinking men
that the attempt to make the Empire a fiscal union had been unwise. The
independence of America, since trade with the former colonies increased, was not felt as a loss. The French Wars, 1793–1815, were not
fought to acquire territory. British interest at the Peace Conference
was to build up French and Dutch strength with the result that only
a few strategic points were added to the British Empire, though all
French and Dutch colonies had been occupied. Trade and sea-power
were preferred to dominions.

Many frontier disputes in America, embittered by the wanton War of
1812, were settled by negotiation during the next forty years, not without some offence to Canadian loyalists. A renewed interest in whaling,
sealing and the fisheries led to the exploration of Arctic Canada. In
spite of the Monroe Doctrine British interests predominated in South
America, especially in the Argentine. A sore point was the British
claim to the Falkland Islands, another whaling base from which penetration into the Antarctic was begun.

Evangelical hostility to the protectionist slave-owners of the West
Indies helped the cause of free trade as well as the cause of liberty. The
abolition of slavery and compensation of the slave-owners was a
triumph of Parliamentary skill and administrative efficiency.

1. WILLIAM PITT AND
THE WEALTH OF NATIONS

WILLIAM PITT the Younger, Prime Minister from 1783 to 1801
and from 1804 to 1806, has already made several appearances in
this history. The struggle over Fox's India Bill was the occasion
of his being summoned to form a ministry, but the first fruit of
his administration, the India Bill of 1784, though a measure of
such importance, was prepared and managed by his colleague,
Robert Dundas. The bills authorising the foundation of New
South Wales and separating Upper from Lower Canada were
under the charge of Lords Sydney and Grenville. Pitt

voted for the impeachment of Warren Hastings as a form of judicial enquiry into abuses, while dissociating himself from the prejudiced violence of Burke. On the question of the slave trade, though he gave his personal support to Wilberforce, he was unable to unite his political followers in favour of abolition, which, accordingly, was not taken as a Government measure. In each of these instances, whether it was a case of providing for plundered loyalists, or oppressed Hindus, or kidnapped negroes, or condemned felons, Pitt's actions were guided by a spirit of philanthropy, not by a policy of empire-building.

He cared more for trade than for plantations. As Chancellor of the Exchequer in Shelburne's administration (1782–3) he had conceived a programme of commercial and financial reforms leading in the direction of free trade, a tendency new and radical at that date though it was to be the commonplace of the nineteenth century. 'Monopoly is always unwise,' said Shelburne, 'but if there is any nation under heaven who ought to be the first to reject monopoly it is the English. Situated as we are between the Old World and the New, and between southern and northern Europe, all that we ought to covet upon earth is free trade and fair equality. With more industry, with more enterprise, with more capital than any trading nation upon earth; it ought to be. our constant cry, let every market be open, let us meet our rivals fairly, and we ask no more.'

Such modes of thought were confirmed by the researches of a quiet scholar, Dr Adam Smith of Glasgow and Oxford. During the crisis of the American Revolution, in 1776, he had published a treatise entitled *An Enquiry into the Nature and Causes of the Wealth of Nations*. Like some others of the world's great books it was remarkable not so much for the enunciation of any strikingly original thesis as for the presentation in plain language of principles which had gradually been forcing themselves upon the notice of all enlightened men. He did not bring about a revolution in the science of political economy, he proclaimed the triumph of the new doctrine in terms so clearly defined and supported by such a mass of evidence that his book instantly became a classic. All progressive thought upon the subject for a hundred years was obliged to begin where Adam Smith left off. All who disagreed with him were thrown upon the defensive. 'Sir, we are all your pupils', said Pitt when Adam Smith was presented to him at a dinner-party. His thesis, that monopoly is always disadvantageous, that the free exchange of commodities benefits both parties, and that the British, although 'a nation of shopkeepers', had grossly mismanaged their business, was built upon a close analysis of the East India Company's monopoly and of the effects of the Acts of Trade upon Great Britain and her colonies.

'Nations have been taught,' he wrote, 'that their interest consisted in beggaring all their neighbours. Each nation has been made to look with an invidious eye upon the prosperity of all the nations with which it trades, and to consider their gain as its own loss. Commerce, which ought to be a bond of union and friendship, has become the most fertile source of discord and animosity. The capricious ambition of Kings and Ministers has not been more fatal to the repose of Europe than the impertinent jealousy of merchants and manufacturers.' Thus 'the sneaking arts of underling tradesmen are erected into political maxims for the conduct of a great empire'.

'It is the interest of the merchants and manufacturers of every country to secure to themselves the monopoly of the home market. Hence the extraordinary duties upon goods imported by alien merchants, hence the prohibitions upon foreign manufactures, hence the restraints upon importation from those countries with which the balance of trade is supposed to be disadvantageous.'

All forms of monopoly fell under Adam Smith's condemnation since their effect, in his view, was to restrict the growth of trade by diverting capital from more profitable markets to some market selected for an 'impertinent' reason. The restrictions upon colonial trade raised the price of colonial products and reduced their volume, thus hampering colonial development; while the encouragement given to the English merchants to trade by preference with the colonies diverted them from better markets nearer home.

'The wealth of a neighbouring nation, though dangerous in war and politics, is certainly advantageous in trade. As a rich man is likely to be a better customer to the industrious people in his neighbourhood than a poor, so likewise is a rich nation.'

'France is the nearest neighbour to Great Britain. France besides is supposed to contain 23,000,000 of inhabitants. Our

North American colonies were never supposed to contain more than 3,000,000, and France is a richer country than North America. France could afford a market at least eight times more extensive and, on account of the superior frequency of the returns, four and twenty times more advantageous than that which our North American colonies ever afforded. Such is the difference between that trade which the wisdom of both nations has thought proper to discourage, and that which it has favoured the most.'

Since on other grounds he condemned the management of affairs by joint-stock enterprises, the East India Company, a joint-stock company controlling a trading monopoly, was the object of his special disapproval. 'The single advantage which the monopoly procures (a high rate of profit which depresses other industry) to a single order of men is in many different ways hurtful to the general interest of the country.' He shrewdly pointed out that the supposed profits derived by the nation from the East India monopoly were in fact paid to the Directors of the Company out of the pockets of other Englishmen, who were not only deprived of the right to trade with Asia on their own account, but were obliged to buy Asiatic goods at an artificially enhanced price.

The trade with India and America in itself, was 'always and everywhere beneficial; the monopoly of that trade always and necessarily hurtful'. Adam Smith's strictures were concerned with finance and commerce, not politics. He wrote to rid the British people of their illusion that it was the mercantile system that held the Empire together. 'It has been not an empire, but the project of an empire, a project which has cost immense expense without being likely to bring any profit; for the effects of the monopoly of the colonial trade are, to the great body of the people, mere loss.'

'To propose that Great Britain should voluntarily give up all authority over her colonies was to propose such a measure as never was and never will be adopted by any nation in the world.[1] If it was adopted, however, Great Britain would not only be immediately freed from the whole annual expense of the peace establishment of the colonies but might settle with them such a treaty of commerce as would effectually secure to her a free trade,

[1] These words have an ironical ring after 1947. C.E.C.

more advantageous to the great body of the people, though less so to the merchants, than the monopoly which she at present enjoys.'

'By thus parting good friends, the natural affection of the colonies to the mother-country, which, perhaps, our late dissensions have well-nigh extinguished, would quickly revive. It might dispose them to favour us in war as well as in trade, and instead of turbulent and factious subjects, to become our most faithful, affectionate and generous allies.'

It should be remembered that these words were published in 1776, before the breach with America was irreparable. They were then far in advance of public opinion. Seven years later when the Thirteen Colonies were lost, such ideas, though bold and revolutionary, were beginning to make headway. So cautious a statesman as Pitt, though he acknowledged the influence of Adam Smith, was not the man to liquidate the British Empire in order to test the validity of an economic theory. In fact the hard necessities of politics obliged him to strengthen the bonds of Empire and to fight a bitter war in its defence. The main task of his administration, until war distracted his efforts, was to reform the whole fiscal system of Great Britain, gradually and prudently, according to Adam Smith's doctrine, by reducing and simplifying all duties which acted in restraint of trade, by a rational system of accounting, by adopting Adam Smith's rules of fair taxation, and by his commercial treaties with France. These were the first moves towards the free trade policy of the next generation; but the full implications of that policy: the suppression of the chartered companies, the repeal of the Acts of Trade, and the eventual dissolution of the Empire were still academic considerations. No practical politician of that age brought them into his programme.

Since 1776, the whole character of the Empire had changed. The three great wars with France, of 1740, 1756 and 1778, had been fought, so far as the British were concerned, largely over colonial rivalry in North America. The stake had been the present security and future prospects of a group of small self-governing communities, the most important and the most populous of which were inhabited by men of British blood and origin. Their value to Great Britain, apart from sentimental considerations of prestige, had been conceived as resting on the control of their trade. The prestige had gone for ever and the best informed students were of the opinion that the attempt to control their trade was an economic error. But all was not lost. The valour of Carleton and Elliot and Rodney and Warren Hastings, had preserved the framework of an empire of a quite different nature. There was Canada with its nucleus of docile French-Canadians, not very numerous and of no great account hitherto in the City of London. This colony must be retained, because of the debt of honour to the loyalists who had migrated into it, and because of the fur trade of Hudson Bay, the fisheries of Newfoundland, and the masts and spars from the Maritime Provinces. These practical shipping and commercial interests gave new strategic importance to the naval base at Halifax. There were the West Indies, the sugar islands, prize of so many battles, though not so prosperous as formerly. Some said that this has been their constant complaint, that their former happy state was mythical, but the West Indian Interest commanded sometimes as many as eighty votes in the House of Commons, and was strongly backed by the Navy. There was Bengal. In the years when we had been losing the sovereignty over two or three million white men in America we had been acquiring the sovereignty over twenty-six million Indians, three times as great a population as that of Great Britain, consisting of impoverished peasants to whom we could sell little or nothing. Could they be regarded as anything but an encumbrance which the impetuous servants of the East India Company had loaded on the shoulders of the Crown? If the Company would pay its way and keep quiet that would be the best of a bad business. As Pitt surveyed the population of the Empire in 1792, the unreconciled French-Canadians, the wretched peasants of Bengal, the slaves in Jamaica, the convicts in New South Wales, there was little cause for imperial pride.

But to turn from plantations to trade was to see a brighter prospect. His nine years of peaceful administration (1783–92) had raised the revenue of the nation to unprecedented heights while, at the same time, the French were lapsing into bankruptcy. 'Our good old island,' wrote one member of the Government, 'now possesses an accumulation and completion of prosperity beyond any example in the history of the world.' The nation of shopkeepers had become aware of their economic destiny and had learned that the loss of the Thirteen Colonies did not at all impair their aptitude for importing raw materials and exporting manufactured goods.

2. THE FRENCH WARS, 1793–1802

UNLIKE the three previous wars, which had been fought for colonial rivalry, the War of 1793 was a war of ideas, though the Prime Minister of Great Britain was slow to notice the difference. Pitt's foreign policy, after concluding the Commercial Treaty with France, had been chiefly concerned with such distant affairs as the dispute with Spain over the Pacific coast of North America and the encroachment of Russia in the Black Sea. His confident hopes of another fifteen years of peace were shattered in 1792, by the fall of the French monarchy, the first victory of the French revolutionary army over the Prussians, and the September Massacres in Paris. Even then, though anti-Jacobin horror was rising in England, he saw no reason for war until the French denounced the treaties which restricted the commerce of the Scheldt and prevented the fortification of Flanders. After some weeks of quarrelling, in which the British demonstrated their ancient sensitiveness about the Flemish coast, and the French appealed from old engagements to new abstract principles, the French declared war on 1 February 1793, a few days after the execution of Louis XVI. To the Jacobin leaders it was a war on 'behalf of all peoples against all kings'. To Pitt and the English middle-classes it was a war for the maintenance of commerce as guaranteed by treaty.

As is customary the British armies and navies were dispersed in ill-contrived expeditions without sufficient preparation or clear objectives. Pitt's 'inveterate prudence and instinctive horror of indiscretion' prevented him from concentrating his forces for some bold stroke, but not from frittering them away. The first year of the war was spent in despatching three combined forces, after much vacillation, to Gibraltar, to the West Indies and to Flanders. A large allied army of Prussians, Austrians and British was formed in Flanders for a victorious march on Paris, but was defeated in detail. The British under the Duke of York fell back from Dunkirk and were eventually withdrawn from Holland, the first of three evacuations which in that war concluded attempts to open a western front. Wellington, who had his baptism of fire under the Duke of York, used to say that the campaign taught him one lesson: how not to do it.

While professional opinion in the services looked to Flanders, the cabinet and the City hoped for solid successes in the West Indies, and on their side the French government was similarly biased. Between 1793 and 1798 each belligerent poured into the West Indies a stream of warships and transports carrying scores of thousands of soldiers, most of whom were destined to die of yellow fever. Almost any sacrifice of soldiers' lives, any diversion of the Navy from other tasks, was thought worth while to protect sugar islands and to seize those of the other powers. Added to the influence of the sugar-importers was now that of the manu-facturers in Lancashire whose raw cotton came chiefly from the West Indies. The cotton importers, like the sugar importers, were firm monopolists unconverted to Adam Smith's principles of free trade.

When Pitt introduced the Income Tax in 1797, in calculating incomes from overseas investments he adjudged that four-fifths of all such incomes were derived from the West Indies. British investments there were worth £70,000,000. One-eighth of all British shipping cleared from West Indian ports. But these com-mercial assets were small compared with the wealth of the French island of San Domingo, or Dutch Guiana, or Spanish Trinidad and Cuba. The Spaniards were at first our allies, though later they went over to the French side. The Dutch were the allies on whose behalf we had entered the war; it was one of our primary objects to protect the Dutch colonies even though the enemy should overrun the Netherlands. We had friends too in the French islands, where the white planters invited British aid to restore the royalist regime, and to suppress the negroes who, in every island, were in a state of rebellion. None of the colonial campaigns was a simple issue. In each, loyalties and motives were divided. In almost every Dutch and French colony there was strife between those who dreaded British commercial competition and those who hated the Jacobin revolutionaries.

In 1794 British fleets and armies arrived in the West Indies to begin the bloodiest of their many wars for the sugar islands.

Since Cromwell's assault on the Spanish Indies every European war had brought about a dismal repetition of these ill-advised

WAR IN THE WEST INDIES
1793-1814

Miles

0   100   200   300

Trade Winds

ATLANTIC   OCEAN

LEEWARD IS.

Virgins
Anguilla
Porto Rico
St. Thomas (U.S.)
Barbuda
St. Kitts
Antigua
St. Eustatius (Dut.)
Nevis
Montserrat
Guadeloupe (Fr.)
Dominica
Martinique (Fr.)
St. Lucia
Barbados
St. Vincent
Grenadines
Grenada
Tobago
Trinidad

WINDWARD IS.

CARIBBEAN   SEA

HISPANIOLA
HAITI
SANTO DOMINGO
Porto Rico

Curaçao (Dut.)

GUIANA
Cayenne (Fr.)
Essequibo
R. Demerara
Georgetown
R. Berbice
Berbice
Br. Surinam
(Du.)
Cartagena
(Fr.)

Gulf of Darien

N

Map 5

George Philip & Son, Ltd.

campaigns. In generation after generation expeditions were launched there by politicians who neglected to learn from past experience. Soldiers and sailors knew only too well what would be their fate in these desirable islands that stretched from Trinidad to Cuba across the path of the trade-wind. Of the British islands Barbados lay farthest to windward, Jamaica farthest to leeward, so that a sailing-ship might make a fair passage in a few days from Barbados to Jamaica, but might beat backwards and forwards in the Gulf for three or four months on the return voyage. Thus the naval campaigns turned on occupying a base to windward of your intended prize. All depended on the trade-wind which blows steadily for nine months of the year until the hurricanes begin in October or November, after which there is no sure sailing. These conditions required that every expedition should put to sea and be firmly based ashore before the hurricane season, a requirement that the planners and the purveyors rarely met.

Since Barbados had no natural harbour, the bay of Castries in St Lucia became the means and the prize of victory. In those days the neutrality of the Windward Islands was forgotten and most of them changed hands several times in the four French wars (1756–1815). Dominica, taken after fierce fighting in 1761, remained in British hands after the Treaty of Paris 1763, as did St Vincent and Grenada. Rodney's great victory over de Grasse in the American War was the culmination of a campaign for St Lucia which was, however, twice receded to the French and twice recaptured before it finally became British in 1814. Between the French wars, the English troops were engaged in fierce contests with the Caribs, most of whom were at last transported, in 1802, to Ruatan Island off the Honduras coast. A few still linger in St Vincent and Dominica.

In those steep, wooded, roadless islands, every tropical disease afflicted the redcoats. Unsuitable food and clothing, plentiful rum, the heat, the rain, drink and the devil did for army after army. They landed, won a victory, pursued their enemies into the Bush, encamped and died of yellow jack. Cromwell's expedition of 1654 was the worst-found of all, perhaps justifiably since it was the first. William III's expedition of 1695 failed because the fleet got to sea too late in the year. Few more shocking stories can be read than that in which Smollett described

(*Roderick Random*) the attack on Cartagena in 1740. Not only the English regulars, but almost all of a contingent of American volunteers died of fever. Of the 12,000 men who took part in the grandiose campaign of 1762, 5000 died and were buried in Havana. The war against the Caribs of St Vincent, in 1772, was almost as deadly. A few years later St Lucia and Martinique were swallowing up soldiers who might have weighed down the scales on the side of victory if they had been with Cornwallis in Virginia. A hundred years of colonial wars with France saw whole armies dissolve and perish in the West Indies. More than 300,000 Englishmen died for the avarice of the sugar-planters and the ignoble lust to plunder the Spaniards. But of all these operations the most futile were the campaigns of the Younger Pitt, which cost 100,000 casualties while contributing nothing to the main course of the war against Revolutionary France.

In 1794 the British got an easy foothold in Martinique and Guadeloupe and restored the royalist regime, to the great gratification of the French planters. It is not surprising that the negroes and the mulattos, unwilling to lose their promised liberty, combined with the Jacobin armies to fight against the British. By July, rebellion, and yellow fever to which the negroes were almost immune, had liquidated the British conquests, except in Martinique. Revolt then broke out in the British island of Jamaica, where the Maroons held the soldiers in check for about two years. An expedition against San Domingo far to the west also proved peculiarly costly and ineffective.

The pressure of the Lancashire cotton-spinners persuaded the government to send out a still larger expedition in the winter of 1795–6, again at the wrong time of year. The operations proved as unsuccessful as before in reducing San Domingo but progress was made in the Windward Islands. This expedition is remarkable for two developments in the history of the British Army, the provision of a medical staff which studied the prevention and cure of tropical diseases, and a reformation in the treatment and training of troops by Sir John Moore, who learned in these campaigns the lessons on which he built up the army that at last defeated Napoleon. Moore's caustic comments did not endear him to his superiors: 'In the West Indies, industry and cultivation do not contribute to the happiness of the inhabitants. All tends to the profit of the master.'

'With a Roman instead of a modern exercise and discipline the troops in the West Indies might, I am convinced, be kept healthy.'

San Domingo, the principal objective, was not subdued. After troublesome campaigns the British withdrew, leaving it under the rule of the negro patriot, Toussaint l'Ouverture.

Early in 1795 the troops of the French republic burst into Holland proclaiming a new age of liberty. The Prince of Orange fled to England, as his descendant was to do when similarly attacked by the Germans in 1940, while the invaders set up at The Hague a revolutionary government which they designated the Batavian Republic. The Prince called upon the Dutch colonies to place themselves under British protection and to maintain the war against France. The very rich colony of Demerara in Guiana, which had largely been developed by British capital, fell in with the Prince's desire and invited British protection, but in other parts of the world, suspicion of British motives and age-old commercial rivalry, even, perhaps, some sympathy with French principles, provoked the Dutch to resistance. The British were so eager to occupy the Cape of Good Hope that their army arrived before the instruction from the Prince of Orange, so that the Dutch Governor made some show at resistance before surrendering. Nelson's keen eye had marked down the harbour of Trincomali in Ceylon as the key to naval warfare in the Indian Ocean; it fell into British hands in 1796, after a tortuous intrigue. A Scottish professor named Hugh Cleghorn hit upon the device of buying over the regiment of Swiss mercenaries whom the Dutch employed to garrison the island. Having struck his bargain in Switzerland with the proprietor of the mercenaries, Cleghorn accompanied him to Ceylon to withdraw them from the Dutch service. Faced with this situation, or perhaps on account of his personal preferences, the Dutch Governor surrendered Colombo after a slight show of resistance.

While the commercial people had kept their eyes on the war in the West Indies and the advantages of occupying the Dutch colonies, the Admiralty had been increasingly concerned with the war in the Mediterranean, where conquests were estimated for their direct strategic value. In 1792 we had no naval base in those waters east of Gibraltar. Our first endeavour to control the French southern coast, by co-operating with the royalists in

Toulon, was a failure. The British fleet was expelled, in 1793, by the Jacobins, largely owing to the efforts of Bonaparte who commanded the artillery.

At this juncture the restless inhabitants of Corsica broke out in civil war. One party, among whom were the family of Bonaparte, adopted the cause of the French Revolution, while their rivals, led by the aged patriot Paoli, threw off the French yoke to elect George III as their king. Thus for two years (1794-6) the island of Corsica was a self-governing dominion of the British Crown. Nelson took part in the Corsican campaign—in which he lost an eye—and recorded his dissatisfaction with the unenterprising conduct of his superior. The French Toulon fleet was allowed to put to sea and to support the operations along the Riviera by which Bonaparte conquered Italy. The British then took a further step forward by occupying Elba, but with no effect.

At this stage of the war (1796) the Spaniards joined the French, supposing theirs to be the winning side, a step which seemed to make the maintenance of British sea-power in the Mediterranean impracticable. Since hostile forces held Minorca and the whole coastline of Spain, France, and Italy, it seemed wise to withdraw the British fleet to Gibraltar. Corsica was evacuated, an unheroic measure which, however, gave the turbulent islanders little cause for regret. Having found already that representative government and trial by jury were inconsistent with devotion to their *vendettas*, they readily lapsed into a simpler state of freedom when the British fleet was gone. Strategically the island was no great loss since it had no port on the north or east coast conveniently placed for naval operations against France or Italy.

But war with Spain meant renewed activity in the West Indies. The British soon got control of the Spanish and Dutch colonies, and of such French islands as were not in a state of negro anarchy. They had already occupied Ceylon and the Cape of Good Hope. Otherwise, after negotiations for peace had come to nothing, they were again, in 1797, fighting alone against the forces of France and Spain. All central Europe was in French hands and the French fleet was unquestioned master of the Mediterranean Sea. This costly and unprofitable war had outlived the anti-Jacobin enthusiasm of 1793 and was most unpopular. The Radicals clamoured for peace, the three-per-cents were down to forty-eight, Ireland was in a state of rebellion, even the Navy mutinied.

At this crisis Bonaparte was preparing to strike at Asia through the Mediterranean. Though still a junior general, without legitimate authority to dictate policy, ambitious fancy led him to follow the eastward path of Alexander the Great. The overthrow of the Venetian Republic, in 1797, had given him control of the Alpine Passes, of the Dalmatian Coast, and of Corfu which guards the entrance to the Adriatic. He secured his flank by seizing Malta, the key of the central Mediterranean narrows,

George Philip & Son, Ltd.

Map 6

and transported an army to Egypt under convoy of the Toulon fleet. The conquest of Egypt was but his first intended step. Far beyond, in the Indian Ocean, the Governor of Mauritius had been at work inciting Tipu Sahib ('Citoyen Tipu') to drive the British from India with the help of a French fleet. These plans for a single co-ordinated offensive based on Malta and Corfu, developed through Egypt and Mauritius as far afield as Mysore, with the intention of breaking the power of England in the East, were bolder, grander in conception, more far-reaching than any earlier combination against the British Empire. It required political imagination, audacity and responsibility in a high degree to meet the threat, in days when there was no electric telegraph for exchanging information and instructions between London and Calcutta; nor were these virtues lacking.

Nelson had already persuaded the Admiralty to send the fleet back into the Mediterranean. Having no suitable base for blockade he failed to intercept the Toulon fleet but, with uncanny insight, guessed the destination of their voyage. His total victory over the French fleet at the Battle of the Nile (1 August 1798) disrupted the whole design. Though it was the decisive blow, it was but one move in a strategic plan which almost equalled Bonaparte's in grandeur, excelling it in one respect, that of being simultaneously improvised by statesmen in three continents.

Another expedition sent from England captured Minorca and drove the French from Malta after a long siege. These naval victories made Nelson supreme throughout the Mediterranean. Naples, Sicily and Malta came under British protection. It was, however, unlucky that Bonaparte escaped to France, leaving his army marooned in Egypt. Meanwhile Lord Wellesley, far away in India, had acted with equal resolution. Tipu was defeated and killed at Seringapatam in 1798. Not content with that, Wellesley had sent an Indian army from Bombay to the Red Sea to co-operate against the French in Egypt; and even Popham, the Governor of the Cape, had been able to spare troops for a similar expedition. As these two armies converged from the far south and the far east upon the doomed Frenchmen, a third and more powerful expedition was launched against them from England and arrived first of the three. It was General Abercromby's force from England that destroyed the French army at the Battle of Alexandria (September 1801). A few days later preliminaries of peace were signed at Amiens.

3. THE BRITISH EMPIRE AND NAPOLEON

THE long wars against the French revolutionary armies had left the nations exhausted and inclined to pacifist sentiments. In Europe the dynasts had been toppled from their thrones, or sat in them uneasily by favour of the French. Elsewhere in the world, the richest islands and plantations had come into British hands through the prowess of the Navy. Though Britannia ruled the waves she longed for peace, for the day when she could disarm. When the day came, she disarmed with indecent haste, without regard to future perils. The pedestrian statesman Addington, who succeeded Pitt as Premier in 1801, was for peace at almost any price. He sent the ubiquitous, invaluable Cornwallis to negotiate terms at Amiens with the dictator of Europe, demanding no conquests, glories, triumphs or spoils. All the colonies of France, Spain and Holland, except Ceylon and Trinidad, were to be restored; even Tobago and Demerara which had been developed by British planters with British capital, even Malta where the inhabitants protested against the restoration. On the Continent, the dictator Bonaparte undertook to respect the frontiers and the liberties of surrounding states. But generosity was wasted on Bonaparte; he had undermined and weakened the authority of every state in Europe; his quislings were appointed, his fifth-columns were ready, in each of the subservient unarmed states adjacent to France. He flooded the world with inflammatory propaganda, protesting with unrighteous indignation at each diplomatic impropriety committed by any nation, at the time when he was violating frontiers, instigating political murders and annexing, one by one, the neighbouring states whose independence he had guaranteed. The inevitable breach with Great Britain came in the negotiations over Malta. Since the sixteenth century the island had been quietly decaying under the somnolent rule of the Knights of St John. These worthies, once an order of crusaders who had defied the Turks from their island fortress, had degenerated into a close corporation of hereditary noblemen, the last Grand Master having been a Frenchman. Their dwindling revenues were too small for administering the civil population, not to speak of garrisoning a military station sought by all the powers. For financial reasons the Knights placed themselves under the protection of the Czar, which further confused the issue. Like other Mediterranean cities, Valetta had some tradition of self-government, of having elected its own *Consiglio Popolare*, long ago before the coming of the Knights; and this tradition had been revived by the Jacobins during the short period of French occupation (1798–1800). By the Treaty of Amiens, the British agreed to withdraw from Elba, Egypt and Malta. Of these three, Malta provided a problem, since it could not be merely vacated. Some provision for its good government and military security must be made, a matter of delicate negotiation between Great Britain, Russia, France and the Maltese. Luckily the British remained in possession, proposing that they should garrison the island pending a settlement and refusing to accept the islet of Lampedusa as an alternative. This provided Bonaparte with the grievance he sought. With outcries about English perfidy he declared war in the spring of 1803. The Peace of Amiens had lasted only eighteen months, but long enough for him to have treacherously occupied Holland, Switzerland and Piedmont.

The restless ambition of Bonaparte (who at this time proclaimed himself the Emperor Napoleon) reached out to all parts of the world. During the interval of peace he had sent great armies to restore French control over San Domingo, but without success. Tropical disease defeated the French as it had defeated the English. Discouraged from further empire-building in the New World by this failure, he attempted to cut his losses by a plan which would ingratiate the Americans. He had acquired from Spain, by treaty, the undeveloped territory west of the Mississippi known as Louisiana. Instead of developing a French colony in this region (which now contains a population of fifty millions and several of the world's greatest cities), he offered to sell it to the Americans, to their great surprise, the agreed price being no more than fifteen million dollars (1803).

The first great crisis of the war, the threat to invade England, falls outside the scope of this book. From 1803 to 1805 the Grand Army lay encamped about Boulogne while the fleets of England maintained close blockade of the ports from which the French convoying squadrons were to sail. When, in August 1805, the Grand Army struck camp to march to the Danube, when in October Nelson destroyed the combined fleets of France and Spain off Cape Trafalgar, the course of events again diverted Napoleon's eyes to the East, persuading him to ignore the Atlantic and to destroy the islanders by boycotting their trade.

Routes to the East again became objectives of strategy. The British still held Malta. In 1806 Napoleon sent his brother to carve out a satellite French kingdom for himself at Naples. The British countered by occupying Sicily which for eight years (1806–14) was under British control. The Treaty of Tilsit (1807) between Napoleon and the Czar, contained provisions for partitioning the Turkish Empire, which led to further advances by the belligerents into the neutral eastern Mediterranean. A British squadron under Duckworth sailed through the Dardanelles but returned when the Turks refused to be drawn into alliance. The clash came in the Greek islands which were ruled by Pashas nominally subject to the Sultan. The French annexed the Dalmatian coast and islands, and threw a garrison into Corfu, the key of the Adriatic (1808). At the request of the inhabitants the British came in to 'protect' Cephalonia, Zante and the other Ionian islands. With sea-power and island bases the British had now stopped Napoleon's advance to the Levant.

All the foreign colonies which had been taken in the 1790's and given back at the Treaty of Amiens were again at Britain's mercy. Before Trafalgar there were no forces available for colonial campaigns, none even for Wellesley's Maratha War; after Trafalgar objectives might be selected at will. The West Indies were reduced during 1808, 1809 and 1810 without much fighting. The Cape was again occupied in 1806, in spite of stronger Dutch resistance on this occasion. The Admiral, Sir H. Popham, knew that the cabinet was dallying with plans for raising the Spanish colonies in revolt. With one eye on friends of his own among the Spanish revolutionaries, and the other on associates in the City, who were watching the South American market, he decided to liberate, or occupy, the Spanish colony at the River Plate. Borrowing some troops from his colleague General Baird, he crossed the South Atlantic and seized Buenos Ayres (June 1806). But since it soon appeared that the *gauchos* had no desire to exchange Spanish for British domination he found himself besieged and was forced to withdraw to Montevideo after a capitulation. The British government was so deeply committed that it was obliged to send a relief expedition, which arrived too late. In June 1807 General Whitelocke again attempted to assault Buenos Ayres, already at that date a city of regular stone buildings. Whitelocke's converging columns lost touch and were defeated by the Spaniards, who showed their historic skill at street-fighting. This shabby affair ended in another withdrawal on terms agreed at a parley. When he returned, Whitelocke was cashiered, and the speculators lost their money. Two years later, when Napoleon's injustice had goaded the Spaniards into war with France, Spain and her colonies were again allied with Britain. The River Plate was to become a profitable field for

British commerce and investment, even for British emigration, but not as a conquered province.

The Dutch colonies in Asia were quickly gathered in, Batavia itself in 1811. East and West, all the tropical colonies of the European powers and all the strategic points defending them were under British protection, and might all have been annexed if that had been the desire of the British government. Meanwhile Napoleon, then at the height of his power, ruled Europe directly from Danzig to Corfu, from Brittany to the Black Forest; his allies and dependants ruled Russia, Sweden, Denmark, Germany, Spain, though the Spaniards backed by British armies and navies were in revolt against him.

The death-blow to all Napoleon's Asiatic schemes was the taking of Mauritius by an expedition from India in 1810. From that base General Decaen had sent expeditions to survey a new colony in 'Terre Napoléon' on the Australian coast. From Mauritius he had supplied Tipu Sahib and sent agents to the Marathas. The Cape route was barred, the Mediterranean was a British sea, the friends of the French in India were defeated. The loss of Mauritius meant that there was no rallying-point left in Asia for French agents or French forces.

4. NEUTRAL RIGHTS AND THE WAR OF 1812

SINCE all wars fought by Great Britain are contests in the use of sea-power, the British, more than any other nation, have been concerned with the growth of international law in respect of blockade, contraband, right of search, and neutrality. Some general principles which emerged during the wars of the Dutch and English against the Spanish monarchy, had developed during the eighteenth century into positive rules of maritime law about which there was a tolerable measure of agreement among the civilised nations. Some of these rules were quoted as valid in treaties and were enforced by admiralty courts of all the great powers, to the general satisfaction. But the growing strength of the Navy, from age to age, enabled the British to conduct war by means of blockade ever more stringently, a process which has implied a steady encroachment upon neutral rights in the interest of belligerents. In the eyes of British lawyers, this has been a normal continuous process in constructive jurisprudence, while lawyers of other nations, whose interest has been intermittent, have often regarded it in a quite different light. Encroachments were championed or opposed according to the momentary status of the nation concerned, whether as an enemy or an ally of Great Britain, or as a neutral. Such has been the weakness of international law that Great Britain could never afford to disarm herself by conceding the right of search, while other powers have protested against it when fighting Great Britain but used it gladly when engaged as Great Britain's ally.

During the great wars with France, the neutral Baltic powers assumed an intermediate status known as Armed Neutrality to resist interference by the belligerents in their regular sea-trade. In effect these alliances operated against Great Britain since it was the British Navy that habitually made war by blockade. Further, the British Navy depended upon the Baltic trade for masts and spars and hemp, a consideration which obliged the government to treat the Northern powers with discretion. Not until the end of the Napoleonic Wars did the output of naval stores from New Brunswick and Nova Scotia arrive in sufficient quantity to provide a substitute.

War by blockade reached a new intensity in 1806 and 1807, when Napoleon attempted to turn the tables on the British by laying an embargo on their whole trade with France and the occupied territories. The British retaliated by declaring an absolute blockade on all the ports of Europe where Napoleon's writ should run. From 1807 to 1812 the trade-war continued, the precursor of the trade-wars of 1914 and 1939, and, like the two later examples, to the great advantage of the maritime over the continental power. So secure was British naval strength that all western Europe was deprived of its external trade by our hold on the Ionian Islands, Sicily, Malta, Gibraltar and Lisbon, to which were soon added Heligoland, and Anholt in the Cattegat. The peoples of Europe could export nothing but, by large-scale smuggling, they imported a fair quantity of British goods through the ports which the British had occupied. At first the armed neutrals of the Baltic were ill-disposed towards Great Britain. The Czar allied himself with Napoleon in 1807, the two together agreeing to seize the Danish fleet. The British forestalled Napoleon's move by raiding Copenhagen, the second such occasion, as Nelson had similarly forced the Danes out of their neutrality, by an unprovoked attack in the previous war. Later, when the British blockade had begun to tell against continental Europe, the Baltic powers saw where their true interest lay. The War of Liberation in the north began with the alliance in 1812 between Great Britain, Sweden and Russia, the Czar having soon quarrelled with his brother-autocrat.

At the moment, when the crisis of the naval war was past, the Americans intervened on the side of the Tyrant of Europe. Surely no event in the history of Great Britain or of the United States is so entirely discreditable to either nation as the War of 1812. In America it is still remembered as a sort of epilogue to their War of Independence; in England it has been altogether forgotten, and better so. It grew out of national prejudices, it was fought with an utter lack of magnanimity by both combatants, it resulted in nothing but bad blood. It is sad that the candid historian should be obliged to exhume so unsavoury an episode.

Washington had bequeathed, as his political testament to the Americans, the doctrine of isolation, advising them not to enter into 'entangling alliances'. This policy had been continued until the trade-war of 1807 had obliged the Americans to define their attitude to the British blockade of Europe. Unfortunately for them, Jay's Treaty of 1794 had accepted the British interpretation of neutral rights in time of war. Now that the British Navy commanded every sea and exercised these rights in an extended form, the Americans, like the Baltic neutrals, began to raise objections. Negotiations, which should have reached an agreement, were compromised by repeated tactless interferences on the part of British naval officers. The American public was irritated when a British warship stopped the American frigate *Chesapeake* and deprived her of half her crew on the score that they were British subjects. On the one hand it might be alleged that right of search was justified by treaty, that the Navy was entitled to impress British seafaring men, and that American ships then, as throughout the nineteenth century, were manned largely by British deserters. American crimps openly seduced them with bounties in every port of the New World. On the other hand so insolent a treatment of a foreign navy was foolish and exasperating. Tempers rose as negotiations progressed, the more hot-headed among the Americans crying out to renew the old war against the British tyrants, and the British infuriating the Americans by treating them still as rebel colonists. Canning, in the House of Commons, alluded to the Americans as 'not a people we should be proud to acknowledge as our relations'. Liverpool, the Prime Minister, condescendingly suggested that the Americans 'ought to have looked to this country as the guardian power to which she was indebted for her comforts, for her rank in the scale of civilisation, for her very existence'.

As an American historian has said, this contest 'was waged by one free people against another free people in the interest of Napoleon, the real enemy of them both'; but it did not appear in that light to firebrands in Congress. Henry Clay of Kentucky demanded war with Great Britain 'because I believe her prior in aggression, and her injuries and insults to us more atrocious in character'. Clay came from the west where they had other causes of quarrel with the British. In the region of the Great Lakes where there was free movement of the tide of new settlers across the unmarked frontier, the British were still the protectors of the Indians, still spoke of creating a wide Indian reservation in the lands that the Kentuckians desired for themselves. 'The conquest of Canada is in your power,' Clay asserted. 'I verily believe that the militia of Kentucky are alone competent to place Montreal and Upper Canada at your feet....Is it nothing to us to extinguish the torch that lights up savage warfare? Is it nothing to acquire the entire fur trade?'

The British government, deeply engaged in the Peninsular War, in the Blockade of Europe, and in the Baltic negotiations, could spare but little attention to this side-issue in America. The general situation had, however, reached a stage where they were able to loosen the Blockade by withdrawing the Orders in Council which the Americans thought obnoxious. This was done on 16 June 1812, the moment in history when Napoleon began his fatal attack on Russia, too late for appeasement. President Madison, a weak inadequate man, more concerned with catching western votes than with any higher consideration, was pushed by the westerners into declaring war, on 18 June. Though he could not know it, the principal *casus belli* had vanished two days earlier.

The dismal story of the war may be told in three phases, the American raids on Canada, the frigate actions at sea, and the British raids on the American coast.

The western frontiersmen began the assault on Canada. Even Jefferson, who should have known better, said it would be 'a mere matter of marching'. An incompetent braggart named Hull led a small army into Canada from Detroit, proclaiming that he would deliver the Canadians from 'tyranny and oppression' and would restore them 'to the dignified station of freemen'. A mixed force of British regulars, British and French-Canadian volunteers and friendly Indians, about 1300 men in all under General Isaac Brock, fell upon a superior number of their would-be deliverers and drove them back in headlong ignominious flight. Hull surrendered Detroit with all the stores assembled for the invasion. Thus western Canada was saved, largely because the Indian tribes had rallied to the side of their British protectors. Troops from New York now attempted another invasion near Niagara which again was hurled back by the Canadians with heavy loss. Brock, the victor of Detroit, was killed in this action.

In the two successive campaigns of 1813 and 1814 the Americans showed more spirit. Realising the value of water communications they built small armed ships on Lake Erie, which were handled skilfully by Commodore Perry. With this advantage they regained the west and brought better-managed expeditions into the field. But though they made at least eleven separate attempts to invade Canada every one was repulsed, the severest battle being fought at Lundy's Lane (1813). Meanwhile the victorious conclusion of the war in Europe had allowed the despatch of many of Wellington's veterans from Spain for service in North America. By midsummer of 1814, 16,000 British regulars ensured the defence of Canada. The honours of war, however, went to the Canadians, a nation of less than 600,000, deeply split by racial differences, who had combined to resist the unprovoked aggression of a powerful nation six times as numerous, until help came. The war had been anything but chivalrous. While the Americans complained of the British employment of Red Indian auxiliaries, the Canadians complained that the American filibusters, who had come with promises of deliverance, had plundered and destroyed whatever they could reach. The village of Newark (now Niagara) and the town of York (now Toronto) had been wantonly burned by the invaders.

The war at sea was equally ineffective. The United States had no battle-fleet, but some useful small craft, and three large, heavily-armed frigates, each of them almost a match for a line-of-battle ship. They fought a number of well-conducted single-ship actions against British frigates and usually had the best of it owing to their heavier broadside. These actions, though very heartening to the Americans, had no effect upon the course of the naval war. No more had the action in which H.M.S. *Shannon* forced the *Chesapeake* to surrender in sight of Boston, to the disgust of

> The people of the port who came out to see the sport
> With their bands a playing Yanky-doodle-dandy-O.

Throughout the war British command of the sea was never challenged. The British could—and did—land troops at any point they chose on the American coast. 1814 was a great year for privateering. The Halifax privateers were busy off the New England coast and the New England privateers off the coast of Old England. The great difficulty of the Americans was disposing of their prizes since the British Navy was ubiquitous. Most of the ships they took were retaken and set free.

By 1814 the war had reached a stage of pitiable futility. But for this malicious pin-pricking the world was rapidly returning to peace. Large sections of the American people had been opposed to the war since its commencement and were anxious only to renew their trade with Britain. Commissioners from New England arrived at Washington in 1814, proposing to contract out of the Union in order to make a separate peace. However, the British had fleets and armies in America and must do something with them. An army landed in Chesapeake Bay and after inflicting a sharp defeat on an American force at Bladensburg (24 August 1814) occupied Washington, then a raw new settlement consisting of a few half-finished government buildings set in the wilderness, among temporary huts and pegged-out streets without houses. After frightening President Madison away and eating his breakfast, the troops burnt the government buildings as a reprisal for the American burnings in Canada, and withdrew. It was a legitimate act of war but, like all reprisals, most ill-advised. One Peninsular veteran, Harry Smith, wrote of the affair: 'At Bladensburg we licked the Yankies and took all their guns with a loss of 300 men, whereas Colborne [his old commander] would have done the same thing with a loss of forty or fifty, and we entered Washington for the barbarous purpose of destroying the city. Admiral Cockburn would have burnt the whole, but General Ross would only consent to the burning of the public buildings.... Fresh from the Duke's humane warfare in the south of France we were horrified.' The Americans began again to build their capital and refurbished the President's damaged house with a coat of white paint, from which it has since been known as the White House.

A still larger expedition was then sent against New Orleans, and ended the war with a complete fiasco. A combined operation, carried out by a squadron under command of one of Nelson's 'band of brothers', and an army of Peninsular veterans under command of one of Wellington's generals, utterly broke down through mismanagement. These troops, who had stormed Badajoz and forced the passes of the Pyrenees, failed to take a temporary fortification defended by Andrew Jackson and the local militia. The Americans were much gratified; while on their part the British Infantry had won such glory in Spain as not to be disgraced by one setback. The worst of it was that peace had been signed at Ghent (24 December 1814) before the battle was fought; New Orleans was but another sample of the malignant folly which characterised the War of 1812 from start to finish.

The Treaty of Ghent settled nothing, merely appointing commissions to adjust boundaries. It contains no reference to neutral rights or impressment of sailors. However, after a war which disgraced both nations, peace was restored. *Esto perpetua.*

5. THE EMPIRE AFTER WATERLOO

NEGOTIATIONS among the allies during the War of Liberation led to a series of treaties which were mostly concluded in 1814 after the occupation of Paris, and were but slightly affected by Napoleon's ephemeral reappearance for the Hundred Days' Reign in 1815. The continental powers gave almost the whole of their attention in these negotiations to the Balance of Power in Europe. It was hardly realised that the most striking effect of the war had been to endow Great Britain with overwhelming commercial and financial power. The British were now, without question, the most secure, the most opulent and the strongest among the nations. They might have retained the captured colonies of France, Spain and Holland if extension of territory had been their aim, but it was not. The objects of Lord Castlereagh and the other British diplomats were to rebuild the ancient kingdom of France under a stable legitimate government, to create a strong monarchy in the Low Countries under the House of Orange, to secure the world-wide British trade and shipping by the military occupation of certain strategic points, and to persuade the other powers to join in suppressing the slave trade.

With a few exceptions, the additions to the British Empire at this time were military outposts and, accordingly, were administered by military or naval officers under the close supervision of the Secretary for War and the Colonies. This Crown Colony government was a new system quite unlike the easy-going representative government of the earlier colonies. Since the American Revolution there had been a wide diffusion of Adam Smith's opinion that colonies should either be released from their allegiance or firmly held in the imperial system so that some real advantage could be got from them.

One colony taken from the Dutch in the earlier war, Ceylon, had been retained throughout the Peace of Amiens and remained in British hands. It had at first been handed over to the East India Company to be incorporated into the Madras Presidency, but the Madras revenue system, which was quite unsuited to the customs of the Cingalese, had produced complete chaos. In 1802 the Government resumed control, converting the island into a Crown Colony. Its first governor, Frederick North, though he got into grave trouble by unwise interference in the politics of the unsubdued kingdom of Kandy, restored the old system of civil administration, with the Dutch code of laws, and relied upon the support of the 'burghers', that is the half-caste Dutch settlers.

Three Dutch colonies in South America had welcomed the British occupying forces sent there at the request of the Prince of Orange. They were Essequibo, Berbice and Demerara. Even before the British occupation many English planters had settled in this rich undeveloped land where Ralegh had once searched for El Dorado. The settlements prospered during the twenty years of occupation and, in 1812, the British renamed the capital of Demerara—Georgetown, treating it as their own. The three settlements were ceded in 1814 and in 1831 were combined into the Crown Colony of British Guiana. It was for long a wilderness of unknown extent perhaps 500 miles in depth behind 300 miles of coast. Its inland frontiers were not delimited until 1904, when the King of Italy acted as arbitrator.

Far more difficult was the case of the Cape of Good Hope, which was desired solely for its position on the route to India. British policy was directed to building up Dutch power in Europe and, while strengthening the frontiers of the Netherlands, seemed justified in taking responsibility for a fortress in the southern hemisphere which the Dutch were quite unable to defend. All the rich islands in the East Indies were restored to the House of Orange and, for the loss of Colombo, Capetown and Demarara, the Dutch willingly agreed to accept an indemnity of £6,000,000. The Dutch negotiator Falck summed it up: 'Our own interest ought to have brought us to abandon properties that are always onerous and compromised by the least chance of war. What good fortune to find people complaisant enough to pay us for abandoning them!'

Two Spanish colonies, Tobago and Trinidad, were retained, frankly in compensation for the great expenses which Great Britain had incurred. Tobago, like Demarara, was one of those colonies with a chequered history of conquests and reconquests, its first white settlers having been British.

The history of Trinidad, a rich island about the size of Lancashire, deserves a backward glance. It was discovered by Columbus and settled by the Spaniards in 1580. Ralegh overran the infant colony at Port of Spain in 1595 and caulked his ships from the Pitch Lake. Some of the grants to courtiers in early Stuart times included Trinidad among the English 'Caribbees' but the island was not settled by Englishmen, nor was it actively developed by Spain.

In 1780 a Spanish governor named Chacon, showing more than ordinary spirit, invited French colonists who raised the white population in a few years from 3,000 to 18,000. In the war of the French Revolution an English squadron under Captain Vaughan became embroiled with these Frenchmen, a breach of Spanish neutrality which provoked Spain into joining the French in alliance against England (1796). The Spanish dons soon found that they had more sympathy with the English than with the

French Jacobins so that, when General Abercromby invaded
Trinidad (1797), there was little opposition. At the Peace of
Amiens the Spanish colonists petitioned against the return of the
island to Spain. Trinidad became a British Crown Colony but
retained its Spanish law, with the mild Spanish slave-code but
the harsh Spanish legal procedure which permitted the examination of an accused person by torture. The first Governor,
Thomas Picton, was severely censured by the humanitarians for
maintaining it. But Trinidad prospered, and in 1834 its 22,000
slaves were valued at a higher price than those of any colony but
British Guiana.

Most of the French colonies were restored to the rule of King
Louis XVIII, except St Lucia in the West Indies, and Mauritius
in the Indian Ocean which were retained as British naval stations.
The unfortified French factories in India, and the fishing rights
off Newfoundland were again restored to France.

In European waters, British naval power was guaranteed by the
occupation of Heligoland, Malta and the Ionian Islands which,
with Gibraltar, ensured for the Navy power to renew the
blockade, a wise measure taken in no other general treaty, and
strongly conducive to the peace of Europe. The good intentions
of governors brought up in the tradition of English liberty produced a curious series of constitutional experiments in these
European islands. Almost every island in the Mediterranean was
held by a British landing-party at some time between 1792 and
1815. Corsica had for a time placed itself under British rule.
The Maltese in 1800, after the expulsion of the French, had invited the sovereignty of the British. The islanders of Cephalonia
and Zante had followed their example in 1809. Sicily was in
British occupation for eight years, Corfu for the last year of the
war. In Corsica the attempt to impose British Parliamentary
institutions upon the islanders had lamentably failed. A similar
attempt was made in Sicily, in 1812, but without success. There
was a party in Malta, the Italianate aristocracy, who likewise
demanded representative government under the British Crown.
In 1812, a commission of inquiry went to Malta charged with the
task of giving the Maltese 'as large a share of civil liberty as is
consistent with the military circumstances of the island'. The
place was a fortress and must be ruled as one. Warned by the
failures in Corsica and Sicily the commission strongly recom-

mended against representative government. 'The majority of
people want nothing better than a more intimate and indis-
soluble Union with Great Britain.' During the war the island,
by doubling its volume of shipping, had acquired a degree of
prosperity never before known. With that and with an efficient,
honest administration the people would be perfectly satisfied.
There was no truth in the assertion that they nourished a tradition of former self-government. In consequence of this report
Malta too became a Crown Colony with a Council including the
Bishop and other Maltese officials, and with a martinet, Sir
Thomas Maitland, for Governor. He was a benevolent autocrat,
tirelessly efficient, scrupulously honest and somewhat con-
temptuous of the people he devotedly served. It was perhaps an
error to replace Latin by Italian as the language of administration, since the bulk of the people spoke neither, but only the
Arabic patois peculiar to the island.

Maitland's advice was taken over the Ionian islands, Corfu,
Cephalonia, Zante, Ithaca, Cerigo, Paxo and Santa Maura. They
had begun by petitioning Great Britain 'to restore their independence'. General Oswald who began the occupation in 1809
had undertaken to 'establish a free independent government', a
pledge which was guaranteed by the powers in a treaty (1815).
The islands were to be 'a free republic under protection of the
King of Great Britain'. Someone produced a federal constitution
on paper for the Septinsular Republic, but 'King Tom' Maitland
pointed out at the beginning that 'the only real and true method
of administring government here for the benefit of the people,
is in fact to maintain all the powers in the hands of His Majesty's
Lord High Commissioner'. 'The old nobles of the head families
look with disgust at anything like protecting the people from
their tyrannical and arbitrary control.' However the forms of the
constitution were preserved with some advantage to the political
education of the islanders.

British rule over the island of Odysseus and its larger neighbours lasted more than fifty years. Obligations in the Ionian
Sea forced British statesmen, somewhat unwillingly, into close
association with the Greeks during their national revival and the
War of Greek Independence. Missolonghi, where Byron died,
Navarino, where Codrington destroyed the Turkish fleet, were
but a short sail from the British Ionian Islands. When Greece

was set free the basis of the Treaty of 1815 was removed, and the British protectorate became an anomaly.

The necessity of interning Napoleon after Waterloo brought into prominence the island of St Helena where, since 1673, a resident officer of the East India Company had provided for the occasional needs of ships. This remote but healthy island[1] in a temperate climate was lent by the Company to the Crown for a few years (1816–21). For greater security against attempts to rescue the Emperor, the garrison of St Helena was supported by outposts on the two nearest islets, Ascension, and Tristan da Cunha hitherto uninhabited and 700 miles away. A time-expired soldier, Corporal William Glass, remained on Tristan da Cunha with his wife and two other families from St Helena. The Colonial Office lost interest in the settlement which was not regarded as a British colony until 1875 when authority was resumed upon a report made by the *Challenger* surveying expedition. Corporal Glass had died in 1853. The little colony, reinforced by a ship-wrecked crew and by other wanderers, reached the number of 225 persons in 1945.

Ascension also was reoccupied, after the *Challenger* expedition, but as a naval station. It has been an important junction on cable routes and may achieve a new importance as an air base. It was administered by the Admiralty, and was rated as a warship. In 1922 the island was resumed by the Colonial Office for the benefit of Cables and Wireless Ltd. and was thereafter administered as a dependency of St Helena.

6. THE INDUSTRIAL REVOLUTION AND THE EMPIRE

READERS of history are familiar with the notion of what is called the Industrial Revolution, though it is often represented as a sudden change accomplished about a hundred years ago. In the stable mid-Victorian age, when the British were consolidating their gains and no other nation was yet industrialised, such a

[1] St Helena is a rugged, hilly volcanic island about as large as Jersey. As well as Napoleon another famous man once lived there, Edmund Halley who used it as an observatory in 1676–7. With the disappearance of sailing ships its value as a port of call has declined. The population in 1946 was 4992, the only industry the cultivation of New Zealand flax.

view of the early nineteenth century appeared to be correct. The development of steam-power by British engineers had given a lead to British industry which the nation maintained and improved by means of its natural advantages: its unlimited coalfields with adjacent beds of iron ore, its soft damp climate uniquely suited to the manufacture of textiles, its geographical position athwart the trade routes of the world. To these gifts of nature were applied the unrivalled technical ability of our metal-workers, the accumulated wealth of the City which had made the saying 'safe as the Bank of England' proverbial, the admitted probity of British merchants, the sea-faring tradition which maintained half the world's shipping under the British flag, and the prowess of the Navy which from Halifax, Gibraltar, St Lucia, Capetown and Colombo ensured a safeguard for the King's dominions and a 'security for such as pass on the seas upon their lawful occasions'. All these blessings, all these achievements had been, and were again to be, multiplied in the new machine age which the British had created. The nineteenth century belonged to Great Britain as surely as the seventeenth century to France, or the sixteenth century to Spain.

Although this wealth was based upon world-wide trading connexions, it was not dependent upon overseas dominions. British merchants had long abandoned, if indeed they had ever approved, the old mercantile system of trade within an enclosed empire. So far had the principles of Adam Smith triumphed, though full free trade was still far off, a Utopian dream. Meanwhile diplomatic action was directed towards opening markets; and fiscal reforms (after the Corn Law of 1815) towards loosening restrictions. Against this tendency, powerful groups of monopolists fought to retain their obsolescent privileges. First should be mentioned the landed interest at home, though their struggle to protect British agriculture against the advocates of cheap imported food and low wages lies outside the scope of this chapter. Next in importance was the West India Interest, by now highly organised to defend the sugar trade with a block of Tory votes in the House of Commons. Through their influence prohibitive duties on foreign sugar kept the price of colonial sugar up to 8d. a pound in the English shops.

The West India Interest was derived from the fusion of two groups, the absentee West Indian proprietors who lived in

England and the London merchants who traded to the West Indies. They had not always seen eye to eye, for example in 1733 when the planters persuaded Parliament to pass the Molasses Act in spite of the Shipping Interest.

As early as 1670 a number of planters met in London to recommend to the government of Barbados the appointment of a salaried agent who should represent their interests at home. The appointment was made in the following year and was soon imitated by Jamaica and other colonies. During Queen Anne's War the Commissioners of Trade and Plantations regularly consulted the colonial agents on such subjects as instructions for convoys. A Planters' Club was formed in London before 1740.

The trading interest first met at the Jamaica Coffee-house, a resort of sea-captains where, before 1700, letters were accepted for despatch to the West Indies. About the year 1750 there came into being a society of West India merchants, whose minute-books survive for the years 1769 to 1843; it was one of many regional trading associations. Monthly meetings were held; membership was by election; funds were raised by a voluntary levy of a penny on each cask of sugar shipped; and a paid secretary was appointed.

Trade dislocation during the American War caused such alarm that public meetings of planters and merchants were held in London and Bristol with the result that a standing committee was formed, in 1782, to represent their common interests. A secretary and treasurer were appointed, and Lord Penrhyn was the first chairman. This was the origin of the West India Committee which has an unbroken history to the present day, as one of the most influential of 'pressure-groups'.[1]

Three important chartered companies had survived into the new age. The East India Company still stood for the monopoly in China tea, and inevitably, since the Chinese Empire admitted no other merchants. Otherwise, after 1813, the Company had become a subsidiary organ of government. The Africa Company, since the abolition of the slave trade, had few functions beyond maintaining its mouldering fortresses on the shores of the Gulf of Guinea. In 1821 it was dissolved, after handing over its responsibilities to the Crown. The Hudson's Bay Company

[1] See L. M. Penson in *Eng. Hist. Review*, vol. 36.

alone survived as a body of traders with sovereign rights. Its territories were inaccessible and inhospitable; its system of trading posts was economical and effective, and it escaped the steady fire of criticism which other companies had to endure.

The newer generation of manufacturers, exporters, ship-owners and investors were turning away their eyes from the old monopoly trades, far afield to expanding markets which Adam Smith had not foreseen. Trading connexions with Europe, broken during the blockade, were not quickly renewed with the impoverished war-weary continental nations. While their commercial strength had been reduced during the wars, British trade had been growing in every other quarter of the globe. Naval superiority made it possible for British ships to carry British goods throughout the world in spite of Napoleon. After the war British capital established the trade and maintained the lead over other nations. The skill of British manufacturers and the wealth of British investors were now so great as to outweigh by far the advantages of a political monopoly. 'We had the ships, we had the men, we had the money too', and could afford to buy and sell in any market, whether the Union Jack flew over it or not. At this stage in British history, the old conception of the Balance of Trade was nullified by the appearance of 'invisible imports' which constituted an ever-growing proportion of the commercial turnover. Payments for shipping, banking and insurance; interest on foreign loans, and salaries to British technical experts residing abroad, all well-earned, were none the less a tribute paid by foreign nations to the British. In this sense several of the United States and large parts of South America were subject to the commercial empire of the City of London almost to the same degree that Jamaica and New Brunswick were subject to the Colonial Office.

In 1810, during the blockade of Europe but before the outbreak of the American War, North and South America took more than half of British exports, amounting in value to £26,000,000 out of £45,000,000, a high proportion in a boom year. After the reopening of the Continent, during the depressed years from 1815 to 1818, the United States alone took about a quarter of a smaller total. In the early 1820's, when the total exports averaged at about £36,000,000 annually, rather more than one-sixth went to the United States, almost one-sixth to Latin America and almost one-twelfth to the British West Indies. Canada absorbed a tiny fraction. Together the exports to the Americas amounted to about £14,000,000, a sum which equalled the exports to the Continent of Europe.

Cotton cloths were much the largest item in the British export trade. Before the war they had been negligible in value; by the 1820's they had risen to about £16,000,000 annually, whereas woollens, so long the staple of export, now came to no more than £6,000,000; Australian wool was not yet on the market. Iron and steel, the next on the list, made up less than £1,000,000. Liverpool, once the port of the slave trade, now prospered on slave-grown cotton, carrying 'Manchester goods' abroad and bringing back timber from eastern Canada in summer, and raw cotton in winter from the Gulf of Mexico. The Lancashire cotton trade had almost entirely grown up since the American Revolution. In 1775, while England still depended upon cotton piece-goods from Bengal, no more than 4,700,000 lbs of raw cotton had been imported, from the West Indies. The demand of the Lancashire mills for raw cotton during the next few years swelled the imports to 33,000,000 lbs in 1792, 57,000,000 lbs in 1802, 143,000,000 lbs in 1822 and vastly greater figures in later years. Three-quarters of this mass of raw material now came from the United States, especially from the 'sea-islands' off the Carolina coast where long-fibred cotton was grown in quality comparable with the finest from Bengal. Only fine muslins such as those which Henry Tilney priced for Catherine Morland were now brought from the East Indies.

While the Company retained its trading monopoly it was not likely to press for an increased export of Manchester goods to India. But, no sooner was the monopoly broken and traders admitted freely to British India (1813) than the people of India, and even of China, began to buy more of the cheap cottons from the Lancashire mills than they had ever bought of the fine cottons from the hand-looms of Bengal.

The Hudson Bay fur trade had given way in importance to the new import of timber from the Maritime Provinces of Canada. In 1802 the Baltic supplied almost the whole demand for masts and spars, in 1820 the Maritime Provinces supplied three-quarters of a demand that was steadily increasing. There were 1500 ships and 18,000 seamen employed in the Atlantic timber trade, a fruitful nursery of men for the Navy, and a great addition to the merchant service, since, in winter, when the St Lawrence was ice-bound, the ships were employed elsewhere. Nova Scotia ships and shipmasters played no small part in the making of a maritime empire. The Canadian trade was small in volume but important for its reactions on the whole naval and shipping interest. It therefore attracted some attention and earned preferential treat-ment. In the long struggle over the Corn Laws, Canadian wheat was brought into the system of imperial protection, though no-body then supposed that the surplus of Canadian harvests could ever be enough to swamp the English market. .

Such preferences were concessions to imperial sentiment and were frowned upon by progressive economists and greedy exporters. Nevertheless the Tories were in office for eighteen years after Waterloo and were not to be rushed into radical experiments in free trade. The two statesmen principally con-cerned, Peel and Huskisson, continued the prudent, cautious methods of Pitt. War finance had been economical. Though the national debt had risen to over £800,000,000, that is seventy pounds per head of the population, imports, exports and revenue had also risen. The revenue (£103,000,000 in 1805, £120,000,000 in 1808, £131,000,000 in 1811), had reached £162,000,000 in 1814, which included £30,000,000 for the service of the national debt. Staggering as these amounts were by the standards of the previous age, the country seemed able to bear them, after the period of post-war disturbance had passed away. Normal trading conditions were reached when Peel, in 1819, stabilised the money market by restoring the gold standard.

Trade was secured by the campaign to suppress piracy in every sea, especially by the reduction—long overdue—of the strong-holds of the Barbary pirates in North Africa. The naval opera-tions by the Americans against Tripoli (1814) and by the British against Algiers (1816) may be considered as episodes in the abolition of the slave trade, since these African states lived by piracy and slave-trading.

Further steps towards a scientific tariff, rather than towards free trade were taken in 1823–5, when Huskisson was at the Board of Trade. The independence of the Latin-American republics was recognised and they were admitted to trade with the Empire on the same terms as the United States. Other nations were allowed to negotiate on terms of reciprocity for a share in the colonial trade. Much of the obstructive tangle of the Navigation Laws was swept away, but the main provision reserving trade within the Empire to ships registered under the British flag was retained, as perhaps it should have been retained to the present day. Preferences were granted to colonial goods, but the colonies were not yet permitted to fix their own tariffs. Though the dominions of the Crown were favoured and protected, their interest was not permitted to overrule the greater advantage to be derived by the mother-country from trade outside the Empire. India and the colonies provided some essential commodities such as tea, and sugar, and naval stores but on such a scale as to be able to buy back no more than one-third of the exports of Great Britain.

Sentiment could hardly count for much when the Empire was composed of such varied and substantially un-English component parts. Only in Canada was there a loyalist population of British origin. If the protected Indian states were taken into account the whole population of the Empire overseas exceeded one hundred millions, but of these less than one million were Europeans and less than half a million were British. The rest were French-Canadians, Cape Dutch, Bengali peasants, negro slaves and aboriginals of savage countries. In 1750 the population of the British Isles had been estimated at eight millions, while there were one-quarter of that number, about two million whites, in the American colonies. In 1821, the population of Great Britain was fourteen millions, with perhaps another six millions in Ireland, twenty millions in all, while the British overseas together made up less than a fortieth of that number, perhaps 250,000 in Canada, 100,000 in the West Indies, 50,000 in India, 30,000 in Australia, and smaller groups in other colonies. It was no wonder that the colonials carried little weight in Downing Street.

No one then living could foresee the future progress of the Industrial Revolution when steam-power should be surpassed by electric-power of which Great Britain had no privileged supply; when coal would be largely replaced by oil fuel of which she had no supplies at all; when Bombay, and even feudal Japan, would snatch away the textile trade from Lancashire, despite their less favourable climates; when America and Germany would be more intensively industrialised than England, and Russia bid fair to outstrip them both; when the population of Great Britain would be stabilised at forty-five millions while the despised colonies in a century would produce between them a British population of at least fifteen millions, a higher proportion of British overseas to British at home than before the separation of America.

7. THE HUDSON'S BAY COMPANY AND THE NOR'WESTERS

ONE effect of the Hudson's Bay monopoly had been to discourage exploration beyond the regular paths of the fur trade. With the exception of one lad named Henry Kelsey, who penetrated the country of the horse-riding Blackfeet Indians in 1690 and was the first European to see the prairie darkened with herds of buffalo, the Company's traders did little to explore the west during their first hundred years. The British conquest of Canada in 1763 opened the field to interlopers who threatened the monopoly. As early as 1768 a Scottish trader from Montreal went far into the west and soon, it was estimated, 500 *coureurs-de-bois* passed annually through Grand Portage at the west end of Lake Superior, taking westward with them the smallpox which killed off most of the Assiniboine Indians.

At last the Governors of the Hudson's Bay Company were stirred into competitive activity and began the systematic exploration of the far north-west which they called Rupertsland. Samuel Hearne was sent from Hudson Bay in 1768 to make a pact with the Athabasca Indians and to find a river flowing west. He wished to travel light, his Indian guides insisted on taking their squaws with them: 'Women,' they said, 'although they do everything, are maintained at very trifling expense, for as they always stand cook, the very licking of their fingers, in scarce times is sufficient for their sustinence.' He found his river and followed it, to the shores of the Arctic Ocean. The elusive North-west Passage had receded again. He also found that the Indians on the banks of his river, the Coppermine, made arrow-heads of pure copper, a new indication of the mineral wealth of Arctic Canada. A result of Hearne's voyage was the establishment of a Hudson Bay Post at Cumberland House on the Saskatchewan River.

The interlopers from Montreal became numerous and energetic, almost all of them Scotsmen. Simon McTavish first formed a group of them into a new fur-trading organisation, the North-western Company, in 1784. The Nor'westers were simply traders, with no royal charters or noble governors, and no legal rights of socage or jurisdiction. Their internal history was stormy with a long succession of amalgamations and schisms which led to fierce rivalries between groups. Agents went about the west competing for the allegiance of Indian tribes with gifts of rum. They fought one another for profitable areas and combined to fight the Hudson's Bay Company to northward and the American fur-traders to southward. In 1800 they reached a degree of equilibrium, moving their headquarters westward to Fort William (named after William McGillivray, one of their leaders) at the head of Lake Superior. 'The partners held a lordly sway over the wintry lakes and boundless forests of the Canadas', wrote Washington Irving with pardonable exaggeration. Their power, he said, was 'almost equal to that of the East Indian Company over the voluptuous climes of the Orient'. In 1800 they employed 50 clerks, 71 interpreters, 1120 canoemen and 35 guides; they exported annually 100,000 beaverskins and 80,000 other furs. One of the Nor'westers, James McGill, used his wealth to found a college at Montreal (1821) which has become a celebrated University.

Another Nor'wester of very independent views was (Sir) Alexander Mackenzie. In 1789, encroaching in undoubted Hudson Bay Territory, he reached and named the Mackenzie River, descending it to the Arctic Ocean. In 1793, portaging from the Peace River to the Fraser, he turned west and made the first crossing of the Rocky Mountains. On 22 July 1793 he reached the Pacific Ocean at Bella Coola, unperturbed among hostile Indians and timorous companions.

Twelve years passed before Mackenzie's discoveries were exploited, perhaps because of distractions in the Company's organisation. Between 1806 and 1811 two exploring parties from the North-western Company revealed the general topography of British Columbia just in time to save it from annexation by American rivals from the south. Simon Fraser, an Empire Loyalist, followed the course of what is now called the Fraser River; David Thompson followed the Columbia down to its mouth where he found the Americans already established in a trading post which they called Astoria (1811).

Until Mackenzie's expedition of 1793 there had been no crossing of the Rocky Mountains north of the Mexican border. Westward progress from the Thirteen Colonies had come to a halt where the tributaries of the Missouri rose in the dry prairie of the Middle West, then inaccurately described as the Great American Desert. Only in the far south had the continent been crossed by the Spaniards from Mexico, and that not long previously. In 1774 the Santa Fé route had been opened from New Mexico to the mission at Los Angeles in California. Otherwise all communication with western America had been by sea. Some account has been given in chapter IV, 1 of Byron's unsuccessful attempt and Cook's successful attempt to trace the Pacific coast in the latitudes which Drake had once visited; but this region in 1790 was a mere coastline on the map with no white settlement north of San Francisco. The effective survey was made by Captain George Vancouver (1792–4) who had learned his business as one of Cook's lieutenants. The coast was disputed by four claimants: the Russians, the British, and the Spanish by virtue of naval discovery, the Americans by virtue of cession from the British. Between 1790 and 1814 there was much diplomatic friction over these claims.

The affair of Nootka Sound, which led to the Spanish Armament crisis of 1790, is of great importance in the history of the west. In consequence of Cook's discoveries ships had come to the coast of what is now British Columbia to hunt for skins of the sea-otter (see page 462). In 1789 John Meares, the pioneer of the trade, was arrested, and his ship confiscated by a Spanish war-ship in Nootka Sound. Pitt took a strong line in Parliament, mobilising the Navy in preparation for war with Spain, a course in which he was strongly supported by the shipping interest in the House. The resulting negotiations, in which the Spaniards gave way on the main issue, led to far-reaching decisions. The attempted monopoly of the South Seas was at last abandoned. The King of Spain limited his claim to dominion 'so far as discoveries have been made and secured by treaties and im-memorial possession', while navigation and fishing in the Pacific were thrown open to British subjects except within ten leagues of coasts occupied by Spain. In the Nootka Sound area the northern limit of the Spanish Empire was fixed at the Columbia River.

Ten years later Spain ceded the whole province of Louisiana to Napoleon, who sold it to the United States (1802). There remained great uncertainty as to the northern limits of Louisiana. The Americans claimed, and acted on the claim, that their purchase included a long stretch of the Pacific slope including what are now the states of Washington and Oregon. By this assumption they became Pacific neighbours to the British at the mouth of the Columbia River if, that is, they admitted the British right to Nootka Sound. Hence the efforts of the fur-traders on either side of the Columbia to stake out a claim for their respective countries, and hence the sudden determination to explore the routes across the Rockies.

About the same time that David Thompson was exploring the Columbia River, the American expedition of Lewis and Clark was wintering in Oregon, having spent two years in traversing America from St Louis on the Mississippi. John Jacob Astor, a Montreal fur-trader and the founder of the Astor family fortune, moved to New York with the intention of repeating the exploits of the North-western Company on the American side of the frontier. In 1810 he founded the Pacific Fur-trading Company with the ambitious plan of first sending his traders round the Horn to the Pacific coast and then supporting them by a chain of overland posts. After severe setbacks Astoria on the Columbia River was thus established. The War of 1812 brought rivalry with the British to blood-heat. The Nor'westers descended the Columbia, captured Astoria and renamed it Fort St George but, at the peace of 1814, were obliged to restore their prize. Thus a temporary frontier was fixed between Oregon and British Columbia under circumstances which left much room for future bickering.

Again the Governors of the Hudson's Bay Company attempted to assert their rights against the encroaching Nor'westers, the moving spirit being now a Scottish philanthropist, Thomas Douglas, 5th Earl of Selkirk (1771–1820). Like his friend Sir Walter Scott, he was a Lowlander deeply moved by the misfortunes of the Highland clansmen. The publication of Mackenzie's *Voyages through the Continent of North America* suggested to him that the displaced Highland crofters might be

George Philip & Son, Ltd.

Map 7

systematically settled in western Canada. The neighbourhood of Lake Winnipeg, he supposed, had a climate 'not more severe than that of Germany or Poland' and more temperate than that of the Atlantic seaboard. 'Here the colonists may, with a moderate exertion of industry, be certain of a comfortable subsistence.' He memorialised the government to this effect, during the Peace of Amiens, and organised a party of 800 emigrants from Skye who went to Canada in 1803. They were, however, diverted by the government from their westward goal, to Prince Edward Island.

Selkirk was by no means satisfied. In 1810, after taking legal advice, he began to buy up Hudson's Bay stock until he owned £35,000 out of the nominal capital of £105,000, a controlling interest. He then acquired from the Company the right to colonise a large tract of land on the Red River, in the district known as Assiniboia. At once there was an outburst of opposition from the Nor'westers who had come to regard this territory as their own, and especially from Alexander (now Sir Alexander) Mackenzie. The view of the Hudson's Bay Governors was that settlement would confirm their prescriptive right, and that an agricultural community would grow food for the trading posts, to which all kinds of stores were carried from great distances by dog-sledge.

The first party of seventy Selkirk emigrants left Scotland in 1811, wintered at Fort York in Hudson Bay and reached the Red River after a 700 miles overland journey in the autumn of 1812. The party was led by Captain Miles Macdonell, one of the Glengarry settlers from the St Lawrence, whom Selkirk had selected for the task.

For nearly ten years there was bloody feud and at one time open war between the Selkirk settlers and the Nor'westers, the one party representing the Hudson's Bay Company's monopoly, the other the commercial interests of Montreal. Since the Red River settlement lay outside the jurisdiction of the Governor-General of Canada, he would not intervene but left the rivals to fight it out. The settlers planted themselves on the west bank of the Red River, building there a fort which they named Fort Douglas. The Nor'westers issued from their Fort Gibraltar, a mile downstream, and scattered them among the Indians. Next year a second party of settlers arrived, every man provided with a musket and bayonet and an Indian pony. They too were driven away and Macdonell, captured by the Nor'westers, was packed off to Montreal. The third party in 1814 still clung to Fort Douglas but not much more. In 1815, a larger and better-organised party arrived from Sutherland led by Robert Semple, while simultaneously Selkirk from Montreal despatched experienced Scots and French-Canadians to their assistance. The Nor'westers, led by Cuthbert Grant, brought matters to a head by a direct assault upon Fort Douglas. Semple rashly sallied forth and was killed with more than twenty of his men in the Battle of Seven Oaks (June 1816).

Selkirk, exasperated at his failure to get support from government, now took the law into his own hands like a true Scottish nobleman of the old times. He enlisted a band of soldiers, largely Swiss mercenaries discharged in Canada at the Peace of 1814, and set off for the west with his fighting tail. He seized Fort William, arrested the partners of the North-western Company, and confiscated their private papers; then despatched Macdonell with men and guns to regain Fort Douglas far away on the Red River. Violence on the most distant frontier might pass unchecked by government but warfare on Lake Superior was another thing. The fur-traders of Montreal got a warrant for Selkirk's arrest; which he refused to accept. The Selkirk settlers were again in possession of their land and could defend it, but the struggle continued in the Canadian courts where charges and countercharges were laid and argued for several years. The dominant faction at Montreal, known as the Family Compact, were hot against Selkirk and resisted the conciliatory efforts of Lord Bathurst the Colonial Secretary. Selkirk was a 'canting rascal and hypocritical villain. He has got possession of our Fort William. Well, we will get him out of it and the Hudson's Bay knaves shall be cleared, bag and baggage, out of the North-west.' 'Fort William', said Selkirk, 'had served, the last of any in the British dominions, as an asylum for banditti and murderers, and the receptacle of their plunder.' Both companies were obliged by the courts to restore their conquests; the charges of murder against the Nor'westers broke down, since the Battle of Seven Oaks had been fought outside Canadian jurisdiction but, after long litigation, Selkirk was mulcted of heavy damages for his seizure of Fort William. He died in 1820 a disappointed man, too soon to see the reconciliation. His happiest years had been spent at Red River (1817–18) administering his little colony.

In 1821, the North-western Company was absorbed into its older rival, giving the Hudson's Bay Company undisputed power over territories stretching from Labrador to Vancouver Island, from the Yukon to Lake Superior. Selkirk's rights to the lands occupied by the Red River settlers were resumed by the Company in 1836 after a composition with his heirs.

The years between their union with the Nor'westers (1821) and the surrender of their vast estates (1870) were the great age of the Hudson's Bay Company; their policy being much en-livened by the ruthless energy of the free traders who had joined them. Sir George Simpson (1792–1860), who became governor of the northern department in 1823, was the driving force of the new trade; he was 'ever the fastest of travellers', and his progress in state on the Red River with a crew of scarlet-liveried Indians and with a Highland piper in attendance was long remembered. In 1841 he crossed the North Pacific in order to make an overland journey round the world through Siberia. He was a good friend to the Indians, not least for restricting the allowance of spirits given to them at the trading posts; though the saying in the west was that 'a beaver-skin was never lost to the H.B.C. for want of a bottle of rum'. The ferocious Blackfeet Indians met Simpson at Edmonton, imploring him with the rhetoric due to a wonder-working chief that 'their horses might always be swift, that the buffalo might abound, and that their women might live long and look young'. His policy was to fix the Indians in certain areas where they might trade with the Company's agents, but to extinguish their vague claims to unde-fined hunting-grounds. A 'Hudson's Bay Company Indian' was always a term of praise in the west.

Later he settled at Lachine, near Montreal, now the gateway of the west, but once the westerly limit of the first French settlement. Thence the French-Canadian *voyageurs* set out for their long journey westward by water, to St Anne's and the Ottawa River, past the Calumet rapids and over the portage into Lake Nipissing, then by the French River to Georgian Bay, through the rapids of Sault Ste Marie (by-passed by a canal in 1855) into the cool, deep waters of Lake Superior, until Thunder Cape brought the prospect of the rude luxury of Fort William.

From the western forts the trains of dog-sledges set out in winter to travel forty miles a day across the snow with pro-

visions for the distant trading posts, some so remote that they
were only visited once a year with their mail and a complete
year's file of the *Montreal Gazette*. Months later the sledges
returned freighted with beaver-skins. At one far post between
Labrador and Hudson Bay a young man named R. M. Ballantyne
was stationed in the 'forties. He returned home to write books for
boys (*The Young Fur-Traders*, 1856, *Ungava*, 1857, *The Dog*

Map 8

Crusoe, 1860) which, though they have not retained the celebrity
of his *Coral Island*, are still known to the present generation of
boys and girls.

The Red River settlement became the central depot for the
Hudson Bay territories. Selkirk's colony never flourished.
Sections of land were laid out along the river bank and sold for a
mere registration fee. Their frontage having been surveyed, their
depth ran conventionally 'as far back from the river as a man could
see looking under a horse'. The few settlers, after enduring every
setback and surviving every plague, began about 1826 to get
bumper harvests, proving that Manitoba could rival the black
soil of Russia in fertility; but as yet they had no more than the

local market and only rudimentary communications with the world. North to York Factory on Hudson Bay, east to Fort William on Lake Superior, south to St Paul on the Mississippi the journey was more than 400 miles by any route, even to the outposts of civilisation. The best outlet was southward over the American border to St Paul by the celebrated York boats designed to cross the portages from Hudson Bay to the Red River, or by the no less celebrated two-wheeled Red River carts which went in caravans across the open prairie through the country of the hostile Sioux.

Those few Scottish settlers who remained were lost among the multitude of buffalo-hunters, H.B.C. traders, French-Canadian boatmen and Indians of many tribes who frequented the settlement, and formed, in two generations, a turbulent, brave, adventurous, half-breed race known as the *métis*. The settlement, which had been known by many names, was best known as Fort Garry, from the great, square, stone fortress with round towers at the angles, built at the junction of the rivers in 1836.

Fort Garry, in the 'forties, had a floating population of about 5000, mostly half-breeds who assembled for the annual buffalo-hunting. Tourists came out from England to take part in it, as their descendants went to hunt big game in Kenya. 'It was not uncommon to see officers of the Guards, Knights, baronets and some of the higher nobility coursing their steeds over the boundless plains and enjoying the pleasure of the chase among the half-breeds and savages.' In 1840, a leaguer of 1200 wagons moved out from Fort Garry for the annual round-up and slaughter of the buffalo herds, under an elected captain and an agreed code of camp rules. The *métis* counted on making more money by riding down and shooting buffalo on these annual expeditions than by the rest of the year's work. The buffalo were killed for their skins and for their tongues, said to be the most delicious meat in the world.

It was a great day for Fort Garry when, in 1844, Dr G. J. Mountain, the Anglican Bishop of Quebec, arrived by canoe to inspect the C.M.S. mission which had laboured there since 1820. He ordained three clergy and confirmed 800 persons. At his instance the diocese (later the arch-diocese) of Rupertsland was formed in 1849. The first Archbishop, Robert Machray who held the see from 1864 to 1904, found 12,000 inhabitants on the Red River, a few hundreds only being of his communion. He was a

powerful organiser of missions and schools, a pillar of the
Anglican Church and of the British connexion in the west, the
true founder of the University of Manitoba, and a wise counsellor
to the Colonial Office on confederation. In the far north the
Anglican missions have made progress among the eskimos who
are mostly attached to that communion, while the Canadian
Indians, through their old association with the French, adhere to
the French-Canadian Catholic missions, established in the north-
west since 1818. Selkirk had found the Red River in the days of
the Nor'westers a place without religion; 'no trace of temple or
idol or place of Christian worship'. He had promised his Highlanders a Scottish minister; but when at last one came in 1851 he
proved of small service as he had no Gaelic. Presbyterian influence in the west came later with emigration from Ontario;
the early Methodists came over the border from the United
States. While Machray was the religious and educational leader
of the British settlers, an equivalent part was played among the
far more numerous *métis* by the French-Canadian, Father A. A.
Taché (1823–94) who, after long missionary labours in the west,
became the first Roman Catholic Bishop of Manitoba in 1871.

8. FRONTIER PROBLEMS IN AMERICA:
NORTHERN AND SOUTHERN SEAS

(1) THE CANADIAN FRONTIER

THE Treaty of Ghent, at the end of the War of 1812–14, left
many outstanding subjects for dispute, of which some were
settled at a further conference in 1818. By what was called the
Rush-Bagot Treaty of that year both nations agreed to disband
their naval forces on the Great Lakes, a triumph for the cause of
disarmament; and progress was made in delineating the Canadian
frontier in those regions where it had been left uncertain at the
Treaty of 1783. While it was not difficult to fix it at the forty-
ninth parallel of latitude across the featureless central plains the
eastern and western extremities were uncertain because the
country was unmapped. The respective rights of British and
American fishermen off Newfoundland were also defined.

As the United States increased in wealth and power, far more rapidly than its northern and southern neighbours, republican fervour produced an expansionist policy. At every corner of the Union, in Maine and Oregon, in Florida and Texas, the Americans seemed anxious to meet the fate foretold for those who remove their neighbours' land-mark. A thousand speeches and newspapers proclaimed the intention to assume, sooner or later, a protectorate over all North America, if not actually to annex it. This was, it was said, the 'manifest destiny' of the New World; it was extended to South America by President Monroe's message to Congress in December 1823.

During the Napoleonic Wars the Spanish Empire in America had withered away. While Spain itself had been liberated with British help, the trade of the Indies and the Spanish Main had passed into the hands of British merchants. By 1822 the southern provinces, the modern Argentine Republic, had virtually been independent for several years, while in Mexico, Central America and Colombia (then much larger than it now is) the Spanish power was moribund. Peru and Chile were in revolt. In that year the United States recognised the independence of the Spanish colonies and Chambers of Commerce in British cities petitioned Canning to do likewise. Though the United States stood forth as their champion it was Great Britain that supplied them with money, shipping and soldiers of fortune, Great Britain alone that could prevent a reconquest from Europe. But to recognise their independence would be an affront to Spain which Canning could not justify, it must be 'a matter of time and circumstance'. He accordingly appointed consular agents in 1823, and despatched commissioners to report on the affairs of South America.

The kingdom of Spain was too distracted and weak to undertake any great campaign for the recovery of *España Ultramar*. It was only when a French army intervened in Spanish affairs in 1823 to restore a despotic king that Canning took action. 'I determined', he said, 'that if France held Spain, it should not be Spain with the Indies. I called the New World into existence to redress the balance of the Old.' He positively warned the French off any attempt to restore the Spanish power in South America. A few weeks later President Monroe announced the policy which came to be known as the Monroe Doctrine, the isolation of the Americas from European imperialisms. Though Monroe appeared to echo Canning's decision he was swayed by other considerations. The message to Congress was not drafted with British collusion and was, in part, a threat to British interests. 'The American continents', said Monroe, 'are henceforth not to be considered as future subjects for colonisation by any European power.' From its context it is clear that he aimed this shaft at the Russians and the British who were staking out claims on the unoccupied North Pacific coast of America. 'With the existing colonies and dependencies', he went on to say, 'we have not interfered and shall not interfere, but with the governments who have declared their independence and maintained it, we could not view any interposition...by any European power, in any other light than as the manifestation of an unfriendly disposition towards the United States.'

This unilateral declaration, though it has come to be accepted as a fundamental rule of international affairs, at first had little effect. The South American governments were far more concerned with what Canning did than with what Monroe said. While Canning made it clear to the Americans that the British would oppose French designs on Mexico, and harboured no designs of their own on Cuba, he pressed on with commercial negotiations. Sir Woodbine Parish (1796–1882), his commissioner at the River Plate, convinced him in 1824 that the new state there (later known as the Argentine) deserved diplomatic recognition. A commercial treaty (1825) of reciprocal free trade between Great Britain and the Argentine not only conferred untold blessings on the people of both nations for a hundred years but convinced Canning that he had deflated the Monroe Doctrine. South America was again drawn into the circle of the older nations. The recognition of the other Spanish-American republics followed in 1825.

The Canadian frontier was the scene of further friction in the 1830's. Not only did Canadians and Americans clash at several points during the Canadian Rebellion of 1837 (see below, page 340), each accusing the other of frontier violation, but the infiltration of American lumbermen over the New Brunswick frontier along the Restook (or Aroostook) River led to something that approached guerrilla warfare. Since the seventeenth century the New England states had maintained claims to this country, which the British resisted on the grounds that it had passed to them with the sovereignty of French Acadie. An arbitration by the King of Holland in 1829 was not accepted by either party. As usual the crux of the question was geographical, to decide which was the 'St Croix river' and where lay the 'north-west angle of Nova Scotia' mentioned in the Treaty of 1783. When Peel came into

George Philip & Son, Ltd.

Map 9

office he despatched Lord Ashburton as a special envoy to settle this and other questions by direct diplomacy. The negotiations leading to the Ashburton-Webster Treaty, 1842, may perhaps be regarded as reasonable since Daniel Webster was bitterly assailed in Congress for giving way to the British while Ashburton was equally abused by the Canadians.[1] The district

[1] It should be remembered that the infiltration across the unknown, unmarked, frontier went both ways. Over a million French-Canadians have made their way into New England and remain unassimilated.

between the Restook and St John Rivers, rather more than half the disputed area but less than the award made by the King of Holland, was ceded to the United States. One positive result was that the American State of Maine thereafter lay across the direct route from Quebec to Halifax, thus hindering the progress of communications. Peel and Ashburton did not regard this as of equal consequence with their success in gaining some American co-operation against the slave trade. Almost at once a new conflict arose over the frontier in the Far West.

The dispute with Russia was settled after negotiation in 1824. The Russians undertook not to extend their settlement southward beyond latitude 54° 40' N. They retained not only Alaska but the coastal strip known as the Alaska Panhandle which barred access to the sea from the northern part of the Hudson's Bay Company's territories. (In 1867 Alaska and its Panhandle were sold by Russia to the United States.) The Spanish territories, limited by the Treaty of 1819 to the coast south of latitude 42°, became a province of the Mexican Republic three years later. Between 54° 40' N. and 42° N. the coastal strip was known as Oregon and was visited by British and American sealing-ships. Inland the country was 'freely open to the citizens of both powers without prejudice to the claims of either'. The Hudson Bay traders frequented the Fraser valley and Vancouver Island, the Astoria traders frequented the Columbia valley.

In the eighteen-forties the first covered wagons reached the west by way of the Oregon Trail. The advent of settlers made it imperative to settle the sovereignty of the fur-trader's Alsatia. The democratic candidate for the presidency in 1844, James Polk, went to the polls on the slogan: 'fifty-four forty or fight', that is: exclude the British from the whole of Oregon up to the Russian frontier; but the British took the prospect calmly. When Polk was safely elected he stopped the agitation since it was not his real aim to multiply the free states of the north-west; it suited him better to support the filibusters of the southern frontier who were infiltrating Texas, New Mexico and California, regions where the southerners might increase their influence by forming new slave-states. The whole of this southern region was ceded to the United States in 1848 after the American invasion of Mexico. Meanwhile, Polk had been glad to negotiate with Great

Britain the Oregon Treaty of 1846 which partitioned the Oregon territory according to the spheres of interest of the fur-trading companies. Some years later the new American state of Washington was formed south of the line, and north of it the new colony of British Columbia, within its present frontiers.

(2) CENTRAL AMERICA

When the Gold Rush of 1849 sent hundreds of thousands of emigrants to California, some plodding over the desert and others tossing round Cape Horn, the old project, talked of since the days of Philip II of Spain, for a canal across the Central American isthmus was brought forward. American filibusters were active both in Nicaragua and Panama, seeking for concessions which might enable them to annex territory as they had annexed Texas and California. In 1846 the Americans got their first concession for a canal through the Isthmus of Panama. By the Clayton-Bulwer Treaty of 1850, Great Britain and the United States bound themselves not to annex territory or extend their dominion at the expense of the Central American republics. On their late record the Americans exposed themselves to deep suspicion, and they, too, were deeply suspicious of British designs on Nicaragua, another possible site for an isthmian canal. The presidential election of 1852 was again fought on the popular platform of restraining British imperialism, which was again challenged in respect of the frontiers of British Honduras.

The English 'baymen' in the seventeenth century ranged along the Caribbean coast of Central America for 600 miles from Campeachy Bay in what is now Mexico to the San Juan River which divides Nicaragua from Costa Rica. At two points, Belize and the Moskito (or Mosquito) Coast, these Englishmen were the first European settlers and could claim effective occupation since the seventeenth century. The British claim to Belize is unquestionable *de facto*; the town was founded more than three hundred years ago by Englishmen in a region which was never occupied by the Spaniards or by their successor states. The basis of the claim *de jure* is the Treaty of Madrid, 1670, by which the king of Spain ceded to King Charles II, in full sovereignty 'all lands, provinces, islands, colonies, and dominions in the West Indies or in any part of America which the said king of Great Britain and his subjects have and possess at present'. During the next hundred years the English interpreted this claim widely, while the Spaniards restricted it to the right of cutting logwood at Belize. In each of the eighteenth-century treaties, the English privilege was more strictly defined and notably at the Treaty of 1783 after the disastrous American War. 'His Britannic Majesty's subjects', declared the treaty, 'shall have the right of cutting logwood between the Rivers Wallis (or Belize) and Hondo. These stipulations are not to be taken as derogatory in any way from the rights of [Spanish] sovereignty.' This was the narrowest definition in the series and, three years later, was modified by a Convention which again widened the British privilege.

In the same year (1786) a 'superintendent' was appointed by the British Government to administer the settlement according to their customary code, known as Burnaby's Laws. There were then about 200 whites, 200 coloured men and 900 slaves engaged in the wood-cutting trade. They asserted their loyalty by manning a flotilla which defeated a Spanish squadron off St George's Bay, near Belize, on 10 September 1798, a day of which the anniversary is still a holiday in British Honduras. At the end of the War, in 1814, a treaty with Spain renewed the *status quo ante*.

Much farther down the coast the British protectorate over the Moskito Indians rested on a different sanction. From Charles II's reign onwards a series of treaties of alliance had been made between British Governments and successive 'kings of the Moskitos', of whom one paid a state visit to London in 1796. The Moskitos had never been conquered by the Spaniards. But the Moskito Coast was very loosely administered by a Captain-general, usually despatched from Jamaica. Whereas on the mainland there were only woodcutters' camps among the Indians, there was in the Bay Islands a long-established colony of English settlers. At the Convention of 1786, the British had undertaken to withdraw from the Moskito Coast and the Bay Islands, but the settlers clung to their homes.

Though the Spanish colonies declared their independence in 1821 it was not until 1838 that the republics of Guatemala, Nicaragua, and Honduras were established in their present boundaries. They soon began to press for boundary settlements with the British Colony. Palmerston took a high line in these negotiations, especially over the Moskito Coast which, he said, 'has for upwards of 180 years been acknowledged as being under the protection of the British Crown'. He intervened several times with naval forces against Nicaraguan filibusters. But after the Clayton-Bulwer Treaty this 'protection' could hardly be maintained. Sir C. L. Wyke was despatched to Central America to negotiate treaties with the new republics. On 30 April 1859, a treaty was signed at Guatemala City, making provision for the demarcation of a boundary between Guatemala and British Honduras, and clearly stating (Article 1) that 'all the territory north and east of the boundary belongs to Her Britannic Majesty'. Article (7) of the Treaty led to prolonged negotiation. It declared that the two parties would 'mutually agree conjointly to make their best efforts for establishing communications between the fittest place on the Atlantic Coast near Belize and the capital of Guatemala'. After seven years the discussions lapsed since the cost of a road deterred both parties. Sixty years later, when a far better line of communication had long been opened to the Atlantic through Puerto Barrios, the Guatemalan Government threatened to denounce the Treaty on the grounds that Article 7 had not been implemented. Again long discussions took place until, in 1938 Lord Halifax proposed to refer the issue to arbitration, which the Guatemalans prudently declined.[1]

After coming to terms with Guatemala, Wyke negotiated next with Nicaragua, the point at issue being to ensure the rights of the Moskito Indians. A Treaty renouncing the British 'protection' but declaring that they should retain autonomy within the Nicaraguan State was signed on 28 January 1860 and, as recently as 1905, the Foreign Office used its influence on behalf of the Indians. The British then withdrew from the Nicaraguan Coast, leaving the isthmus free for the American imperialists of the next generation. Less reputable was the withdrawal of British authority from the Bay Islands. The Government withdrew; the British settlers did not. A visitor in 1937 described the islanders as being about 4000 in number, half of them of pure British stock. They were engaged in trading fruit and copra in their own schooners and were stubbornly resistant against the efforts of the Honduran government to latinise them.

[1] After 1814, British Honduras was regarded a colony by the Colonial Office, though not brought under normal 'Crown Colony' administration until 1870. The trade in logwood was superseded by a trade in mahogany, and later by that in *chicle*, one of the constituents of chewing-gum.

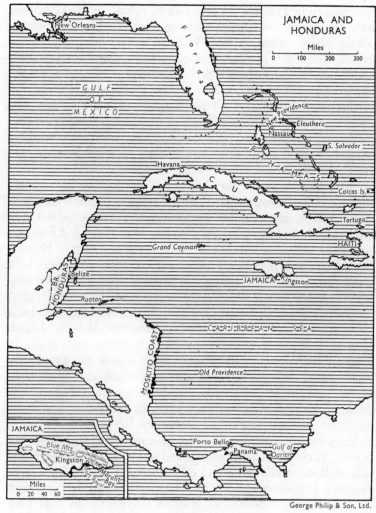

Map 10

(3) THE ARCTIC

A renewed interest in polar exploration may be traced to the development of the whale-fisheries, both in northern and southern waters, after Cook's demonstration that long voyages could be made without loss of life. Exchequer bounties were given as an inducement to Greenland whalers, and a special award of £5000 was offered in 1776 for the first ship to operate north of latitude 80°. More than 200 English ships were engaged in the northern whale-fisheries when, in 1806, William Scoresby qualified for the award. His many voyages seemed to show that there was open water at very high latitudes, perhaps even at the Pole, so that the old dream of a navigable North-west Passage was revived. A further reward of £20,000 was offered in 1818 for the first ship that should make its way through to the Pacific. From that year a series of authorised voyages of discovery was begun, bringing to the fore the names of two naval officers, Sir W. E. Parry (1790–1855) and Sir John Franklin (1786–1846).

Since knowledge of the Arctic regions had actually waned since the Elizabethan voyages, Parry's first expedition served to confirm the accuracy of Baffin's 200-year-old map on which they were recorded. Then between 1819 and 1821 Parry and Franklin simultaneously attacked the icy region north and west of Hudson Bay. Parry evolved the art and science of polar voyaging; by a careful study of diet, clothing and hygiene, he wintered his ship among the ice-floes in comparative comfort and sent out sledging parties to survey the frozen channels. He extended geographical knowledge westward from Baffin Land to Melville Island. Meanwhile Franklin marched overland from the most westerly Hudson Bay posts to the Arctic shore which had previously been visited only by Hearne and Mackenzie at two isolated points. In spite of shocking hardships he traversed the northern coast of the American continent through thirty-five degrees of longitude east and west of the Mackenzie River.

Parry's route had taken him far to the north through Lancaster Sound, leaving vast areas unexplored to southward. The peninsula of Boothia and the island called King William's Land were discovered by John and James Clark Ross in an expedition financed by Felix Booth, the distiller (1829–31). In 1831 they claimed to have identified the position of the Magnetic Pole. The outline of the coast westward from Hudson Bay to the limit reached by Franklin was filled in by Thomas Simpson, an official of the Hudson's Bay Company, in 1836–7. The general shape of the land-masses in the Arctic was by this time pretty well understood.

During the next few years Clark Ross was leading an expedition to the Antarctic under the patronage of Franklin who had

been sent as Governor of Tasmania. In 1845 Franklin returned
to the north with Ross's two ships, to complete the series of
expeditions by an attempt to force the North-west Passage.
Three years later, since no news of him had been received, the
Admiralty sent a relief expedition. While no certain trace was
found, the rumour grew slowly into a certainty that Franklin's

Map 11

voyage had ended in disaster. His wife raised funds for a search-
party, and then for others. Not less than seven fully-equipped
expeditions and many lesser ones were organised to discover the
fate of Sir John Franklin; by the Admiralty, by Lady Franklin,
by the Hudson's Bay Company, and by American sympathisers.
Though his ships were never found, evidence accumulated that
Franklin had discovered, but had failed to force his way through,

a westward channel south of Prince of Wales's Island. In 1846 he died. After two winters his men had abandoned their ice-bound ships intending to make their way overland to Canada, but all perished on the journey. The story was revealed at last by Sir F. L. McClintock (1819–1907), a masterly exponent of sledge-travelling, in 1859. Another of the searchers, Sir R. McClure (1807–73) demonstrated the existence of the North-west Passage though he reported it ice-bound (1850).

Arctic exploration since the voyages of Parry has been continuously developed. The search for Sir John Franklin initiated a succession of seamen and pioneers into the craft of polar travel. The Arctic islands northward of Canada had all been discovered by British travellers in two active periods (1578–1631 and 1818–59); and all were assumed to be part of British North America. Later travellers were concerned either with pure scientific research or with the merely adventurous design of 'breaking records'. Two dreams still dazzled the eyes of explorers: to reach the Pole itself and to sail a ship—however unprofitably—through the North-west Passage. After all that the British had done in practical exploration they were not to have the barren glory of these spectacular feats.

In 1879 an international Polar Conference was held at Berne to organise scientific investigations. It resulted in the establishment by the northern nations of a chain of circumpolar stations for taking magnetic and meteorological observations. Sea-voyages into the Arctic by the ships of all these nations were frequent in the 'eighties and 'nineties. The most brilliant exploit was that of Nansen (1893–6) whose ship, the *Fram*, was carried in drifting ice to a point which stood for many years as Farthest North. Another Norwegian, Roald Amundsen, similarly took a small ship through the North-west Passage with the drifting ice (1903–5).[1] The Pole, a geographical point on the frozen sea, was reached (1909) by the American, Robert Peary, who trained his team of Eskimo and European assistants as for an athletic contest.

---

[1] In 1937 the Hudson's Bay Company established a post at Fort Ross in Bellot Strait. Occasional trading voyages east and west from that post by the Company's ships have actually put the North-west Passage to commercial use.

(4) THE FALKLAND ISLANDS
AND THE ANTARCTIC

The exploration of the Southern Seas also was due to the activity of the whalers. In addition to the extension of geographical knowledge they were largely responsible for the early settlement of the southern colonies. Many voyages were despatched through the enterprise of Messrs Enderby, the shipowners, into the seas southward of the Falklands where Cook had noted the existence of South Georgia. The South Shetlands were discovered by the whalers in 1819, South Orkney in 1822. So many ships frequented the Falklands in these years that they became a subject of dispute among the powers; and it will be convenient to recapitulate their history at this point.

As early as 1592 the Elizabethan navigator, John Davis, discovered a lonely rainy group of islands 400 miles north-east of Cape Horn. They were rarely visited for a hundred years until another English sailor, Captain J. Strong, called there in 1689 and named them the Falkland Islands. On his voyage round the world (1740–4) Anson remarked upon their strategic value for controlling the South American trade routes, whereafter they received attention from the British, French and Spanish admiralties. The French navigator, Bougainville, landed a few settlers on one island of the group, which he called Les Malouines, in 1764. Without knowledge of this French move the British Government instructed Admiral Byron to annex the islands on his way to the Pacific in the following year. His formal act of annexation was confirmed by the building of a blockhouse on another of the islands, at which a small party of British soldiers were left, in remote isolation, to show the flag (1765). Two years later France ceded her claim upon the islands to Spain. So soon as he heard of the British outpost the Spanish Governor of Buenos Ayres took steps to crush it, by a show of force in the islands and by diplomatic pressure in Europe, with the result that the little garrison was withdrawn. The British government was sharply criticised in London for this compliance and all the more because they still claimed theoretical sovereignty over the Falkland Islands, even after removing the evidence of its reality (1774). For some years afterwards the islands were unoccupied and their sovereignty in dispute. The Spaniards claimed that the British relinquished their pretension to possess the islands by the Nootka Sound Convention (1790).

When Buenos Ayres revolted from Spain the nascent national feeling of the Argentine Republic was reasserted in the Falkland Islands which were proclaimed a dependency in 1820, under the name of Las Malvinas. Settlers sent from the Argentine found a fleet of fifty British and American whalers in the anchorage. But at that time there was friction between the Argentine and the United States. When the Argentine authorities arrested the crew of an American whaler for riotous conduct, an American warship bombarded and destroyed the Argentine settlement, leaving the Islands again desolate and in dispute. The British claim had never been allowed to lapse but was maintained by Sir W. Parish. In 1832 at the instance of the Royal Navy it was again asserted and has since been maintained. The Colonial Office took charge of the group in 1843 setting up an administration at a new settlement which was named after Stanley, the Secretary of State (1844). Again a tiny garrison was established, its strength (according to a return made in 1858) no more than thirty-five soldiers. At first a whaling-station and a strategic *point d'appui*, the Falkland Islands were then developed as a great sheep-run. S. F. Lafone, the merchant and rancher of Montevideo acquired a large estate (1845), which he stocked with sheep and managed with Scottish shepherds and South American *gauchos*. In 1851 his interest was bought out by the Falkland Islands Company which G. T. Whittington had founded some years earlier in London.

Crown Colony government on normal lines dates from 1892, the year which also saw the foundation of an Anglican bishopric. In 1938–9 the population was estimated at 2378, 'mostly British'. The islands contained 600,000 sheep, which produced about four million pounds of wool annually. But in recent years a new importance has come to the Islands from the whale-fisheries. Since northern waters have been over-fished the whalers have returned to the south and now get about five-sixths of the world's supply of whale-oil from the Antarctic. Dundee whaling-steamers began to make their base at the Falklands in 1892.

In 1923 the Colonial Office appointed a research committee to investigate the distribution and habits of whales, in order to preserve them, and the whaling industry, from extinction. It was generally known as the Discovery Committee, from the name of

Captain Scott's ship, *Discovery*, which was acquired for its use. The work of research and the consequent control of the whalers was administered by the Governor of the Falkland Islands whose authority was extended, in 1917, to cover all the islands and territories to the southward of the Falklands between the fiftieth and eightieth degrees of west longitude. On the island of South Georgia a resident magistrate was sent to preside over the most southerly settlement in the world.

In the two German Wars the Falkland Islands proved their worth as naval bases. Old Anson's prudence was justified five generations after his death by two naval victories, at the Falkland Islands, December 1914, and at the River Plate, November 1939.

The general exploration of the South Polar regions was not much advanced for sixty years after Cook crossed the Antarctic Circle, at several points, in 1772–3. A naval expedition under Sir James Clark Ross established the fact, in 1839–42,[1] that a mountainous mass of high land lay within the Great Ice Barrier. He penetrated the wide inlet known as the Ross Sea, and saw the two volcanoes which have been named Mount Erebus and Mount Terror, in honour of his two ships. Ross had demonstrated that, after all, there was an Antarctic Continent, part of which he annexed under the name of Victoria Land. Sixty years passed before any systematic attempt was made to investigate it. This long period was bridged by the life of the botanist, Sir Joseph Hooker (1817–1911), who accompanied Ross as a young man and survived to give his advice upon Scott's first and second voyages.

In 1898 an expedition under the Norwegian, Borchgrevink, wintered on the Antarctic Continent, and thereafter voyages of discovery were frequent. Three large expeditions were organised by British scientific bodies with help from the Royal Navy in 1901–4, 1908–9, and 1911–12, the first and third under Captain R. F. Scott, R.N. (1868–1912), the second under his lieutenant (Sir) E. H. Shackleton (1874–1922). Those who were best qualified to know gave the highest praise to Shackleton for his journey by sledge, in 1909, over the high plateau of Antarctica to a point within two degrees of the Pole. Since these expeditions were

[1] Wilkes's American expedition (see p. 786) visited the other side of the Antarctic Continent during the same years. He was probably the first to sight the land mass.

concerned with investigating the geography, climate and natural resources of the Antarctic, the race for the South Pole was incidental. Nevertheless the heroism of Scott's last journey, in which he and his four comrades lost their lives, is not likely to be forgotten. Amundsen, who had prepared Nansen's old ship,

EXPLORATION OF
THE ANTARCTIC
Miles
0   200   400   600   800   1000

George Philip & Son, Ltd.

Map 12

the *Fram*, for a secret record-breaking exploit, unhampered by any intention of scientific research, had reached the Pole on 14 October 1911, a few weeks before Scott.

The systematic exploration of the Antarctic Continent was carried on by Shackleton in a series of voyages which placed him in the front rank of explorers. After his death, in South Georgia

in 1922, his work was, in part, continued by the Discovery Committee which has been already mentioned. Hardly less valuable
were the explorations carried out between 1911 and 1931 by Sir
Douglas Mawson (b. 1882), an Australian scientist. In 1928 the
Americans entered the field, despatching a series of expeditions
under Admiral Byrd who first used aircraft for Antarctic exploration, working from a base which he called Little America.

The discovery of some signs of useful minerals, the growth of
the whaling industry and the need for meteorological stations in
the Antarctic led to disputes over sovereignty where seamen of
several nations had declared annexations though none had
effectively occupied the territories they claimed. In addition to
the Falkland Islands Dependency another sector lying between
longitudes 160° E. and 150° W., from New Zealand southward to
the Pole, was formally annexed to New Zealand in 1923, under the
name of the Ross Dependency. Similarly, in 1933, the Commonwealth of Australia declared that the sector between Australia
and the Pole, that is between the 45th and 160th meridians of
East Longitude, was the Australian Antarctic Dependency.
These sectors of the southern continent were uninhabited. In
January 1948, it was announced that Australia had annexed Heard
Island south of Kerguelen and South Africa Prince Edward
Island far to the south-east of the Cape.

9. THE ABOLITION OF SLAVERY: THE EVANGELICALS

WHEN the British slave trade was abolished in 1807 the Evangelicals indulged in the hope that slavery would wither away.
By cutting at the root of the supply they would oblige the slave-
owners to study the welfare of slaves who could not easily be
replaced. Marriage and the nurture of children would be encouraged. Domesticity, they believed, would raise the moral
level of the slaves, inculcating habits of industry and a desire for
self-improvement until eventually the planters themselves would
realise that hired free labour was in every way superior to forced
labour. The next step of the abolitionists was accordingly the
foundation of the African Institution (1807), to form a general
staff for the army of pioneers, merchants, and missionaries who

were to repair the wrong done to the peoples of Africa in the past, by bringing them the blessings of civilisation. At the same time their political influence was turned to the field of diplomacy where all other nations were to be persuaded to follow the British example.

The gradual realisation that the prohibition of the slave trade in British ships was not enough led to the revival of agitation in 1823. Clarkson and Wilberforce were growing old though, in retirement, they lived to applaud the passing of the Act of Abolition in 1833. The lead was now taken by Sir T. F. Buxton, Joseph Sturge of Birmingham, and a rising light of the Clapham sect named James Stephen. These were the founders of the Anti-Slavery Society, an influential body with a royal duke as President. Their intention was 'amelioration' of the conditions of slavery leading to gradual emancipation or, as Stephen put it, 'an emancipation of which not the slaves but the masters themselves would be the willing authors'.

Demerara was the scene of their first attempts to ameliorate the conditions of slavery, with the immediate effect of an outbreak by the slaves, who thought that the reign of anarchy had begun (1823). The planters complained that the missionaries were preaching sedition. Even in sedate Barbados a 'party of respectable gentlemen' assembled to destroy the Wesleyan chapel. But the Evangelical tide was flowing in Whitehall. Lord Bathurst, the amiable undistinguished Colonial Secretary, was persuaded to issue draft instructions to colonial governments, which they were to issue as ordinances for preventing the ill-treatment of slaves. A register was to be kept and returns made to the Colonial Office. Protectors of slaves were to be appointed for each colony; and two new bishoprics were created, at Barbados and Jamaica. These proposals met with a poor response from the Colonial Assemblies, especially from Jamaica, the colony where slavery was most extensive. The 30,000 whites of Jamaica, standing on their chartered rights of self-government as proudly as the planters of Virginia in 1776, declined to be overruled by the Colonial Office. Far worse than the recent example of British Guiana was the anarchy prevailing in Haiti and San Domingo, their near neighbours, where concessions to the slaves had led to the massacre of their French masters and a generation of bloody misrule. The Jamaican Assembly would show no sign of weakness lest their 300,000 slaves should make another Haiti of their island. From 1824 to 1827 the Colonial Office urged concessions which the Jamaica Assembly found means of nullifying.

English politics were too feverish during the next two or three years for the Anti-Slavery Society to make headway. The issue turned on property rights; the same defence, which property owners made for the right to nominate members in a pocket-borough, served as a defence of slave-owning. The fifty-six votes which the West India Interest commanded in the House of Commons were votes alike for slavery in the colonies and for an unreformed Parliament. The Anti-Slavery Society by agitating against the West India Interest, threw the nonconformist middle-classes into the struggle for reform. Nomination boroughs and West Indian slavery were to be swept away together.

When the Whigs came into power in 1831 hopes of emancipation rose. The new government tried to bargain by offering adjustments in the tariff in favour of Jamaica, if the island would remodel its slave-code. The offer of this bribe was repudiated by the Assembly and the rumour of it produced a slave-rising in 1832, the year of the Reform Bill. In the first reformed Parliament Buxton moved and carried a motion for the Abolition of Slavery. Negotiations between the Colonial Office and the colonies on the form of the bill occupied the early months of 1833. The bill (3 & 4 Will. IV, cap. 73), drafted by James Stephen (who sacrificed his sabbatarian principles to complete it between a Saturday and Monday), became law in August 1833 and took effect on 1 August 1834.

Some of the more extreme abolitionists had desired to free the slaves without compensation, on the ground that there was no common-law right to slave labour which, they said, was no better than stolen property; but the view prevailed that England shared with the colonies the guilt of the slave trade and would suffer with the colonies if the sugar-plantations were ruined. It was expedient, in the words of the Act, 'that provision should be made for promoting the industry and securing the good conduct of the persons to be manumitted'. Slaves of working age were therefore to be retained as indentured apprentices by their former masters and still held, for a provisional period, to compulsory labour; but the hours of labour would be restricted to forty-five a week, a reduction by one-quarter from the sixty hours usually enforced on slave-plantations. In compensation for the loss of this quarter of their labour, and for the expectation of the labour of slave children (who were finally emancipated on 1 August 1834), the government first proposed a loan of £15,000,000, which was raised after some shrewd bargaining to a grant-in-aid of £20,000,000. On the other hand the period of apprenticeship was reduced from twelve years to six, and eventually to four years, at the instance of the Anti-Slavery Society. The last slaves in the colonies were emancipated in March 1839.

The payment[1] of this vast sum in cash to thousands of claimants in many countries presented an administrative problem which was solved with great skill and economy, but with inevitable delay. The first necessity was to provide the funds, a sum equal to two-fifths of the national revenue, in a time of financial depression. After several banking-houses had declined the task Rothschild undertook to raise a loan of £20,000,000, by instalments, on the principle that the money would be deposited with the Commissioners of the National Debt, until payment with accumulated interest, to the particular slave-owners was authorised. The subscribers to the loan received annuity bonds which were charged to the Consolidated Fund. The adjudication of claims and the distribution of compensation were placed in the hands of a body of five Commissioners from whose decision there was no appeal except to the King-in-Council.

The chairman was Mr C. C. Pepys, afterwards first Earl of Cottenham. James Stephen was one of the commissioners. They met, in rooms rented from John Murray the publisher, on 14 October 1833. Their first task was statistical: dividing the slave-colonies into nineteen 'units' they prepared from the current slave-registers the number of slaves in each 'unit' at the most recent return. Next they prepared a valuation of the average price of slaves of various classes during the eight years, 1822–30, arriving at the preliminary figure of 780,993 slaves with an aggregate capital value of £45,281,738. To arrive at these figures it was necessary to invite the co-operation of Assistant Commissioners appointed and paid by the governments in each 'unit'. The allotment of slaves to various classes: headmen,

[1] Historians, for the most part, are reticent on the method of emancipation. The only succinct account I have seen is in an unpublished thesis in the Library of the University of London, *The History of Slave Compensation* by R. E. P. Wastell (1932). I am obliged to him for permission to use his statistics.

field-workers, tradesmen, domestics, superannuated old people, young children, etc., proved a complex task since conditions varied in different colonies. 'Appraisers' were next appointed to visit every slave-owner in order to classify his slaves, an easy task in a small concentrated colony like Barbados, a difficult one among the scattered Bahama Islands or on the rugged frontier of Cape Colony, where one appraiser was killed in a Kaffir raid. Having gathered and analysed this information, which occupied them throughout 1834, the Commissioners in London could calculate what sums of money were due to each colony for slaves of each class at the average local price for that class. Claims for compensation were to be filed by slave-owners, before 1 March 1835, with the Assistant Commissioners who certified them and sent them to London. The great fault of the system was that claims were payable only in London, the intention being that slave-owners should collect their money through their London agents.

The first claim was paid, to a Jamaican claimant, on 10 September 1835. The total number of claims filed was 44,441, a number somewhat in excess of the actual number of slave-owners since some filed more than one claim. The Commissioners, when the procedure was running easily, dealt with 160 claims a week but, even at that rate, five years were required for settlement. By 31 October 1840, £15,125,347 had been paid on account of 39,790 uncontested claims. Correspondence about the contested claims dragged on for several years longer until, by 1845, the whole sum of twenty million pounds with the accrued interest had been disbursed, less the cost of administration which did not exceed the modest figure of £150,000. No more than six appeals were carried to the Privy Council and in only one case was the decision of the Commissioners reversed.

The process required the co-operation of the colonial legislatures at every stage and won it inasmuch as the slave-owners wanted their money. The unpopularity of the measure made it difficult everywhere to persuade men of character to act as appraisers. Some colonies had been remiss at keeping their slave-registers and now suffered for it. In Mauritius, and perhaps elsewhere, the returns had been falsified in order to avoid taxation; the planters were punished by qualifying for so much the less compensation. Meanwhile, before the claims were paid, it was everywhere admitted that apprenticeship was a failure.

Antigua and Bermuda cancelled it, giving their slaves full emancipation from the first day of freedom. On the other hand Jamaica, where two-fifths of all British slaves were concentrated, made the rules of apprenticeship so harsh that it was indistinguishable from slavery. By 1838 the abolitionists were in full cry against the Jamaica planters, persuading Parliament to sweep away apprenticeship without further delay. The Jamaica Assembly refused to co-operate further and talked of secession from the Empire. Lord Melbourne's threat, in 1839, to suspend the constitution of Jamaica was the issue on which his tottering administration was turned out of office. That point, and that alone, was scored by the West India Interest, with unwonted help from the Radicals who rallied to defend colonial self-government, as well as from the Tory Opposition.

The effect of adjusting the rate of compensation to the local price of slave-labour was to help the new colonies where land was cheap and labour scarce, but to handicap the old colonies where the soil was exhausted and the slaves numerous. The highest rate paid for any class was £230 for each 'headman' in British Guiana, a territory with boundless resources then rapidly being developed. The lowest rate was for 'inferior field labourers' in the worn-out over-populated Bahamas, the beggarly sum of £19. So sad was the plight of the Bahama planters that they petitioned the King for a special rate, but without success. The colonies with an expanding agriculture received more than those which had seen better days.

All the colonies were short of currency since in slave-economy men lived by barter. The distribution of a substantial part of twenty million pounds sterling, in small payments throughout the Empire, had a steadying effect upon their banking systems. Not the least of the obstacles which the Commissioners surmounted was the lack of any standard currency. In many colonies Spanish dollars (pieces-of-eight) passed as a token coinage with a most uncertain rate of exchange. The Commissioners arbitrarily valued the Spanish dollar at four shillings and fourpence with advantage to some colonies and disadvantage to others. In the long run the sterling payments and the fixed rate of exchange were a benefit to all.

The unknown factor is the proportion of the payments that actually reached the colonies. What was the value of a sterling draft on London to a boat-builder employing three or four slaves as carpenters in Bermuda, to a logwood cutter working on the Honduras coast for a merchant in Jamaica, to a Boer farmer about to trek inland with a train of Hottentot herdsmen? These men had no London agents, perhaps no banking accounts; the Boer farmers had no contacts with London of any kind. All they could do was to sell their claims to some speculator at a discount. On the other hand in the old colonies many of the plantations were owned by absentees who spent the money in London, while many more were mortgaged to London agents who collected the compensation money by power of attorney. Again it was the older colonies that had the worst of the bargain. Not only were they paid at the lowest rate, but their receipts were most reduced by the exactions of absentees and mortgagors. New plantations in Trinidad, Mauritius and British Guiana were more likely to get the benefit of the money.

Thus slavery in the colonies was abolished at great expense to the British tax-payer. Where the British flag flew there was freedom for men of every creed and colour. Let a foreign slave set one foot on British soil, touch with his extended hand the timbers of a British ship, and his freedom would be guaranteed by all the might of Britain's arm.

The Emancipation Act did not apply to the territories of the East India Company. The importation of slaves to British India had been ended in 1811, but the institution of domestic slavery survived much longer. It was deeply embedded in the social organisation of the people, and was regulated by Mohammedan Law. Further it did not display the hideous features of economic exploitation which were essential to plantation slavery in the colonies. The principle of Permissive Emancipation was introduced by the ordinance of 1843 which merely abolished the legal status of slavery, thus placing master and slave under the same rules of law as employer and employee. Slavery in India then diminished and disappeared. Not till the issue of the penal code of 1861 was slave-holding made a criminal offence. Permissive emancipation followed the same course in Malaya (1843), Ceylon and Hong Kong (1844) and in other Eastern dependencies. Domestic slaves held by bush tribes were emancipated in Burma as recently as 1925 and in Sierra Leone (by an irony of history) later still.

The men who had abolished slavery soon looked for new worlds to conquer. During the years of agitation, reports had come in from the missionaries in South Africa of the wrongs inflicted, as it was alleged, by the settlers upon the natives. Lord Glenelg, Colonial Secretary from 1835 to 1839, had picked a quarrel (see page 316) with Sir Benjamin D'Urban, the popular Governor of South Africa, over the Kaffir War of 1835, which led to a new philanthropic movement in London. Sir T. F. Buxton of the Anti-Slavery Society was appointed chairman of a Parliamentary committee on the state of the aborigines in the British settlements. The report of the committee, largely based on missionary evidence, was a mine of information upon the state of many savage races. It drew attention, for the first time, to the distinction between such primitive races as the Australian Blacks who hardly seemed capable of civilisation, and more adaptive races, such as the Polynesians of New Zealand and the South Seas, over whom the missionaries had soon gained a favourable influence. It recounted the history of the Hottentots and the Kaffir Wars in terms most reprehensive to the Boers and to the British governors, and proposed some definite recommendations. The protection of natives in the colonies should not be entrusted to the colonial legislatures but should be the prerogative of the imperial government. Indentured labour and 'pass-laws' forbidding the free movement of natives should be condemned as a form of slavery. The right to buy tribal lands from natives should be denied to the settlers and confined to the agents of the imperial government. Above all, the missionaries should be supported and maintained by the government as the natural protectors of the natives against exploitation.

Although these recommendations were never codified in any act of Parliament they were adopted by the Colonial Office as rules of guidance so long as the Evangelicals dominated its counsels, especially when Lord Glenelg held the seals. An easy lethargic man, he was confirmed in the faith and stirred to activity by the appointment of James Stephen as Permanent Under-Secretary in 1837. Outside the Office their efforts were supported by Buxton's new organ, the Aborigines Protection Society (1837), a body of philanthropists as powerful as the Anti-Slavery Society had been.

These years were the heyday of that surge of religious emotion which the ungodly characterised as 'Exeter Hall'. The Evangelicals, no longer an obscure group of pietists meeting at a villa in Clapham, had grown into a multitude of earnest and devout Bible-Protestants, of whom an increasing majority were radical and non-conformist, not Tory High-Churchmen like their founders. The May Meetings held annually at Exeter Hall in the Strand were religious conventions, of a type more frequently seen now in America than in England, where devotional fervour was concentrated on some field of Christian endeavour, most constantly upon foreign missions. Empire, to the crowds at Exeter Hall, was an opportunity for civilising and converting the savage and the slave, and under that flag the Colonial Office marched for many years.

The two ancient societies (S.P.C.K., 1698 and S.P.G., 1701) had languished during the free-thinking eighteenth century. They were now surpassed in enthusiasm by the new evangelical societies: the Baptist Missionary Society (1792), the undenominational London Missionary Society (1795), the Scottish Missionary Society (1796), the Church Missionary Society (1799), the Wesleyan Missionary Society (1813). All this activity was supported by the British and Foreign Bible Society (1804), and was equalled by a parallel activity in the United States. At the end of the nineteenth century British Protestant Missions were spending an income of £4,000,000 a year. In the Pacific islands, in Central Africa, and especially in China the social and political influence of the Protestant Missionaries was profound, not only because they converted the heathen, but because all missionaries were teachers and the most successful were often medical men.

In thus describing the Protestant missions it is not intended that the even greater efforts of the Roman Catholics, should be underrated. Since the foundation of the 'Propaganda' by Gregory XV in 1622 there has been no time when the Missionary Orders have not encircled the globe; but their work falls largely outside the scope of this book. The historian of the British Empire must however be aware of a noble rivalry, in the great age of Protestant missions, between them and the French missionary bodies, especially the Marists (1816) and the Society of Picpus (1817) in the Pacific, the Oblates of Mary (1845) in North-western America, and the White Fathers (1868) in Central Africa.

VI

THE BRITISH AT THE CAPE,
TO THE YEAR 1852

Argument: The Dutch evolved a characteristic society at the Cape in the eighteenth century, with the help of imported slaves; they had little to do with the Bantu peoples. Traditionally hostile to the monopoly of the Dutch East India Company, they resisted British administrative reforms after the cession of 1814, and especially those prompted by the Evangelicals.

Extension eastward engaged the colony in Kaffir Wars, all the more after the plantation of a British settlement near Grahamstown in 1820.

Boer dissatisfaction with British rule promoted the Great Trek, the first penetration of the interior by European settlers in any considerable number. After complex disputes three new states were formed. Natal as a British colony, the Orange Free State, which was at first under a shadowy British suzerainty, the Transvaal as an independent republic.

1. THE CAPE OF GOOD HOPE, 1488–1826

BARTHOLOMEW DIAZ passed the Cape of Good Hope on a voyage of discovery, probably in May 1488. Nine years later Vasco da Gama, with a larger expedition equipped for military and diplomatic exploits, was driven off the Cape by storms and made a landfall farther up the coast, at a place which he named Natal, the day being Christmas, 1497. But his concern was with India, the Arab Sultanates, and the realm of Prester John. Then and thereafter the Portuguese passed on from the stormy Cape to the good hope of empire in the East; though Almeida, one of the makers of that empire perished, as it happened, in a scuffle with Hottentots at the foot of Table Mountain. The first Portuguese holding in East Africa was Mozambique (1508) from where they dominated the coast as far south as the Zambezi by the end of the sixteenth century. On the west coast their first holding, a true colony, was founded at St Paul de Loanda in 1575. Strange to relate they made little use, in their great century,

of the anchorage at Table Bay, though ships of all the maritime
nations called there occasionally for water and fresh meat
which they bought from the Hottentots. Lancaster was there in
1591, and in 1620 two English captains took possession of the Cape
for England, without effect since the government repudiated their
action. Negotiations, which came to nothing, were even then in
progress for a joint occupation by the Dutch and English East
India Companies.

The prize lay there for any man's possession. The hippo-
potamus wallowed in the marshes of the Cape flats; lions ranged
the slopes of Table Mountain when, in 1647, the crew of a Dutch
East Indiaman wintered in Table Bay, having lost their ship.
After their rescue in the following year, they reported on the
healthy climate, the fertile soil, the friendly disposition of the
Hottentots, and the amenities of their life when camping at
Green Point. The Dutch Company, which had found St Helena
(1633) too near home, and Mauritius (1638) too far afield for
half-way ports of call, then sent Jan van Riebeeck to occupy the
Cape. On 6 April 1652 his three small ships cast anchor in Table
Bay. His business was to provide victuals and refreshment for
Dutch East India shipping, and no more. In his first report he
pressed for the despatch of settlers to raise crops and cattle, but
was severely snubbed. Their High Mightinesses wanted no more
than could be grown by his garrison and servants, and would not
hear of the admission of outsiders to their chartered territory.
Not till 1657 was van Riebeeck permitted even to settle nine
families of his people on farms of their own, and then only on
condition that they traded exclusively with the Company. His
attempts to develop his little colony were consistently overruled
by inspecting officers sent out from Holland. Though he dutifully endeavoured to enclose the settlement by a line of forts and
ditches, its growth could not be restrained. By 1658 the handful
of settlers united seditiously against the restrictions, and by 1660
he was at war with the Hottentots who felt the encroachment of
the white men upon their narrow grazing-grounds.

In 1662, when van Riebeeck relinquished his command, the
colony numbered 1394 persons, of whom thirty-six were 'free
burghers' settled with their families. There were some white
labourers and a few Malayan slaves brought from the Dutch
East Indies. Cattle-breeding, which meant further encroachment

on Hottentot land, was the most promising trade, if we except selling provisions illegally at high prices to British and French ships, when all should have been preserved for the Dutch ships at a fixed rate. The colony grew in strategic importance during the French and English wars of the 1670's. Capetown Castle was built by 1674. Between 1672 and 1677 conclusions were reached with the Hottentots; by a deed between the Company and various tribes, all the land as far north and east as the 'Hottentots Holland' Mountains and Saldanha Bay was ceded to the Company in return for trade goods which, the Hottentots alleged, were not paid to the rightful vendors. Hence another war which ended in a dispersal of these tribes beyond the confines of the colony.

The age of restriction ended with the coming of Simon van der Stel as Governor in 1679. Setting himself at once to the task of colonisation and expansion he planted thirty families with a minister and a teacher in the fertile inland valley which he named Stellenbosch (1683). The policy of the Company was now to attract Protestant emigrants who would form a local militia to garrison the fortress; and accordingly some approved families of Dutch, German and French Protestants were admitted, among them about 200 Huguenots after the Revocation of the Edict of Nantes. These French refugees, besides improving the culture of the vineyards and the quality of the wine, added a lively flavour to the phlegmatic Dutch temper of the settlers. The Afrikaner race would have been the poorer without that sparkling admixture of Gallic blood, and African history different without such names as Marais, de Villiers, Delarey, Joubert, Duplessis, Malan.

Van der Stel retired in 1699 to the dignified white manor house of Constantia which he built and which still stands among his oak-trees and vineyards on the sunny eastern slope of Table Mountain. His vintages carried by the India ships east and west soon attained worldwide fame. He loved the land and the cultivator, the *land bouwer*, somewhat distrusting the new generation of cattlemen; for in South Africa with its long dry seasons and periodic droughts every cattleman must be a rover like the Hottentots before him. But the wandering *trek-boer*, not the husbandman of the old Western Province around Capetown, became the national type.

Two hundred years ago the well-known comment was made that Boer farmers feel crowded when they see the smoke of a neighbour's chimney, a sentiment encouraged by their land laws. New farms were granted by the Governor well spaced-out. The farmer, in addition to his cultivated ground could buy a grazing licence for about 6000 acres round the farm at a nominal price, marking off its boundary, or so it was said in jest, by the rough test of 'riding-off' from the farmstead for half an hour at a walking pace.

During the eighteenth century the population grew rapidly, more by a high birth-rate and a healthy environment than by immigration. There may have been 500 Boer families in 1700; there was a white population of 21,746 in 1798 expanding out-wards from four centres: 6000 about Capetown, 7000 about Stellenbosch and 4000 in each of two new settlements Swellendam (founded 1743) and Graaff-Reinet (founded 1785). There were also 25,000 slaves, many of them imported Asiatics, mostly in the neighbourhood of Capetown, the progenitors of the unfortunate 'Cape Coloured' race. The older farming districts were largely self-supporting and but little affected by the obstructive rule of the Company's Governors. In such settlements as Stellenbosch might best be seen the great farms built in the characteristic colonial style, which is now so much admired. These were the homes of a sober secretive frugal race, outwardly calm and in-wardly passionate, notable for shrewdness and subtlety and a stubborn unbending courage; a nationality distinguished from the 'Hollanders' with whom they were already losing contact. The golden age of Boer legend, when this simple society enjoyed halcyon days, was the time of Governor Tulbagh (1751–71).

On the frontier the less disciplined members of this intractable race, the trek-boers, lived another life. Mounted on hardy ponies, they moved easily in search of pasture and of 'game' to settle always farther out, bringing on their family and goods in covered ox-wagons with Hottentot drivers and 'coloured' slaves walking alongside, until they chose a home where sweet water could be drawn from some 'fontein'. The first great trek was the eastward movement to the Fish River in the 1780's which led to the settlement of Graaff-Reinet.

The farther they were removed from the paternal hand of the Governor at Capetown the more republican became the settlements. Early in the century the outlying groups had developed the two characteristic organs of Boer self-government, the Commando and the Church-session (*Kerkraad*). Strict Calvinists of the Heidelberg Confession, it was natural for the elders of the *Kerk* to assume control over the local welfare of the community, though the minister was, in the early days, appointed by the Governor. The annual assembly of the Church for the *Nagmaal*, or Communion, became too a secular function where politics, marketing and matchmaking flourished. Defence was provided by the local militia in which every man served, bringing his own horse, gun and rations. Each local band, or commando, elected its officers. Commandos were first raised in the early Hottentot wars and were systematically organised during the eighteenth century for the war of extermination against the Bushmen. In 1778 the trek-boers first came into contact with Bantu Africans of the Xosa tribe, a foe that could give real opposition. After war and negotiation the Fish River was taken as the eastern boundary, which the Graaff-Reinet settlers defended against Xosa raiding parties, with little or no support from the Governor. There was not much expansion northward over the mountain ranges. The Orange River was discovered in 1760 but its banks were not settled until many years later.

At least twice during the eighteenth century the 'free burghers' were irritated into sedition by the petty despotism of the Company's Governors; they were exasperated when the Governor tried to check the Kaffirs on the Fish River with fair words instead of hard blows. Always conservative and unenterprising, the Company declined in wealth and power throughout the century, abating nothing of its oppressive demeanour. The dividend was reduced from 25 per cent to 12 per cent and then was left unpaid. The volume of Dutch shipping at the Cape dwindled so that Capetown rarely knew prosperity unless a French or British fleet revictualled at this 'tavern of the Indian Ocean'. When de Suffren left a garrison at the Cape in 1781 his French officers brought an air of frivolity to the little town with the gaiety and fashion of the old regime. That ended in collapse when the British naval victories, at the end of the American War, disposed of de Suffren and destroyed Dutch trade. From this blow the Dutch East India Company never recovered, but lapsed into bankruptcy. The French Revolution had its echoes in the far south where the settlers at the Cape grew restive against their moribund rulers. When the British forces under General Craig arrived in 1795, the settlers on the eastern frontier were already in revolt, having thrown off their dependence upon the Governor at Capetown.

The relations of British and Dutch in the French Wars have been discussed above (see page 240). The allegiance of the Cape was most uncertain since Craig brought a letter from the exiled Prince of Orange calling on them to admit an English garrison, producing a situation somewhat like the Dakar Incident of 1940, though with a different ending. The tradition of the Dutch Company, always suspicious of British rivalry, led the Governor to make at least a token resistance which deeply embarrassed General Craig. The Governor capitulated only when British reinforcements arrived. Soon a Dutch naval force arrived to restore the situation but achieved nothing because the sailors proved loyal to the House of Orange and joined with the British.

For seven years British military governors found themselves faced with just the same problems as their Dutch predecessors. Their interest was in making the Cape into another Gibraltar, which brought a boom of wartime prosperity to the Capetown merchants; they were much averse to frontier wars against the Kaffirs in the eastern districts. The attempt to wave an olive-branch in the face of Kaffirs on the war-path soon raised some of the burghers of Graaff-Reinet in revolution against the British for the same reasons that had raised them against the Dutch Company. But, at the peace of 1802, the Cape was receded to the Dutch, that is to the Jacobin Batavian Republic which was maintained in Holland by French money and French arms. The new Governor announced a programme of administrative reforms, alarming the conservative Boers by a promise of secular education and equality for all religions, but had neither time (February 1803 to January 1806) nor funds to accomplish much before the second British conquest by Sir Home Popham. Again, after a show of resistance, the Governor capitulated on terms of a guarantee to the inhabitants of their property, privileges and legal system.

At first the only change made in the Dutch system of administration was the sending of justices on circuit to the outlying districts. Although they were Dutchmen administering Roman-

Dutch law, their actions caused deep resentment among the frontier farmers. The missionary influence already felt in the last decade of Dutch rule was far more powerful after the British annexation. Reports were finding their way to London about the treatment of the Hottentots by their white masters, with the result that the justices made it their duty to investigate complaints. The circuit of 1811, long known as the Black Circuit, was felt by the burghers to be an insolent attempt to stir up a rebellion of native and 'coloured' servants. The British, like the Dutch before them, raised a Hottentot corps of military police. A crisis came in 1814 when a frontier farmer named Bezuidenhout refused to appear in court to answer charges of cruelty to a native. Having fired on the sheriff who attempted to serve a summons, he was killed in the resulting scuffle. His brother then formed a band of armed men and declared open rebellion, inviting the alliance of Kaffir chiefs. Most of his sixty followers surrendered to a burgher commando backed by troops, when the outbreak had manifestly failed; but Johannes Bezuidenhout made a running fight until he too was mortally wounded. Five of the rebels were sentenced to death and hanged at Slagter's Nek (1815). These unsuccessful rebels have been elevated by some extremists into a high place in Afrikaner martyrology. Bezuidenhout's myth, like John Brown's, goes marching on, though neither legendary hero gets much glory from the addict of factual history.

The affair of Slagter's Nek was determined by the stern decision of Lord Charles Somerset (1767–1831), a new Governor who left his mark on South Africa. His appointment was a Tory job, or so said the Whigs at Holland House: 'he was a horse-jockey who went to the Cape to make money'. To be sure his salary was the enormous sum of £10,000 a year and he anticipated it largely. He was an arrogant, overbearing aristocrat quite out of sympathy with Evangelicals or intellectuals of any colour, not an attractive figure. But much was done in his day, perhaps the better because this horse-jockey rode rough-shod over obstructors. He quarrelled with Sir John Cradock his predecessor in office, with Sir Rufane Donkin who acted as his deputy, with Dr Philip the agent of the London Missionary Society; but he knocked the colony into a shape that endured, held the frontier, settled the eastern province, and promoted agricultural improvement at a model farm.

When Somerset arrived, the frontier had been brought into better order than for years past by Colonel J. Graham, who founded the military post of Grahamstown (1812), covering it by a chain of forts along the Fish River. The new Governor proposed to hold this line with mobile columns of mounted infantry; and would have done so, had not Whitehall suddenly withdrawn his cavalry establishment, as an economy after Waterloo. It was ridiculous, in their eyes, that he should want 3000 troops at the Cape 'to guard against a few Caffres'. However, the garrison of Grahamstown, 500 miles to the east, was obliged to fight for life against a determined attack by 10,000 natives in 1819. After their defeat Somerset pushed back the frontier to the next river valley making a 'neutral zone' beyond the Fish River. He next began to demand settlers to form a militia—an English militia—in the Albany province on this side of the frontier.

Several projects had been formed, some speculative and some philanthropic, for settling parties of labourers at the Cape, as a remedy for post-war unemployment; and some hundreds of emigrants had actually sailed when a comprehensive proposal was launched in July 1819. The Chancellor, Vansittart, moved a vote of £50,000 which was to be spent by Bathurst, the Secretary for War and the Colonies, on assisted emigration to South Africa. *The Times*, not usually favourable to such schemes, gave its support with an enthusiastic account (18 June 1819) of 'our noble station at the Cape of Good Hope which has the finest soil and climate in the world'. The scheme for an organised emigration was that intending emigrants were to apply for permits to the Secretary of State, each head of a family making a deposit of £10 which would be returned to him by instalments in the colony. The first to apply from any town or village was appointed 'head of a party' and was authorised to select suitable emigrants from the other applicants in that locality. No party of less than ten persons was accepted. Within a few weeks fifty-six parties were formed comprising 3487 men, women and children with a combined capital of £14,000 deposited in cash. The smallest party was composed of fifteen persons from Carlisle, one of the largest was 220 from Cork. Twenty-four ships of about 400 tons burthen were chartered in various ports. The London fleet was delayed by ice in the river, this being the last occasion (December 1819) when the Thames was frozen at London Bridge.

The Irish party went to Saldanha Bay, the Welsh to Caledon, but the main landing was on the open beach of Algoa Bay in the early months of 1820. Two or three thousand emigrants spent the southern autumn in tents among the sand-hills waiting for wagons and ox-teams to draft them away to the settlements around Grahamstown. Thomas Pringle, the poet of the 'Eighteen-Twenty Settlers', thus described the camp on the seashore:

> It consists of several hundred tents, pitched in parallel rows or streets, and occupied by the middle or lower classes of the emigrants.... There were respectable tradesmen and jolly farmers, with every appearance of substance and snug English comfort about them. There were watermen, fishermen, and sailors from the Thames and the English seaports, with the reckless and weather-beaten look usual in persons of their professions. There were numerous groups of pale-visaged artisans and operative manufacturers from London and the large towns, of whom...a proportion were squalid in their aspect, slovenly in their attire, and discourteous in their demeanour.... Lastly there were parties of pauper agricultural labourers sent out by the aid of their parishes, healthier perhaps than the class just mentioned, but not apparently happier in mind.

Within a few months all were settled south and south-east of Grahamstown between the Kowie and the Fish Rivers. The most remote settlement was that of 400 Highlanders led by Captain Grant. They had particularly asked 'not to be mixed in with any others as speak a different language'.

Since Somerset was on leave of absence in England the colonists were received by his deputy, Donkin, who named the landing-place Port Elizabeth, after his wife. Donkin found himself obliged to issue rations against deductions from the settlers' deposits and, when these were exhausted, at government expense. Though the settlers were located before the coming of the spring the wheat crop failed for three successive years 1821, 1822 and 1823. Persistent blights, in spite of experiment with rustproof varieties, made it clear that this was not a district favourable for wheat growing; nor were many of the settlers expert cultivators. As always in a new colony some of the immigrants were ne'er-do-wells and many more, known as 'cockney gardeners', were incorrigibly urban in habit. When the deposit money and even the government rations were exhausted they drifted off into the older settlements to become tradesmen or objects of charity in

the towns. By May 1823 the original thousand families had
dwindled to 438. The leaders of parties stayed, the labourers
drifted away.

When Lord Charles Somerset came back, his masterful love of
interference led him to tyrannise over the settlers, often spitefully
undoing what Donkin had done for them. He kept his eye on
them as suspect 'radicals', a term of abuse in his vocabulary;
but on the other hand he secured their land-titles and eased their
burden of financial obligation. Donkin had allowed pasturage
leases which Somerset refused. Keeping cattle led to dispersal of
the settlers and tempted the Kaffirs to raid. Sheep-walks were not
permitted until 1825. The settlers were forbidden to hold slaves,
though their Dutch neighbours were slave-owners, as was the
Governor himself.

It has been customary to say that the 'Eighteen-Twenty Settlement' was a failure, because the settlers failed to make their
fortunes out of wheat in the first few years. Many of the best of
them stayed on the land. Some took up trading in ivory and
ostrich feathers with the Kaffirs; others, in 1827, introduced fine-
woolled sheep, thus finding what thereafter remained the true
pastoral wealth of the eastern province. The settlement was
decried by men with short views and mean minds. Time and
working capital are needed to found a colony. In their first three
years the 1820 settlers fared better than the first Virginians and
no worse than the first Dutch at Table Bay. To judge the worth
of the seeds planted on the open beach of Algoa Bay we must
look to-day at Port Elizabeth with its harbour-works and heavy
industries, at Grahamstown with its justly celebrated University
College and schools. By 1842 Grahamstown was a flourishing
town of 700 houses with 5000 inhabitants, a church, a school,
two newspapers and a bank.[1]

[1] See Isobel Edwards, *The Eighteen-Twenty Settlers.*

2. SOUTH AFRICA, 1820–38

WHEN Lord Charles Somerset returned to the Cape for his
second term of office (1821–6) his manner was more overbearing
than before. He watched what he supposed to be subversive
movements, through agents among whom moved obscurely the
mysterious figure known as 'Oliver the Spy'. Still the military
governor of a fortress and of its victualling area, he saw no reason
for allowing political privileges to the inhabitants. Under the
changed conditions, as population and prosperity increased, his
arbitrary behaviour provoked hostile criticism from two sides.
The Eighteen-Twenty settlers demanded civil rights, advancing
their claim through a newspaper which the Governor, and the
Colonial Office, severely restricted. But the agitation was felt in
England and fomented there; the first number of the *Manchester
Guardian* (5 May 1821) featured an article on the oppression of
the settlers in Cape Colony. Even more effective was the
influence of the Rev. John Philip, the agent of the London
Missionary Society at the Cape, who began, soon after his arrival
in 1819, a long crusade on behalf of the Hottentots and, as if it
were *a priori*, against the Boers.

In 1823 the Colonial Office sent a Commission led by J. T.
Bigge (who had already made a similar investigation in New South
Wales) to report and advise upon administrative reforms,
whereupon the tongues of the critics were loosened. The effect
of Bigge's Commission was the granting of the elements of civil
rights and constitutional procedure in 1825. Some check was put
upon the arbitrary action of the Governor by the provision of a
nominated advisory council. Trial by jury was instituted, and an
independent judiciary appointed. With the growth of liberties
the criticism of Governor Somerset grew louder. Further
attempts to restrain the liberty of the press led to his recall.
His long survival as Governor had been due to the influence of
the Somerset family which commanded twenty-two votes in the
House of Commons. He and his patron Bathurst fell together in
1826, when attacked by Sir Rufane Donkin in the House and
denounced by *The Times* newspaper.

The colony was divided some years later for administration
into an eastern and a western province, the eastern province in-

cluding the Kaffir frontier and the new English settlements, under Sir Andries Stockenstrom as Lieutenant-Governor.

A less prudent reform was the replacement of Dutch by English as the language of administration and of the law courts (1827). It seemed justified since the Boers were now completely cut off from the culture of the Netherlands and had no system of Afrikaans education. Their dialect, which varied locally, had not yet crystallised into a literary language. Even the Dutch Reformed Church with its tiny establishment of seven congregations (1795) languished for lack of a succession of ministers. The scarcity was remedied by an appeal to the Scots who were of the same communion and whose racial character agreed well with the canny, dour, and yet essentially generous Boers. A powerful contribution to Afrikaner culture was made by the Scottish ministers who went to the Cape in response to this appeal. Among them Andrew Murray and his two sons should be specially mentioned; though strictly orthodox Presbyterians they brought into the Dutch Church a liberal and devout spirit and a respect for learning which the 'doppers' of the old age had lacked. The young Andrew Murray was the first minister at Bloemfontein; John Murray was a principal in founding the University of Stellenbosch (1859), for a long time the chief source of Afrikaner culture.

Though some slight attempts had been made by one of the ubiquitous Moravian missionaries (1737–44), and by Dutch Evangelicals (1786–95), to convert slaves in the colony, systematic missionary endeavour began to flourish with the intervention of the undenominational London Missionary Society in 1799. These English missionaries formed a Hottentot community near Algoa Bay, at Bethelsdorp (1808), which the Boers regarded with suspicion, and all the more when John Philip (1775–1851) began his polemical career as agent for the Society. He maintained a correspondence with Wilberforce and the other Evangelical leaders in England, influencing through them the policy of the Colonial Office, at least so long as Lord Glenelg was Secretary of State (1835–9). Philip frequently made tours of inspection of the mission stations which multiplied through Africa in the 'thirties and 'forties, conferring with tribal chiefs upon political as well as upon religious matters. Sometimes he seemed to show an almost malignant hostility to the Boer frontiersmen, yet it would be unjust to underrate his disinterested passion, his lifelong struggle, for justice on behalf of his native clients.

The gravamen of his charge against the Boers was their treatment of the Hottentots. In the full fervour of the Evangelical Revival he blamed the Boers for behaving as white men behaved to almost every aboriginal race until his own generation. The older Boers never doubted that the heathen savages were a lower order created to serve the Chosen People, and were deserving of kindness in proportion to their docility. They were good masters to their domestic slaves—liberal masters in Capetown where slaves owned property, practised crafts and traded on their own account. There was even a recorded case of a Dutch boy bound apprentice to a slave to learn his trade. But manners were rougher in the pastoral districts and on the frontier, where few farmers were so poor as not to own a tail of Hottentot herdsmen, not slaves by law but none the less forcibly held to labour, a system defended by precepts from the Old Testament.

The nickname 'hottentot' means 'stammerer' and alludes to the peculiar use in their language of palatal 'clicks' similar to those used for encouraging horses. By European standards they were an ugly race with yellowish skins, everted lips and strangely protruding buttocks, but they were tamable and were skilful with cattle. The first generation of Boer settlers had broken up their tribal system and reduced a large part of the race to servitude, but unknown numbers, perhaps 30,000, still wandered round the outskirts of the settlements, living largely by cattle-raiding. Among them, since the early Boer settlers were not so fastidious as their descendants, were many half-breeds who formed themselves into new tribes known as Griquas, or more bluntly as 'Bastards'. So scattered and interbred were they by the middle of the nineteenth century that it was said that no pure Hottentots remained. The Griquas were the peculiar care of the London Missionary Society.

In the dry scrub of the western province there lingered still more primitive tribes of 'Bushmen', so stunted in appearance, so secluded in habit that they seemed hardly human. Among the Bushmen the Old Stone Age survived—and still survives—as it once was in palaeolithic France and Spain. The drawings in a free bold style, which may be seen in Pyrenean caves, of animals long extinct, are paralleled by the hunting-scenes which the Bushmen draw on their rock-shelters in South Africa. They possessed nothing to tempt European cupidity, having neither landed property nor cattle but, being predatory hunters, they regarded the settlers' herds as fair game and so provoked reprisals. Before the British came they had been extirpated from the colony by systematic 'drives' and massacres. Hottentots and Bushmen were neither numerous nor formidable. The new tribes of Xosa[1] Kaffirs, whom the settlers confronted across the Great Fish River, were men of a different mettle.

Kaffir is an Arabic word meaning 'unbeliever', used by Moslems to describe all non-Moslems and especially heathen slaves. It came to be applied in a more limited sense by the Portuguese to the negro peoples of Central Africa who were the perpetual prey of the Arab slave trade, and finally by the Dutch to those tribes with whom they came in contact in south-east Africa.

The *Bantu* peoples were for long the dominant race of south-east Africa. Their prototype is the Ethiopian of Scripture, 'black but comely', who has not changed his skin these 3000 years and may be seen to-day just as he is represented in Egyptian frescoes of the wars of Pharaoh Rameses. The Bantu are a tall, strong, upright people with skins of chocolate brown to deep black. They use spears of hammered iron, wear girdles of oxtails, and delight in bracelets or anklets of copper wire. They are people of the savannahs, following the game-herds and the cattle-pasture in the dry uplands of thorn-scrub and sparse trees, where there are no lakes, few navigable rivers and but rare patches of forest. Men's work is herding cattle since wealth is counted only in numbers of cows. The women hoe the mealie-patch while the men squat on their heels beside the reed-thatched beehive huts. Legitimacy and the permanence of domestic life are secured by the custom of *lobola*, the ceremonial pledging of cattle from the bridegroom's to the bride's family. But cattle are a form of currency, not a consumable commodity, so that numbers, not quality, matter. Some tribes live largely on milk, and few of the Bantu, though cattle are all their care, make beef a staple diet.

[1] The name begins with a click introduced into a Bantu dialect from the language of the adjacent Hottentots.

For his food the Ethiopian, like the lion and the leopard, was parasitic on the countless herds of giraffe, zebra and quagga; the gazelles and antelopes of many species, which ranged over the Veld until times within living memory, but which now are rare except in parks and reservations. Deprived of their former food supply by the destruction of the game, the Bantu cow-herds have not learned to breed cattle for beef. Unwilling vegetarians, they subsist on an inadequate diet of mealie porridge which has lowered their resistance against disease.

Herding cattle, hunting game, and making war they held to be the proper occupations for a man. They were as fierce and predatory as the Europeans who appeared in South Africa simultaneously with them. Among the Bantu, in general, young men were of no account until they had won in war the cattle which meant the price of a bride. Wars were cattle-raids and were very bloody, so that the death of many warriors made polygamy the rule.

In private character men and women are simple, loyal, good-humoured, docile and brave. They are extremely superstitious and suffer much from mental persecution by witch-doctors. Among their *taboos* is commonly one against using the names of the dead, a prohibition which precludes records of the past, so that the Bantu have no recorded history. Perhaps the dynasty bearing the obscure title of Monomotapa, with whom the Portuguese trafficked from Mozambique in the sixteenth century, were a Bantu dynasty of superior abilities. They may have built the dry stone walls about the mysterious ruined citadel of Zimbabwe in Rhodesia, but no tradition was recorded; no other Bantu tribe with which we are acquainted was capable of the task.

During the eighteenth century Bantu tribes were drifting southwards through the Transvaal in numerous small warring bodies, among whom there arose a military genius, quite untaught by the lore of Europe or Asia, in Chaka, King of the Amazulu (died 1828). He formed a standing army of young warriors organised in regiments (*impis*) and armed with short stabbing spears (*assegais*). They were drilled to march in double time and to fight in a loose formation not unlike that of the Roman legions. No young man might settle down with a wife until he had served in an *impi* and blooded his spear, a rule which, for a hundred years, made the Zulus awkward neighbours.

Chaka established his dynasty in Zululand, ruled the greater part of what is now Natal, and raided all South Africa, setting in motion a wave of migration that was met by the contemporary Boer migration on the banks of the Great Fish River.

Tension between the Boers and the British missionaries grew over three distinct native problems: the treatment of the Hottentots, the abolition of slavery, and the defence of the Kaffir frontier. The Hottentot policy had been propounded in Governor Caledon's ordinance (1809) which declared that every native should have a fixed place of abode and not leave it without permission from the *landdrost* (district magistrate). This honest attempt to 'locate' the nomadic tribes was the first of the 'pass-laws', still so hotly discussed in South African politics. Missionary agitation against this restrictive ordinance had led to an inquiry into the treatment of natives and in consequence to the Black Circuit (see above, page 306) which so offended Afrikaner pride. 'Nearly one hundred of the most respectable families on the frontier' had been implicated by their coloured servants in charges which were sometimes false or frivolous. When a reaction set in, John Philip went behind the back of the Governor to Wilberforce and Wilmot Horton, the Evangelical leaders through whose influence Bigge's Commission was sent to Africa. In 1828 Philip had the signal success of instigating Buxton, the chairman of the Anti-Slavery Society, to denounce the pass-laws in the House of Commons with the result that the Governor was obliged to withdraw them. By the '50th Ordinance' (1828) he gave equality of status to all free men in the colony, irrespective of colour, an even greater affront to the patriarchal Boers.

Philip's hour struck when slavery was denounced throughout the Empire on 1 August 1834. The act of emancipation had been long foreseen and was but the climax of a gradual series of legal changes. No slaves had been introduced into the colony since the Batavian Republic took control in 1803. The visits of slave-ships to Table Bay had been forbidden since 1808. The slave-code had been ameliorated in the 1820's by legal restrictions upon the power of the slave-owner and by the appointment of an official Protector of slaves, as in the British West Indies. Further the appearance of a white labouring-class had somewhat relieved the perennial demand for hands. The effect of the Proclamation of 1834 was to convert the 39,021 slaves in the colony, mostly of Asiatic or mixed origin, into apprentices under indentures which held good until 1838, a change of legal status rather than of economic or social position. The masters were annoyed but not ruined, their chief concern being that compensation, in the form of drafts payable in London, amounted to no more than £1,247,701 or rather less than half their expectation. Five-sixths of the slaves thus emancipated were in the old-established western provinces.

Emancipation was administered by a new Governor, Sir Benjamin D'Urban (1777–1844), like most governors in that age a military man with a distinguished record in the French Wars. Philip at once began to urge upon him a new frontier policy. They were to set up a Griqua state and a series of Bantu states protected by the British missionaries against exploitation by the Boers. At this moment (December 1834) the eastern frontier flared up in one of its periodical conflagrations. Cattle-raids, which the Kaffir chiefs condoned as common form, led to reprisals, which the settlers similarly condoned, and so to a fierce frontier war in which the eastern province was saved from desolation by the brilliant and ruthless operations of Colonel Harry Smith. D'Urban's difficulties were increased by a sharp despatch from the Colonial Office rebuking him for carrying the war into the enemy's country. 'The Kaffirs', wrote Lord Glenelg, 'had right and justification on their side.' Glenelg obliged D'Urban to withdraw the frontier to the Fish River, abandoning the new province which D'Urban had just annexed. He also forbade settlers to take up land north of the Orange River. These weak concessions, this truckling to men and measures that the Boers detested, brought the frontiersmen to a decision to migrate beyond the reach of the British Governor.

3. THE GREAT TREK AND ITS
CONSEQUENCES

FOR some years past adventurous parties of *voortrekkers* had
made exploring and hunting trips through what is now the Transvaal, as far north as the Limpopo. One of the boldest of them,
Hendrik Potgieter, after a brush with the formidable Matabele
tribe had fallen back to Thaba 'nchu at the foot of the mountains
of Basutoland. Here was the rendezvous to which assembled in
1837 about 3000 Boers in a vast camp of covered wagons. They
had trekked north from all parts of the frontier, but mostly from
the Graaff-Reinet district, a journey of about 300 miles. Harry
Smith, who knew and liked them well, wrote of the *trek-boers* as
men 'of strong prejudices, most credulous in all respects, especially where the government is concerned, jealous to a degree of
what they regard as their rights, constantly at variance with one
another, and evincing a want of mutual confidence'. When Piet
Retief, who planned an eastward march towards Natal, was
elected 'Governor of the United Laagers', Potgieter and his
followers broke away and trekked northward into the country
he already knew. His mounted men engaged the Matabele *impis*
in a running fight along the River Marico (November 1837)
driving them into regions so remote that they were hardly heard
of at the Cape for another fifty years. While Potgieter's party
entered into possession of the treeless, sparsely-inhabited High
Veld around Potchefstroom, Retief's wagons had moved on to
Winburg, where they halted while he scouted ahead to find a pass
down the high scarp of the Drakensberg into the coastal plain.
Coming here by land, he met again the intrusive British, who some
years earlier had reached Port Natal by sea. English guides led
Piet Retief to the royal *kraal* of Dingaan, who had succeeded
the great Chaka as King of the Zulus, in the land upon which
the trekkers hoped to settle. The kraal stood in the hot coastal
belt not far from the mouth of the Tugela river. Retief sought to
win the favour of the King by leading a commando against a
rival chief to recover stolen cattle; but Dingaan, having seen the
skill of the Boer warriors, thought it all the more reason for
getting rid of them. Having allayed Retief's suspicions by granting him a concession of land, the King enticed him and his men,

sixty-nine in number, into the kraal unarmed and murdered them.
The deed of gift was found on Retief's dead body. At the same
time Dingaan's *impis* fell upon the scattered trekkers struggling
through Natal, and murdered all they could master (6 February
1838). To make a clean sweep he also drove the English settlers
from Port Natal.

Map 13

The Great Trek and its consequences made painful reading in
Downing Street. Glenelg endeavoured to shift the blame by
recalling D'Urban on the grounds that he had failed to stop the
Trek. The next Governor, George Napier, was held in impo-
tence by a succession of impracticable instructions. He was to
stop the trekkers but was not to fight. Even the reoccupation of
Port Natal, reluctantly ordered in January 1839, was counter-
manded in December; for the Boers, with epic courage had
settled their own account with Dingaan. The trekkers who were
still assembled on the High Veld, under a new leader, Andries

Pretorius, invaded Zululand, provoking Dingaan to attack. They formed a *laager* in a bend of the Blood River, protected on two faces by the deep stream and on two by the interlocked and barricaded line of fifty wagons. On 16 December 1838, always remembered in South Africa as Dingaan's Day, the Boer elephant-guns were ranged behind the barricade against the assault of the Zulu spearmen. Three thousand Zulus were slain for a loss of three Boers; Dingaan fled a fugitive to the Bush leaving all Natal in the power of the trekkers. Pretorius at once formed the first of the Boer free states, the Natal Republic (1839–43) with its capital at Pietermaritzburg. He solved the Zulu problem by setting up, as a rival to the discredited Dingaan, his brother Umpanda who was duly enthroned upon a sacred stone at the Boer capital, and was properly subservient to the Boers. Dingaan was hunted by his tribal rivals and killed in 1840.

English adventurers by sea had long previously secured a foot-hold on the coast of Natal. In 1823 a retired naval officer, Lieut. F. G. Farewell, had taken a ship up the coast from Port Elizabeth with a party of traders among whom the most striking figure was H. F. Fynn, an innkeeper from Capetown. They formed a little settlement at Port Natal on the rich warm coastal plain which had been swept bare of inhabitants in Chaka's wars. Fynn visited the Zulu tyrant (1824) and won his favour by curing his wounded leg. In a hazy, ignorant fashion Chaka thereafter favoured the handful of English traders, giving them some sort of title to their settlement and even exchanging compliments with the Governor at the Cape; though he permitted no trade except with himself upon his own terms. They never numbered more than forty white men, mostly elephant-hunters who lived an easy half-savage life such as is described in Rider Haggard's early romances. In 1835 they devised the plantation of a colony, laying out the site of a city which they called Durban in honour of the Governor; but the plan was cancelled by Glenelg who saw no profit in it. On the other hand he went so far as to send a magistrate to Natal with authority under an Act of 1836 to exercise criminal jurisdiction over British subjects anywhere south of the twenty-fifth degree of latitude, another offence to the Boers, who saw it as an extension of British sovereignty. In 1835 three American missionaries arrived at Port Natal, and two years later an English clergyman, the Rev. F. Owen, sent by the Church Missionary Society, was actually allowed to live at the royal kraal of Dingaan. Owen drew up the deed granting a concession to Retief's Boers and was the horrified witness of their murder.

The whole short life of the Natal Republic was occupied in futile disputations with the British government and quarrels among the republican leaders. In the panic of 1838 the settlers at Port Natal had withdrawn by sea, leaving to the Boers possession of the whole country, after their triumph on Dingaan's day. Two years of negotiation followed (with two changes in the office of Secretary of State) while Downing Street, blowing now a little hotter or a little colder, maintained the divergent propositions that Natal was not British territory, that some of its native inhabitants were under British protection, that the Boers in Natal were British subjects, and that British subjects remained subject to British jurisdiction anywhere south of the twenty-fifth parallel.

Lord Stanley (Peel's Colonial Secretary), while stoutly refusing either to annex Natal or to admit Boer independence, went so far as to send troops to reoccupy Port Natal in April 1842 with the object of protecting tribes who complained of Boer oppression. A local commando of Boers took arms, besieging the little British garrison until a youth named Dick King brought aid from Grahamstown after riding inland 600 miles through the wild Kaffir country. This little war forced the issue. The Cape Governor sent as Commissioner an Afrikaner, Henry Cloete, to come to terms with the Natal Republic. The Boers, however, solved the problem for themselves by trekking again. While in Natal there was endless trouble with fierce and numerous tribes, and endless irritation by the feeble-forcible British government, up on the High Veld there was freedom for the trekkers. The Natal Republic dwindled and disintegrated, as the farmers straggled north again over the passes of the Drakensberg. In August 1843 Natal became a British colony after some heated conferences with the republican remnant at Pietermaritzburg.

The same forces which obliged the British to intervene in Natal equally drove them to intervention north of the Orange River. Though this was the political frontier, beyond it were allied native kingdoms, under the influence of British missionaries and now threatened by the encroachment of the trek-boers. There were the Griquas and, beyond them, the most virile native race in South Africa, the horse-breeding Basutos, securely based upon their healthy highlands. The British made their first treaty with Moshesh, the Basuto king, in 1843. All through the High Veld, from the Orange to the Vaal and far beyond, there were now 10,000 Boer settlers loosely organised in commandos which formed petty republics, then split and trekked again. Parties of settlers took up land at will, determined to subdue the heathen to honest labour and to be free of the vexatious British. These little states had neither revenue nor administration, hardly even a fixed abode, and were constantly engaged in native wars. Into this confusion there was thrown a new Governor of the Cape, Sir Harry Smith of the Rifle Brigade (1787–1860) who was also appointed the Queen's High Commissioner for all South Africa.

In February 1848 Smith, who knew and liked the Boers and had great self-confidence, took the bold step of declaring British sovereignty over the area between the Orange and the Vaal. Some form of unity for South Africa was already seen as an inevitable goal by the wisest observers. This method might have led to the establishment of free Boer states and protected native kingdoms under the British flag, had not Pretorius the hero of Dingaan's Day, determined to fight. He led a commando to Bloemfontein, where a British agent had resided since 1846, and was neatly and soundly defeated by that very old soldier, Harry Smith, at the smart little action of Boomplatz, 29 August 1848, 'one of the severest skirmishes' he ever saw. Pretorius then fled north across the Vaal River in an irreconcilable mood.

Smith was chosen by the historian of the British Army as the pre-eminent fighting soldier of his generation. After a baptism of fire at Buenos Ayres, he served through the seven campaigns of the Peninsular War. He was present at the burning of Washington and the repulse from New Orleans, and yet returned to Europe in time to have two horses shot beneath him at Waterloo. Throughout the 'thirties he was busily engaged in the Kaffir Wars. Next serving in India he won the brilliant action of Aliwal against the Sikhs, and then returned to the Cape as Governor. After the storm of Badajoz he had rescued two Spanish ladies from the licence of the soldiers. One of them, a young and spirited girl, became his wife and accompanied him on all his campaigns. Her gaiety and courage, his shrewd sense and cool bravery, and the risks they encountered together made the favourite romance of the Peninsular veterans. Their names are commemorated in the two South African towns of Harrismith and Ladysmith.

After the annexation of the north the whole colony enjoyed a brief period of calm under Smith's vigorous and popular administration. The Cape itself was now the centre of a prosperous colony with an expanding home market and a useful export trade in wool. Full self-government, for which the colonists had frequently petitioned Downing Street, had not yet been granted though Smith and the Secretary of State were corresponding over a draft constitution (at last promulgated in 1853). Meanwhile the administration had been progressively improved. The Governor's advisory council had been converted (1833) into a legislative council of the normal Crown Colony type. The larger towns were provided with elective municipal government in the 1830's, the country districts with elective road boards in 1843. A comprehensive educational system, including some schools for coloured children had been instituted in 1839. The South African College, which grew into the University of Capetown, dates from 1829; Victoria College, Stellenbosch, the first Afrikaans university from 1859. The Dutch Reformed Church was given self-government in 1843; the Anglican bishopric of Capetown dates from 1847. One heavy storm blew up over the threat to introduce convict labour, which Smith light-heartedly had invited. When a shipload of convicts arrived in 1849, such a flurry of petitions and threatened resignations blew up that he was forced to refuse them admittance and to divert them to Van Diemen's Land.

In 1850 war broke out again on both frontiers. A renewed struggle with the Kaffirs proved so prolonged and expensive that Smith (like most of his predecessors) was recalled (1852), though the Duke of Wellington protested in Parliament that no man could have done better. While he fought his last campaigns on the eastern frontier other British troops had been forced to intervene in a quarrel between the Boers and the Basuto. Small British columns were twice repulsed by Moshesh from the Basuto highlands to the disgust of the British taxpayer and *The Times* newspaper, which complained lustily of the expense incurred in these never-ending frontier wars. Successive governments had grown heartily sick of the South African problem and all, of whatever political complexion, were anxious to limit their liability. At the time of Smith's recall a conference was taking place at Sand River between the Boer leaders and two British commissioners to define precisely what was the sovereignty proclaimed in 1848. A tardy but reasonable agreement was reached in January 1852 disclaiming British authority over the more distant area beyond the Vaal River. There the British had neither rights nor obligations and there the *voortrekkers* might at last be free. Thus the four rudimentary unorganised Boer states in the far north gained their independence and eventually (1860) coalesced into the Transvaal Republic. But the expenses of the Kaffir war were not yet over and the Basuto were still untamed. The British taxpayers fretted while a great European war threatened in the Near East. The next government went further in limiting liability. In February 1854 at another conference at Bloemfontein the British abdicated their sovereignty over the Orange Free State.[1] The Sand River Convention gave a legal definition to an existing situation and relieved the Transvaal Boers of the threat of unjust persecution. The Bloemfontein Convention was a mere confession of weakness, an act of negation, which persuaded the Boers that a bold front could bluff the British out of any position. There were many British settlers in the Free State, especially in Bloemfontein which was already the seat of an Anglican bishopric, and there is no evidence that the Boers desired independence. Numerous mission stations were centres of British influence among the natives. Two powerful nations, Griqua and Basuto, were deeply embroiled in complex disputes with Boers and British. From these entanglements the British could by no means withdraw.

> Weep, Britain, for the Cape whose ill-starred name,
> Long since divorced from Hope, suggests but shame,
> Disaster, and thy captains held at bay
> By naked hordes. . . .

So wrote a minor poet, considering Kaffir and Basuto victories, governors disgraced after splendid careers, ministers of the

[1] Previously known as the Orange River Sovereignty.

Crown weakly abdicating lawful power; but finding consolation in the story of a shipwreck. Off that rocky, stormy, south-east coast of Africa haunted by the spectre-ship of Vanderdecken,[1] scene of countless piracies and wrecks and founderings in deep water; where so long ago as 1782 the *Grosvenor*, East-Indiaman, took to the bottom a million pounds in gold, while the English men and women who sailed in her were cast away and lost among the savages; where so lately as 1909 a modern liner, the *Waratah*, vanished in a calm sea, on a course that should not have taken her out of sight of land, leaving no trace of her 150 passengers; between Capetown and Port Elizabeth the troopship *Birkenhead* struck a reef in 1852. She carried drafts of young recruits from four British regiments on their way to join the columns fighting in the Kaffir war. In order to hold her on an even keel while the civilians took to the boats, the soldiers were paraded on the quarter-deck and stood in their ranks until the ship went down; 357 out of 506 officers and men perished. That is all, but the story has never been forgotten. The King of Prussia gave orders that it should be read out on parade before every regiment of his army.

[1] Several accounts of the Flying Dutchman are given in Martin's *History of the British Colonies*, vol. IV (1835). She was twice reported from H.M.S. *Leven* in 1823.

VII

THE COLONIAL REFORMERS, 1830–46

Argument: The Malthusian theory led to discussion of relieving unemployment by emigration and, eventually, to Wakefield's theory of systematic colonisation. Lord Durham's report on Canada, largely inspired by Wakefield, was the gospel of the Colonial Reformers. Planned emigration to Australia under control of a Board of Commissioners overcame much opposition and many unexpected difficulties. Wakefield carried out a series of experiments in colonisation on the model of the seventeenth-century colonies, the first in South Australia, the last at Canterbury in New Zealand.

1. EDWARD GIBBON WAKEFIELD

PARLIAMENT was plagued, in the 'thirties and 'forties of last century, by the activities of some persons called the Colonial Reformers. They can hardly be described as a group or party since they rarely acted in concert; at first drawn from the Radicals they later found support among the enlightened Tories. What they had in common was a determination to take the British Empire seriously even if its destiny were disintegration. What they opposed was the idle indifference of British politicians, expressed by one of their number in the truism that 'any government would rather lose a colony than lose a division in the House'. When they first appeared, the Empire, so far as it came into the calculation of politicians, was estimated at its strategic value. There were good naval and military reasons for retaining Gibraltar, Malta, Corfu, the Cape, Mauritius, Ceylon, Newfoundland, Halifax, Bermuda and the Windward Islands. Though free trade was the fashionable doctrine of the new age there were also grounds for protecting the fisheries, the North American timber trade, and West Indian sugar even in despite of the economists; or, at any rate, there were strong interests in favour of their protection, in the House of Commons. Nor could certain sentimental considerations be excluded. There was a debt of honour to the

Canadian loyalists, and even some sort of a duty towards those of our neighbours whom we had exiled to Botany Bay. But on the whole the population of these strategic outposts and other casual dependencies, consisting largely of disaffected Frenchmen, disaffected Dutchmen, white convicts and negro slaves, was felt as a burden rather than a blessing to the imperial government.

With the flowing tide of Evangelical Revival there came a change in this view of the colonies, taking its most definite form when Lord Glenelg, the son of Charles Grant who first sent missionaries to India, was Secretary of State (1835–9). He, and Sir James Stephen, his Permanent Under-Secretary from 1837, gave policy a new direction. It was their glory to free the slaves, and to protect savage races in several parts of the world from exploitation by land-hungry settlers.

But settlers also have rights, and their case was put by the Colonial Reformers. The new factor in the problem was the growing belief that emigration might be a cure for unemployment. The economic principles of the Reformers were utilitarian, deriving from the Malthusian doctrine (1798), that population, which tends to increase by a geometrical progression, must always outrun food supply, which can at best only be increased by an arithmetical progression.[1] This was the basis of Ricardo's theory of marginal rent (1817) and McCulloch's theory of the fixed wage-fund (1826) which together established the new Political Economy as the 'dismal science'. Low wages and chronic unemployment appeared to have been entailed upon the human race as the conditions of material progress. All the evidence then to hand, from the few and imperfect censuses, supported these theories. The population of Great Britain was rising at an astonishing rate: from 10,000,000 in 1801, to 12,000,000 in 1811, 14,000,000 in 1821, and 16,000,000 in 1831. And, although trade was expanding, unemployment seemed to be growing still more rapidly. The Poor Law of 1834, felt by humane men to be a desperate remedy, a cruel necessity, was not the end; the 'Hungry 'Forties' were to follow. Among the Classical Economists the link with the Colonial Reformers was John Stuart Mill (1806–73) who propounded the maxim that 'colonisation, in the present state of the world, is

---

[1] 'When goods increase, they are increased that eat them: and what good is there to the owners thereof, saving the beholding of them with their eyes?' Ecclesiastes v. 2.

the very best affair of business, in which the capital of an old and wealthy country can possibly engage'.

The plain answer to the problem of unemployment seemed to be emigration. To a generation that thought badly of the Americans and never read colonial history, the names of Governor Winthrop, Penn, Baltimore, and Oglethorpe, meant nothing at all. The reasons why some colonies had succeeded while others had failed were quite forgotten, if indeed they had ever been understood in Whitehall. Colonisation was conceived as meaning no more than shipping paupers overseas; and very enlightened colonisation no more than paying their passage overseas to some place where there was already a British governor. The exponent of this simple plan was Sir Wilmot Horton (1784–1841), a philanthropist, who was Under-Secretary for the Colonies in the 1820's. Though he achieved something in the way of providing cheap unskilled labour at the ports of entry in established colonies, his methods could not create new settlements for which capital and skill and organisation and patience were needed. In fact, less than one-seventh of the emigrants from the British Isles in those years were transported by his efforts, to which the Treasury contributed about £20,000 a year. Of that great and growing wave of emigrants (which will be further discussed in chapter IX), some went in conditions of great misery from the slums of British towns to similar marginal employment in Canada or the United States; some were shipped off as paupers at the expense of the parish in accordance with a provision of the new Poor Law; some luckier families were drawn overseas by the attraction of relatives who had already established themselves in a colony; some went in one of the organised parties which are described elsewhere in this book.

The beginnings of a systematic plan of land development in the colonies were to be seen in 1826 when the Canada Land Company was incorporated by Royal Charter under the provisions of an Act of Parliament of 1825. An area of 2,400,000 acres between Lakes Huron and Ontario was sold to the Company for 3s. an acre with the stipulation that one-third of the purchase price was to be spent on bridges, roads, schools and other improvements. The land thus thrown open was to be sold as a commercial transaction to immigrants brought in by the Colonial Office. The originator of this scheme, which made steady progress for many years, was John Galt (1779–1839), the Scottish novelist, who paid

two visits to Canada in 1824 and 1826. Though he made no fortune for himself, he began the settlement of western Ontario.
Seven years later the British American Land Company was similarly incorporated but, taking up land at Sherbrooke in the eastern
townships of Lower Canada, it provoked bitter opposition from
the French-Canadians to whom English land-titles and English
settlers were equally unwelcome.

These were schemes that partially succeeded among many that
failed utterly. Land speculation in the colonies was a byword
among investors who learned painfully that colonisation schemes
were usually Utopian and sometimes fraudulent. New light on
the subject was derived from researches made by a convict in
Newgate. In March 1827, a young man of fashion named Edward
Gibbon Wakefield stood his trial at Lancaster Assizes for abduct-
ing an heiress from a girls' school. Brougham prosecuted and
Scarlett defended in a case without parallel. Wakefield's own
statement, put in as evidence, revealed in him extraordinary elements of recklessness, ingenuity, and bad judgment. He was
thirty years old and this was not his first elopement. When very
young he had made a runaway match and had loved his first wife
dearly. After her death, his brother and his young stepmother
urged him to marry a fortune which would enable him to stand
for Parliament, in the liberal interest. Together they plotted the
abduction of Ellen Turner, a girl of sixteen who was quite unknown to them except by repute. She was inveigled from her
school on some pretence and persuaded to set off with Wakefield,
who now saw her for the first time, on a journey in a post-chaise
which actually brought them to Gretna Green. In those few hours
Wakefield's eloquent tongue revealed the imposture and persuaded her to marry him. The celebrated blacksmith of Gretna
gave evidence of her willing gaiety at the ceremony (and died of a
chill caught on his way home from the trial). Wakefield was sentenced to three years' imprisonment in Newgate. His Parliamentary ambition was restricted to an appearance at the Bar of the
House to protest unsuccessfully against Sir Robert Peel's Bill for
annulling the marriage. This was the end of Wakefield's public
career, his last performance, in a blaze of lurid light, before
fashionable society.

Three years later a changed man was released from Newgate, or
rather a man who showed the other side of his nature. The *flâneur*

who had known Lord Byron in Italy and seconded a duellist in Paris was also the friend of Francis Place the Radical, and was first cousin to Elizabeth Fry. As a convict he studied the reform of the penal code and wrote pamphlets in picturesque and rather violent language upon capital punishment and convict transportation, this last being the bridge that brought him to colonial reform. The reviewers spoke warmly of his work, especially Rintoul of the *Spectator*, with whom he was thereafter closely associated. But his method was to work, he said, like the mole in obscurity. He was, as Ellen Turner knew, remarkably persuasive and, for the next thirty years, was somewhere in the background of every colonising venture and every agitation for colonial rights, rarely showing himself, not often signing his innumerable essays and pamphlets, but preferring to speak through the mouth of some unexceptionable young politician who was free of the taint of Newgate.

The *Letter from Sydney* (1829), fathered upon a young colonist named Robert Gouger, was actually written by Wakefield in prison. It can hardly be believed that the author was a young man who had never seen a colony. It purports to describe the life of a settler who has land and capital in New South Wales but no labour. The English artisans whom he has taken out have left him to set up on their own account as mere subsistence farmers; the convict servants assigned to him are idle and dishonest. He is alone and helpless in the midst of his fine estate surrounded by timber which would be worth a fortune if he could fell it and cart it to Sydney seventy miles away. There may be minerals underground but to what advantage? He cannot 'hew down a tree with a banknote or cleave the soil with a sovereign'.[1] Returning to Sydney he finds society utterly corrupted by sycophancy to the despotic Governor and by the wretched vices of the convicts, a society where he 'must needs associate familiarly with depraved men and women; where to break the law is a merit, and to elude its grasp an honourable achievement; where, above all, human beings are continually hanged in rows, as cattle are slaughtered in the French *abattoirs*'. The shortage of women leads to a prevalence of immoral habits over which he does not mince words. And what is the remedy for all these evils? To supply free labour

---

[1] This graphic and oft-quoted phrase is used by Wakefield's first biographer, Dr R. Garnett. I cannot trace it to Wakefield's writings.

in a fixed ratio to the amount of land occupied. Sydney capitalists, feeling the shortage of labourers, demand that more convicts should be imported but 'however earnestly we may desire it, we cannot expect that the increase of crime will keep pace with the spread of colonisation'. How otherwise can labourers be attracted to the colony and prevented from dispersing into the bush as small proprietors, with no market for their produce and no civilised society for their families?

All can be accomplished if the simple rule is kept of disposing of the public land at a uniform fixed price, and applying the land-fund thus created to paying the passage-money to the colony of selected young emigrants of both sexes, preferably newly-wed couples. This was the doctrine of the 'Sufficient Price' which Wakefield maintained against all critics for the rest of his life. Karl Marx, in a diatribe marked by his usual sardonic perversity, described the Wakefield plan as a new method of capitalist exploitation, whereas it was the opposite in intention and in effect. It aimed at preventing any man, rich or poor, from monopolising more land than he could use; it produced close settlement by resident proprietors, assuring them of a home market. Wakefield's mistake was to suppose that it was a panacea for all colonial ills. *'Concentration'*, he said, 'would produce what never did and never can exist without it—*Civilisation.'*

Within a few years the Wakefield doctrine became the common form of all colonial land-laws. His supporters and his critics alike used his terminology; colonial statesmen accepted or diverged from his norm. The doctrine was adopted, with some hesitation by the Colonial Office for New South Wales in 1831, was approved by a Committee of the House in 1836, and was ratified in an act of Parliament in 1842, though never with sufficient firmness to satisfy its author. Wakefield would never admit that the price had been fixed at a high enough rate in any one instance to demonstrate the full effect of his principle; but when pressed he would never name a standard figure. It must vary according to the local demand for labour. Experience taught him, in the course of years, to shift his ground, to take some few steps to meet critical attacks from this or that quarter, but his main position he doggedly defended.[1] It became an obsession, a *'cacoethes colonizandi'*,

[1] The development of his ideas and their gradual effect upon policy are closely studied in *The Colonisation of Australia*, by R. C. Mills.

said Sir William Molesworth,[1] 'for which he would send to the devil any person or thing that stood in his way'.

If this were all, the Wakefield plan would be a dry corner of history, interesting to economists only, but the gaol-bird who formulated the doctrine of the Sufficient Price had a deeper insight into human affairs. He saw that colonies are made by women as much as by men, that the settler's wife is as valuable a figure as the settler in building a new nation. He first appreciated that a new plantation requires families not single men. He looked forward to a day when the proportion of children to grown-up people in the colonies 'would be greater than ever was known since Shem, Ham and Japhet were surrounded by their little ones. The colony would be an immense nursery, and would offer the finest opportunity that ever occurred, to see what may be done for society by universal education.' This was neither a question of relieving the English Poor Law unions nor even of founding raw new societies; 'they would be so many *extensions* of an old society' requiring not only pauper labourers, but surveyors, architects, engineers, miners, botanists, chemists, printers, schoolmasters, publishers, 'and even reviewers'; surgeons, lawyers, bankers, clergymen, singers, milliners, 'and at least one good Political Economist at each settlement, to prevent us from devising an Australasian tariff'.

Could such a society be conceived without self-government? Would such men as William Penn and Lord Baltimore have crossed the Atlantic if they had known that they would remain subject to the whims of an Under-Secretary at the Colonial Office? The settlements recently attempted in Western Australia and at the Cape were the first examples, in the long history of the Empire, of colonies begun without representative institutions. The errors of the struggle with the American colonies might be avoided in the new Empire for which he pleaded. The colonists 'might either take a share in framing the general laws of the empire, by means of their representatives in the British Parliament; or they might frame their own laws in a Colonial Assembly, under

---

[1] Sir W. Molesworth, Bart. (1810–55) was an independent and a *franc-tireur* in politics, who had been expelled from Cambridge for offering to fight a duel with his tutor. He was the reputed leader of the Colonial Reformers in Parliament after the deaths of Lord Durham and Charles Buller. He, too, died young, shortly after Palmerston had made him Colonial Secretary.

the eye of a viceroy, incapable of wrong and possessing a veto like the King of England, but whose secretaries, like the ministers of England, should be responsible to the people'.

The modern reader of Wakefield's *Letter from Sydney* may well be astonished at his foresight (though neither Wakefield nor any other political economist could foretell the vagaries of the birth-rate in the ensuing century). He is not least illuminating when he writes of political geography: of the errors of diet formed by con-servative Englishmen who have settled in a new province which is the antipodes of Naples; of the emergence of a new physical type in the 'Mediterranean' climate of New South Wales; of the central position of Australia facing the great arc of south-east Asia where lives the greatest mass of the world's peoples; and, as an afterthought, of the possibility of peopling Australia with Chinese coolies if it cannot be peopled with free white men.

2. FIRST EFFORTS OF THE COLONIAL REFORMERS

WAKEFIELD formed the first of his Colonisation Societies in 1831 and reconstituted it as the National Colonisation Society two years later. There were not more than about forty members, then young obscure men but, in several instances, marked for future distinction. They included John Stuart Mill, George Grote the historian, Rintoul of the *Spectator*, Hobhouse who had been Byron's friend, Sir Francis Burdett, Charles Buller, Sir William Molesworth, and other liberal M.P.'s. Robert Gouger, Wake-field's stalking-horse, was secretary. Several Radicals, whose in-terest in the Empire was disruptive rather than creative, though not members of the Society, must be numbered among the Colo-nial Reformers. J. A. Roebuck, a harsh critic of Wakefield's theories, which he did not understand, was London Agent for the restive French-Canadians. Joseph Hume, always to be found with every small minority, actually moved in the House during the debates on the Reform Bill that the colonies should send their representatives to Westminster, a proposal which the honourable members received with shouts of laughter. A few years later, he had swung round and was speaking openly for colonial indepen-dence, as did a much saner man, Sir William Molesworth. Indeed

it would be difficult to find any statement of colonial policy by a
front-bench politician in the eighteen-thirties, putting aside the
utterances of extremists, which did not assume that independence
was the goal of the colonies, whether temporary adjustments in
the imperial connexion were thought desirable or not.

Wakefield had first to persuade his own circle that a constructive policy might make the colonies worthy of preservation, his
own nucleus of disciples who stood by him faithfully being Mill,
Rintoul, Buller and Molesworth. They had a signal triumph in
converting Jeremy Bentham, then in the last year of his long life
(1831), to the doctrine of the Sufficient Price. Less successful was
the attempt to convert Wilmot Horton who attended one of the
early meetings but broke out in furious opposition on finding that
Wakefield's principles of emigration were destructive to his plans.
An early convert was Lord Howick, son of Lord Grey of the Reform Bill and afterwards an energetic Secretary of State. As
Under-Secretary in 1831, he was responsible for the decision that
free grants of land in New South Wales should be forbidden and
that all unappropriated land should be put up for sale at a uniform
price of 5s. per acre. Though the mischief was done as regards the
best land round Sydney which, long previously, had been given
away to favourites of the government, and though Wakefield
thought 5s. a miserably insufficient price, here at least was a
beginning.

In 1829, a somewhat hare-brained scheme was launched for
settling a colony at Swan River in what is now called Western
Australia. Robert Gouger intended to join the party until Wakefield convinced him that the scheme must fail. It combined all the
errors in the art of colonisation which he had already demonstrated. It failed; and Wakefield thereafter used it, not always
quite scrupulously, as the standard example of how not to do
it.[1] Several of the Colonial Reformers then proceeded to plan
an experiment in systematic colonisation on Wakefield's model,
selecting for the site of the experiment the fertile lands discovered
(but not yet explored and mapped) by Captain Sturt near the
mouth of the Murray River. There were six changes in the office
of Secretary of State in the seven years (1830–6) required to
launch the colony. Each of the six successive rulers of the Empire
had to learn the doctrine anew, each must be convinced, and each

[1] For the history of the Swan River Settlement, see chapter VII, 6, page 363.

be stimulated into forcing Parliamentary action in the busy times of the Great Reform Bill. Whatever their party and however faint their interest, the six Secretaries of State were agreed on two points: the colonists should not be released from control by Downing Street, and the colony should not cost the British government a penny.

The first inquiry was politely repulsed by Wellington's government on the grounds that colonies were an expense and we could afford no more of them. In August 1831, three members of the Society, Colonel Torrens, Major Bacon and Gouger, approached the next government, Lord Grey's, with an elaborate plan for founding a joint-stock company with the double role of financing a 'Wakefield' colony and appointing a governor, to control it until it should include 5000 citizens after which it should receive self-government. Sir James Stephen, the permanent Under-Secretary, persuaded his chief to reject this plan as 'wild and unpracticable', unsound financially and above all 'republican'. His opposition, maintained throughout the transitory reigns of several phantoms in the Secretary-of-State's chair, won him the enmity of Wakefield, who never forgot an injury. They should have thought of introducing a House of Lords into Australia, he said, with 'a Viscount Kangaroo and a Bishop of Ornithorhyncus'.

In March 1833, when Lord Stanley was at the Colonial Office, they tried again. Wakefield had just written a new work, *England and America*, in which he compared the generous charters of Penn's and Baltimore's colonies with the petty restrictions imposed by nineteenth-century governments. The reformers now asked for a Chartered Company, not financially interested, but controlling both the finances and the government of the infant settlement through trustees. Stanley positively refused to relinquish political control. Luckily the next incumbent, Spring-Rice, was a school-friend of Wakefield and was persuaded to adopt the financial provisions; though the hope of getting self-government for the new settlement was abandoned. To get a bill through in the busy session of 1834 would have been an impossible task had not Wakefield by some means won the good offices of the Duke of Wellington who now gave his support to the scheme. No sooner had the South Australia Act become law, in August 1834, than the ministry went out, so that no action was taken for another year. The appointment of commissioners became a party matter, most of the original enthusiasts being put out to make room for friends of the ministry. By this time Wakefield's patience was exhausted; he had quarrelled with Gouger over the price of land which, at 12s. an acre, he thought far too low. The new men on the commission were, in his opinion, ignorant amateurs, though their secretary, Rowland Hill (afterwards the postal reformer), was one of the Wakefield school.

For a long time he was abroad at his beloved daughter's death-bed and, in 1835, when he returned, he affected to wash his hands of South Australia which could be regarded as a 'Wakefield' Colony only in an imperfect sense.[1] The settlement, at last planted in 1836, was not called after Wellington as the claims of gratitude should have required, but after Queen Adelaide in the hope of earning the favour of King William IV.

The next activity of the Colonial Reformers was to brief the Parliamentary Committee on Colonial Lands, 1836. Here Wakefield departed from his usual custom of pulling strings in the background. His public evidence before the Committee triumphantly displayed the causes of failure at Swan River and the dangers of failure at Adelaide inasmuch as the Sufficient Price had not been enforced. Though Sir George Grey (of Fallodon[2]), the government representative, voted against each proposal of the reformers, the general sense of the Committee favoured their views. They recommended 'that the whole of the arrangements connected with the sale of land should be placed under the charge of a central Land Board, resident in London', a salutary proposal which was carried out by Lord John Russell after no more than three years' delay.

In the next session the reformers raised the question of the evils of convict transportation. Public attention had been roused by a thoughtful book which Archbishop Whately had published in 1834. He argued that the strongest objection to transportation was that in many cases it meant not punishment but reward. All

---

[1] For the settlement of Adelaide see chapter VII, 6, page 365.

[2] The student of colonial history may be confused by the intermittent appearances of three statesmen named Grey in the mid-nineteenth century. Henry, 3rd Earl Grey (known in his father's lifetime as Lord Howick), was Colonial Secretary in 1846. His cousin Sir George Grey of Fallodon was Colonial Secretary in 1854. Sir George Grey, the Colonial Governor, was of another family.

convicts were brutalised and degraded, but many eventually made their fortunes at Botany Bay and lived in vicious luxury ever after. Transportation failed either to reform or to punish. The work of the Parliamentary Committee of 1837 emerged as a landmark in the history of penal reform, then actively pursued by many who were not much concerned about the colonies. Peel, Russell, Howick and Sir George Grey of Fallodon sat on the Committee as well as Buller and Molesworth, the last-named being chairman. Upon the main issue there was little difference of opinion. It was agreed that the system of transporting convicts in the mass to the colonies should be discontinued as soon as possible, but that penitentiaries should be maintained abroad as well as at home for the reception of convicts sentenced to hard labour. The foreign convict stations, which should be located where there were no free settlers, were required solely because of the lack of accommodation in English prisons. The planting of colonies with exiled criminals ended on 1 August 1840, to the great disgust of the Legislative Council in New South Wales, where ruin for the colony was gloomily predicted.

From 1788 to 1836, 75,200 convicts had been sent to New South Wales; 27,759 had been sent to Van Diemen's Land since 1817. In 1836 there were 25,254 men and 2577 women held as convicts in the former, 14,914 men and 2054 women in the latter. At Norfolk Island there were, in the year 1837, about 1200 convicts, mostly transported again after committing further crimes in New South Wales. There were also 1500 convicts in Bermuda, mostly soldiers and sailors detained for offences against military law.

Van Diemen's Land, Norfolk Island and Bermuda were retained as penitentiaries; no fewer than 35,378 convicts were transported to Van Diemen's Land between 1841 and 1852 when at the urgent request of the free colonists the island was at last released from this burden of depravity. Norfolk Island was abandoned in 1855. The government was hard put to it to find a home for convicted criminals and the Colonial Office was often pressed by the Home Office to accept some batches. In 1846 when Gladstone was at the Colonial Office he varied the procedure by founding in Queensland a settlement for ex-convicts, emancipists from New South Wales. When Lord Grey succeeded him the scheme was abandoned, though the township of Gladstone survived. Here

Plate 9

A MEETING OF THE ANTI-SLAVERY SOCIETY

At Freemason's Hall in 1840. Thomas Clarkson, eighty years old, is speaking. The figure
with dark hair at the top, on the left, is Daniel O'Connell. Beneath and in front of him
is Sir T. F. Buxton. Joseph Sturge is on Clarkson's left. Painted by B. R. Haydon.
See p. 292.

Plate 10

LORD DURHAM (1792–1840)

'Radical Jack.' An engraving after a portrait by G. Richmond. *See p. 341.*

and there capitalists, finding themselves without labour in the days of emancipation, sighed for slaves or convicts, and even begged the Colonial Office to provide them. In general, as free emigration progressed, the decent feelings of the settlers everywhere revolted against accepting the off-scouring of the criminal class. In 1849 an attempt to ship ticket-of-leave men to the new colony of Melbourne was met by the stern refusal of the settlers to admit them and, what is more, they were refused admittance at Sydney also. New Zealand also kept its shores clean.

In the same year a shipload was turned away from Capetown. Lord Grey (formerly Howick), then Colonial Secretary, thought this attempt at transportation justified. 'What will be the consequence when two or three thousand convicts are turned loose upon society in the United Kingdom?' That they should be turned loose among honest men at Melbourne or the Cape seemed to him a matter of less consequence. The Parliamentary debates of 1849 reveal an enlightened approach to the problem, with much sensible discussion of the punitive, deterrent, and reformative effects of transportation. The Tory opposition on the whole denounced it, while the Whig ministry made a guarded defence of the policy of transporting small numbers of selected convicts under careful control. *The Times* took a large part in the controversy with much pregnant quotation from Gibbon Wakefield, but came down on the side of Lord Grey. 'If you do not transport to South Africa', asked the Thunderer in a leader that is often misquoted (27 March 1849), 'whither will you transport your convicts? If you do not send them to your colonies what will you do with them?' English society was saved by the weakness of one colonial governor, Fitzgerald of Western Australia, who expressed his willingness to receive his quota. Accordingly, 9720 male convicts were sent to Western Australia between 1849 and 1868, when the iniquitous system ended.

Naval requirements had brought about the despatch of convicts to Bermuda. The loyal conservative Bermudans had been shaken in their allegiance during the American War. The schooners they built and rigged so skilfully were used for the inter-colonial trade, and the islanders were sorely tempted to maintain the supply of Washington's army, until the rival influence of the King's Navy prevailed when Bermuda was required as a blockading station. The dockyard was not founded, however, until 1810. Not long afterwards the capital was removed from St George to the new township of Hamilton (1815). The population fell in times of peace. From 15,000 in 1780 it declined to 8500 in 1837. Since there were no plantations, slavery in Bermuda was merely domestic; the 4000 negroes worked for 1000 white proprietors and were not available for public works, even after the abolition of slavery. As early as 1824 gangs of white convicts were employed in making the dockyard. Until 1863, an establishment of 1500 convicts, military and naval offenders, was maintained there, each batch returning to England on completion of sentence, so that the islands were rid of them.

The Andaman and Nicobar Islands, the home of very primitive tribes, were occupied, for use as a penitentiary, by the Indian Government in 1857. The Andamans won notoriety for the murder, by a convict, of Lord Mayo, the Viceroy (1872).

3. THE CANADAS AND LORD DURHAM'S MISSION, 1822–39

POLITICAL life in Canada had not developed happily under the constitution of 1791. Though there was often a single Governor-General for the two provinces of Upper (or British) and Lower (or French) Canada, there was constant friction between the two provincial governments and the two races; friction in each province between the elected assemblies and the nominated councils; friction between the legislatures and the executive officers.

In Lower Canada the issue turned on control of the public purse. From 1818 onwards, every session took the form of a wrangle between the Governor and the Assembly over voting the civil list, which the Governors wished to be allocated as in England for a term of years, but which the Assembly attempted to grant or withhold, item by item, at will. The leader of the popular party was Louis Joseph Papineau (1786–1871), the Speaker of the Assembly. After numerous changes of Governor, references to Downing Street, debates in the House of Commons, and after the failure of a Royal Commission to adjust grievances, a complete deadlock was reached. From 1831 to 1835 the Assembly was repeatedly prorogued without transacting any legislative business, having refused to vote Supply. Their grievances were put forward in a series of demands (February 1834) for unconditional control of the revenue, for an elective upper chamber, for repeal of the imperial statutes which had modified French feudal tenures, for cancellation of the charter of the British American Land Company, and for various restrictions upon Crown patronage and the power of the executive. The Whig government in London made some concessions to these demands but authorised the Governor to pay the overdue expenses of government by appropriating the funds then in the Colonial Treasury. At the news of this decision the Assembly protested furiously and was prorogued for the last time (August 1837).

Meanwhile a parallel agitation had been felt in Upper Canada though there the issue was not embittered by a racial feud. An enthusiast named Robert Gourlay had struck at the root of the matter, at a political convention at Toronto in 1822, by making suggestions for public control of land settlement which found their way into the plans of later reformers. The deadlock in Upper Canada was formed by the permanent composition of the Governor's Executive Council, the 'Family Compact', which persisted, unchanged and irresponsible through the terms of office of governor after governor. Control of the revenue and the land-grants was theirs, it seemed, for life. The strongest man among them was an Anglican clergyman, John Strachan, a Loyalist and great Church organiser but a tactless politician, who was determined to maintain the rights of his own communion in a province which was increasingly Scottish and Presbyterian. In 1839 he became Bishop of Toronto.

The leader of revolt against the Family Compact was William Lyon MacKenzie (1795–1861), a somewhat violent journalist who became the first Mayor of Toronto when it was incorporated as a city, in 1834. He drifted away from the more moderate reformers to make common cause with Papineau in Lower Canada and with the Radical, Joseph Hume, in the British House of Commons. Hume gave great offence to the loyal Canadians, who wanted only an improved constitution, by foretelling a crisis in Canada 'which will terminate in independence and freedom from the baneful domination of the mother-country'. A new Governor, Sir Francis Head, failed as all his predecessors had failed to come to terms with the reformers, though he did work for a time with the most able of them, Robert Baldwin (1804–58), the reputed inventor of the device later known as responsible government. Similar crises had repeatedly occurred in each of the three Maritime Provinces and in Newfoundland, the most eminent reformer in the east being Joseph Howe, the editor of the *Nova Scotian*.

In the autumn of 1837 Lower Canada was in a state of passive rebellion. The Assembly was prorogued, the revenues were not collected, the administrative machine had run down and stopped. Actual bloodshed was limited by the preventive measures of the military commander Sir John Colborne, who in his day had delivered the decisive counter-attack at Waterloo and was not to be caught unaware. He concentrated troops at Montreal and was ready for anything. On 23 October, when the movement of reinforcements from England was stopped by the freezing of the St Lawrence, a republic was proclaimed at St Charles, on the Richelieu River, the road to the United States, by an English Radical named Nelson. Colborne sent a party of troops who dispersed these rebels almost without fighting and took Nelson prisoner. Papineau, who had gone to join with Nelson, fled over the American frontier rather ignominiously. Stimulated by the rumour of these doings a few villages west of Montreal had armed and entrenched themselves. In December Colborne marched against these misguided peasants and defeated them, killing about seventy in a skirmish at St Eustache, which ended the rebellion in French Canada. Montreal was calmed by the efforts of Mgr Martigue the Bishop, who denounced rebellion as sin.

It seemed more alarming that a revolution should begin at Toronto in the land of the loyalists. There MacKenzie assembled a band of frontiersmen, some of them filibusters from the American side, with the intention of seizing the city which had been denuded of troops for the concentration at Montreal. But at the first show of force his followers melted away and he, too, fled over the American frontier. A 'provisional government' for Canada was then formed on American soil and, for some months, riots and raids were reported from several points on the unpoliced border.

The news from Canada provoked Lord Melbourne to characteristic action. Something must be done, and two nuisances might be cured together if a dangerous rival could be sent to do it. He therefore decided, in January 1838, to send the Earl of Durham to North America with a multiple authority as Captain-General, High Commissioner and Governor-in-Chief of all the provinces, including Newfoundland. Lord Durham (1792–1840), the first of his line to accept a peerage, was head of an ancient family, the Lambtons of Lambton Castle, whose wealth had been vastly increased by the development of collieries. As a young man in Whig society he had been celebrated for his off-hand remark that a man should be able to 'jog along on £40,000 a year'. He had made his name in Parliament as one of the committee appointed to draft the Great Reform Bill, and had broken with Lord Grey, his father-in-law, when the passing of the Bill was not followed by further radical reforms. Marked down as an extreme liberal he was nevertheless too proud, too pure-bred a Whig, to be classed as one of the doctrinaire Radicals. A brilliant, queer-tempered man and a bad colleague, he was admired and feared and excluded from office. Guizot, the French ambassador 'perceived in his haughty melancholy a strong imprint of egotism and vanity'. *The Times* described him as 'vainglorious, perverse and reckless'. Melbourne sent him as ambassador to Russia in 1836 and was glad to be able to send him next to Canada. The first statesman of cabinet rank ever to be made governor of a colony, Durham had no intention of submitting to departmental instructions from the Colonial Office. Conceiving his mission as a Viceroyalty, he used pomp as an instrument of power, laid careful preparations, travelled in state at great personal expense, and proposed to act with bold decision when he should be quite ready. He selected his staff with care and deliberation, choosing as confidential secretary Charles Buller (1806–48), a young liberal M.P., the friend and pupil of Carlyle. Buller's lively critical memoir is the best account of Durham's mission. He also wished to appoint two expert advisers, Wakefield for the public lands and Thomas Turton for the judicial system; but the high-minded Glenelg positively forbade the appointment of the disreputable Wakefield who, nevertheless, accompanied Durham privately, with 'no ostensible employment'. Turton's career, like Wakefield's, had been clouded by a domestic scandal which was disinterred and flaunted in Durham's face by his political enemies. The long delay from January to April before Durham sailed for Canada was an error which 'took the bloom off the mission'. The crisis seemed to have subsided and the pomp which Durham affected seemed superfluous, all the more as it was tarnished by the Turton scandal.

On reaching Quebec Lord Durham was well received by the British-Canadians but with 'sullen and distant apathy' by the French. He set himself at once to the actual routine of government in Lower Canada where all was anarchy. At the end of six weeks his imperious activity had so far restored order that he took the step of celebrating the young Queen's Coronation day (28 June 1838) by proclaiming a general amnesty to the hundreds of rebels who were under arrest, excepting eight named leaders whom he banished to Bermuda, forbidding them to return on pain of death. Those other rebel leaders who were still plotting further rebellion from their retreat in the United States were also threatened with death if they should re-enter Canada. The amnesty gave general satisfaction throughout North America, even going some distance towards mollifying the French. According to Buller it was approved in a despatch from Glenelg to which was added an autograph letter from the Queen.

In July, Durham visited Upper Canada, making a short stay at Niagara where he impressed the filibusters by holding a review of troops. He minimised the importance of the petty tumults on this unruly frontier, setting himself to secure cordial relations both with Washington and with the neighbouring Americans. He had already sent his brother-in-law on a complimentary visit to President Van Buren and now took pains to pay courteous attentions to American visitors at Niagara, a welcome change from the haughty aloofness of earlier British officials. 'A million of money would have been a cheap price', wrote Buller, 'for the glass of wine which Lord Durham drank to the health of the American President.' Next he turned his attention to the affairs of the Maritime Provinces which sent deputations to represent their grievances to him at Quebec.

He was now at the height of his career, busy and triumphant when rumours reached the Dictator (as his staff affectionately nicknamed him) that renewed attacks had been launched against him in Parliament by his rival, Brougham, as well as by his opponents, the Tories. Lord Melbourne's government, basely giving way, passed an act restricting the scope of Durham's commission and disallowed his ordinance of 28 June, on the grounds that he had exceeded his authority by the banishments to Bermuda. Addresses poured in to the Dictator from all parts of British North America assuring him of much loyal support, but Durham's pride would not allow him to remain in office after such a snub. He instantly resigned and went further by attacking his political enemies in a proclamation (9 October 1838) announcing his departure. He assured the Canadians that he would defend their interests against 'some persons too apt to legislate in ignorance and indifference'.

On 1 November 1838, Durham sailed from Quebec in a ship with the ill-omened name of *Inconstant*. 'The sky was black with clouds', wrote Buller, 'bearing the first snow-storm of the winter, and hardly a breath of air was moving. The streets were crowded; the spectators filled every window and every housetop; and though every hat was raised as we passed, a deep silence marked the general grief for Lord Durham's departure. His own presentiments depressed him and those about him, for he had told me and others that he did not expect to reach England alive.' No sooner was he gone than rebellious outbreaks were renewed in both provinces and were again suppressed by Colborne without much difficulty (November 1838).

Durham's health, never strong, had broken down under the strain of his efforts and disappointments. Commissioned in January 1838, he had reached Canada in May; he resigned in October and was back in England in December. The Durham Report which refashioned the British Empire, was debated in Parliament on 11 February 1839. After completing his report he took little part in public life. He died eighteen months later at the early age of forty-eight.

4. THE DURHAM REPORT AND ITS CONSEQUENCES

IT was not to be supposed that Lord Durham's report was all original or all new. Since he had taken pains to consult the most enlightened opinion in Canada and England no one need be surprised that many of his recommendations had been anticipated by students of Canadian affairs. He would have been foolish indeed if he had not taken their advice. He even appealed to the sym-

pathy of the young Queen by pointing out that her father, the
Duke of Kent, had foreshadowed one of the recommendations
when serving in Canada in 1799. Nor is there any truth in the
bitter jibe made by Brougham to Macaulay as they walked
together in Lincoln's Inn Fields on 13 February 1839: 'The
matter came from a swindler [Wakefield], the style from a
coxcomb [Buller], while the Dictator furnished only six letters,
D.U.R.H.A.M.' The Report is graced here and there with
flashes of Buller's lively wit and is strengthened with the close
contexture of Wakefield's forceful argument in those passages
dealing with subjects in which he was expert; clearly Durham
would not have employed these men if he had not intended to
make use of their talents. He was no niggling bureaucrat, but a
bold statesman with a contempt for small views and petty vanities
and selfish interests. The breadth of vision, the nobility of sentiment in the Report are his own. His prescription for producing
a free, prosperous, and loyal nation was threefold: he called for
political union, administrative reform, and the device which is
known, not very lucidly, as responsible government.

The Report is lengthy; it extends to more than 300 pages, excluding the appendices, in the standard edition prepared by Sir
C. P. Lucas, nearly one-half of it being devoted to the future of
the French in Lower Canada. Were they to be absorbed into
a common citizenship with the British or were they to become
(as in fact they have become) a *nation canadienne*? Of Lower
Canada Lord Durham wrote: 'I expected to find a contest between a government and a people: I found two nations warring
in the bosom of a single state: I found a struggle, not of principles,
but of races; and I perceived that it would be idle to attempt any
amelioration of laws or institutions until we could first succeed in
terminating the deadly animosity that now separates the inhabitants
of Lower Canada into the hostile divisions of French and English.' Lord Durham was far from displaying any national prejudice against the character of the French, who were not wanting
in those virtues which 'common consent attributes to the nation
from which they spring. They are mild and kindly, frugal, industrious and honest, very sociable, cheerful, and hospitable, and
distinguished for a courtesy and real politeness, which pervades
every class of society.' He paid a particular tribute to the Catholic
clergy who 'to a very remarkable degree, conciliated the goodwill

of persons of all creeds'. 'I know of no parochial clergy in the world whose practice of all the Christian virtues is more universally admitted.' But, having paid these tributes, he enlarged upon the conservative habit of mind of the French; deplored their obstructiveness against all forms of improvement and especially those forms of improvement which extended British influence into French-Canadian districts; and described the breakdown of all administration and the loss of public confidence which the recent rebellion had brought about. The French were irreconcilable. 'I feel confident that the accuracy and moderation of my description will be acknowledged by all who have seen the state of society in Lower Canada during the last year. Never again will the *present generation*[1] of French-Canadians yield a loyal submission to a British Government; never again will the English population tolerate the authority of a House of Assembly, in which the French shall possess a majority.'

The causes of dissension among the British in Upper Canada were altogether different, and not deep-rooted. Theirs were faulty institutions which could be remedied by a return to the true English principles of government. The rebellion in Upper Canada was not a national movement but the 'foolishly contrived and ill-conducted attempt' of a handful of persons in an exasperated country. 'Almost the entire body of the reformers of this province sought only by constitutional means to obtain the objects for which they had so long peaceably struggled before the unhappy troubles occasioned by a few unprincipled adventurers and heated enthusiasts.' At the threat of an invasion by ruffians from across the border the general population 'turned out with unanimity to defend their country'.

The disorders were occasioned by defects in the constitution which were common to Upper and to Lower Canada, even though there were underlying and graver causes in the case of Lower Canada only. 'It may fairly be said that in all these colonies [including Prince Edward Island, New Brunswick, Nova Scotia and even Newfoundland] the natural state of government is that of collision between the executive and the representative body. In all of them the administration of public affairs is habitually confided to those who do not co-operate harmoniously with the popular branch of the legislature.'

[1] My italics. C.E.C.

In addition to these two principal weaknesses—the racial feud
and the inadequate political institutions—there were many particular defects in all parts of the administration and all of them
aggravated in Lower Canada by the hostile attitude of the French.
The judiciary was insufficient; the juries were corrupt—in Lower
Canada so partial that civil justice was no longer administered;
there was no police force, except in Quebec and Montreal where
Durham himself had instituted it. Stipendiary magistrates and a
Supreme Court of British North America were much to be desired. There was no general system of public education except,
and this is the one exception in their favour,[1] among the French
whose Church made itself responsible for parish schools. It was
no credit to the British, as good Bishop Macdonell pointed out in
a letter couched in courteous and loyal terms, that the government, having suppressed the Order of the Jesuits (1774) in
Canada, had applied their educational endowments to the Secret
Service fund. A fundamental defect was the absence of municipal
institutions. 'The people should have been trained for taking
their part in the concern of the Province, by their experience in
the management of that local business which was most interesting
and most easily intelligible to them. But the inhabitants of Lower
Canada were unhappily initiated into self-government at exactly
the wrong end.'

Durham made an acute remark upon the parochial character of
politics in a colony. 'I know of no greater difference in the
machinery of government in the old and new world than the
apparently undue importance which the business of constructing
public works appears to occupy....If an individual is asked how
his own legislature has acted, he will generally say what roads or
bridges it has made, or neglected to make, in his own district.' In
this respect the British provinces were far more backward than
the neighbouring American states where public works were developed by self-governing municipalities. The report frequently
turns aside to draw unflattering parallels between the two sides of
the frontier. (It is fair to say that the author of *Martin Chuzzlewit*,

[1] Durham appears to be confining these strictures to the British minority in
Lower Canada. A common-school system on the American, or Scottish, model
had been instituted in Upper Canada in 1816, in Nova Scotia even earlier.
Canadian Education, perhaps, owes more to Egerton Ryerson (1803–82), the
Methodist leader, than to any other man. He was Superintendent of the schools
of Upper Canada from 1844 to 1876.

who visited Canada and the United States a year or two later, did
not find conditions in the Great Republic so rose-coloured.) 'On
the American side, all is activity and bustle. The forest has been
widely cleared; every year numerous settlements are formed, and
thousands of farms are created out of the waste; the country is
intersected by common roads; canals and railroads are finished or
in course of formation. Good houses, warehouses, mills, inns,
villages, towns and even great cities, are almost seen to spring up
out of the desert.... On the British side of the line, with the exception of a few favoured spots, where some approach to American
prosperity is apparent, all seems waste and desolate.' There were
only fifteen miles of railway in Canada; the roads were so bad that
wheat could be shipped more cheaply from Toronto to Liverpool
than from the farm where it was grown, ninety miles away, to
Toronto. Local improvements were made the instruments of
political jobbery. The development of roads and canals from the
seaports of Lower Canada to the rich resources of Upper Canada
was obstructed by the French who refused to contribute to the
cost. The revenue of Lower Canada, deriving largely from
customs-duties, showed a surplus which was never usefully employed; the finances of Upper Canada were burdened with debt,
partly as a result of French unhelpfulness but partly the consequence of their own improvidence.

The backwardness of public works was closely connected with
the misuse of public lands, and here Wakefield contributed his
quota to the report. On the other side of the frontier the 'system
of the United States appears to combine all the chief requisites of
the greatest efficiency. It is uniform throughout the vast federation; it renders the acquisition of new land easy; and yet, by
means of a price, restricts appropriation to the actual wants of the
settler; it provides for accurate surveys; it gives an instant and
secure title; and it admits of no favouritism. That system has promoted an amount of immigration and settlement, of which the
history of the world affords no other example; and it has produced
to the United States a revenue which has averaged about half a
million sterling per annum.' On the other hand, excepting the
experiments of the Canada Land Company, there had never been
any regular system in the British North American colonies.
Grants of land, far larger than the requirements of any settler, had
been made profusely to the favourites of government without

accurate survey, without secure titles, without access or communications. The practice of reserving one-seventh of the land for the clergy had merely sterilised one-seventh of the land, since the clergy could not take it up. Both large and small grants were commonly sold off to speculators for a nominal price when it was found that there were no facilities for cultivating them. Even the grants to loyalists and old soldiers had been made at the maximum expense to the government and the minimum advantage to the grantees. Not one-tenth of them had persevered to cultivate the land granted. The most shocking case was Prince Edward Island which had been entirely alienated, in sixty-seven grants to proprietors who were mostly absentees, with the effect that of nearly 1,400,000 acres in that fertile island only 100,000 were under cultivation. Emigration to Canada had dwindled from 50,000 in the year 1831 to 5000 in 1838 because of the political disturbances, the appalling reports of misery in the emigrant ships, and the failure to settle the newcomers effectively on the land. And of the emigrants who landed, an unknown number—perhaps half—had drifted over the border into the United States.

This accumulated record of lethargy and corruption did not oppress the buoyancy of Lord Durham. His recommendations were few and practical and he closed his report with an optimistic forecast. Having considered and rejected the confederation of the North American colonies he decided 'that tranquillity can only be restored by subjecting Lower Canada to the vigorous rule of an English majority; and that the only efficacious government would be that formed by a legislative union'. This would deprive the French of no political liberty or privilege but would tend to absorb them into the English majority, in the course of time, as the French of Louisiana had been absorbed into the English-speaking majority of the United States, an analogy which he developed at some length. He proposed to solve the problem of the relations between executive and legislature by 'precisely that limitation of their respective powers which has been so long and so easily maintained in Great Britain'. Each colonial governor should be instructed, 'by a single despatch' requiring no legislation, 'to secure the co-operation of the Assembly in his policy, by entrusting its administration to such men as could command a majority'. This was the device known as responsible government, the Governor under such a system being made responsible to the Assembly in the colony rather than to the Secretary of State in Downing Street. Responsible government was the crux of the matter and became the subject of fierce controversy at home and in every colony. It implied the discontinuance of that vexatious interference by the Colonial Office in the affairs of the colonies, excepting in certain matters of high policy which were reserved for the imperial government. Durham proposed to reserve three subjects only, the form of the colonial constitution, the regulation of foreign affairs and external trade, and the disposal of the public lands which should be held, he said, as the birthright of the crowded millions of Great Britain rather than the private property of the first-comers to a new settlement.

He intended that the Union should embrace all the British colonies in North America including Newfoundland, since all had common problems of communications and defence and almost all were separately concerned in diplomatic disputes with the United States. 'The preservation of the present general sympathy of the United States with the policy of our Government is a matter of the greatest importance'; but the disposition of the American frontiersmen towards filibustering could not be neglected. Whether all the colonies were to be united or not, the immediate union of Upper and Lower Canada was urged as a measure that would admit no delay, while the establishment of a common currency, a postal union, a customs union and a supreme court for all the colonies were hardly less desirable. Municipal administration should everywhere be introduced on a uniform plan. The public lands should be taken under imperial control and administered on the principles discussed above. The clergy reserves should be abolished. Several useful suggestions were also made for preventing corruption in the assemblies and the law-courts.

But the most unexpected feature of Lord Durham's recommendations is his forecast of what might be done by centralising the public works under a single government. 'The great discoveries of modern art [*sic*], which have entirely altered the character and the channels of communication between different countries, will bring all the colonies into constant and speedy intercourse with each other. The success of the great experiment of steam navigation across the Atlantic (1833) opens a prospect which will materially affect the future state of all these provinces. ...The formation of a railroad from Halifax to Quebec would

entirely alter some of the distinguishing characteristics of the
Canadas...it would supersede the lower part of the St Lawrence,
as the outlet of a great part of the Canadian trade, and would make
Halifax, in a great measure, an outport to Quebec.'...'The
great natural channel of the St Lawrence gives all the people
who dwell in any part of its basin an interest in the government of
the whole.'

Here was a country, wrote Lord Durham, where 'an almost
boundless range of the richest soil still remains unsettled. The
wealth of inexhaustible forest and the most valuable minerals
have as yet been scarcely touched. Around each island and in each
river, are to be found the greatest and richest fisheries in the
world. The country which has founded and maintained these
Colonies at a vast expense of blood and treasure, may justly expect
its compensation in turning their unappropriated resources to the
account of its own redundant population; they are the rightful
patrimony of the English people.'

'I cannot participate in the notion', he wrote in his peroration,
'that it is the part either of prudence or of honour to abandon
our countrymen when our government of them has plunged them
into disorder, or our territory, when we discover that we have not
turned it to proper account. The experiment of keeping colonies
and governing them well ought at least to have a trial.'

The Durham Report was received in French Canada with dismay,
in British Canada with bitter criticism from those who feared
that it would deprive them of the spoils of office. The Colonial
Reformers everywhere accepted it as a new gospel. It was avidly
read in South Africa, Australia and the West Indies, but at Westminster attention was diverted by a storm in a political teacup.
Lord Melbourne's government went out in May 1839 and was
reconstituted after the incident known to students of the
constitution as the 'Bedchamber Question'. Nothing could be
done for North America at such critical times. However, when the
political shuffle and the new deal were completed, the colonies
were found to have benefited by the appearance of Lord John
Russell at the Colonial Office. Though Molesworth had moved a
vote of censure on Glenelg in 1838 the latter clung to his job until
February 1839, unmoved by the Great Trek and the Canadian
Rebellion which, said Brougham wickedly, 'must have cost him

many a sleepless day'. Yet he could not be displaced until a sufficiently fat sinecure was found as a consolation for him. Russell
persuaded the cabinet to accept the greater part of Durham's
recommendations but not 'what is absurdly called responsible
government'. He either did not understand or would not accept
Durham's revelation that self-government for the colonies implied an abdication of power by the Colonial Secretary. He still
intended that colonial governors should be guided by his instructions and not by the advice of a colonial ministry; and, when the
Tories returned to office in 1841, his successor Lord Stanley was of
the same opinion.

Between 1839 and 1845 Canada was ruled successively by
three able and eminent governors-general: Poulett Thomson
(afterwards Lord Sydenham), 1839–41, who was killed in a riding
accident; Sir Charles Bagot, the negotiator of the Treaty of 1818
with the United States, who died after holding office for only
a few months; and Sir Charles Metcalfe, 1843–5, who, after
thirty-seven years in India, was slowly dying throughout his
term of office. Between them they carried out many of Durham's
administrative proposals and moved cautiously towards his
constitutional policy.

Sydenham scored a great personal success by persuading the
administrations of Upper and Lower Canada to accept the union.
An act was accordingly passed through the imperial Parliament in
1840 and a joint Canadian legislature was summoned in 1841 at
Kingston. Under the new constitution the Civil List was assured
to the Governor. With the aid of a loan of £1,500,000, negotiated
by Russell's aid, Sydenham established a Public Works Department and launched a programme of improvements. The system
of allotting Clergy Reserves was abolished[1] by the Union Government which, in spite of Wakefield's theories and Durham's
recommendations, was given unhindered control of public lands.
County courts and rural district councils were instituted tenta-
tively in Upper Canada. So far so good, but the clash between the
executive and the legislative branches of government was post-

[1] In spite of Sydenham's efforts, the influence of Bishop Strachan in London
secured the retention of the Clergy Reserves system until 1854. The seigneurial
tenures were also commuted upon reasonable terms in that year.

I take the opportunity of mentioning the researches of Mr Paul Bloomfield.
His life of *Edward Gibbon Wakefield* (1961) throws new light on the policy of
these Governors.   C.E.C.

poned only by tact and compromise. Bagot's term of office was chiefly taken up with diplomatic affairs. This was the period of the American Presidential election fought on the issue of annexing much British territory in North America (see chapter v, 8, page 278). The Ashburton-Webster Treaty, 1842, delimiting the frontier between New Brunswick and Maine, owes something to the steadying influence of Bagot. He did his best to rally moderate men from the English and French parties in the legislature into a popular administration, and lost the confidence of the Colonial Office by doing so. Metcalfe was sent out as a strong man to retrieve the position by reasserting the authority of the Crown. His method was to act as Prime Minister, forming a Cabinet and appealing to the country to support his policy. At the bitterly contested election of 1844 he got a bare majority. It was a gallant fight which brought Sir James Stephen of the Colonial Office to the gloomy opinion that 'Canada appears to have shaken off, or laid aside, the colonial relation to this country, and to have become, in everything but name, a distinct state.... There are this moment, in Canada, almost as many Europeans as there were in the United States when they declared their independence—a very pregnant fact.'

While Whig and Tory leaders in England agreed in confusing this simple issue, the plain way out was again demonstrated by a colonial statesman, in the little province of Nova Scotia. The principle of responsible government, which Robert Baldwin had propounded and which Durham had recommended, was flatly demanded by Joseph Howe in his published *Letters to Lord John Russell* (September 1839). His six years' struggle followed the same lines as that in Canada but achieved an earlier victory. In 1846 the Whigs again returned to office in England with Russell now as Prime Minister, and Henry, 3rd Earl Grey (1802–94) as Colonial Secretary. Now at last the office at Downing Street was in the hands of a statesman who neither regarded the colonials as an encumbrance to the garrison of his fortresses, nor assumed that missionaries were always right and settlers always wrong, nor subordinated colonial reform to party advantage. On 3 November 1846, Grey instructed the Governor of Nova Scotia, Sir John Harvey, to apply the principle of responsible government, his despatch being quoted as 'applicable to all colonies having a similar form of government'. The triumph was due to the steady,

Plate 11

SIR JAMES STEPHEN (1789–1859)

'Mr Mother-country', from a bust by A. Munro, said by his daughter
to be an excellent likeness. *See p. 390.*

Plate 12 A

W. C. WENTWORTH
(1793–1872)

Leader of the popular party in
New South Wales. *See p. 354.*

Plate 12 B

JOHN MACARTHUR
(1767–1834)

Founder of the pastoral wealth
of Australia, leader of the 'exclusives'. *See p. 213.*

loyal and constitutional propaganda of Howe and to the support given him by Charles Buller in the House of Commons.

Lord Elgin introduced responsible government in Canada in 1848, the first ministry being formed by Robert Baldwin and the moderate French leader, Louis Hippolyte Lafontaine. Such was Grey's confidence that he even suggested the admission to office of Papineau, the returned rebel—if the majority should ask for him; but Papineau's influence had faded. The frenzy of Canadian politics could not be expected to be calmed for ever by so simple, though salutary, a change. In 1849 Governor Elgin incurred unpopularity with the Tory Canadians by signing the bill for reparation to French sufferers in the late rebellion. In the ensuing riots he was stoned in the streets, and the public buildings at Montreal were burned. Another cry, for secession from the Empire, was raised when Canadian preferences were abolished by the successive movements of the imperial government towards Free Trade. The answer to this complaint was provided by Elgin's Treaty of Reciprocity with the United States, 1854 (see pages 545–6).

5. LIFE IN THE AUSTRALIAN COLONIES,
1820–50

AT the census of 1828 Sydney town was found to contain 13,000 inhabitants, about one-third of the population of the colony. A thriving port with a considerable trade in ship-chandling, it was better supplied with public works, the result of convict labour, than other colonial capitals. Though Governor Phillip began with some notions of town-planning they were forgotten during the corrupt days of the New South Wales Corps, with the result that the city grew up planless in the gullies sloping down to Sydney Cove. Governor Macquarie (1809–21), a man of a liberal and improving turn of mind, encouraged educated men among the 'emancipists' to come forward and take their place in society when released from the status of convicts, a policy which Macarthur and the older generation of 'exclusives' bitterly resented. Among the emancipists whom Macquarie favoured was a Bristol architect, Francis Greenway (1777–1837), transported for fraudulent bankruptcy. He was encouraged to build several public offices and churches (notably St James's, Sydney) in a severe but

elegant Regency style that can still be detected here and there in
the older settlements of New South Wales. Had Greenway remained in favour Sydney would have been a more spacious city
today, for he prepared street-plans and even indulged in a fancy,
a hundred years before his time, of bridging the harbour. But his
schemes were obstructed by the 'exclusives' and finally stopped,
on grounds of economy, by Commissioner Bigge. Greenway
died in obscurity and Sydney grew haphazard, depending for its
singular beauty upon its natural surroundings, not its architecture.

The emancipists found a voice in William Charles Wentworth
(1793–1872) when, as a result of Bigge's Commission, a limited
measure of civil liberty was granted. The New South Wales Judi-
cature Act (4 Geo IV, c. 96) checked the Governor's sole authority by providing a nominated Legislative Council, a Supreme
Court, and trial by jury in civil causes.

Wentworth was not, himself, an emancipist; he was born at
Norfolk Island, the son of a lawyer who had made his own way to
Australia to avoid disgrace. As a young lad, Wentworth was
selected by Macquarie for the post of Deputy Provost-marshal
which must have inured him to the harsher features of life in a
convict colony. In 1813 he accompanied Blaxland at the crossing
of the Blue Mountains, a contrasting experience from which he
returned a convinced enthusiast for the wealth and greatness of
a free colonial empire.

Pausing, like Rhodes fifty years later, in his colonial career, he
visited England, became a fellow-commoner at Peterhouse, Cambridge, and was called to the Bar. On his return he founded a
newspaper, *The Australian* (1824), which conducted an agitation
for reform. Though he appeared as the leader of the despised
emancipists he was at heart an aristocrat, as ruthless as Strafford
whom he claimed as his ancestor, as greedy for power as Ralegh
whom he greatly admired. Two successive governors (Sir T.
Brisbane, 1822–5, and Sir R. Darling, 1825–31) endeavoured to
come to terms with Wentworth, as their contemporaries in
Canada were endeavouring to do with Papineau, but without success. They were successively recalled after failing to reconcile
their obedience to the Colonial Office with their duty to their
turbulent subjects. The former had fallen foul of the exclusives,
the latter of the emancipists. A more subtle effort for reform was
made by the Chief Justice, Francis Forbes, who recommended in

a confidential letter to the Colonial Office (October 1826) the same remedy that Robert Baldwin prescribed for the woes of Canada, perhaps the earliest suggestion of responsible government. Like Baldwin's, Forbes's appeal fell on deaf ears. New South Wales was not yet self-supporting in food nor could it show a balanced revenue-account. Convicts cost the imperial government £24 a head per annum, a subsidy to the colony which destroyed the claim to self-government.

Van Diemen's Land was separated from New South Wales in 1824 and made a distinct colony under Sir George Arthur, a puritan and a martinet. This beautiful and fertile island with its soft English climate was made hell by 'man's hate'. Nearly half the population (7449 out of 16,924 at the census of 1828) were convicts, many of them second offenders in punishment camps; the other half, the settlers, waged a perpetual war of extermination against the blacks, pathetic relics of the Old Stone Age with whom no civilised contact seemed possible. Nothing could make them understand the white man's notions of property in land or the difference between untended sheep and wild game. No considerable effort was made to come to terms with them until Governor Arthur decided to bring them to parley and to locate them for their own protection. To do this he was obliged to drive the country, at a cost of £30,000. Elusive to the last, they slipped through his cordons, vanishing into the Bush; or merely died to avoid the menace of civilisation. The survivors, penned at last in one peninsula, were removed to Flinders Island where forty-four still lived in 1847. The last full-blood died in 1876.

Between the settlers and the convicts in each of the penal colonies was a marginal population of runaways who had taken to the Bush, and lived by stealing sheep or raiding the remoter homesteads. These were the bushrangers—the name is first recorded at Sydney in 1806—who reached their prime in Van Diemen's Land. Michael Howe, the worst of them, was hunted down and killed in 1818. An atmosphere of false romance idealised these southern Robin Hoods; among them Martin Cash, who twice escaped from the punishment camp at Port Arthur, came nearest to deserving it. Governor Arthur was obliged to wage a regular campaign against the bushrangers of his day. For two years Matthew Brady, 'governor of the ranges', defied the Governor of Hobart Town until he was taken (1826) by a bold pioneer,

John Batman, afterwards renowned as the founder of Melbourne. The colony, so cursed in its birth, now knew tranquillity and the free settlers blessed the name of Governor Arthur. He reappeared in imperial history as the 'timid and inert' governor of Upper Canada who brought that province to disaster in 1838, having found that ruling free men was a harder task than ruling prisoners and savages. As Wellington said of Governor Brisbane, 'there are many brave men not fitted to be governors of colonies'. The most popular of the island's Governors (1837–43) was Sir John Franklin the explorer, a founder of schools and public works.

Hobart, beneath its snowy mountain and beside its blue harbour, grew up an Italianate town with buildings of dressed stone. Like Sydney it took shape before the Gothic Revival reached Australia. Settlement in Van Diemen's Land spread northwards from Hobart and southwards from Launceston, which was founded in 1806. The older districts contain several stone mansions, built a hundred years ago, where run-holders lived magnificently, like Virginia planters, upon the labour of assigned convict servants. While there was some settlement on the warm east coast, the rugged, harsher west coast remained (and remains) undeveloped.

Under the squatter aristocracy who began to enjoy an easy generous life in Tasmania and New South Wales, with more luxury than comfort or refinement, framing their social round upon the wool-sales, the horse-shows and the race-meetings, the work of the station-hands was monotonous and lonely. A sheep-run (which in England would have been called a sheep-walk) was merely a string of 'stations' at each of which a shepherd lived alone in a bark hut guarding his flock against drought, bush-fires, dingoes, and marauding blacks, his only variety being made by the periodic visit of the overseer with his week's or month's rations. When he could endure the isolation no longer, the shepherd threw up his job, drew his cheque—at a rate of no more than £25 a year in the 'thirties—and cashed it at the nearest public-house. There he stayed in drunken oblivion until his cheque was 'out', when he took the road as a 'sundowner' or 'swag-man' to tramp in search of another job. The wandering swag-man bearing a bundle, like Christian in the old woodcuts of the *Pilgrim's Progress*, boiling his 'billy' of tea and cooking his 'damper' of kneaded flour in the ashes of a wood-fire, claiming as a right a night's lodging in his own blankets under any roof, is perhaps the typical figure of pastoral Australia, immortalised in the jargon of *Waltzing Matilda*,[1] the national song. Though many an immigrant tried his hand at shepherding, or tramped as a swag-man in search of employment, the greater number of those who worked for wages in the stations, out back, were old hands spoiled by the convict system for any more civilised way of life. Shepherding was no occupation for a married man. For roughing it in the bush the squatters preferred men 'without encumbrances', drawing single rations. Later in the century came the migratory gangs of shearers, the aristocracy of Australian labour, who moved from station to station at shearing-time.

With the extermination of the wild black-fellows and the dingoes from the south-east, it was no longer necessary to fold sheep at night. The older type of shepherd was replaced by the mounted boundary rider, whose talk was of horses and dogs and the state of fencing, which became general in the 'fifties. Wages rose steeply on the stations when labour was drawn off to the gold-diggings, and native-born Australians now made the majority up-country. Known as 'wild colonials', 'currency lads' (by con-temptuous contrast with the 'sterling English') or as 'cornstalks', they had been marked down early in the century as a new physical type. The author of the *Letter from Sydney* had grown lyrical over the grace and sparkle of the 'currency lasses'. The men were taller than the English but sparely built; loose-limbed and small-featured, plain-spoken, irreverent, equalitarian, impatient of dis-cipline. Rovers rather than settlers, they were natural horsemen, addicted to racing and gambling; they lived by overlanding stock, bullock-driving, horse-breaking. The literature of colonial Australia, rich in picturesque tales of the squatters, preserves an admirable account of the type in *Robbery Under Arms* (by 'Rolf Boldrewood', 1888).

Fresh-faced immigrants from feudal English villages had thriftier habits and a more cautious temperament. Station life with black-fellows lurking in the scrub was too lonely; debauchery at the bush public-house, where the landlord might be in league with

---

[1] The words are by A. B. Paterson (1864–1941) whose ballads are more truly redolent of Australian life than those of the better-known Adam Lindsay Gordon (1833–70). Though Gordon adventured and died in Australia, he was essentially an English writer.

the bushrangers, was too reckless. They tended to remain at first in Sydney or within the limits of settlement. These 'New Chums' or 'limeys' (not yet known by the expressive modern nickname of 'pommies') were at first treated by the old hands with pitying contempt, but not for long. 'Every first emigrant to a colony', the Colonial Reformers used to say, 'regards the second as his enemy.' Within a few years the New Chum had become a colonial and was ready in his turn to resist the influx of newer chums whose arrival might be expected to lower the rate of wages.

MRS CAROLINE CHISHOLM

The census of 1841 revealed still twice as many men as women in Australia, with the result that young women who arrived at Sydney often went astray. The care of female immigrants was undertaken as a voluntary task by Mrs Caroline Chisholm, an officer's wife (1810–77), who found herself unoccupied in Australia when her husband went off to the China War. She prevailed on Governor Gipps to provide her with a building which she managed as an immigrants' hostel; then, in spite of ridicule, she undertook to chaperon parties of young women up-country to respectable situations where they were likely to find good husbands. She arranged to seek out and bring to Australia the wives of men who had emigrated or had been transported alone. With untiring energy she united broken families, sent for relatives of colonists who had made good, found places for the lethargic and timid and, in the course of six years (1841–7) is said to have 'settled' 11,000 immigrants. All was done by direct personal influence and contact, without regulations or administrative expense. She travelled all over New South Wales in a bullock-dray to see for herself that her girls found good homes.

In 1847 she returned to England to force her schemes upon Lord Grey. Her connexion was not with the Colonial Reformers but with pure philanthropists such as Shaftesbury and Sydney Herbert. Through their help she founded the Family Colonisation Loan Society for advancing small sums of money to families of emigrants, who were pledged to return their borrowings by instalments remitted from the colony. By 1854 she had despatched 3000 emigrants and, a fact which is more remarkable, the Society was solvent with £15,000 in hand. She interviewed intending emigrants, giving advice on their needs, inspected emigrant ships, and finally took over the whole responsibility, chartering ships in the name of her Society, and conducting a party personally to Australia in the first ship. Next she appointed her obliging husband as her agent for the reception of immigrants in Sydney while she despatched more ships from London. The total number of those she assisted is unknown. In 1854 she returned to a less active life in Australia. The changed circumstances there, brought about by the gold-rush and the grant of self-government, were bringing to an end the period of philanthropic colonisation.

The attitude of the British public towards emigration had also been completely changed by the practical endeavours of such workers as Mrs Chisholm no less than by the preaching of the Colonial Reformers. The change may be observed, for example, in the works of Charles Dickens between the publication of *Martin Chuzzlewit* (1843), in which emigration to America is painted in the blackest colours, and of *David Copperfield* (1850) in which Australia has become the land of promise. The kindly fun made of Micawber's preparations is reminiscent of Mrs Chisholm's advice to emigrants. Dickens was one of her strongest supporters, giving much space to her propaganda in *Household Words* (1850–2). It may also be noted with regret that the character of Mrs Jellyby (*Bleak House*, 1852) has been thought by some critics to present some features of an unkind parody of Caroline Chisholm.

EXPLORATION

The 1820's saw a great impulse outwards from the narrow bounds of coastal New South Wales, at first around the coasts and later across the ranges. Melville Island in the far north, which had been surveyed by a naval expedition, was occupied in 1824 with the hope that a trade-route to the East Indies might be opened. The settlement was discontinued when the trade came to nothing. Other annexations were made when Governor Darling took alarm at the appearance of a French scientific expedition, under Dumont d'Urville, in Australian waters (1826). He hastily sent parties of soldiers and convicts to occupy Westernport (in what is now Victoria), King George's Sound (Western Australia) and Moreton Bay (Queensland). A regular convict settlement was formed at Moreton Bay a few years later (1833); the other settlements were abandoned when no longer serviceable. The west coast was proclaimed British territory by Captain Fremantle in 1829, as a preliminary to the Swan River settlement. Australia was never formally annexed to the dominions of the Crown as a single territory. Lord John Russell used to relate that when he was at the Colonial Office (1839–41), 'a gentleman attached to the French Government' called on him to ask how much of the continent was British. 'I answered him "the whole", and with that answer he went away.'

In the same generation the overland routes were explored from Sydney. When Blaxland had found a way through the mountains a settlement was formed beyond the pass, at Bathurst. Though there was a growing desire to penetrate into the grassy plains which rumour reported beyond the ranges, not much, except unauthorised squatting, was done in Governor Macquarie's time. The interior of Australia was quite unknown and its character misjudged by early explorers. In 1817 and 1818 the government surveyor, John Oxley, traced the course of some of the rivers running north and west from the rugged bush-clad slopes of the Blue Mountains, until he lost them among swamps; from which he deduced that all central Australia might prove to be a salt-marsh. Later the pressure of the flock-masters on more accommodating governors led to the despatch of several exploring parties. They set out in ox-wagons (known in Australia as 'drays'), sometimes carrying whale-boats dismantled in sections, and accompanied by gangs of convicts who were spurred on with promises of early release and grants of land. Not far behind the exploring parties, and sometimes ahead of them, went the 'overlanders', the roving pioneers, driving their mobs of sheep in search of well-watered grassland.

In 1824 Hamilton Hume's party crossed the Murrumbidgee on a raft and worked south-west through the snow-clad ranges until they emerged at the western end of Port Phillip near the site of Geelong, to find sealing-gangs, landed from ships, already encamped there with huts and planted gardens. Three years later Allan Cunningham, a botanist from Kew, struck north from Bathurst into the fertile tableland, which was to be known as the Darling Downs, and reached them again by another route over Pandora's Pass from Moreton Bay. But the river-system, the topographical key to south-east Australia, remained hidden until it was revealed by the chivalrous Captain Charles Sturt (1795–1869), the knight-errant of Australian history. He correctly divined that the Murrumbidgee, and the Darling which he discovered, were tributaries of a greater river which must flow into Spencer's Gulf; then found the river and named it the Murray (1829). For twenty-six days he floated down the torrent in a whale-boat, which he had brought overland from New South Wales, until he

EXPLORATION AND
EARLY SETTLEMENT OF
AUSTRALIA
The north and west coasts
were known to the Dutch
in the 17th century.

George Philip & Son, Ltd.

Map 14

saw the breakers of Encounter Bay. Then he and his men rowed back against the flooded stream for fifty-six days, on rations reduced to half a pound of flour a day for each man.

Sturt's deductions were questioned by another Peninsular veteran, Major Thomas Mitchell, who was not convinced until he had made several journeys through the Murray basin. From the junction of the Darling with the Murray he struck south to the ocean at Portland Bay, finding there a settlement of unauthorised squatters from Van Diemen's Land. On his return journey Mitchell surveyed the route afterwards used by the overlanders who brought stock from New South Wales. From the top of a mountain he saw, through the heat-haze of an Australian mid-summer (December 1836), 'white objects which might have been tents'. It was the camp of John Batman who had just come from Van Diemen's Land as agent of the Port Phillip Association.

The topography of New South Wales was now revealed. Under the easier rule of Governors Brisbane and Darling the flock-masters were following hard behind the explorers. In 1820 no more than 300,000 acres of land had been appropriated; by 1830 more than 3,000,000 acres had been granted away to sheep-men. Far beyond the limits of surveyed land, for which title from the Governor was required, squatters were driving sheep and cattle to occupy newly discovered pasturage, either paying a nominal quit-rent for a pasturage licence or merely occupying what they could find. This was a situation outside the calculation of eco-nomists in England. Like the trek-boers on the Veld the squatters desired to disperse and not to concentrate. As at the Cape there were two zones of colonisation: the inner settlements, fenced and surveyed and amenable to regulation; the outer zone, beyond the ranges, where possession was ten points of the law.

The north-western coast of Australia, well-known to mariners but rarely visited by landing-parties, was traversed by Lieutenant George Grey (afterwards the distinguished colonial governor), when a very young man. In 1836 he went ashore in Dampier Land from a naval surveying-ship and made his way south-west towards Swan River until he was baffled by the dry sandstone country. After the foundation of Adelaide, E. J. Eyre (also a colonial governor in later life) brought cattle overland from Port Phillip. He led two expeditions from the new settlement, reaching Lake Torrens to the northward and King George's Sound (1841) far to the westward along the shores of the Australian Bight. In 1844 Captain Sturt went north-east from Adelaide over the un-suspected mineral wealth of Broken Hill. He returned from the wilderness with ruined health to confirm Eyre's reports that cen-tral Australia was a desert. Eyre and Sturt had shown exemplary leadership and resolution but had found no new pastoral paradise.

The mountainous south-east corner of Australia was first penetrated by a Pole, Count Strzelecki, who gave the name of Mount Kosciusko to the highest peak (1840). Another European adventurer, Ludwig Leichhardt, made three journeys (1842–8) from Queensland to the tropical north. He crossed the continent from Sydney to Port Essington, east of the site of Darwin. From his third expedition he never returned. As in the case of Sir John Franklin, the relief expeditions sent in search of Leichhardt were productive of much practical knowledge. One of the searchers, A. C. Gregory, crossed the continent on the other diagonal, from Brisbane to Adelaide (1858). Sturt's lieutenant and admirer, J. M. Stuart, took up his master's quest from Adelaide and at a third attempt (1862) reached the northern coast. It was largely generous rivalry on the part of the citizens of Melbourne that led them to launch another expedition with the object of crossing the continent on a parallel course farther to the east, from Melbourne to the Gulf of Carpentaria. Burke and Wills, to whom the leadership was entrusted, mismanaged the journey. 'Then the wood failed, then the food failed, then the last water dried.' Both lost their lives (1861), a tragic story better remembered in Australia than some more fruitful but less dramatic tales of travel. Professor E. Scott drily remarks of John McKinlay's later expedition, which reached the Gulf of Carpentaria, finding the relics of Burke and Wills by the way: 'The most picturesque exploits were not always the most valuable. A good bushman like McKinlay did not produce so readable an account of his travels as did George Grey; but the object of exploration was not to add to the literature of adventure.'

6. AUSTRALIAN LAND AND EMIGRATION IN THE 'FORTIES

THE colony at Swan River, which Wakefield selected as the target of his scorn, was first planned in 1828. As early as 1697 the river had been visited by the Dutch navigator, Vlaming, who discovered there the real existence of the black swan, a bird formerly known to fable only. Swan River estuary, opening into the Indian Ocean, 2000 miles from Sydney, was otherwise forgotten until it attracted the attention of a naval officer, James (afterwards Admiral Sir James) Stirling (1791–1865). It was his ambition to emulate Raffles by making at Swan River another Singapore. Getting no sort of encouragement from the Colonial Office, he managed to enlist the aid of John Barrow, Secretary to the

Admiralty and, after much lobbying, was appointed military governor—with one company of soldiers—of the country annexed by Captain Fremantle, in 1829 (see above, page 360).

Just then Thomas Peel (cousin of Sir Robert) and others came forward in London with a scheme for taking up land and importing settlers, a plan which Stirling hurried into execution without proper preparation. The coastline was annexed on 2 May 1829; in June Stirling proclaimed the colony; and in the next nine months thirteen ships arrived with 1500 immigrants, to find that there was no anchorage, no survey, no currency and no treaty with the aboriginals. The soil was light and the fertile patches lay inland. The natural tendency to disperse was intensified by huge land-grants, to the Governor among others. The food-supply was precarious because the settlers arrived at the wrong time of year for sowing. For some years the colony was half-starved between ships' visits. Peel brought out 300 settlers, 60 of them indentured labourers, to work on his estate of 250,000 acres; all had drifted away in six months, to squat on other fertile land, or to try their luck in the other colonies. The Sydney press was bitterly hostile to the Swan River scheme and did all in its power to draw away the precious labourers to New South Wales.

Meanwhile Stirling made the best of things, with robust good-humour and a sailor's inventiveness. He laid out the town-sites, of Perth a few miles inland beside a broad lagoon, and Fremantle on the dusty shore. The settlers grumbled that these towns were good for nothing but 'sand, sorrow, and sore eyes', a description which will surprise those travellers who have seen the flowery banks of Swan River, a century later. The colony cost the British Government £41,000 for a commencement, and a grant-in-aid of £6000 a year, which was put on a regular basis when a constitution, of the type then usual in Crown Colonies, was granted in 1834. Three years later, when Stirling retired, the population had crept up to 2032 whites, of whom 688 were women. The black-fellows had been driven off by the 'Battle of Pinjarra' (1834), a punitive raid led by the Governor against a marauding tribe. Of 1,500,000 acres allotted to holders of land-grants, only 1400 were under crop. The settlers were already talking of the advantages of convict labour. In 1848 the population had crept up to 4600, who lived without much prosperity. Their plea for a reinforcement of convicts was gladly granted when the Colonial

Office in 1849 could find no other place in the Queen's dominions where convicts were welcome.

The story of the obstacle race run by the South Australia Association has been told in an earlier chapter. Long before the settlers sailed, the projectors, especially Wakefield, had despaired of founding the model colony they had first proposed. Twice had the first body of settlers been assembled and twice dispersed before the progress of negotiations with Downing Street permitted their despatch. Land sales flagged amid these deferred hopes until an enterprising banker, G. F. Angas, floated a commercial company with a capital of £200,000 to give the colony a start. The 'sufficient price' had at last been fixed at £1 an acre.

In May 1836 the Surveyor, Colonel William Light (the son of Francis Light of Penang), sailed to Spencer Gulf and chose the site of Adelaide in the open country recently discovered, but not explored, by Captain Sturt. Those who thought the project fantastic might observe with irony that an earlier explorer, Captain Lemuel Gulliver, had located the kingdom of Lilliput just here on the map. The first batch of 600 colonists arrived too soon (December 1836), before the survey was completed. Within a few months there was complete deadlock between the Resident Commissioner for land sales and the Governor, Sir John Hindmarsh. The site and the survey were sharply criticised, and the settlers could not or would not take up their land. Meanwhile hypothetical sales of land in England continued and new batches of colonists continued to appear, one of the most useful groups being 600 German peasants sent out by Angas. By 1838, Wakefield's doctrine of concentration seemed only too successful; almost all the 3600 inhabitants of South Australia were still at the capital, living on rations provided at the expense of the Company. Hindmarsh and the Resident Commissioner were then recalled and replaced by Colonel George Gawler, who was invested with the powers of both. Light had resigned in disgust after planning the garden city of Adelaide, and the survey of the interior was taken over by the explorer, Charles Sturt. Gawler struggled with the unbalanced finances of the settlement for two years, drawing bills on the Commissioners for current expenses, while all the revenue was diverted to bringing out from England a stream of emigrants who could not be absorbed into the infant economy of the settlement. This was the Wakefield plan reduced to an absurdity.

In 1839 Lord John Russell, who had reason to doubt the integrity of the Commissioners, dissolved the Commission, replacing it by a Land and Emigration Board which for the next thirty years administered the sale of Crown lands and the despatch of 'assisted' emigrants throughout the Empire, a useful administrative reform. Colonel R. Torrens (1780–1864), one of the founders of South Australia,[1] became chairman of the Board.

By 1841 Adelaide was taking root as a colony but was bankrupt as a financial concern. Gawler demanded and got a loan of £155,000 to meet current expenses. But he, like so many colonial governors of that age, was held responsible for the chaos he had inherited and was recalled. To meet the crisis Russell took the audacious step of appointing as Governor a young soldier not yet thirty years old, Captain George Grey,[2] who had distinguished himself as the explorer of north-western Australia. Grey had the advantage of coming in as the luck was turning. More than half the inhabitants had already moved out of Adelaide on to the land. More than 7000 acres were under cultivation and more than 200,000 sheep were grazing in South Australia before Gawler departed. The new Governor worked no miracles other than those always achieved by economy, promptness, and resolution. Since there was now food in the land he stopped the issue of free rations, a decision which soon drove the labourers into the fields. But he was no more able than Gawler to pay his way without drawing bills on London. Already 16,000 emigrants had been despatched when, in 1842, the next Colonial Secretary, Lord Stanley, obtained an act of Parliament for constituting South Australia a colony of the normal type, and for writing off the loan of £155,000 as a grant-in-aid, a modest price for such a settlement. In that year copper was discovered at Kapunda. In 1845 when Grey was transferred to New Zealand the population of South Australia was 38,000, the revenue £82,000 and the aggregate land sales had reached half a million sterling. What meant more, as Grey noted, was 'the calibre of the new settlers. There was a worth, a sincerity, a true ring about them, which could not fail of great things.'

[1] His son Sir R. R. Torrens (1814–86), South Australian statesman, was author of the Torrens Act for registering land-titles, 1857. Later, returning to England, he was M.P. for Cambridge.
[2] See footnote above, page 335, for the Grey family.

South Australia has generally been taken as the test-case of systematic colonisation, and has been quoted by Australian writers in condemnation of the Wakefield plan. In spite of the obstructions and delay of the Colonial Office which foisted upon it an unworkable constitution, in spite of the misuse of funds by the Commissioners, whom Wakefield had condemned as 'ignorant and careless', it was a striking advance upon all earlier experiments in that generation. Its birth-pangs were slight indeed compared with those of Swan River. But colonies are made by men, not by agrarian laws. The quality of the settlers was the difference, and that was as essential to Wakefield's system as the Sufficient Price.

The Colonial Reform movement began to attract attention in New South Wales in these times of outward expansion. Systematic colonisation by means of the land-fund appeared to Australian sheep-farmers as a restrictive attempt by doctrinaires in Downing Street to interfere with natural growth. They were vociferous against the Colonial Office throughout the 1830's, on account of its supposed subservience to the Wakefield school at the same time when South African farmers were complaining of its subservience to the missionaries. The Colonial Office pleased nobody, and would please nobody, until it accepted the logic of responsible government for the colonies. Successive Governors at Sydney, with increasing reluctance and diminishing effect, tried to confine the squatters to the 'limits of settlement', the original nineteen counties of New South Wales. As well might they try to confine the Arabs of the desert or the trek-boers of the African Veld. New land, discovered every year, was taken into possession by the overlanders. Wentworth, himself a squatter on a great scale, promoted the squatting interest in the press and at public meetings, since there was not until 1842 any representative assembly in which he could form a constitutional opposition. Macarthur and the other 'exclusives' in the nominated Legislative Council found themselves in sympathy with him on this issue, so that, with the growing preponderance of the new generation of freeborn Australians, the distinction between 'emancipists' and 'exclusives' slowly died away.

Sir Richard Bourke, Governor from 1831 to 1837, was obliged to administer the regulation of 1831 though he disapproved of it. It obliged him to ear-mark the revenue from land sales

Map 15

for subsidising emigration; and, after 1834, he had to pay the cost of gaols and police from colonial funds. Macarthur in the Council (until his death in 1834) and Wentworth in the press combined to denounce these instructions, demanding control of their own revenues through an elective assembly. Wentworth, with Dr J. D. Lang and others, founded the Australian Patriotic Association, whose London agent was Charles Buller, the reformer. In 1836 Bourke persuaded the Colonial Office to allow him to throw open Port Phillip to settlement on the same terms as the nineteen counties and to grant licences to squatters outside the 'limits of settlement'. With this incentive the squatters dispersed more rapidly than before. A thousand of them took possession of 44,000,000 acres of land. Bourke was long remembered in Sydney as the most popular of governors and, like most popular governors, was recalled for displeasing the Colonial Office. The Australians gave him the credit for founding religious equality, trial by jury, and the freedom of the press.

Sir George Gipps, a man of great force of character, was Governor at the crisis of the fever for land (1838–46). It was one of his tasks to prepare the negotiations with the Maori chiefs, in 1840, which made them subjects of the Crown. Wentworth took a hand in that, securing for himself by a private bargain with one of them a grant of half the South Island of New Zealand. In disgust, Gipps denounced and nullified this deal, making it his reason for excluding Wentworth from public office. Not at all abashed, Wentworth gloried in the attempt, saying that Drake or Ralegh would have done the same.

In a climate subject to periodic droughts, wool prices tended to fluctuate violently and all the more when arbitrary changes in the land-regulations led to speculative buying. During the great slump of 1843, when all parties in the colony were clamouring for Gipps's recall, he made regulations for preserving the rights of the Crown (that is of posterity) against mere land-grabbing, while securing genuine sheep-farmers in possession of their runs. Every squatter was obliged to buy a section of 320 acres within five years of occupying a run, in order to secure his right to pasture his sheep on the rest of it. Otherwise his claim lapsed. In spite of fierce opposition Gipps held to this principle until a compromise, not essentially different, was embodied in an imperial Act of Parliament (1846), giving to squatters in 'unsettled lands' a leasehold of fourteen years with rights of pre-emption. This was on the whole a triumph for the pastoral over the agricultural interest and for the practical experience of the colonists over the theories of the Colonial Reformers. Control of the waste lands of the Empire from Whitehall had proved impossible. Wherever responsible government was granted, control of undeveloped land quickly passed to the colonial parliament and became the focus of colonial party politics.

A proportion of elected members were at last added to the Legislative Council of New South Wales in 1842, with no distinction in the franchise between emancipists and free emigrants. In forming an administration Governor Gipps brought forward a young English lawyer, an Oxford man named Robert Lowe (1811–92), whom he thought the ablest man in the colony, as a counterpoise to the influence of Wentworth. Lowe proved to be an independent of advanced views. During the 'forties, politics at Sydney took the form of a duel between Wentworth, the leader of the squatters, who became increasingly aristocratic in his outlook, and Lowe, who led the new democratic interest of the free immigrants, opposing the claim of the squatters to unlimited land, and protesting against the continued importation of convicts. Lowe's most useful achievement was to organise the schools of the colony. In 1850 he returned to the wider world of London, becoming Chancellor of the Exchequer in Gladstone's administration and Lord Sherbrooke. His colonial experiences made him bitterly cynical on the subject of democracy without literacy; he first said of the English electorate: 'We must educate our masters.'

When Lord Grey was at the Colonial Office (1846–52) self-governing institutions were granted to all self-supporting colonies. He made some motions towards federating Australia, a cause which received little support, except from Wentworth who was a man of large ideas. Out there the general tendency was centrifugal and the social cleavage between New South Wales, South Australia and Swan River too wide for adjustment, as wide as the geographical distance between them. In 1850, Grey obtained an Act of Parliament for giving each of the Australian colonies an elective legislature with a limited power of constitutional amendment, but reserving control of the waste land and the land-revenues to the Crown. Wentworth and the squatters received this offer without enthusiasm. During the next five years, in which no less than seven gentlemen held the office of Secretary of State, Downing Street yielded concessions step by step to the colonies. Control of the waste lands was transferred to the new legislatures by an act of 1855. Responsible government was hammered out in practice, not formally granted.

Wentworth's policy in New South Wales was to restrict the franchise and to restrain the assembly by a nominated upper house, even by a hereditary House of Lords. But the electorate, consisting largely of new immigrants with Chartist notions, insisted on a wide franchise, an elective upper house, and the ballot. Finding himself out of sympathy with the new democratic Australia, Wentworth retired to England. He is remembered as the founder of the University of Sydney (1849–52), the first true university in the British dependencies.

Port Phillip was separated from New South Wales as the self-governing colony of Victoria (1850). This was the one example in Australia, one of few in the whole Empire, of successful colonisation without a plan. In 1834 Edward Henty had left the fiasco of Swan River to set up a shore-whaling station in Portland Bay. In 1835 John Batman, an unauthorised squatter from Van Diemen's Land, had obtained a concession of 600,000 acres at Port Phillip from an aboriginal chief, who was certainly unaware of the nature of the bargain. Batman was the pioneer of the Port Phillip Association, a group of adventurers who brought in stock from the confined valleys of Van Diemen's Land to the wide plains of Port Phillip. They were soon joined by overlanders following Mitchell's track, known as 'the Major's path', from New South Wales. Governor Bourke persuaded the Colonial Office to permit land sales and pasturage licences at Port Phillip on the same terms as at Sydney. In 1836 he sent a magistrate to Port Phillip where a township of squatters had sprung up.

Early in 1837 Governor Bourke arrived at Port Phillip and instructed the government surveyor, Robert Hoddle, to lay out the site for a town on gently sloping ground, overlooking the Bay, beside the River Yarra. Hoddle's original sketch (now in the Savage Club at Melbourne) is the noblest conception of all town-plans in the Dominions, a rectangle described about four parallel avenues, each one hundred feet wide, interspersed by narrow service streets. Bourke named the new colony Victoria after the young Queen (1839) and the town (incorporated in 1842) Melbourne after her first Prime Minister. At the last census before the discovery of gold, which set the town booming, the population of the district was over 32,000 and of Melbourne itself over 10,000 (1846).

All this progress came by infiltration of voluntary settlers neither planted by the Crown nor by any colonising company. It cannot, however, be justly compared with the settlement of Adelaide, a new plantation on a virgin site. Land, capital, stock and willing pioneers were available for development at Port Phillip. The first stage of colonisation was over in New South Wales and Van Diemen's Land, the next region for settlement was explored, and the frontier was ripe for a forward move when John Batman took the initiative. This was not, as the foundation of Sydney and Adelaide had been or as the foundation of Massachusetts and Maryland had been, a first venture into a new land; it was a second step like the advance of the Americans into the Ohio basin. It was carried forward by the boom in sheep-farming and enormously advanced in the next generation by the discovery of gold. Behind the advancing squatters moved up the rank and file of the invading colonists. Between 1831 and 1842 land sales had produced £1,090,000 of which £950,000 had been spent on providing passages for 50,000 free immigrants. Without this steady stream Port Phillip might have grown as slowly as Swan River.

Van Diemen's Land shed its unhappy past and was reborn as the free self-governing colony of Tasmania in 1855. Moreton Bay was separated from New South Wales in 1859 as the self-governing colony of Queensland. Western Australia (or Swan River), lapsing into the status of a convict colony from which the others had just emerged, was not yet qualified for self-government.

7. NEW ZEALAND AND THE MISSIONARIES, 1792–1848

COOK'S annexation of New Zealand, ignored by successive governments, was nullified by an Act of Parliament of 1817 which alluded to the islands as a place 'not within His Majesty's Dominions'. Occasional visitors to New Zealand noted chiefly the ferocity of the natives who, on several occasions, cut off boats' crews and devoured them. The massacre of the whole ship's company of the *Boyd* in 1809 had an alarming effect; yet white men did visit the islands and even settled there. The first recorded residents, a sealing-crew, spent the summer of 1792 ashore, in the far south where no native tribes were settled.

As early as 1791 efforts were made from Sydney to develop a trade in timber for spars and in the tenacious fibre of the New Zealand flax. These shipping stores attracted the British and American sperm-whalers to the Bay of Islands, a region broken by deep-water inlets among the forests of gigantic *Kauri* pines. Here dwelt numerous natives, children of the sun, who throve better in the sub-tropical north than in the cool windy south. Deserters from the ships and runaway convicts from Botany Bay sometimes made their way ashore at the Bay of Islands where, if they were not quickly knocked on the head and eaten, they might hope to make themselves useful to some chief as boat-builders, blacksmiths or interpreters. The first of these 'white [pakehà] maoris' was George Bruce, who married a chief's daughter in 1807. In the 'twenties and 'thirties every chief aspired to keep a tame white man, a *pakehà*, perhaps a mere pimp and bootlegger who got rum and muskets for his master in return for sending native women aboard the ships, perhaps an honest trader, or even something more. The great chiefs regarded the missionaries as their *pakehàs*, their agents with the outside world, much as a Frankish or a Saxon king regarded his bishop in the seventh century. Thus English civilisation at its worst and best began to penetrate New Zealand.

But the Maoris were far too virile and intelligent to wait for civilisation to come to them; many shipped before the mast to discover the world for themselves, and so came to the notice of the Apostle of New Zealand, the chaplain to the convict establishment at Sydney. The Rev. Samuel Marsden (1764–1838) of St John's College, Cambridge, was a straightforward practical Christian of the old school, not an enthusiast from Clapham. Since he could not obtain the services of ordained clergy he agreed with the Church Missionary Society to establish two respectable laymen, William Hall a carpenter and John King a rope-maker, at the Bay of Islands to prepare the way for Christianity. 'Till the attention of the heathen is gained, and moral and industrious habits are induced, little or no progress can be made in teaching them the Gospel.' In December 1814 Marsden conveyed his party to New Zealand under protection of two friendly chiefs, inaugurating his mission on Christmas Day with a sermon preached, through an interpreter, upon the text: 'Behold I bring you tidings of great joy.'

Since Hall and King were not sufficiently well-educated to master the Maori language, Marsden's next step was to despatch one of the two chiefs—his name was Hongi—to England. He stayed at Cambridge in the house of Samuel Lee, the Professor of Arabic (1820) who prepared a Maori grammar and dictionary in which the language was transliterated with elegance.[1] Until his death in 1838 Marsden supervised his missions in New Zealand, visiting the country seven times and, when sixty years old, making adventurous journeys on foot into the unknown interior. There was little evidence of progress until the arrival (1822) of Henry Williams, a naval officer turned clergyman, who impressed the savages with that quality of moral greatness (*mana*) which they instantly appreciated. 'This island was a very hard stone', said a Maori chief, 'and Archdeacon Williams broke it.' He and his brother, William Williams, were the patriarchs of a clan which has served New Zealand faithfully in Church and State for a hundred years. The Williams family has given bishops to the Anglican Church of New Zealand in three successive generations.

In his anxiety to find clergy, Marsden had invited the Methodists to send a mission. When it came (1823) he aimed at co-operation, with the result that spheres of influence were agreed upon, the Anglicans taking the north-east and the Methodists the north-west

[1] Readers may note the different effect of the elegant transliteration of aboriginal place-names in New Zealand and the commonplace transliteration of aboriginal place-names in Australia. The apparent ugliness of some Australian names is a fault of the Europeans who reproduced them in writing, not a defect in the native language.

coasts. In London there was no such happy issue since the two societies failed to come to terms. Those who doubt the efficacy of missionary endeavour would do well to study the change in the habits and morals of the Maori people achieved by the influence of a handful of missionaries in a single generation (c. 1820–50). Tribal warfare, cannibalism and slavery gradually disappeared without the exertion of political or economic pressure. The Maoris were neither conquered nor expropriated, but converted.

Before the consummation of this change, which Marsden did not live to see, the Maoris indulged in a last orgy of bloodshed. The chief, Hongi, whose 'mild manners' had made so good an impression, did not restrict his English acquaintance to Cambridge professors. He had been escorted to England by Thomas Kendall, one of Marsden's lay missionaries, who very improperly helped him to sell land-concessions to speculators for cash with which he bought guns. On his return to New Zealand he revolutionised the art of war. His raids and conquests, until his death in 1831, devastated the North Island, exterminating whole tribes, and greatly complicating for posterity the titles to tribal lands. The pressure of his campaigns affected, among others, an audacious and cunning chief named Te Rauparàha ('The Convolvulus Leaf') who took the war-path southwards. Making his headquarters on an island in Cook Strait, he dominated all the central region of New Zealand, almost annihilating the few and scattered tribes of the South Island. Gun-running for these wars led to a greater and even more disreputable trade between Sydney and the little Alsatia at the Bay of Islands, where the missionaries competed for the attention of the natives against the worst ruffians of the South Seas.

Rumours of land sales to missionaries and *pakehà maoris* had drawn the attention of speculators in colonisation to the possibilities of New Zealand. Mr Lambton (not yet Earl of Durham) had sent out a ship-load of emigrants who were frightened away by the mere aspect of a Maori war-dance (1826). There was also a cosmopolitan adventurer called the Baron de Thierry[1] who, as an undergraduate at Cambridge, had obtained some sort of land-concession from Hongi, and had notions of carving himself out a

[1] C. P. de Thierry (1793–1864) of Magdalen Hall, Oxford, and Queens' College, Cambridge, son of the Baron de Thierry, a French refugee. Born at Brussels, he had served in the British Army.

kingdom in New Zealand, with Dutch or French if not with English help.

Land-speculation, gun-running, escapes of convicts, increasing trade, and complaints by the missionaries about the outrageous proceedings in New Zealand at last obliged the Governor of New South Wales to intervene. The final abomination was the case of the brig *Elizabeth* (Captain Stewart) which was hired by Te Rauparàha to convey his war-party on a marauding expedition (1830). The English sailors, having decoyed a hostile chief and his family on board to be kidnapped and murdered, allowed the murderers to cook human flesh in the brig's galley and to enjoy a cannibal feast on the deck. It proved impossible to fix any charge against Captain Stewart except that of taking service under a foreign potentate in contravention of the Foreign Enlistment Act, and on that count the evidence proved insufficient. In 1831 Governor Darling decided to send James Busby as British Resident at the Bay of Islands. Since he had no more than moral authority either over whites or Maoris he could do little beyond rallying the support of the respectable inhabitants to the cause of law and order. He encouraged the formation of a confederacy of native chiefs, the United Tribes of New Zealand, for their own defence against exploitation (1835), and especially against the pretensions of the Baron de Thierry.

In his evidence before the Parliamentary committee of 1836 (see chapter VII, 2, page 335) Wakefield began his campaign for the colonisation of New Zealand. 'Very near to Australia there is a country which all testimony concurs in describing as the fittest country in the world for colonising, as the most beautiful country with the finest climate, and the most productive soil.' In 1837 he formed the first New Zealand Association with a strong committee including most of the Colonial Reformers. Their first draft of an enabling bill for colonising New Zealand received the usual short-shrift from James Stephen. He thought the project 'vague and obscure' and that it would 'infallibly issue in the conquest and extermination of the natives'. Here he expressed the view of the Church Missionary Society which, at last, was beginning to receive good reports from its agents in New Zealand. A sharp duel of pamphlets and addresses to the Colonial Office ensued between Wakefield and Mr Dandeson Coates, the secretary of the Church Missionary Society. Coates refused an interview with a deputation from the Colonial Reformers, sending them word that he proposed to thwart them by every means in his power. Nevertheless the missionaries and their parent society did not intend that New Zealand should remain a scene of chaos and anarchy. They, too, desired annexation by the Crown in order to create a missionary paradise of meek, unworldly converts under their own spiritual direction. Both parties alike demanded that the Crown should intervene to impose law and order. It was the failure of the Colonial Office to act that incited Molesworth to propose his vote of censure (March 1838) against Lord Glenelg, already deeply discredited by the collapse of his policy in Canada and in South Africa.

As in the case of South Australia, the only terms on which the Colonial Office would approve an experiment in colonisation were that they should retain absolute control while incurring none of the financial risk. And, on these terms, some encouragement was given to the New Zealand Association just before Glenelg was at last ejected from Downing Street. The Association, a philanthropic body, was accordingly replaced by a joint-stock company to the great mortification of Wakefield who was again forced to appear, against his will, in the character, which his enemies falsely attributed to him, of a land-speculator. The project, he said, had been begun by men with large minds and small purses and would be continued by men with small minds and large purses.[1]

During the greater part of 1838 he was with Durham in Canada. The Durham Report was no sooner issued than the Reformers turned to the formation of the New Zealand Company with a nominal capital of £200,000 and Lord Durham as Governor. But alas! the new Colonial Secretary, Lord Normanby, flatly refusing to be bound by his predecessor's decision, would give no direct or indirect sanction for the formation of a colony. The Directors accordingly decided to force the issue. They had bought a ship of 400 tons, the *Tory*, and had appointed, as leader of the colony, Wakefield's younger brother William, who had outlived the disgrace of his share in Ellen Turner's abduction as

---

[1] Presumably a hit at Joseph Somes, the great shipowner, who became chairman of the Company after the death of Lord Durham. I acknowledge here my debt to the memory of Somes whose estate provided endowments in New Zealand, to which I owe my education. C.E.C.

a colonel in the Spanish service, and had fought with distinction in the civil wars in Spain. Since preparations were well advanced, the elder Wakefield posted to Plymouth, on 4 May 1839, to despatch his brother with the *Tory* before the government could find means to prevent it. The sailing of the *Tory* on 5 May had the desired effect. Lord Normanby was now obliged to issue an instruction 'with extreme reluctance' for the annexation of New Zealand if only to protect the natives from the British colonists. On 13 June he informed Lord Durham that he had decided to send Captain William Hobson, R.N., to negotiate with the United Tribes of New Zealand for a cession of sovereignty. The one benefit he conferred upon the infant colony was an instruction that no convicts should be sent there.

Colonel Wakefield in the *Tory* sighted the South Island of New Zealand on 16 August 1839; in September he negotiated an agreement for the purchase of a wide tract of land from Te Rauparàha and other chiefs; Captain Hobson arrived at the Bay of Islands on 29 January 1840; and by this time there was also a French champion in the field. The story of the French designs on New Zealand has been somewhat confused by romantic exaggeration, in the local legend of the 'Race for Akaroa' between French and English warships. There was a race, but it took place in Europe between Edward Wakefield and a similar projector in France, a Captain Langlois, who was also trying to stimulate his government to action. He too formed a colonising company and despatched a shipload of emigrants without authority. Wakefield was the winner, both in getting his expedition under way and in forcing the hand of his government. Supposed French designs upon New Zealand were used by the Colonial Reformers as a means of bringing pressure on the English government. About the real activities of French free-lances there could be no doubt. Baron de Thierry in New Zealand was negotiating with the French government through his brother in Paris. Far more weighty was the work of French missionaries at the Bay of Islands. As in Canada a hundred years earlier, the missionaries, however innocent their motives, were regarded both by the savages and by most Europeans as the agents either of the Catholic or the Protestant power.

Jean Baptiste Pompallier (1802–70) was a learned and pious French priest who founded a missionary order (now generally known as the Marist Brothers) for the evangelisation of the Pacific

islands, under the authority of a brief from Pope Gregory XVI.
Having been consecrated a bishop *in partibus*, he arrived in New
Zealand as Vicar-general in January 1838, with a letter of intro-
duction to de Thierry. He made an error in not striking out a new
claim but settled at the Bay of Islands in open rivalry with the
Anglicans, who received him as an enemy.

As soon as Captain Hobson arrived at the Bay he commenced
negotiations with the Maori chiefs for a treaty which was drawn
up at Busby's house near the estuary of the Waitangi River.
Williams the Anglican missionary, as interpreter, urged the chiefs
to give their assent. Bishop Pompallier, who appeared at the conference in his canonical robes, was plainly hostile to the treaty but,
on being assured that the British would guarantee freedom and
protection to all Christian sects alike, he abstained from active
opposition.

On 6 February 1840, the first signatures were obtained to the
Treaty of Waitangi, the method being that each chief drew on the
paper a copy of the design tattooed upon his face. Duplicates of
the treaty were then carried by the missionaries to several parts of
the islands for the collection of further signatures. Forty-six chiefs
made their mark at Waitangi, and 456 others during the next few
months, constituting a large majority, but by no means all, of the
magnates of the Maori nation. The Treaty, to which the Maoris
attached and still attach great respect, is a short document in three
articles:

(1) The signatory chiefs 'cede to Her Majesty the Queen [*Te
    Kuini Wikitoria* in the Maori version] all the rights and
    powers of sovereignty which the said chiefs...exercise or
    possess...'.
(2) H.M. the Queen 'confirms and guarantees to the chiefs and
    tribes...undisputed possession of their lands...but the
    chiefs yield to Her Majesty the exclusive right of pre-
    emption'.
(3) Her Majesty extends her protection to the natives of New
    Zealand and 'imparts to them all the rights and privileges
    of British subjects'.

The Treaty was, in a sense, a counterblast to the action of
Colonel Wakefield who had already begun to occupy the lands he
professed to have bought, several hundred miles to the southward
of the Bay of Islands. The site of a town had been selected and

named Wellington, as a belated tribute to the old Duke who had helped the Colonial Reformers to steer the South Australian Bill through Parliament. The first shipload of emigrants had arrived, a fortnight before the signing of the Treaty. Hobson expressed his intention of visiting Wellington but was prevented by a paralytic stroke which left him an invalid, a dying man. But when the settlers, following the old model of the Pilgrim Fathers, held a meeting and formed a provisional government, the news alarmed him into action. He felt this to be a sort of declaration of independence and denounced it as high treason. He resolved to implement the Treaty of Waitangi by proclaiming British sovereignty over the North Island (21 May 1840). As if this trouble were not enough a French corvette appeared in June to protect the French emigrant ship which was then on its way to the South Island. Hobson thereupon despatched H.M.S. *Britomart* to the South Island to proclaim British sovereignty there also (17 June 1840). Further signatures were obtained to the Treaty of Waitangi including that of the redoubtable Rauparàha.

The site selected by the French colonists was the lovely secluded bay of Akaroa. The French corvette arrived there on 11 August to find that the *Britomart* had cast anchor in the harbour on the previous day, and that a magistrate had held a court, as formal evidence that the proclamation of 17 June was effective. A shipload of sixty French immigrants, arriving shortly after, decided to remain under the British flag, at Akaroa where some of their descendants still dwell. The French naval officers accepted the *fait accompli*, as did the French government, some years later, after an acrimonious debate in the Chamber of Deputies at Paris. So ended the French designs on New Zealand. Pompallier confined his labours to the mission field and became a British subject. The Baron de Thierry lived in obscurity at Auckland until his death in 1864.

Note: The account of Wakefield's dramatic visit to Plymouth, to despatch the *Tory*, was given by his early biographers. It is fair to say that doubts have been cast on the story by later students. There is no doubt that he used all the means at his disposal to force the government's hand.   C.E.C.

8. EARLY SETTLEMENTS IN
NEW ZEALAND

MEANWHILE several shiploads of emigrants had arrived at
Wellington. Their way had been smoothed by the whaling-
parties which, since about 1830, had settled in Cook Strait and
the South Island. In 1840 there were 600 of these shore-whalers,
making sixty boats' crews dispersed at about thirty settlements.
Unlike the deep-sea whalers who hunted the toothed sperm-
whale, they slaughtered the whale-bone whales who came to calve
in the shallow water, usually killing the calf because the cow-
whale would never leave its body. Such wanton destruction could
but result in a short life for the trade. Though the fishery soon
declined, a single shore-whaling station still operated a hundred
years later, in 1932, at Te Awaiti. This station had once been the
home of 'Dicky' Barrett, the doyen of the shore-whalers, who
directed Colonel Wakefield to the site of Wellington and
negotiated between him and the Maoris.

Colonel Wakefield claimed to have acquired a property in about
twenty million acres of unexplored land on either side of Cook
Strait. It was described in the deed of purchase merely in geographical terms as lying between certain degrees of latitude and
longitude; it was paid for in two ways, by complimentary gifts
to the chiefs of trade goods to the value of £9000, and by the
guarantee that one-eleventh of the land, when surveyed and
developed, would be formed into native reserves. The New
Zealand Company always maintained that the reserves, immensely
increased in value by the coming of civilisation, were the important consideration.

From the beginning of the story there was open conflict between the missionaries, who supported the Treaty of Waitangi,
and the settlers, who supported the Wakefield land-purchase. On
the one hand it was asserted that the settlers were mere 'land-
sharks' expropriating the natives by a fraudulent contract which
no law-court would uphold; on the other hand the settlers
claimed that all reasonable native rights were scrupulously
guaranteed by the New Zealand Company, whereas the Treaty
of Waitangi was merely a legal fiction, a 'device to amuse and
pacify savages for the moment'. When Lord John Russell became

Colonial Secretary (September 1839) he sent instructions to Governor Hobson to treat the Wellington settlers with 'kindness and consideration'. Their action, right or wrong, had preceded the signing of the Treaty and could not therefore be treated as a breach of it. In February 1841, after long negotiation, he gave a charter to the Company, thus justifying Wakefield's action in despatching the *Tory*. Notwithstanding the Treaty it was agreed that the Company might occupy four acres in New Zealand for every pound it had spent in colonisation. This would have been an equitable solution had events not moved in a contrary direction in the colony. There was a delay of three to six months between the issue of a despatch in London and its reception by the Governor at the Bay of Islands, and perhaps as long again before the Governor's action took effect at Wellington. The Letters-patent setting up New Zealand as a distinct colony, no longer subordinate to New South Wales, were issued in November 1840, but not promulgated in New Zealand until May 1841.

Not finding a suitable site for a capital city in the Bay of Islands, Governor Hobson cast about until he hit upon a commanding position, the isthmus between the two harbours of Waitemata and Onèhunga (October 1840). Here he decided to build a city, calling it Auckland after the Viceroy of India, his former patron at the Admiralty. It was a stroke of genius, or would have been, if either funds or labour had been available to develop it; but to foist an official capital, a Washington or a Canberra, upon a tiny struggling community was financially absurd. The population for some years consisted of officials and their families, with a few speculators from Sydney who manufactured a highly profitable boom in town lots, although there were no genuine settlers and no prospect of any. Nine-tenths of the paltry revenue of the country was spent on Governor Hobson's 'Folly'. His efforts in his last year were spent in trying to persuade the Wellington settlers to remove to Auckland, theirs in trying to persuade him to remove the capital to Wellington. So far from moving north the settlers were spreading into new areas in the south, rejecting Hobson's choice.

In 1841 the Company despatched two new ready-made colonies to different parts of the vast domain they claimed to have bought. A subsidiary company, formed in the west country under the patronage of the Earl of Devon and the Mayor of Plymouth, sent a small but select body of emigrants to found New Plymouth at the foot of the giant volcanic cone of Tàranàki (or Mount Egmont). Another colony occupied a site on the southern side of Cook Strait, and called it Nelson.

In July 1841 there arrived at Wellington a government commissioner armed with authority to arbitrate upon land-claims. Within a few days the settlers were convinced that his interest and intention was to urge the natives to repudiate their bargain with Colonel Wakefield. Two years of desultory negotiation were required for the allocation of the land to which Lord John Russell had declared the Company entitled. Long before that time had passed, the exasperated settlers were squatting where they could, while the natives had realised that strong factions among the white men would support them in repudiating any land sale. Hobson died in September 1842, a well-meaning honourable man, but unequal to the office he held, even if he had been in good health. During the full year required to arrange for a successor the Governorship was held by a deputy, Lieutenant Shortland, R.N., an incompetent underling whose reign was chiefly marked by jobbery, extravagance and delay. When at last the new Governor arrived, disaster had overtaken the colony.

The leader of the Nelson settlers was Captain Arthur Wakefield, R.N., another sprig from that remarkable family-tree, but unlike Edward and William, a man of blameless, indeed distinguished, reputation. After a long dispute with the ferocious Rauparàha about the ownership of a block of land at Wairau, the Nelson settlers determined to arrest him on a charge of arson since he had driven away a surveying party and burnt their hut. The warrant was served by Arthur Wakefield, a police magistrate and a posse of special constables, upon this renowned barbarian in the midst of his armed followers. High words led to fighting in which the civilian constables cut a poor figure. In an endeavour to stop the bloodshed Arthur Wakefield surrendered, and was massacred with several other Englishmen as a reprisal for the death of a Maori woman who had been accidentally shot during the brawl.

The Wairau Massacre has many counterparts in the long history of the relations between savages and civilised men, but the sequel is unparalleled. The action of the Boers after the murder of Retief in 1838 was in striking contrast. Far from leading to war and reprisal the news of the massacre led to an instant revulsion of feeling against the settlers. The Company's three little colonies began to put themselves in a state of defence until they were sternly forbidden by the Acting-Governor to form Home Guards. To their request for protection he let it be known that he was far more concerned with protecting Rauparàha against their reprisals. The captain of a warship which was sent to the Chief's village, though an old shipmate of Arthur Wakefield, addressed his murderer as 'Friend Rauparàha', taking him by the hand. No claim was made for recovery of the property stolen from the dead men. The missionaries, one and all, took the side of the natives. When the news reached England, Lord Stanley, the Colonial Secretary, declared in the House that the victims had 'violated the rules of the law of England, the maxims of prudence and the principles of justice'. How he came to this conclusion is not evident as no investigation had been held and the material witnesses on the other side were dead. Since Stanley himself had disallowed the Governor's ordinance granting municipal government to the settlements there was no means of empanelling a coroner's jury at Nelson.

Great hopes were entertained from the arrival of the new Governor, Captain R. Fitzroy, a celebrated scientist and navigator. As soon as he arrived (December 1843) he visited Wellington and, after upbraiding the leading settlers at his levee, passed on to a more congenial interview with Rauparàha, whose account of the massacre he instantly accepted as conclusive.

On the one hand stood an old bloodthirsty cannibal, renowned among his fellows for treacherous cunning, who for twenty years had been bargaining with white men, treating them with a nauseous alternation of bluster and fawning, who had signed the Treaty of Waitangi, and the Wakefield land-concession, and had repudiated both; whose sole claim to the Wairau lands lay in the fact that he had killed and eaten the former owners; whose tribe, not having occupied the lands, would suffer no material loss by their sale. On the other hand lay the dead bodies of a naval officer, a magistrate and twenty special constables killed in the execution of what they believed, however 'imprudently', to be their duty. The Church, the State, and the historians have agreed to blame the dead men. Such was the strength of early Victorian philanthropy.

During the two years when Governor Fitzroy held sway (1843–5) New Zealand lapsed into chaos. The Maoris every-

Plate 13

SIR GEORGE GREY, K.C.M.G. (1812–98)

'Good Governor Grey'. An engraving after a painting by G. Richmond,
about 1841. *See p. 386.*

Plate 14

GEORGE AUGUSTUS SELWYN (1809–78)

Bishop of New Zealand. An engraving after a painting by G. Richmond,
about 1842. *See p. 387.*

where repudiated land sales, obstructed surveys, and treated the English with the contempt due to cowards. In the north they truculently declared that Rauparàha should not be allowed to monopolise the glory of killing *pakehàs*. Progress at the Company's settlements, though emigrants continually arrived, was exceedingly slow. At Auckland the land-boom had collapsed, leaving the government sorely embarrassed. Governor Fitzroy, like the early Governors at Adelaide, was forced to draw bills on New South Wales without authority or backing. Being a convinced free-trader he abolished the customs duties, the sole reliable source of revenue, intending to replace them by direct taxes, which he could not collect. Being an honest man he quarrelled with his subordinates, from Deputy-Governor Shortland downwards, since there was not one of them who was not speculating on his own account. Yet the whole machinery of government at Auckland was so corrupt that he could not keep his hands clean and was actually blackmailed by one of his own officers. Suddenly, in desperation, he tried to solve all his problems by overruling the statutory price of land and reverting to the bad old principle of making grants for a nominal fee. This was too much for Lord Stanley who dismissed him with ignominy in 1845. The man selected to revive the bankrupt disorderly colony was Captain George Grey, who had just completed a similar task in South Australia. He was no more than thirty-three years old.

Grey's first problem was a native campaign at the Bay of Islands. In sheer high spirits, one of the tribes, spoiling for a fight, had repeatedly cut down the flagstaff bearing the Union Jack at Koro-ràreka (now called Russell), the old whaling-port. In March 1845 the defence of the flagstaff developed into a battle in which the Maoris sacked the town, allowing the inhabitants to escape by sea to Auckland. Troops from Sydney, and a naval brigade conducted a little bush campaign, not very successfully, against the Maori warriors, who then revealed their prowess. They based their tactics upon building at each suitable point a fortress (*pa*), sited, entrenched, and stockaded with a skill that won the admiration of regular officers, and defended with a courage that defied their efforts. After several failures under other officers, George Grey took personal command. He established his prestige (*mana*) as a great warrior by taking the *pa* of Rua-peka-peka ('the bat's nest') which brought the campaign to a close in January 1846.

From that day the northern tribes have maintained friendly relations with the British.

All observers reported a change in the habits of the Maori. In the northern war there was no cannibalism and no massacre of non-combatants. The tribesmen were Christians, observing the rules of civilised warfare. They complained ruefully that Ruapeka-peka fell only because the Governor launched the assault on Sunday morning when the Maori warriors were at church parade.

Grey had that quality which unsuccessful commanders describe as 'luck' in the successful commanders who supersede them. He had a sense of timing and the resolution to act only when the time was ripe. He was able to do what Hobson and Fitzroy could not, because he insisted upon being given the necessary resources. Whereas Hobson had been expected to make New Zealand self-supporting with its own revenues, and secure with an escort of five policemen, Grey demanded and got 2000 soldiers and a grant-in-aid to cover an estimated deficit of £25,000, his whole budget being £49,000. He set to work briskly at settling land-titles, reverting to the high-price system, and soon came to an agreement with the Company about their claims. Utterly ruthless when confronted with corruption or inefficiency, he discharged most of the officials who had served under the previous Governor.

His greatest success was with the Maoris whose language and traditions he studied, finding time to write a standard work on *Polynesian Mythology*. It was his custom to honour the leading chiefs with public and private attentions, usually inviting one or two to attend him on his journeys. After his success in the northern war he went south to Wellington and taught the tribes who adhered to Rauparàha a salutary lesson. Having defeated them in two or three skirmishes he set them to road-making for good wages. When one chief proved recalcitrant, Grey quickly brought him to another mind about the uses of a road by presenting him with a horse and trap. As for Te Rauparàha, the Governor had taken his measure. A party of sailors was sent ashore by night to kidnap the old warrior. They carried him, kicking and biting, aboard a warship where he was held in honourable captivity for several months. Though the Colonial Office was deeply shocked by such a deed, it was instantly effective. All the Maoris understood that the Governor had greater *mana* than the old chief, who died at a great age, in 1848, soon after his release.

The estimated population of New Zealand about the time of Grey's arrival was 120,000 of whom nine-tenths were natives.[1] Most of the white minority lived in the south, most of the native majority in the north. Grey was obliged, like his predecessors, to give most of his attention to the north and, accordingly, to Auckland rather than to Wellington.

The same point of view was taken by another Englishman, of hardly less moral and mental stature than Grey. This was George Augustus Selwyn (1809–78) who became Bishop of New Zealand in 1842. He was ideally qualified to reconcile Maoris with English, and missionaries with settlers. Not only was he a scholar and a High Churchman, but the Maoris were quick to recognise him too as a great chief. He had all the powers of body and mind required to dominate a community of pioneers. He would make stupendous journeys on foot, alone, from one settlement to the next, swimming the rivers, and sleeping rough. He loved the whalers and visited their camps to marry them to their native wives and to baptise their half-caste children. In return they paid him the compliment of saying that the Bishop could handle a sailing-boat better than any man in the South Seas. It was the Bishop who intervened in the fight at Koro-ràreka in an attempt to prevent the destruction of the town.

Among the problems he had to solve was the complaint that the missionaries themselves were not clear of the taint of land speculation. Even the saintly Henry Williams had provided an estate for his own family, and stoutly asserted that he had acted with honour in doing so. Marsden's policy of civilisation before conversion had made every mission station a farm colony by which the missionary was expected to earn his livelihood. He could not therefore escape the benefit of the general rise in land prices.

[1] Approximate figures 1844–5:

Natives (of whom 40% were Anglican; 15% Methodist; 5% Roman Catholic; and the rest heathen)		109,000
Whites: Bay of Islands	500	
Auckland	2000	
Wellington	4000	
Nelson	3000	
New Plymouth	1000	
etc.	500	
		11,000
		120,000

EARLY SETTLEMENTS
IN
NEW ZEALAND

Miles

0   50   100   150

Land over 3,000 feet

BAY OF ISLANDS

Waitangi
KORORAREKA
(Theatre   (Russell)
of First
Maori   Waipu
War)

Auckland

L. Rotorua

L. Taupo

Cook's
Landfall
1769

New Plymouth

Mt.
Egmont

Wanganui

Tasman's
Landfall
1642

Whaling Stations

Wellington

Nelson

WAIRAU

Mt.
Cook

CANTERBURY

Christchurch

Banks
Pen.

Akaroa

Christchurch

Lyttelton

Akaroa

Canterbury Plains

Whaling
Stations

OTAGO   Dunedin

CANTERBURY SETTLEMENT
LAND TAKEN UP IN 1856

Miles

0   10   20   40   60

Land over 3,000 feet

George Philip & Son, Ltd

Map 16

Selwyn's contribution to Church History was the organisation of the New Zealand Church on an elective basis. He and Governor Grey, mindful of similar experiments in Upper Canada, drew up a constitution for an autonomous colonial Church in communion with Canterbury, placing the temporalities in the hands of lay trustees, a device which, through Selwyn's influence, has spread throughout the whole Anglican Church. Selwyn and Grey, fast friends and allies, were a pair whose like could not easily be found even in that age of great Englishmen.

9. THE COLONIAL REFORMERS AND NEW ZEALAND

WHILE his two brothers, William at Wellington and Arthur at Nelson, were practising the art of colonisation in New Zealand, Edward Gibbon Wakefield had paid two visits to Canada, on private business in connexion with the North American Colonisation Company of Ireland, a land and irrigation company which had bought the Seigneurie of Beauharnois on the St Lawrence as a commercial speculation.[1] None of his biographers has much to say of this period of his life (1841–3). But Wakefield could never abstain from political activity. He was elected to the second Canadian Parliament for the district of Beauharnois, a predominantly French constituency which had been the scene of bloodshed and sedition throughout 1838, the revolutionary year. As was his custom he exercised his powers most vigorously behind the scenes as confidential adviser to Governor Metcalfe urging him to 'finish what Durham began'. The news of his brother's death in the Wairau Massacre recalled Wakefield to England (1843) as champion of the New Zealand settlers.

Since the death of Lord Durham (1840), and especially while Wakefield was abroad, the leading position among the Colonial Reformers had been taken by Charles Buller who, until his early death in 1848, was regarded by his own generation as a politician of great promise. His career, like that of his contemporary, the young Disraeli, was retarded only by an excess of wit which sometimes degenerated into flippancy. He made it his business to

[1] *Bulletin of Dept. of Hist. and Pol. Science.* Queen's University, Kingston, Ontario, December 1925.

deride the Colonial Office and its Permanent Under-Secretary, James Stephen, whom he caricatured under the figure of 'Mr Mother-country'. Despatches from Downing Street and speeches at Westminster made a practice of exhorting the inhabitants of the British colonies to submit dutifully to a mysterious fiction called the Mother-country. Buller set himself to discover who or what was this Mother-country to whom colonials did in fact pay a pathetic and unrewarded tribute of loyalty. It was not the young Queen whose actual power was no greater in imperial than in domestic politics; it was not the British public whose ignorance of the colonies was equalled by their unconcern with them; it was not the House of Commons which could hardly be persuaded to make a quorum for discussing a colonial bill; it was not the Secretary of State, a transient party-hack who never held office long enough to master the multifarious business of his office. In the last resort some irresponsible and obstructive clerk in Downing Street was all the Mother-country that a colonial could identify. 'We will not flatter the pride of our colonial readers', wrote Buller, 'by depicting the real arbiter of their destinies as a person of lofty rank or of the first class among what we call states-men.... He has a modest home in the outskirts of London with an equally modest establishment; and the colonist who is on his road to "the Office" little imagines that it is the real ruler of the colonies that he sees walking over one of the bridges, or driving his one-horse shay, or riding cheek by jowl with him on the top of the short coach, as he comes into town of a morning.... Mr Mother-country's whole heart is in the business of his office. He alone knows on what principle the predecessors of the noble or Right Honourable Secretary acted before: he alone, therefore, can point out the step which it is incumbent to take.'

Colonists who wait in the dismal ante-room of 'the Office', in the belief that they are appealing to the sovereign, find that this right of appeal is 'a mere device for prolonging the tortures of the unhappy victim who, bandied about from colony to England, from Secretary to Secretary, from Under-Secretary to Under-Secretary, from clerk to clerk, wastes away hope and existence, as a subject of Mr Mother-country's systematic procrastination'.

This and much more like it was no doubt personally unjust to James Stephen, a shrewd, prompt civil servant with a legal training and an evangelical conscience, but as a denunciation of the principle of Colonial Office rule it was fully justified. Neither Stephen nor anyone else was competent to direct the government of forty scattered provinces, some of them distant by the length of a six-months' voyage, and all known to him by hearsay only.

Repeated attacks by Buller, and the representations of the New Zealand Company Directors, led to the appointment of a Parliamentary committee on which the Reformers were strongly represented. In April 1844 the committee made a report which gravely embarrassed the government. After examining, and publishing, a mass of evidence largely supplied by Wakefield, they declared that the action of the Company in despatching the *Tory* to New Zealand had been 'highly irregular and improper', but that the Treaty of Waitangi, on the other hand, had been 'injudicious'. The implication that all the land of New Zealand, whether occupied or not, was the property of the sparse Maori tribes had been 'an error productive of injurious consequences'. Lord Stanley, the Colonial Secretary who had stoutly championed the Treaty of Waitangi, was obliged to accept this rebuff, but beyond informing the Governor of New Zealand, he took no further action.

The growing strength of the Reformers during the next few months must be considered as a phase of the revolution in English politics. Free Trade, an issue which was to affect the colonies as profoundly as the mother-country, was bringing about the break-up of the old Whig and Tory parties; and the agitation over New Zealand was used as another wedge to split Sir Robert Peel's majority. Buller took an active part in the Corn Law debates, surprising the House by blurting out: 'You advocates of Free Trade wish to bring food to the people. I suggest to you at the same time to take your people to the food.'

In June 1845 he achieved a triumph by moving a resolution that was, in effect, a vote of censure on Lord Stanley. The importance of the debate is not so much in what was said as in the fact that a colonial question was discussed for three whole days in a full House, an event that is rare in imperial history. When the House divided, Buller mustered 173 votes against a Government majority of 233. The Whig leaders Russell and Palmerston, the 'anti-corn-law' leaders Cobden and Bright, supported Buller, as did Disraeli, who was then working up his vendetta against Peel. Gladstone supported the Government. Peel himself spoke powerfully in defence of his subordinate, justifying the Treaty of Waitangi and assuring the House that all would be well now that Governor George Grey had taken charge. But the debate was so damaging to the administration that Lord Stanley soon resigned, ostensibly because of a difference with Peel over the Corn Laws.

When at the crisis of the Irish famine the Tories split and the Whigs returned to office (July 1846), Lord John Russell gave the seals of the Colonies to the third Earl Grey, who, as Viscount Howick, had adopted the Wakefield theories in 1831 and had voted for Buller's motion in 1845. Unfortunately he was one of those many people who disliked Wakefield and whom Wakefield hated. Lord Melbourne said of Grey, explaining his character to Queen Victoria, 'he is a very clever man but a very obstinate man, and excessively eager about what he takes up, and very angry when everybody don't immediately adopt his views'. He was now determined to solve the New Zealand problem in his own way, in consultation with his namesake, Governor Grey, and without reference to the intriguing Colonial Reformers. An interview between Lord Grey and Wakefield in August 1846 ended in a personal quarrel which the two participants described in flatly different terms. A few days later Wakefield was removed from the scene by a paralytic stroke—which confined him to private life for about a year. Physically he never recovered from this attack—he was fifty years of age—mentally he grew more violent, quarrelsome and secretive. In his absence the New Zealand Company had lost its grip on political affairs and had been degraded into a commercial company for administering the Crown's right of pre-emption over the central and southern parts of New Zealand. The government of the country was to have been regulated by a new and highly democratic constitution which Lord Grey had prepared and offered to the Governor. To the surprise of all concerned, the Governor instantly rejected it on the grounds that such a constitution would enable the whites, who formed one-tenth of the population, to tyrannise over the natives, who formed nine-tenths. Even more surprising was the fact that Lord Grey acquiesced. The settlers in New Zealand now began to regard Governor Grey as their enemy and no better than his predecessors; while the Colonial Reformers in London began to think that Lord Grey was a renegade from their principles.

A plan had long been germinating in Wakefield's fertile brain for interesting the Churches in colonisation, outflanking thereby the opposition of the missionaries. At Adelaide, Wellington, Nelson and New Plymouth there had been something wanting to complete the parallel with Maryland and Pennsylvania. The missing factor was religion as a motive force. He had begun to consider Anglican, Presbyterian, Irish Catholic and Jewish settlements, which involved him in a network of new intrigues. The foundation of New Plymouth, by a philanthropic association acting as an extension of the moribund New Zealand Company, foreshadowed the method by which Church Associations might found colonies. The Otago[1] (1848) and Canterbury (1850) settlements concluded Wakefield's career with a degree of success attained by few political projectors.

Mr George Rennie of Edinburgh had for some years been urging the New Zealand Company to found a Scottish colony, when the Disruption of the Scottish Church (1843) provided the necessary impetus. A Lay Association of the seceding Free Churchmen was formed in 1845 to organise a Free Church colony, the promoters being the Rev. Thomas Burns (the poet's nephew) and Captain William Cargill, a Peninsular veteran. Little progress was made until 1847 (the time of Wakefield's return to active life) when an agreement was reached between the Lay Association and the New Zealand Company. The former body was to select and despatch Free Church emigrants, the latter was to acquire and survey the site, and settle the emigrants upon the land. 2000 sixty-acre sections were to be sold to settlers at £2 an acre, while 400 additional sections were to be reserved as an endowment for churches and schools.

In November 1847 the first ship sailed from Gravesend with 100 Scottish emigrants, the second from Greenock with 240. In April 1848 they landed at Otago harbour in the south of New Zealand and founded the township which they called Dunedin. The harbour was renamed Port Chalmers after the hero of the Free Church. As in all the Wakefield colonies progress was much slower than had been anticipated. By December 1852 only about one-eighth part of the allotted land had been sold. The population consisted of hardy Lowland labourers (2000 in 1852, 3800 in 1856) who accepted the patriarchal rule of honest old Captain Cargill;

[1] Pronounced to rhyme with 'virago'.

and found the climate and the landscape not unlike their native Scotland. But for some years the colony languished, though its future was to exceed the hopes of its founders.

In November 1847, while convalescing at Malvern, Wakefield had become acquainted with a young Irish squire, John Robert Godley (1814–61), who proved to be the ideal promoter for a Church of England colony. Godley was a Tory and a High Churchman, a classical scholar of Christ Church, Oxford, and a friend of Gladstone (who, it should be remembered, was at that date still a Tory). He had travelled widely and had recently published a thoughtful book on his experiences in America. It was reported that he had almost persuaded Peel, in 1845, to anticipate the Irish Famine by advancing £10,000,000 to trustees who would transfer a million Irishmen to Canada. Godley brought into the circle of the Colonial Reformers a new group of young men whose ideals were very different from those of the matter-of-fact young Radicals of Wakefield's youth. Godley's friends were earnest, pious and enthusiastic, the products of the reformed public schools, the Oxford Movement, and the Romantic Revival. Wakefield had little difficulty in inspiring Godley with his enthusiasm for a Church colony, which Godley was to organise on the Wakefield plan. Twenty years of propaganda and experiment at last· bore fruit. One Church dignitary alone, Dr Hinds, the Bishop of Norwich, had from the beginning stood with the Colonial Reformers; now many of the most dignified clergy gave their support to Mr Godley's scheme. Archbishop Sumner joined them as chairman of what was known as the Canterbury Association (March 1848). The membership was far more eminent than that of Wakefield's previous colonising bodies. In addition to two Archbishops, Sumner and Whately, seven other bishops lent their names. The lay members, many of them Godley's college friends, included Lord Shaftesbury, Lord John Manners, Sidney Herbert, the Earls of Lincoln and Devon, several other peers and fifteen members of Parliament. Among these notables, two now threw in their lot with the Colonial Reformers and devoted much of their public life to colonial questions; these were the fourth Lord Lyttelton (1817–76) and Mr C. B. Adderley,[1] afterwards Lord

[1] Perhaps best remembered by the main street of Capetown which bears his name, in gratitude for his Parliamentary efforts to save the Cape from being made a convict colony, 27 March 1849.

Norton (1814–1905). Godley was managing director of the Association until, in 1849, he was ordered abroad for his health. He then undertook to go to New Zealand as leader of the Canterbury Settlement, leaving the management of the Association at home largely to Lyttelton and Adderley.

Though Wakefield's name did not appear among the notables of the Canterbury Association he was never more active than in 1848 and 1849. His letters reveal a network of negotiations of extraordinary complexity. No one observing a stout florid John-Bullish figure, riding slowly over the Surrey Downs, followed by a pack of the rare Talbot hounds and beagles which it was his hobby to breed, would have supposed that this was the Machiavellian Mr Wakefield, whom *The Times* denounced as a dangerous and discredited swindler, whose past history was unmentionable, whose present activities were a spider's web of doubtful intrigues. Yet Wakefield was indispensable. He boasted that thirty-six members of Parliament called one week-end at his little house at Reigate to consult him on colonial questions. He had to manage the press, to write the propaganda, to appoint the officers of the Association, even to select a bishop for Canterbury, though he was a better judge of a prize bulldog than of a colonial bishop. He drafted the constitution of New Zealand one afternoon sitting with Adderley in the garden of the latter's house. Provided that he remained in the background all went well. In 1849 he instituted a new Colonial Reform Society to which he attracted his new Tory friends[1] from the Canterbury Association, as well as his old Radical associates. Colonial Reform was now respectable as was proved by the belated adherence of *The Times*. For twenty years every project connected with the hated names of Durham or Wakefield had been belaboured by the Thunderer. In 1849 the tune was changed, the Canterbury Settlement with its episcopal backing could not be denounced in the old clap-trap style.

The proposal was to transfer, to some part of New Zealand where there were no native inhabitants, what *The Times* described as a 'complete slice of England cut from top to bottom'. The settlers were to comprise not only labourers as at Otago, but gentle and simple, professional men in due proportion, teachers and clergy and at the top of the social scale a nobleman and a bishop

---

[1] Hume and Roebuck, Cobden and Lowe joined the Society, Peel and Disraeli refused Adderley's invitation to join.

as the natural leaders of an English, and Anglican, society. Two and a half millions of acres of land were to be purchased from the New Zealand Company and sold to settlers at the price of £3 an acre, which even Wakefield thought sufficiently high. The land-fund derived from sales would be disposed of at the rate of 10s. for the purchase price of the land, 10s. for survey and development, £1 for the emigration fund and £1 for the endowment of churches and schools. Every buyer of a fifty-acre section would be entitled to a quarter-acre town-lot in the capital city, and to a pasturage lease over the undeveloped land beyond the limits of settlement. At first, only members of the Church of England were admitted as land-purchasers.

Lord Grey somewhat grudgingly approved the scheme, though he took exception to some details, for which a royal charter was issued in November 1849. The New Zealand Company was dis-solved in 1850 after disposing of its assets to the Canterbury Asso-ciation, the whole transaction being legalised by the Canterbury Settlement Land Act (13 & 14 Vict. cap. 70) which became law on 14 August 1850.

While Godley was preparing to receive the settlers in New Zea-land, Wakefield urged on the land sales in London. During the summer of 1850 the first band of settlers was chosen. Meeting fre-quently at their office in the Adelphi they formed a constitutional association, discussed their plans, heard lectures on New Zealand, and assembled the necessities of civilised emigration. Several settlers took with them frame houses in sections; a committee was appointed (under another of Wakefield's brothers) to acclimatise English plants and animals; and among other accessories the first ships carried an organ, a church bell, school equipment, and a printing press. The first actual achievement of the settlers was to collect a reference library of 2000 volumes from a grant made by the University of Oxford. Their keenest enthusiasm was for the foundation of a cathedral and a college, at the first commencement of the colony, to be 'a centre from which arts and morals should be spread through the southern world'. This combination of cathedral and college was derived from the constitution of Christ Church, Oxford, and Christchurch was accordingly to be the name of the principal town in Canterbury Settlement.

In spite of support from all quarters, and publicity hitherto un-paralleled, the land sales again fell short of expectations. In the first year land to the value of £39,450 was sold whereas the terms of the charter required £50,000. The Association was saved from insolvency in May 1850 by a personal guarantee given by Lord Lyttelton and some others. They were now so deeply committed that they decided to launch the colony on a smaller scale than had been first intended and without the exalted leadership of a noble-man. Four shiploads of settlers were assembled in London and were dubbed by Martin Tupper, the popular poetaster of that day, the 'Canterbury Pilgrims', the name by which they are still re-membered in New Zealand. A public dinner to the whole party was given by the Association at a cost of £742; and a farewell sermon was preached to them by the Archbishop in St Paul's. The First Four Ships sailed from London River on 7 and 8 September and arrived at the New Zealand harbour which they were to call Port Lyttelton between 16 and 27 December 1850. They carried 127 cabin passengers (at £42 a berth), 85 intermediate pas-sengers (at £25 a berth), and 534 steerage passengers (at £15 a berth). No party of emigrants so well-chosen, well-prepared and well-led had landed in any colony since the golden days of Charles II. Never had any emigrants arrived to find such com-plete arrangements for their reception. Godley stood there to re-ceive them on a wooden jetty. Four large 'barracks' had been erected on the hillside for temporary shelter. A hundred Maori labourers were at work making a road inland. The million acres had been roughly surveyed and three town-sites, Christchurch, Lyttelton and Sumner had been laid out. Governor Grey and Bishop Selwyn, both inclined to dislike Wakefield colonies, had been won over by Godley's transparent honesty, and both arrived to welcome the settlers. At first the Utopian dreams of the projectors seemed to have come true; but as a matter of fact the Canterbury Association was penniless and deep in debt.

10. CANTERBURY SETTLEMENT, 1850

EVERY new colony produces some new problem which the planners have not foreseen; in Canterbury it was the road from the port to the capital. The Canterbury block was a shelving alluvial plain formed by the outfall of torrential rivers from the Southern Alps, with a landscape and a climate like northern Italy. There was no harbour or anchorage off the surf-beaten sandy beach. Midway along the shore and projecting into the sea there rose a humped volcanic mass of hills, named Banks' Peninsula, penetrated from seaward by four deep-water inlets. One of these harbours was Akaroa where the French settlers had made their home in 1840; another was Port Lyttelton where Godley received the First Four Ships. But the exit from Port Lyttelton (or from Akaroa) to the fertile plains was over the crest of the range, a journey which Godley compared to a crossing of the Ogwen Pass from Bettws-y-Coed. Lack of funds compelled him to curtail construction of a mountain road so that for some years the settlers carried their goods by packhorse over a rocky trail, or transhipped them into whale-boats which must cross a dangerous sand-bar before rowing up the swampy stream to Christchurch, five miles inland. This was the first taste of 'roughing it', which dispelled the rosy dreams of the gentlemen in tall hats and ladies in crinolines among the Canterbury Pilgrims.

A school was opened, and a newspaper—vehemently demanding self-government in its early issues—was published at Lyttelton within a few days of landing. In February 1851 the centre of activity shifted over the hills to Christchurch where land was selected by the purchasers in order. While the settlers took up their sections, built huts of the scanty timber, and began to till the ground, Godley, as resident magistrate and as agent of the Canterbury Association, was responsible for law and order; for the survey and road-making; for the issue of land-titles and pasturage leases; for negotiating the limit of their reserves with the handful of Maoris who occupied three or four villages in Canterbury; for coming to terms with the French at Akaroa; and for regulating the position of some settlers from Wellington who had squatted in Canterbury before the coming of the 'Pilgrims'. Godley welcomed them, in spite of the displeasure of the land-purchasers, since they could sell provisions which would tide the 'Pilgrims' over to their first harvest.

Such tasks as these, which in every other new colony had led to bickerings and disputes, Godley carried out with firmness and patience. The foundation of churches and schools, which had bulked so large in the prospectus, took much of his time. The bishopric proved very troublesome since the bishop-designate fled at the first glimpse of colonial hardships, to the great disgust of Bishop Selwyn. The college (later known as Christ's College) made a start with a grammar school, a hospital, a library, and primary schools in each township but all on a tiny scale and under rough conditions. Godley's plan for the control of the Church endowments by a body of lay trustees proved to be the solution of the vexed problem of providing for the clergy from the waste lands of a new colony.

As political leader of the Canterbury settlers, Godley placed himself at the head of the opposition to Governor Grey, demanding the constitutional rights which the Governor withheld. On the other hand, although he was the agent of the Canterbury Association he declined to be bound by instructions from London if he found them unsuited to the conditions of the colony. He would not submit to regulation either by the Governor, 500 miles away at Auckland, or by the Association, 13,000 miles away in London. 'The form of the constitution', he said, 'might be a question for discussion, but it must be *localised*. I would rather be governed by a Nero on the spot than by a board of Angels in London, because we could, if the worst came to the worst, cut off Nero's head, but we could not get at the board in London at all.' Having realised very soon that pastoral farming, not agriculture, would make the wealth of Canterbury he began to grant pastoral leases to sheep-farmers from other colonies, who brought their stock and their experience to the new settlement. As this was in flat defiance of the original plan which allowed grazing-rights only to land-purchasers, he found himself at loggerheads with the Association in London. In Godley's view it was time for them to abdicate in favour of the settlers.

The Canterbury Settlement, founded with such high hopes, had already been written off as a failure by the faint-hearts, and as a failure it has been described in several histories. The mistake made by the promoters had been to suppose that it could be established in a year or two. In December 1852 Godley returned to England, where Gladstone gave him a high appointment in the Civil Service (see chapter x, 2, page 536). His farewell speech to the Canterbury settlers, a decent thriving community of 3400 persons, propounded his own faith. 'Now that I have been a practical colonist,' he said, 'I often smile when I think of the Ideal Canterbury of which our imagination dreamed. Yet I am not sure that the reality is not in many respects sounder and better than the dream.' He defended the Wakefield plan, claiming that at Canterbury there was a more concentrated population, a larger proportion of resident landowners and, consequently, a more civilised society than in earlier colonies, none the less because 'a barrister was not ashamed to dig nor an army officer to drive cattle'.

Six years later he was able to announce to a meeting of sympathisers in London, as agent for the Canterbury settlers, that the population had reached 7000, with 2000 immigrants coming in each year, that the debt to Lord Lyttelton had been repaid, that the colony had been self-supporting from its third year and was exporting food to the Australian gold-fields, that revenue at the rate of £14 per head was raised without hardship and that exports were valued at £30 per head. Between 1861 and 1867 the little colony was able to finance from its own resources a railway, piercing the hills between Port Lyttelton and Christchurch with what was then the longest tunnel in the world. Within thirty years the Cathedral and College were built much as they had been planned, and the Canterbury block now sustains about 250,000 New Zealanders with a remarkably high standard of comfort.

The New Zealand Constitution Act (15 & 16 Vict. cap. 72) had been initiated by Governor Grey who thought the time ripe, at last, for giving the colony a democratic and federal constitution. Though Lord Grey concluded his policy of granting self-government to the 'white' colonies by preparing the New Zealand Bill the Whig government fell before it was enacted. The next Colonial Secretary, Sir John Pakington, a Tory and a friend of the Colonial Reformers, saw it through Parliament. The colony became a federation of six strong provinces, five of them Wakefield settlements, and the sixth the 'official' settlement of Auckland.

Plate 15

EDWARD GIBBON WAKEFIELD (1796–1862)

The founder of six settlements in Australia and New Zealand. From a portrait by
C. A. Collins painted for the New Zealand Company in 1849 and now in the Canterbury
Museum, New Zealand. The dogs are said to be by Landseer. *See p. 325.*

Plate 16

HENRY, 3RD EARL GREY (1802–94)

Authorised responsible government in several colonies. 'A very clever man but a very obstinate man.' *See p. 392.*

With this happy ending to the struggle for systematic colonisa-tion and self-government, Wakefield's life-work seemed to have been completed. His political testament, *A View of the Art of Colonization*, had been published in 1849, a book full of wise reflexions, marred by bitter personal attacks on Lord Grey. The governing classes had at last been converted, as was demonstrated by the last of Wakefield's foundations, the Colonial Reform Society. Wakefield now fulfilled an old promise of ending his days in the colony he had founded. He arrived in New Zealand soon after Godley's departure. 'I would have fancied myself in England,' he said of Canterbury in 1853, 'but for the hard work-ing industry of the upper classes and the luxurious independence of the common people.' It was however in Wellington, which his brother William had founded, that he spent his last years, fated, to the end, to provoke suspicion and dislike. When one of the Wellington constituencies elected him to the first New Zealand Parliament (1853) he was accorded the honour of moving a reso-lution calling upon the Acting-Governor to institute responsible government. For Governor Grey had gone on furlough, dis-creetly avoiding an encounter with Wakefield. Not many weeks passed before Wakefield's inveterate love of intrigue had alienated all his friends. The champion of responsible government was bitterly denounced for exercising a malign secret influence over the Acting-Governor.

He was now growing old and soon retired from public life. For some years he lived quietly at Wellington and died, in 1862, at the age of sixty-six, almost a forgotten man. The graves of the two brothers, William and Edward Gibbon Wakefield, are in the old cemetery overlooking Wellington harbour. They have no monu-ment other than the Dominion of New Zealand itself.

VIII

EMPIRE IN THE EAST, 1814-79

Argument: The demands of trade and sea-power established British authority first in the seaports and then in the adjacent territories of Ceylon, Burma, Malaya, Borneo and the China coast. Singapore was the creation of one man who forced the hand of the British government, Sarawak of one man who played a lone hand.

The dynamic of the West broke through the fragile crust of conservatism that protected the old kingdoms of Asia. China and Japan were violated and forced to move with the times. Liberals and Evangelicals set out to reform India on Western lines. Less justifiable were the diplomatic intrigues that led to wars and conquests on the North-West Frontier. British India was integrated by Lord Dalhousie, against whose system the ill-organised spontaneous 'Indian Mutiny' reacted in vain, with the effect only of stiffening the ruling British caste.

1. CEYLON, BURMA, SINGAPORE, SARAWAK

CEYLON

AFTER seizing Ceylon from the Portuguese in 1658 the Dutch had occupied three or four seaports on the coast, but had never penetrated the interior. There were, as there still are, considerable settlements of Europeans and half-castes recruited from both nations at Galle, Colombo and Trincomali. Of these the Dutch element, known as 'burghers', made the deepest mark upon the life of the island. The settlements, under good Dutch laws and a Dutch system of administration, exported cinnamon and pearls.

The cupidity of rival nations was directed towards Ceylon, during the eighteenth-century wars, chiefly on account of the harbour of Trincomali which all strategists remarked upon. Nelson and Wellington had each made note of it. It had been held in turn by Hughes and de Suffren in the seventeen-eighties, and passed to Great Britain at the final cession of the island in 1814. Meanwhile the interior was held by the kings of Kandy who, generation by generation, excelled other oriental tyrants in pride, cruelty, and treachery. This was the island where every prospect pleased but only man was vile. The Dutch left the kings of Kandy alone. The East India Company, on many occasions, tried to come to diplomatic terms with them but were always repulsed with contempt. When they accredited an envoy to Kandy in 1762 he found his representations somewhat hampered by being obliged to approach the King's throne on all fours through a long hall and under a barrier. Prostrate on the ground, he then conveyed his message through four intermediaries to the royal ear. As was usual at such courts intrigue and bribery were the only ways to favour.

The story of the British occupation of Ceylon (1796) has been told in another chapter. Since the island had been occupied by troops of the East India Company it was for three unhappy years subjected to the Madras Presidency. But when the Madras revenue-system proved so unsuited to the customs of Ceylon as to provoke rebellion, it was decided (1798) to convert the island into a Crown Colony on the new model. Accordingly Frederick North, a man of talent and energy, was sent as Governor under the Colonial Office. His domestic policy was liberal and practical. Abandoning the Madras system he won the confidence of the cultivators and enlisted the support of the 'burghers', by restoring Dutch principles of administration and by introducing a specially prepared code of Roman-Dutch law. Externally he engaged his government in disgrace and disaster by intervening in the affairs of the kingdom of Kandy. He supported a candidate for the throne during a palace revolution and, naturally enough as politics went in that country, was cheated by the upstart whom he thought to make his tool. A peculiarly revolting series of treacheries and tortures was concluded by the massacre of a party of British soldiers, isolated at Kandy, who tamely surrendered on promise of their lives (1803). Since war against Napoleon was just then being renewed, no troops were available to avenge the massacre until 1815. The King of Kandy had filled the interval with sadistic acts of cruelty which provide material for bazaar story-tellers to this day. He overreached himself by seizing and mutilating a party of Cingalese merchants who were British subjects and, when a punitive expedition was sent against him, could think of no better means of resistance than by executing the messengers who successively brought news of their approach. His kingdom was overthrown and annexed to the colony of Ceylon. The

George Philip & Son, Ltd.

Map 17

forests and hills of the interior were not pacified until 1824, perhaps not securely until the completion of the military road from
Colombo to Kandy in 1831 (reinforced by a railway in 1867),
since when the political history of the island has been for the most
part uneventful.

Among the administrative troubles of the government were
some arising out of duties and privileges inherited from the

former dynasty. For more than 2000 years the kings of Kandy had
enjoyed great temple revenues as guardians of the sacred relic
reputed to be Buddha's tooth. These temporalities were now
attached to the British government, which for some years received
the rents and administered the estates until, in 1844, the Colonial
Office repented. 'A Christian administration must not be associated with the practices of an idolatrous religion.' The decision
caused much offence in Kandy and led to a local insurrection.

At that time there was also economic unrest in Ceylon. Formerly cinnamon gardens and pearl-fisheries, both coastal industries, had formed all the commercial wealth of the island. Coffee
had been introduced in 1836. In the few years before Peel's Free
Trade government reduced the protective duties (1845) there was
a boom in coffee-planting, in the virgin lands of the kingdom of
Kandy. A few British planters moved in, followed by Tamil
labourers from the Malabar Coast, to the number of 70,000 in a
year. Unrest at this economic revolution, all the more when a
slump came in 1846 and 1847, contributed to the outbreak of disorders. Nevertheless plantation coffee (exports to Great Britain
were worth £363,000 in 1845, £2,750,000 in 1870) soon became
the main source of Ceylon's wealth, while exports of cinnamon
declined in quantity and more in quality. Though an increasing acreage of the best coffee-plantations was developed by
the skill of British planters a substantial proportion (a third in
1850, a seventh in 1870) was owned by natives of the island. Rice
was also cultivated intensively on the coast. The rising standard
of living of the cultivators was marked by the increasing imports
of foodstuffs and cotton cloth. Tea-planting was begun by the
government of Ceylon to save the island from disaster, when, in
1876, a disease of the coffee plant killed off all the plantations.
During the eighteen-eighties tea-planting extended and prospered
until by the end of the century 390,000 acres of plantations
produced, in a year, 146,000,000 lb. of tea. This was a more
highly organised industry than coffee-planting. Tea-plantations
required British supervision and the investment of £10,000,000.

BURMA

The kings of Ava, the inland part of what is now called Burma, resembled the kings of Kandy. Like most Asiatic rulers their origin was reputed to be divine and their sovereign powers accordingly unquestioned. In general, diplomatic relations were impossible since the Burmese monarch would converse with no one but the ambassador of a heaven-born king and then only if the ambassador first abased himself before the throne. Notwithstanding this arrogance, the Burmese kings were, in diplomatic theory, subject to the Chinese Empire.

In 1823 the King of Ava ordered his armies to march into Bengal and conquer the English, though, it appears, he did not very well know what or where Calcutta might be. Very ill-found expeditions took the field against him, suffering heavy losses from malaria, but there was little fighting. A sea-borne expedition to Rangoon made little progress up the rivers; a column from Manipur failed to penetrate the jungles of Assam; while a third combined operation under command of Captain Marryat, the novelist, led to the capture of the Akyab peninsula. The provinces of Arakan, Manipur and Tenasserim, which were inhabited by jungle tribes, not of Burmese race, were occupied, ceded to the British in 1826, and incorporated into the Presidency of Calcutta.

Prosperity soon came to the Arakan district from the cultivation of rice for the Indian market, which made Akyab the greatest rice-exporting seaport in the world. Administration was, however, bad. Direct government from Calcutta led to alternate neglect and delay, and to niggling interferences with the Resident. (Fanny Burney's brother, Admiral Burney, was the first to hold the office.) No funds and no forces were available to suppress *dacoity*, the form of brigandage which has always flourished when times are bad in Burma. There were no overland communications with India then, or a hundred years later when they were so sorely needed. The roads from the coast to the interior were jungle trails across parallel ranges of wooded mountains. Inland the kings of Ava were as intransigent and truculent as ever.

The second Burmese War broke out in 1852 over disputes between British merchants and the Burmese Governor of Rangoon, a cosmopolitan seaport. Repeated acts of petty tyranny against British citizens led to intervention by the Viceroy, Lord Dalhousie, who was then actively engaged in his policy of annexing misgoverned provinces as though the propriety of British expansion were a Law of Nature. The operations against the southern coast of Burma were carried out, again without meeting serious resistance, by Admiral Austen (Jane Austen's brother); and were followed by the annexation of Rangoon, Martaban, and Pegu. Again the expedition stopped short of invading Burma proper, the inland districts where the Burmese race dwelt. The trade with Rangoon was in hardwoods, and the annexation led to the growth of a prosperous shipbuilding industry at Moulmein. Teak was also exported for building ships on the Clyde.

THE STRAITS SETTLEMENTS

The great island of Sumatra imposed a barrier, a thousand miles long, across the sea-ways to China from the West. Though the Sunda Strait at its southern extremity was commanded by the Dutch port of Batavia, the Malacca Strait at the northern extremity had never been brought completely under Dutch control. The old fort of Malacca, once Portuguese, then Dutch, was declining; its trade with Sumatra dwindled, as the sultans of that island successfully maintained their resistance against commercial or any other progress. As early as 1771 Francis Light, the master of a 'country ship', had approached Warren Hastings with a proposal for a British post at Penang but nothing was done until peace was restored. Intervention in the American War brought no advantage to the Dutch. On the contrary by the treaty of 1784 the Dutch renounced their exclusive claim to the trade of the East Indies. Thereafter for about ninety years there were repeated disputes between the British and Dutch governments, and repeated claims and counter-claims by British and Dutch empire-builders on the spot, before the division of spheres of influence was completed. Sumatra, at first treated as neutral ground on which both nations had some paltry trading-posts, was a contentious region.

In 1785 Francis Light renewed his efforts, making a private treaty with the Sultan of Kedah who ceded him the island of Penang, 'as long the sun and moon should give light' for a pension of 6000 dollars a year.[1] This was a commercial transaction and lovers of the romantic must abandon the old fictitious tale that

---

[1] By a further Treaty in 1800 a strip of coast on the mainland of Kedah, Wellesley Province, was added to Penang and the payment raised to $10,000. Later still, in the general treaty of 1826, another foothold on the coast, known as the Dindings, was ceded to the Company, and was receded to Perak in 1934.

Light received the island as a dowry upon his marriage with the Sultan's daughter. Light then persuaded the acting Governor-General of India, Sir John Macpherson, to take over Penang as a province under the name of Prince of Wales' Island (1786). From the beginning Macpherson proposed that it should be a free port for the trade of all nations. For many years Penang showed a large annual deficit, and was valued chiefly as a naval station. Macpherson refused to be drawn into a defensive alliance with Kedah against the king of Siam, though Francis Light had promised an alliance to the Sultan.

When the Dutch Republic was forced into alliance with the French Jacobins, the rivalry between Dutch and British grew hotter in the Indies. The seizure of the Dutch colonies was more strongly resisted there than in Ceylon or at the Cape where the Orange party favoured a British alliance. Malacca was taken by a British force in 1795, receded at the Peace of Amiens, taken again in 1807 and receded once again after Waterloo. It was the base in 1809 for Lord Minto's hard-fought campaign for the conquest of Java in which Stamford Raffles (1781–1826) made his name as intelligence officer.

The extension of British trade and British sea-power into Malaya was brought about by the personal efforts of far-seeing pioneers and not by acts of policy such as those which led to the occupation of Ceylon and Lower Burma. These acts, though they substituted the rule of law for frantic tyranny, peace for perpetual strife, and wealth for poverty, were somewhat high-handed: but Singapore and Sarawak were occupied by the British without intrusion upon any man's rights. The work of Stamford Raffles and of 'Rajah' Brooke was entirely advantageous to the peoples of the archipelago and to the commerce of the world. Though both men were exposed to the ignorant abuse of partisans in England, both earned the lasting gratitude of the Asiatic nations whom they served.

When Lord Minto found Raffles invaluable, he was appointed administrator of Java, and set himself to mitigate the harshness of Dutch rule. He was a linguist, a student of oriental life, devoted to the Malayan peoples. 'The Malay races', he said, 'when treated with sympathy, are of all eastern peoples, the easiest to rule.' He prohibited the slave trade, regulated the conditions of slavery, abolished forced labour and the legal use of torture and mutilation, and attempted a settlement of the revenue on the Madras system. Like his contemporaries in India he favoured direct administration in European style, failing to appreciate the method of the Dutch which, though severe, was a kind of Indirect Rule. These sudden reforms assumed that Java would remain in British hands and were brought sharply to a close when the Dutch colonies were, in 1814, restored to the kingdom of the Netherlands. Raffles was marked down as a hasty and domineering young man who moved too fast and incurred unjustified expenses. However he was appointed Lieutenant-Governor of Bencoolen, a decayed trading-post in Sumatra, where he continued his researches and studies, in strategy as well as in the natural sciences. He made botanical discoveries and sent home ethnological specimens for the British Museum.

He was convinced, and repeatedly urged his conviction upon the governments in London and Calcutta, that the Dutch 'animosity against British trade was never greater than at this moment', that they were still determined to monopolise the East Indies. The remedy was for the British to occupy some strategic point: 'a port which should have a commanding position at the southern entrance of the Straits of Malacca, in the track of our China and Country trade...which might give us the means of supporting and defending our commercial intercourse with the Malay States, and which...might enable us to watch the march of Dutch policy'. 'There are ports of which we may take possession...and princes at liberty to make treaty with us in favour of our commerce. To the Dutch intimidation of the natives we can oppose protection. To their imposition of heavy duties...we can oppose the facility of obtaining our goods free of duty.'

When on a visit to Calcutta, he was encouraged by the Governor-General, Lord Hastings, to pursue his schemes. ' Sir Stamford, you may depend upon me.' This seemed enough. On 30 January 1819 he signed a treaty with the Sultan of Johore for ceding the island of Singapore to the East India Company. 'You have only to glance at the map...', he wrote, 'our station completely outflanks the Straits of Malacca, and secures a passage for our China ships at all times and in all circumstances. It has also been my good fortune to discover one of the most safe and extensive harbours in these seas....' 'What Malta is in the West, that may Singapore become in the East.'

But Raffles's enthusiasm and a hint from Lord Hastings were not enough. The Dutch took deep offence, which even the British Governor of Penang thought well-justified. Each nation accused the other of breaches of the treaties of 1784 and 1814 and with good cause, since the agents of the Dutch Company were at

Map 18

least as active as Raffles. The matter was referred to diplomatic negotiation in London which took its leisurely course during the next four years. At this time Canning was much engaged in discussions with the Dutch minister Falck over a wide range of subjects, and noted that

the fault of the Dutch
Was offering too little and asking too much.

However, in 1824 an amicable treaty was signed. The British ceded to the Dutch their factories in Sumatra, the Dutch to the British their factories in India. The Dutch recognised the British claim to Singapore, and both governments agreed to allow no new settlements in the East Indies without authority from Europe. Canning wrote with typical British complacency to Raffles: 'Your extreme activity in stirring up difficult questions . . . did oblige me to speak my mind to you in instructions of no very mild reprehension. But I was not the less anxious to retain the fruits of your policy. . . .' Raffles had contracted with the Sultan of Johore for the site of a factory and an area within range of a cannon-shot about it. Compounds were to be surveyed for European, Chinese, and Malay inhabitants. The English were to advance money for building 'a respectable mosque' near the Sultan's palace. The town was to be administered jointly by the English Resident and the Sultan's representative. British common law was to be enforced 'with due consideration to the usages and habits of the people'. In return for a final cession of the island the Sultan was paid 60,000 dollars and a pension of 2000 dollars a month. Though the island contained the ruins of an ancient city, the site had been deserted for many hundred years and was, when Raffles came there, uninhabited but for a few families of fishermen and pirates. Raffles had indeed committed the government without their knowledge to the founding of a city which would rival Batavia. Though the chancelleries of Europe were satisfied for the moment, the competition between Dutch and English empirebuilders never slackened in the East.

The founder of Singapore returned to England in 1824 still a young man of forty-three and full of restless energy. On the way he lost, by shipwreck, his savings and his ethnological collections. His reward for service was to be presented by the East India Directors with a bill for £20,000 which he had overspent in their interest. The last two years of his short life, for he died in 1826, were devoted to the encouragement of foreign missions and, as first President of the Zoological Society, to the foundation of the London Zoo.

When Raffles left Singapore the population was said to be about 10,000, including many Chinese merchants. From its foundation it was a free port open to the trade of all nations, a new feature in the political economy of Asia. The slave trade, slavery,

and even debt-slavery, the oppressive Malayan system that enabled a creditor to seize the person of his debtor, had been abolished. It had been Raffles' intention to administer his city on
English rather than on Indian principles and to associate the mercantile community with the government. Merchants had already
been commissioned as Justices of the Peace. But, in 1826, when
the government of the three 'Straits Settlements', Singapore,
Malacca and Penang, was organised by the East India Company
and the last holdings in Sumatra were surrendered to the Dutch,
a change took place for the worse.

After they had lost their monopoly of the China tea-trade, in
1833, the East India Company lost interest in the Far East. These
outposts, with their Malayan peasantry and Chinese townsfolk, had
little in common with Bengal and brought it no advantage. Malacca,
once a rich city and for centuries the outlet for the trade of Sumatra,
was now cut off from that trade and dwindled in importance. By
contrast no mere neglect could stop the port of Singapore from
growing, so long as there was free trade. In 1832 the population
was returned as 22,000 including 91 European men, 28 European
women and 8500 Chinese. About 5000 Chinese arrived annually
to disperse themselves throughout Malaya and, in 1832, 420 full-
rigged ships aggregating to 120,000 tons cleared the port, carrying
a trade worth over £3,000,000. Thirty years later the population
was 90,000. But no thanks were due to the East India Company.

Penang, after a brief appearance as a separate Presidency
(1804–5) when it had been the base of naval operations, also sank
into obscurity. No progress was possible outside the British and
Dutch seaports in the East Indies until there was common
security for life and property. Throughout the archipelago all the
sea-ways were infested by Malay and Dyak pirates, whose swift
prahus could outsail most merchantmen and many warships. The
war against the pirates, a concern for the Admiralty, not the East
India House, was the chief British activity in the Straits Settlements. It was this that brought James Brooke as a volunteer to
Sarawak. Only steamships could solve the problem and steam
required coaling-stations. In 1844, reports of coal in the island of
Labuan led the Admiralty to take it over as a naval station for re-
fitting and refuelling ships, by treaty with the Sultan of Brunei.
The measures against piracy had become effective by about 1852
when the sea-ways through Malaya were reported clear.

SARAWAK

Sir James Brooke (1803–68) of Sarawak, though a mere gentle-man-adventurer, did more good than most of his contemporaries. Having fought gallantly as a young soldier in the first Burmese War, and spent some roving years, he returned home to inherit a fortune which enabled him to indulge his fancy for voyaging. He loaded his own schooner, the *Royalist*, with trade goods and set sail for Singapore (1838), where he heard tales of the archipelago which fired his curiosity. Most of the larger islands were ruled by Moslem sultans, and inhabited by simple aboriginals. The *Dyaks* of Borneo, for example, were dark-skinned savages, living com-munally in huge thatched huts raised on piles above the tidewater, each hut housing a whole clan. They were so easily at home in the water as to be almost amphibious. Their chief occupation, their sport, their religion was head-hunting. Their rulers, the Malay in-habitants of the larger settlements, lived by slave-raiding. Beside the more or less legitimate sultanates were many villages of mere pirates recruited from Dyak head-hunters and Malay slavers in-discriminately.

The Sultan of Kuching eagerly fastened upon Brooke, asking his advice about Dutch and English strength. The English from Singapore sought trade, the Dutch forbade him to engage in it. 'Which was the cat and which the rat?' Brooke was at first un-willing to take part in Malay politics but, when begged to assist a vassal of the Sultan against a usurper, he reluctantly agreed to make a demonstration. The mere sight of a body of English sea-men was enough to put the usurper's men to rout. Brooke made himself so useful that the Sultan invited him to become Rajah of the subordinate state of Sarawak. 'The principal people were assembled and the agreement being read to them, the Raja in-formed them that henceforth I was to hold the government. I expounded my principles, and really I believe they were well pleased. We had great firings and rejoicings' (29 September 1841). But neither Malay landlords nor pirate chiefs rejoiced so heartily when they discovered that Brooke really meant to enforce even-handed justice and preserve the peace. He protected the cultivators against oppression and began to wage war against the pirates. 'What', said one pirate chief when tried and found guilty, 'am I to be put to death only for killing a few Chinamen?'

To change the character of two nations was no light task. 'I work like a galley-slave,' he wrote, 'I fight like a common soldier, the poorest man in England might grumble at my diet, luxuries I have none, necessities are often deficient. I am separated from civilised life and educated men.... Could money tempt a man to this?'

His campaign against the pirates drew the sympathy of the naval officers at Singapore, who on two or three occasions sent warships to help him, so that some degree of regularity was gradually given to his position. In 1847 he returned to England for a visit, was knighted, and was appointed Consul-General for North Borneo. Protests from the Dutch, that his activities were a breach of the treaty of 1824, were rebutted by the government.

When Brooke returned to Sarawak in 1848, he had to fight harder than before against new pirate bands which had arisen during his absence. He was not helped by an agitation worked up against him by a dishonest assistant, who denounced him to the Aborigines Protection Society. 'He had gone out as a private adventurer, had seized a territory as large as Yorkshire, and then drove out the natives. Under pretence that they were pirates, he subsequently sent for our fleet to massacre them.' His career was so odd that a Parliamentary enquiry was reasonable, but commissioners, who sat for three months at Singapore, abandoned further enquiry when they failed to find any evidence that was not entirely in Brooke's favour. He had pacified all the coast of North Borneo under legitimate authority and without incurring expense to the British government. The true test of his beneficence was that the population of Sarawak had more than doubled in ten years.

In 1857 he retired to England, hoping to persuade the government to give recognition to his rule over Sarawak. This proved so difficult a task that in despair he even offered the territory to France, but at last, in 1864, he achieved his end. His nephew succeeded as Rajah under British protection and founded the dynasty which ruled unchallenged until 1941.

2. WARS WITH CHINA, 1833–60

EAST of Suez most kingdoms were exclusive; they went further than the empires of the West, which endeavoured to monopolise trade, by endeavouring to close their frontiers absolutely against all contacts with the outer world. In Japan, from 1638 to 1853, the exclusion was complete, and in other kingdoms would have been so if the kings had been masters of their own frontiers. To these balanced societies with their self-sufficient economy, the very idea of progress, if it ever occurred to men's minds, was abhorrent. All changes, all *novae res*, were alike undesirable. Undoubtedly the universal belief in the Divinity of Kings contributed to this conservatism. The physical and moral order of society depended upon the rites of kingship so that aliens who would not submit to the system were indeed 'foreign devils'.

Hast thou not signed a decree that every man that shall ask a petition of any God or man...save of thee, O king, shall be cast into the den of lions? The king answered and said, The thing is true, according to the law of the Medes and the Persians, which altereth not.

Until the nineteenth century the kings of the East were able as a rule, to maintain their inviolability. Then there burst in upon them an influx of foreign devils: the British being the most powerful owing to their ubiquitous navy; the Americans, the Dutch, the French not far behind; the Russians and the Germans following. All alike were innovators, despisers of authority, anxious to turn the world upside-down. All demanded, as if they had a moral right to it, access for traders, access for missionaries, access for diplomats who scorned to perform the *kow-tow* and blasphemously insisted upon coming as equals before the thrones of the Divine Kings.

Rightly or wrongly, the energy of the Western nations prevailed. When once the frontiers were pierced, when Western traders, or missionaries, infiltrated into the forbidden lands, no power on earth could stop the disintegration of the old rigid societies. Whether the penetration was economical or ideological or military, the destructive effect was the same. The old way of life could not be maintained, the new culture must replace the old.

After a hundred years the process is almost complete, though two small and inaccessible countries, Tibet and Nepal, have still

(1949) resisted infiltration. Among those which have dissolved and recrystallised, no sentimental regrets need be wasted upon such bloodstained anachronisms as the kingdom of Kandy, nor upon Japan, which was adjusted to the new age with such shocking efficiency. The great drama is the dissolution of the Chinese Empire which, since the T'ang dynasty in the seventh century A.D., had sheltered one-quarter of the human race, in a rigid constitutional frame, under the rule of the 'Son of Heaven'. The peoples of the river valleys of China were cut off from the rest of the world, on the north and west by mountains and deserts, on the south and east by seas and by the tributary kingdoms of Korea, Annam, Siam, Burma and Tibet. When the Empire lost its protective crust of tributary states it was soon infested with the seeds of decay. The emperors knew little of the outer world and saw little good in knowing more, since the 'foreign devils' were, throughout the period, inferior to the Chinese in most of the arts of life. After resisting, with a fair measure of success, the encroachments of traders and diplomats, the crystalline structure of Chinese life was dissolved by an even more powerful solvent, the influence of Protestant Christianity.

The East India Company never succeeded in establishing diplomatic relations with the emperors of China. Like the traders of other nations the Company's servants were held off at arm's length, and were admitted (see chapter III, 7, page 187), on sufferance only, to a temporary foothold at Canton. Though officially treated with contempt by Chinese governors, they were actually received on friendly terms by the Canton guild of exporting merchants, known as the 'Hong'. The Chinese government reluctantly allowed its merchants a restricted commerce with the 'foreign devils', only on condition that they remained in isolation, outside the Chinese system of law and administration. It will be seen that this is a variant from the Moslem custom of permitting to foreign traders a right of local self-government by 'capitulation'.

In spite of these humiliations, the Company's servants were comfortable and prosperous at Canton. They found the Hong merchants, who were no less anxious to sell tea than the British were to buy it, so businesslike as to give the Chinese people a lasting reputation with the nation of shopkeepers as good customers when their national characteristics were understood. The

Plate 17

SIR STAMFORD RAFFLES (1781–1826)

The founder of Singapore. From a painting by G. F. Joseph, dated 1817.
See p. 408.

Plate 18

'RAJAH' BROOKE (1803–68)

From a painting by Sir F. Grant dated 1847. *See p. 413.*

Chinese government imposed a tax of 6% on all dealings with the
foreigner, allotting the proceeds to a fund from which bad debts
incurred by their own merchants were paid. The difficulty was to
find a way of balancing the trade, since the Chinese desired little in
the way of British goods. As an alternative to paying for the tea in
coined silver, the Company (in 1773) hit upon the unlucky device

THE CHINA COAST
TREATY PORTS

Map 19

George Philip & Son, Ltd.

of importing opium from Bengal to China, thus fixing the trade in
drugs upon both countries. The use and abuse of drugs, though
almost unknown in the West, was widely spread in the East;
eighteenth-century traders were not likely to have been squeamish
about dealing in it, even if a moral objection had been raised, but
at first there was none. Country traders, Portuguese from Macao,
Americans and Dutch, joined freely in importing opium from

Turkey and Persia as well as from Bengal; but the British, owing
to their firm trading connexions at Canton, had the best of the
market. A new method, introduced from the Dutch Indies, of
smoking opium as a habitual indulgence, instead of occasionally
eating it as a remedy against fatigue or hunger, began to fasten
itself as a national vice upon the Chinese, and provoked an edict
of prohibition by the Emperor in 1800. Neither the Hong merchants, nor the imperial Governor of Canton paid the slightest
attention. Imports of opium and exports of tea continued to increase in volume, while unknown quantities of the drug were
smuggled in by Chinese bootleggers.

  This was the situation when, in 1833, the Act abolishing the
East India Company monopoly made it necessary to negotiate a
new agreement for the trade with Canton. Twice before had
British embassies been sent to the emperors of China. On each
occasion the ambassador (Lord Macartney in 1793, and Lord
Amherst in 1816) had returned, without achieving anything, after
a series of deliberate public humiliations. Luckily their ignorance
of Chinese characters prevented their understanding the insulting
notices on banners borne before them. The attempt to negotiate
was renewed by Lord Napier,[1] who appeared at Canton in 1834.
The Governor haughtily refused to see his letter of credence, re-
ferring him to the Hong merchants. When Napier attempted to
assert his diplomatic status he was ordered to leave Canton; and
when he refused to do so the English trade was stopped. Eventually he withdrew to the Portuguese colony at Macao, having
failed in his mission, and, shortly after, died there. Three or four
years of bickering ensued. Brawls between sailors and Chinese
officials led to lawsuits in which it became the rule of all the
Western trading peoples not to surrender their nationals to trial in
Chinese courts, where torture was normally used to extract evidence. The breakdown of the monopoly brought many new
dealers into the trade, largely Americans, whose fast clipper-built
ships were, at this time, getting supremacy at sea. Napier's successor, Sir C. Elliot, though acting for the British only, assisted
all the 'foreign devils' by the presence of a British naval squadron
which lay in the sheltered anchorage behind the uninhabited
island of Hong Kong, at the mouth of the Canton River. Quar-

  [1] William, 8th Lord Napier (1786-1834), not one of the celebrated Napier
brothers.

rels about jurisdiction and prestige did not prevent an increase in the exchange of opium for tea. Elliot's reports stimulated Palmerston to insist upon a new settlement, but the ministry was so bitterly opposed in parliament that they could secure a majority of only nine votes for their Chinese policy.

In 1838 the Emperor sent a new Governor to Canton to root out the opium trade. Without warning he shut up the British merchants in their factory, seized the stock—20,000 cases of opium, worth more than £2,000,000—and destroyed it without compensation. After repeated attempts at compromise and repeated snubs from the Chinese Governor, Elliot broke off negotiations and returned to Macao. A final breach was made when a fleet of Chinese junks demanded the surrender of some British sailors for trial in a Chinese court. Attempting to seize the men by force, they were fired upon by two British warships at Hong Kong. In February 1840 the British were formally excluded from the trade of Canton, and retaliated by blockading the port. Thus began what has been called the 'Opium War', a shabby business indeed, but not half so disreputable as the enemies of Britain have represented. The cause was not British determination to import the drug, but a blank refusal on the part of the Chinese government to meet other governments on terms of equality, to discuss informally, to negotiate officially, to make binding agreements on commercial matters, or to admit that 'foreign devils' had any rights whatsoever.

A brigade of British troops from India, under Hugh Gough, operated with naval support along the coast (August 1841–June 1842), forcing the surrender of successive towns. Wellington, the oracle, described the skill with which these combined operations were conducted as 'unparalleled'. When the force sailed up the Yang-tse to Nanking, the southern capital, Chinese intransigence gave way. Three imperial commissioners were sent to sue for peace on the deck of a British warship. For centuries the Chinese had made no agreements with the outside world save in the form of 'unequal treaties', the other contracting party being obliged to accept what the Chinese contemptuously offered through subordinates. The Treaty of Nanking, 1842, between the Chinese Emperor and the Queen of Great Britain, was the first of a series of 'unequal treaties' biased in the other direction. It was described as a treaty of 'peace and friendship' and might have merited the description if it had been interpreted with goodwill on either side, since the principle of friendly negotiation was admitted. In fact it inaugurated a long contest between the European powers for commercial and strategic advantages, each tending to weaken the authority of the Chinese Emperor. The Chinese agreed to pay an indemnity of about £5,000,000 for damages at Canton, and ceded the island of Hong Kong to Great Britain. They admitted European traders to five 'Treaty' ports (Canton, Amoy, Foochow, Ningpo, Shanghai), and granted foreigners in those ports the right of trial in their own consular courts, the rule of 'extra-territoriality'. A supplementary treaty also contained a clause granting, in advance, to Great Britain any advantages which might thereafter be granted by treaty to any more-favoured nation. France and the United States (whose government had heartily supported the British action) were not slow to negotiate similar treaties, each demanding the 'most-favoured-nation' clause, a perpetual stimulus to competitive encroachment; and other nations followed. As an American historian has written: 'The nationals of countries which did not resort to war with China enjoyed all the privileges of the countries which assumed the burden of war and Chinese resentment.' The resumed opium trade trebled in volume during the next twenty years, though still, from the point of view of Pekin, a trade in contraband goods.

Since this illegitimate trade was conducted by connivance with corrupt officials beyond the reach of the Emperor's feeble grasp, since the Treaty Ports were invaded by unruly foreigners who were hated the more for their extra-territorial privileges, since each of the foreign nations was always on the watch for claims to be advanced under the most-favoured-nation clause, relations between provincial governors and 'foreign devils' steadily deteriorated. The success of the British in the 'Opium War' led to what was called the 'gunboat policy'. A show of force, even the bombardment of a Chinese town by light naval craft which could penetrate the navigable rivers, proved the simplest way to intimidate a truculent governor. Such warlike acts might be undertaken without reference to Europe and without fear of Pekin.

Among the Western nations, the Americans have the best diplomatic record in the Far East. They claimed extra-territorial rights, enjoyed most-favoured-nation treatment, and smuggled opium, but always urged moderation. They deplored the 'gunboat policy', and until the end of the century annexed no territory in the East. On the other hand they sent Protestant missions to China at an early date (1830), introducing the ferment of liberal democracy through the channel of the mission schools.

The French, whose policy was more aggressive even than that of the British in the 'forties and 'fifties, came into the field as champions of the Roman Catholic missions, which had been established in China since the sixteenth century. In 1845 they persuaded the Emperor to issue an edict granting, though in vague terms, a general toleration to Christians. Thereafter missionary influence flourished, and their extra-territorial rights in remote inland provinces became a fruitful source of conflict.

Chinese good sense and Western adaptability combined, at the Treaty Ports, to set local government and commerce upon a business footing, especially at Shanghai. It was British enterprise that established the Foreign Settlement in 1845, as a quarter of the town where the consular courts of the Treaty Powers held exclusive jurisdiction. Four years later the French obtained a concession for a similar quarter, for their own nationals only. When, in 1854, a minor rebellion put the Chinese administration to flight, an improvised Board was set up by Chinese and foreign merchants to control the customs. Since in efficiency and honesty it was so far superior to the official establishment as to render a much larger revenue to Pekin, the Board was extended to cover all the ports, after the suppression of the rebellion. In 1863, Robert Hart, a servant of the Board, became Inspector-general of the Chinese Customs Service, the one branch of the imperial administration which remained efficient through all the revolutions of Chinese affairs until the Japanese invasion in 1937. The Foreign Settlement at Shanghai prospered and attracted population by its honest government. Similarly the rocky island of Hong Kong soon became a thriving city, with suburbs on the adjacent mainland.

Hong Kong, Singapore, Bombay, three of the world's great cities, are alike tributes to the blessings of British rule. Each of the three was an almost uninhabited island until developed by British industry; each was also an island in a sea of anarchy. The oppressed peoples of the neighbouring mainlands flocked to enjoy, under the British flag, the security, the justice and the equal laws which their own governments were unable or unwilling to provide. Each of the three islands was acquired by treaty without injury to any earlier inhabitants, and there is no reason to suppose that any of the three cities would be more than a village to-day if the British had not made it so.

While the Treaty Ports prospered, inland China was collapsing. All the southern provinces were scourged by the Taiping rebellion, which brought slaughter and famine behind it. A fanatic and mystic, who had been baptised by an American missionary, proclaimed himself a Messiah, born to establish the Kingdom of Heaven in China. At first the missionaries regarded him with some favour as a reformer until he raised mercenary armies, over-threw the government of provinces, and massacred the inhabitants of cities. He captured Nanking in 1853, with much bloodshed. Chinese civil servants, rotten with venality and sloth, and drugged with opium, could not cope with the Taiping fanatics; Chinese soldiers, miserably equipped members of a despised profession, could make no stand. The harassed Emperor lost province after province to the rebels while, in the same years, the British were encroaching upon his tributary kingdom of Burma (1852), and the French upon his tributary kingdom of Annam (1858).

To add to these troubles the Western powers renewed their pressure for further trading and diplomatic privileges. The French produced a list of grievances culminating in the murder of a French missionary priest, while Palmerston called upon the House of Commons for action against China on twenty-two distinct counts, the most serious being the seizure of the British ship *Arrow*. An official named Yeh, the imperial Commissioner at Canton, had thrown the British captain and Chinese crew into prison where several of them died. The state of the Chinese prisons was the only genuine grievance, for the case against the *Arrow* was justified. Palmerston's aggressive patriotism was then potent in British party politics, as he well understood. Public indignation against Commissioner Yeh, who actually behaved with dignified propriety but whom *Punch* made into a slightly comic ogre, helped to put 'Pam' in office with a larger majority after the election of 1857, and precipitated the second China War. Lord Elgin and a French colleague were sent to present demands to the court of Pekin. 'Fifty-seven was the Mutiny year. Though Canton was blockaded by the Navy, the troops designed for China had to be diverted to India, so that it was not until 'fifty-eight that military pressure could be applied. Like the first war, this was a struggle for prestige, correctly summed up in Sir F. H. Doyle's celebrated verses upon the *Private of the Buffs*, who was taken prisoner when drunk and executed out of hand near Canton, for refusing to perform the kow-tow. He too, like the Great Earl of Elgin, was Britain's ambassador. 'Let dusky Indians whine and kneel, an English lad must die.' Though ignorant, rude and drunken, 'he only knows that not through him shall England come to shame'.

Canton was again occupied by British troops and Commissioner Yeh carried off to exile in India. But the state of China was so chaotic that, while these operations were taking place in the south, the foreigners at Shanghai in central China were organising the imperial campaign against the Taipings, and in the north Elgin and his French colleague were attempting to negotiate with Pekin. They demanded the establishment of permanent legations at the Emperor's court; extra-territorial rights for Europeans, wherever they might be; a guaranteed toleration for all Christians whether Chinese or foreign; and more Treaty Ports.

The British contention upon the opium question was that it was useless and unjust to attempt to prevent the drug habit by legislative action against a single foreign source of supply, when much opium was home-grown, and more smuggled through other channels not protected by commercial treaties. The Chinese must begin by internal reforms, by stopping the demand and disciplining the corrupt officials who openly encouraged the trade. It was the American envoy who proposed a new solution to the opium problem, that the trade should be regulated, not ineffectually prohibited. This proposal was accepted, with the consequence that the opium trade became legal. Since administrative reforms did not follow, no action was taken for many years to decrease the consumption of the drug, or the demand for it.

It may be convenient to recapitulate here the later history of the opium trade between India and China. An agitation against opium-smoking was begun in 1906 by missionaries in China, backed by the new Liberal majority in the British House of Commons. The Chinese government then undertook to restrict the sale of opium to the addicts and to prevent the further extension of the habit. Cultivation of the opium poppy in China was to be reduced by one-tenth every year, so that the country would be ready for prohibition in ten years' time. The Indian government immediately concurred in reducing the export of opium to China by one-tenth annually. Such great progress was made in suppressing the habit that the Indian government was able to put an end to the trade in 1913, four years earlier than was expected, a serious loss to the Indian revenue. When the Japanese invaded Manchuria in 1931 one of their first actions was to restore and encourage the growth of the opium poppy, with the deliberate intention of debauching the Chinese population.

Though a treaty had been negotiated at Tientsin in December 1858 the representatives of the powers were determined that, as a matter of prestige, it should be ratified at the Emperor's court. This led to further diplomatic bickering throughout 1859, and to renewal of the war. The Chinese barred the approach to Pekin by strengthening the Taku Forts at the mouth of the Peiho River. Naval squadrons then forced an entrance after bombarding the forts; and despatched a small mixed expedition to occupy Pekin (August 1860). This was the occasion when the American Commodore Vatnall, though commanding a neutral squadron, cheerfully joined in the action with the words, 'blood is thicker than water'.

The Emperor fled from his capital, taking with him as hostages the British consul, Sir H. S. Parkes and other British and American diplomats. All were ill-used and some died, which added to the indignation of the Treaty Powers. Accordingly, as a reprisal, Elgin ordered the destruction of the Emperor's Summer Palace, a piece of architecture built to the plans of French Jesuit architects during the eighteenth century, in the Chinese Rococo style which was not fashionable in 1850.

The Emperor was forced to submit to the treaty, although the price of submission had risen still higher. Tientsin itself, the harbour of Pekin, became a Treaty Port, to ensure access for the Powers to the fortified legation quarter which they established at Pekin. The British colony at Hong Kong was enlarged by the cession of the mainland suburb of Kowloon. The Powers also exacted a large indemnity. It is worth noting that the Americans afterwards restored a large part of their share.

China was now 'open', and was ready for reconstruction. An

American officer was employed to organise measures against the Taipings, with success until he was killed in action. His place was taken, in 1863, by Colonel Charles Gordon, R.E., who suppressed the rebellion. In the same year, Robert Hart became Inspector-general of the Chinese Customs Service. China now entered upon a new phase of history. The powers vied with one another, all in turn using the most-favoured-nation clause to extend their spheres of influence and to get railway contracts for their nationals. Missionaries penetrated deeper, protected by extra-territoriality, spreading belief in Western education and distrust of the age-old Chinese learning, the path to promotion in the Imperial Service. The more the Treaty Ports prospered, the greater the unrest in the unexploited provinces. But the new culture was anarchic, giving no impetus to constructive reform at the Emperor's court.

Very different was the history of Japan. During the years of exclusion, the Dutch (like the British at Canton) had been allowed to visit Nagasaki for a restricted trade under humiliating conditions. As in China so in Japan, several attempts by Western nations to accredit ambassadors had been rudely repulsed. In 1853 the barrier was broken by an American naval mission under Commodore Perry, who scrupulously avoided the use or even the threat of force. A coaling-station on the way to China, and a promise of commonly humane treatment for shipwrecked American sailors were his first objectives. By tact and firmness he extracted from the Shogun, the hereditary vizier who then ruled Japan, a Treaty Port and a most-favoured-nation treaty. The Dutch followed with similar demands. Since the Crimean War was then being fought, the Russian and British naval squadrons in the East were deeply concerned, and each negotiated a similar treaty with Japan in the hope of scoring off the other. When commercial relations were established, the Treaty Powers were surprised to find that the Shogun was not the sovereign of Japan. There was in the background a concealed Divine Emperor, the Mikado, whose courtiers were bitterly hostile to the 'foreign devils'. Many incidents occurred in which the hired bullies of the conservative nobility murdered unarmed traders who relied on treaty-rights. Against the wishes of the American government the 'gunboat policy' was used against Japan. In 1864 a combined squadron, in-

cluding an American ship, bombarded the naval port of Shimonoseki. The sufferer in the contest was the Shogun who lost face
with the imperial court, by submitting to the Western Powers
when they demanded an indemnity for the murders. A new
Mikado, Mutsuhito, who had just ascended the throne (1868),
took advantage of the situation, to resume the royal power which
the Shogun had misused and to treat with the Western powers for
his own advantage. These were no 'unequal' treaties. There
would be no opium trade, no special privileges for missionaries,
no loopholes through which 'foreign devils' could creep to dis-
rupt the Japanese economy; but unlimited trade, so that the
Mikado's men could buy such weapons as had trounced the
Shogun at Shimonoseki.

3. BRITISH SOCIAL REFORMS IN INDIA, 1813–56

WHEN the charter of the East India Company had come before
the House of Commons for renewal in 1793 an effort had been
made by Wilberforce to authorise the foundation of Protestant
missions to India, but in vain. The interest of the Company was
opposed to any such disturbing factor; their policy was to protect
the laws and customs of their Indian subjects. Behind Wilberforce
stood Charles Grant, an Evangelical, lately returned from the
Company's service and now devoted to the uplifting of the
peoples of the East. Pushing his interest in Leadenhall Street he
became a Director and returned to the charge when the charter
was again to be renewed for a second period of twenty years. By
1813 the two causes of evangelicalism and free trade had prospered, with the result that the power of the Company over the
moral and material welfare of India was whittled away. No longer
had the Directors a monopoly over the trade between England
and India, but all British citizens, and accordingly the missionaries,
were at last admitted freely to any of the Company's ports.
Furthermore the Governor-General was authorised to apply some
part of his funds to the promotion of learning in British India.
Christian missions and Western education in India, trace their
origin to the charter of 1813, though they had some earlier
foundations to build upon.

Round the coasts of India there had long been Christian settlements of various kinds: Portuguese Catholic missions which the English still regarded with suspicion and even hostility in the early nineteenth century; remnants of the ancient Churches of the East, known as Syrian Christians, on the Malabar Coast; and even a few evangelical Protestant missions which had infiltrated where the Company could not prevent them. Lutheran Protestants had been working for a century at the small Danish[1] factory of Serampur, sixteen miles from Calcutta, chiefly among the Eurasians. In 1793 an English Baptist named William Carey had gone alone as a missionary to Bengal. After rebuffs from the Company he settled at Serampur where he exhibited a talent for Church organisation, founding schools for Eurasian and native children, translating the Scriptures into vernacular versions which he printed and distributed, and conducting his mission so economically that it paid its way. He received help and encouragement, unofficially, from Lord Wellesley.

All that the Company had done for Christianity was to provide English chaplains at its own factories and when, in the new age of religious revival, an English bishopric at Calcutta was founded, the bishop's status was that of a chaplain-general subordinated on the one hand to the Governor-General and on the other to the Archbishop of Canterbury. Though all the missionary societies had combined in urging his appointment, the government did not send him abroad with a general mission to convert the Hindus. The first bishop, Thomas Middleton, was not able to do more than found some Mission schools around Calcutta. The second bishop, Reginald Heber (1783–1826), the author of the missionary hymns and of an account of travels in India which was widely read, made a great impression as an ecclesiastical statesman and as a pastor. He was much concerned with uniting the efforts of all the Protestant bodies and with bringing the Syrian Christian Churches into communion with them. The evangelising of India, or at least of the low-caste Hindus and the outcaste peoples, began to be spoken of as a possibility. As in other parts of the Empire the mission schools had an effect which extended far beyond the ranks of their converts.

A parallel movement in secular education began with the foundation of the Presidency College in Calcutta by David Hare, a

[1] Serampur was sold to Great Britain by Denmark in 1845.

free-thinking English tradesman, and Ram Mohan Roy, a learned Brahmin (1823). The Presidency College was the source of the flood of Western liberal ideas which has so profoundly changed the intellectual life of India. Ram Mohan Roy (1772–1833) was the first Brahmin scholar to be deeply versed in European languages and culture. A man of saintly life and sincere wisdom, he desired, as the dilettante Mogul emperors had desired, to make a synthesis of Eastern and Western thought, to reject the superstitious beliefs and vicious practices which had accrued to Brahminism, and so to regenerate the life of India. In 1833 he died while on a visit to England, where he had been received with honour and had given evidence before a committee of the House of Commons.

The arrival of Bentinck as Governor-General in 1828 implied that government would now begin to liberalise the laws and institutions of the Indian peoples. Lord William Bentinck (1772–1839) was a specimen of that characteristically English type, the aristocratic Radical; he combined liberal principles with a despotic temper. When he came to Calcutta, he had long experience of war, diplomacy and administration. He had been a soldier, and a martinet. Twenty years earlier, in Madras, his enforcement of the *minutiae* of military parade had been a principal cause of the Sepoy mutiny at Vellore. He commanded a division in Spain under Wellington who had a low opinion of his judgment and capacity, yet he was advanced to higher command. He conducted an invasion of Sicily and was responsible for providing the island with the stillborn parliamentary constitution of 1812. In Sicily, as afterwards in Bengal, Bentinck was remembered as the patron of liberty. He returned to the East pledged to 'found British greatness upon Indian happiness'.

The first part of his term of office was occupied with a firm consistent campaign against cruelty and oppression. He found himself obliged, much against his will, to take over the administration of two provinces in the south which were misgoverned by their protected native rulers. Of these two, Coorg remained part of the Madras Presidency, while Mysore, after fifty years of British rule, was restored in 1881 to its historic dynasty. Bentinck also forbade the internal trade in slaves in India, though the status of slavery was not abolished until 1862. The censorship of the press was discontinued in 1836.

Since time out of mind the peoples of India had suffered—and suffered almost willingly—from the misdeeds of the *thugs*, a sect whose cult of the hideous goddess Kali defies Western credulity. They were a secret society who worked in gangs to provide themselves with victims for human sacrifice. Having ingratiated themselves with solitary travellers, they lured them into lonely situations, and murdered them, with no other motive than religion, of the kind that is so potent to persuade men to do evil. Fear and superstition and perjury combined to render conviction for *thuggee* almost unobtainable in the courts. The *thugs* were sought out and hunted down by the long and patient efforts of Colonel William Sleeman, though they cannot be said to have been completely extirpated.

Almost more horrible because so widely spread and widely approved was the Hindu custom of *suttee* or widow-burning, which was no part of the pure religion of the original Aryans, but an older superstition prevalent among many primitive races. Perversely, the exalted view of the marriage vow taken by caste Hindus led to the incorporation of this vile custom into the Hindu religion. It was a pious duty, and a duty often joyfully embraced, for a widow to reunite herself with her lost husband, through the fire. The propriety of such behaviour was hotly defended by the consensus of Brahmin opinion, and would have been capable of defence on grounds not quite irrational if the custom had been confined to voluntary suicides. But the effect of another antisocial custom, child-marriage, deprived the defenders of *suttee* of what rags of decency they affected to shelter behind. A large proportion of the sacrificed widows were girl-children thrust into the flames before crowds of sightseers who assembled to gloat over the spectacle. Europeans since first they came to India, had protested against *suttee* and occasionally interfered to protect the victims. Job Charnock, the founder of Calcutta, is said to have married a Hindu widow whom he had rescued from the fire. But the politic necessity of respecting Indian religious rites had prevented British governors from putting an end to this practice.

The early Protestant missionaries, especially William Carey, had set themselves to force the issue. They remonstrated with organisers of *suttee*, usually in vain, begged mercy for involuntary victims and tried to dissuade volunteers. The British generation that abolished slavery was horrified at the revelation that little girls were burned alive by hundreds annually in British India; but the Governor-General was placed in a dilemma which has reappeared a dozen times in the history of Christianity. He was pledged as an enlightened ruler to respect the laws and customs of the Indian people, but equally pledged as a civilised man and a Christian to protect the helpless from cruel oppressors. What if cruelty to children were a religious rite held in great honour? Even Ram Mohan Roy, who denounced *suttee* in his teaching, thought its legal prohibition unwise. Lord William Bentinck made the decision, in 1829, to prohibit the practice of *suttee* by law, declaring all 'abettors in the act guilty of culpable homicide'. The abolition caused a wave of resentment among the more devout and conservative Hindus. Sir Charles Napier met the objections of the Brahmins of Sind with characteristic plainness. 'You say *suttee* is the custom. Well, we too have a custom which is to hang men who burn women alive. You build your funeral pyre and I will build a gallows beside it, and let each of us act according to custom.'

It is doubtful whether Bentinck won much gratitude, even from the Hindu women whose lives he saved, since they had been taught to regard *suttee* as a heroic duty which might fall to their lot, such a chance as human beings often face with equanimity. As with the slaves who were set free, so with the young widows whose lives were saved, the act of philanthropy produced a new problem, of providing for the released unfortunates. Since the abolition of *suttee*, the fate of the despised widows, deprived of martyrdom and left without social status, has been the shame of India.

In 1833 the charter of the East India Company came up to be renewed for a fourth period. The renewal followed upon the passing of the Great Reform Bill and was inspired by the principles of the new age. Respect for its 200 years of history preserved the Company, as yet, from dissolution but not from drastic reconstruction. It now entirely ceased to be a trading company. The last relic of the old commercial days, the monopoly at Canton was swept away with its perquisites, leaving the Directors as an auxiliary organ of the British government, in modern phrase a Public Utility, which undertook to rule British India by contract, under supervision of the Board of Control in Whitehall. The principles of Free Trade, invoked to condemn the monopoly, were based upon the secure right of private property, and therefore afforded no threat to the Proprietors, the holders of the gilt-edged East India stock. A guaranteed 10% dividend on every share of the nominal value of one hundred guineas was made a first charge upon the revenue. On the other hand public control was strengthened by an increase in the authority of the Governor, who was henceforward designated Governor-General of India. Bentinck during the two last years of his term, was the first to whom the title properly belonged.

The new charter contained the memorable words: 'No native of the said territories or any natural-born subject of His Majesty resident therein, shall by reason only of his religion, place of birth, descent, colour or any of them, be disabled from holding any place, office or employment under the said Company.' The tendency since the time of Cornwallis had been to restrict the higher appointments under government to civil or military officers brought out from England and, since the time of Wellesley, to train them for their duties at one of the Company's colleges. In order to reverse the tendency, education of Indians for the public services became an urgent need if the words of the charter were to lead to action.

The problem of Indian education came to the notice of Thomas Macaulay (1800–59) who went out to Calcutta in 1834 with a new appointment as Legal Member of the Council. He was a cocksure young parliamentarian and lawyer, the son of Zachary Macaulay who had been Governor of Sierra Leone. But unlike his father— that pillar of the Clapham Sect—young Tom Macaulay was a decided Whig and not in the least degree a pietist. So recent were the days when men had prospered by 'shaking the pagoda-tree' that Macaulay saw nothing indiscreet in announcing that he had sought the appointment in India with the primary intention of making money. He would save enough of his salary of £10,000 a year to provide himself in three years, with an independent income for life. Whatever his motives during his three years' service, he did more than many a Governor-General to mould the character of the Indian nation, by his labours in devising a penal code and by his recommendation that English should be the medium of instruction in India.

In some remote past age the dominant race of Hindustan had formed its character upon the Sanskrit literature, and had made the Laws of *Manu* the customary basis of land and village life. Then had come centuries of Moslem domination, reaching their

climax in the age of Akbar when Persian was the language of the
court and Urdu the dialect of camp and market. Persian was still
the language of diplomacy and of legislation under the East India
Company. The most cultured of the early governors, such men
as Warren Hastings, successors of Moslem rulers in Bengal, had
admired and had encouraged Moslem culture. As successors to
Mogul governors and rivals of the Mogul's nawabs their view
of India was tinged with a Moslem colouring. Meanwhile the
break-up of the Mogul Empire had been accompanied by, and
partly caused by, a Hindu revival. Conquests in central India had
altered the balance, bringing the British into contact with Hindu
dynasties and sects, while the Moslem minority, no longer the
rulers of the land, ceased to impose their culture upon it.

The rationalist theology and law of the Moslems might well
have been adapted to the needs of the nineteenth century, but for
the vitality of the Hindu undercurrent. Warren Hastings had
founded a Moslem Madrasa (or college) at Calcutta for the training of a governing class among the Bengalis. A few years later, in
1792, a Sanskrit college was founded at Benares with the support
of Lord Cornwallis; but the antiquated mythology which passed
for learning among the Brahmins was of little value in the modern
world. Bishop Heber, after attending a lecture in 1824, 'wondered
that such rubbish should be taught in a government college'. This
was the object of Macaulay's scorn in his 'Minute on Education'
(1835): 'Medical doctrines which would disgrace an English
farrier, astronomy which would move laughter in the girls of an
English boarding-school, and history abounding with Kings
thirty feet high.' Was such literature and such philosophy capable
of being modernised? Were the languages of India adequate to
express the notions of the modern world? Macaulay treated the
suggestion with derision. Others were of a different opinion.
B. H. Hodgson (1800–94), an orientalist of repute, argued vainly for
Bengali, the language of 37,000,000 people, 'competent to express
any imaginable mode of thought'. The great advantage of Bengali
was the existence of a system of vernacular instruction; there were
said to be 100,000 village schools in Bengal. But to what advantage,
said Macaulay, when one considered the nonsense taught in them.

On 7 March 1835 the decision was taken by the Governor-
General in Council that 'the great object of the British government ought to be the promotion of European literature and science

Plate 19

LORD DALHOUSIE (1812–60)

Governor-General of India. From a painting by Sir J. W. Gordon dated 1847.
See p. 443.

Plate 20 A

JOHN, LORD LAWRENCE
(1811–79)

Governor-General of India in
1864. From a drawing by E. G.
Lewis. *See p. 448.*

Plate 20 B

LORD CURZON
(1859–1925)

Governor-General of India in
1899. From a painting after J. S.
Sargent.

among the natives of India and that all the funds appropriated would best be employed on English education alone'. The appropriation was at first no more than £20,000 per annum rising to £70,000 in the 1850's, and was spent chiefly on the provision of text-books. Small as this sum now appears, it was as much as was appropriated for education in England in the 1830's. Bishop Heber had already noticed that the desire to learn English was widespread in the mission schools, and that the less enlightened followers of Ram Mohan Roy merely showed an apish tendency 'to imitate the English in everything'. Candidates for government office soon found that a knowledge of English was an advantage worth striving for; they were officially notified in 1844 that English-speaking applicants would be preferred. The cleavage between the old and the new learning widened. It was remarked that both Hindu and Moslem aristocrats, the old governing class, were holding aloof from government service under the new conditions, while a middle-class of half-educated *babus* with a pedantic smattering of government-English was arising. But the English language was never forced upon the *babus* of Bengal; they strove for it at their own expense as a means to employment. Neither in India nor in England was universal education by the state yet thought practicable or desirable. At last, in 1854, the Board of Control in London instructed the Governor-General to frame a 'properly articulated scheme of education from the primary school to the university'—articulated though, of course, neither universal nor compulsory. One of the last acts of the government before the Mutiny was to found examining universities at Calcutta, Bombay and Madras, on the model of the University of London.

The tendency of the Victorian English to despise the native culture of India was partly due to their own abounding self-confidence. Britain so patently led the world in all that the age regarded as progress. Partly too it was justified by the corrupt state of the Province of Bengal when the British first acquired it. The conquerors could not doubt that physically, mentally and morally they were the better men, possessing advantages that might be conferred upon the Indians. The missionaries assured themselves that by their efforts idolatry would die out in a generation. The teachers believed that Macaulay's system would create an educated upper-class with English notions of politics and ethics. The lawyers believed that the penal code would inculcate English notions of legality. They were hardly aware that their contempt for native Indian culture depressed the status of the Indian upper-classes. Either the Indians must ape the British or lapse into dependence. As early as 1817 Sir Thomas Munro, in recommending eventual self-government, reproached the Company for debasing the natives of India. The Victorian philanthropists hastened the process. Since India was to be Westernised, her indigenous products fell into contempt. Indian handicrafts were ruined, undersold by Free Trade in cheap manufactured goods. Architecture and the Fine Arts, which the Mogul Emperors had patronised, were neglected by the British philistines.

4. WARS IN THE NORTH-WEST, 1839–49

THE peaceful and progressive administration of Lord William Bentinck was followed by the unhappy times of Lord Auckland (1836–42), when a foreign policy which was always aggressive and often unscrupulous led the Indian government into unjustified and unsuccessful war. He bequeathed to his successor Ellenborough a strategic tangle which could be straightened only by further and still more ruthless campaigns. Lord Auckland was prim, earnest and weak. His mission in India was to second the foreign policy of Palmerston by checking the growing influence of the Russians in Central Asia. Since the Treaty of Tilsit (1807), Russia rather than France had become the rival to British power in Asia and throughout the century the Russian frontier was steadily advanced (see chapter XVIII, 1, page 921). Wellesley had sent Sir John Malcolm in 1799 on the first of a series of diplomatic missions to Persia but without attracting it into the British sphere of influence. On the other hand the Russians compelled the Persians to cede territory in 1813 and when, in 1838, further Russian advances were made towards Bokhara the pressure began to be felt in regions where the British too had interests. Herat in western Afghanistan was next menaced by Persia, a threat which was thought in India to be a concealed Russian move. Auckland began to prepare strong diplomatic action largely on the advice of Alexander Burnes, an adventurous young political agent with a reputation for Central Asian travel.

The kingdom of Kabul, through which run so many celebrated lines of communication, has not always been the debatable ground that it was in the nineteenth century. Once it was the secure patrimony of the dynasty of Timur and only lapsed into anarchy on the decline of the Mogul Empire. Tom Coryat and other early travellers plodded their way through Kabul and the Khyber Pass without any sense of particular peril in that part of their journey. But since Nadir Shah of Persia had stripped the Moguls of these hereditary provinces (1739), all that lay between the Sutlej and the Oxus had been the prize of rival military chiefs.

The Sutlej is the most easterly of the five tributaries of the Indus which give their name to the Punjab, a wide corn-growing plain. Here the Khalsa, the military brotherhood of the Sikhs, lorded it over a largely Moslem peasantry. These robust puritans, the most stout-hearted race encountered by the British in India, valiant as foes and faithful as friends, had been united under the rule of Runjeet Singh, in friendship with the British government since the treaty of 1808.

In the peaceful years river traffic down the Indus grew in importance and promised much for the future. Its limitation was the tribute levied upon the trade by a group of Moslem robberbarons who had possessed themselves of certain fortresses commanding the stream, especially the walled city of Sukkur. Their title was based only on recent conquest, their sole interest in the river-valley was predatory, their sway was admitted by all to be tyrannous in the extreme; they ruled three confederate provinces, Khairpur, Hyderabad and Mirpur, through tributary chiefs, the whole body being known as the Amirs of Sind. In 1838, when arbitrating between Runjeet Singh and the Amirs, Lord Auckland obliged the latter to accept a British agent by the first of a series of treaties which the Amirs always accepted with reluctance and always violated. There was in short no ground for an agreement; Auckland wished to extend British influence and to safeguard the commerce of the Indus; the Amirs wished to live by preying upon it without his well-meaning interference.

The third party to the struggle was the Amir of Afghanistan who held the wild Pathan tribes with a most uncertain grip. Afghans and Sikhs were hereditary foes by race, religion and history. The fluctuating frontier between them became, when the Punjab was annexed, the turbulent North-west Frontier of India.

Runjeet Singh had long maintained at his court at Lahore an exiled Amir of Afghanistan named Shah Suja from whom he had extracted the Koh-i-noor, the fetish of the empire of Hindustan. While Runjeet had no intention of burning his own fingers he was

Map 20

quite willing that the British should go to the trouble of replacing Shah Suja on the Afghan throne. Auckland first sent Alexander Burnes to negotiate with Dost Mohammed, the reigning Amir, but later overruled him, on the advice of Macnaghten, a rival political agent, and decided to restore Shah Suja to power. It was agreed with Runjeet Singh that a British army should march with Shah

Suja to Kabul, but not pass through Sikh territory; the Army of the Indus must go through the Bolan Pass—that is through territory of the Amirs of Sind. Pressure was again brought on the Amirs to give them right of way which was reluctantly permitted. Karachi, an ancient, silted-up, ruin of a seaport was occupied as a base in 1839. At first all went well; the march to Kandahar and Kabul was accomplished. The military administration was good and the only opposition, at Ghuznee, was overcome in a smart little action. Shah Suja was placed on the throne in place of his rival, who fled. The military operation was completed by a return march, north about, through the Khyber Pass. British garrisons were entrenched at Karachi, Quetta, Kandahar, Kabul and Jelalabad with the intention of retiring as soon as Shah Suja should be firmly seated. Two years later the garrisons were still in position. Shah Suja's authority extended not a yard beyond the reach of the British bayonets. While the soldiers, always unhappy when engaged on police work, would have been glad to withdraw, the political officers, especially Macnaghten, pressed for a forward policy, attempting to pacify the mountain tribes, alternately with bribes and punitive expeditions.

The morale of the army, or at least of its higher command, was low, since relations were strained between the civil and military powers. The Commander-in-Chief, who held that the British frontier should remain at the Sutlej, and refused responsibility for adventures in the 'Far West', was overruled by Auckland's political officers, the most offensive among them being Macnaghten, whom Wellington in England described as 'the person employed to command the army'.

In November 1841 the city of Kabul rose in rebellion. Shah Suja's authority vanished and Dost Mohammed reappeared. Burnes was murdered in the first onslaught, Macnaghten a few weeks later while attempting to divide the Afghan chiefs by a dubious intrigue. The garrison commander, an elderly invalid named Elphinstone whom Macnaghten had consistently snubbed, would have built a fort, had not Auckland disallowed the expenditure. Finding that he had no means to stand a siege, Elphinstone capitulated, agreeing to quit the country with his army under safe conduct. Since the state of the passes would not permit a withdrawal southward to his base he set out northwards for Jelalabad in the depth of winter (January 1842) with a column

consisting of 700 English soldiers, 4000 sepoys, 12,000 camp-
followers and a few English ladies. Whether Dost Mohammed
intended that the army should escape is of slight importance, he
could not have prevented the Pathans from harassing the retreat.
All through the snowy passes the tribesmen attacked the column
with increasing audacity. At one of many attempts to parley,
Elphinstone and the Englishwomen surrendered to Dost Mohammed on the undertaking that they would be protected and
that the attacks on the column would cease. The first condition
was observed, the second was at once violated. In the rearguard
the one British regiment, the 44th (Essex), making repeated
counter-attacks, fought and died to the last man. The column
straggled, dissipated and was destroyed. A solitary survivor, Dr
Brydon, an army surgeon, reached Jelalabad.

Meanwhile the two authors of the war had disappeared from
the scene. Runjeet Singh had died in 1839 leaving no legitimate
heir to control his regular army of 50,000 men, trained by European soldiers of fortune and supported by 300 guns of a type
more modern than those used by the British. 'Jealous of our
power and contemptuous of our mismanagement', they observed
the disaster at Kabul with pugnacious interest. Auckland too had
gone, in February 1842, on the expiration of his term of office, a
sadly discouraged statesman.

The next Governor-General, Lord Ellenborough, had exalted
ideas about prestige. As soon as the passes should be open in the
spring, Afghanistan was to be again invaded so that 'face' might
be saved by a token victory. The southern garrisons which had
been firmly held, produced a column under General Nott while,
in the north, a column from Peshawar under General Pollock
forced the Khyber Pass and relieved Sir Robert Sale in Jelalabad.
The two columns converged on Kabul. The prisoners, excepting
Elphinstone who had died, were released unharmed through the
exertions of Sir R. Shakespeare, the reputed original of Thackeray's
Colonel Newcome. Prestige having been restored, as Ellenborough supposed, by this promenade, the troops were withdrawn,
leaving Dost Mohammed in possession of Afghanistan. As a
symbol of victory Ellenborough ordered that the gates of Ghuznee should be brought back to India, supposing that they were
trophies carried off by the Moslem conqueror Mahmud in the
thirteenth century. The gesture was somewhat ineffective since

the antiquaries decided they were not authentic; and in any case the Hindus had long forgotten their existence. To crown his victory Ellenborough issued a medal to all ranks who had taken part in the campaign, the first such issue. The custom spread until, after agitation in the press, a belated medal was issued even to the survivors of the Peninsular War, against the wish of Wellington. Time had been when he had represented the most powerful of the world's kingdoms at the Congress of Vienna, wearing dark well-cut plain clothes which marked him out among the beribboned and bejewelled courtiers of the European monarchs. He would have hated to see the British soldier's breast gaudy with stars and crosses as if he were a Portuguese or a Prussian.

Fate struck a blow at the Amirs of Sind by sending Sir Charles Napier in 1842 to command the Bombay Army. Although the forward policy had just been abandoned, after the disastrous retreat from Kabul, Napier had no intention of allowing that to influence his behaviour in Sind where he had troops deployed at Karachi and the crossings of the Indus. The most brilliant member of a handsome, gallant, pugnacious family, Charles Napier (1782–1853) was an elderly soldier who had done a hundred things but had never fulfilled his ambition of commanding an army in battle. In politics he was an advanced Radical, in character a pure dictator. During the Chartist troubles he had kept the peace in the north of England by assuring the Chartist leaders that he supported the whole of their policy but would shoot them without a qualm if they provoked riot and disorder. To deal with the Amirs was a simpler problem; if they would not act fairly by him he would 'knock them over like ninepins', and would welcome the chance. Our erroneous policy had led us into difficulties from which there was no way of escape without the use of force. 'Auckland began by an act of injustice', said Napier. 'A course of injustice cannot be closed without hardship on someone. It is likely to fall on the Amirs and on a crew more deserving to bear it hardly could it alight.. . .I do not think the Amirs fools, I think them cunning rascals. They saw our defeat which encouraged them to break treaties. They hoped to have a second Kabul affair. Now what is to be done? That which is best for. . .the good government of the population, and we must not sacrifice it to an endeavour, utterly hopeless I may say, to give to these tyrannical, drunken, debauched, cheating, intriguing, contemptible Amirs a due portion of the plunder they have amassed from the ruined people.'

Napier kept his political officer, James Outram,[1] under control; he first nicknamed him the 'Bayard of India', and afterwards over-ruled and abused him. Outram was for peace and was still nego-tiating hopefully when Napier and the Amirs were openly arming. It is hard to say who struck the first blow. On 17 February 1843 with a small force of raw unseasoned troops, Napier defeated ten times as great a force of Baluchis at Miani, a battle picturesquely described by his brother, William. 'Thick as standing corn, and gorgeous as a field of flowers, stood the Beloochs in their many-coloured garments and turbans; they filled the broad deep bed of the Fullailee, they clustered on both banks, and covered the plain beyond. Guarding their heads with their large dark shields, they shook their sharp swords, beaming in the sun, their shouts rolled like a peal of thunder, as with frantic gestures they rushed for-wards, and full against the front of the 22nd [Cheshires] dashed with demoniac strength and ferocity.' Charles Napier now reached his ambition by winning a battle in the field, which gave him the mastery of Hyderabad. He followed it up by a desert march in the hot weather to Mirpur where he subdued another of the Amirates. These two were annexed as the province of Sind. The third, Khairpur, whose Amir had observed the treaty and remained friendly, became a protected native state.

This brilliant little campaign was a masterpiece of Indian war-fare, as the old Duke of Wellington declared. Napier was the idol of his men, restoring their confidence in their leaders and the con-fidence of the government in its generals. He was a forceful ad-ministrator with a strong sense of justice and complete indiffer-ence to criticism, the creator of the model province of Sind. To his foresight India owed the port of Karachi, the commerce of the Indus, and the future prospect of the irrigation of the Indus basin. And yet the Sind campaign is the most blatant example of mere aggressive warfare in British history. Napier had no misgivings about his work. He did not say of it *'peccavi'*, 'I have sinned';

---

[1] Sir J. Outram (1803–63). 'His life was given to India. In early manhood he reclaimed wild tribes by winning their hearts; Ghazni, Khelat, the Indian Caucasus witnessed the daring deeds of his prime; Persia brought to sue for peace; Lucknow relieved, defended, and recovered, were fields of his later glories. Many wise rulers, many valiant captains, hath his country sent hither, but never any loved as this man was by those whom he governed or led on to battle.' (Epitaph.)

though a contemporary witticism suggested that he might have said it. His comment was that it was 'a very advantageous, useful, humane piece of rascality'.

All his work and all his words were characteristic and original, as was his appearance. 'Beneath a huge helmet of his own contrivance' he revealed 'a fringe of long hair at the back and in front a large pair of round spectacles, an immense hooked nose, and a mane of moustache and whisker reaching to the waist'. His men affectionately called him Old Fagin from a character in a recent best-seller. Some indications of that eagle's beak, that lion's mane, are conventionally represented on his monument in Trafalgar Square 'to which the most numerous contributors were private soldiers'.

The Sind campaign was by no means the last of the troubles in the north-west. Lord Ellenborough was obliged to intervene in Scindia's state of Gwalior because he dared not leave so powerful a prince in doubtful friendship on his flank when troubles with the Sikhs was blowing up. Dissatisfaction over these campaigns led to Ellenborough's recall and replacement by Lord Hardinge (1844), but not to any settlement with the Sikhs. British victories in Sind and Gwalior brought the British armies in greater force upon their frontiers and provoked the trial of strength which they desired. In 1845 the Sikhs crossed the Sutlej with the intention of marching on Delhi.

Hardinge was an old soldier and, more in the manner of a knight-errant than a viceroy, he accompanied the army as a subordinate to his friend Hugh Gough, the Commander-in-Chief. Gough had made a reputation by his combined operations on the China coast in 1841, so that much was expected of him. But war against the Sikhs with their well-served artillery, their European staffs, and their stout Punjabi infantry proved a very different matter from hunting Chinese coolies led by mandarins. This was war between well-matched opponents, the only advantage to Gough being the leavening of British infantry in his army. After two costly combats with a doubtful outcome at Moodkee and Ferozeshah, Gough forced an issue at Sobraon (10 February 1846), a furious and bloody triumph for the British infantry. The campaign was fought by a force which would now be reckoned at three infantry divisions, whose nine British battalions lost 3400 men in killed and wounded. Sobraon enabled Hardinge to impose the Treaty of Lahore on the Sikhs, restricting their frontiers and obliging them to accept a British Resident, Henry Lawrence, at Lahore. His team of assistants were men of such force of character, such manly honour as the world has rarely seen.

Hardinge deprived the Sikhs of the mountainous tracts, outside the Punjab proper, which Runjeet Singh had taken from the Afghans, and imposed a war indemnity of £1,500,000. Part of the hill-country, the principality of Jammu, was ruled by a Rajput client of Runjeet Singh, named Gulab Singh, who assisted the British cause and negotiated the terms of the treaty. Gulab undertook the payment of the indemnity in return for the principality of Kashmir of which he became first Maharaja. By this rather shabby bargain the backward Moslem state of Kashmir, renowned for its natural beauty, passed under the control of a Hindu court and aristocracy.

The Treaty of Lahore was never more than an armistice. When the next Governor-General, Lord Dalhousie, arrived in 1848, his hope was for another period of peace and progress like Bentinck's term, but his first great effort was required against a Sikh national revolt. The first Sikh War had not produced so decisive a British victory as to reconcile the warlike Punjabis to a union with British India.

The cause of the second Sikh War was the murder of the British agent at Mooltan, the signal for a general uprising against the other British political officers. Dalhousie again unleashed Hugh Gough, a fighting Irishman who never had enough. 'Unwarned by precedents, uninfluenced by examples, the Sikh nation has called for war', declared Dalhousie, 'and they shall have it with a vengeance.' Again the Sikhs displayed their valour; they very nearly got the better of Gough at Chillianwalla (1848) where the British troops lost two colours, four guns and 2000 men. In response to public agitation Napier was ordered out to supersede him, but Gough 'never was bate and he never would be bate'; he finished the whole epic struggle by a crushing victory at Gujerat (1849), and by a pursuit to the banks of the Indus before Napier arrived.

The Punjab was now annexed and reorganised as a province of British India. Politically the most striking effect was to advance British rule to the line of the Upper Indus and thus to present the problem of the North-west Frontier which remained unsolved for a hundred years. John Lawrence, Henry's brother and successor, wished to stop at the river-line, since no practical advantage came of pressing on into the barren hills beyond. The military view tended to the orthodox strategic doctrine that all river-lines are weak unless covered by strong bridgeheads. Peshawar, which had been so often disputed between Sikhs and Afghans, at least should be held. It was occupied in 1850 and secured by the extension of the Grand Trunk Road, westward to Lahore and eventually to Peshawar, where George Lawrence, a third brother, was Deputy-Commissioner. The Punjab was quickly pacified by the personal influence of Lawrence's men over the Sikh soldiery. A Corps of military police was formed and then a new army, the Punjab Irregular Frontier Force whose reputation as the 'Piffers' is not yet forgotten in India. Their leaders, Herbert Edwardes, John Nicholson, Hodson of Hodson's Horse, were to see their work justified in 'fifty-seven.

5. LORD DALHOUSIE AND THE INDIAN MUTINY

THE organisation of Sind and the Punjab should be considered part of the achievement of James Ramsay, Marquess of Dalhousie (1812–60), who was Governor-General from 1848 to 1856 and one of the three or four greatest in that long and famous line. The unwieldy Bengal Presidency was also reorganised under his direction as two provinces each under a Lieutenant-Governor. He fostered commerce and the communications on which it depends. In addition to his two great roads, the Grand Trunk from Lahore to Peshawar and a hardly less vital artery from Agra to Bombay he linked the whole country with 4000 miles of public telegraphs, a more complete service than there was at that date in England; and introduced a halfpenny rate for letter-postage. He lighted the coasts and improved the harbours. He built the first railways in Asia, two short lines running inland from Bombay and Calcutta. Exports and imports were doubled and the revenue, though much enlarged, showed a surplus in his last year. At the end of his time his government was planning a comprehensive scheme of Indian education. He had arrived in India an active young man of thirty-six; he departed an old man of forty-four, worn out by incessant travel and responsibility but confident that India was set in the path of progress.

Politically he was no less enterprising but on far more dangerous ground. After the second Sikh War he found himself faced with a second Burmese War (see chapter VIII, 1, page 406) and, forcing the issue with spirited efficiency, annexed Lower Burma without compunction. He took a firm line with that superannuated phantom, the King of Delhi who still preserved some of the trappings of the Great Mogul. Thirty years before Dalhousie's day Bishop Heber had described the fantastic squalor of the court of Delhi, where hordes of beggars bivouacked in the purlieus of a palace greater than the Kremlin, where nothing was ever mended and nothing cleaned, where the King's throne was so coated with filth that its ornaments could not be distinguished. Princely gifts were exchanged between the Bishop and the old King according to the rule of oriental courtesy, but all was pretence since the government at Calcutta prescribed and provided what each English visitor should offer to the King, and confiscated the King's present in order to balance the account. The monarch had nothing to say except to complain fretfully that Lord Amherst had insisted on taking a seat in his presence. 'At Delhi,' wrote Heber, 'all was dirty lonely and wretched; the baths and fountains dry; the inlaid pavements hid with lumber and gardener's sweepings, and the walls stained with the dung of birds and bats.' The Mogul Empire had been a fiction since that day when Shah Alam had thrown himself upon the mercy of Clive, 'a fugitive without money, without troops, dependent on the English for his daily bread'. But fifty years passed before Viscount Hastings took the step of discontinuing the pretence that as ruler of Bengal he acted in the name of the Mogul. Amherst declined to do homage in 1827, meeting him on equal terms as the viceroy of an equally dignified monarch. Still the royal title, the pension of twenty-six *lakhs* of rupees (£200,000 a year) and the mysterious prestige of monarchy survived when Dalhousie took the decision that the Mogul monarchy should end with the life of the present incumbent. The last King of Delhi, Bahadur Shah, was eighty years old when Dalhousie left India.

This deferred sentence was not felt to be so significant as the annexations made in accordance with Dalhousie's doctrine of 'lapse'. The immemorial rule of Indian law gave to an adopted heir all the rights of a natural heir including that of succession to a throne. Dalhousie decided not to admit the principle in newly-created native states where the rulers held solely by an act of grace from the British *raj*. In such instances, when the legitimate family died out, the principality would lapse to the British government and not pass to an adopted heir. Cases occurred in Satara (1848), Nagpur (1853) and Jhansi (1854), each being a principality granted by the British to a conquered enemy after the Maratha Wars. The fourth case was the great and rich kingdom of Oudh which, since the days of Clive, had been intricately associated with the Bengal Presidency. The kingly title, first of its kind in India, had been assumed by the Nawab of Oudh upon British authority. The Company's troops had garrisoned the province and guarded the King's person for near a hundred years. And though Oudh was rich, its government remained in the scandalous state of all Indian governments in the eighteenth century. One Governor-General after another had urged reforms upon the kings of Oudh but without visible result. Corruption and misrule grew worse until it was commonly said that our own troops protected the King from the vengeance of his subjects. In 1856 Dalhousie was so heartened by the progress in Sind, the Punjab and the three lapsed Maratha states that he decided to intervene in Oudh under the terms of the treaty of 1837. Upon the advice of Outram and Sir Henry Lawrence, both of whom were opposed to annexations in general, he forced the King to abdicate, and placed Lawrence as British Commissioner at Lucknow, the capital of Oudh.

Dalhousie's momentous term of office was now drawing to a close. His successor, Lord Canning, had already arrived in India when the annexation was completed. In the same year (1856) the Persians had taken advantage of the diversion caused by the Crimean War to resume their encroachments towards the east. After long, unfriendly negotiation the British declared war to prevent their occupation of Herat. Outram was sent with the Bombay Army to Bushire on the Persian coast. After defeating the Persians in several small engagements, he obliged them to withdraw from Herat and to give an undertaking that the slave trade would be suppressed in the Persian Gulf. Having completed his task, Outram and his army returned to India (March 1857) in time to take part in the campaigns of the Mutiny year.

What was the Indian Mutiny, that fierce conflict which so profoundly moved our great-grandparents? It was not a proletarian revolution like those which began to agitate Europe in 1848; no general strike precipitated the urban workers into direct action; no agrarian riots threatened the property of the landlords; no national guard sprang into life. Nor was it a feudal tumult like those in which Clive and Dupleix had so audaciously intervened during the decline of the Mogul Empire; the greater princes held aloof, excepting two or three who nourished personal grievances, or used their influence discreetly in support of the government. Nor was it a communal struggle, though it began among the high-caste Hindus; nor a revolt of the newly conquered provinces, for Sind and the Punjab remained calm. It was not a general protest against British administration, for the unrest scarcely spread into the Bombay and Madras Presidencies. And yet it was something more than a mutiny of the Bengal Army.

Acute observers had been foretelling for years past that the pace of reform had been dangerously forced. 'The crusading improving spirit of the last twenty-five years', said Outram shortly before the Mutiny, 'would cause a resounding clash.' English law, English teaching, English religion, English interference with age-old customs pointed the way to a new India which would be Anglicised and centrally administered by means of road, rail and telegraph in despite of caste and race. The vernacular press, uncensored since Bentinck's day, harped upon grievances and denunciations; it was free to agitate and obstruct, but impotent to inform the illiterate masses. Bentinck had alarmed the orthodox by his liberal intentions; Dalhousie had threatened vested interests by strengthening the hand of government. The Evangelicals were at work in the civil departments and the officers' messes, speaking hopefully of a day when heathen practices should be extinct in India, and the English no longer be required to act as 'churchwardens to Juggernaut'.

But unrest does not make revolution, without resolute leading and a plan of action. Only in the Bengal Army does it appear that there was any conspiracy to revolt, and the mercenary armies of the East India Company had been chronically mutinous. It should be remembered that there was not one Indian Army but three, under separate administration and command, in the three Presidencies, with the nucleus of a new fourth Army in the Punjab. At one time the Mutiny looked rather like a civil war between the Punjab irregulars and the Bengal sepoys.

The Bengal Army, recruited largely from high-caste Hindus, had all the faults common to idle mercenaries. Since the Sikh Wars, when some regiments had behaved badly, they had been unemployed. Discipline was relaxed, the officers were elderly and easy-going, the sepoys chafed at military infringements of their caste rules. Service overseas in Persia or Burma was disliked and resisted. Grievances accumulated, to reach a climax in the rumour that their new cartridges were wrapped in paper greased with cow's fat as a deliberate British affront to caste. Early in 1857 the greased cartridges led to several minor mutinies in Lower Bengal which were suppressed without difficulty. The High Command was slow to take alarm, supposing that the withdrawal of the greased cartridges would restore tranquillity. Then and later, British officers, with pardonable pride, refused to believe that their own men would break faith, whatever the rascals in other regiments might have done. Some shrewd observers, noticing the faulty distribution of troops in the Bengal Presidency had foreseen the greater danger. Napier had pointed it out, and Henry Lawrence, fourteen years earlier, had published an accurate forecast of the events at Delhi. But the sudden bloodthirsty outbreak of the garrison at Meerut on that hot Sunday evening (10 May 1857), came as a surprise to the British residents and the Commander-in-Chief at Simla.

The mutinous sepoys had two obvious alternatives before them: to restore the military kingdom of the Marathas or to restore the Mogul Empire. They chose the latter. Marching off to Delhi in the night, they occupied the Palace and placed themselves under the allegiance of the bewildered, purblind Bahadur Shah, thus associating the Moslems with their cause. Letters had been passing between the court of Delhi and the Shah, from which arose a whole new crop of rumours that a Persian army would soon be marching to Delhi as it had done 120 years earlier. Moslems and Hindus were soon at loggerheads. The rebellion produced no statesman, so that the sepoys who fought bravely enough for the capital were championing a hopeless cause. The so-called siege of Delhi resembled the siege of Troy. Within the walled city were thousands of warriors and an old doomed feckless King. The engagements took the form of turbulent sorties by the garrison against the camp of the besiegers who were few, headstrong and heroic. It seemed that by nothing but a miracle could they take the city. Meanwhile in May and June the Mutiny spread like an epidemic through the Ganges valley. Sepoy regiments murdered their officers and marched off to join the mutineers at Delhi. Civilians, if they could not hold their districts, gathered the European residents in a body in some stronghold. The administration vanished. Petty princes armed their retainers to take vengeance on personal enemies, or on their creditors. Landlords, dispossessed in the revenue settlements, resumed their old estates. The police took to *dacoity*. But the villagers, the overwhelming majority of the Indian people, showed no resentment to the British, often helping them to places of safety.

From the first the conflict was ruthless and bloody. The repeated treacherous murders of officers by their men led to uncontrolled reprisal. All the main centres of communication between Calcutta and Allahabad were held or recaptured by small bodies of British troops, often by the personal authority of solitary British officers, who gave no quarter to sepoys or their associates. Beyond Allahabad all the countryside was dominated by the rebels and all the larger towns except Cawnpore, and Lucknow, as far west as Agra. Cawnpore surrendered on 27 June to Nana Sahib, the adoptive heir of the long-deposed Peshwa and therefore a claimant to the leadership of the Maratha confederacy.

At this crisis, when Lord Canning at Calcutta was separated by two anarchic provinces from his Commander-in-Chief, who lay outside Delhi with a handful of British troops, while the infection of mutiny was still spreading, India was saved from a relapse into chaos by the firmness of two brothers, John Lawrence (1811–79) at Lahore and Henry Lawrence (1806–57) at Lucknow. The sons of an Irish Protestant soldier, both had spent many years in India fighting in Lord Auckland's wars and afterwards reorganising the conquered provinces. They had much in common, both being rugged, simple, headstrong, unyielding men with firm notions of duty; and Lahore had not been large enough to hold them both. After a disagreement Henry had been posted away to other appointments and had arrived at Lucknow, the capital of Oudh, only a few weeks before the Mutiny. He found that province in turmoil after the annexation of 1856, seething with complaints that the monetary compensation promised by the government had not

been paid. The aristocracy, a body of 300 hereditary landowners
known as the *Talukhdars*, Rajputs of great wealth and feudal influence, had been deprived of all their rights pending a revenue
settlement which had not yet been adjusted. Such a state of affairs
was not disconcerting to Henry Lawrence who knew the land and
the countryfolk of India better than any Englishman alive, and had,
in fact, quarrelled with his brother by asserting the rights of a
similar class in the Punjab. In the first days of the Mutiny he made
the Residency at Lucknow a firm bastion, and even maintained
some personal influence over the Talukhdars. But by the end of
June the Residency was a besieged fortress and the only outpost
held by the Government in Oudh. Lawrence was mortally
wounded on 2 July and died urging his officers never to surrender.

The relief of Lucknow was the first step to be undertaken by
the government in Calcutta before a way could be opened to
Delhi and the west. A psalm-singing old ironside general named
Havelock first undertook this campaign, smiting the Amalekites
without mercy as he fought his way up-country. On 17 July
1857 he discovered the bodies of 200 British women and children
treacherously murdered at Cawnpore, and took exemplary vengeance. But when he reached Lucknow he could do no more than
reinforce the garrison with part of his small column under James
Outram.

Meanwhile 500 miles away John Lawrence had acted at Lahore
with resolution founded on the clearest vision. When the news
from Meerut reached the north-west by telegraph his officers on
the frontier had instantly formed a 'movable column' of reliable
British and Sikh troops to march to any threatened point. Herbert
Edwardes ensured the friendship of the Amir of Afghanistan,
John Nicholson quieted the frontier tribes and so schooled one
sepoy regiment which mutinied that his name is still a legend in the
hills. Some Hazara tribesmen insisted on worshipping him as a
god in his lifetime, though he did his best to flog them out of their
creed. Before the end of May the movable column was swinging
down the Grand Trunk Road to Delhi, the Guides marching a
steady twenty-seven miles a day through the hot weather in their
new dust-coloured (*khaki*) uniforms. Lawrence urged the Commander-in-Chief to audacious action. 'Reflect on the whole history of India. Where have we failed when we acted vigorously?
Where have we succeeded when guided by timid counsels? Clive

with 1200 men[1] fought at Plassy, in opposition to the advice of his leading officers, beat 40,000 men and conquered Bengal.' Lawrence would have abandoned Peshawar to save Delhi had that been inevitable, but so firm was the frontier that it proved unnecessary. 'Hold on to Peshawar to the last', telegraphed the Viceroy on 7 August. The new roads and telegraphs vastly increased Lawrence's resources. Bartle Frere in Sind, and Elphinstone at

THE PUNJAB
AND
INDIAN MUTINY
Miles
0   100   200   300   400
Grand Trunk Road

George Philip & Son, Ltd.

Map 21

Bombay, kept open his communications with the west and sent him troops after quieting their own provinces. The princes of Rajputana and Kashmir, even the great Maharaja Scindia, held firm to their treaties with the British and to their faith in Lawrence. With tact and firmness he anticipated mutiny by disarming and disbanding many regiments of unreliable sepoys, so releasing 10,000 British troops for the campaign at Delhi. These he reinforced with more than 30,000 Sikhs, who never swerved from their military allegiance.

[1] Actually 3000.

The little British force on the Ridge overlooking Delhi fought every day throughout the summer against vastly superior numbers. It was reinforced in June by the movable column from the Punjab and later by other troops who brought with them a bewildering succession of commanders. In the heated discussions of policy the strong men from the Punjab dominated the councils, urging an assault on the city which was delivered against terrifying odds in September. John Nicholson was mortally wounded while leading one of the storming columns. On the day after the fall of Delhi, a dashing leader of irregular cavalry, Major Hodson, was sent to seize the person and family of the old King, Bahadur Shah, who was arrested, tried and transported to Rangoon for the remainder of his inglorious life. Hodson also arrested his two sons and, when a crowd of palace retainers threatened, or seemed to threaten, an attempt at rescue he shot the two princes with his own hand. Thus with the death of the last heirs of Tamburlaine the Great ended the ill-considered attempt to restore the Mogul Empire. Hodson's plea that the princes were 'shot to prevent their escape', a plea so sadly familiar in the revolutions of our own day, has never quite rung true.

After the recapture of Delhi the mutineers were thrown on the defensive. The Punjab movable column pushed on, and in October 1857 made contact with the loyal troops near Lucknow. The next problem was to reduce the province of Oudh where alone the Mutiny had assumed the form of a national rising against the British. Lord Canning, while always attempting to spare the lives of rebels who submitted, had made an error in declaring forfeit the lands of those Talukhdars of Oudh who had not stood by the Government. His mercy earned him the scorn of the soldiers who called him 'Clemency' Canning, a name he accepted as an honour; his confiscations drove the Talukhdars to join the mutineers. A year's hard fighting (October 1857 to October 1858) was required before Sir Colin Campbell, the new Commander-in-Chief, restored order in Oudh by the employment of numerous troops from England. The withdrawal of Canning's proclamation and the promise of a new land-settlement perhaps had more effect than Sir Colin's battles.

Until the last phase the Mutineers remained anonymous. The old King of Delhi had been no leader; for a time Nana Sahib cast himself for the part but proved as irresolute as cruel and treacherous.

A mere idle voluptuary, his sole interest had been a quite un-justified claim that the British should have added to his vast wealth by paying him the Peshwa's pension. His troops were scattered in the hills where he escaped the gallows by vanishing. His lieu-tenant, Tantia Topee, a Maratha soldier, broke away south into the hills of Central India. Here he was joined by the sole heroic figure among the rebels, the Ranee of Jhansi, girl-widow of a Maratha prince whose territory had lapsed by Dalhousie's rule. While Colin Campbell pacified Oudh, the Bombay Army under Sir Hugh Rose fought the last Maratha War against Tantia and the Ranee who were joined by mutinous soldiers from the armies of Scindia and Holkar. The Ranee was killed at Gwalior in May 1858, fighting in soldier's uniform at the head of her troops. Tantia held out till April 1859 when he was hunted down and very properly hanged for his share in the massacre at Cawnpore. Long before these smouldering embers were trodden out the East India Company had been dissolved and the Queen's government pro-claimed throughout India.

6. BRITISH INDIA, 1858–76

WHEN the charter of the East India Company came before Par-liament in 1853 for its fourth periodic renewal, it was generally felt that the system of 'double government' could not last much longer. Forty years had passed since the trading monopoly had been withdrawn from the Company, twenty years since the com-mercial branch had been closed, so that the position of the Pro-prietors had become anomalous. They merely held shares in what might be described as part of the funded debt of the British Dominions. Now their authority was further whittled away; the Crown strengthened its control by assuming the right to nominate one-third of the Directors, and weakened the Company by taking away the patronage. In accordance with current reforms in the home civil service, new appointments to India, after 1853, were made on the results of competitive examination. Old Haileybury College was closed down in the Mutiny year after celebrating the fall of Delhi in its last term.

Public opinion tended to fix the blame for the Mutiny upon the Company. The Directors defended themselves in a dignified petition to Parliament composed by John Stuart Mill, pointing out that political sovereignty had already passed away from the Company so that the servants of the Crown must be held responsible. In its day the Company's government had been 'not only one of the purest in intention, but one of the most benevolent in act, ever known among mankind'. During the last generation it had been 'one of the most improving governments in the world'. It had governed and defended India 'without the smallest cost to the British exchequer, which cannot be said of any other of the dependencies of the Crown'. The Company had constantly held that 'its first duty was to the people of India' and had 'seen with the greatest pain the demonstrations of indiscriminate animosity towards the natives of India' which the events of the Mutiny had provoked.

There was much truth in these assertions but not enough to justify the control of an Empire by a casual group of investors, as Palmerston jauntily pointed out in proposing a new India Bill on 12 February 1858. Before the Bill got through, his administration was overturned on quite another count, so that the short-lived Derby administration was responsible for the Government of India Act 1858 (21 & 22 Vict. cap. 106), which differed from Palmerston's Bill in some particulars. The government of India with all territorial rights and revenues and all tributes previously enjoyed by the Company was transferred to the Crown. The powers formerly exercised jointly by the Board of Control and by the Directors were to be exercised by an additional Secretary of State, acting upon the advice of a council of fifteen members. Seven councillors, in the first instance, were to be nominated by the Directors; the remainder by the Crown. Strict financial provisions prevented either the Secretary of State or the Governor-General from waging aggressive wars. The Secretary of State was instructed to render an annual financial statement to Parliament. The Company's armies and navy were absorbed into the armed forces of the Crown.

The Company submitted gracefully with a farewell message to its servants in India, September 1858. 'Let Her Majesty appreciate the gift—let her take the vast country and the teeming millions of India under her direct control, but let her not forget the great corporation from which she has received them nor the lessons to be learned from its success.'... 'The Coy has the privilege of transferring to the service of H.M. such a body of civil and military officers as the world has never seen before.'

The winding-up of the East India Company was a lengthy process since the dividend to stock-holders had been guaranteed by the Act of 1833 for a period of forty years. This sum, £630,000 a year, remained as a first change on the revenues of the Indian government until 1873, when the stock-holders were paid off in cash or in Indian government bonds. Until that final settling-day John Company retained a shadowy existence in the form of a chairman, five directors, a secretary, and a clerk, with no duties other than distributing the dividend. The palatial East India House in Leadenhall Street was taken over in 1858 by Lord Stanley, the first Secretary of State for India. Two years later he found it more convenient to remove to Whitehall whereupon the old house was sold and demolished.

On 1 November 1858, while war still raged in Central India, the Queen issued a proclamation to the 'Princes, Chiefs and the People of India':

We have resolved to take upon ourselves the government of the territories in India, heretofore administered in trust for us by the Honourable East India Company....

We announce to the native princes of India that all treaties and engagements made under the authority of the Company will be scrupulously maintained....

We desire no extension of our present territories....

We declare it to be our royal will and pleasure that none be in any wise favoured, none molested or disquieted, by reason of their religious faith or observances...that our subjects of whatever race or creed be freely and impartially admitted to office in our service...that in framing the law due regard be paid to the ancient rights, usages and customs of India....

Our clemency will extend to all offenders save those convicted...of the murder of British subjects....

When internal tranquillity shall be restored, it is our earnest desire to stimulate the peaceful industry of India, to promote works of public utility and improvement, and to administer the government for the benefit of all our subjects resident therein.

The last President of the Board of Control, Sir Charles Wood, later first Lord Halifax (1800–85), became Secretary of State for India in 1859. He in London and Canning as Viceroy reconstructed the administration in its new form after the turmoil of the Mutiny. Though much of the old system remained unchanged there was a new spirit in India. The old heroic age when adventurers like Nicholson ruled provinces by sheer force of character, without regard to precedents or regulations, had passed into a new age of efficient centralised administration. Much fun was made of the 'competition-wallahs', the discreet bureaucrats of the new dispensation by the salted, liverish, rough-and-ready 'quahais' of the old school. Everyone was tied by a telegraph-wire to Calcutta where lived the Viceroy, who was tied (after 1870) by a telegraph cable to Whitehall.

Although the Queen had proclaimed equality the sahibs more than ever constituted a new caste in India. As government grew more efficient and more impersonal the gap widened. The bad blood of the Mutiny lay between the sahibs who could not forget Cawnpore and the natives who could not forget the hangings and the shootings and the blowings from guns. The old easy relation between rulers and ruled was never resumed, at least not in the Ganges valley. It was quite out of the question for a sahib to set up a native domestic establishment. The British had reasserted their status as the master-race of India more firmly than ever. In mere physical courage, in endurance, resource and audacity, in unselfish co-operation, loyalty to their leaders, and in defiance of overwhelming odds they had proved themselves unquestionably superior to all the Indian peoples.

Before the Mutiny the task of the rulers had been to subdue the warlike races of the north and to restrain ambitious princes. Now the direction of the British effort was altered. The Princes who had been faithful to the treaties were the strongest buttress of the British *raj*. The virile martial races of the north, who had never swerved from their military allegiance, had earned the faith and friendship of the sahibs, while the mutinous 'pandies' of Bengal remained objects of suspicion and dislike. So small a share had they shown of military virtue that for two generations after the Mutiny few if any recruits for the Army were drawn from Bengal. But the history of British India in those years was not much concerned with war.

On their part the Indian intellectuals also withdrew from intercourse with the British. The Brahma Somaj of Bengal languished while a new reforming sect, the Arya Somaj founded by Dayanand Saraswati (1827–53) gained strength among the Hindus. This was not an attempt to reconcile East and West but a return to the pure undefiled religion of the early Vedas.

IX

MARKETS, MONEY AND MEN IN THE AGE OF FREE TRADE

Argument: In the old economy, staple trades in commodities not produced at home were protected by various devices. These monopolies and protective duties were swept away in an age when voters demanded cheap food and low production costs. Colonial interests were overlooked while trade with all the world expanded. Yet Royal Mail contracts, acting as a bounty to British steamships, gave them a new advantage. Steamships, coaling-stations and deep-sea cables were the nervous system of the new commercial empire. Its life-blood was the flow of capital for overseas investments. British commerce enjoyed continual prosperity from the 'fifties to the 'seventies. A series of gold-finds (all but the first in British territory) stimulated expansion, allowing several colonies to finance their own development. The United States was Britain's best customer, both as a buyer and a borrower, in mid-Victorian days; she also received the largest share of British emigration.

The first Empire had been made by Englishmen; Scottish and Irish emigration came later. A majority of the English race, a large majority of the Scots and an overwhelming majority of the Irish now live outside their lands of origin.

1. FREE TRADE

THE extent of this book does not permit a full enquiry into the effects of the policy of Free Trade, important though they are to the history of the Empire. Few will now deny that Free Trade was a prudent policy for English merchants to support during the period of commercial expansion between 1850 and 1875. Then, improved communications were opening new markets daily in every part of the world. Then, British mechanised industry was far in advance of all its rivals. If unrestricted imports led to an increasing return from unrestricted exports, then the British could hold the markets of the world against all rivals. Cheap coal and cheap labour could and did produce and distribute textiles and machinery for all markets at competitive prices. The surplus of a sure home market formed the broad margin for export; and the export market, in turn, was insured by the invisible export of shipping, services and capital loans (which will be discussed in the succeeding chapters). Even the surplus of population gave no trouble since the emigration of men had become as easy as the emigration of capital. America was a better market for British goods than was Australia. It therefore followed that emigration to America was a more advantageous means of disposing of the unemployed than emigration to Australia. Such, at least, seemed to be the belief of Mr Gladstone's government in 1870. The whole economy was unified by the gold standard. Successive finds of gold throughout the century brought each of the commercial nations into line and into closer relations with the dominant money market of London. The economics of Free Trade seemed unanswerable.

Though the academic economists preached *laissez-faire* as a panacea for all social ills, practical men tended to make a reservation in respect of their immediate concerns. While paying lip-service to Free Trade on principle, they were inclined to think that an exceptional preference should still be imposed to maintain the price of the particular line of goods they wished to sell or the particular rate of wages they had secured; just as their successors, a hundred years later, while admitting the theoretical necessity of a Planned Economy, still claim the right to bargain for better prices or wages in their own industry.

The first effect of mid-Victorian prosperity was to sweep away such slight enthusiasm for the Empire as had been engendered by the Colonial Reformers. Their work was done. The colonies were set free, and sentimentally associated with the mother-country only by common allegiance to the Crown. And the influence of the Crown ran low during the early years of Queen Victoria's widowhood. Free Trade and the utilitarian outlook were expected to weaken the irrational bonds of Empire while they strengthened the rational links of mutual commerce between all the nations of the world. Meanwhile the purchasing power of the colonies was but small. Since they bought less than one-third of what Britain exported and were not developing as rapidly as the United States, it was not to be supposed that the nation of shopkeepers would take much interest in them. British shipping required naval supremacy, that is to say coaling-stations. Otherwise the Empire was valued in terms of West Indian sugar, softwoods from Canada, Australian wool, and tea from the East Indies, until a cheaper supply should crop up somewhere else. The most interesting prospect lay in India, a vast potential market for textiles and not yet fit for self-government. When the Manchester men spoke indifferently of letting the colonies go they had no intention of losing their grip on India.

In general the colonies showed (as some still show) the instability and weakness of every economy based upon the export of a single crop. This Huskisson had recognised in his enlightened tariff reforms of the 1820's, giving preference to the colonial staples, and refusing to admit American goods at the same rate. But the colonies were not then self-governing, and Huskisson insisted that their tariffs should be determined by the British Parliament.

Other countries he met on terms of reciprocity, especially in making exceptions to the Navigation Laws.[1] He extended to the Latin-American republics the privileges given to the shipping of the United States, thus developing a brisk trade with the Spanish Main; but British and Nova Scotian shipping got the best of it. Guano from Peru was brought in great quantities to England as early as the 1820's. Huskisson's commercial treaty with the Argentine (1825) almost amounted to a fiscal union, admitting British merchants to Buenos Ayres on an equal footing with denizens. When steamships came into use in the 1840's the Pacific Steam Navigation Company established coaling-stations all along the coast of the continent. The value of British exports to Latin America in 1830 was £5,000,000, not far short of the goods worth £6,000,000 sent to the United States. British ranchers who began to raise sheep and cattle in the Argentine in mid-century were largely responsible for opening up the cool, empty grasslands of Patagonia.

West Indian sugar-planting had always been a chancy trade, exposed to violent fluctuations in the market and natural disasters by hurricane or earthquake. Perhaps it never had flourished except during the French Wars when scarcity produced high prices. Even before the abolition of slavery the older colonies were languishing.

The Whigs were determined to cheapen sugar which the working-classes consumed in ever greater volume. After a

[1] When they were finally repealed in 1849 little was left but a confused mass of exceptions and amendments.

long Parliamentary struggle Gladstone succeeded, in 1854, in removing the colonial preference, a step which reduced the planters to despair. They were saved from collapse by the general rise in prices in the 'sixties. Though impoverished by well-intentioned philanthropists, neglected on principle by utilitarians, they continued to grow sugar and to live. The excellent Cape wines also felt the weight of Gladstone's hand. Until he swept away the preferential duty (1861), 10% of all the wine drunk in England came from the Cape; thereafter very little

The soft-wood trade of the St Lawrence had no defender when the Admiralty turned to iron hulls and steam. Baltic pines would content English buyers as well as those of New Brunswick or Quebec and, in this case, no question arose of slave-labour in either trade. The preference which Huskisson had allowed on timber from British North America was swept away by Gladstone in 1860. In spite of protests from the colonies he seemed justified by the imports of the next few years. So great was the demand for soft-woods that the annual import from the colonies steadily increased under Free Trade until 1867. But imports from the Baltic increased more rapidly. Thereafter two-thirds of the British supply came from the Baltic while the greater part of the Canadian output went to the United States.

The great struggle over the Corn Laws touched the Empire at one point only. The merchants of Montreal had prospered by shipping their surplus of wheat from the St Lawrence to Great Britain, and Peel had given them a preference of one shilling a bushel in 1843. In spite of pressure from the Colonial Reformers he refused to extend this preference to Australian wheat. The whole advantage was abolished with the English Corn Law in 1846. Canadian wheat was a trifling consideration at that time, hardly enough to sway the market price. No one foresaw the day when England would depend for bread upon the harvest of the prairie. No advantage accrued to England from the Canadian preference. A *douceur* to a struggling colony, it could not survive the storm that swept away the Corn Laws.

It seems to posterity complacent in the extreme that the men who withdrew colonial preferences and granted colonial self-government should have still attempted to control colonial tariffs. The Whigs took it very much amiss that Galt's government in Canada, regarding the withdrawal of the preference on wheat as a betrayal, should discriminate against British goods in the Canadian budget of 1859. They were still angrier when the Indian government attempted to discriminate against Manchester goods in the same year.

The East Indian trade is less easy to analyse. In the later days of the Company's commercial branch the only trading on a large scale had been the exchange of Bengal opium for China tea. India proper exported luxury goods and imported little, until English textiles, piece-goods woven in Lancashire of American cotton, began to find their way into Asia soon after Waterloo. An early visitor to Singapore reported the prevalence of English cotton cloths in Malaya even in 1830. Singapore and (after 1841) Hong Kong were free ports from which trade was distributed to all parts of the East. As soon as the new Indian government was formed it began (1859) a tariff struggle to protect the Indian industry against imported cotton goods. The prospect was changed by the American Civil War which put a stop for four years to the supply of raw cotton from the Southern States. Accordingly Lancashire bought up the Indian crop, the first large-scale importation of any form of Indian goods. When trade was resumed with the cotton-states of America the Indian merchants lost their short-lived trade and looked about for a substitute. Rice first came to England in quantity in the 'sixties and rice-pudding was then first seen in nurseries. Indian teak was also brought to England to build hard-wood ships which helped to drive the American clippers off the seas.

As the consumption of tea in England increased throughout the nineteenth century, the price fell steadily. When the China trade was thrown open in 1833 there was keen rivalry among ship-owners to seize this profitable trade from the slow East Indiamen. Samuel Cunard had been shipping direct to British North America since 1825 and now the Yankee Clippers came into the race. As in the southern wool trade the British ships had the best of it in the end. The great year of the tea-clippers was 1866 when nine Greenock ships left Foochow on a single tide. Three of them tied up together in London docks, having made an even passage round the Cape in ninety-nine days.

But by that date tea grown within the Empire was coming into the market. The wild tea-plant of Assam was noticed as early as 1820. After twenty years the first large plantation was made by the Assam Company which sent to London an inferior bitter tea consumable only when blended with Chinese. It was long before Indian tea improved in quality. By 1874 only 8% of British imported tea came from India, which now supplies much more than half. Tea-planting in Ceylon had not then begun.

Of Australian economy there is little to say here. Between 1820 and 1850 the export of wool, almost all of it to London, was multiplied tenfold. By the end of that period it was half the British supply and the best half in quality. The gold-rush of 1852 placed Australia on such a footing that the various states could finance their own development. Australia was less dependent than Canada or India upon the British investor, a fact which may have encouraged the self-reliant democracy of the Australians. The settlements scattered round the fringe of a continent trafficked by sea with one another and with England. Unlike the Canadians they were not burdened in their infancy with the cost of trunk railways.

The year 1860 saw the general triumph of free trade, the policy of the Open Door which for two generations was accepted by most progressives as a part of morality. It was clinched by Cobden's commercial treaty with France, the first of several treaties extending most-favoured-nation treatment to Continental countries. Great Britain thus deprived herself of the power to give preferences to colonial trade if ever thereafter she should wish to do so.

2. BRITISH SHIPPING AND CABLES

CAPTAIN COOK's achievements, which revealed the shape of the Pacific Ocean, also showed that long sea-voyages need not be prodigal of life. From the days of Magellan to those of Anson and Byron the hazards of a voyage to the Pacific had been so adverse as to deter commercial speculators. Cook was two years at sea without losing a man from preventible disease, and merchant ships soon imitated his measures against scurvy. It was not long before English ships came to be known as 'lime-juicers' and English seamen as 'limeys'.

The first commercial voyages into the Pacific, as it appears, were made by country-ships from the East Indian ports. On

Cook's third voyage his men had enriched themselves at Macao by selling skins of the sea-otter which they had brought from the Pacific coast of America. The news filtered through to Calcutta, into the receptive ear of John Henry Cox, an interloping trader. With connivance from friends in the East India Company he found his way to Canton, circumventing the Chinese authorities; and financed a series of voyages to seek for sea-otter skins. Cox was the backer of John Meares whose misadventures at Nootka Sound (see chapter v, 7, page 267) provoked the Spanish Armament in 1790. It is noteworthy that the Spanish Governor, after confiscating Meares's ship and goods, sold them obligingly to a Yankee skipper who was standing by to jump Meares's claim. Pitt's spirited reaction against the Spanish threats led to the opening of the Pacific to the trade of all nations. It was promptly invaded, in the 1790's, by numerous British and American whaling-ships, coming from East Indian ports or round the Horn.

The whalers were prepared to cruise for two or three years and to return only when their holds were filled with oil. In the words of the chantey, the whalemen 'never see the corn in the ear'. Though every whaler was a factory and depot-ship, it was common practice to leave a boat's crew for a season at a beach-whaling station on some prolific shore. As we have seen at Cook Strait, at Port Phillip, and in the Falkland Islands, shore-whaling stations sometimes grew into colonies. The whalers have no chronicle or statistics. Their activity and their profit grew with the demand for fine oil to lubricate the new machines, and declined as one species of whale after another was annihilated. Their contribution to the expansion of the British Empire must be indicated not computed. Though obscure in the records of the scientific historians it is clear enough in romance as the subject of a score of adventurous tales for boys.

The throwing open of the Pacific was followed by the abolition of the monopoly in the Indian trade (1813), and the China trade (1833–40); the repeal of the British Navigation Acts (1849); and the opening of Japan (1864).

Shipping plied on the old trade-routes, not much affected, for two generations, by the coming of steam-power. An engine had been put into a boat on the Clyde, by Symington, as early as 1789, but the first practical use of steamships derived from Robert Fulton's experiments and demonstrations in America, from 1807 onwards. Steamboats found their first opportunity on the American inland waterways. In the 1820's the celebrated stern-wheelers and side-wheelers, built like house-boats, were already plying up and down the Mississippi on wood-fuel. There was a steamer at Red River in 1839. In England inland water transport did not call for steam. The first British steamships were tugboats like that which for ever tows the *Fighting Téméraire* in Turner's picture (1839). The oldest sea-going steamship line in the world is the General Steam Navigation Company of London, founded in 1824 to carry passengers down to Margate, a run which was extended to the east-coast ports and Scotland.

Deep-sea voyages were beyond the capacity of the early steamships, simply because the ratio of fuel-consumption to engine-power was far too high. The ships could not carry enough coal to drive them across the Atlantic Ocean. Thus the claim to have made the first crossing by steam-power is put forward on behalf of several ships which carried auxiliary engines while depending in the last resort on sail. An American ship, the *Savannah*, crossed the Atlantic in 1819 with auxiliary steam, in seventeen days. It was a mere *tour de force*, leading to no further development. In 1833 the *Royal William*,[1] built and manned at Quebec through the endeavours of Samuel Cunard, made what is described as a crossing by steam which led to competitive attempts. The merchants of Calcutta and Bombay were also beginning to clamour for quicker communications than were provided by the slow East-Indiamen. It was indeed a great triumph for machinery when the *Enterprise* (470 tons and 120 h.p.) struggled round the Cape, mostly under steam, in 1825. She was piloted up the river to Calcutta by a young man named Thomas Waghorn (1800–50).

Logical progress towards steam communication pointed to carrying mails in fast steamships with a few passengers, while unhurried emigrants and bulky goods travelled under sail. The

[1] According to a writer in the *Mariner's Mirror* (January 1948) she was a paddle-steamer, schooner-rigged, with three tall masts; her length 176 feet, her engines developing 300 h.p.; her tonnage estimated at 363 tons 'burden' but actually much greater. Built for the St Lawrence trade she called at Boston in 1833, the first British steamer to visit an American port. Having been sold, she was despatched to England for disposal and left Pictou (Nova Scotia), 18 August 1833. When a gale disabled one engine she ran for ten days on her port engine only, and reached Gravesend on 12 September having averaged six knots, 'mostly under steam'. Sold as a warship to Spain she was the first steamship to fire a shot in action, 1834.

Admiralty had provided packet services of fast sailing-ships to carry mails since the seventeenth century. The regular services to Calais, the Hook of Holland, and Lisbon date from 1689, to Jamaica from 1702. Like most other public services in the eighteenth century they lapsed into an easy corrupt system of management by deputy. In the nineteenth century Post Office reform was begun by experiments with steam. The mails went from Liverpool to Dublin by steam-packet from 1819.

The first of the Royal Mail steamship companies is the 'P. & O.' which was founded by Arthur Anderson (1791–1868). He began his career as a blockade-runner in the Carlist Wars and specialised in taking light, fast ships from Falmouth to Lisbon. In August 1837 he advertised a service of five steamships to carry passengers and mails to Lisbon, Cadiz and Gibraltar, by contract for the General Post Office. His largest ship was of 900 tons with engines of 300 h.p. From Gibraltar the Admiralty already ran a steam-packet service in naval vessels to Malta but, for some years, the weak link was the run from Malta to Alexandria where the Overland Route began.

Thomas Waghorn, fascinated by steam and speed, had persuaded the Indian government to make some experiments in speeding the mail service, for which he agitated in Liverpool and London, making himself heartily disliked among the slow-coaches at the G.P.O. He plumped for the Overland Route. In Wellesley's day, despatches had been conveyed to India through Beirut and Basra, a road much beset by Bedouin robbers; Waghorn thought better of the route through Egypt and made a record trip from London by Trieste and Alexandria to Jedda in the Red Sea, in order to demonstrate its advantages. *The Times* now took up his case, threatening the East India House with awkward questions about its dilatory service of mails, until at last the Overland Mail was established in 1838. The Post Office extended its steam-packet service from Malta to Alexandria where Waghorn set up a travel agency for conveying passengers by stages through the desert to Suez. There they caught the mail-steamer, provided by the Indian government, to Bombay. The average time taken eastward to India was seventy-four days, and westward to England sixty-four days; the record run was fifty days.

Waghorn's service was conducted for five years (1838–43), the period from which dates the tourist traffic to Egypt, and the English 'colonies' at Alexandria and Cairo. Shepheard's Hotel was opened in 1844 as a rival to Waghorn's establishment. But the Post Office authorities disapproved of these interlopers. The Peninsular Steam Navigation Company was given a new contract in 1840 to take the mails through to India, which justified them in changing their name to the Peninsular and Oriental (P. & O.). In 1843 they floated a subsidiary company to manage the crossing of the desert, and put Waghorn out of business. He had transported 800 passengers in his last year.

Though he had lost all his money, Waghorn retained his energy and enthusiasm for rapid travel. He continued to harass the Post Office with schemes for sending the mails overland through Trieste. In 1845 and 1846 he was employed by the government to make further experiments. He twice achieved the timing of thirty days from Bombay, via Alexandria and Trieste, to London; but had great difficulty in recovering his expenses. He died in poverty in his fiftieth year (1850), having worn himself out with tropical voyaging. His furious energy and passion for speed were favourite subjects for the humorists of the age. He may well have supplied the model for Jules Verne's eccentric Englishman who went *Round the World in Eighty Days* (1872).

The organisation of the P. & O. Company in the days of the Overland Route was threefold. In Western waters they ran ships with English crews. East of Suez, after 1854, they used ships built for tropical seas and manned by Lascars (the hereditary caste of Moslem seamen from the coasts and islands of the Bay of Bengal). In Egypt they maintained resthouses, and caravans of 2500 camels and 400 horses, until they in their turn were supplanted by the Egyptian State Railways, which Robert Stephenson built for the Khedive (1858). The opening of the Suez Canal in 1869 was a sore blow to the P. & O. Company since their ships must now be refitted to make the whole voyage from England to India but, for many years more—until 1888—the mails and the passengers disembarked at Alexandria to go swiftly overland while the ship passed through the Canal dead slow, by daylight only.

The P. & O. Company designed steamships for comfort, even for luxury, on long voyages. In 1842 their crack ship was the *Hindostan*, a wooden paddle-steamer of 2000 tons with engines developing 520 h.p. at a pressure of 7 lb. Ten years later they could boast of the *Himalaya*, an iron-built screw-steamer of 3000

tons and 2500 h.p., able to carry 200 cabin passengers. A traveller
to India described a voyage in the *Nyanza* (1800 tons) in 1869,
with enthusiasm about the saloon and fitted cabins, for the P. & O.
was the line of the empire-makers, the new governors going out
to the scene of their triumphs. The fare, £95, included wines and
spirits *gratis*, either at meals or when required. Dancing and
games were enjoyed on deck but the other relaxations of modern
cruising were not allowed. 'Strict etiquette was observed in
clothing.' Since there were neither refrigerators nor electric fans,
a cabin on the windward [1] side of the ship was a consideration.

The mail contracts were extended to China (1845), Australia
(1856) and Japan (1864), until the P. & O. held something like a
monopoly of Eastern travel. When competition came, the security of their government contracts enabled them to defy it and to
lag behind in consideration for their passengers.

The year 1838 saw a contest for the Atlantic crossing by steam.
Brunel of the Great Western Railway had built a ship named the
Great Western, to extend his line of transport from Bristol to
America. It made the round trip in fifteen days out and thirteen
days home, but was preceded by a rival ship the *Sirius*. Among
the observers of the contest was Joseph Howe of Nova Scotia who
used his influence with the Home Government to give the mail
contract to a steamship. Tenders were offered and the contract
secured by Samuel Cunard, the Nova Scotian, for his Liverpool
ship the *Britannia* which made the passage from Liverpool to
Halifax in 15 days (1840), against Brunel's *Great Western*, a
triumph for the Mersey as well as for Cunard. Regular sailings by
four ships of the British and North American (Cunard) Line provided a fortnightly service to Halifax and Boston from September
1841. The P. & O. and the Cunard contracts were followed by
the issue of mail contracts to steamship lines sailing to all parts of
the Empire. The Royal Mail Steam Packet Company took over
the Admiralty packet service to the West Indies; the Union Company (now Union Castle) to the Cape in 1857; the Allan Line, in
opposition to the Cunard, obtained a contract for Canadian mails
to Quebec in 1855. By 1860 the British government was paying
a million pounds a year to steamship lines for carrying mails, a

---

[1] Port-side Outwards, Starboard-side Homewards. P.O.S.H. With regret I
abandon this popular derivation, which is not substantiated, of the slang word
'posh'. C.E.C.

concealed subsidy which placed the British far ahead of their rivals in marine engineering; for steamships could not yet be made to pay without a subsidy. The Whigs had repealed the Navigation Acts in 1849, as an act of devotion to the fetish of Free Trade, and never noticed the protection they gave to the new shipping industry in another way.

Yet all but the smallest steamships still depended upon auxiliary sail in the last resort and, until the end of the century, were mostly rigged with masts and spars. The first true ocean-going steamships, moved by steam-power and nothing else, were the ironclad warships of the 'sixties. The Anglo-French rivalry of the years 1858–60 led to a race in naval armaments, similar to the Anglo-German contest of fifty years later. Though French inventiveness at first placed France in the lead, British superiority in marine engineering and British industrial strength prevailed. Something was learned from the improvised ironclads used in the American Civil War, and more from the fast commerce-raiders fitted out in European ports, but the problems of design were solved by naval architects in the older countries. H.M.S. *Devastation*, launched in 1869, may be regarded as the model ironclad of the new age, an 'all-big-gun' ship with her armament in turrets placed amidships and without masts or spars for carrying sail. Such ships produced a revolution in naval strategy and tactics. Dispositions for war were based on coaling-stations so that the value of the old naval stations now depended upon supplies of coal. Cheap English coal was towed about the world in hulks and stored at strategic bases for the Navy. Similarly the Royal Mail Lines, especially the P. & O., organised auxiliary fleets of coal-hulks.

While the British services turned to steam, the Americans, not yet an industrial nation, concentrated on increasing the size, speed and efficiency of their sailing-ships. The *Mayflower* had crossed the Atlantic in sixty-six days. The news of the Declaration of Independence, 150 years later, reached London by the easier east-bound route in forty-four days. A substantial improvement had been begun (1816) by the Blackball Clippers, actually the first of all shipping 'lines'. Running to a schedule in fair weather or foul, between New York and Liverpool, they averaged twenty-three days eastbound and forty days westbound. Their ships were built in progressively larger size, from 500 to 1200 tons; and at last, in a few instances, reached 2000 tons. These were great four-

or five-masted sailing-ships, clipper-built, longer than British
ships in proportion to their beam, and schooner-rigged to eco-
nomise man-power. Though they held their own against the
steamers in carrying emigrants and freight, their limitation was
the difficulty of finding forecastle hands with sufficient stamina
and strength. Yankee skippers were proud of their reputation for
hard driving, which even British seamen admired and envied. It
was no disgrace but good cause for pride to be

> mate of a bucko ship
> That always killed one man per trip.

On the longer runs they outsailed the mail steamers. The great
days of the Blackball Line were the 'fifties when they grasped the
Australian trade, going out with emigrants and coming home with
wool. Driven recklessly before the westerly winds, with the land-
lubbers battened under hatches for days on end, they logged a
steady sixteen knots through towering seas, a speed that no steamship could then achieve. British shipowners went into the trade,
buying ships in New England and Nova Scotia or, later, building
them on the Mersey or the Clyde. Some were celebrated, such as
the *Cutty Sark* which is still afloat, or the even faster *Thermopylae*
which carried mails to Melbourne under contract to pay a heavy
forfeit for every day taken on the voyage in excess of sixty-eight.
During the gold-rush of 1852 the two first steamships to reach
Melbourne were sixty days out from London. The Blackball
Liners, bought by Thomas Ismay of Liverpool, formed the
nucleus of the White Star Line (1867), but teak-built British ships
proved better than the soft-wood Americans.

As early as 1862 the Holt Line had built an economical steam
cargo-ship, the first of many which at last drove the Stars and
Stripes almost off the seas. The advantage of steam was certainty.
Too often a sailing-ship, having made a record run from Cape
Horn to the Lizard, lost its advantage beating against adverse
winds in the Channel. Furthermore no less than 3% per annum
of sailing-ships were lost at sea in the 'sixties. The proportion of
steamships lost was less than half of 1%.

In 1830, American ships carried 90% of American trade; by
1890 they carried no more than 9%. The British had a million
tons of steamships afloat in 1870 and held their lead well into the
twentieth century. In 1910 Great Britain owned 40% of the

world's shipping, her nearest rival being—not the United States—but Germany with 10%. Men were scarcer than ships. The unhonoured stokers and deckhands of the steamship lines inherited little of the glamour that had once surrounded the jolly tarpaulins who had been England's glory. The Merchant Service employed, in 1910, 280,000 seamen, of whom 80,000 were foreigners.

While speed in travel had obvious advantages, punctuality did not seem of equal importance in earlier days—could not until the addressee of a message or consignment had some means of knowing that it had been despatched. Perhaps the significance of the deep-sea cables has not been sufficiently noticed in history. Of all the mechanical devices introduced in the Great Century, surely these sensitive wires, sunk a thousand fathoms below any means of care or maintenance along an unsurveyed path of several thousand miles, are the most amazing. Merchants were sceptical of their use for many years, with good reason since they faded or failed intermittently.

Practical telegraphy was a by-product of railway-building and therefore, in the English railway age, was developed by private enterprise. The first telegraph line, built beside the Great Western Railway according to Wheatstone's patent of 1837, was thrown open to the public for sending outside messages in 1846. Telegraph lines multiplied with the new railways and surpassed them in 1851 by diving under the Channel from Dover to Calais. To stretch a cord across the Atlantic Ocean seemed too fantastically difficult a task, the crux of the problem being that no ship then afloat could carry a sufficient length of it. When a line was established from New York to New Brunswick, to Cape Breton Island and even to Newfoundland, an American engineer named Cyrus Field undertook to extend it across the Ocean (1856) with a financial guarantee from the British government. A ten years' struggle ensued, first on the principle of loading two ships with cables which were to be spliced together in mid-ocean and, when that failed, by packing the whole load into the hull of Brunel's *Great Eastern*, the ship built fifty years before her time. She was ten times as large as any other ship of her day, a 20,000-tonner of the same dimensions as the old *Mauretania*, but unmanageable since her engines could not develop sufficient power to hold her against bad weather, even though she was fitted with screws and paddles, and carried six masts rigged for auxiliary sail. A useless hulk, Brunel's Folly, she found her purpose as a cable ship.

When the line was at last laid from Land's End to Trinity Bay, Newfoundland, in 1866, transmission was so uncertain that it was still pronounced a failure. Not till the line was re-laid in 1872 was there regular communication. In the same years the deep-sea cables were rapidly extended, linking London with Bombay in 1870, with Melbourne in 1872, with Wellington in 1876. The world-wide linkage of London with the outer seas was completed in 1893–4, by the Eastern Telegraph Company, a British company controlling the main services to the Far East and the Islands. Some very lonely places gained a new importance as cable stations, among them Cocos Island, Norfolk Island, Fanning Island, and Ascension.

The reorganisation of the Post Office seemed to run counter to the *laissez-faire* principles of the age, so that it was odd to find Chambers of Commerce agitating in 1856 for cheap rates through the public ownership of telegraphs. This was achieved in 1868 in respect of inland telegraph lines. By an agreement between parties in Parliament the six telegraph companies were bought out for £6,000,000 and placed under management of the Post Office. The cable-services, excepting the Anglo-French cable which the Post Office took over in 1889, were still privately owned (as were telephone and radio services when, much later, they came into general use). In Canada, where the Far West looks across the sea to the Far East, cables round the world were more to the point than cables radiating from London. It is to Canada and especially to Sir Sandford Fleming, one of the builders of the Canadian Pacific Railway, that the Empire owed the conception of 'all-red routes', that is to say world-embracing links between all the countries coloured red on the map. This was the theme of the Ottawa Conference on imperial communications in 1894. A standard postal rate of one penny, or two cents, between all parts of the Empire as proposed by Sir W. Mulock, the Postmaster-General of Canada, and supported by Sir J. Ward, the Postmaster-General of New Zealand, was readily accepted. The 'all-red' cable route was more difficult. Though Canada and New Zealand were enthusiastic, Australia was lukewarm since her economy was nearer to the old world than the new. One of the triumphs of pioneering in Australia had been the overland telegraph line from Adelaide to

Darwin, linked to Java and the main Asiatic services, and completed in 1873. Having this service the Australians did not relish
the expense of providing an alternative route across 6000 miles of
ocean. However, the proposal for completing the circuit of the
world by a trans-Pacific cable was strongly supported by Chamberlain when he came to the Colonial Office in 1895. Departmental committees in 1897 and 1899 urged its construction in
spite of opposition from the Post Office and the Treasury. They
were for leaving such matters to private enterprise, which won for
them the influential backing of the cable companies. In 1900
Chamberlain got his way, overruling the other departments and
securing the support of Australia. Tenders were issued for the
laying of a cable to be managed jointly by the governments of
the United Kingdom, Canada, Australia and New Zealand through
a Pacific Cable Board. The cable was laid in 1902, at a cost of
£2,000,000, from Vancouver to Fanning Island, Suva (Fiji), and
Norfolk Island whence it divided into two branches running
respectively to Queensland and northern New Zealand.

At the Imperial Conference of 1911 the Dominion premiers
raised the question of applying the new technique of wireless telegraphy to 'all-red' communications. They were assured that the
Postmaster-General, Mr Herbert (now Viscount) Samuel, was
already negotiating contracts for an imperial wireless chain.
Tenders were issued and agreements signed in 1912 with the
Marconi Company. It was the suggestion that some members of
the government had used their secret information to 'bull the
market' in Marconi shares that caused one of the nastiest scandals
of the age.

Modern commerce dates from the institution of the submarine
cables which put the importing merchant in direct touch with his
source of supply. He was now enabled to buy raw cotton or wool,
sugar or tea, before shipment and to estimate the date of its
arrival. Accordingly transactions on the exchanges at London,
Liverpool and Manchester assumed the form which has become
familiar.

Another consequence of regular sailings on the shipping-routes
was the appearance of that typical English figure, the 'globe-
trotter'. The English had long been known as a race of travellers
but not of travellers round the world. Until the nineteenth century circumnavigations were still so rare as to be placed on record.

Seamen and emigrants went their ways but travellers for pleasure rarely strayed beyond the Grand Tour of France, Italy and the Rhineland. When the Travellers' Club was formed in 1819, the qualification for membership was to have travelled 'out of the British Islands to a distance of at least five hundred miles from London', this being the limit of mere commonplace touring. In the 'thirties and 'forties trips to America became fashionable. Literary men went there, like Dickens in 1842, to write a travel-book. Young men of fashion, like Lord Stanley when out of office in 1834, toured North America, took a glance at the Far West, perhaps even went to Red River for the buffalo-hunting. Twenty years later the steamship lines took them on to Melbourne and California. Lord Salisbury (then Lord Robert Cecil) was one of the first among young noblemen to extend the traditional Grand Tour to a trip round the world (1851–3). He thought poorly of colonial life. Sir Charles Dilke, after an extensive tour in 1866 and 1867, published his views in *Greater Britain*, a curious jumble of acute observation, perverse politics, and reckless prophecy.

J. A. Froude was another globe-trotting literary man whose descriptions of the colonies may still be read with profit; but the best among them was Anthony Trollope who combined business with pleasure by travelling to make reports for the Post Office. His robust, unsentimental books on *The West Indies* (1859), *North America* (1862), *Australia and New Zealand* (1873), *South Africa* (1878) are the best contemporary accounts of the colonies before imperialism came into fashion. The first royal tours were the visit to Canada in 1860 by the Prince of Wales, and a voyage to all the colonies in 1869–72 by his younger brother, the Duke of Edinburgh. After the 1880's globe-trotting had become so normal and easy as to deserve no further mention here.

3. THE EXPORT OF BRITISH CAPITAL[1]

BEFORE the French Revolution Amsterdam had been the financial capital of Europe. Dutch capitalists were believed to have held one-quarter of the shares in the British national debt, and Dutch bankers advanced money at a low rate of interest to London merchants who invested it at a high rate in the British West Indies. After Waterloo London became, for a hundred years, the unchallenged money-market of the world, with surplus capital always available for investment.

In the older wars the British had financed their allies by subsidies from the Treasury; the first foreign loan, as distinct from a subsidy, was that to Austria in 1794. When peace came, twenty years later, the agents of foreign governments flocked to London for money on commercial terms, and got it—perhaps too easily—from the great banking houses, among which Baring's was the most eminent. Many years passed before this new form of trading was accepted as worthy of political support. Neither Castlereagh nor Canning nor Aberdeen nor Palmerston regarded foreign investment as anything more than speculation by private persons or groups. Loans were rarely supported by a public guarantee, nor was any help given to the investors in collecting debts.

The first phase in the export of British capital was the financing of reconstruction in Europe after the wars, for which about £50,000,000 was pretty securely invested between 1815 and 1830. It was not by the wish of the Tory administration that a second phase followed of financing revolution in Greece and Latin America. The boom began with an advance to the republicans of Colombia in 1820 and continued until the bank failures of 1826, by which time about £20,000,000 had been subscribed for seven or eight revolutionary juntas. The shareholders for the most part lost their money. Two loans, nominally amounting to £2,800,000 had also been raised in 1824 by enthusiasts in London, for the Greek patriots. These also proved most unprofitable to the subscribers though very lucrative to the financial houses that issued

[1] In writing this slight essay upon an abstruse and contentious subject I have in general followed L. H. Jenks' *Migration of British Capital*, 1927. While paying a tribute to this scholarly and penetrating book I venture to dissent from the thesis which the author implies with delicate irony in almost every chapter, that few men and no Englishmen act on other than mercenary motives.

them. Joseph Hume the Radical made himself a rich man by commissions on the Greek loans.

The general history of these proceedings was that money was
raised in London, and mostly spent there, on ships and arms and
retaining fees to soldiers of fortune. When the financial houses
had covered their own risk by deducting commission and interest
in advance, the remainder was placed at the disposal of the revolutionary leaders. About one-tenth of the Greek loan was spent in
Greece. So, in the case of the Mexican loans at the same date,
about one-third of the £6,000,000 nominally subscribed was
transferred to Mexico. But these were war loans which the revolutionaries accepted with open eyes. The difficulty was that affairs
remained too unstable in Greece and Latin America for the burden
of debt to be carried. In almost every instance the liability was
repudiated at the next turn of the revolutionary wheel. When a
new junta came, hat in hand, to the London bankers the terms for
a new loan would be found to include some adjusted responsibility for the old one, with a mortgage upon the revenue to ensure
payment of interest. This arrangement too would be repudiated
at the next change of government, and would make the terms
offered to future borrowers still more onerous. Thus the liability
of Mexico to the bond-holders was doubled between 1821 and
1857 without any tangible advantage to the Mexicans; whereas the
bond-holders received dividends only in the intervals between
revolutions and only by foreclosing their mortgage on the Mexican
customs.

In addition to these government loans much British money was
invested in South American mining and engineering projects,
beginning with a speculative boom (1825–6) when young Benjamin Disraeli was employed to write prospectuses for bubble
companies, when Robert Stephenson went to Buenos Ayres to
construct mine tramways, when Cornish miners were shipped to
the Andes to improve mining techniques, and Scottish milkmaids
to the Pampas to teach the *gauchos* to make butter. Though the
bubble burst, these schemes were not entirely unproductive.[1]
British capital, British technicians, and even some emigrants continued to find their way to South America and particularly to the

[1] Mr Dombey considered that to break one's heart on account of an adverse
speculation in Peruvian mines was 'a very respectable way of doing it', as well
he might when Dombey and Son grew rich by negotiating the loan.

River Plate. Commercial and banking houses established their agencies in South America to handle the exports from Great Britain. The financial connexion was supported by the shipping connexion, which was almost a British monopoly, and in due time the South American railways were built, largely with British capital and British skill. By the end of the century British investments in Latin America were worth not less than £300,000,000.

The 1830's saw an investment boom in the United States. About £30,000,000 was advanced by the London bankers to the agents of several states of the Union, with the effect of creating an inflationary movement in the South. Reckless finance produced the American banking crisis of 1837–9 which obliged nine states to repudiate their debts, three of them (Michigan, Arkansas, and Mississippi) finally and absolutely. American credit sank so low that the federal government itself was unable to raise a loan anywhere in Europe. 'Not a dollar', said Rothschild. It was against the background of this speculative misuse of surplus capital that Wakefield brought forward his plan for the simultaneous exportation of surplus men and money. Very little capital had been invested in the colonies during those years, the most noteworthy issues being for land development companies in Canada and Australia. The largest and most successful were the Canada Company (1826), the British North America Company (1834) and the South Australian Association (1834). It is hard to say how much capital they actually exported. In the case of the Emancipation Loan (1835) which was raised by Rothschild in London and charged to the British national debt, perhaps £10,000,000 was actually distributed in the colonies.

Overseas investment passed into a new phase with the boom in railway construction. Observers noted that it brought a new set of men into the money-market, raising the firm of Glyn Mills to the first rank among the banking houses. Even before the bad times of 1846–8 the railway contractors had begun to reach out into France and Belgium. Later, in the great age of expansion which we may attribute to the effect of steam, free trade, or gold discoveries, they carried their efforts into all parts of the world. The trunk lines were financed with British money, equipped with British rails and engines, surveyed by British engineers and, in many instances, constructed by British navvies. Greatest of the railway contractors, greater even than the Stephensons in the

scope of his achievement, was Thomas Brassey (1805–70) who
undertook 170 contracts for 8000 miles of railway in five continents between 1840 and 1865.[1] He employed 80,000 men in all,
sending them abroad in organised parties of labourers with
teachers, doctors and clergy. There were 4000 British navvies
working for him on the Paris-Rouen railway alone. This was
solid productive work quite unlike the speculative finance of the
eighteen-twenties. It enabled him to survive the great crash of
Overend Gurney in 1866 which brought down so many railway
financiers. His foreign customers got value for money while
Great Britain benefited by the direct earnings of the capital, by the
sale of iron rails and locomotives, and by the wages paid to
British engineers and labourers. But the monopoly was too rich
to last. After the 'fifties and 'sixties industrial expansion was
world-wide. Under the Second Empire Napoleon III tempted the
savings of the frugal French out of the proverbial stocking into
productive investment. The French began to finance their own
railways and then to export their own surplus capital in competition with the British. No sooner was the Civil War over (1865)
than the wealth of America began to be felt in the financial world.
From year to year the Americans were less dependent upon
importing British machinery, better able to finance their own
expansion, more inclined to invest their occasional surplus of
capital abroad, especially in Canada. Germany appeared as a third
competitor after 1871. The Utopian dream of Free Trade had
faded. Protective tariffs, strategic railways and guaranteed loans
were the dominant factors in the politics of the late nineteenth
century, even in the British Empire, though England itself clung
to the doctrine of Free Trade.

One of the first of these imperialist projects was that for the
Grand Trunk Railway of Canada (1852–64). Should the trade go
by the American canals to the Hudson River and New York;
or by the earliest Canadian railway—then the only international

---

[1] For example: 1841 Paris-Rouen Railway.
                   1852 Grand Trunk Railway of Canada.
                   1854 Turin-Mont Cenis Railway.
                   1858 Eastern Bengal Railway.
                   1862 Mauritius Railway.
                   1863 Queensland Railway.
                   1864 Central Argentine Railway.
                   1864 Lemberg-Czernowitz Railway.

railway in the world—from Montreal to Portland, Maine (1853), or by a new route through British territory to the Maritime Provinces? The merchants of Montreal and Upper Canada were disposed to look southwards to the United States for their commercial routes, and to develop that trade on terms of reciprocity, though the easy route between Lower Canada and the open sea had been blocked by the Ashburton-Webster Treaty of 1842. The Colonial Office (under Lord Grey), and the influence of the Colonial Reformers, were for a railway through British territory at whatever cost. An Act of the Canadian legislature was passed to guarantee a British loan, financed by Barings and Glyn Mills, whereupon Brassey hurried to Canada to supervise the contract. The Grand Trunk Railway was routed for strategic rather than commercial reasons and never paid its way in sixty years. It cost the British investor about £12,000,000. Perhaps the best purpose it served was to induce the recalcitrant electorate of Nova Scotia to accept confederation with Canada.

During the early railway boom several proposals were made for railways in India. When Dalhousie became Governor-General (1848) they were revived but on a new principle. Watching with interest the methodical planning of state railways in France by Napoleon III he proposed for India a similar system which should avoid the haphazard speculative method of the English. His plans, which were approved in 1853, had made some progress when they were interrupted by the Mutiny. By that time about £14,000,000 had been invested by British shareholders who found that the price of stock stood firm. The settlement of India in 1858 was followed by a large increase in trade, particularly in cotton during the American Civil War. Accordingly India became the best field for the investment of capital. By 1870 about £150,000,000 of British money had been committed there, half of it in railways. It was noticed that Indian capitalists who invested freely in government bonds showed a strange unwillingness to take up guaranteed railway shares. Dalhousie's intention had been to limit Indian liability, to control costs, and to grant railway concessions only for a term of years. These safeguards were whittled away, through the influence of the moneyed men and the *laissez-faire* economists, in spite of the efforts of John Lawrence to preserve them. The Indian lines were well built and well designed, but at great expense. Too large a proportion of the Indian tax-revenue was always withdrawn to London in the form of 'Home Charges', which amounted in the 'sixties to £10,000,000 a year, mostly interest on guaranteed loans.

Personal control by a few great banking-houses over the market in foreign loans was never so great after the Overend Gurney failure of 1866. On the one hand the influence of governments was more directly applied; on the other hand the interest, and political power, of the small investor was beginning to be felt, owing to the principle of Limited Liability which was consolidated in English practice by the Act of 1862. With his liability limited and his interest secured by a government guarantee, the small investor found colonial bonds, paying 5% or 6%, increasingly attractive, though they were not classified as Trustee Stock until 1900. Except in rare instances, foreign holdings were still not secured by the British government but, after 1868, investors' rights were upheld by the influential Corporation of Foreign Bondholders, representing capital valued at £800,000,000.

All statistics of the export of capital are estimates and those of earlier date than 1854[1] are mere conjectures. Thereafter, accurate figures of new issues are available. The annual export of British capital in the 1830's may have averaged £30,000,000; in the 1860's it was £60,000,000. In 1872 it reached a record high figure of £83,000,000; and slumped in the succeeding years of depression. Between 1875 and 1880 more capital was withdrawn to London than was exported. Since by this date the United States and Germany were beginning to finance their own expansion, British investment went farther afield, largely to South America and to Australia which in the 1880's, for the first time, attracted capital in great quantities. It was in these years that the English became dependent for more than half their foodstuffs upon distant sources of supply, and paid for them in part by financial services. In 1890 the export of capital again reached the figure of £82,000,000. After a decline during the Boer War which swallowed up the available surplus, the export was again renewed in the twentieth century at a vastly increased rate, reaching the figure of £246,000,000 in 1912. During this phase Canada and the Argentine received the largest share.

In 1854 the total holdings of British investors overseas may have been as much as £500,000,000. In 1875, at the end of the first

---

[1] The figures in the following paragraphs are mostly derived from *The Migration of Capital* by C. K. Hobson.

great period of expansion, the sum has been estimated with a fair degree of probability at £1,300,000,000, of which £125,000,000 was in Indian and colonial railways, £118,000,000 in colonial government bonds, and £115,000,000 in other investments within the Empire. By 1909 the total sum exceeded £2,330,000,000, of which perhaps half was held within the Empire, one-fifth in the United States and one-fifth in Latin America.

Taking a longer view it may now be seen that investment within the Empire has been in every way more advantageous to Great Britain than investment in foreign lands. Not only was there no repudiation in the colonies, no writing-down of the value of shares for political reasons, no confiscation by revolutionary juntas, but colonial investments brought immediate and positive returns. Foreign loans were spent either on public works which brought no advantage to the lender beyond the interest on his money, or on armaments which were a menace to him. In the case of railway loans some part of the capital might be spent on British equipment, but of this there was no certainty. On the other hand much of the money lent to the Canadian Pacific Railway never left England; it was at once invested in British rails and locomotives. 'Of the loans for Indian railways, about one-third went to pay the Home Charges in London; something under one-third was spent on wages and administrative expenses, largely paid to English engineers; something over one-third on British rails and engines and in paying British ships to bring them to India.'

'Even those loans raised in New Zealand to pay for the Maori Wars and by the Indian Government to pay for suppressing the Mutiny went largely to people likely to increase the direct demand for British goods. Much went to produce, at lower prices, raw material for the industries of Britain and food for her people.' Still more valuable was the export of young men of the middle classes to the agencies of shipping, banking, and commercial firms. These men with the engineers, surveyors, doctors, and other technicians were the makers of the mid-Victorian Empire.

The years between 1850 and 1875 are a period unique in history for rapidity and magnitude of economic expansion. The export values (from Great Britain) increased by 40% between 1840 and 1850, by 90% in the next decade, and by 47% between 1860 and 1870. Wages, which had been almost steady between 1830 and 1850, rose by almost 56% between 1850 and 1874. Whatever method of computation is used, the national income and the amount of

capital were growing prodigiously during these years. Between 1865 and
1875 the amount of capital increased by nearly 50%. The explanation of this
efflorescence has been found in a great variety of circumstances: factory legislation, trade unions, the new railways and the new gold from California and
Australia. But none of these by themselves explains satisfactorily the substantial rise in real wages. An important part of the explanation is to be
found in the character and extent of English overseas investment between
1850 and 1875 and further in the fact that so large a proportion of it was to
new and undeveloped countries within the Empire.[1]

At the conclusion of the third great phase of British expansion
the total sum of British investments overseas was estimated
(December 1913) at £3,763,000,000,[2] of which about 47% was
invested in the British Empire, 20% in the United States, 8% in the
Argentine, 6% in Continental Europe, 3% in China and Japan,
1% in Egypt. The proportion invested in the British Empire,
47%, was made up as follows: 14% in Canada and Newfoundland,
11% in Australia and New Zealand, 10% in India and Ceylon,
nearly 10% in South Africa, 1% in West Africa and less than 1%
in Malaya. Or, if the whole sum of £3,763,000,000 is classified
by the nature of the investment, about 40% was invested in
railways, 30% in government and municipal bonds, 5% in public
utilities, and the rest in industry and finance. The annual income
earned by these investments was, in 1913, about £200,000,000.

During the first German War British overseas investments were
reduced by about £850,000,000, two-thirds of the reduction being
securities sold in the United States. This was one of the steps
which converted the United States from a debtor country, to
the amount of £500,000,000 on balance in 1914, into a creditor
country, to the amount of about £1,200,000,000 in 1922. These
figures take no account of the war-time credits which France and
Great Britain advanced to their weaker allies, or of the credits
which the United States advanced to France and Great Britain,
since almost all were, sooner or later, repudiated.

British investment overseas was resumed during the 1920's, too
lavishly, in the view of some economists, in proportion to the progress of trade, though never on the scale of the pre-war years. By
1930, when the shadow of world-wide economic depression was
deepening, the total figure of British overseas investments was

---

[1] H. J. Habbakuk in the *Cambridge History of the British Empire*, vol. II.
[2] Estimated figures, based on *The Problem of International Investment*, Royal
Institute of International Affairs, 1937.

back to something like the pre-war figure, but with a difference. Of the holdings 60% were now in Empire countries and only 5% in the United States. Canada, still a debtor country though highly industrialised, now owed more to the United States than to Great Britain. The older British investment (£540,000,000), mostly in government and railway securities, had been surpassed by the new American investment (£720,000,000) mostly in municipal bonds, public utilities and industry. Australia, on the other hand, had borrowed heavily, perhaps too heavily. Her indebtedness to London amounted to £494,000,000, 13% of the whole British overseas investment and a heavy burden on the Australian economy in the depressed 1930's.

4. THE GOLD-RUSHES, 1848–98[1]

DURING the eighteenth century the main source of the European supply of gold was Brazil which produced, at best, about 500,000 ounces annually. Production from the Gold Coast, averaging perhaps one-tenth of this amount, was not enough to sway the world market. The South American gold rushes, about the years 1730–50, saw the beginnings of that customary code of miners' law which spread through the whole world a century later. Though Brazilian gold was a Portuguese royal monopoly the restricted ownership of bullion proved illusory. It was used to finance the export to Brazil of goods, largely of English origin and handled by English commercial firms. There is little doubt that much of the advantage and some of the actual bullion drawn from the Brazilian mines helped to build up England's expanding trade.

The gold of the Ural Mountains, produced by servile labour in provinces remote from Western commerce, was used to finance the eastward march of Russia. The greater fields in Eastern Siberia were producing 900,000 ounces annually in the 1840's. Distances were long and roads were bad to the swamps and forests where the gold was found. Russia's backward industries could not provide machinery for mining until the opening of the Siberian Railway in 1891, yet the output steadily rose, to 1,400,000 ounces a year in the 'eighties, and to 1,900,000 ounces in 1914.

[1] For the information in this chapter I am obliged to Professor W. P. Morrell, who has allowed me to draw upon his standard work, *The Gold-Rushes*.

The mechanised mining which was made possible by railway development was largely financed by British capital. But this steady increase in gold production was part of the gradual growth of the world's industries which gives the nineteenth century its general character. The gold-rushes of the English-speaking peoples to California and Australia, to British Columbia and New Zealand, to South Africa and the Klondyke were phenomena of a distinct sort.

The Californian and Victorian gold-rushes of 1849–53 multiplied the world's total annual output six or seven times over. The stimulus of so great an increase in the gold backing to the currencies promoted an age of expanding trade and rising prices which lasted about twenty years. After 1866 the output of gold fell by a third but was still much higher than in the years before 1849. France and Germany adopted the gold standard; while the United States, which fought the Civil War on paper 'green-backs', was able to stabilise them at a rate convertible with gold. After twenty years of less rapid expansion the second group of gold-rushes, to the Rand and the Klondyke, produced another period of expansion. Between 1893 and 1913 the world's stock of gold was doubled.

The financial effects are surpassed in interest by the social and political effects. Whole new nations were called into existence by the emigration to the gold-fields in America and Australia, where a new type of society emerged. It is hardly too much to say that until 1849 the typical emigrant was a peasant in search of land, a natural conservative; after 1849 the typical emigrant was a digger, a man who would turn from working with pick and shovel on his own mining-claim to working with pick and shovel for a capitalist mine-owner or railway company. Such a man was a natural Radical strongly moved by the lessons of the hungry 'forties in Europe, sometimes a Chartist or revolutionary from the barricades of 'forty-eight. The prospector and the mining-engineer were now the leaders of the host, men very different in stamp from the *voortrekkers* of the older age. Thus the mining-camps of California pointed the way to the social changes which, with local variation, would appear successively in each of the British Dominions.

The gold-rush of 1849 was a by-product of the filibustering activity which added Texas, New Mexico, and California to the

United States. Settlers of the type that infiltrated these Latin-American provinces, overthrew their government, and seized control by force of arms were the most adventurous even of the frontiersmen. There were prospectors among them who had learned the technique of gold-hunting in the smaller fields of North Carolina. California was still under martial law, without settled government, when gold was found on the Sacramento River (24 January 1848). By the end of the year 10,000 men had flocked to the scene of the discoveries, but the main force, numbering over 80,000, the "forty-niners', of whom only one-tenth were women, did not reach this wilderness beyond the Rocky Mountains until the following year. They raised about 2,500,000 ounces of gold in the first season. Half the immigrants arrived by land from the Middle-Western states, over the newly-opened Oregon Trail. A quarter came by sea round the Horn in ships from New England, the remaining quarter by way of Panama. There was a railway across the Isthmus in the 'fifties, and talk already of an isthmian canal (see chapter v, 8, page 280). The Pacific Steam Navigation Company ran ships from Panama to San Francisco.

The miners, mostly Americans from the North, showed from the first their intention to make California a white man's country. There was no negro slavery, which put them out of favour with the dominant party at Washington: and, when Chinese immigrants appeared, they were met with plain hostility. Nor were other foreigners welcomed. The celebrated Vigilance Committee of San Francisco was formed largely to discipline certain unruly Australians, known as 'Sydney Coves' or 'Sydney Ducks', who had found their way across the Pacific. But the true character of the Californian miners was shown in their instant spontaneous organisation of democratic forms of government. The astounding fact is not that there was so much violent disorder, but that there was so little. At every new gold-field a diggers' committee enforced the two fundamental laws: 'jumping' another miner's claim or stealing his gold were instantly punished by the hand of popular justice. The extensive literature of the gold-fields—Bret Harte (1839–1902) was the first writer of repute—gives the impression that the miners themselves were industrious and law-abiding, though the chances of their profession disposed them to reckless gambling. Life at a new mining-camp was decent though rough. It was in the mushroom cities like San Francisco, which sprang into existence as depots for supplying stores and buying gold, that the harpies and the parasites, the swindlers, the card-sharpers, the confidence-men and the racketeers congregated. Since California had no law and no administration, these evils flourished unchecked, but not for long. As early as November 1849 the miners' committees elected a constituent assembly and formed themselves into a state. Their sternest trouble was to persuade the politicians at Washington to help or even recognise them, since the admission of another free state to the Union was a sore blow to the defenders of slavery.

By 1853 the number of miners had reached 100,000 and the output of gold 4,000,000 ounces. This was the climax of the boom from which California relaxed slowly into a less feverish condition. The independent diggers and prospectors had moved on by 1860, to carry into every continent the tradition of the 'forty-niners.

The diggers, who flocked to Australia when gold was reported there, wore characteristic costume: a red shirt open at the neck, moleskin trousers stuffed into the boots, a wide-brimmed slouch hat and an ostentatious pistol in the belt. Their jargon was already creeping into popular speech, with its talk of life at the diggings: of staking claims, and making lucky strikes, and getting down to bedrock, and watching how things panned out, and finding an expected Bonanza already a wash-out, and going stony-broke. The routine of a gold-field follows a typical course. First comes the solitary prospector, 'in a cavern, in a canyon, excavating for a mine', a pioneer of secretive habits, with an eye for country, washing samples of alluvial mud in every likely creek until the shining particles left in his pan satisfy him as 'payable gold'. He must keep his secret and register his find with the competent authority, often many hundred miles away, before pegging out a claim according to the lie of the land and the custom of the country. Now the secret is out and shrewd observers will be close on his track to peg out claims as near as possible to the original 'strike'. Claims in California were no more than ten feet square on some fields, and rarely more than thirty feet square, by diggers' law. If the first-comers strike it lucky, washing out an ounce or more a day for each hand in a gang of three or four, a rush soon sets in. Experienced diggers are followed by hordes of amateurs ('greenhorns', 'tenderfeet', 'new chums', 'cheechakos'—according to the jargon of the country), who may 'shout on seven-ounce nuggets' or may flinch at the hard labour of digging, starve through not knowing how to 'rough it', be bullied, or be cheated out of their claims. Soon the camp burgeons into a boom-town of tents and huts, vaingloriously named Eureka or Eldorado City, largely composed of saloons and gambling-booths where little sacks of gold-dust pass as currency. Now speculators in claims begin to make more money than diggers, and the price of a claim may be less than the price of the site for a provision store where a trader 'grub-stakes' the mining gangs. The cost of food and transport soars in a society that lives on an increasing flow of easy money. Inevitably, as the best sites are washed out, and the population grows, the profits of labour show a diminishing return, until the old hands begin to slink away in search of a new field. When the nuggets embedded in the superficial mud of the creeks have all been found, payable gold must be sought deeper where ancient watercourses have been buried, sometimes, as at Ballarat, beneath layers of hard clay, or, as in New Zealand, under beds of gravel, or, as in Alaska, deep in frozen mud. It becomes worth while to gather the smallest particles of gold by washing in a tank containing quicksilver with which the gold forms an amalgam; to sluice down and wash away the sides of ravines under hydraulic pressure; to break up frozen ground with jets of steam; and to pursue the veins of gold into the auriferous rock with drills and crushing machines. The speculators, the amateur miners and the human parasites who prey on them abandon the goldfield to the workers in a mechanised industry. Last of all, when that has ceased to pay, comes the 'fossicker', often an old solitary, who makes a meagre living picking over the 'tailings' of the mine for the crumbs of gold that have been overlooked, in a landscape stripped and scraped and scarred.

The finding of gold had several times been reported in Australia before 1851, but prospecting had been discouraged by governors who feared the anarchy of a gold-rush in a convict country. The Californian boom made such a restrictive policy untenable. Edgar Hammond Hargraves (1816–91), an Australian who went to California, returned convinced that he could find gold in his own land. According to an apocryphal story an American shouted after his departing figure, 'There's no gold in the country you're going to,

and, if there is, that darned Queen of yours won't let you dig it.'
Hargraves replied with mock dignity, 'There's as much gold in the
country I'm going to as there is in California, and Her Most
Gracious Majesty, Queen Victoria—God bless her—will appoint
me one of the Gold Commissioners.' He was right. In the spring
of 1851 he reported several finds, and in May a gold-rush began
to the Turon field in New South Wales. Sydney poured forth its
citizens even though it was race-week.

The Turon goldfield, though it will be familiar to readers of
that old-fashioned classic tale, *Robbery Under Arms*, was soon exhausted when 4000 diggers had washed 100,000 ounces of gold.
The most notable episode in the rush was the finding of a block of
quartz containing 1200 ounces by an aboriginal shepherd whose
master rewarded him with gifts of a flock of sheep and a team of
horses. Later in the year much more lucrative finds were made at
Ballarat (August) and Bendigo (September 1851). These were in
the new squatters' state of Victoria, lately separated from New
South Wales, and inhabited by 97,000 settlers and 6,000,000 sheep.
Only a few months earlier Lord Grey's Act had enabled the Vic-
torians to draft a constitution. Nothing had yet been done and
Governor Latrobe found himself obliged to control an unruly influx of diggers without adequate revenue or constitutional support. In September there were 7000 diggers at work; by December 20,000; by February 1852, 40,000 at Bendigo Creek alone. In
June 1852, 70,000 men at the various Victorian diggings were
washing out 30,000 ounces a month, at the time when the output
of California, too, was at its climax. One twenty-four-foot claim
at Ballarat produced gold worth £55,000, in five weeks during
which its ownership five times changed hands. By 1854 the population of Victoria had reached 400,000 and, by 1861, 540,000, of
whom half were immigrants from the British Isles. The Victorian
gold-miners were not experienced pioneers and prospectors as
were the 'forty-niners of California; they were for the most part
'new chums', including many Irish labourers, and some English
Chartists. They found no municipal government at Ballarat and
Bendigo, and a narrow freeholders' franchise for the legislative
council, while law was enforced by an armed corps of police who
were accustomed to disciplining convicts. No publicans' licences
were issued at the goldfields with the result that 'sly-grog-shops',
and the petty corruption that accompanies them, flourished. Yet

there was law and order. The miners' code was observed, and maintained by the police.

Governor C. J. Latrobe (1801–75), with no means of raising revenue except from miners' licence-fees (thirty shillings a month), in an empty capital city from which dockers, civil officials, Government House servants, and even policemen had decamped to make easy money at the diggings, yet did pretty well. He sent Gold Commissioners (of whom Hargraves was one) to allot claims; organised an escort for conveying gold to Melbourne; and established an Assay Office. In the time of his successor Sir C. Hotham (1806–55), the system broke down on the score of objection to paying licence-fees. A poll-tax that fell as heavily on the unlucky as on the lucky digger, in a community without responsible government, could not be collected without disorder. While dilatory plans were being made for constitutional reform, a riot provoked by a petty miscarriage of justice broke out at Ballarat. Impatience, ebullient democracy, and dislike of the police—who have never been popular in Australia—led to the growth of a republican movement, largely Irish in sentiment. A flag, with four silver stars on a blue ground, was adopted and a rude fortification built at Eureka near Ballarat, with no clearly defined purpose. Governor Hotham, acting promptly before the affair should get out of hand, sent a company of soldiers with some police, who stormed the Eureka Stockade on 3 December 1854. This violent irrational episode, in which four soldiers and thirty miners were killed, is the only land-battle ever fought on the Australian continent. Hotham insisted on prosecuting the defenders for treason but the juries refused to convict. The leader of the rebels Peter Lalor (1823–89), an Irishman bred at Trinity College, Dublin, having lost an arm in the Eureka fighting, lived to be the highly respected Speaker of the Victorian Legislature. The story of the diggers' stand for democratic rights is an honoured legend and the silver stars of the Eureka flag are still to be seen on the flag of Australia.[1]

---

[1] Since, at that date, there was no submarine cable east of Suez, the incident at Eureka on that southern summer morning was not quickly recorded in England, where all eyes were turned towards the Black Sea. The battle of Inkerman had been fought a few days earlier. Florence Nightingale had just arrived at the theatre of war, and a great storm which scattered the ships lying off the beaches announced the onset of winter. During the early months of 1855, the miseries of the Crimean campaign filled the newspapers.

The agitation died away when a democratic constitution that recognised the diggers' interests was proclaimed, in 1855. Mining constituencies were set up with a special miners' franchise. Elective assessors were added to the courts on the goldfields, which heard cases arising from disputed claims. The unpopular miners' licence was superseded by an export-duty on gold. Thus Australian democracy was born. Two previous eras, the age of the convicts and the age of the squatters, had come and passed. The future of Australia belonged to the new men whom the goldfields had formed into a type, the Australians who still familiarly hail one another as 'Diggers'.

The democratic forms claimed unsuccessfully by the English Chartists were freely adopted by the new state governments. Manhood suffrage was first introduced in 1855, in South Australia and, shortly after, in the other colonies. The secret ballot soon followed. The interests of the 'small men' were promoted by the agitators for easier access to the land which the great squatters monopolised. Hence the demand for Free Selection (see chapter x, 7, page 586) which became the law of New South Wales in 1861. But the miners tended to become urban rather than rural workers. Before the end of the 'fifties there were twenty factories making agricultural machinery in Australia and the agitation for an eight-hour day in industry had begun. Among the first acts of the new democratic government in Victoria was the laying of a poll-tax on Chinese immigrants. Though Palmerston had just concluded a treaty of friendly intercourse, at the end of the second China War, the miners would have none of it, but were already determined to preserve a White Australia.

In ten years (1851–61) gold worth £124,000,000 had been raised and the population of Australia had risen from 437,000 to 1,168,000. While the inevitable rise in wages and prices had threatened to ruin the farmer and the squatter, the actual effect had been to double the annual value of the wool-clip, which was worth £4,000,000 in 1861, and to increase the annual value of the external trade of Australia from £13 per head to £30. A great difficulty at first had been the difference between the cash price of gold, usually sold at a heavy discount, and the mint par value of the sterling currency. After some misgivings the Colonial Office, in 1855, permitted the establishment of a mint at Sydney where gold was freely bought at £3. 17s. 10¼d. per ounce, a fixed price which endured as long as the international gold standard. Prices then grew steadier, though intercolonial jealousy tended to disparage Sydney currency at Melbourne. As for the miners themselves, some had made fortunes, but few had made more than a bare living. It appears that in Victoria the earnings of the first 35,000, the men of 1852, were about £500 on an average. In 1853 the number of miners rose to 73,000 and the average earnings dropped to £170. Thereafter when there were more than 100,000 miners it is estimated that their annual earnings never reached the average figure of £100 a year.

The third gold-rush to a new country will be further discussed in chapter x, 3. In March 1858 Governor Douglas of Vancouver sent prospectors who confirmed reports of gold in the Fraser River. During the summer a rush of 25,000 miners, by sea from San Francisco, inflated the village of Victoria on Vancouver Island into a boom-town. Douglas asserted the right of the Crown by appointing a Gold Commissioner and charging licence fees to diggers at the rate of five dollars a month. In spite of opposition from unruly Americans, he got his way, founded his colony of British Columbia, and maintained the Queen's peace. In 1862 when the wagon-road had been driven far up-country, a second rush took place to the Cariboo district north of Lake Quesnel. It produced 200,000 ounces in 1863. But these proved not to be 'poor mens' diggings'. The extraction of gold from auriferous rock required machinery and capital, which were not then available, since more profitable gold and silver mines were booming in Nevada at the Comstock Lode.

In all the colonies prospectors were now at work and rewards were offered by speculators for finds of 'payable gold'. After British Columbia the next was in the antipodes where Gabriel Read reported a find beneath a bed of gravel in the South Island of New Zealand. In July 1861 the phenomena of a gold-rush startled the dour Scottish settlers of Dunedin, not then a prosperous colony. In the southern summer of 1861–2, 7000 miners went up to 'Gabriel's Gully' and found 400,000 ounces of gold; and larger crowds, deeper among the bush-clad mountains, found more in the following season. The Scottish colony had no sooner been inflated into a mining city and province, than the same fate came to the Anglicans of Canterbury Settlement. In the summer of 1864–5, even richer goldfields were found on the rainy west coast across the Southern Alps, a country so inaccessible, with no harbour and no road across the mountains, that a literary man among the Canterbury settlers had just imagined there the fantastic polity which he called *Erewhon*. In 1866 it was invaded by 30,000 miners, mostly from Australia, who risked the crossing of the bar at Hokitika, where many stout ships were wrecked, to win half a million ounces of gold in a season. Once ashore they found good order; it is reported that New Zealand miners did not carry guns.

The Victorian miners' code was legalised by the New Zealand Parliament, and the local government was administered (until 1873) by Canterbury Province, which undertook the construction of a mountain road over the high Southern Alps in 1865. Canterbury had already taken root and flourished before the west coast gold-rush brought an influx of new capital and labour. The prosperity of the province was then assured. But a state with strong foundations has a cohesion and stability of its own. The Canterbury settlers absorbed the new emigrants and used the new capital in directions that their founders would have approved. They now had the wealth to build the city with its cathedral and college which had been devised in the original plan. Close settlement continued on the plains; wheat was exported to neighbouring colonies; and sheep spread over the foothills of the Southern Alps. Similarly the Scottish element reasserted itself at Dunedin, to which Lowland and Highland emigrants continued to be attracted. Fifty years after the gold-rush to Gabriel's Gully, Christchurch was still aggressively English and Dunedin aggressively Scottish.

The gold-rushes of the 'sixties ended with the finds of 1866 and 1867 at Gympie in Queensland. Although the prospectors passed over the site of the rich Mount Morgan mines which, later in the century, were to be developed by machinery, at that date they only reproduced on a smaller scale the story of Bendigo and Ballarat. The finds were chiefly important for bringing 100,000 white immigrants into a colony which was beginning to depend on imported coolie labour.

Optimists could hardly doubt that the land of King Solomon's Mines would provide discoveries as rich as those of Victoria. In the 'sixties the prospectors were penetrating deeper into the Veld of South Africa until, looking for gold, they found diamonds. The first payable finds were in 1869, on either side of the River Vaal, the boundary between the two Boer republics. The British government had expressly repudiated all claim to sovereignty over the Transvaal, while still asserting a shadowy right to a protectorate over native races in the Orange Free State. A rush of British miners to a Boer farm named Vooruitzigt ('foresight') obliged the Governor of the Cape to organise a temporary administration like that of a goldfield, by virtue of his supposed obligation to the Griqua tribe (see chapter X, 10, page 622). In 1871 this district was annexed to Cape Colony and named Kimberley after Gladstone's Colonial Secretary. In that year 'a Mr Rhodes of Natal' found 110 carats of diamonds in twenty days. The character of the diamond-fields differed from that of the Australian goldfields in two respects. Though prospectors began by doing their own digging they generally brought in native labour for the heavier work when a claim was established. The European rush was succeeded, at every South African find, by an African rush of labourers in search of high wages. By 1872 there were 16,000 Europeans and 21,000 African natives at Kimberley. The other feature of the diamond-fields was the speculative nature of the product which could not, like gold, be converted into currency at a standard rate. The diamond industry was largely in the hands of Jewish traders among whom the most successful was Barnett Isaacs of Whitechapel ('Barney Barnato'). Very early in the history of Kimberley it became apparent that a glut of diamonds was spoiling the market. If profits were to be made after the first lucky strikes they would accrue to the men who cornered the claims and restricted the output. The richest mine was that of the De Beers Company who bought the freehold of 'Foresight' farm for £6000 (and later sold it to the government for £100,000). In deep pits, like the craters of volcanoes, 3600 separate claims were worked. From every one a rope and windlass was rigged to draw up samples of diamond-bearing clay to the pit's rim.

The Kimberley mine (on the De Beers estate) is said to be the deepest hole ever made by man. Claims were first pegged out on the 16th July 1871, 31 feet by 31 feet....In 1815 the greatest depth of the open working was 450 feet, the cavity excavated representing 9,000,000 cubic yards....The open area was stated to be 38 acres....Owing to the continual falling in of the sides the apparent depth is now somewhat reduced but

the existing hole is still a remarkable sight....Mining was afterwards
carried on by underground workings to a depth of 3601 feet, but has been
discontinued since 1909.[1]

The De Beers Company steadily year by year bought out the
claims until, by 1885, they were reduced in number to ninety-
eight. Cecil Rhodes's masterstroke was to amalgamate all the
De Beers holdings into a single mining-company, with financial
backing from Alfred Beit and Rothschild. By 1888 he was in a
strong enough position to force Barnato, his principal rival, to
come into the combination. Thereafter Rhodes and his associates,
controlling the diamond-fields, could keep the output steady at a
value of about £4,000,000 a year.

Kimberley was a raw mining-camp in a desert, and retains the
appearance of such a place to the present day. The railway reached
it in 1885 but brought little in the way of the amenities of civilisation. Kimberley lived (and lives) by digging and trading diamonds
and by little else. Beneath the surface of society an underworld
lived on smuggling and illicit diamond-buying (I.D.B.), since
diamonds, of all valuables, are the easiest to conceal. When in
control of the whole capital and labour-force, Rhodes was able to
put a check on I.D.B. by supervising the recruitment and the
movement of native labourers who, for the period of their contract,
live under strict discipline and are confined to closed locations
behind barbed wire.

In the heyday of the diamond-fields, gold had been reported
from several parts of South Africa, but generally in auriferous
rocks which offered no easy return to individual prospectors.
Several finds had been reported along the Witwatersrand before
the attention of the Kimberley capitalists was attracted. In March
1886, J. B. Robinson (backed by Alfred Beit) bought land which
contained a great part of the main reef, and began to develop deep-
mining with native labour. In September 1886 the Rand was proclaimed a goldfield and prospectors flocked into the area. Within
a year the new town of Johannesburg, named after the government surveyor, Johannes Rissik, had a population of 6000. But
this was a rush of speculators rather than diggers. Prospectors
staked out claims with the intention, not of working them, but of
selling them to some great mining company with resources sufficient to organise excavation. The output even in 1888 was no

[1] *South and East African Year Book*, 1938.

more than 230,000 ounces and the main reef, 2400 feet below the
surface, was reached only in 1893, after long technical experiment.
By this time there were 35,000 native labourers in the mines; by
1899, the year when the Boer War put a stop to further progress,
the number was over 100,000. The main reef proved to be 'an
immense body of low-grade ore requiring elaborate large-scale
work', quarrying not treasure-hunting. As at the diamond-fields
the output could be regulated to suit the state of the market and
the amount of available labour. In 1898 the 100,000 native miners
produced 3,500,000 ounces of gold to justify a capital investment
of £40,000,000.

Simultaneously with the prosperity of the Rand, industrial
gold-mining reached great importance in Australia and New Zealand. In 1886 the Mount Morgan mines in Queensland began to
employ profitable wage-labour, and in 1892 new gold-rushes took
place in Western Australia. Coolgardie, 1892, and Kalgoorlie, 1893,
attracted 70,000 emigrants, but these were not 'poor men's diggings'. The lack of water for washing gold in this dry country
required irrigation works, organised by the state government on
a great scale. The investment of £8,000,000 in three years implied that there was more speculation in shares than in claims; but
the output reached 2,000,000 ounces in 1903. In Australia, unlike
Africa, all the labour was done by white men and was propor-
tionately expensive. Industrial gold-mines were also developed in
the North Island of New Zealand. Advanced scientific techniques
for extracting gold were notably introduced at Waihi near
Auckland, from 1878 onwards. With an output of 500,000
ounces in 1902, this was the most profitable mining concern in
the world.

The last of the great gold-rushes, to the Klondyke, presents the
interesting feature of American and British methods side by side.
Soon after the Alaska purchase (1867), Californian prospectors began to search for gold within the Arctic Circle, finding it at various
points in the basin of the great navigable Yukon River. In winter
they thawed out the frozen ground by lighting fires which enabled
them to penetrate down to the 'pay-streak' at bed-rock; in
summer they washed out the gold dust from the accumulated
'dirt'. In 1886 came a rush to Circle City. When (1894) the
Canadian government found that disorderly American miners
were flocking over the frontier, a mere unmarked meridian, they

sent Inspector Constantine with forty troopers of the North-West Mounted Police to the Yukon. Two years later, in August 1896, an Indian found eighty ounces of gold in the narrow muddy Bonanza Creek which flowed into the Klondyke River, a tributary of the Yukon—in Canadian territory. Before winter set in, a 'city' had sprung up at Dawson. In the spring of 1897 a few hundred miners cleared $2,500,000; and in July the torrent of fortune-hunters began to appear. It is estimated that 100,000 persons set out for the Klondyke that year, but that only one-third of them reached the goldfield before winter. Some came by steamboat up the Yukon from the Arctic harbour of St Michael to Dawson City; some overland from Canada by way of the Peace River; the great majority came in ships from Seattle and San Francisco to Skagway, a 'mushroom' port in the Alaska Panhandle. Thence, equipped with stores and dog-teams, they had to climb the snow-bound Chilcoot Pass before crossing the divide into the valley of the Klondyke. Even among old prospectors, few were experienced in arctic travel; among the thousands of 'cheechakos' (amateurs) who passed through Skagway, the vast majority were unaccustomed to any form of pioneering.

Alaska was anarchic until the arrival (1900) of federal officers. Skagway was a 'wide-open' racketeers' town without law or government, controlled by a gangster named 'Soapy Smith', who, until he was shot by a rival, took toll of all comers. All forms of corruption, dishonesty and violence flourished as far as the top of the Chilcoot Pass where the 'Mounties' maintained a frontier post. Since food was scarce and dear at Dawson City they turned back every immigrant who was not provided with 1000 lb. of supplies.

Inside Canada there was law and order, thanks to the 'Mounties'. The Dominion government sent a Commissioner of cabinet rank, Clifford Sifton, and a Supreme Court Judge, to administer the goldfields, and to collect a royalty of 10% on exported gold. Lawless as they were, the Americans yet showed great enterprise. They chafed at Canadian control, resisting the payment of the royalty, but they invested capital in irrigation and in methods of thawing the ground by jets of steam. Between 1898 and 1900 they built a railway from Skagway over the White Pass to a navigable tributary of the Yukon, thus bringing freights down from $1 to 4½ cents a pound. By 1900 when individual mining was giving way to industrial processes the output of the goldfields reached 2,500,000 ounces. During the next few years payable gold was found in several parts of Alaska.

5. POPULATION CHANGES

EACH wave of migration has three phases. First come the pioneers, the 'legion that never was listed, that carries no colours or crest'. They are almost without exception men of strongly-marked individuality and force of character. Among them are always to be found a high proportion of traders, 'merchant-adventurers' in search of new untrammelled markets. In the seventeenth and eighteenth centuries the pioneers were largely seamen, lone hands like Henry Hudson or leaders of authorised expeditions like Captain Cook. In lawless places and unsettled times the pioneers included many hard-handed self-seekers and some mere ruffians, but it betrays a poor understanding of men and affairs to condemn out-of-hand even the buccaneers of the Spanish Main and the founders of the African slave trade; they took the world as they found it. The nineteenth century also had its characteristic types. As prominent then as the traders and the sea-captains were the prospectors and the missionaries. There were also the soldiers and sailors who hunted down and destroyed the slave-traders. Among the philanthropic pioneers of the nineteenth century, women appeared as well as men.

In our own day a new type, who may be regarded by posterity as the characteristic pioneer of the twentieth century, the scientific investigator, has entered the field. Anthropologists, ecologists and other research workers, men and women alike, now penetrate deepest into the wilderness to learn its secrets and master its afflictions.

Until the pioneers have blazed the trail there can be no colonisation but, such are their habits, no statistics are kept of their coming and going. I have found no way of making even a useful guess at the distribution throughout the world of the isolated traders, missionaries, prospectors, seamen, research workers and 'rolling stones' in general, whose place of origin is in the British Isles. Their irregular journeys are not recorded in the shipping returns, they haunt regions where censuses are often deficient, they pass easily from country to country. Quantitatively, their numbers are a lost item in the sum of the British population overseas; qualitatively they are more significant than any other group.

The second phase in the history of migrations is that of systematic colonisation. Those who have accompanied me so far as this chapter will probably agree that the common belief in an Empire which casually grew without direction is quite unjustified. Almost every British colony was deliberately founded by a formed body of settlers according to a preconceived plan and, generally speaking, the more complete the plan the more successful the colony. The settlers, for the most part, were groups of families and fairly representative of the society from which they had come. Their early success was the better assured if they were inspired by a common political or religious impulse. These systematic colonies may be classified in two groups: before the American Revolution (1607–1749), the best examples are Virginia, New England, Maryland, Pennsylvania, Georgia and Halifax; after the Revolution (1783–1850), Ontario, Red River, Albany (South Africa), the Australian settlements and the New Zealand settlements.

The third phase of colonisation, which persisted into the twentieth century, was the outward thrust of the frontier by the pressure of a growing population. After filling the temperate lands, or at least after exploiting their primary products, the colonists, whose numbers were everywhere swollen as much by the excess of births over deaths as by a torrent of new immigrants, flowed out into lands which previously had not been considered 'White Man's Country', into Texas, Arizona, Queensland, Rhodesia and even Arctic Canada. The lure was, in many instances, the prospect of finding gold, silver or diamonds. Boom-towns growing up where there has been a rush to the diggings seem to be the only exceptions to the rule of systematic colonisation. Of the great cities of the Commonwealth, Melbourne, Winnipeg and Johannesburg alone were not planned settlements, but even they did not spring up suddenly in the wilderness. They 'hived-off' from other thriving settlements within the jurisdiction of existing colonies. Apart from the gold-hunters, the emigrants in the third phase of colonisation are, for the most part, labourers in search of better conditions of work, perhaps driven out by adversity at home, perhaps led on by the rumour of prosperity abroad. But this casual migration of the third type can only follow upon the first and second phases. If the ground is not prepared before them, the casual migrants are a mere horde of refugees.

Until the end of the eighteenth century there are, generally speaking, no reliable statistics of the growth or movement of population. The first census of the United States was taken in 1790, of Great Britain in 1801, of Ireland in 1831. Before the establishment of the Colonial Lands and Emigration Commission in 1840 there are no reliable figures of the shipment of emigrants from the British Isles. Even after that date the reported figures are deceptive to the student unversed in the analysis of statistics. The gross figure of departures must be offset by the return of temporary visitors and dissatisfied emigrants, by the unknown number of passengers in transit from some other country through Great Britain, and of those in transit through one new country to another. To take an example, there has been, for more than a hundred years, an ebb and flow of migrants across the open frontier between Canada and the United States in the direction where greater prosperity was to be found for the time. This increase in the population of one country or the other is not indicated by the shipping returns from Europe.

Ten generations ago, in the age of Shakespeare and Ralegh, it is estimated that the inhabitants of England and Wales numbered about five millions, of Ireland something more than one million and of Scotland something less than one million. These seven millions (whom we shall call for brevity the British race, without implying thereby any ethnological doctrine) have increased and multiplied, in ten generations, about eighteen or twenty times over. Their descendants now number about 140,000,000 of whom rather more than half live in the United States and not much more than one-third in the British Isles. This is physically the most remarkable phenomenon in British history. While the British race has been so prolific, it is conjectured on scanty evidence that the population of Europe as a whole has multiplied no more than four or five times; and (on still scantier evidence) it is thought that the population of the world has increased at about the same rate as that of Europe.

Until the middle of the eighteenth century British emigration overseas was almost entirely English and agricultural. The two Scottish attempts at settlement, Nova Scotia and Darien, had failed miserably. The Southern Irish did not go far afield except

by twos and threes to Newfoundland. On the other hand the
Presbyterians of Ulster began to move to America when the pressure of the English Acts of Trade bore hardly on their industries.
Some 20,000 are said to have crossed the sea before 1700. Bitterly
anti-British, the Scotch-Irish, as they were called in the colonies,
formed the backbone of Washington's Continental Army and
provided several leaders to the Revolution. Still, at the first
American census (1790), returns of the white population have
been analysed as 80 % English, 8 % Irish (mostly Scotch-Irish) and
4 % Scottish, while the other countries of Europe provided no
more than 8 % between them.

The mass-movement from the Highlands of Scotland to the
colonies began in the middle of the eighteenth century. Maclean
of Coll was endeavouring to ship away his clansmen as early as the
foundation of Georgia (1733). The reduction of establishments
after each European treaty of peace (1748, 1763, 1783, 1802, 1814)
produced a flow of discharged Highland soldiers to the colonies.
The pacification of the Highlands had put an end to the days when
each proud chief was followed by a 'tail' of fighting men who
lived on his bounty. When Dr Johnson made his tour of the
Hebrides in 1773 he found the whole country inflamed with a
fever for emigration, which he deplored. 'The lairds', he said,
'instead of improving their country diminished their people.' He
spoke of rapacious chiefs 'making a wilderness of their estates' by
their greed in demanding too high rents. It was the 'tacksmen',
the better class of tenants, who were forced to emigrate. The
depopulation of the Highlands, which Karl Marx selected as his
classic example of the expropriation of the poor by the rich, makes
an ironic commentary on the romantic legend of the north. The
very chiefs who revived the tartans, the kilted dress, the bagpipes
and the Highland games, who luxuriated in the sentiment of the
Waverley Novels, were engaged at the same time in destroying the
clans and driving away their kin. The crofts were first turned into
sheepwalks and then by a further degradation into deer-forests
which, in the fulfilment of time, must be leased to alien capitalists
when the degenerate lords could no longer even boast their
sheep. The descendant of that Maclean of Coll whom Boswell
had criticised petitioned the Colonial Office in 1827 'for aid towards emigration. He himself sent out 300 souls from one of his
islands, and he can now *spare* 1500.' The clearances of Coll,

Skye and Sutherland have been often selected as examples but I know no means of tabulating the general effect of the emigration, except by studying where the Scottish race now lives. To this I shall return later.

A single example will show the tenacity of Highland purpose and the fluid character of the statistics. A party of McLeods evicted from Sutherlandshire migrated to Pictou, Nova Scotia, and from there went on to St Anne in Cape Breton Island, but did not prosper. In 1851 their leader, the Rev. Norman McLeod, then an old man of seventy, ordained a further migration on the advice of his sailor son who wrote to him of the superior advantages of South Australia. Whereupon 130 Highlanders set off in a barque of 500 tons, which they themselves had built and manned, but, finding South Australia also not to their liking, they migrated again, to New Zealand (1854). Governor Grey settled them on land at Waipu north of Auckland, where several more shiploads followed from Nova Scotia, making a colony of 900 souls. The old patriarch, McLeod, long survived to preach to them in Gaelic. Their women used the spinning-wheel at least into the twentieth century, and their young men distinguished themselves in the German Wars.[1]

All attempts to estimate the numbers of Scottish, or of Irish, migrants are vitiated by the unchecked flow of internal migration between the three kingdoms. At all times in history there has been a reciprocal flow of population between Ulster and the Clyde. In the seventh century it set strongly towards Scotland, in the seventeenth century towards Ireland, and in the twentieth century towards Scotland again. Similarly there has long been a seasonal movement of unskilled labour across the Irish Sea towards England. Many return but many stay and are absorbed into the English population. Since the first Union with Scotland, in 1603, the drift of the Scots southward across the border has been remarked in every generation. There are a hundred columns of names beginning with 'Mac-' in the London telephone directory for 1947,

---

[1] I am obliged to my brother-in-law, the Rev. D. B. MacGregor, for drawing my attention to the part played in the emigration by the Scottish Episcopal Church, always closely associated with the American Episcopal Church. When the potato famine of 1847 assailed the Highlands, Episcopalians in the U.S.A. sent relief to their fellows in Scotland. Some of them chartered a ship, loaded it with food, and despatched it to the Bishop of Argyll, recommending that he should send it back to Portland [Maine?], laden with Scottish emigrants.

an observation which suggests, by a cursory comparison of the frequencies of certain surnames in proportion to the population, that there may be many more Scots in London than in Edinburgh.

There is however a difference between Scottish and Irish migration. Apart from the one Lowland colony (Otago, New Zealand) and certain mass-movements caused by the Highland clearances, the Scottish migrants, whether to England or abroad, are strongly individual. No traveller in the Empire can fail to observe how high a proportion of the leaders of colonial life are Scots. Doctors trained in the Scottish universities are (or seem to be, for there are no statistics) far more numerous than English or Irish doctors overseas. Many technologies, especially marine-engineering, seem almost Scottish monopolies. Very different is the status and repute of the Southern Irish. Though a peasant people they become town-dwellers when they go overseas. As in Liverpool and Glasgow, so in New York and Chicago and in the cities of the Dominions, the Catholic Irish form the urban proletariat, while the Scots everywhere are in positions of responsibility.

The rapid increase of the Irish population in the eighteenth century was not accompanied by the growth of industry, by agricultural improvement, or by any form of social insurance. When the population reached 8,000,000 in 1841, the island was grossly overpopulated. This is not the place to recount the wrongs of Ireland before the Union or the fallacious belief of English reformers that all would be set right by representation at Westminster, Roman Catholic emancipation and Free Trade. A wave of emigration, or rather of refugees escaping from misery, began about 1820 from Southern Ireland to North America. At first the rural slums of Connaught were merely decanted into the urban slums of New York and Quebec, in utter wretchedness. The pitiable conditions on the emigrant ships and at the docks were denounced in an appendix to Lord Durham's Report. But very soon observers noticed that the flow was strengthened and the intake rapidly absorbed. Of all emigrants the Irish have done most in the way of family self-help. One Irishman would no sooner find wage-labour at the high colonial rate than he would save money to bring out his friends and family. Thus the migration gained momentum and the newcomers found friends to receive them in the new lands. Wakefield said bitterly, 'the Irish do not colonise, they only emigrate miserably', a true statement but an insufficient one. They did in fact transport the majority of their race by their own efforts to another land. They were never pioneers and never founded a new settlement; they followed in the third phase of colonisation as proletarians. As in Old Ireland, so in the Dominions, the Protestants of Ulster have taken a different course. Ulstermen have taken as prominent a part in the commercial and professional world of British Canada as did the 'Scotch-Irish' in the Thirteen Colonies. Orange Lodges, preserving the Ulster tradition, have been prominent in politics, especially in Ontario.

Between 1815 and 1840 the gross total number of emigrants from the British Isles was about a million, of whom 499,000 went to British North America, 417,000 to the United States and 58,000 to Australia. The largest number in any one year was 103,000 in 1832. The export of Irish paupers had begun in 1823 but was not more than a small fraction of the whole emigration at this period.

Under the new Poor Law of 1834, English paupers were also shipped to the colonies at the expense of the rate-payers until, in 1840, the Wakefield system was partially adopted. In that year the South Australian Commission (see chapter VII, 6, page 366) was reconstituted as the Colonial Lands and Emigration Commission[1] with authority to collect the receipts of land sales and to apply the proceeds to despatching selected emigrants of good character. For twelve or fifteen years the Commissioners did useful work in issuing reports on colonial life, advising emigrants about their requirements, warning them against 'bubble' schemes of settlement—especially fraudulent attempts to divert emigrants to Latin America—and in publishing statistics. The conditions of life on emigrant ships were gradually improved, though the Irish rush of 1847–52 overwhelmed all attempts at organisation. The worst abuses disappeared after the shipping regulations had been consolidated in the Act of 1855. The gross number of passengers who left the British Isles during the thirty-three years that the Commission lasted was about 6,500,000, of whom nearly two-thirds went to the United States.

The North American emigration was uncontrolled. Most of the millions who crossed the Atlantic in those years paid their own passage-money (aggregating to £15,000,000) or were subsidised by their friends already in America. The Irish who went to the

[1] See W. A. Carruthers, *Colonial Lands and Emigration Commission*.

United States, nursing the memory of their oppression, fanned the flame of anti-British prejudice and remained bitterly hostile to all that reminded them of Britain. The United States until the 1840's had been violently Protestant in tendency. The Irish exiles created the first pressure-group and perhaps the strongest in American politics, the Catholic anti-British vote.

The year 1847 saw the beginning of the great Irish emigration. Flood-tide was reached in 1851 when 336,000 passengers, of whom 257,000 were Irish, left the British Isles. In 1852 the gross total figure was higher, 368,000, but the Irish element had dropped to 225,000. The attraction that year was the gold-rush to Melbourne. After 1854 the stream of migrants slackened off for a few years. No new goldfields were discovered, and the Crimean War provided employment for potential emigrants. But the strongest reason was the absolute decline in the population of Ireland. At a time when all other European populations were rapidly increasing, that of Ireland sharply fell, partly from actual famine but much more from the removal of so large a proportion of the men and women of marriageable age, as is proved by the great fertility of the Irish-Americans. Within a few years the Irish in America were far more numerous than the Irish in Ireland had ever been.

While hordes of miserable Irishmen were fleeing across the Atlantic to escape starvation, the Commissioners were conducting an orderly system of emigration to Australia. By good management they reduced the death-rate on the voyage from 5% to 0·5%. In 1847 they began to charter ships of their own for the long voyage and, by 1869, had carried 339,000 emigrants, in 1088 shiploads, at a cost of £4,864,000. More than £4,000,000 of this sum had been raised by land sales in Australia. But since the colonies had matured to self-government in the 'fifties, acquiring control of their own land sales, the spending of the fund by a Board in London had become an anomaly. After long agitation by Adderley, the Colonial Reformer, the Commission was terminated in 1872, its duties being divided between the Board of Trade and the agents of the colonial governments in London.

The statistics of inward as well as outward migration were first analysed and issued by the Board of Trade in 1873, from which date it is possible to quote a net figure of the annual loss to the British population by emigration. But it was not until 1912 that detailed particulars were recorded of the country of origin and intended residence of each ship's passenger. The annual net loss to the population of the British Isles by emigration, according to the Board of Trade returns, is as follows:

Net migration from the British Isles to places outside Europe, 1876–1930.

British nationality—excess of outward over inward passengers (numbers in thousands).

	Annual Averages				
Period	United States	British North America	Australia and New Zealand	All other places	Total
1876–80	47	8	28	4	87
1881–85	124	24	36	3	187
1886–90	110	20	22	7	159
1891–95	66	11	4	8	89
1896–1900	38	7	4	7	56
1901–05	58	36	5	18	117
1906–10	70	84	20	5	179
1911–13	49	132	67	9	257
1921–25	38	45	37	4	124
1926–30	31	39	24	5	99

That is an aggregate total of between six and seven millions. Again taking annual averages the net annual loss by migration is, generally speaking, about one-quarter of the net annual increase by the excess of births over deaths. Changes in the population of the British Isles during the last hundred years are shown in Fig. I overleaf, but the decline of the population of Scotland and Ireland should be accepted with reserve since it takes no account of Scottish and Irish migration to England.

The net annual average gain of the British Dominions and the United States in persons of British origin is given in Fig. II which shows the excess of outward over inward passengers between the British Isles and these countries during the period from 1876 to 1930.

It thus presents a general picture of the net emigration from the British Isles. The three pronounced dips in the curve (1884–5, 1894 and 1908) are each related to financial crises in the United States. The high peak of 1883 was a time of depression in England but of prosperity in the United States. The outward movement

Fig. I. *Population 1831–1931. England and Wales,
Ireland, Scotland.*

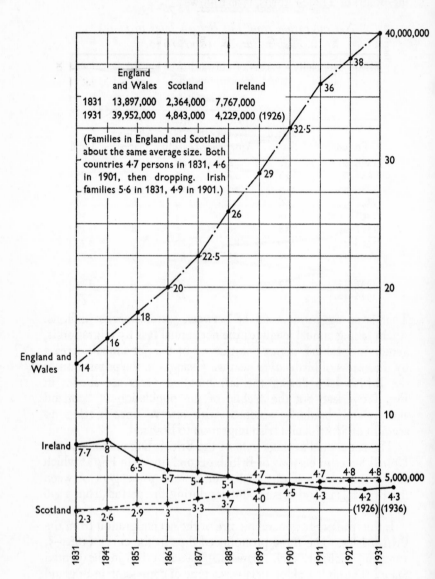

	England and Wales	Scotland	Ireland
1831	13,897,000	2,364,000	7,767,000
1931	39,952,000	4,843,000	4,229,000 (1926)

(Families in England and Scotland about the same average size. Both countries 4·7 persons in 1831, 4·6 in 1901, then dropping. Irish families 5·6 in 1831, 4·9 in 1901.)

Fig. II. *Excess of outward over inward movement of British passengers between the British Isles and non-European countries, 1876–1930.*

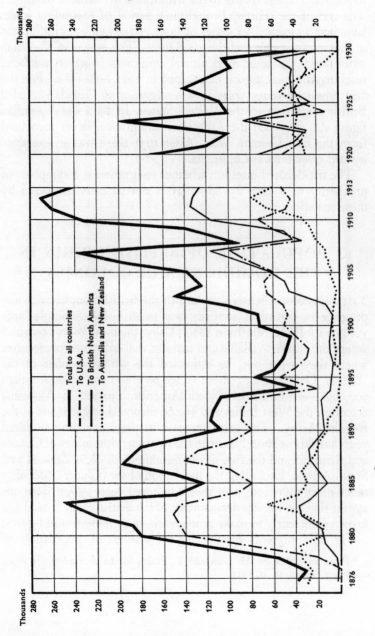

Legend:
- Total to all countries
- To U.S.A.
- To British North America
- To Australia and New Zealand

of the middle 'eighties was a further Irish flight from agricultural depression. The early 'nineties were in general a period of contracting trade both in Europe and in the Dominions. Emigration to Australia lapsed owing to the withdrawal of 'assisted passages'. The end of the century brought in a period of expanding trade, launched by great discoveries of gold. Renewed emigration was in this instance a sign of the good times. The boom in Canadian wheat-lands attracted agricultural emigrants in great numbers, reaching the peak figure of 260,000 in 1911 and 1912. For the first time in seventy years British migration to Canada exceeded British migration to the United States. In 1912 the Australian figure also exceeded the American. Emigration never recovered from the first German War. After 1931 there was an excess of inward over outward migrants.

The oft-debated question whether emigration is a symptom of prosperity or a cure for adversity is not patently answered by these statistics.

6. POPULATION OF BRITISH ORIGIN IN THE DOMINIONS AND COLONIES

THE first comprehensive account of the British Empire with any pretence to statistical accuracy was published in a single large volume by R. M. Martin in 1839. Using the most recent censuses where they were available and making well-informed conjectures where they were not, he estimated the whole number of the 'British Overseas' as about 1,200,000, of whom more than 900,000 were in British North America, 130,000 in Australia, 60,000 in the West Indies and 56,000 disposed as garrisons of the Regular Army. The great increase in the succeeding hundred years has almost entirely been in the two older dominions of Canada and Australia and the two newer dominions of New Zealand and South Africa. Excluding the lost legion of the pioneers, probably much more numerous now than a hundred years ago, it does not appear that the smaller detachments of the British race abroad have grown sufficiently to make much mark upon these round figures.

Fig. III[1] presents graphically the growth of population of

[1] From an article by H. Leak and T. Priday in the *Journal of the Royal Statistical Society*, pt. II, 1933.

FIG. III. *Population of British origin in four Dominions compared with the population of Ireland and Scotland.*

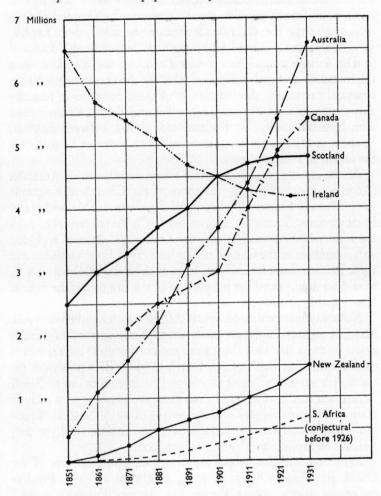

British origin in these dominions according to the census returns from 1850 to 1931. Since smaller numbers are in question the height of the scale is doubled in proportion to that of Fig. I and, for convenient reference, the populations of Scotland and Ireland are reproduced on the same enlarged scale.

The first complete census of Canada was taken in 1871. Since

the Canadian constitution was designed to protect minority rights
the censuses distinguish French- from British-Canadians and
classify the British into English, Scottish and Irish. The figures
of the total British population may therefore be accepted. In the
census of 1931 the 5,381,000 British were classified as English
50%, Scottish 24% and Irish (including 'Scotch-Irish') 22%.

The Australian and New Zealand censuses are complete since
the foundation of each colony. Excluding the aboriginals who are
separately returned, the population of these countries is remarkably homogeneous, showing a smaller non-British element even
than England itself. No distinction is drawn between English,
Scottish and Irish. A rough estimate may however be made by
the return of religious sects.

At the census of 1933 the total white population of Australia
(6,630,000) included 39% members of the Church of England;
18% Roman Catholics (almost all Southern Irish); and 11%
Presbyterians (Scottish and 'Scotch-Irish'). At the census of 1936
the total white population of New Zealand (1,485,000) included
40% members of the Church of England; 25% Presbyterians; and
13% Roman Catholics. Other sects, such as the Methodists, 9%
would no doubt swell the proportion of the English, if the figures
were capable of analysis.

No analytical census of South Africa was taken before 1926.
Martin's figures imply no more than 10,000 settlers of British
origin in 1839. By 1865 there were 100,000 'whites' but no means
of distinguishing British from Dutch origins. The passenger returns give no indication of extensive British emigration to South
Africa before the 1890's and even then the gross figures include
many temporary visitors. At the census of 1936 the total 'European' population was returned as 2,003,000, the Bantu as 6,597,000,
Asiatics as 217,000 and 'others' as 770,000.

Religious statistics, which are very full, give members of the
Dutch Reformed Church as 57%, Anglicans as 19%, Presbyterians as 4·45%, other Protestants (largely English) as 9%,
Roman Catholics as 4·8% and Jews as 4·7%. The small proportion of Presbyterians may be due to their absorption into the similar Dutch Church. Throughout South Africa there are many
Afrikaner families of Scottish origin. The small proportion of
Southern Irish may be due to their failure to compete against
cheap native labour. Out of the two million who constituted

the European population of the Union in 1936, perhaps 800,000 may be described as of British origin.

Three other 'white' settlements are worth noting precisely: Newfoundland with Labrador contained a population of 289,000 at the census of 1935; Southern Rhodesia contained 58,870 'Europeans' at the census of 1938; Kenya contained 20,894 'Europeans' at the census of 1930.

The aggregate figures for the populations of British origin in the four great dominions, and in Newfoundland, Southern Rhodesia and Kenya, will then amount to about 14,600,000, making no allowance for inter-censal increase, but taking in each instance the census nearest to the year 1935. To this must be added a figure, hardly more than a random guess, for the people of British stock in the British West Indies where races have been mingling too long for statistical analysis. R. R. Kuczynsky[1] gives an estimate of about 100,000. The Indian census of 1931 returned 300,000 'Europeans', 155,000 'British subjects' and 138,000 of the race euphemistically described as 'Anglo-Indians'. I know not how to regard these figures. Adding a random allowance for the unreturned numbers of the scattered pioneers throughout the world it seems that the British overseas in about the year 1936 numbered not less than 15,000,000.

Taking the figure of 1,200,000 for the decade ending in 1839 and the figure of 15,000,000 for the decade ending in 1939, and basing estimates at intermediate dates upon the census of the four dominions, we can now surmise the growth of the population of British origin in the Empire. Fig. IV presents as a graph the decennial census returns for the British Isles from 1831 to 1931 with a conjectural estimate of the whole 'British' population of the Empire, the total for 1931 being shown as 65,000,000. It also includes an estimate of the other half of the 'British' race no longer living under the protection of the British Crown. The decennial censuses of the United States (1790–1930) have distinguished, though not consistently, between 'white' and 'coloured' Americans. The graph of white Americans, also shown in Fig. IV, gives a starting-point for enquiry. In 1790 the white population was 92% British. It was not until the 1850's that the immigrants from the Continent of Europe began to outnumber those from the British Isles. The conscious endeavour of the

---

[1] *Population Movements*, 1936.

FIG. IV. *Estimate of the growth of populations resident or originating in the British Isles, 1830–1931.*

American people to mix the ingredients (or at least the white ingredients) in the melting-pot of the great republic makes it increasingly difficult to estimate the proportion of British stock.

The net emigration from the British Isles to the United States between 1830 and 1930 cannot be much less than 7,500,000. In the same period we know that about 2,300,000 emigrated to Australia and New Zealand and increased naturally to 8,000,000. Assuming that the 7,500,000 British emigrants to America increased at the same natural rate as those to Australasia and that the resident 'British' population of the United States increased at the same rate as the population of the British Isles, the total population of British origin in the United States in 1930 would be about 75,000,000.[1]

In conclusion I must refer to the scattered groups of persons of British origin living in other foreign lands, perhaps 200,000 in all. From the Argentine 1797 men and 532 women served as volunteers in the British forces in 1939–45 and another 1000 from other South American states. The British Argentine Society estimates that there are about 50,000 persons of British descent domiciled, and mostly naturalised there, among them the Welsh settlers at Chubut (see Appendix IV, pages 1048–9). The mercantile colonies in Egypt, China and elsewhere contain many British citizens who have not severed their connexion with home. In the Baltic and the Levant small and often ancient settlements of Englishmen and Scotsmen maintain their individuality. Finally there are the residential colonies in beauty spots and spas, mostly in France, Italy, Switzerland and the Atlantic Islands.

ASIATIC EMIGRATION

The great European emigration of the nineteenth century was paralleled by an Asiatic emigration produced by similar causes. The abundant population of south-east Asia also overflowed, the Chinese south-eastwards into Malaya and the Islands, the Indians south-westwards into the coasts and islands of the Indian Ocean. Statistical information of these folk-wanderings is scarcer even than of those previously discussed. The Asiatic emigrants appear

[1] These are indications not statistics. Another estimate by Julian Huxley and A. C. Haddon (*We Europeans*, 1935) gives the percentage of persons of British origin in the population of the U.S.A. as 53·6% in 1920.

generally as a discordant factor in the history of the British overseas. Sometimes, as with the Chinese at the goldfields or the
Hindus in Natal, they came as direct rivals to the European emigrants; sometimes, as in the West Indies, Asiatics were introduced
as indentured labourers upon terms which aroused the suspicion
of philanthropists. To summarise emigrations which will be
alluded to elsewhere in this book, mention should be made of the
attempted infiltration of California and Australia by Chinese gold-
diggers, the successful colonisation of Malaya by Chinese merchants and tin-miners, the settlement of Ceylon with Tamils from
Southern India, and of Burma with coolies from Bengal and the
colonisation of the East African coast from Durban to Zanzibar
with Indian settlers of several castes and creeds.

But greater in scale was the importation of low-caste Indian
coolies to the sugar-colonies, where labour was scarce after the
abolition of slavery. The first experiment was made in Mauritius,
which received 24,000 coolies between 1834 and 1839. A similar
transportation to the West Indies was begun in 1837 but was
stopped by the government of India, two years later, as an abuse.
Herman Merivale of the Colonial Office said that 'in everything
but the compulsion and the cruelty the immigration trade is but a
repetition of the slave trade'. The whole history of indentured
labour in the colonies repeats the same story. At its worst it de-
generates into something not far different from slavery, but this
worst has not often been seen under the British flag. At its best
the labourer is still far from freedom. In many, perhaps in most,
instances food and quarters and hygiene are well attended to because it is the employers' interest to keep the workers healthy and
contented. But all indentured labour implies a one-sided contract,
which the coolies were often obliged to accept under pressure of
poverty, and which conveyed them to a distant land where there
could be no economic liberty for them. Payment often took the
form of truck, and repatriation depended on the goodwill of the
employer. In fact coolies did not often return to India, with the
result that families were divided and, since men very largely outnumbered women, morals deteriorated.

In 1844 the West India Committee approached Lord Stanley,
then Colonial Secretary, to ask for a controlled migration, which
Stephen the Under-Secretary resisted until his retirement. Stanley,
also, was 'determined to prevent the institution of any order

approaching slavery' but obtained the consent of the Indian government for the transportation of 12,500 coolies a year under careful supervision by the Land and Emigration Commissioners. The movement went, naturally enough, to the prosperous new colonies rather than to the old exhausted plantations. By 1872, 80,000 Indians had been sent to British Guiana, 44,000 to Trinidad, 16,000 to Jamaica and 6000 to the other West Indian islands, while the far greater number of 350,000 had made the short journey to Mauritius, where efforts were also made but with little success to attract free African natives. In another direction, many thousand Indians emigrated to Fiji. Some 12,000 Chinese also found their way to British Guiana. In the 1860's negotiations for a steady flow of Chinese coolies broke down because the Chinese government demanded a clause in the contract guaranteeing a free return passage to China for each emigrant, and this the planters would not undertake.

7. THE WEST INDIES IN DECLINE,
1839–75

THE sugar colonies had not yet adjusted themselves to an economy without slaves when the second blow was struck by reformers in England. The preferences given to West Indian sugar were weakened and soon abolished. From the point of view of political economists at home, though not of planters in Jamaica, the new Crown Colony of Mauritius deserved the same treatment as its competitors, the British West Indian islands. As early as 1825 it had been admitted to a degree of preference; in 1835 the duties on sugar from the East Indian and West Indian colonies were equalised. Next an attempt was made during Peel's administration to discriminate by a tariff against sugar grown in countries where there was still slavery, although this led to diplomatic difficulties with Brazil. When Russell became Prime Minister in 1846 a general policy of free trade was adopted, to the dismay of the sugar planters. The West India Committee even found themselves allied with the Anti-Slavery Society on this issue in opposition to free trade in sugar. The two interests, strongly represented on a committee with Lord George Bentinck as chairman, held off the threatened blow. Russell had intended to reduce the preference by stages until a flat rate of 14s. a cwt., a mere revenue tariff, was reached. Through the efforts of Bentinck's committee the last stage was postponed until, in 1854, when Gladstone was Chancellor, an equal rate for free- and slave-grown sugar was fixed. Without much doubt the preference had been so high as to subsidise incompetence in the colonies and to restrict consumption at home. Yet to remove it altogether and to abandon the colonies to their own resources seemed to them a death-blow.

It was immediately followed by the banking crisis of 1847 which brought down the principal banks of Jamaica, British Guiana, Trinidad and Mauritius, in the train of their greater associates in London. The evils of plantation-colonies, their dependence upon a single cash-crop, their tendency to fall into the power of absentee-owners, their sensitivity to booms and slumps, were then peculiarly apparent. Wages in the West Indies fell by 50 % and, in several colonies, the attempts to reduce public expenditure led to struggles between governors and assemblies. Perhaps Trinidad, a Crown Colony governed just then by Lord Harris who had both ability and tact, came through the crisis with the least suffering, since he had instituted a systematic reform in local government, authorising the collection of rates for schools and police. Trinidad also preceded the other colonies in attempts to establish the free negroes as peasants on Crown land.

Jamaica was the worst afflicted of the islands. Hard times were followed by pestilence; in addition to the endemic yellow-fever, there were epidemics of cholera in 1850 and smallpox in 1852. The historic constitution of Jamaica, founded under King Charles II, was quite unequal to these strains. Since its foundation there had been intermittent struggles between the Governor and the Assembly over control of the revenue. In 1839 an attempt to reform this ancient model had led to the fall of Melbourne's government in England; in 1854 after some months of deadlock in Jamaica, the pride of the planters was abated and the island voted itself a new constitution. The Assembly was induced to give up its proud and reckless irresponsibility in return for a loan guaranteed by the British government. During the next five years Tobago, St Kitt's, St Vincent, Nevis and Antigua adopted similar constitutions which somewhat resembled the responsible government of the Australian and North American colonies.

The root of the economic problem in the sugar colonies was

shortage of labour since the abolition of the slave trade. When the introduction of indentured labour was authorised (1847), the Office reluctantly submitted to the demands of the planters that contracts for three or even five years should be permitted under the strictest supervision. There was some evidence, and the opinion of Lord Harris to back it, that long contracts were more humane since they enabled the labourers to settle down under supervision. The expense of shipment, and repatriation at the end of the indenture, fell heavily on the employers and most heavily where the voyage was longest. In these respects also Mauritius had the advantage being nearest to the source of supply in India. The planters of Mauritius financed their own immigration while the West Indians were obliged to raise loans in London with a guarantee from the Treasury. In Trinidad and British Guiana, where the largest numbers were introduced, they were encouraged by bonuses to remain as settlers when their indentures were out.

Of the other colonies, Barbados received very few; it differed from the other British islands in being overpopulated (1000 inhabitants to the square mile), with the result that there was no labour problem. Barbadians were said to be averse to travel; their pride in their island and its long loyal history was famous, and exclusive. Jamaica, on the other hand, was always short of labour. Wanting indentured labourers more than any colony, it received few because the missionaries and the coloured voters resisted their importation. The largest and richest of the older colonies,[1] Jamaica was always the most prominent in the view of the public at home, yet it was not a typical West Indian island. Though sugar-planting was the staple industry, the export of raw sugar made only 41 % of the island's external trade. There was an almost equally valuable trade in the celebrated Jamaica rum, and a

[1] Annual exports of sugar:

	Average of the years 1853–5 (cwt.)	Average of the years 1868–70 (cwt.)
British Guiana	931,000	1,567,000
Barbados	719,000	772,000
Jamaica	459,000	551,000
Trinidad	421,000	860,000
(No other British West Indian island had an output half as great as the lowest of these figures)		
Mauritius	1,951,000	1,984,000

considerable trade in coffee grown by peasant-farmers. Jamaica planters were the aristocracy of the West Indies but Jamaica also had more small-holdings than the other islands. The administration, even under the constitution of 1854, was inefficient and corrupt. Wages were low and public services almost unknown. The government of the island, and the planters individually, were, as a rule, in debt.

During the last years of slavery and the first years of free labour the West Indies were described by many travellers.[1] The travellers concur in picturing a highly characteristic society. The exuberant beauty of the islands with their gaudy flowers and fruits forms a background to the indolent luxurious life of the planters, inclined to careless profusion and wasteful methods of using the land, but by no means deficient in the virtues of high caste, not unlike the aristocracy of old Virginia. Their life was clouded by the sense of slow decay. Living among abandoned plantations upon which the negro peasantry squatted they tended to assume that there had been better times in some half-mythical yesterday. Between the masters and the slaves (or ex-slaves) there was a patriarchal relation; West Indians never cringed as negroes did in the United States, but spoke up boldly to assert their loyalty and, especially in Barbados, their island pride. The negroes are described by all visitors as high-spirited, good-natured and idle, gaily dressed in coloured cottons, living as easily as they can, if the 'buckra' does not make them work, in a land where providence gives food for the lightest labour. Yet, 'between the idea and the reality...falls the Shadow'. The curse of slavery and caste lay on the islands. Social *malaise* expressed itself among native Christians, not far removed from African savagery, by relapses into the bloody rites of 'obeah'; in outbreaks of terrified cruelty by the white men against seditious negroes.

Charles Kingsley's account (*At Last*, 1870) is the most picturesque; Anthony Trollope's (*The West Indies and the Spanish Main*, 1859), written in his thumping downright style, is more to our purpose. Between the bombast of the patriots and the wishful thinking of the philanthropists his philistinish comments find a useful mean. Trollope arrived at St Thomas (then a Danish and

[1] A collection of their views may be found in an amusing essay entitled *West Indian Summer* by James Pope-Hennessy, 1943.

now an American possession) in the Virgin Islands in 1858. Since the coming of the steamships this first-rate harbour, though far to leeward, had superseded all the harbours of the Windward Islands to become the distributing centre of the West Indies. He thought it 'a niggery-hispano-dano-yankee-doodle place'. From there he made his way to Jamaica in burning heat, and disliked it, especially its towns. The naval dockyard was at Port Royal near the site of the old city, once the richest and wickedest city in the world, but drowned since the earthquake of 1692 beneath eight fathoms of water. The commercial port of Kingston four or five miles away was an insanitary slum without architectural pretension or decent streets, a wretched place compared with Havana or Martinique. Though the metropolis of Jamaica it was not the capital, which was placed at Spanish Town, a torrid empty city from which fled to the hills all whom the business of government did not detain.

At the great plantation houses among scenes of natural beauty the planters lived like squires and kept open house with crowds of domestics who managed to be both insolent and servile. All that was English was fashionable and all that was colonial, even their gorgeous fruits, despised. The colour-line was strictly drawn in every English house, 'except at the Governor's table'. It was the curse of politics, in Trollope's opinion, that had done most to reduce the wealth of the island. 'Her roads are almost impassable, her bridges are broken down, her coffee plantations have gone back to bush, her sugar-estates have been sold for the value of the sugar-boilers. Kingston as a town is the most deplorable that man ever visited, unless it be that Spanish Town is worse, and yet they have Lords and Commons. It has availed them nothing.' The Assembly largely consisted of coloured men and the white gentry tended to withdraw from it. 'Every man might vote who paid tax or rent', though few in fact took up the qualification. They would be much better off, he thought, under direct Colonial Office rule like British Guiana.

Barbados with its large population and fertile soil had no distress. There 'no coloured man votes at all. A coloured man or negro is doubtless qualified to vote if he owns a freehold; but then care is taken that such shall not own freeholds.' The future of the islands lay neither with whites nor blacks. A brown race, fitted for the climate with European energy and Asiatic physique, would emerge in the course of many generations and would inherit all.

Trinidad and British Guiana were lively commercial colonies filled with bustling vigorous Asiatic coolies, and not hampered by a corrupt 'lords-and-commons'. The Anti-Slavery Society before agitating against indentured labour should compare the progress of these Crown Colonies with the decadence of Jamaica. British Guiana, says Trollope, 'is the land of my choice when I settle out of England'.

Nevertheless the 'fifties, 'sixties and 'seventies were a period of modest progress in the West Indies as the increase in the export of sugar demonstrates. The calm was broken by one deplorable outburst, the rebellion associated with the name of Governor Eyre. Among the coloured voters of Jamaica was a man named George William Gordon, the son of a Scottish planter and a slave-woman. He made money in trade, attracted a following by his liberality and eloquence, was appointed a magistrate and was elected to the Assembly. Early in the 1860's he came to the fore as a dangerous critic of the government. He caused some alarm among the whites by comparing the state of Jamaica with that of Haiti, the negro republic, and was heard to make unguarded remarks about the future when the white men should no longer own the land. His enemies called him a seditious agitator, his friends a patriot. His clients spoke of his charities, which the opposite faction denominated bribes. After making rash charges against the officers of St Thomas parish at the south-east corner of the island and failing to sustain them, he was imprudently removed from his magistracy by Eyre, the Acting-Governor. Eyre and Gordon were thereafter political enemies.

A wave of unrest was passing over Jamaica. The American Civil War had raised the price and shortened the supply of foodstuffs which meant hardship to the thousands who lived improvidently on small-holdings and casual labour. More important perhaps was a religious revival which swept through the native population, an emotional explosion far removed from rationality. The new sect was known as the Native Baptists and their ceremonies, according to hostile critics, differed little from 'obeah'. But the powerful Baptist Missionary Society took the Native Baptists under its protection and, when Gordon joined the Native Baptists, Dr E. B. Underhill, the Secretary of the Society in London, took up the cudgels for Gordon. A petition was sent to the Queen asking her to relieve the sufferings of her Jamaican subjects, and was referred to the Colonial Office. Cardwell, who was then Secretary of State, rejected the advances of Dr Underhill and snubbed the petitioners in plain terms. He wrote that they 'must look for an improvement in their condition to their own industry and prudence'. This reply infuriated Gordon who spent the summer of 1865 moving about the island, making inflammatory speeches. It was not however proved that he ever crossed the bounds of treason or incited to violence. On 11 October 1865 a brawl broke out at Morant Bay in the parish of St Thomas which was regarded as the hub of Gordon's influence. It was the most backward of the twenty-one parishes into which Jamaica was divided, and had long been seething with unrest. The volunteer militia was called out, shots were fired, and the brawl grew into a bloody riot in which the court-house was burnt down and fifteen or twenty whites were murdered, among them a local magistrate who was Gordon's rival and enemy. The ringleader was Paul Boyce, a negro client of Gordon's.

The news reached Kingston forty miles away the next day. Governor Eyre had no more than 1000 regular troops, under General L. S. O'Connor, at hand. They were disposed with great skill and speed to close the road along the southern coast and the passes through the Blue Mountains to the north. Having thus prevented the rebellion from spreading beyond St Thomas's parish, the troops closed in upon Morant Bay, giving no quarter to negroes who could give no good account of themselves. Within a week order was restored. About eighty-five negroes were shot without trial; no less than 354 were executed by authority of courts-martial. On the day of the outbreak Gordon had been at his house in Kingston, quietly engaged in issuing propaganda leaflets. He made no attempt to join the rebels or to escape. By order of the Governor he was arrested, taken to Morant Bay and court-martialled on board a warship on 21 October. He was sentenced to death and hanged two days later. So skilful had been the dispositions of the Governor that it had not been necessary to extend the operation of martial law beyond a single parish, and the rising was over.

Eyre was quite unconscious of the storm he would arouse. Strong in his understanding of that which he had already quelled he met the Assembly on 7 November and, taking advantage of the state of panic which prevailed among them, he persuaded them to abdicate their powers to the Colonial Office. As there was no submarine cable as yet to the West Indies, Eyre's despatch describing the rebellion and its suppression did not reach London until 16 November. Cardwell at once congratulated Eyre on his promptness and vigour but warned him that the despatch contained 'many passages that will require to be explained'. As soon as 'the news was published a torrent of indignation was poured out, particularly in *The Times*, and by all the channels known to 'Exeter Hall'. On 16 December Cardwell recalled Eyre to London, pending the report of a Commission which was to go to Jamaica with the Governor of Malta, Sir Henry Storks, as chairman.

The fury of the philanthropists was unabated for six months and it was heated seven times hotter when the Commissioners reported in June 1866. They were by no means plain in their condemnation of Governor Eyre's actions. They decided somewhat equivocally that there had not been 'a general conspiracy' and that it had not been 'consciously provoked' by Gordon; but that there had been 'planned resistance to lawful authority'. Eyre was praised for his 'skill, promptitude and vigour' but blamed for maintaining martial law 'longer than was necessary'. Punishments had been excessive and in some cases 'positively barbarous'. The trial of Gordon was censured not so much as an act of tyranny as for technical irregularities. Not only had the defendant been arrested in an area where martial law was not proclaimed, but the court had also been irregularly constituted. Storks was then confirmed by Cardwell as Governor of Jamaica and Eyre retired on pension.

But this was not enough for the British public. The nation took sides for or against Governor Eyre, who was either the saviour of the white colonists or the cruel oppressor of the blacks. A strong committee, including John Stuart Mill, Herbert Spencer, T. H. Huxley, Thomas Hughes and Goldwin Smith, continued to assail him while he was powerfully defended by Carlyle, Ruskin, Tennyson and Kingsley. Several actions were begun against him in court, without success, for murder and other crimes, and the agitation did not subside for five years or more. Eyre maintained silence and lived in retirement for more than thirty years.

The riot at Morant Bay, the bloodshed, the panic, and the vindictive reprisals have many parallels in the annals of race-pre-
judice. Much crueller tales were told of the Jamaican slave-revolt
of 1760. Much worse deeds than the execution of Gordon have
since been done in nearer and more civilised lands. The reaction
in London is the striking feature of this story. Eyre's persecutors
and champions alike were imbued with a sense of responsibility
towards the blacks that other ages and other conquering races
have not known. It would not have been thought necessary in
some great states to go to the trouble of preparing an apology for
him.

Edward John Eyre (1815–1901) is now remembered, if at all, as
an oppressive governor. His tragedy is that he was a life-long
humanitarian. His youth had been spent as a pioneer in Australia
where he accomplished the most exhausting desert journeys by his
skill in placating the shy, suspicious black-fellows. Almost alone
among Australian pioneers he had understood and loved them.
Later, in New Zealand, as Lieutenant-Governor under Sir George
Grey, he had emulated that great native administrator in managing
the high-spirited Maori with sympathy and respect. He was an
impulsive man, a hero in any physical crisis, and when left for
years in Jamaica as a make-shift Deputy-Governor he gave rein
to his impulses, acted, and bore the brunt of his action. In happier
times, with a manageable constitution, he might have been a great
colonial statesman, and Gordon his right-hand man.

Jamaica thus reverted to Crown Colony rule in 1866, with a
nominated legislative council after 200 years of self-government.
The other self-governing colonies in the West Indies followed
suit until, in 1875, Barbados, Bermuda and the Bahamas alone retained their ancient liberties. The Leeward Islands were federated
in 1870 under a single governor with a council elected by the
nominated councils of the several islands.

Under the rule of the Colonial Office the islands were more
efficiently and honestly administered and that is all. They continued to be neglected in all those respects where progress required
the investment of capital with no immediate return in sight. All
continued to suffer from too great dependence on a single cash
crop in a highly competitive market. All lacked the steadying
effect of a self-supporting peasantry, as every critic had pointed
out since Rodney, who wanted to colonise St Lucia after its

capture in 1783. Here and there some local enterprise made an exception, like the trade in lime-juice which brought prosperity to Montserrat. Every visitor commented on the uneconomic system whereby each planter was also the manufacturer of his own sugar. They ordered this better in the French colonies where the planters sold their cane to large centralised sugar-factories. Not until 1874 was the first sugar-factory opened in an English colony (St Lucia).

Among other changes may be mentioned the disestablishment of the Anglican Church in Jamaica where its adherents were a minority (1870); in Barbados Anglicanism still prevailed.

Outside the general run of the sugar islands, the Bahamas followed their own fortunes, prospering by the contraband trade and blockade-running during the American Civil War. The American tourist trade began soon after the peace. Bermuda, after a wartime boom, suffered an eclipse when the steamships captured the old coastal and island trade from her famous sailing-boats. In 1869 she began to supply early vegetables by steamship to the New York market. Otherwise she lived upon the dockyard.

APPENDIX I

RULERS OF THE COLONIES

DATE	PRIME MINISTER	SECRETARY OF STATE		PERMANENT UNDER-SECRETARY
1768	Duke of Grafton	Lord Hillsborough		
1770	North			
1772		Lord Dartmouth	for the American	
1775–82		Lord G. Germain (afterwards Lord Sackville)	Department	
1782 Feb.	Rockingham	(American Department abolished by Burke. Until 1801, colonial affairs were usually referred to the Secretary of State for the Home Department)		
1782 July	Shelburne			
1783 Feb.	Portland (Coalition of Fox and North)			
1783 Dec.	Pitt			
1801	Addington (Tory)	Lord Hobart	S. of S. for War and the Colonies	
1804	Pitt (Tory)	Lord Camden	„	
1805		Lord Castlereagh	„	
1806	Grenville (Coalition)	W. Windham	„	
1807	Portland (Tory)	Lord Castlereagh	„	
1809	Perceval (Tory)	Lord Liverpool	„	
1812	Liverpool (Tory)	Lord Bathurst	„	
1827	Canning (Liberal Tory)	F. Robinson (later Viscount Goderich)	„	1825 R. W. Hay
1827	Goderich (Liberal Tory)	W. Huskisson	„	
1828	Wellington (Tory)	Sir G. Murray	„	
1830	2nd Earl Grey (Whig)	Viscount Goderich	„	
1833		E. Stanley (later 14th Earl of Derby)	„	
1834 July	Melbourne (Whig)	T. Spring-Rice	„	
1834 Dec.	Peel (Conservative)	Lord Aberdeen	„	
1835	Melbourne (Whig)	Lord Glenelg	„	
1839		Lord Normanby	„	1836 (Sir) J. Stephen
1839		Lord John Russell	„	
1841	Peel (Conservative)	Lord Stanley (later 14th Earl of Derby)	„	
1845		W. E. Gladstone	„	
1846	Russell (Whig)	Henry 3rd Earl Grey	„	
1852 Feb.	Derby, 14th Earl of (Conservative)	Sir J. Pakington	„	1847 H. Merivale
1852 Dec.	Aberdeen (Coalition)	Duke of Newcastle	„	
		(1854 War Office separated from Colonial Office)		
1854	Aberdeen (Coalition)	Sir G. Grey of Fallodon		H. Merivale
1855 Feb.	Palmerston (Whig)	Sydney Herbert		
1855 May		Lord J. Russell		
1855 July		Sir W. Molesworth		
1855 Nov.		H. Labouchere		

INDEX

Figures in bold type after personal names denote a main entry